ID0974950

TODAY'S
BEST
NONFICTION

TODAY'S
BEST
NONFICTION

THE READER'S DIGEST ASSOCIATION, INC.
PLEASANTVILLE, N.Y., MONTREAL

TODAY'S BEST NONFICTION
Editor-in-Chief: Barbara J. Morgan
Executive Editor: Tanis H. Erdmann
Senior Managing Editor: Marjorie Palmer
Managing Editors: Jean E. Aptakin, Thomas Froncek,
Herbert H. Lieberman, Joseph P. McGrath, James J. Menick
Senior Staff Editors: Anne H. Atwater, Angela H. Plowden-Wardlaw,
Ray Sipherd
Senior Editors: Dana Adkins, M. Tracy Brigden, Catherine T. Brown,
Linn Carl, Thomas S. Clemmons, Maureen A. Mackey, John R. Roberson
Senior Associate Editors: Catharine L. Edmonds, Ainslie Gilligan
Associate Editors: Christopher W. Davis, James R. Gullickson,
Barbara M. Harrington, Paula Marchese, Julie E. Sanders
Senior Staff Copy Editors: Jeane Garment, Jane F. Neighbors
Senior Copy Editors: Maxine Bartow, Claire A. Bedolis, Rosalind H. Campbell
Senior Associate Copy Editors: Jean S. Friedman, Jeanette Gingold,
Tatiana Ivanow, Marilyn J. Knowlton
Associate Copy Editors: Daphne Hougham, Heidi Kalnitzky, Charles Pendergast,
Miriam Schneir
Editorial Administrator: Ann M. Dougher
Art Director: Angelo Perrone
Executive Art Editors: William Gregory, Soren Noring
Art Editor: George Calas, Jr.
Associate Art Editor: Katherine Kelleher
Assistant Art Editors: Marcelline Lowery, Todd D. Victor
Director, Book Rights: Virginia Rice

INTERNATIONAL EDITIONS
Executive Editor: Gary Q. Arpin
Associate Editors: Bonnie Grande, Eva C. Jaunzems, Antonius L. Koster

The condensations in this volume have been created by The Reader's Digest
Association, Inc., and are used by permission of and special arrangement
with the publishers and the holders of the respective copyrights.

The original editions of the books in this volume are published
and copyrighted as follows:

In the Wake of the Exxon Valdez: The Devastating Impact of the Alaska Oil Spill
published by Sierra Club Books
distributed by Douglas & McIntyre Ltd. at $24.95
© 1990 by Art Davidson

Murder of Innocence: The Tragic Life and Final Rampage of Laurie Dann
published by Warner Books, Inc., a Time Warner Co.
distributed by Random House of Canada Ltd. at $26.00
© 1990 by Joel Kaplan, George Papajohn and Eric Zorn

*In All His Glory: The Life of William S. Paley, the Legendary Tycoon
and His Brilliant Circle*
published by Simon & Schuster
distributed by General Publishing Co., Ltd. at $41.95
© 1990 by Sally Bedell Smith

Guerrilla Prince: The Untold Story of Fidel Castro
published by Little, Brown & Co., (Canada) Ltd. at $28.95
© 1991 by Georgie Anne Geyer

© 1991 by The Reader's Digest Association, Inc.
© 1991 The Reader's Digest Association (Canada) Ltd.

ISBN 0-88850-264-8
FIRST EDITION
Volume 9

All rights reserved. Unauthorized reproduction, in any manner, is prohibited.

Printed in the U.S.A.

Contents

IN THE
WAKE
OF THE
EXXON VALDEZ

The Devastating Impact of the Alaska Oil Spill

ART DAVIDSON

. . . At 12:04 a.m. the *Exxon Valdez* shuddered. Hazelwood raced to the bridge. After first impact, the tanker advanced 600 feet before it ground to a halt on Bligh Reef.

Hazelwood didn't try to back off the reef. With the engines running full speed forward, he ordered a hard right, then a hard left. For fifteen minutes he held the throttle forward, spinning the wheel right to left. The ship swung slightly and groaned as rock ground metal, but Hazelwood could not dislodge the tanker. The stench of crude oil filled the air. Control-room gauges confirmed that they were rapidly losing oil. Hazelwood turned to Chief Mate Kunkel and said, "I guess this is one way to end your career."

—In the Wake of the Exxon Valdez

INTRODUCTION

THE fateful journey of the *Exxon Valdez* begins, in a sense, with the discovery of oil-saturated sands 8708 feet beneath the tundra of Alaska's North Slope, in January 1968. Further test wells confirmed a pool of at least 10 billion barrels of oil and 26 trillion cubic feet of gas—one of the world's largest accumulations of these resources. Within three years oil companies had paid a record $900 million to the federal government for leases on the North Slope.

The oil companies wanted to build an 800-mile pipeline through the heart of Alaska—from Prudhoe Bay, at the edge of the Arctic Ocean, to Valdez, in Prince William Sound. Supertankers would pick up the oil at the pipeline's terminus, in Valdez, and carry it through the remote and incredibly abundant waters of Prince William Sound. With storms, drifting ice, narrow passages, and submerged reefs, these were treacherous waters for oil-laden tankers the length of three football fields. An accident could devastate colonies of seabirds and kill eagles, sea otters, seals, salmon, whales, and many other creatures.

At the time, 1970, I was working for Friends of the Earth, and we filed suit against the proposed pipeline. This would be the first test of the Environmental Policy Act of 1969, which requires an assessment of the social, economic, and environmental implications of activities on federal lands. We felt there were safer alternatives to the oil industry's proposal. For example, an all-overland pipeline through Canada would eliminate the need for tankers, and thus would avoid the risk of oil pollution at sea. Fishermen also filed suit against the pipeline.

Having already invested nearly $3 billion in North Slope leases and development, seven oil companies formed a consortium called Alyeska and pleaded their case for building the pipeline before a sharply divided Congress. It took intensive lobbying from the state of Alaska and a tie-breaking vote by Vice President Spiro Agnew to clear the way for the Trans-Alaska Pipeline and the tanker route. Congressional approval rested on an oil industry pledge to spare no effort to protect the environment. To make certain the industry kept this pledge, the state of Alaska created its Department of Environmental Conservation (DEC).

The pipeline was the largest and most expensive private construction project in history. When oil started flowing through it in 1977, I knew that it would take persistent monitoring to ensure the industry maintained the required safeguards. Despite their gestures toward wildlife and wild places, the oil companies hadn't come to Alaska to nurture caribou. They'd come to make money.

The stances of the federal and state governments were harder to predict. The U.S. Department of the Interior and the U.S. Coast Guard are supposed to help safeguard Alaska from oil spills, but would their resolve be firm? The state has a constitutional obligation to protect its lands and waters. After being ardently pro–oil development, could Alaska transform itself into a conscientious guardian?

In any event, like other Alaskans, I soon became accustomed to the benefits of having the oil industry in the state. With the advent of North Slope oil money, state income taxes were abolished, and each resident began receiving an annual windfall check of at least $800 from oil revenues. Oil development was soon producing 85 percent of state revenues, creating jobs, and paying for new highways, schools, and libraries. For nearly twelve years we enjoyed the oil wealth without having to face its trade-offs—until the wreck of the *Exxon Valdez*.

CHAPTER ONE

PRINCE William Sound is a region shaped by water in many forms. Glaciers sculpt sharp granite ridges along the coastal range. Turbulent rivers, swollen with spring melt, rush to the sea. Waterfalls tumble through timeworn grooves cut into cliffs. And wind-driven breakers roll and explode against rocky islets and headlands.

Here in the northernmost reach of the Pacific Ocean, spring stirs in the sea before it is felt on land. In late March of 1989 snow lay deep among the spruce stands and along the beaches, but migrations were under way out in the sound. Salmon drawn landward from the open sea had begun their restless search for spawning streams. Gray whales from Mexican waters would soon breach in the swells of the sound. Seabirds were coming in from across the Pacific. Swans, geese, cranes, and flocks of shorebirds were flying the coastal winds. Tiny humming-birds were on their way from Central America; terns were coming from Antarctica.

Humans share Prince William Sound as well. Fishing families and villagers make their homes among its quiet bays and thickly wooded islands. Waters of the Gulf of Alaska slip past Hinchinbrook Island, at the southern entrance to the sound. This has been a favored route of mariners since Captain Cook sailed here in search of the elusive Northwest Passage. Cook found no route to the Orient, but he named the sound for England's young Prince William. He named one island for his trusted mate Hinchinbrook, and another for his friend the great navigator Captain Bligh. Now sailing ships have faded into the past, and oil tankers ply this passage to the pipeline terminal at Valdez.

Once a small village ringed with mountains, Valdez became wedded to oil when Alyeska chose it as the base port for shipping North Slope oil. Nowadays seventy to seventy-five tankers come to Valdez each month, and local bumper stickers and baseball caps sport the phrase VALDEZ, HOME OF THE SUPERTANKERS.

On Thursday, March 23, 1989, at the port of Valdez, under gray evening skies, the crew of the *Exxon Valdez* readied the ship for the five-day run to Long Beach, California. The three-year-old, 987-foot tanker was the newest ship in Exxon's fleet. Its captain, forty-two-year-old Joseph Hazelwood, had sailed for Exxon Shipping for nineteen years and had made the Valdez–Long Beach run many times. By 6:00 p.m. that Thursday, the *Exxon Valdez* was loaded with 1,264,164 barrels of North Slope crude, and Captain Hazelwood was anticipating a routine passage through Prince William Sound and down along the West Coast.

Meanwhile, Alyeska oil executives were celebrating a "safety dinner" at the Valdez Civic Center. Two months earlier the British Petroleum tanker *Thompson Pass* had lost 1700 barrels of oil while berthed at the

Alyeska terminal. Over the years there had been many spills, but none as large as that one. Alyeska employees had corralled most of the oil, and the celebrants were now congratulating themselves on a job well done.

However, not everyone was happy with the way Alyeska had handled the *Thompson Pass* spill. The tanker had been leaking before coming to Alaska, but British Petroleum had sent her north anyway. When the *Thompson Pass* berthed at the terminal, "they placed a boom around the ship, but they didn't watch her," said Chuck Hamel, a former tanker broker. "Suddenly there was a lot of oil in the water, but it took them fifteen days to lift seventeen hundred barrels from the water to the dock. And Alyeska called it a textbook response."

When Valdez mayor John Devens heard what had happened, he assembled a citizens committee to investigate safety problems at Alyeska. "Now, I've always been prodevelopment," said Devens, "but these tankers are getting out of hand. We've got to make sure they don't hurt our fisheries and tourism."

Devens' committee learned that ships making the Valdez run constituted 13 percent of the nation's total tanker traffic but accounted for 52 percent of its accidents. This discovery confirmed long-standing fears. Devens said, "In 1982 Alyeska dismantled its team dedicated 100 percent to oil spill response, and workers started coming to us saying, 'Don't use our names, but we don't like what's happening. Alyeska's cutting corners to save money.'

"We planned to build up our own oil spill protection—just in case," Devens continued. "We instituted a new property tax to raise money to buy our own boom and skimmers. Pretty soon Alyeska told us, 'You all don't really need that stuff.' Then the state tried to talk us out of getting it. We went ahead anyway and collected about twenty million dollars, but the state sued us to cease and give it the funds. So while the lawyers argue over it, that money sits in a bank instead of buying oil spill equipment."

ON THE same evening that the *Exxon Valdez* crew readied their tanker, Devens convened a town meeting to discuss the risks oil development might pose to Valdez. When Alyeska declined an invitation to send a speaker, Devens invited Riki Ott, from the town of Cordova, to voice her concerns about tankers passing through the sound. Ott is a fisherwoman who each summer dons rubber boots and rain gear to fish the treacherous channels of the Copper River delta. She is also Dr. Fredricka Ott, with a master's degree in oil pollution and a doctorate in sediment pollution.

Fog prevented Ott from flying the 70 miles from Cordova to Valdez, so she spoke by teleconference line to the thirty people gathered in the Valdez council chambers. Riki recalled the 1973 suit initiated by her fellow Cordova fishermen to block the pipeline from exiting in Prince William Sound. They had simply wanted to protect the sound and the fisheries that supported their way of life.

The town of Cordova had once been a port for shipping copper to market, but when the ore played out, fishing became the mainstay of the community. For more than eighty years now, life in Cordova has revolved around the herring that spawn in spring, and the summer runs of pink, red, chum, coho, and king salmon. The harbor is the center of town. Houses look out over multicolored fishing boats, and streets wind down to the water's edge.

"Congress overrode the fishermen's lawsuit in 1973," Riki Ott pointed out, "but not the fishermen's concern about water quality. Congress acknowledged these concerns and stipulated in legislation that there would be an oil spill contingency plan. We were assured that the best available technology would be utilized."

Ott then questioned Alyeska's ability to handle a large spill. "We have already had a close call in 1980," she cautioned. "We're playing Russian roulette here. It's not a matter of if. It's just a matter of *when* we get the big one."

WHILE Ott was voicing her concerns Captain Joseph Hazelwood was taking shore leave as the *Exxon Valdez* loaded oil. He had pulled into port at 11:00 p.m. the previous evening. For six months of the year, on rotations of sixty days on and sixty off, Hazelwood's home was the ship. A few hours' relaxation in town helped to relieve the monotony.

At 5:00 p.m. Hazelwood and his chief engineer, Jerzy Glowacki, stopped in at the Pipeline Club, a popular bar and dining room. With a seaman's cap set over his prominent forehead and his dark beard laced with silver, Hazelwood's appearance reflected his experience. After graduating from maritime college, in 1968, he had advanced quickly through the Exxon ranks. He had earned his master's license at age thirty-two, ten years earlier than most Exxon captains.

Hazelwood, nursing vodka straight up, told Glowacki that there had been a report of a heavy flow of Columbia Glacier ice into the sound. They discussed the possibility of waiting for daylight before setting out. They had already lost time on the northbound leg of the trip, but Exxon had allowed them three extra days, so a delay was feasible. Still, Hazelwood wanted to set out. He had been making the Valdez run for ten years and had encountered ice in the dark before.

On the way back to the tanker, Hazelwood and Glowacki stopped at the Club Valdez for pizza to go. The captain ordered another drink. At 8:10 p.m. they called a cab to run them back to the terminal.

By 9:00 p.m. the *Exxon Valdez* was ready to depart. At 9:12 the last mooring line was detached from the pier, and two tugs nudged the tanker from her berth. On the bridge were harbor pilot Ed Murphy and Captain Hazelwood. Coast guard regulations require that harbor pilots—who know about navigational hazards in local waters—guide tankers from port to open water. Earlier, Murphy had smelled alcohol on Hazelwood's breath, but he had said nothing about it.

At 9:21 p.m. Murphy, directing the vessel's speed and course settings, began to steer the *Exxon Valdez* out of the harbor, toward Valdez narrows, seven miles from port. The narrows, a channel that forms the entrance to Valdez bay, is 1700 yards wide, but a rock in the middle reduces the usable width to 900 yards. With Murphy at the helm Hazelwood left the bridge, which was highly unusual and against company policy. But Murphy said nothing; he knew Hazelwood well and respected his seamanship.

Fourteen miles out of port, the tanker reached Rocky Point, where harbor pilots normally transfer command of a ship back to the captain. Murphy had to order Hazelwood called back to the bridge. When Hazelwood returned, Murphy again noticed the smell of alcohol on the captain's breath. However, he decided that Hazelwood looked fit and focused enough to assume command. At 11:20 p.m. Captain Joseph Hazelwood took control of the *Exxon Valdez*.

In the dimly lit radar room atop the three-story coast guard station in Valdez, civilian radarman Gordon Taylor watched a bright orange ring on the radarscope. The ring represented the *Exxon Valdez* as it moved out through the narrows. At Rocky Point, radar coverage became fainter, and Taylor found the scope difficult to read. As the tanker approached the edge of radar coverage Hazelwood radioed the coast guard that he was "heading outbound and increasing speed." At 11:24 harbor pilot Ed Murphy left the tanker and boarded a pilot boat that would speed him back to the port of Valdez. Hazelwood radioed Traffic Valdez, the coast guard's radio monitoring station.

> HAZELWOOD: We've departed a pilot. At this time hooking up to sea speed. And ETA [estimated time of arrival] to make it out [past Naked Island] on 0100 [1:00 a.m.]. Over.
>
> TRAFFIC VALDEZ: Roger. Request an updated ice report when you go down through there. Over.
>
> HAZELWOOD: Okay. Was just about to tell you that judging by our radar, I will probably divert from TSS [Traffic Separation Scheme] and end up in an inbound lane. Over.
>
> TRAFFIC VALDEZ: No reported traffic. I got the *Chevron California* one hour out and the *ARCO Alaska* is right behind him. But they are an hour out from Hinchinbrook.
>
> HAZELWOOD: That'd be fine, yeah. We may end up over in the inbound lane, outbound track. We'll notify you when we cross over the separation zone. Over.

SHORTLY after Hazelwood notified the coast guard that he was going to divert from the one-way inbound and outbound tanker lanes, he radioed that he was going to angle left and reduce speed in order to work through some floating ice. "I am going to alter my course to two hundred [degrees] and reduce speed about twelve knots. Once we're clear of the ice, we'll give you another shout. Over." However, despite Hazelwood's assurance to the coast guard, the ship's speed was not reduced.

At 11:40 p.m. the night shift took over at the coast guard station. Before heading home, radarman Taylor told his replacement, Bruce Blanford, that the *Exxon Valdez* was crossing into the separation zone—possibly into the northbound lane—to avoid the ice.

However, Hazelwood did not notify the coast guard when he left the traffic separation zone. And instead of ending up in the inbound lane, he went on through it, taking the tanker farther off course. In one transmission he mistakenly identified his vessel as the *Exxon Baton Rouge,* and his speech was slurred.

At the coast guard station it was now Blanford's responsibility to track tankers and warn of impending danger. Instead of trying to locate the *Exxon Valdez* on radar or monitoring its movements by radio, Blanford began to track its progress on a traffic data sheet and to move a stack of papers representing the vessel around the room.

By the time Blanford had arranged his stacks of paper to represent all the vessels going to and from the port, the *Exxon Valdez* was nearing the ice. "After I got things squared away, I went down and got a cup of coffee," Blanford would report. "I may have been gone a couple of minutes. I really couldn't say how long."

Meanwhile, on the *Exxon Valdez*, Third Mate Gregory Cousins had joined Hazelwood on the bridge to make a navigational fix on the vessel's position. The night was too dark to see any icebergs, but ice was silhouetted on the radar screen. It was an extensive floe—thousands of chunks of ice had broken from the Columbia Glacier and were being massed together by the current. Some the size of a house and larger could be out there in the night.

Cousins and Hazelwood discussed skirting the ice. The northern edge of the floe appeared to be two miles dead ahead. At their current course setting they would run into it. The ice was backed up to the glacier, so they couldn't pass the floe to the right. To the left was a gap of nine tenths of a mile between the ice and Bligh Reef. They could wait until the ice moved, or reduce speed and work their way through it. Hazelwood chose another option: turn and enter the gap between the ice and the reef. The ship was still accelerating.

Hazelwood ordered the helmsman to alter course to 180 degrees— to turn left across the 2000-yard-wide zone separating inbound and outbound traffic and continue across the inbound lane. A well-timed right turn would be necessary to avoid Bligh Reef, which lay six miles ahead in the darkness. There would be little room for error. The vessel needed at least six tenths of a mile to make the turn, and the gap between the ice and Bligh Reef was only nine tenths of a mile wide. The tanker would have to start its right turn well before the gap if it was to make it through.

At 11:46 p.m. Maureen Jones left her cabin to go on lookout duty on the bridge wing. As she came on duty helmsman Harry Claar's shift was ending. Hazelwood gave him two last orders: to accelerate to sea speed and to put the ship on automatic pilot. Both commands were highly unusual. Speed was normally reduced when ice was encountered. The automatic pilot—almost never used in the sound—would have to be released if any course changes had to be made.

Though puzzled by Hazelwood's orders, Claar increased speed and locked the controls on automatic pilot. He was then replaced at the helm by Robert Kagan.

On the bridge, Hazelwood told Third Mate Cousins he was going below and asked if he felt comfortable navigating alone. Cousins had made only a few voyages with Hazelwood, and he had never maneuvered the *Exxon Valdez* in tight quarters. Nevertheless, he replied, "Yes, I feel I can manage the situation."

Standard coast guard procedure dictates that in the presence of danger, two officers must be on the bridge. The junior of the two is responsible for fixing the location of the vessel, the senior one for directing the vessel's course. Before leaving the bridge, Hazelwood told Cousins to make a right turn when the ship was across from the Busby Island light and to skirt the edge of the ice, but he neither gave Cousins an exact course to follow nor plotted a line on the chart. If he had, Hazelwood might have noticed that it was virtually impossible to turn abeam the Busby light and also miss the ice.

Hazelwood left the bridge at 11:53. Moments later Cousins, who had not heard Hazelwood's orders to Claar, discovered that the vessel was on automatic pilot, and he shifted it back into manual mode. The ship was still headed on a 180-degree course toward Bligh Reef, and Cousins faced a critical maneuver: he had to avoid the ice but couldn't wait too long before turning. The vessel was increasing speed.

At 11:55 Cousins called Hazelwood to say, "I think there's a chance that we may get into the edge of this ice."

Hazelwood said, "Okay." They talked for less than a minute, and neither mentioned slowing the vessel down.

Once more Cousins turned to the radar as he tried to locate the leading edge of ice. He was peering at the radar screen when the tanker slipped past the Busby Island light without beginning to turn.

It was nearly midnight, the beginning of Good Friday, March 24, when Maureen Jones noticed that the red light on the Bligh Reef buoy was to the ship's right. Red navigational lights should be to the right of ships returning to port. Since the *Exxon Valdez* was leaving port, the light should have been on the left side. Jones alerted Cousins that "a red light was flashing every four seconds to starboard."

At the same moment, Cousins immediately ordered a 20-degree right turn.

Jones called Cousins a second time. She had a more accurate count on the red light; it was flashing every five seconds. It was still on the wrong side of the ship.

Cousins ordered a hard right and called Hazelwood, saying, "I think we are in serious trouble."

At 12:04 a.m. the *Exxon Valdez* shuddered. Hazelwood raced to the bridge. After first impact, the tanker advanced 600 feet before it ground to a halt on Bligh Reef.

Hazelwood didn't try to back off the reef. With the engines running full speed forward, he ordered a hard right, then a hard left. In the engine room, the chief engineer did not know they had grounded; he couldn't figure out why the system was overloading.

Chief Mate James Kunkel had been sleeping in his quarters but awoke at first impact. "The vessel began to shudder, and I heard a clang, clang, clang." Realizing they might capsize, Kunkel went to the bridge and quickly calculated their stability on the ship's computer. The vessel was listing 4 to 5 degrees to starboard. "We weren't stable enough to move."

However, Hazelwood continued his attempts to force the tanker ahead. For fifteen minutes he held the throttle forward, spinning the wheel right to left. The ship swung slightly and groaned as rock ground metal, but Hazelwood could not dislodge the tanker from the reef. The stench of crude oil filled the air. Control-room gauges confirmed that they were rapidly losing oil. Hazelwood turned to Chief Mate Kunkel and said, "I guess this is one way to end your career."

At 12:27 a.m., twenty-three minutes after grounding, Hazelwood finally radioed the coast guard traffic control in Valdez. "Yeah. It's *Valdez* back. We've fetched up, run aground north of Goose Island, around Bligh Reef. And evidently we're leaking some oil. And we're going to be here awhile. We'll give you the status report as to the changing situation. Over."

At 12:30 the coast guard officer on duty woke Commander Steve McCall, the ranking coast guard officer in Valdez. "This is the big one. We have the *Exxon Valdez* aground at Bligh Reef."

"What? You must be kidding," McCall said. "Okay, I'm on my way."

The coast guard officer then radioed the *Stalworth,* a tug in the

Valdez harbor, "for possible assist" and closed the port of Valdez to all commercial traffic. He then called for the *Silver Bullet,* a speedy pilot boat, to run out to Bligh Reef.

Commander McCall sped through the empty streets of Valdez. As soon as he arrived at the coast guard traffic-control center, he radioed Hazelwood, with whom he had gone to maritime school many years before.

McCall: *Exxon Valdez,* this is the captain of the port, Commander McCall. Do you have any more of an estimate as to your situation at this time? Over.

Hazelwood: Oh, not at the present, Steve, but we are working our way off the reef. The vessel has been holed. Right now we're trying to steer off the reef. And we'll get back to you as soon as we can.

McCall: Roger on that. You know, we've got all our planned mechanisms in place to give you what assistance we can. Take it, take it slow. Take it slow and easy, and we are getting help out as fast as we can.

Hazelwood: Okay. We're in pretty good shape right now stability-wise. We're just trying to extract her off the shoal here. Once I get under way, I'll let you know.

McCall: Roger. Yeah. Another thing, before you make any drastic attempt to get under way, you make sure you don't . . . start doing any ripping. You got a rising tide. You got about an hour and a half worth of tide in your favor. Once you hit the max, I wouldn't recommend doing much wiggling.

Hazelwood: Okay. Yeah, I think the major damage has kind of been done. We've kind of rolled over it, and we're just kind of hung up in the stern here. We'll just drift over it, and I'll get back to you.

CHAPTER TWO

MOMENTS after Captain Hazelwood radioed Valdez, ringing phones began to break the early morning quiet.

At 12:30 a.m., March 24, the coast guard called Alyeska and alerted night-shift superintendent Dave Barnum that the *Exxon Valdez* had run aground and was leaking oil. Barnum notified a crew that was loading a tanker.

Before Alyeska began tightening its budget in 1981, the oil spill response team had operated much like a firehouse—running drills, maintaining equipment, and staying on duty twenty-four hours a day. Commenting in retrospect on the dismantling of the team, Alyeska's managing engineer, William Howitt, said, "The idea was that personnel assigned to other jobs would be available to fight an oil spill." On the morning of the spill, therefore, Alyeska had no trained spill response team in place and ready to act.

At 12:35 a.m. Alyeska terminal superintendent Chuck O'Donnell was awakened by the phone. Told that a tanker had "possibly gone aground," he called Alyeska marine supervisor Larry Shier and sent him to the coast guard office to see what was going on.

At 1:23 a.m. Darryl Warner, president of the Exxon Pipeline Company, in Houston, was notified of the spill. He immediately called Frank Iarossi, president of Exxon Shipping, also in Houston, who, at his bedside phone, initiated Exxon's response.

At 1:59 a.m. coast guard commander McCall radioed the *Exxon Valdez* for a status report. He was told that no one knew how many of the tanker's oil storage compartments had ruptured or how much oil had been lost.

By 3:00 a.m. coast guard lieutenant Thomas Falkenstein and Dan Lawn, of Alaska's Department of Environmental Conservation, had arrived at the *Exxon Valdez* aboard the *Silver Bullet*. Falkenstein asked Captain Hazelwood the nature of the problem. Hazelwood said, "I think you are looking at it."

Lawn ascended the pilot's ladder and saw a turbulent pool of oil rising two feet higher than the surrounding water. He would later describe what he saw as "a boiling cauldron."

At 3:19 a.m. Falkenstein radioed McCall that at least 138,000 barrels of oil had been lost already and that 20,000 barrels were escaping every hour. As the oil rushed out, the tanker balanced precariously over Bligh Reef. Falkenstein warned McCall that the vessel was in danger of either breaking apart or capsizing, and that an additional one million barrels of oil might escape. McCall, in turn, warned Alyeska of this crisis and advised that lightering (transferring the *Exxon Valdez's* oil to another tanker) be commenced as soon as possible.

Alyeska's contingency plan stated that a vessel with containment boom and skimmers would arrive at the scene of a spill in no more than five and a half hours. By 5:00 a.m. that period was nearly over. DEC's Dan Lawn called Alyeska from the tanker's satellite phone. "What's going on? This ship is still leaking. You need to send out every piece of equipment you've got right away."

At Alyeska, Larry Shier replied that the equipment was on its way.

However, the boom required to contain the oil, and the skimmer attachments needed to suck it up, were not on the response barge—and the barge itself was in dry dock awaiting repair to a crack in its bow. The large skimmers and deep-sea boom lay in a warehouse, buried under tons of other equipment. A forklift and a crane were deployed to begin sorting the equipment and loading the large skimmers and sections of boom onto the barge. However, for several hours there was only one operator for both the forklift and the crane.

An observer likened the scene to a slapstick movie: "The operator would snag containers of boom with the forklift, drive to the barge, climb into the crane to swing each container onto the deck, jump from the crane to the forklift, and speed back to the warehouse for another pickup."

As soon as the boom and skimmers were loaded onto the barge, it was discovered that the barge and its tug were needed for a task even more urgent—getting lightering equipment to the stricken tanker. The tug stood ready to run the large inflatable fenders and other lightering gear out to Bligh Reef, but first the equipment had to be found. After an hour's search, someone noticed the fenders buried under a snowdrift. The barge was unloaded to make room for the lightering equipment.

At 6:00 a.m. Mayor John Devens was awakened by a call from the local radio station. "You'd better put on your mayoral hat. We've got an oil spill."

"It's six o'clock, for God's sake," Devens mumbled, half asleep. "We've had others. They'll take care of it."

"No, no, John. This is a different kind of spill. This is big."

Before rushing to his office, Devens tried to call Alyeska and Exxon, but couldn't reach anyone. He left messages on their answering machines requesting calls back. He never got any.

Shortly after 6:00 a.m., as dawn crept over Prince William Sound, Alyeska officials flew over the spill for the first time. They saw a slick three miles long and two miles wide, drifting south from the tanker.

They couldn't see the depth of the black pool from the air, but rising fumes stung their eyes.

At 6:30 a.m. Dan Lawn, still on the *Exxon Valdez,* called Larry Shier again at Alyeska. "You need to get that equipment to Bligh Reef. The oil has to be contained immediately."

Shier assured Lawn that boom and skimmers were en route. In fact, they would sit on the dock in Valdez for another four hours.

AT 7:00 A.M. morning light was flooding into the Cordova home of Jack and Paula Lamb when their phone rang. The Lambs run a tender that collects salmon from fishermen in the sound, and for the past weeks they had been readying their boat for the salmon runs. When Lamb hung up the phone, his wife recalled, "He looked like someone had died."

After telling her what had happened, Jack Lamb went straight to the union hall, home of Cordova District Fishermen United. CDFU director Marilyn Leland was already there. The two tried to call Riki Ott, but her phone was off the hook. Jack left to get her.

At 7:30 a.m. Riki Ott flew downstairs in her nightgown to answer the banging on her door. "How long will it take you to get dressed?" Lamb panted, out of breath. Ott ran upstairs to throw on her clothes, yelling to Lamb to build a fire in her wood stove so her cabin would be warm when she returned. It would be more than five weeks before she got home.

At the CDFU office, Lamb, Ott, and Leland began making phone calls. Personnel at the coast guard office in Valdez "were noncommittal and provided little information," Leland said. She called the Alyeska emergency number, but no one answered. She and Lamb began to alert the fishermen. Ott ran out to the airport to find a small plane that would take her out into Prince William Sound and to Valdez.

It took Ott's pilot eight minutes to circle the slick. "It was perfectly calm. But I was stunned," she said. "There was no boom, no containment. Just a tanker on the rocks, with two fishing boats coming up to it. Where *was* everybody?"

They flew through a blue haze that was lifting from the slick, the air thick with the stench of oil. By the time Ott reached Valdez, government officials and reporters were already pouring into town.

Back in Cordova, thirty fishing boats were ready to leave the harbor.

"The fishermen weren't asking about being reimbursed. They just wanted to help, get some boom out there, run the skimmers, do whatever they could," Leland said.

Shortly after 9:00 a.m. someone answered the phone at Alyeska and told Leland, "We are putting together a list of boats that can get out on the spill immediately. We'll get back to you." When Leland hadn't heard by noon, she called to tell them that seventy-five boats were now ready to help. Alyeska told her, "We have a person on this, and he'll call you back." He never did.

AT 9:30 A.M. Hazelwood was given a sobriety test aboard the *Exxon Valdez.* He told a state trooper that he had drunk only one beer before reboarding the ship, but had drunk a low-percentage alcoholic beverage after the accident.

By 10:00 a.m. the *Exxon Baton Rouge,* en route to load oil in Valdez, was diverted to Bligh Reef to take on oil from the *Exxon Valdez.* Before tying the two ships together, the pilots wanted to survey the seabed for submerged rocks.

By 4:00 p.m. Alaska's governor Steve Cowper had arrived in Valdez from Fairbanks, and Dennis Kelso, the commissioner of the state's Department of Environmental Conservation, had flown in from Juneau. Together they boarded a float plane, flew out through the narrows, and landed near the *Exxon Valdez.* A small coast guard boat ferried them to the crippled tanker. Acrid fumes burned their eyes. Commissioner Kelso told the governor that "Alyeska's contingency plan is very specific about what kind of equipment they would have here within five and a half hours. It's quite clear that what was promised has not been delivered."

The Alyeska barge, loaded with boom and skimmers, hadn't set out from Valdez until 11:00 a.m. It arrived at Bligh Reef at 2:30 p.m.— more than fourteen hours after the accident. Kelso and the governor did see two open skiffs with skimming apparatus mounted on their bows that were crossing and recrossing the oil. However, Alyeska had sent no storage barge. In minutes the skimmers were filled to capacity, with nowhere to unload their collected oil. The men saw no boom around the tanker.

Cowper said that they would have to consider using chemical dispersants wherever the environmental risk would be acceptable. Kelso responded that the state had already preapproved their use in off-shore areas in order to reduce the likelihood of oil moving into more ecologically sensitive areas. But since the chemicals might be as damaging to the environment as the oil itself, state approval was still required for near shore areas.

By now the oil had spread out to the southwest farther than Cowper and Kelso could see from the deck of the tanker—over 200,000 barrels spread over more than 18 square miles. As he was leaving the *Exxon Valdez* Governor Cowper said, "I've never seen such a god-damned mess in my life."

By that evening Kelso had assumed overall command of the spill for the state. At forty-one, the commissioner emanated a relaxed charm that masked a sharp command of detail. With an undergraduate background in sciences and a law degree from Harvard, Kelso had become commissioner of the Department of Environmental Conservation in 1987. His responsibility was to direct the state's three-part role in the crisis: to oversee the industry's spill response, assess the damage, and monitor the cleanup. That night Kelso had no idea that another response had been generated—by Exxon—thousands of miles away.

AFTER receiving word of the grounding early Friday morning, in Houston, Frank Iarossi, president of Exxon Shipping, said, "My first thought was that I couldn't believe this was happening to us just two weeks after the other one."

"The other one" was the *Exxon Houston*. Exxon Shipping had sailed through more than twenty years without a major oil spill—until March 1989. The *Exxon Houston* had been discharging oil at Oahu, in Hawaii, when heavy winds had picked up and the terminal's mooring chain had broken. The vessel was blown onto a reef, where it spilled 200 barrels of fuel. Disconnected terminal lines spilled 600 barrels of oil.

"We initiated our response plan, and it worked effectively," recalled Iarossi of the *Exxon Houston* incident. "The coast guard called it a model response, and we were absolved of any blame." Iarossi had visited the site and returned from Hawaii feeling that his people had performed well. Two weeks later he awoke to the *Exxon Valdez*.

Iarossi had faced challenges before. After graduating from the U.S. Coast Guard Academy, in 1959, he had remained on active duty for ten years, earning master's degrees in mechanical engineering and naval architecture. After leaving the coast guard, he had gone on to earn an M.B.A. and ended up taking a job with Exxon.

At Exxon he supervised tanker construction in Japan and helped the company develop its oil spill response plan. In 1982 Iarossi was made president of Exxon Shipping, responsible for eighteen tug-and-barge units and nineteen oceangoing tankers.

At 1:30 Alaska time on Friday morning Frank Iarossi began making phone calls from his bedside, in Houston, waking executives and oil spill specialists. "The real shock came at 3:30 a.m. Alaska time, when George Nelson [Alyeska president] called to say the vessel had lost an estimated one hundred and thirty-eight thousand barrels. I didn't feel panic, just a tremendous sense of urgency. I told him that we were going on full mobilization. He was obviously relieved to know that we'd be in Alaska that evening."

Before driving to his office, Iarossi recalled a few moments of quiet. "I'm not sure what I was doing, maybe praying or trying to gather my strength," he said. No one had ever faced a spill like this before. It was the largest spill ever to occur in North American waters, and it had not occurred on the high seas, where the oil might have more easily dispersed and broken down. This oil was loose in Prince William Sound, where the tides, currents, and wind could carry it into some of the most ruggedly beautiful coves and fjords in the country.

At 7:00 a.m. Texas time (4:00 a.m. in Alaska) Iarossi arrived at his office to meet with his top managers. Calls were made to mobilize skimmers and boom in San Francisco and Southampton, England. Harvey Borgen, Exxon Shipping's West Coast fleet manager, called Commander McCall to ask if dispersants could be used. Borgen understood McCall to say that they could. Iarossi contracted two 707 jets to transport dispersants to Alaska. A C-130 equipped to spray them was also sent.

At 11:36 a.m. Texas time Iarossi and Exxon oil spill response coordinator Craig Rassinier left Houston for Valdez in an Exxon corporate jet. They were accompanied by Gordon Lindblom, a scientist who had helped pioneer the use of chemical dispersants on oil spills, as well as a lawyer, a claims adjuster, and one of Exxon's senior mariners. As they flew north the executives discussed strategy and made periodic air-to-ground calls. Gordon Lindblom called Valdez and was disturbed to learn that Alyeska was going to make a dispersant test with a large bucket slung from a helicopter. Iarossi later recalled that "Lindblom came back muttering, saying that they were going to use a helicopter and that that was a mistake."

Meanwhile, data from the grounded tanker was being relayed to Houston so that an Exxon marine expert could evaluate the stability of the *Exxon Valdez*. He foresaw problems. The tanker was unbalanced. Divers would have to determine how firmly it was lodged on the reef. Lightering was delayed because withdrawing oil would further unbalance the ship.

At 5:37 p.m. Alaska time Exxon's corporate jet landed in Valdez, and Frank Iarossi immediately opened the company's command post at the Westmark Hotel. On his way to a press conference, Iarossi ran into coast guard commander McCall. "He said we needed to test dispersant. That was the first time we heard that we were required to do tests," Iarossi said.

That afternoon Alyeska had made the first dispersant trial from a helicopter, and as Gordon Lindblom had predicted, the test failed. "A helicopter using a drop bucket never works," Iarossi said. "It's really not enough to make a noticeable difference on a large spill. Between that failed test and all the pressure he was starting to get from the fishermen and from the governor, McCall began to have second thoughts about dispersants."

At the press conference, Iarossi announced that Exxon accepted responsibility for the spill. He then drove to the Valdez tanker terminal and assumed responsibility from Alyeska for the lightering operation, dispersants, and public relations. Exxon let Alyeska remain in charge of the existing skimmers.

DEC commissioner Kelso was puzzled. He believed that Alyeska was still in charge legally, because its obligation was clearly spelled out in the contingency plan. This was the first of many confusions regarding actual, legal, and moral responsibility—not to mention authority. Together they would add up to the most profound unanswered question surrounding the cleanup: Who, in fact, was in charge?

The state expected Alyeska to act, as specified in its contingency plan. However, Alyeska's parent companies, anxious to disassociate themselves from the disaster, looked to Exxon to take over. Exxon said it was responsible for the spill and, according to a prior agreement with Alyeska, was mobilizing. When the state expressed surprise, Iarossi was surprised in turn. "We clearly stated all the way back in 1982 that in the event of a major spill we would mobilize the spill response."

In 1982 Exxon had written to the Alaska DEC that "for most tanker spills the response outlined in the Alyeska plan will suffice. However, in the event of a major spill by an Exxon owned and operated vessel it is anticipated that Exxon Company, U.S.A.'s oil response team would be activated."

Now, in response to a crisis, Exxon had to mobilize from thousands of miles away. "We started from ground zero," Iarossi said. "First, Exxon shipped its equipment to the Anchorage airport. Then the company set up a feeder airline and trucking system to transport equipment from Anchorage to Valdez. Finally, the equipment had to be deployed by boat, float plane, and helicopter to the oil slick twenty-five miles out in Prince William Sound."

While the Exxon people scrambled to mobilize equipment, state and local observers were beginning to sense what one called "a nightmare within the nightmare." Not only was a tremendous amount of oil loose on the waters of Prince William Sound, but Alyeska, which they had counted on to recover the oil, was disappearing. Kelso had expected fast and effective action from Alyeska, whose contingency plan even listed the names and phone numbers of employees who would fight a spill. However, Valdez mayor John Devens noted, "For some reason these people, who were trained and ready to work, were never called."

At 10:00 p.m. Friday, Captain William Deppe, Exxon's marine expert, boarded the *Exxon Valdez* to take charge of the precarious job of salvaging the tanker without losing more oil. Hazelwood was being relieved of command and, after questioning by authorities in Valdez, would be free to return to his home in Huntington, New York.

Captain Deppe quickly met the various state and coast guard officials aboard ship and began formulating a plan to save the vessel. Deppe had commanded the *Exxon Long Beach,* the sister ship to the *Exxon Valdez,* and had been chosen by Exxon to supervise four vessels in its West Coast fleet. Maneuvering the *Exxon Valdez* off Bligh Reef would be his most harrowing experience in nearly twenty years at sea.

BY SATURDAY morning, March 25, estimates of the amount of oil spilled had risen to 240,000 barrels. This spill was 140 times larger than the *Thompson Pass* spill, which Alyeska had taken fifteen days to clean up right in Valdez harbor; 300 times larger than the *Exxon Houston* spill in Hawaii; and 1000 times larger than most terminal-related spills.

Exxon took command of what barges, boom, and skimming equipment Alyeska had, and Frank Iarossi pressed for permission to do controlled burning—the ignition of a floating pool of oil cordoned off with fireproof boom—and to use chemical dispersants. However, Iarossi faced an even more pressing problem than the oil already in the water. Perhaps only he and his closest advisers realized how close the tanker was to capsizing and dumping the remaining 1 million barrels—42 million gallons—of oil into the sound.

Throughout the early hours of Saturday morning, divers descended into the dark waters beneath the *Exxon Valdez* to assess the damage and help determine the vessel's stability. "We felt our way in the darkness while this enormous ship was creaking and groaning," diver Mark Dione said. "The hull is seven-eighths-inch steel, but it was like a tin can with holes punched in it, some large enough to drive a truck through. There was a boulder in there the size of a Volkswagen."

The divers' survey revealed "very substantial underwater damage over about 50 percent of the vessel's bottom." Half of the tanker's cargo compartments were ruptured, and more than 600 feet of hull lay cracked or broken. The divers also found that the ship's stability was more precarious than had been thought at first: "The vessel is balanced on a rocky pinnacle at about its midsection." It sagged where it hung over the reef. At low tide the vessel would flex further, possibly cracking apart and disgorging the remaining oil.

"We had to proceed very very carefully," Iarossi said. "The first real decision I had to make was, With between thirty and forty people on the ship, do we risk lightering at all? It's one of those decisions that was made instinctively. We just had to go all out to get the oil off the ship."

By dawn Saturday morning the waiting *Exxon Baton Rouge* had tied up next to the *Exxon Valdez*. William Deppe began the removal of the remaining oil with extreme caution. To counterbalance any weight shift, seawater had to be used to displace oil removed by lightering.

Meanwhile, Exxon was trying to mount a three-pronged attack to retrieve the oil from Prince William Sound: burning, skimming, and dispersants. Burning required specialized fireproof boom, of which there was hardly enough in Alaska to make an appreciable difference.

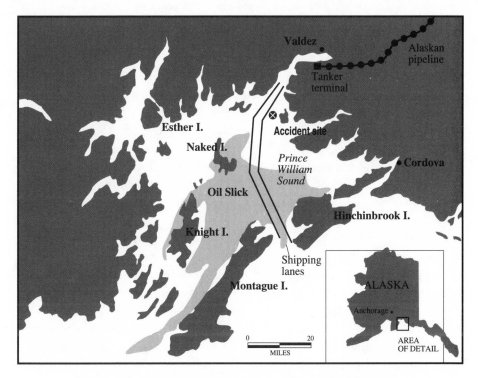

Driven by spring storms and tides, the oil spreading from the
Exxon Valdez eventually covered more than 10,000 square miles.

However, by noon Saturday, Exxon had transported 2500 feet of fire
boom to Valdez, and a test burn was scheduled for that evening.

Twenty-four hours into the spill, Alyeska's skimming boats had re-
claimed fewer than 1000 barrels of oil. Exxon's skimming attachments
were arriving from San Francisco and England, but no one had yet
developed an effective method of transferring oil from the skimming
boats to a collection barge—even though such a transfer had been a
foundation of Alyeska's contingency plan. Dispersants appeared to be
the only real hope of controlling the spill. However, dispersants are
controversial. They do not remove oil from the water; rather, they act
like dishwashing detergent, breaking the oil into tiny droplets that
descend into the subsurface water directly below the spill, where they
can harm marine organisms.

"Dispersants act as an aid to the natural weathering process of oil in
water," said Dr. Alan Maki, Exxon's chief environmental scientist in
Alaska. "But," Maki cautioned, "the circumstances that dictate their
use are seldom clear cut."

U.S. Environmental Protection Agency scientists have determined that "one state or region placing a high priority on its shellfish industry would have very different policies from a state or region assigning highest priority to waterfowl protection."

Recognizing that trade-offs are often involved, the U.S. Environmental Protection Agency (EPA) devised a national contingency plan that allowed each state to decide if and when dispersants would be used. Still, for dispersant use to proceed, a coast guard on-scene coordinator must obtain agreement from both the affected state and the regional representative of the EPA.

Alyeska's spill response guidelines, which the state approved, note that "dispersants will be considered as a possible response option only when mechanical containment and recovery response actions are not workable." Alaska DEC commissioner Dennis Kelso explained: "They are a tool to be kept in the kit—and used in the right circumstances."

So that this tool could be used quickly in an emergency, the state established three dispersant-use zones. Regions far from sensitive shorelines were designated zone 1; for these the EPA and the state of Alaska gave the coast guard's on-scene coordinator preapproval to use dispersants. The large, open areas in Prince William Sound, including the tanker route from the narrows to the open sea, were identified as zone 1.

In the more ecologically sensitive zone 2 areas, dispersant use was to depend upon case-by-case EPA and state approval. In zone 3, places such as intertidal areas, small coves, and fjords, the use of dispersants was not recommended at all. But as in zone 2, the use of dispersants required EPA and state approval.

Bligh Reef, onto which the *Exxon Valdez* crashed, was designated zone 3. However, the oil was spreading through a zone 2 area and soon would be extending into the more open waters of zone 1. Within hours of the grounding, Exxon had phoned Commander McCall, the coast guard's on-scene coordinator, to ask if dispersants could be used. Iarossi had understood McCall's answer to be yes, and since only McCall's approval was necessary for zone 1, Iarossi had called for dispersant and for planes to spray it on the slick.

However, Alaska's dispersant guidelines also state that "in all cases the use of dispersants will be based on the determination that their impact will be less harmful than that of non-dispersed oil." McCall had yet to make that determination, and he was neither a chemist nor a marine biologist. Assailed from all sides, he was in a very difficult position—caught between the urgency to use dispersants and concern that they might do more harm than good. He decided he needed further trials.

It was noon Saturday before McCall approved a test run. At 4:00 p.m. Exxon's C-130 plane, equipped with dispersant spray, took off from Valdez loaded with 3700 gallons of dispersants. It laid down a 150-foot-wide swath just south of the *Exxon Valdez.* "The test in my view clearly was successful," said Iarossi. "Two important things happened. Light reflection was different where sprayed. And the surface action was different, a clear rippling effect where dispersant had been sprayed."

McCall, however, saw it differently. "We couldn't really tell how well it was working, mainly because of the lack of wind and lack of surface action in the water." He told Iarossi he needed "unequivocal" proof that dispersants were working.

"Not using dispersants because the water is too calm is a fallacy," said Dr. James Butler, a Harvard University professor who had chaired a National Research Council oil spill study. "When the wind came up, the dispersant would mix with the oil, and the slick would begin to disperse. Even if the slick didn't disappear, oil washed ashore with some dispersant wouldn't stick to shoreline surfaces so much."

As night fell, the unseasonably calm weather held. A fisherman anchored near the slick watched the setting sun ripple red-orange over the water, then saw a wall of flame shoot suddenly into the sky. "The ocean's on fire!" he yelled to his crew. "Let's get the hell out of here!"

The fishermen escaped unscathed, but residents of the nearby village of Tatitlek reported sore throats and stinging eyes from the smoke of Exxon's first test burn. This prompted the state to require Exxon to obtain a permit from DEC before doing any further burning.

The company had hoped this test would clear the way for continued burning. The test had successfully burned off 15,000 gallons of oil in less than an hour, and now Exxon had enough fire boom in Valdez to run four simultaneous burns. If its permit came in time, Exxon could work through the night, burning off approximately 50,000 gallons (nearly 1200 barrels) per hour. Said Frank Iarossi, "Getting that permit right away was absolutely critical. Once you let the oil emulsify and it begins to take on water content, you can't burn it."

By midnight Saturday, forty-eight hours after the grounding, mechanical cleanup had made little headway and Exxon had yet to receive permission to proceed with burning and dispersants. Response to the spill was becoming paralyzed by indecision, a struggle over authority, and vastly different expectations as to which measures would work. Said Frank Iarossi, quoting Dr. Butler, "It's like arguing whether to use water to put out a fire while the house is burning."

CHAPTER THREE

EASTER Sunday crept coral pink over Prince William Sound as sharp white mountains emerged from the darkness. In Valdez, Easter celebrations were overshadowed by the ominous presence of oil drifting southwest from Bligh Reef. Most of the oil was concentrated in a 15-square-mile pool, but thick tendrils swirled out over more than 100 square miles. Two dead sea otters were sighted, as were seventy-five oiled seabirds.

According to Alyeska's prespill projections, more than 100,000 barrels of oil should have been recovered by now, but total recovery stood at fewer than 3000 barrels. Skimming boats were still scooting over the slick, like water bugs on a pond, with no effective means of transferring skimmed oil. Exxon was still awaiting a burning permit, but the main question at hand was dispersant authorization. The decision-making process, much like the town of Valdez and the state of Alaska, was being consumed by strained emotions and conflicting information.

By Sunday, Exxon's employees in Valdez were outnumbered by radio and television crews and journalists, who became part of the general turmoil. As the media relayed images of the spill to people around the world, they both reported and fueled the atmosphere of growing anger, frustration, and mistrust.

"The crowds are getting angrier and nastier," said Alyeska spokesman Tom Brennan. "Valdez has become a black hole, sucking in every nut and screwball in the universe. Some clowns tried running our people off the road." Brennan even discreetly asked about getting a bulletproof vest.

Tumultuous general admission–style press conferences were now being held morning and evening, and these became a forum for public debate. Some Exxon managers considered these press conferences distractions from the work of fighting the spill, but many people saw them as a means of pressuring Exxon into more decisive action.

"Those so-called press conferences were Roman circuses," observed coast guard admiral Edward Nelson after he arrived in Valdez that weekend. Nelson was now the ranking coast guard officer in Valdez. While Commander Steve McCall served as on-scene coordinator, Nelson became a behind-the-scenes coordinator.

It was at the press conferences that the public had its say regarding dispersant use, and Nelson considered the outcry to have a significant impact. "The attitude was, You're going to throw these dangerous chemicals in the water and they are going to destroy our fish. No one is concerned about the environment. If you allow dispersants, you're letting big oil off easy."

It was not only the press conference turmoil that was stalling the decision making; it was also the fact that definitive answers did not really exist. "The effects of dispersants depend on a lot of different factors—spraying technique, sea-surface state, ocean currents, water depth, and the biological communities being impacted," Dr. James Butler said. However, enough was known about dispersants to warrant their use in open-water areas. As Dr. Butler added, "Even if the oil were dispersed in the upper layer of water over a large area, it would be rendered much less harmful than the untreated slick."

Commander McCall, ever cautious, requested further dispersant tests. At 2:00 p.m. Sunday a C-130 dropped 5100 gallons of dispersants on the slick, and in Iarossi's opinion the results were "spectacular." A breeze that had begun stirring the water's surface may have helped to catalyze the dispersant. McCall acknowledged that "the test seemed to work pretty well."

Meanwhile, at 3:00 p.m. Sunday, Iarossi received word that the state had finally granted a permit for controlled burning. But permission to use dispersants was still being withheld.

At 5:00 Iarossi was still trying to persuade Commander McCall to approve dispersants when DEC's Dennis Kelso, his staff, and additional coast guard and Exxon officials arrived to join the discussion. Kelso said that the state was not ready to permit an open-ended use of dispersants. He was concerned about the trade-offs between dispersing oil into the water versus allowing it to wash ashore.

Iarossi feared that the decision makers were "slowly being consumed with political issues versus spill issues. We were fighting amongst ourselves rather than fighting the oil spill."

By 6:45 p.m. McCall had deliberated long enough. "We finally have agreement to use dispersant in zone 1," he told Iarossi. The question of whether to use dispersants was finally answered—sixty-six hours after the grounding. Yet as dispersants were flown in from around the world it became apparent that there were not enough *anywhere* to treat a spill of this magnitude.

At Bligh Reef, lightering of the *Exxon Valdez* had commenced, although the stricken tanker still contained 940,000 barrels of oil.

Before returning to his hotel room Sunday night, Frank Iarossi said, "Starting tomorrow, we are going to have all three tools—skimmers, burning, and dispersants—at our disposal. We'll be going all out."

However, that night the weather turned. For three days the wind had stayed below 15 knots, keeping the oil pooled close to Bligh Reef. The waves had been less than three feet high, ideal for oil recovery. The sun had shone brightly Sunday morning, but in the afternoon a high overcast had seeped into the sky and the wind started picking up. By nightfall small-craft warnings were posted. Gusts up to 25 knots buffeted the port of Valdez, and in the fading light whitecaps raced across Prince William Sound.

BY DAWN Monday a spring blizzard was howling down out of the Chugach Mountains, driving snow and sleet through the streets of Valdez. Boats were pinned in the harbor. Planes were grounded. Twenty-foot waves raced across Prince William Sound. Gale-force winds whipped the heavy crude into a frothy mixture of seawater and oil. The massive oil slick was spreading out, breaking into separate slicks and running southwest with the wind.

"The slick is moving like it's on a superhighway," said Frank Iarossi. "Our worst fears happened. The wind just shot us down."

The main pool of oil moved 40 miles overnight. Stygian waves, heavy with oil, hammered the headlands of Knight Island. Purplish black tendrils twisted along the tidal rips. The beaches of Smith and Naked islands were awash with the black crude; in places waves tossed oil 40 feet above the tidal rocks. Within twenty-four hours the spill had grown from 100 to approximately 500 square miles.

It had been a long night for Captain Deppe, his crew, and the coast guard and DEC officials gathered on the *Exxon Valdez*. Dressed in survival suits, they had stood watch through the hours of darkness, listening to the steel hull groan as it shuddered and twisted upon the reef. The *Exxon Valdez* had been tied to the *Exxon Baton Rouge* and four giant tug boats. By morning the storm had turned all six vessels 12 degrees, as if, lashed together, they had become a giant weather vane pivoting on the rock. On the vessels' decks, sea spray had frozen into sheets of ice.

Out on Prince William Sound, globs of oil-soaked debris, barely recognizable as birds, began washing ashore. Cormorants and ducks became coated when they dove into the sea to feed. Eagles ingested oil as they fed upon weakened creatures and contaminated carrion. Spring migrations of geese, swans, and shorebirds had just begun.

Sea otters were suddenly finding the clear waters of their marine world black, thick, and deadly. A strange substance they could not comprehend burned their eyes and lungs and soaked into their fur as they struggled to stay afloat. Many otters swam to exhaustion and drowned. Some managed to crawl ashore, where they died of exposure. Along the poisoned shorelines, deer grazed on oil-stained seaweed and grass. Bears coming out of hibernation were seen scavenging blackened birds and otters washed up on the beaches.

The storm had churned much of the oil into the frothy sludge called mousse. In this emulsified state, the oil was too weathered to be treated with either burning or dispersants. Skimmers, which had proved ineffective under ideal conditions, were now the sole means of recovering oil before it washed ashore.

Those fighting the spill found themselves in a vacuum of authority. Alyeska, which the state had relied on for spill response, had disappeared. Exxon was trying to respond but needed official authorization. Most of Exxon's people, having flown up from other parts of the country, had little knowledge of Alaska. They didn't know Alaska's weather, Alaska's waters, Alaska's shoreline, or Alaska's people. But the state and the coast guard, both of which could have provided direction, strained against the limits placed on their own authority.

The state wanted to direct Exxon, to draw up and enforce priorities of where to go, what to do. However, as Governor Cowper acknowledged, "It is not by any means clear that we have the authority to direct Exxon to do anything." DEC Commissioner Kelso clarified: "We have enforcement sanctions we can impose if a spiller fails to do something. But there is no sanction we can use to make sure spillers do what they say they are going to do, or what the law requires them to do."

Admiral Nelson echoed Kelso's frustration: "The rules of the game are that unless the spiller is irresponsible or unresponsive, we don't take over. This is wrong. Without relieving the spiller of financial responsibility, we have to be in charge at the beginning, not after things have gone to pot."

By Monday the spill response had done just that—gone to pot. The oil that Alyeska and Exxon had recovered represented little more than 1 percent of the spill. The wind had scattered the boom that Exxon had positioned on the leading edge of the slick. Governor Cowper wanted the coast guard to call Exxon's response inadequate and federalize the spill, but Admiral Nelson resisted, explaining that it would take weeks for the coast guard to set up the government's cumbersome contractual procedures.

Nevertheless, Frank Iarossi himself encouraged Admiral Nelson to take charge amid the confusion. "Oil was running loose, and instead of being able to act decisively, we were caught up in committee activity," Iarossi recalled. "I encouraged Admiral Nelson to use his authority to decide what had to be done and when. I think he really wanted to, but he had to check with Admiral Yost first."

However, coast guard commander Admiral Paul Yost did not federalize the spill, which meant that Admiral Nelson could not take command. "As long as we weren't going to federalize," said Nelson, "we could only stand back and watch and let Exxon do it. It wasn't that Frank Iarossi wasn't trying—he certainly was. But all the needed equipment—pads, absorbent materials, boom, skimmers, barges, and so forth—just wasn't around. The worst part was, nobody knew where to get it all."

To bring some sense of order and direction to the spill response, Iarossi, Nelson, and Kelso set up two working groups: a steering committee composed of Iarossi, Nelson, and Kelso, and an operations committee composed of key people from the state, Exxon, and the coast guard. The operations group was to meet at 8:00 a.m. and 8:00 p.m. each day, and then report to the steering committee. However,

Kelso, Iarossi, and Nelson found they had to attend the operations meetings as well. This working group soon swelled to forty-six members, and its meetings began lasting proportionally longer.

"We'd be crammed into this room," Iarossi said. "One night there were two Exxon people, five coast guard officers, thirty-nine representatives from the state, and a whole bunch of local community groups. There wasn't a lot of arguing, just endless discussions by the same people who were supposed to be out coordinating the spill activities. It really turned into a disaster, a hopeless situation."

It was a disaster that the world was watching, and regardless of the problems Exxon faced, the public would hold the oil industry accountable for what was quickly becoming the nation's most devastating oil spill. "How can the public feel comfortable with how you would handle a spill off the coast of California, South Carolina, Florida, or any other coastal state?" asked California Congressman George Miller. "If the industry can't respond to this spill on a timely and effective basis, I don't think the public is going to buy into new offshore development that expands the risk and expands the opportunity for failure."

CHAPTER FOUR

As OIL surged through Prince William Sound one central question rang through the general confusion: How could such an accident have happened? The world's largest oil company, the "jewel of the fleet," an experienced captain, open waters, and yet . . .

Many Exxon officials, particularly liability-conscious lawyers, had a vested interest in dismissing the wreck as a tragic but unpredictable and virtually unpreventable incident. However, reports began to surface of watered-down regulations, oil company budget cuts, coast guard cutbacks, rules violations, alcohol abuse, fatigued tanker crews, and governmental negligence, and it soon became clear that many factors besides chance had contributed to the accident.

Bob LeResche, who had been appointed by Governor Cowper to be Alaska's oil spill coordinator, traced the roots of the *Exxon Valdez* incident back ten years to "a thousand little mistakes and inattentions."

Another who tried to fit the multitude of pieces together was Andy Santos, British Petroleum's port captain and the most experienced

Within days of the spill, the pristine waters of Prince William Sound, above, were covered with crude oil several inches thick. Right, Captain Joseph Hazelwood.

Right, Third Mate Gregory Cousins was at the wheel when the *Exxon Valdez* ran aground. Below, the crippled oil tanker under tow.

Seabirds, like the murre at left, were returning to Alaska to nest when the spill occurred. Below, a sea otter and pup on the shore of the sound before the spill.

Three who battled the oil spill under different banners. Center left, Alaska governor Steve Cowper. Above, Cordova environmentalist Dr. Riki Ott. Bottom left, Exxon Shipping's Frank Iarossi.

mariner in Valdez at the time of the wreck. "The fatal mistake," said Santos, "was Hazelwood leaving the bridge. Cousins knew the ship, knew how to run it. Unless he was a complete chowderhead, Cousins should have known they were heading into the reef. But the ultimate responsibility lies with the captain of the ship. When Hazelwood went below deck, something fell between the cracks that was god-awful."

JOSEPH Hazelwood's character and abilities emerged in his youth. At New York Maritime College, a rigorous school with a 60-percent drop-out rate, he was capable enough to earn good grades and party on weekends. A former roommate recalls the time he and Hazelwood got so drunk they pretended their convertible Volkswagen was a skateboard. Driving down a steep road, they turned off the engine, jumped into the back seat, and shifted their weight to try to steer the vehicle. Nevertheless, Hazelwood breezed through maritime college with honors. The motto printed next to his yearbook picture reads, "It can't happen to me."

Later, in the merchant marine, Hazelwood's seafaring instincts made an impression on his superiors. "Joe had what we old-timers refer to as a seaman's eye," recalls a retired Exxon captain. "He had that sixth sense that enables you to smell a storm on the horizon, or watch the barometer and figure how to outmaneuver it."

A 1985 incident off Atlantic City, New Jersey, highlighted Hazelwood's seamanship. On a trip south from New York, Hazelwood's ship encountered a freak storm. High winds snapped the ship's mast, and it toppled, along with the ship's radar and electronic gear. With 30-foot waves and 50-knot winds overpowering the vessel, several sailors prepared to abandon ship. Yet Hazelwood calmed the crew, then turned the ship back to New York.

However, Hazelwood's reputation as a drinker developed along with that as a seaman. "It was almost like Joe was trying to get caught," said a shipmate who knew him well. "He'd close his cabin door, but everyone knew what went on. He always said that everything was fine, but then why was he drinking? The guy was begging for help."

The wreck of the *Exxon Valdez* abruptly threw Hazelwood's drinking into the open. Nine hours after the grounding, the state of Alaska's lab report revealed that his blood-alcohol level had registered .06. A toxicologist calculated that the level could have been .20 at the time of grounding, five times the legal limit for vessel masters. What wasn't clear was precisely when Hazelwood consumed the alcohol—before or after the crash.

One piece of the puzzle had to do with the renewal of Hazelwood's master's certification. At the time of the accident his driver's license had been invalid, revoked as a result of a drunk-driving incident the previous fall. In all, the license had been suspended for drunk driving three times since 1984. Why had the coast guard made the renewal without checking Hazelwood's motor-vehicle driving record? Exxon denied knowledge of the license suspensions, but the company was well aware of Hazelwood's past drinking problem.

In April 1985 Hazelwood had voluntarily entered a private alcohol-treatment program. A year later former Exxon employee Bruce Amero had sued Exxon for $2 million, claiming that from 1980 through 1982 Hazelwood had been abusive while drinking aboard ship. "There's a bad joke in the fleet," Amero had said, "that it's Captain Hazelwood and his chief mate, Jack Daniels, that run the ship."

Exxon had evidently disregarded Amero's allegations.

After the accident Hazelwood's employment with Exxon was terminated. The state of Alaska charged Hazelwood with misdemeanors for operating a ship while intoxicated, reckless endangerment, and negligent discharge of petroleum. The charges carried combined maximum penalties of two and a half years in prison and $11,000 in fines. Hazelwood also faced one felony charge of criminal mischief—maximum penalty of five years in prison and a $5000 fine.*

When the National Transportation Safety Board (NTSB) analyzed the *Exxon Valdez* accident several months later, it came to view Hazelwood's drinking in light of a larger issue: oil industry control of substance abuse. As NTSB investigators compiled detailed reports, alcohol use and abuse emerged as problems in the shipping industry. When asked at the hearings how strictly alcohol was controlled on the *Exxon Valdez*, the tanker's helmsman Harry Claar said, "It's probably not any different than any others—stricter than some and looser than others." Katie Hite, a Valdez bartender, recalled having to stop serving drinks to tanker crewmen and put them in cabs to get them back to their ships.

---

*In March 1990 Joseph Hazelwood was convicted of negligent discharge of petroleum, a misdemeanor. He was acquitted of all other charges.—THE EDITORS

Exxon's alcohol policy states that employees may be required to submit to drug and alcohol testing, and some surprise checks had been done on a number of tankers. However, when Iarossi was asked if Hazelwood had ever been tested to follow up his rehabilitation, he replied, "Not to my knowledge."

After the wreck of the *Exxon Valdez*, Exxon announced that officers who volunteered for rehabilitation would not be permitted to return to their original positions. With this decision Exxon confronted a dilemma that faces many corporations. Confidentiality encourages employees to enter rehabilitation but also shields them from being moved to less critical positions. However, Exxon's prohibition "may just drive [the alcohol problem] underground," said Frank Iarossi.

In fact, in Exxon's 1982–83 review of officer performance it was recommended that Joseph Hazelwood be reassigned to shore duty. However, this appraisal was never signed or forwarded to Exxon headquarters for review, and the seriousness of his drinking problem escaped management's attention until the morning of March 24, 1989.

"Lots of the captains are alcoholic," observed a Cordova fisherman who worked for Exxon, in Valdez, in the early 1980s. "It's a lonely life out there. I think all that time away from families and friends may drive some of them to drink."

"After the wreck," said Valdez mayor John Devens, "a couple of tanker captains called me. They told me, 'Sure, Hazelwood did something wrong, but when we get into port, we often have to work for twenty-four hours straight. We're dead tired. There's pressure to turn the ship around. Time is money. The deed is done, but don't make Hazelwood the scapegoat.' "

Others who appeared before the NTSB also cited crew fatigue. Helmsman Harry Claar reported that he sometimes felt so tired his performance was impaired. Chief Mate James Kunkel testified that seamen were allowed to work up to eight hours of overtime per day.

To ensure that crew members are well rested while on duty, the U.S. Congress established guidelines for regulating overtime hours and required periods of rest. One rule prohibits an officer from active duty unless he or she has had at least six hours of rest during the previous twelve hours. Third Mate Cousins was working overtime when the tanker crashed. In his first report to the NTSB the state's Bob LeResche wrote, "Cousins had only three and a half hours of rest in the twelve hours prior to departing Valdez—a violation of Coast Guard regulations."

However, Frank Iarossi countered, "By our count, Cousins had six hours off duty in the previous twelve hours, and he had ten hours of sleep in the twenty-four hours prior to the grounding. We're quite comfortable with Cousins' work schedule, and he was too. He even decided to take an extra hour of watch. I'm sure he now wishes he hadn't. We do too."

Violations aboard the *Exxon Valdez*, such as having only one officer on the bridge while exiting Prince William Sound, also raised the question of how well the coast guard was enforcing its regulations regarding manning levels. Under query by the NTSB, Commander McCall acknowledged that the coast guard's capability to monitor tankers was limited.

Budget constraints were at the root of a number of coast guard problems. One casualty was a program to monitor ice, long recognized as a hazard on the Valdez route. During one week in 1984 ice conditions had forced eighteen tankers to reduce speed or divert from designated traffic lanes, passing as close as 500 yards to Bligh Reef. "There is no observation system in place," said Commander Steve McCall, acknowledging that "any ice is a hazard to navigation."

An accurate ice report on the night of March 23 might have averted the grounding of the *Exxon Valdez*. Moments before impact Third Mate Gregory Cousins had been studying the sketchy outline of ice on the ship's radar. Cousins may have lost track of precious time while trying to figure out the ship's position in relation to the ice.

Hindsight revealed another contributing factor to the accident: tanker-crew reliance on coast guard monitoring. Tanker crews believed that the coast guard plotted their progress at six-minute intervals out to Bligh Reef—this is a requirement detailed in the coast guard operations manual. However, the coast guard had discontinued the practice without informing tanker crews. If the radarman in Valdez had been plotting the course of the *Exxon Valdez*, he should have been able to warn Cousins of the tanker's imminent collision with the reef.

When pressed to explain the coast guard's failure to warn the *Exxon Valdez*, McCall said, "All we can do is advise. We can't direct a vessel to make a course change." This response reflected the coast guard's deference to an ancient mariner's rule that the master of a ship holds the ultimate responsibility for his ship's safe passage.

However, the coast guard's own manual states that in critical situations the coast guard should actually "direct or prohibit vessel movement." And the manual provides an example of what a traffic controller should say: "This is Valdez traffic. Our radar shows you 100 yards to the left of traffic lane, inside the separation zone. You are *directed* to take corrective action."

Some federal, state, and private investigators who pored over the evidence cast blame in many directions. A few even raised the possibility of a conspiracy to account for the myriad things that shouldn't have gone wrong but did. That suggestion aside, it is certain that a conspiracy of sorts *was* at work—an unconscious conspiracy of denial. A tanker captain denied his drinking problem. Crew members denied their responsibility to report breaches of safety regulations. Company officials denied the potential consequences of crew fatigue and of placing an alcoholic captain in command of an oil tanker. Coast guard officers denied the necessity of following their own safety procedures. It seemed as if everyone involved had adopted Joe Hazelwood's yearbook motto: It can't happen to me.

Meanwhile, as gale-force winds blew on through Prince William Sound, across the Kenai Peninsula to Kodiak Island and the Aleutian Islands, no one knew how far those winds, the tides, and the currents would carry the oil along those wild coasts.

THE grounding of the *Exxon Valdez* was precipitated by individual, industry, and government errors. But once the oil was loose, where did responsibility lie for the failure to contain and recover it before it spread along Alaska's beaches?

During the first hectic days of the spill, most of the blame fell on Exxon, which was trying to mount a response virtually from scratch. "There's no doubt that all this contingency planning did not anticipate having to respond to a spill this big," Iarossi said. "Clearly, no one ever anticipated trying to handle a quarter million barrels of oil on the water."

Nevertheless, Exxon was a major partner in the Alyeska consortium, and from its inception Alyeska had reassured the public that it was prepared for a major oil spill.

"Alyeska's contingency plan is the greatest work of maritime fiction since *Moby Dick*," said Alaska's DEC commissioner, Dennis Kelso. He was incensed that after claiming it could recover 100,000 barrels of oil in seventy-two hours, Alyeska actually recovered barely 3000 barrels within that time.

However, both the state and Exxon had counted on Alyeska as the first line of defense in an oil spill. A contingency plan had, in fact, been required when the seven oil companies that formed Alyeska applied for a permit to build the pipeline in 1970. When lobbying Congress for the permit, the companies committed themselves to such a plan. This agreement was no less than a contract between Alyeska and the people of the United States to protect and preserve the quality of the air, water, and environment.

The contingency plan was not a promise of good intentions, but a document that spelled out precisely how Alyeska would respond to a spill—the equipment that would be available, the names of cleanup personnel, response times, lists of subcontractors, and so on.

"It is supposed to be Alyeska who is responsible for a cleanup and no one else, because that was the Great Promise the oil companies made to the people of the United States," said Dan Lawn, DEC's longtime representative in Valdez. "I believed Alyeska was going to live up to its promise. I know more now. Where the hell were they?"

Dan Lawn, who describes himself as a meat-and-potatoes guy, stands well over six feet tall and weighs around 250 pounds. With his gray beard and long silver hair he looks more like a maverick than a career bureaucrat. An Alyeska executive once denounced Lawn as "that jerk." Some of his own co-workers have called him a troublemaker. Others have viewed Dan Lawn as a lone voice of caution.

In a 1984 memo Lawn warned his supervisor in Anchorage: "There has taken place a general disemboweling of the Alyeska Valdez terminal operational plan. Most knowledgeable and competently trained individuals have either quit, been terminated, or transferred up the line. This has left inadequately trained people to maintain the facility and an insufficient number of people to operate it.

"As you know, [we have] been underbudgeted and understaffed to adequately inspect the terminal and keep in touch with Alyeska's day-to-day operations," Lawn continued. "Unfortunately, this has been a, signal to Alyeska that the state is no longer interested in the Trans-Alaska Pipeline project."

A review of DEC files and Alyeska's track record reveals an overall pattern of denial marked by both the oil industry's tightfisted resistance to making good on its promises and the state's lack of perseverance in requiring it to do so.

• *December 1976.* The coast guard "strongly recommended" that the industry position appropriate cleanup gear in Prince William Sound. Alyeska did not comply.

• *March 1977.* The Alaska Department of Fish and Game declared Alyeska's containment boom insufficient, its maximum spill estimate of 74,000 barrels too low, and its cleanup crew too small. Alyeska took no corrective measures.

• *May 1977.* DEC and the coast guard urged that Alyeska permanently anchor barges loaded with boom, lightering pumps, skimmers, and dispersant at Bligh Island and Hinchinbrook Island. Alyeska's parent companies did not want to incur this expense, and the state did not require them to.

• *March 1978.* The coast guard again urged Alyeska to deploy cleanup equipment in Prince William Sound. Alyeska refused.

• *March 1982.* DEC asked Alyeska to address spills larger than 74,000 barrels in its plan. Alyeska appealed DEC's request in court.

• *October 1984.* Alyeska performed a spill drill. State observers reported that "response efforts failed to contain the hypothetical spill." The Environmental Protection Agency concluded that "Alyeska is not prepared."

• *November 1985.* DEC stated that Alyeska "consistently failed to follow up on commitments" made after spill drills.

• *May 1986.* At DEC's insistence, Alyeska finally worked into its plan a scenario for a 200,000-barrel spill. It protested that such a spill would happen only once in 241 years.

• *March 1989.* The once-in-241-years spill happened. And Alyeska disappeared.

THE federal government—the third player, along with the oil industry and the state—made its own contribution to the Great Promise. When the proposed Trans-Alaska Pipeline route was criticized because it involved tanker transport, the government promised to require double-bottom tankers. This commitment was a key factor in Congress' approval of the pipeline route. Nevertheless, oil industry officials continued to argue that in some situations single-hull tankers are safer. Cost was an underlying motive. Construction of a double bottom can add up to 5 percent to the cost of a new tanker—about an additional $6 million for the *Exxon Valdez*—and a complete double hull runs 1 or 2 percent more. In addition, ships with double hulls can carry only about 60 percent as much oil as tankers with single hulls.

The double-hull debate reached a crescendo in 1975. In January of that year a study by a naval architect concluded that in thirty tanker groundings from 1969 to 1973 double hulls would have contained 97 percent of the oil that was spilled. But by the end of 1975 the coast guard was siding with industry. The bottom line was keeping costs low enough for American vessels to be competitive with foreign tankers.

In any event, the federal government did not require more than a single hull. As a consequence, 73 percent of the tankers in the Alaska trade, including the *Exxon Valdez*, are single-hull vessels. After the *Exxon Valdez* grounded on Bligh Reef, the coast guard estimated that 25 to 60 percent of the spilled oil could have been contained if the vessel had had a double hull.

The wreck of the *Exxon Valdez* revealed that Alyeska's Great Promise represented nothing but the wishful thinking of those who favored oil development. Tragically, the oil industry, the state, and the federal government were all failing to live up to the commitments they had made when the pipeline was built.

CHAPTER FIVE

THE people of Cordova reacted as if there had been a death in the family. "It was like a funeral," said Marilyn Leland, director of the fishermen's union. "After the service everyone brings food to the family's home. After the spill everyone came to the union hall. They brought doughnuts, cakes, meat, and cheese. Everyone wanted to do something."

Soon after reports of dead otters and birds began appearing on television, letters started arriving from children all over the country. "Seeing the dead animals day after day really got to me," Marilyn said. "I found myself standing in the middle of Main Street crying."

Tension had been mounting for days when Exxon made its first appearance in Cordova. A town meeting was called. The high school gym was packed.

"Do you think the oil is worth the risk?" someone asked Exxon spokesman Don Cornett. "In light of this event, would you reconsider the Canadian pipeline route?"

"This [pipeline] has been a phenomenal success," Cornett responded. "It's hell to say that today, but this has been one of the greatest successes we've ever been involved with. But I would reconsider it. . . . Yeah, I would reconsider it."

"Has Exxon considered shutting down the pipeline?" a fisherman asked.

"I don't think that's an option," Cornett said.

"Shut the damned thing down!" someone yelled.

"It's just not an option." Cornett tried to continue as people jeered. "It is not going to happen."

"Is Exxon prepared to reimburse commercial fishermen for damage to the fisheries in Prince William Sound?" one fisherman asked.

"You'll need to have records of what you have earned," Cornett replied, "and demonstrate that you did not earn that this year to some reasonable degree. And—"

"Don't give us that 'reasonable' crap," another interrupted. "To us, fishing's—"

"You have had some good luck and you don't realize it," Cornett shot back. "You have Exxon. And we do business straight."

"How far has the oil gotten down the bay?" asked an older fisherman. "We make our living fishing. We want to know what's going to happen to our livelihoods."

"All of the boom that was in stock as required by the contingency plan was deployed," Cornett replied.

"That is entirely untrue," a man yelled. *"Entirely untrue!"*

"Just a second, folks," Riki Ott broke in. "On the first day, the boom material was off-loaded from the barge because the barge was under repair. Okay?"

"That's correct," Cornett said.

"We asked, 'Why isn't that boom material being loaded into our fishing boats and being taken out?' "

"I think that's a real good question," Cornett said.

"Yeah! Right!" responded Ott.

On that first Friday of the spill, Jack Lamb and thirty other fishermen had stood ready with their boats. "We kept trying to contact Alyeska and Exxon, in Valdez, to offer our help. But call after call went unanswered," Lamb recalled. "In the beginning I felt no anger. But the anger began to build when our offers to help were totally ignored."

When the wind rose on Monday, March 27, Lamb heard reports of oil rushing through the sound. That night he attended the strategy session of the three-party steering committee formed out of desperation by Exxon's Frank Iarossi, coast guard commander Steve McCall, and Alaska DEC commissioner Dennis Kelso. Lamb found Kelso clearly agitated at the lack of palpable results. To provoke action, Kelso asked Lamb to represent the fishermen on the operations committee, the group composed of key people from the state, the coast guard, and Exxon.

At the first operations meeting Lamb attended, later that night, the committee heard the report on the action out on the sound. The wind was dying down, but oil was drifting toward Eleanor and Naked islands. Sheen and mousse were swirling into coves, estuaries, and onto rocky shorelines. Some areas would have to be sacrificed in order to save others.

Lamb found himself thinking about the beautiful Bay of Islands—its deep, clear waters, its cliffs and tidal pools. "It's my favorite spot in the sound, and here I am, hoping the oil gets trapped in there because the hatcheries at Sawmill Bay and Eshamy Lagoon have to be protected."

At the time of the spill, the Koernig Hatchery, at Sawmill Bay, had been about to release 117 million salmon fry, which workers had been nurturing since the previous summer. When the silvery, inch-long fry had hatched in early March, they were flushed through large transparent hoses into net pens floating in Sawmill Bay.

But Armin Koernig and his managers knew they couldn't release the fry into the sound that spring. Even if many of the fry skirted around the main front of the slick, oil was likely to pool up in the intertidal zone, where the fingerlings feed over the summer. Some thought that if the oil didn't kill the young salmon outright, it would still knock out the plankton upon which they feed. However, the most immediate threat was to the rearing pens. Just a few gallons of oil, the fishermen feared, could wipe out an entire generation of salmon.

At the operations meeting in Valdez, Lamb told Iarossi what Exxon had to do: boom the facilities at Eshamy Lagoon, Main Bay, Esther Island, and Sawmill Bay. "Those hatcheries have got to be saved."

Frank Iarossi said he'd get the fishermen some boom and asked, "How soon can you have boats available?"

"Immediately," Lamb said as he started to dial the union hall in Cordova.

"We'll take 'em all in one whack," Iarossi said, committing Exxon financially. Later he summed up his position on the money. "It's going to be a helluva bill, but right now I'm not stopping to count."

At 10:00 p.m. that Monday night, Lamb called for five boats to be deployed to each of the four threatened hatcheries. Ten minutes later four boats were under way. By 2:00 a.m. Tuesday another fourteen boats would stream out of the Cordova harbor. The "Mosquito Fleet," a makeshift armada of seiners, long-liners, and skiffs, was on its way.

Commissioner Kelso lingered after the meeting to speak with his staff. Despite Iarossi's willingness to spend money, Kelso wasn't convinced that Exxon appreciated the full magnitude of the problem. "It doesn't look like Exxon's thinking big enough," he said.

"We could respond faster than Exxon," said one of Kelso's deputies.

"We could get a state ferry," Kelso said, realizing that the Mosquito Fleet would need a large supply boat to serve as an operations center. Knowing that he was pushing the limits of his authority, he said, "I think we should change our responsibility from monitoring to actually going out and starting our own recovery operation."

That key decision made, Kelso and his staff targeted a major objective: within forty-eight hours they'd have boats, men, and equipment recovering oil. They would bring in the state ferry *Bartlett* from Cordova until the much larger *Aurora* could arrive from southeast Alaska.

Meanwhile, Jack Lamb had been sitting alone thinking. Iarossi had promised to send over skimmers to scoop up oil too, and barges to store it in. But there really was no efficient way to transfer oil from the small skimming boats to the barges. Still thinking out the problem at 4:00 a.m., he called a friend, a contractor familiar with heavy equipment. "Larry, we need something big to suck up oil."

Larry told Lamb they had "trucks kinda like big vacs on wheels, called supersuckers." There were six of them on the North Slope.

Lamb asked, "What'll it take to get them here?"

Larry explained that the supersuckers were all under contract to oil companies. "But I'll see if I can get you one."

Larry phoned Prudhoe Bay. A truck driver got out of bed to answer the phone. "You want to do what? You must be crazy." But at 6:00 a.m. the driver sneaked one of the supersuckers out of the security yard.

Lamb called a friend in Homer. "Get us a boat to put this baby on."

By 8:00 a.m. the supersucker was a hundred miles down the road, and a barge was on its way to Seward to meet it.

Later Tuesday morning Lamb boarded a helicopter. He was accompanied by Rick Steiner, a marine biologist and half owner of a Cordova fishing boat. The two flew over the spill and saw the boats of the Mosquito Fleet speeding toward the hatcheries. And they saw the oil. "I was shocked," Lamb said. "The massive oil slick extended down as far as Herring Bay, on Knight Island. The water between Eleanor and Lone islands was pitch-black and looked thick enough to walk on."

They flew to the small island called Applegate Rock and landed. Oil oozed through the beach grass and lichen growing above the high-tide line. Among the slippery, oil-coated rocks lay dead and dying scoters, auklets, cormorants, and oystercatchers.

They spotted twenty harbor seals huddled together 50 feet from shore, heads sticking out of the oil. "They wanted to come ashore," Steiner said. "They kept looking at us with their big brown eyes, as if they were asking, 'What's happening? Why?' They were ingesting oil and were going to die slowly."

Steiner and Lamb made their way toward blobs of oil that were actually sea otters that had managed to crawl ashore before dying. A two-year-old otter was frantically licking oil from its fur. Its eyes were bright red from trying to see in the oily water. Steiner caught it easily, and both his and Lamb's first reaction was to bring it back to Valdez to try to save it. "Jack and I looked at each other," said Steiner. "We realized he'd be dead very soon. We let him die where he'd lived."

After releasing the otter, they plodded silently back toward the helicopter. Out of sight of each other and separated by a large rock, each man began to cry.

Tom Copeland was another fisherman deeply affected by what was happening. While other fishermen sped toward the hatcheries, Copeland spent $5000 of his own money on a pump, gas, and five-gallon buckets. Then he went looking for oil. When he and his crew reached the slick near Knight Island, they just started dipping buckets and pulling out oil, five gallons at a time. The first day they scooped up 1500 gallons, and on their best day 2500 gallons. Exxon's most effective skimmer collected just 1200 gallons a day.

Still, the oil was approaching Sawmill Bay. "All you could see was black," said Eric Prestegard, manager of the Koernig Hatchery. "I was truly scared. I knew the boats were coming, but I didn't think they'd make it in time."

But they did. The Mosquito Fleet reached the hatchery a full day before the oil. The fishermen's first task was to figure out how to use the boom Exxon had flown out. "It was a joke," said one fisherman of the flimsy harbor boom. "A two-inch chop or a boat driving past could push oil right over it. We were constantly trying to keep this stuff together. It ripped in half all the time."

Rick Steiner returned to Valdez to urge Exxon to send better equipment to the Mosquito Fleet. "The disaster was unfolding minute by minute," said Steiner, "but the company was still our biggest hassle those first few days. We'd say we needed something, and they'd say, 'Yes, it's on the way.' Then it took days. At first we believed them. Then we realized they were just trying to get us off their backs. There simply wasn't enough equipment available."

Meanwhile, on Saturday morning, April 1, the state ferry *Bartlett* arrived at Sawmill Bay. The supersucker Jack Lamb had called in from the North Slope arrived that afternoon. The makeshift armada that converged at Sawmill Bay was a cooperative effort—some boats were under contract to DEC and others to Exxon, and there was a large skimming boat borrowed from the navy.

When Exxon finally located some heavy-duty boom, it was flown out to the Mosquito Fleet at the Koernig Hatchery. It didn't break as easily as the lightweight boom, but oil still slopped over the edges. Any oil that got through was met by a second and then a third ring of boom protecting the cove's mesh pens full of fingerling salmon. Beyond these barriers, fishing boats towed lengths of boom to encircle patches of oil. The collected oil was sucked up by the large navy skimmer.

"Everybody's nerves were raw from getting only two or three hours of sleep a night," said Jim Hayden, who coordinated DEC operations. "Tempers were strained. I had to settle several disputes."

"Most of the fighting was over who was in charge," Hayden explained. "The hatchery people had their oil spill crews, and Exxon had theirs. Then all of a sudden DEC comes storming in with a ferryboat, a barge, a scow, and a bunch of fishing vessels. So there was some jostling for control. But we worked it out. We had to."

With a shortage of skimmers some oil still slipped under the boom or washed over the outer barriers. The mariner's instincts of the fishermen solved the problem. Much as a helmsman will angle his ship into waves instead of hitting them straight on, they redeployed their boom at an angle to the prevailing waves and current.

By mid-April the main body of the slick had been deflected from the hatcheries. However, patches of oil continued to appear, and the fishermen's hatchery association continued to protect the fingerling salmon with barriers of boom.

"If they were going to continue the defense of Sawmill Bay, they needed money," said Frank Iarossi, recalling the Sunday the association's president came to see him. "We had set up a ten-million-dollar fund in an Alaskan bank the previous Friday, but we had no checks. So I pulled out one of my business cards and wrote 'one million dollars' on the back. I walked in to meet the hatchery president, shook his hand, and said, 'This is my card. It's as good as my word.' I told him to come back and collect the one million dollars on Monday morning when the bank was open."

With the fishermen working twenty hours a day, the state providing logistical support, and Exxon paying the bills, the Koernig Hatchery and the three other hatcheries in the sound were saved. Exxon paid more than $100 per gallon for the 100,000 hard-won gallons of oil recovered. Meanwhile, however, well over 9 million gallons had swept through the sound. "There was no power on earth that could recover that oil once it had broken loose," Iarossi said.

CHAPTER SIX

SAVING the salmon hatcheries was a victory not only for the fishermen but also for the coast guard, Exxon, and the state of Alaska. However, that victory marked the end of their cooperation as an emergency response committee. Mistrust had begun to hamper the three-party command as it wrestled with complex and controversial decisions. While Kelso and Iarossi were trying to help save the hatcheries, the state and Exxon were already competing to secure the best lawyers, economists, and scientists, who would serve as witnesses for the legal battles that lay ahead.

"It's our very strong desire to settle all of the damage claims, without resorting to lawsuits," said Exxon president Bill Stevens. "But we have about a hundred and fifty lawsuits filed against us by individuals—primarily fishing interests. We had a preliminary hearing in Anchorage a couple of weeks ago. I'm told sixty-five law firms were represented. So the newspaper article about Alaska covered by a slick of lawyers is certainly true."

To diffuse the tension, Exxon began making partial claim payments, with the balance of the claims "to be determined later." This gave fishermen some money to pay immediate bills, and it gave Exxon time to decide what it defined as a legitimate claim. If a fishing season was lost to a community, it was clear that the fishermen deserved compensation. Exxon recognized a secondary impact among fishing-related businesses, such as canneries. However, the company was reluctant at first to acknowledge that cafés, bakeries, and day-care centers were also affected when the primary source of a town's income dried up. With the first hints of dissent, lawyers appeared.

"Frankly, I'm appalled at the way many of my colleagues are descending on this spill like vultures," said Anchorage attorney Paul Davis. "I think it is counterproductive for a fisherman, processor, or café owner to initiate litigation without trying negotiation first. But I'm afraid a lot of attorneys see Exxon as the big fish to fry, and they are scrambling to see who can get a pan over the fire first."

Melvin Belli, the flamboyant California lawyer, was one of many heavyweight attorneys to enter the fray. On behalf of fifteen Alaskan residents who depend on Prince William Sound's resources, and all others similarly injured, Belli filed a $20 billion class-action suit against Exxon, Alyeska, the Trans-Alaska Pipeline Liability Fund, and the state of Alaska.

Flurries of lawsuits created layers of overlapping litigation. Individuals, such as fishermen, who had suffered direct losses, would stand first in line for compensation. Next came participants in class-action suits, such as Melvin Belli's, which represented such groups as sport fishermen or tour-boat operators. Then there was the umbrella suit pressed by the state of Alaska that sought to cover losses to all Alaskans—and a suit by the federal government that extended that umbrella to cover the interests of all Americans.*

Virtually all losses that could be quantified were equated to dollars as potential damages. But establishing values for lost wildlife raised debate over such matters as the monetary value of a cormorant and what to pay for a puffin. If a sea otter is worth $20, is a seal worth more because it is bigger, or less because seals are more common? What's a sea lion worth? A whale? And how can a dollar value be placed on the loss of wilderness along hundreds of miles of coastal Alaska?

To help assess the wide-ranging environmental impacts of the oil spill, the Alaska Department of Fish and Game established a new Oil Spill Impact, Assessment, and Restoration Division. Its director, Greg Erickson, a petroleum economist by training, said, "Exxon seems to be saying, 'Sure, this is a regrettable disaster, but it's only temporary— nature is resilient and self-cleaning.' We expect the damage could be far more long lasting than Exxon may be willing to accept."

The litigation itself revolved around two questions: Who had been at fault, and whether there had been negligence regarding the spill and attempted cleanup.

"It looks as if Exxon is going to try to pin it all on [Third Mate] Cousins," said one attorney representing the state of Alaska. "We didn't even name Hazelwood and Cousins in our complaint, on the theory that they really aren't the responsible parties. They made mistakes, but obviously they can't pay us very much. There is always the chance for human error. However, the state sees the accident as something that was bound to happen because of the way the tankers were being operated. The crews were too small. The crewmen were often overworked and fatigued. Some of them weren't properly trained or licensed." The state sued not only Exxon and Alyeska but all the other owner companies that form the Alyeska consortium. This reasoning held that companies such as ARCO and British Petroleum were as responsible as Exxon for the failed response, and that British Petroleum, as majority owner, was perhaps most responsible for Alyeska's failure to contain the oil.

*The facts surrounding the grounding of the *Exxon Valdez*, the resulting oil spill, and subsequent cleanup efforts remain the subject of several state and federal lawsuits as this volume goes to press.—THE EDITORS

When the state filed its lawsuit against Exxon and Alyeska, Exxon countersued, charging that the state should pay much of the oil spill's costs because it had interfered with the use of dispersants. "The state knew, or should have known, that its vigorous and active opposition to the use of dispersants would cause the coast guard to delay granting permission for the use of dispersants," the complaint said.

In an interview in *Fortune* magazine, Exxon chief executive officer Lawrence Rawl claimed that had the use of dispersants been permitted, up to 50 percent of the oil could have been kept from ending up on the beaches.

"The facts are quite different from Exxon's fabrication," Commissioner Kelso insisted. "Exxon didn't have enough dispersant in Alaska to treat more than about nine percent of the spill. And they didn't have the equipment on hand to spray the huge amount that the Exxon chairman now claims they would have used. These statements are part of a deliberate disinformation campaign. Exxon's apparent strategy is to try and hide from the public the industry's disheveled state of unreadiness."

Amid the crossfire of accusations, it became apparent that both the state and Exxon were partially right. The effective use of dispersant was thwarted by two failures. There was not enough to handle a spill this size, and it was clear that if Exxon had been given prompt approval, use of its dispersant stock would have lessened the impact of the oil. As to how much the impact would have been reduced, the answer probably lay somewhere between Kelso's 9 percent and Rawl's 50 percent.

All the prevailing conditions—the decision-making paralysis, the infighting within the steering committee, the lawsuits and resulting confusion—emphasized the need for strong, clear leadership of the spill response. Someone had to give orders, direct the players. "What we need," said Frank Iarossi, "is a dictator."

"I'M HERE to take names and kick butts," said sixty-one-year-old Admiral Paul Yost, commander of the U.S. Coast Guard. He arrived in Valdez three weeks after the grounding and announced, "This spill is a war. And I intend to fight it like a war.

"The toughest part of this spill is to get everything started from a dead stop," said Admiral Yost, who had commanded a combat unit at the height of the Vietnam War. "There're ten million gallons of oil in the water. We have to try to move from ground zero with very little equipment up here. Very little capability. No communications."

Yost proceeded deftly, with a combination of tenacity and diplomacy. When he took over, Exxon and the Department of Environmental Conservation had been haggling for days over a cleanup plan. Yost correctly identified Exxon's central concern: that anything it offered to do at this point might be used against it later in the courtroom. To reassure Exxon, Yost set up a short review process by which the company could submit its proposed cleanup plan to state and federal agencies to get their approval on the record before proceeding. Less than twenty-four hours after his arrival in Valdez, Yost held Exxon's first detailed cleanup plan in his hands. With a showman's sense of timing he waved the plan in front of the television cameras. Exxon would have the oil cleaned up by September 15—nearly six months after the spill.

Given the unpredictable weather, unproven techniques, and logistical difficulties of supervising crews on remote islands, however, Yost himself had reservations about the September 15 completion date. Since the plan did not address the oil-fouled beaches outside Prince William Sound, Yost gave Exxon until May 1 to expand the plan.

Yost also faced a gyre of confusion that turned on the politics of science. Chemists, pathologists, veterinarians, biologists, oceanographers, anthropologists, archaeologists—many of each had set up shop in Valdez. And each had a different idea of what ought to be done.

"There we were, all working on a common goal—to mitigate the spill's effect—but getting tunnel vision, having our own agenda," said Larry Kiester, a scientist for the National Oceanic and Atmospheric Administration (NOAA). "Admiral Yost came in and cut right through the crap. He got everyone to wear the same baseball caps."

Rosanne Smith, a young public-radio reporter, accompanied Yost's task force to a beach-cleaning demonstration on Eleanor Island. "He went right to the heart of the problem," she said. "Yost was asked if he thought Exxon had enough men and equipment out there. Instead of rattling off the numbers of men, planes, boats, booms, blah, blah, blah, he said, 'Look, all of this equipment is new. It's never been tested under conditions like these before. A lot of this stuff has been jerry-rigged for this operation. I'd like to be able to stand here and tell the

American public that this is going to work, but I can't do that.'

"Everybody was asking Admiral Yost all these technical questions, and he just struck me as an interesting guy," Smith recalled. "So I asked him how old he was. And he must have loved a simple little question like that, because ignoring everyone else, he said, 'I'm sixty-one. How old are you?'

"It touched me," said Smith. "Here's this admiral up to his eyeballs in numbers and men and equipment, and President Bush, and God knows what else—and he was still able to take a moment just to get us to smile again in the middle of all that madness."

By week five of the spill, Yost had organized his troops. He left to oversee the spill's political front in Washington, D.C., turning over the day-to-day supervision to coast guard vice admiral Clyde E. Robbins, who would face a daunting task. The spill now covered 6000 square miles, an area roughly the size of Massachusetts. Oil was spreading in long reddish brown fingers, far out into the Gulf of Alaska. Oil was heading toward Resurrection Bay and the picturesque town of Seward. Oil was nearing Gore Point and the rich coastal waters of Kachemak Bay. Oil was sighted near Kodiak Island and the outer islands of Kenai Fjords National Park, areas with large populations of seals, sea lions, otters, and seabirds.

The war Admiral Yost had come to fight was now being waged on separate, far-flung fronts. Public relations battles were being fought in the press and at congressional hearings. Legal skirmishes were pitting fishermen against corporate lawyers, the state of Alaska against Exxon. And the oil was still flowing out of Prince William Sound, forever hitting new waters, beaches, and communities.

As he left Alaska for Washington, Admiral Yost gave his parting assessment: "There will be no miracles here."

CHAPTER SEVEN

"THERE are whole populations of birds endangered out there, and I can't save them all," said Jay Holcomb. Alyeska had called Holcomb, of the International Bird Rescue Research Center, to Alaska in the early hours of March 24 to rescue oiled birds. "On the other hand," he continued, "if we save one little puffin in Alaska, it will represent what people are concerned about, what the whole country is feeling."

Holcomb had become involved with distressed birds in 1971, when two oil tankers had collided under San Francisco's Golden Gate Bridge. Then a twenty-year-old student, he had seen pictures of oiled birds on TV and had rushed to San Francisco Bay to help save them. There he had met Alice Berkner, who was beginning to see a need for a worldwide organization to care for birds caught in oil spills. Her dream was eventually realized in the International Bird Rescue Research Center, based in Berkeley, California. Holcomb became involved.

The center would face the test of its life in Alaska, where the spring migrations were about to commence. In the few weeks following the spill, trumpeter and whistling swans and great flights of geese and ducks would be passing through the sound. More than thirty-five varieties of shorebirds—terns, plovers, and sandpipers—would funnel through before spreading out across Alaska. Puffins, cormorants, kittiwakes, auklets, oystercatchers, peregrine falcons, and others would remain in the sound in the path of the oil.

Realizing that the bird rescuers would face great difficulties, Holcomb brought along Jessica Porter, a veterinarian with a passion for helping wild creatures. At the time of the spill, Porter was running the Wolf Hollow Wildlife Rehabilitation Centre, in Friday Harbor, Washington, where she cared for an ever changing menagerie of injured animals.

"We flew over the spill our first morning in Valdez and were stunned by how much oil was out there," Porter said. "This spill was unlike any we had ever seen." Not only were Porter and Holcomb and the Alaskans they hired going to have to treat lots of oiled birds but they faced the problems of authority and responsibility that were plaguing so many aspects of the spill response. On other spills the U.S. Fish and Wildlife Service had always brought oiled birds to the cleaning centers. The bird rescue center people had cleaned them and decided when they were ready for release. Now Holcomb and Porter were told they would have to find the birds and bring them in.

Dr. Calvin Lensink, who before his retirement the previous November had worked for the U.S. Fish and Wildlife Service for thirty-three years, expressed dismay at its lack of involvement in the rescue efforts. Commenting on what he observed to be a gradual deterioration of the government's ability to protect wildlife, he said, "The Fish and Wildlife people were ready to go out to the sound, but they weren't being given the authority to go. The advice from Washington was that 'anything you do on the spill comes out of your own pocket.' And I'll be damned if I know why they have this attitude."

Dr. Lensink was far and away the agency's most experienced biologist on the spill. Though retired from the service, he went to Valdez as a volunteer. "I told Fish and Wildlife I'd just as soon not be on salary, so I could do what I thought had to be done the most," Lensink said. "And I didn't take the nice safe jobs, either. I took some of the nasty jobs. Working with dead animals is a nasty job."

While Dr. Lensink set up a makeshift lab to study dead birds, Jessica Porter and Jay Holcomb tried to find a way to rescue those still living. As Porter said, "All of a sudden we had to find boats and planes, organize an armada, get equipment, train people to catch birds. We knew nothing about Prince William Sound. Fish and Wildlife knew all the bays and coves, all the estuaries, currents, rivers, rookeries, and marshes. But they wouldn't help us. We felt isolated—adrift."

At this point the frustration was so great that Alice Berkner considered calling off their rescue efforts altogether. Jay Holcomb replied, "Alice, this spill is killing thousands of birds. Somebody has to go out there and try to get them."

"But we've never set up a program like this," Alice answered.

"I know how to catch birds," Holcomb said. "We'll have to find somebody who really knows the sound."

MEANWHILE, Kelly Weaverling, a long-haired and bearded Cordova bookseller who often dressed in a camouflage jacket and a baseball cap, was anxious to put his unusual skills to work. Since he was probably the only person who had walked every beach of Prince William Sound, he knew where the winter birds were, and where and when the migrants would arrive. When the spill hit, Weaverling had called friends in Valdez to say, "I want to help. Call me."

Weaverling's love for the mountains and the sea, which had drawn him to the sound, had been nurtured during childhood in California. "My mother's Cherokee, and she instilled in me her own great love of the outdoors," he said.

Weaverling came to Alaska in 1976. He spent his first summers guiding sea kayakers through Prince William Sound, and after he married, he and his wife, Susan, decided simply to live out there during the summer months. "We'll be out there from the first of May until the end of August, and always explore places we haven't seen before," Weaverling said. "I've kept notes and records of every beach I was on, every stretch of coastline I've paddled."

On the morning of March 29, five days after the grounding, somebody told Jay Holcomb about Kelly Weaverling, and Holcomb called the Cordova bookstore. "Weaverling, can you help us find and collect oiled birds?" he asked.

Weaverling immediately put out the call for bird-catching equipment. "People started bringing things in," he said. "They gave us their plastic travel kennels for cages, they brought in cardboard boxes. I said, 'I need dip nets,' and they brought me their dip nets. It all came together, just like that."

By nightfall Weaverling and some companions were headed from Cordova to Valdez with three boats. They arrived at 6:30 the next morning and roused the bird rescue people.

"Weaverling was real defensive toward us at first," Jessica Porter recalled. "He viewed us with suspicion because we were under contract to Exxon. But he could see that we wanted to save birds as much as he did."

Weaverling and his teams took off for Knight Island, which had been heavily hit with oil the night of the storm. Jay Holcomb went along to teach them how to catch the oiled birds. On the ride out Weaverling described what he and his wife loved about coming to the sound in spring. "We'd always try to get out there before the bird migration begins," he said. "Twenty million birds go by in a period of about two or three weeks—golden plovers, sandpipers, snow geese, swans, all kinds of ducks and small shorebirds. In early May we'd watch the songbirds arrive, see them select their territory, court and mate and gather nesting material. Later we'd watch their chicks, see them fledge, learn to fly, and feed themselves. And toward summer's end we'd see them fly away."

That's how Weaverling remembered the sound. But on the cold April evening when they tied up in Snug Harbor, oil was a foot and a half deep on the surface of the water. "It was grim," Weaverling said. "Dying animals were floating around. Dead animals. Just the worst. You can't tell what it's like from television or from a boat. You have to actually get on a beach and try to walk through the oil. You have to reach down into that oily water and pull out a bird."

"No matter where you went, it was black," Jay Holcomb added. "Kelly and I went onto this one beach where the oil was almost over the tops of our boots. We heard a noise. It was a big loon. All we could see was its head sticking up out of the oil. Its eyes were red, and it made that eerie loon call. I grabbed him and pulled him out of the sludge. He was just covered. Kelly just stood there in shock. Then he started to cry."

"We cried a lot," said Weaverling. "All of us did. You'd just have to stop and sit down. People would come up and say, 'We can't catch any more birds,' and they'd break out sobbing. It's just beyond imagination. Oil everywhere. Snow falling. Dead otters. Dead deer. Dead birds."

At first Weaverling's team of boats consisted of three salmon seiners, a charter halibut boat, and a boat with a low transom at the stern. The three seine boats leapfrogged their way down the shoreline of Knight Island, stopping at each beach to put people ashore. Several team members would cruise close to shore in another boat to pull birds from the water. At the end of the day, the crews would take the charter boat (their fastest vessel) on a night run to Valdez. There they would drop off the collected wildlife and head back out to start again in the morning.

As Weaverling's team brought oiled and injured seabirds into the Valdez bird center, Dr. Porter and her co-workers put them through the cleaning process. Before being cleaned, each bird was force-fed fluids to counteract dehydration. Then it was placed in bath after bath of warm water and detergent and gently scrubbed until the water was dirty—sometimes for more than ten washings. The last step was rinsing the feathers with a high-pressure hose.

"If you don't get all the soap out, you can have a very clean bird but one that won't float," Porter explained. "A bird floats because its feathers form a basket around its body. Once dry, we put the birds into a pool to see if they can float. We're not going to let a bird go if it can't float."

To begin their recovery, many birds had to overcome their instinctive urge to escape. Volunteers, talking quietly and moving slowly, placed injured birds in settings where visual stimuli had been minimized. "A few of the birds lie on their backs while we clean them," said Porter. "They're so relaxed it's almost as if they know it's going to be all right. But the common loons, which are huge birds with rapiers for beaks, always fight. I have wounds all over my hands."

After repeated washings and, in some cases, just forty-eight hours of intensive care, birds appeared ready to return to the sound. However, to release the birds was to risk their getting reoiled. Common sense suggested holding them until their environment was clean. But that might be a very long time, and every day the birds remained penned up increased their risk of dying from contagious diseases. One night ten of the fifty murres being held at the center suddenly died of a latent fungal disease, which had apparently been activated by the stress of captivity.

"Rather than risking an epidemic, we decided to release the surviving birds," said a Fish and Wildlife officer assigned to monitor bird rescue efforts in Valdez. "If nothing else, it was a real morale booster for the staff. The birds chirped on their way out into the sound, and the staff cheered 'em on."

But as oil spread beyond the sound, reports of dead seabirds and eagles began coming in, like news of fatalities from some distant war. Sheets of oil reached Montague Island, and the leading edge of the spill approached the murre and puffin rookeries on the seawalls of the Chiswells, at the outer reaches of Kenai Fjords National Park. To cope with the spread, Kelly Weaverling took out his map and sectioned off seven bird-capture areas. Each was larger than the state of Delaware, and each one needed its own team of bird search-and-capture boats.

In addition to finding vessels and crews, Weaverling had to broker their contracts with Exxon, a process that often tested his patience. "We've had eight different people in charge of Exxon operations in Cordova alone," he said. "They come up here in cowboy boots, with names like Skeeter and Bubba, and work here for a week or two, and then they're gone. We never see them again."

Jessica Porter shared Weaverling's frustration with Exxon. She said, "We didn't feel Exxon really wanted us here. Oh, some of their people were helpful, but mostly they just didn't seem to care about Alaska or the birds or other people trying to help.

"But the local people were absolutely fantastic to us," Porter added. "They came in and gave, even if it was just encouragement. And schoolkids wrote us letters: 'Don't worry. We know you are sad. Save as many birds as you can.' "

Meanwhile, oil began hitting the outer coast of the Kenai Peninsula, which made Seward the logical place for another bird rescue center. Jay Holcomb went there to organize it. On the way, he would stop at Cordova and Whittier to contract boats.

Holcomb flew to Cordova with Exxon's Tom Monahan, whose task it was to deal with the fishermen. "We got there and the fishermen came at us with death in their eyes," Holcomb said. "I tell you, it was scary. I wanted them to know I wasn't with Exxon. I told them, 'I'm the birdman. I save birds.' They let up on me but really bore down on Tom, hitting him with a lot of pent-up anger. Tom's a nice young guy. I kept saying, 'For God's sake, he didn't cause the spill.' But Tom couldn't even get a word out without somebody yelling at him."

Tom Monahan signed up a number of fishing boats to rescue birds. Then he and Holcomb headed for Whittier, where another group of fishermen was waiting for them. Holcomb recalled that as soon as they landed, a policeman showed up and said, "I'm giving you a ride. There's a guy in town who's got a gun and is screaming about Exxon. We want to protect you."

"This was so crazy," Holcomb said. "Tom didn't know what to say— the guy was in shock. Anyway, the cop rushed us into this meeting, and it was like being in a movie. Everyone had despair in their eyes. These people rely on fishing, and all of a sudden they can't fish.

"When they found out Exxon was hiring people to catch birds, they wanted a part of it," Holcomb explained. "At one point the big, burly guy who was leading the meeting leaned over and asked me, 'Did you know Crazy Joe's in town?' So I asked if the guy was really dangerous.

" 'Well, I'll tell you,' the big man said. 'While he's around, I ain't going out of this building with you.'

"At this point the mayor came in. She's kind of a rugged type who could obviously handle these guys. She said, 'Stay away from Crazy Joe. There's nothing we can do about him.'

" 'Well, if he has a gun, I guess I could arrest him,' the policeman said. 'But I don't know, he's kind of hard to deal with. You never know with Joe.'

"The police took us back to the helicopter," Holcomb said. "I thought for sure we were going to get a bullet, but we got out of there without running into Joe."

Monahan returned to the relative safety of Valdez, and Holcomb went on to Seward with his assistant to set up a bird rescue center there. After days of looking they found an empty warehouse on the outskirts of town. It was large but needed some work. Exxon was willing to pay for renovations and the rent. However, for the electricity to be hooked up, the building had to pass a code inspection, which the building's owner and the city had been fighting over for years.

"Guess who gets caught in the middle of it?" Holcomb said. "The birds. When oiled birds started showing up, we put them in boxes in our apartment. We had no place to wash them, and our kitchen smelled horrible." Then he told the Exxon supervisors that he was going to move some oily birds into *their* apartments—and the code problems cleared up. Renovation work began on the warehouse.

By April 16 it was ready to receive birds, and a group of volunteers was ready to help clean them. Then Rex Colter came to town. Colter was Exxon's new man in Seward, and before meeting Holcomb, or even returning his phone calls, he asserted his authority by cutting off the center's food and water.

"We're three days into this," Holcomb told Exxon's Seward office. "Our supplies have been stopped. We can't get any food for the birds. Tell Colter I'm looking for him."

That afternoon Holcomb saw a stranger on the street, a short man wearing cowboy boots. It was Rex Colter, and he demanded that Holcomb give him an organizational chart of his employees immediately.

"I've been looking for you," Holcomb said. "Our people can't eat. We don't have food for the birds. Our building's been shut down. Birds are dying. And you're telling me you want a goddamned list?"

Nevertheless, he got an organizational chart to Colter, who then restored food and water to the bird center. But next Colter went after the rescue fleet, which was headed by fisherwoman Linda Herrington. Since most of the birds were found in tidal rifts floating with oily kelp and driftwood, rescue crews were gathering up the debris along with the birds. Colter ordered them not to pick up the oily kelp. Holcomb spoke up for the rescuers. "They can't leave that stuff floating around to get another bird," he told Colter.

In defiance of Colter's order, Holcomb instructed the rescue fleet, "Go ahead and pick up the oily debris."

When Colter observed that the boats were still bringing in oily debris, he sent an assistant to see Holcomb. As Holcomb recalled, "This man handed me a letter and said, 'I want you to take care of this for me, okay, Bubba?' When he called me Bubba, I almost puked. His letter directed me to fire Linda Herrington because they had numerous complaints about her work.

"How can I fire Linda?" Holcomb asked Exxon's man. "She's great. She hasn't done anything wrong."

"Well, Bubba, just do it for me, will you?" said Exxon's man.

When Holcomb learned that Exxon was blaming Herrington for the picking up of oily debris, he made sure Exxon knew that it was he who had directed the fleet to defy Colter. But Exxon still persisted, and Holcomb began to suspect an underlying motive. "Then I realized that if they got rid of her, the whole fleet would fall apart," Holcomb said. "Exxon would save money, fewer birds would be found, and the spill would appear less devastating."

Holcomb stood his ground. "I'm not going to do it," he told Exxon. Eventually the order to fire Linda Herrington was rescinded, and she remained in command of the rescue fleet.

Later Holcomb reflected on how Exxon went to great lengths to fire some people, while lavishing money on others. "I've really learned a lot about greed up here, and it's been a rude awakening for me." Holcomb continued, "I think this is probably how Alaska was built. This oil spill is just another gold rush.

"I can't believe how rich some people got," Holcomb said. "One guy took a chance and bought a charter boat for a hundred and fifty thousand dollars. Exxon hired him. In four months he had made enough money to pay that boat off and buy another one."

CHAPTER EIGHT

"**K**NIGHT and Latouche islands are an eerie death zone," said Dr. Ken Hill, a young veterinarian from Cordova who concentrated his efforts on rescuing otters. "Oh, there are a few little niches out there where otters haven't been hit by oil. But the toxic effects go far beyond the slick. There are fumes, and there's oil in the food chain."

When otters arrived at the Valdez shelter, which was sharing space with the bird rescue operation, volunteers immediately scrubbed oil from the otters' fur. After an initial examination they were put into small, plastic airline-kennel cages, where handlers could watch over them. Many otters died within a few days. From colleagues who performed autopsies on them, Dr. Hill learned that many were suffering internal injuries. "Only a few of the hundreds brought in here are going to make it," Hill said. "And we are finding only a fraction of those that are dying."

The widespread death of sea otters occurred shortly after the species had staged a remarkable comeback from the edge of extinction. When Vitus Bering sailed to Alaska in 1728, otters had rolled in the waves from the Aleutian Islands down through the Pacific Northwest to Baja California. Then Russian fur traders had coerced Aleut natives into hunting the otters, which then numbered an estimated 200,000 in Alaska alone. By the time the Fur Seal Treaty afforded sea otters protection in 1911, only about 400 otters had remained in Alaska. Strictly enforced hunting bans enabled the species to recover in many areas. Before Good Friday, 1989, when the *Exxon Valdez* grounded, an estimated 10,000 otters had lived in Prince William Sound.

Unlike whales, seals, and other marine mammals that have insulating layers of fat, sea otters rely on their fur—long brown guard hairs and dense silvery underfur—to keep them warm in the frigid waters of the North Pacific. In the wake of the *Exxon Valdez* spill, their fur acted like a sponge, soaking up the oil. The otters' finely regulated buoyancy became imbalanced. Struggling to stay afloat, many otters crawled ashore. To keep from freezing to death, they needed to burn more calories, which meant eating two to three times their usual amount of food. However, to eat, the otters had to return to the sea, where they would be further chilled and were likely to be reoiled.

Kelly Weaverling found the otters easy to catch onshore because they were so preoccupied with trying to lick the oil from their fur. Normally otters groom themselves for hours each day to maintain the air that provides their fur both warmth and buoyancy. These unusually fastidious animals became frantic when oil clogged their fur, matting it into sticky clumps.

Weaverling had been instructed by the Fish and Wildlife Service to place each otter in its own cage. However, he was finding lots of oiled otters. "We opened up the hatch over the empty fishhold [in the boat] and turned the otters loose in there," Weaverling said. "They immediately bared their teeth and screeched. But after a few minutes they huddled together and began grooming each other."

Weaverling and his crews began sending their oiled otters to Valdez along with the birds they had rescued. But after three days he was told not to send any more otters, that the otter facility was full. "They had no place to receive the otters," Weaverling said after visiting the Valdez otter center. "They were just stacking them up in cages and kennels. Boxes of otters lined the hallways."

Directing otter rehabilitation was Dr. Randall Davis, a physiologist whom Exxon had called up from Sea World Research Institute, near San Diego. Kelly Weaverling found Davis as he was trying to talk with an assistant and two television newspeople at the same time. Commotion, ringing phones, reporters, and onlookers prevented them from talking, so Davis said, "Come on, I know a quiet place," and steered Weaverling into the men's restroom.

"He closed the door and locked it," Weaverling said. "This was the only way we could talk." Closeted in the men's room, Davis and Weaverling tried to figure out what to do with the growing number of otters collecting at the center. Davis mentioned the new Exxon-funded otter center that workers were scrambling to open in Valdez. There would be larger pens and a less hectic atmosphere. The center would be operational in a week and would be able to handle three times as many otters as the present site, being shared with the bird rescue team.

But Weaverling wasn't reassured. He explained that he had been sending in otters from just one team of three boats. Seven more teams of boats were now heading into the sound. By the time the new center opened, there would already be too many otters for it to handle. Davis agreed that another otter facility was needed, and urged Weaverling to start a new one if he could.

"I think Davis might have encouraged me because he underestimated me," Weaverling said. "To some people I may not appear very capable. I look kind of goofy, you know. I wear my hair long. I've got a beard. I don't have any business cards to pass out."

Nevertheless, with Davis' backing, Weaverling sought out Exxon spokesman Don Cornett for financial support. "I'll say this in Cornett's behalf," Weaverling said. "Once he found out there was a legitimate need, he was all for it."

A week earlier Kelly Weaverling had been running his bookstore, the Orca, on Cordova's main street, talking fish and philosophy over cups of coffee, and selling an occasional book. Now his extensive knowledge of the sound had thrust him into a position of leadership. "I might be more effective than some agency," Weaverling mused. "Bureaucracies can't move with much speed. Too many people have to be consulted. They have to fill out requisition forms, go through committees, do studies and tests. I can just walk next door and say, 'I need some lumber and this many guys with hammers. Let's meet two hours from now and start pounding nails.' "

After establishing the need for a new otter center in Cordova, Weaverling lined up a location, carpenters, and building materials in less than thirty-six hours. He instructed his foreman to "build an otter facility so we can get a couple of washing stations and holding pens operational right away."

However, since sea otters fell under the jurisdiction of the U.S. Fish and Wildlife Service, the agency had to approve the project first. "The only officials I could find to talk to were a couple of lower-echelon people," Weaverling said. "I told them the whole story. They took a few notes, and then they said, 'Wait here. We'll be right back.' "

When the officials returned four hours later, they agreed that a new otter facility was needed, but stated it had to be in Seward. "This went against the advice of otter experts out there in the field and my own experience," Weaverling said. "Maybe a center would be needed in Seward later, but we needed a second center in the sound right away."

"Then they dropped the sledgehammer," Weaverling added. "These Wildlife guys told me that my rescue boats had to 'cease and desist' from capturing otters. They said we were unauthorized, untrained, and not inspected by the Fish and Wildlife Service.

"I didn't know what to make of it," he continued. "Here it was the height of the otter rescue, and they had only four boats out there to cover more than a thousand square miles. I had another forty-four boats that could have been bringing in oiled otters.

"But the result has been self-fulfilling," Weaverling said. "By limiting the number of people bringing in otters, the Valdez facility wasn't going to overflow, and what little they were doing for wildlife didn't look so bad. Maybe they figured, Well, the otters would survive as a species, so why worry about saving a few individuals?"

In response one Fish and Wildlife Service official, who asked not to be identified, said, "In retrospect, we shouldn't have shut down Weaverling. We created a public relations disaster for ourselves. Here was a guy trying to save otters, and we stopped him."

Chuck Monnett and Lisa Rotterman, wildlife biologists who had studied sea otters for years, were also angry at the Fish and Wildlife Service for the unnecessary death of thousands of otters due to political and bureaucratic machinations. "We may see ten thousand otters threatened," Monnett said. "Nevertheless, Fish and Wildlife took the position that there wouldn't be any significant biological consequences, so no action was taken. It's as if the service's guideline for emergencies was to deny there *was* an emergency."

"We do have plans and guidelines to deal with emergencies, but this oil spill overwhelmed us," said Wally Soroka, a Fish and Wildlife enforcement officer in Anchorage. "We simply didn't have the personnel or equipment to handle a situation like this."

Funding for regulation enforcement is part of the problem. While the addition of new Alaska refuges since 1980 has more than doubled the size of the national refuge system, the Fish and Wildlife enforcement budgets have not been increased. There are more areas to protect, more recreational hunters, and more industrial activity, but the agency's enforcement capability remains geared to the "homesteader shoots a moose out of season" days.

Under the Bald Eagle Act and the Marine Mammal Act anyone causing the death of eagles or otters is subject to seizure of his vessel and/or cargo. However, Fish and Wildlife enforcement vessels in Alaska consist of one 12-foot inflatable raft and one canoe. "Imagine us paddling up to the *Exxon Valdez* and calling out, 'Hey, Hazelwood! Your boat's killed a lot of eagles and otters. So hand over the tanker and the rest of your oil,' " Soroka said.

Although not apprehended for killing otters, as a hunter might have been, Exxon paid for those needing treatment. To replicate their natural diet, they shipped fresh oysters, clams, mussels, and crabs—at a cost of $60 per day for each otter. In all, Exxon spent more than $20 million to treat 350 otters. The 220 otters that were saved cost Exxon $89,000 apiece.

These high costs raised the question of what an animal's life is worth. To some, every individual life was precious, and saving an otter's life was worth virtually any cost. On the other hand, some, such as Dr. Calvin Lensink, questioned the amount of money spent. "We have only so many resources we can expend," Lensink said. "If we start thinking in terms of individuals, we can waste all of our resources."

Nevertheless, as millions of American television viewers watched the cuddly-looking creatures struggle against the oil, sea otters became a symbol of the spill. Exxon, well aware that their investment would generate good publicity, continued to pay for otter centers and tons of fresh seafood. One result of Exxon's otter centers was a unique collaboration between one of the world's largest corporations and a group of volunteers. At the height of the oil spill, the Alaska governor's office received up to 2000 calls per day from people wanting to volunteer. "Literally thousands of people were calling from all over the world," said a woman who helped organize the volunteer hotline. "Not all of them could come to Alaska, but each wanted to do something to help. We were able to put several hundred volunteers in the field; many of them helped rescue birds and otters."

One volunteer was Suzanne Marinelli, who flew in from Hawaii in late May. In her home on the island of Kauai she had seen the television images of dying birds and otters day after day. She and her friends had discussed the spill at Sierra Club meetings. Then she saw the Sierra Club ad in *The New York Times* that read, "If you can help on the spill, then we need your help."

"I thought maybe I could make just a little difference," Marinelli said. "I decided I had to go. Sometimes you've just got to take a leap of faith."

When Marinelli and several friends arrived in Alaska, they were assigned to the Seward otter center. "Volunteers had come from all over the country—Minnesota, Colorado, New York, Texas, Florida— lots of them from the West Coast states. We worked alongside people from Australia, Germany, Switzerland, and China too."

Many of the volunteers lived in tents down by the beach. Marinelli and her friends, who had gone into debt in order to help the otters, received some help themselves from schoolchildren in Nottingham, New Hampshire, who raised several hundred dollars from bake sales and washing cars.

"My job was taking care of twelve otters," Marinelli said. "Being a mom, I wanted to make each of these little hurt beings feel better. You know, they are a lot like kids. Some liked squid. Others wanted shrimp and clams. Some wouldn't eat their haddock. Some ate out of their bowls and some dipped their food in the water."

The otters were fed five times a day. All otter food had to be lightly iced and kept for no more than four hours. Crushed ice or snow had to be available at all times. Volunteers meticulously recorded the type and amount of all food consumed, and monitored such behavior as appetite, sleeping, grooming, vocalization, and swimming.

Tom McCloskey, manager of the Seward center, cautioned volunteers not to form close attachments. "When looking into a cage, move slowly and avoid direct eye contact. Avoid 'imprinting' between you and the otters. The otters are wild animals and must remain so. If they place too much trust in us, it will reduce their chance to return to the wild successfully."

By October young otters that had not learned how to survive in the wild were sent to zoos. Most of the others were returned to the sound, where the otter count was expected to restore itself in five to ten years.

THE wildlife rescue effort was the beginning of the healing process for many of the humans involved. Individuals who took part were both restoring the sound and reaffirming that wild creatures had to be protected. But their participation yielded new insight and a deepened commitment as well. Marinelli recalled, "One day I heard a young man singing, 'Forgiving won't come easy in Prince William Sound,' and that line really stayed with me, because if we are going to heal ourselves, we must forgive. I've seen a lot of heartbroken people," Marinelli said. "But our memories are short. Everyone's hurting over the spilled oil now. But in a year, five years? It's the limit of our memory that frightens me. If we don't remember what happened in Prince William Sound, it will happen again."

"WHEN the spill first happened, nobody was thinking about eagles. Everybody was talking seabirds and otters. Then all of a sudden we started to find dead or wounded eagles," said Anchorage veterinarian James Scott. "People started saying, 'Something has to be done. This is our national symbol.' "

With more than 2000 bald eagles Prince William Sound is one of the few places where the outstretched wings of these great birds gliding on the wind have remained a common sight. One often sees a bald eagle high in a weathered tree, waiting for the tide to turn. The bird slowly spreads those huge wings, lifts lightly into the air, wheels, and then circles over the sea. Wings suddenly fold. The eagle dives and hits the water. With a fish clutched in its powerful talons, it rises into the sky.

To many Native Americans an eagle rising into the sky links heaven and earth. "Seeing an eagle lying in that oil makes me physically ill," said Maria Williams, a Tlingit woman. "Some people say, 'Oh, don't worry. They're not all dead; they'll come back.' That makes me furious. The death of an eagle is like the death of a friend. A part of me dies with each one of those birds."

Eagles whose feathers were oiled lost their ability to fly and often crippled themselves lurching into rocks or trees. Those that became completely flightless were easy prey for bears and foxes. Those escaping that fate eventually starved to death or were poisoned by contaminated carrion.

By June, fifty-three dead bald eagles had been recovered from Prince William Sound. "The loss of adult bald eagles is a greater tragedy than poor reproduction in a season," said Dr. Scott, who treats eagles and other wild creatures at his veterinary clinic. "Only five to seven percent of young eagles make it to adulthood. When adult eagles are killed, it takes many years for the population to reestablish itself. Eagles face a very hard winter every year, and after going through a summer like this, a lot of them aren't going to make it."

Scott organized eagle rescue efforts from his Arctic Animal Hospital, in Anchorage, where books, letters, reports, and tools spill over every shelf and counter in his office. In twenty-nine years of practice he has treated moose, bear cubs, seals, otters, owls, hawks, and a host of other wild creatures, in addition to the regular flow of puppies, cats, parrots, rabbits, and guinea pigs. "We once raised a baby moose in the backyard," Scott said. "And when our kids were little, they had a bear cub in their bedroom."

By early May, the first eagles had arrived at his clinic—Big Female and One-Wing. In their brilliant yellow eyes, the thin, dark pupils remained attentive to every movement near their pen.

"Old One-Wing, what an eagle!" Scott said admiringly. "He ate some oiled birds and became disoriented. He flew into a rock and broke a wing. It had to be amputated. But what a fighter—the epitome of what we want for a symbol, and the kind of eagle we want out there breeding. Now he's going to spend the rest of his life in captivity."

In the operating room, lights were dimmed to calm an immature bald eagle lying on the table. With its head hooded, the young eagle was fighting the anesthesia-induced drowsiness. Its wings were wrapped in layers of reddened gauze, and its long flight feathers were tarred with oil. After cutting away some gauze, Dr. Scott used tweezers to clean the raw skin on a wing. Then he lifted and flexed the bird's toes. "There's plenty of blood in there," he said. "His feet are stiff, but warm. He's got some swelling."

A young assistant took the eagle's foot in her hand and carefully massaged each toe. "This is only the second time I've worked with him," she said. "He's doing much better."

As the number of oiled eagles increased, Exxon asked Dr. Scott for advice on setting up an eagle rescue center. "I figured out what was needed," Scott said. "Judging by the number of injured and oiled eagles reported, we were going to have to handle two hundred to three hundred eagles. We would have to have a long-term-care facility, both to heal the eagles and to hold them until their habitat was safe for their return. Scott believed that badly oiled eagles needed to be held in captivity until they molted and grew new feathers, which usually takes a year, at a cost of approximately $7500 per bird.

To stretch available funding Scott sought volunteer help to build fly pens for the injured eagles. "The pens were built by the most wonderful set of volunteers you've ever seen in your life," he said. "With a dozen of them we built the best raptor-holding facility I've ever seen. Housewives had paintbrushes in their hands, and a colonel from the air force base was pounding nails.

"But we ran into a wall," Scott said. "I think Exxon was willing to pay whatever it had to. But when it comes to eagles, Exxon is going to do what the Fish and Wildlife Service says. And they said, 'We don't want a facility for more than twenty eagles.'

"I told them that wasn't enough. But I think word came down from Washington, D.C., that twenty oiled eagles were the maximum number expected, and that's all we had to be prepared for. It was outrageous."

Dr. Scott was mystified at how agency people sitting in their Washington offices could predetermine how many eagles would need treatment. Nevertheless, under his agreement with the Fish and Wildlife

Service and with Exxon he readied his new eagle facility to receive oiled and injured birds. Then Fish and Wildlife informed him that they had decided it was best to do just an initial exam in the field, take a blood sample or two, and turn the eagles loose.

"It was just what Exxon wanted to hear," Scott fumed. "It would cost less. I knew it was the wrong decision. I get regular reports that there are eagles dying out there on the sound. Oil had gotten down in the rocks and sand. It's killing the ecosystem, just as if you poured poison out there.

"I told Fish and Wildlife that if they insisted on this quick release, they should at least have the eagles examined by a veterinarian," Scott said. "We had more than two hundred young veterinarians volunteering to fly to Alaska at their own expense to help. I mailed the list to Fish and Wildlife and it was 'lost.' I sent it again, and it was misplaced a second time. The third time, I hand-delivered the names of vets who wanted to help, along with a list of essential things to be done.

"Before you turn an eagle loose, you need to know if it is fit," Scott went on. "Are its eyes clear? Its wings? Remember, we are talking about our national symbol. There are people in the Lower Forty-eight who drive hundreds of miles to see an eagle."

Dr. Pat Redig, widely respected as the most knowledgeable raptor biologist in the world, echoed Scott's frustration. "I think Scott's treatment program is a sound one," he said, "and I'm disappointed it wasn't used more. There are going to be more oil spills, and we need to know as much as we can about the effects of oil on eagles. Basically, we have been deprived of this opportunity."

"In the context of all the eagles in Alaska, the loss is not devastating," said Phil Schimph, a Fish and Wildlife Service biologist. "On the other hand, we know of more dead eagles here than many states have eagles altogether. We've made a mess, and it's going to take a long time to set it right, if we ever can. I expect it will take five years or more for the Prince William Sound eagles to rebound."

But Dr. James Scott remains incensed. "At first I expected the Fish and Wildlife people to do everything in their power to protect wildlife, but I came to realize they have other priorities," he said. "They are mandated to take care of wildlife. It's easy for them to say, 'Well, we have a whole lot of eagles, so losing a few won't hurt that much.' But eagles died. And a lot of those birds died because of bureaucracy."

CHAPTER NINE

A s the wildlife rescue efforts were mounted, oil continued to stream through Prince William Sound and along the outer Kenai coast toward Katmai and Kodiak. The death of otters and birds was only one of many effects of the oil on the coastline, each stretch of which had its own distinct physical characteristics and ecosystems.

"We have all seen the heartbreaking images of dead or dying wildlife. But oil contamination also affects fish and wildlife in other less obvious ways," cautioned Frank Rue, director of habitat for Alaska's Department of Fish and Game. "Oil's toxicity lowers resistance to disease, reduces reproductive success, inhibits normal growth and development, and interrupts normal biochemical processes. Long after most of the obvious signs of the spill have disappeared, these subtle, complex effects can prove lethal to animals.

"Shoreline cleanup is not an easy task," Rue said. "In places, oil has penetrated four feet into beach sediments. It will go deeper, becoming more inaccessible to surface cleaning methods. But we can't throw manpower and equipment at it without regard for wildlife and its habitat," Rue continued. "Cleanup techniques must be thoroughly tested to avoid additional mortalities. Cleanup crews must minimize their disturbance of animals."

Exxon's extended shoreline-cleanup program began on April 4. That morning, at 5:30 a.m. local time, Otto Harrison, then managing production for Exxon-affiliated Esso in Australia, received a phone call from Exxon. "They asked would I come to Alaska, and I said yes. I did my income taxes that night and flew out the next day," Harrison recalled. He was soon to replace Iarossi as director of Exxon's cleanup.

When Harrison arrived in Alaska, coast guard admiral Edward Nelson and Frank Iarossi were trying to rescue the spill response from the morass of indecision and committee meetings. To that end, the two discussed investing the coast guard with authority to direct the cleanup. "We had an agreement drawn up and we were going to sign it," Nelson said. "At this point Frank thought he was going to be relieved, so he and I hashed out [the agreement] until we were pretty happy with it. But then these other guys from Exxon came in. Otto Harrison wanted to change a word here, a little bit there. I thought they were petty, but I said, 'We need to formalize it. Let's do it.' "

By this time Ulysses LeGrange, senior vice president of Exxon U.S.A. and Iarossi's boss, had flown to Valdez, and he too reviewed the agreement. Remarked Admiral Nelson, "I couldn't get this dog-gone agreement from LeGrange. He said their attorneys back there on the East Coast had to approve the coast guard and Exxon working together. They were clearly playing games.

"I never lost my respect for Frank Iarossi," Nelson continued. "He stayed with that ship and kept the other million barrels of oil from getting in the water. My problem was that I didn't think Exxon was bringing in the right people to run this thing. There was no coherent direction. It was an absolute zoo."

In April, Admiral Nelson survived an apparently stress-induced heart attack and retired from active service. It was then that coast guard admiral Paul Yost came to Valdez to hammer out the first of many cleanup agreements and designated Vice Admiral Clyde E. Robbins the on-scene coordinator. And it was then, after the lightering and refloating of the *Exxon Valdez*, that Frank Iarossi was sent back to Houston.

"I felt bad about leaving," Iarossi said. "I didn't want to walk away, because the job wasn't finished." This changing of the guard was reportedly to give Iarossi relief from the high-stress situation and time to prepare for hearings about the spill. However, Exxon may have wanted to bring in someone who hadn't been emotionally involved since the early days of the spill and who would therefore be more disposed to take a tough company stand during the long, liability-laden cleanup ahead.

When Iarossi left Alaska in mid-April, Otto Harrison settled into his job of directing Exxon's cleanup. By April 14, three weeks after the spill, the coast guard had approved Exxon's initial cleanup plan. However, as would happen time and again, the spreading oil was rendering the plan obsolete, and Harrison found himself continually revising to catch up.

Exxon's first step was to dispatch a Shoreline Cleanup Assessment Team (SCAT). There were two members of this original SCAT team: an archaeologist and a biologist. According to plan, they landed on

Left, a cleanup worker's hand reveals the oily sludge that soiled miles of shoreline.

Bathtime for a sea otter, right, at the Valdez otter center

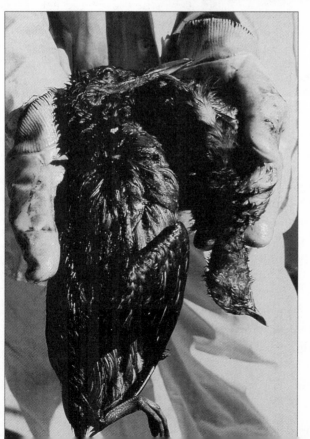

A wildlife rescue worker arrived too late to save the oil-coated seabirds at left, some of many hundreds that were casualties of the spill.

The effort to clean beaches that had been covered by the oil included laboriously wiping individual rocks with absorbent pads, as shown at left.

Right, bags of oily debris await removal from Kenai Peninsula. Below, workers with high-pressure hoses attack a badly damaged beach.

Naked Island three hours before the first cleanup crews and divided the beach into segments, noting significant amounts of oil. Then they developed cleaning guidelines for the crews.

Exxon added a geomorphologist to the SCAT team, and eventually contracted enough professionals to form seven teams of three. As the elaborate system of surveys, recommendations, and procedures evolved, the SCAT team's field findings were no longer passed directly on to crews on the beaches. Instead, they were sent to Exxon's command center, in Valdez, where they were shaped into recommendations. These, in turn, were passed to interagency shoreline-cleanup committees—composed of representatives from such agencies as DEC, state parks, and the U.S. Forest Service—who reviewed and modified them, and passed them on to the coast guard. After coast guard review, the recommendations were returned to Exxon as approved plans of action.

By the end of April all of Exxon's crews had cleaned less than two miles of beach. A revised plan issued on May 8 called for the cleaning of 364 miles of shoreline. But tension developed between Harrison and DEC over Exxon's objective "to environmentally stabilize" beaches rather than actually clean them. "We are not removing all the oil," Harrison said in his good-old-boy Texas drawl, "but removing enough so the environment can stabilize and restore itself."

DEC continued to argue for a more thorough cleanup. Meanwhile, Exxon worked with the coast guard to refine and update the May 8 cleanup plan. Exxon U.S.A. president Bill Stevens said, "Specific milestones have been set for shoreline cleanup, which has commenced and is expected to be completed by mid-September." By June a revision of the May 8 plan expanded the cleanup to more than 700 miles of shoreline, and divided the spill into sectors: Valdez-Cordova, Seward, Homer, and Kodiak.

The oil now extended over more than 10,000 square miles, an area so large that flying around it in a small plane would take all day.

IN ACCORDANCE with its revised plan, Exxon delegated much of the shoreline cleaning to VECO, a private contractor that had served the oil industry in Alaska for years and had earned a reputation for fighting environmental regulations. "VECO is basically a construction outfit servicing the oil-and-gas industry," said Bill Luria, a former planning director for the city of Anchorage. "That's how they got rich and famous." Now VECO was running an intensive high-tech cleanup along hundreds of miles of the nation's most remote and ecologically rich shoreline.

VECO drew its workers from a core of transient laborers, out-of-work plumbers and carpenters, secretaries, college students, housewives, and people from small villages. After running recruits through a two-hour safety course, VECO dispatched them to scrub oil from rocks with large paper towels, hose down cliffs with high-pressure nozzles, rake beaches, or bag dead animals and debris. Crews worked from a flotilla of skiffs, fishing boats, yachts, coast guard clippers—and even an old navy warship.

"We were there to be on-site advisers," said Bill Luria of the participants in the environmental monitoring program he helped organize to guide VECO's cleanup efforts. "We hired about eighteen pretty good people—biologists, science types, technically trained people. And when they got into the field, they saw a lot of things happen that just weren't right. For example, VECO crews were using diesel fuel to wash the rocks. Sure, diesel is a solvent, but it's mighty toxic too. Our field people were telling the VECO supervisors, 'Hey, this ain't right, so don't do it.' And VECO got ticked off. They began telling our field people to just document the good stuff.

"The VECO supervisors wanted to review everything our people wrote. If something looked bad on one of our reports, they'd say, 'You can't put that in. Give me that piece of paper.' We either had to put down what they wanted or get canned. They fired fifteen people, including myself, in one day. Essentially VECO made the decision to can the whole environmental monitoring program."

"I found oiled birds while cleaning up the beach," one VECO worker reported, "and my supervisor told me to hide them in oil bags—that Exxon did not need the publicity."

In another incident, journalists were impressed with a beach that had been "cleaned," until a young man working for VECO pushed the nozzle of his pressurized hose a foot into the gravel. Oil gurgled up.

"After those reporters left, a VECO foreman grabbed the kid," said the young man's uncle. "They twisted his arm and said, 'What the hell do you think you're doing? We don't need this kind of crap around here. You're fired!' "

Here again consequences of the convoluted chain of authority were unfolding. Because the government maintained its stance as monitor only, the cleaning of hundreds of miles of sensitive, pristine shoreline had been delegated to a company that showed gross disregard for both the local people and the environment.

"As far as actual authority over the cleanup, I have none, unless I take over the spill," Vice Admiral Clyde E. Robbins said. "My only hope is to get Exxon to do what I want through jawboning and coercion."

Even so, Robbins had his hands full. He became the mediator between Exxon and the state of Alaska, which began disagreeing on almost everything—from which beaches needed cleaning to which cleanup methods would be used. Robbins remarked that in the future "we have to make sure that the spiller is not in charge of deciding how much work to do, how long to do it, or even how to do it."

A VECO supervisor, who asked not to be identified, agreed. "What we really need is a professional oil spill cleanup company, like a fire department that's on twenty-four-hour call."

WHILE debates about shoreline cleanup raged on, an unexpected source of potential help arrived in the form of oil-eating bacteria.

Oceanographers at Alaska's Institute of Marine Science found an abundance of oil-eating microbes in Prince William Sound. The possibility arose that they could serve the cleanup effort in a process termed bioremediation. However, it was by no means clear that they would consume North Slope crude. After the spill, the federal EPA committed $5 million to assess the oil-eating ability of the bacteria. "It's based on good, sound science," said EPA administrator William Reilly. "They are native Alaskan bugs. It's all local hire."

EPA researchers found that oil-eating microbes run short of phosphorus and nitrogen, so on the EPA's recommendation Exxon ordered a dietary supplement of 500 metric tons of fertilizer from France. Exxon's plan was to fertilize up to 700 miles of Alaskan beaches to encourage the bacteria to eat their way through the oil. But some scientists questioned this rush to stimulate oil-eating microbes with fertilizer, concerned that it might also stimulate other parts of the microbial population. No one was certain, either, how effectively the fertilized bioremediation process would clean the shorelines. Dr.

Jacqueline Michel, of NOAA, explained that the microbes "eat the easy stuff first, leaving the asphalt and waxes—the black residue that's going to stay behind." Nevertheless, Exxon continued to view bioremediation as one of its most promising means of dislodging the oil and went on to spread great quantities of fertilizer.

IN MID-JULY, Congressman Wayne Owens, from Utah, visited Alaska to see for himself whether beach cleanup might actually be counter-productive. At a May 6 congressional field hearing in Valdez, Owens had heard rumors that Exxon's high-pressure hoses and army of workers were doing more harm than good. He decided to see for himself, and returned to Alaska in July, slipping in unannounced. For a guide and boatman he chose Kelly Weaverling.

"He's a politician, so he's somewhat suspect, you know," Weaverling said later. "A lot of them are junketeers. They don't really listen. But Owens was genuinely concerned.

"So we went out and poked around. Surprised a few people," Weaverling recalled. "Here's Owens—clean-shaven, wears glasses, short hair, dressed like a fisherman. A pretty average looking guy. No one knew who he was. We'd mosey up to a beach-cleaning crew and watch them blasting everything from barnacles to limpets with jets of water," Weaverling said. "Owens started seeing some of the things I'd already found on the beaches—graffiti scratched on rocks, orange peels, cigarette butts, oily gloves."

At some locations, they found barges equipped with oil-fired burners that heated 100 gallons of seawater to 160 degrees in one minute. The steaming water was then shot at oil-covered rocks at a pressure of 80 pounds per square inch. The blasting did dislodge oil, but it also exterminated virtually all the living organisms it struck.

When he returned to Washington, D.C., Congressman Owens, now clad in a suit and tie, spoke to Bill Stevens, president of Exxon U.S.A. "In Northwest Bay, on Eleanor Island, where I visited ten days ago, you have four hundred to five hundred people in thirty-five to forty-five vessels," Owens said. "Unannounced, I talked to your foreman there, after having reviewed a lot of what's going on with all of those high-pressure water hoses. And I said to him, 'How much oil are you collecting here with this massive operation?'

"His answer was seven barrels of oil a day," Owens said. "I am convinced, quite frankly, that those operations, though well intended, are doing more damage than good."

While debate on cleanup methods ensued, time and the weather were having their own effects on the oil. As it weathered, it became thick, tarry, and, when the weather cooled,. tacky to the touch. Warmed by the sun, it would soften and become stickier. Oil penetrating the beach surface remained fluid longer, and it drained down between rocks and permeated the fine sands. Oil in this form might seep into the marine environment for years. There appeared to be only one way to remove oil from beach substrata: to wash every cobble and nubbin of gravel, every grain of sand.

Too often the cleanup effort appeared to be driven more by public relations strategies than by scientific considerations. Vice President Dan Quayle's brief visit was typical of what Associated Press writer Paul Jenkins described as Exxon's "daily dog and pony show." Quayle helicoptered onto Smith Island's north shore, where he observed hundreds of Exxon workers flushing thick crude from the beach. Quayle walked the beach on a hastily constructed boardwalk so he wouldn't slip in the oil, sprayed oil-coated rocks for a few minutes, and then left for a press conference, where he said, "I have a very good feel for what's going on."

Two days later Paul Jenkins inspected the same beach and found it empty, but still covered with oil. The army of Exxon cleanup workers had vanished. "All that was left of the cleanup effort were some booms and stacks of orange plastic garbage bags," Jenkins reported.

One Exxon cleanup strategist, who asked not to be identified, acknowledged that for Exxon "the actual recovery of oil and the money spent became secondary to its public image." This official said that by early June, Exxon felt the cleanup had "hit a point of diminishing returns. But quitting was not politically acceptable. Cleaning may have been causing more destruction than leaving the oil. But anytime Exxon voiced that, DEC would say, 'Oh, Exxon is just trying to get out of their responsibility.' Sometimes the truth is not publicly acceptable."

In any event, by the September 15 deadline, Exxon had spent well over $1 billion to treat 700 miles of beach, but there was no consensus on the results.

"Yes, there are still some shorelines that have some oil on them. But

I find the progress very remarkable," said Exxon's Bill Stevens. However, neither Stevens nor anyone else at Exxon would commit to further cleanup work in the spring. They said they would wait to see what the beaches looked like and to hear what the coast guard had to say. Exxon's commitment to complete the shoreline cleanup finally rested on the words of oil pollution expert Dr. John Farrington. "It all comes down to this. How clean is clean? And who decides what is clean?"

PUBLIC relations efforts can alter reality just so far, and Exxon still had to deal with the observers' judgments of how clean they were actually getting the shoreline. In the Valdez press conferences immediately after the spill, Frank Iarossi had said, "We are going to clean it up if it takes months, many months." Three days later Exxon spokesman Don Cornett said that "We are going to pick up, one way or another, all the oil that's out there."

At Exxon's annual meeting on May 18, CEO Lawrence Rawl had assured shareholders that Exxon would clean the shorelines and that "our objective is to complete the job by mid-September." However, later in May "completing the job" had come to mean not cleaning, but "treating" the beaches.

Rawl had also assured Exxon shareholders and the public that Exxon was committed to returning the next spring to finish the cleanup. However, Exxon's embattled executives were feeling a great need to get this nightmare behind them. As management they had to consider the interests of their stockholders. They had come to realize that no amount of money could make the beaches as clean as they had been before March 24, 1989. They were looking for a way to cut off the hemorrhage of funds.

On July 19 Exxon's commitment to "finish the job" was thrown into doubt by a memo written by Exxon's cleanup chief, Otto Harrison. The terse memo informed Exxon managers that the company's "only commitment for the spring of 1990 is to survey the shorelines." It said that Exxon alone would select the dates for curtailing cleanup operations.

DEC commissioner Dennis Kelso responded that the most important thing to the state was Exxon's commitment to continue the work. He charged that the Harrison memo "breaches the promises the company made to Alaskans and the country. This is outrageous and totally unacceptable."

To ascertain Exxon's intentions, California Congressman George Miller called a congressional hearing on July 28. "We want you to know that we will not be satisfied until the cleanup is complete," Miller told Exxon U.S.A.'s president, Bill Stevens. "That's the kind of assurance that we heard from you when we were in Alaska earlier this year. Then along comes the Harrison memo, which suggests that Exxon is now going to take a series of unilateral steps." The most alarming implication of the memo, Miller stated, was that Exxon was "only going to come back in the spring for the purpose of a survey."

As a reply to Miller, Bill Stevens said, "The wording in Mr. Harrison's memo was unfortunate, and he would be the first to say so, were he here. He doesn't take a lot of time to carefully word memos, but more importantly, what we're doing every day, in terms of the operation up there, would say that we will follow through."

However, that same week Exxon Corporation president Lee Raymond, who was considerably above Stevens in Exxon's hierarchy, said, "Well, I don't know if we'll be back next spring. There has to be an end to this. And no matter when we say there has to be an end, we're going to have an argument about it." Raymond made it clear that if the coast guard made unreasonable requests for further cleanup, Exxon would not come back. "I can tell you right now," he said, "that even if there's something to be done next year, we're not going to have ten thousand people working on the thing."

DEC commissioner Kelso said in the first week of August, "There is still too much oil on shorelines where even the gross removal has been completed. As a practical matter, it may well be that the question is not, How clean is clean? but rather, At what point do you have to make the practical decision that you can't get sufficient recovery of oil any longer?"

Nevertheless, the state was able to make a clear, unequivocal determination of how clean is clean for Alaska fishermen. To protect fish products from oil contamination, and also to protect the perceived quality of Alaska's seafood products, the state initiated a zero-tolerance policy: if any oil was sighted in a fishing district, that district would be closed.

"Zero tolerance is a marketing decision, not an environmental decision," charged Otto Harrison. He considered this state policy a public relations ploy to protect the image of Alaska's fish products. Zero tolerance was closing tens of millions of dollars' worth of fisheries in areas where only small amounts of oil were found. In each of these areas, claims would be made against Exxon for lost seasons.

At a meeting in Valdez, a fisherman from Ketchikan challenged Harrison. "The state's salmon industry was almost crippled a few years ago because of a few contaminated cans that led to a botulism scare. There's no way that the state or the fishermen are going to let that happen again because one or two salmon get on the market tainted by oil."

The state's zero-tolerance policy was designed to protect the fishing industry, but the state failed to establish equally clear and decisive standards for the overall cleanup of Alaska's coastline. Commissioner Kelso attributed this to the state's lack of authority. However, Patti Saunders, an environmental lawyer not affiliated with any of the oil spill litigants, charged that "the state was simply afraid to direct Exxon through a series of compliance orders. It's outrageous that we had to sit around and wait for Exxon to agree to do things. Dennis Kelso has put himself in a position where he can play being Mr. Rough Tough. He says all this stuff in the press, but he doesn't do anything about it. The state was pulling its punches because of the legal ramifications. The state knew that if it began directing the cleanup, Exxon could come back with a counterclaim." It could claim interference and thereby reduce its liability for damages.

Still, even the staunchest environmentalists, including Patti Saunders, agreed that further cleaning should not be required if it caused more harm than good. With a sense of resignation Alaska's governor Cowper said he feared that "there will come a time when Exxon and the state of Alaska and the federal government, all three of us, are going to have to go to the public and say, 'Everything that can be done has been done. It's still a mess. But we can't clean it up anymore.' "

Remarked Dr. Jacqueline Michel, of NOAA, "Exxon did a good job. Better, I think, than anybody else in the world could have done. At times [Exxon's people] felt that they weren't getting that much oil removed from the beaches, but they kept going. Eventually this oil will break down and go away. It's not something like PCBs or DDT, which accumulate through the food chain. Prince William Sound is going to recover. The sound was pristine, and now it's going to have oil on it. Oil won't be everywhere. There are going to be some problems, but it's not the end of the world."

However, many Alaskans felt that a part of the world they loved had indeed come to an end. Don Moore, city manager of Cordova, said, "Prince William Sound was one of the two most beautiful places on earth. I leave it to each of you individually to decide what the other one is. We all have a special Shangri-la in our hearts and minds. Think of yours when you contemplate what happened to ours."

CHAPTER TEN

IN THE series of communities that were impacted as the oil spread along the coast, Valdez was, of course, ground zero. And although prevailing currents carried the oil away from Valdez, the town was immediately inundated by an influx of divers, oil recovery specialists, biologists, bureaucrats, reporters, and television crews. Within a week its population had swelled from 2300 to more than 5000. Hotel rooms that had gone for $45 a night sold out at $100. All the rental cars were taken. Phone lines were jammed. The sleepy Valdez airport, which normally handled about a dozen flights a day, averaged 300 to 400 a day, reaching a peak of 687 flights on March 30.

"This means millions for us," said a Valdez cabdriver whose pay tripled after the spill. Gas stations, motels, cafés, bars, and liquor stores reported doubling or tripling their normal income. However, as soon as Exxon began hiring oil spill workers at $16.69 an hour, local businesses started losing employees and had a hard time replacing them.

The flow of Exxon's cleanup money into Valdez sent the town's economy reeling. Apartment rents rose by as much as $500 a month, causing hardships for many residents. In contrast, some kids on their first job made $35,000 scrubbing beaches over the summer—more than some of their parents made all year. And one young man who leased his skiff to Exxon, along with his services as a skipper, earned $700,000 by the end of the summer.

By mid-April a second wave of immigrants began arriving in Valdez, drawn by the millions of dollars Exxon was spending on the cleanup. Men with tattoos, battered cowboy hats, and a week's worth of stubble on their faces milled about on the sidewalks and around the hiring hall. Some drove pickup trucks to town, some hitchhiked in. Bars and camper parks overflowed.

At the peak of the summer's frenzied spill response, the population of Valdez reached 12,000, more than five times its original size. The townspeople feared outbreaks of disease among the tightly packed campers and squatters. They feared the infiltration of drug dealers, and they watched the rate of serious crime rise 300 percent. City Manager Doug Griffen said, "We're fearful that there are a lot of crazies coming in. One guy, drawing a gun, almost got the drop on one of our cops. That doesn't usually happen around here."

Alyeska and Exxon came to fear vandals and assassins even more than the press. Exxon stationed security guards wherever its employees worked or lived. "The rent-a-cops aggravated us no end," said Valdez mayor John Devens. "It irritated me to have to tell some stranger in my community why I was going into a building, who I wanted to see, what I wanted to do."

"We needed security guards," said Alyeska spokesman Tom Brennan. "Every morning when I got out of bed, the first thing I'd do is inch my way over to the window and peep through the curtains to see if a sniper was waiting for me."

For many longtime residents the loss of control over their community combined with the trauma of the spill itself proved overwhelming. "The stress down there in Valdez is incredible," said Tom Scott, director of the region's Emergency Medical Services Council. In April he set up a twenty-four-hour crisis telephone line. The mental health professional staff began taking calls from people suffering from increased drinking, anxiety, depression, and domestic violence.

"We're experiencing a lot of social problems—fights, depression, divorces," Mayor Devens said. "We asked for a counselor, but Exxon turned us down and then gave the twenty thousand dollars we requested to Seward to enhance its summer celebration. A community shouldn't have to come begging to a company."

In an attempt to make Exxon accountable for the social as well as the environmental problems of the oil spill, the leaders of twenty-five separate coastal communities formed an association in April. The mayors faced Exxon united, asking for fair treatment for villages that couldn't afford lawyers and lobbyists to press for help. At first Exxon refused to work with the association, preferring to deal with each community separately. When the mayors held firm, Exxon was forced to consider their request for an overall agreement to reimburse spill-related costs. Many of the towns had spent much of their available funds paying for log boom, anchors, tools, fuel, and other emergency supplies. They also faced mounting costs for increased crime, mental health problems, as well as extra demands for water and waste disposal.

Instead of making direct reimbursements for these costs, Exxon proposed that the communities become subcontractors to Exxon. As subcontractors, they were supposed to promise not to do anything that was not in "Exxon's best interest." Attorneys for the association said, "Exxon is trying to buy the silence of the municipalities."

The outraged mayors refused to accept Exxon's proposal, and overall agreement was never reached between the communities and Exxon. Each community was on its own to confront the oil and deal with Exxon.

CORDOVA was also ground zero, but in a different way from Valdez. While Valdez was overwhelmed with people, the residents of Cordova were so deeply connected with Prince William Sound that they felt personally wounded by its devastation. Environmentalist and fisherwoman Riki Ott described seeing them go through several stages of emotion as the spill unfolded. "First there was all this positive energy to do something—'Let's go! Let's get that oil!' When we made repeated calls to try to help and ran up against Alyeska's stone wall, our feelings turned to anger and frustration. Then when the oil took off, Cordova hit rock bottom. That's when people were mad at everything."

The tension was so great that CDFU, the fishermen's union, kept a "decompression" room, where they sent people who were so stressed they felt they were about to explode. Kelly Weaverling recalled, "When Exxon and Fish and Wildlife were driving me over the edge, a woman from CDFU whisked me across the street and put me in a room at the Prince William Hotel. She said, 'Look, CDFU keeps this room for people who get too hot. We stick them in here and close the door for a while, until they cool down.' "

After being frustrated in the bird rescue operation, Weaverling started a volunteer corps for Prince William Sound. Operating solely on private donations, the corps patrolled for injured wildlife and kept a watchful eye on the operations of Exxon and the various government agencies. For his persistence *Newsweek* magazine made Weaverling its unsung hero of the year for Alaska. "It's a great honor," he said, "but it's kind of an embarrassment—so many people exceeded themselves out there."

The fishermen of the Mosquito Fleet—who, full of anxiety and determination, went out to save the hatcheries—were also widely regarded as the heroes of the early days of the spill. One visiting Congressman compared them to the English fishermen who went out in skiffs and dories to rescue stranded soldiers after the World War II Battle of Dunkirk.

The lives of many people in Cordova were torn apart, not just by the oil but by the cleanup effort itself. Fishermen of the Mosquito Fleet had gone out as volunteers, with little thought of compensation. When Jack Lamb asked Exxon for help, Frank Iarossi had said, "How many boats do you have? Twenty-six? Okay, I'll hire them all."

Iarossi's response helped the fishermen protect the hatcheries, but it also brought them onto the payroll of a company they despised. Exxon began contracting fishermen to clean up the oil, and many of those who had gone out initially as volunteers started getting paid quite well. The first contracts required them to sign a statement saying that they would not talk to the press about what they saw in Prince William Sound. The fishermen found this outrageous, and nearly all refused to sign. When the attempt at censure was eliminated, many did sign up. But the money itself gave rise to conflicting feelings. A person who refrained from signing on might have to watch his friends get rich. One fisherman, not from Cordova, believed that his boat was worth $500 a day. He decided to ask for $1000, but before he could do so, Exxon offered him $3000 a day.

People who fish for a living are competitive by nature. Some went after Exxon contracts as if they were beating one another to the catch, and wound up with $200,000 to $300,000 for the season. This created a new division of wealth in the community, not to mention a new brand of jealousy. Those with a bundle of Exxon money could suddenly buy faster boats, better sonar, more nets. Those who avoided Exxon's money as a matter of conscience hoped they could pay their bills and stay competitive with their old equipment.

As the people of Cordova lived through the tension and torment of the spill, their despair and frustration deepened. To reaffirm their connection to the sound, they set aside a day to focus on positive feelings about it and its place in their lives. The event was called Sound Love and was held on April 23 in the high school gymnasium. Letters and crayon drawings received from children all over the world were taped to one wall. On another wall hung an enormous scroll painted by the children of Cordova. Each child, from kindergarten through sixth grade, had been asked to "try to turn your anger and hurt into a picture of the way you'd like the sound to be." At the very bottom of the scroll, preschoolers had scattered their handprints, like so many shells in the sand. Over their outstretched fingers danced sea urchins and crabs, and octopuses with dozens of arms. Up through the water swam red fish, blue fish, pink fish, polka-dot fish, and one fish with a green plaid tail. Whales broke through the surface of the sea. Eagles and gulls flew over the waves. There were fishing boats with families waving their arms. There were rainbows and smiling suns in the sky. And above it all was written, PRINCE WILLIAM SOUND—OUR HOME.

Children of different ages crowded into the gym with their parents. One elderly lady sat in a wheelchair. Groups of students sat together in the bleachers. Many wore small paper hearts reading SOUND LOVE. Grade school children sang a song they'd composed for the sound. Then, one at a time, people rose to share their feelings.

One woman played her guitar and sang, "I'm proud to be a fisherman's daughter. . . ." Another woman gave an emotional reading of the Declaration of Independence. As she spoke the words of the nation's founding fathers trying to liberate themselves from British oppression, everyone felt their own need to throw off the oppression that had descended upon their lives.

DEC commissioner Dennis Kelso, much loved because of his support of the fishermen, described going out to Knight Island after the oil had passed through. "I stood there on a spring morning when one would expect the sounds and smells of spring. But it was quiet, and there was only the smell of the oil. I felt very sad. But as I was standing there I heard breathing—the deep, explosive breathing of a large pod of killer whales. They passed close and headed out to open water, leaving the oil behind. We must go like the whales, leaving this sadness behind us."

The oil did move on. It spread southwest, toward the Kenai Peninsula, and no one knew how far it would go. Prevailing sea currents and winds made the oil spill a continuing calamity. Every time it reached a new region or community, the spill became a new and separate disaster. While the people of Valdez and Cordova felt the first impact, others would also have to deal with the grief and frustration, and the dilemma of not knowing what to do.

CHAPTER ELEVEN

On MARCH 30, six days after the grounding of the *Exxon Valdez*, a small notice in the Homer *News* said, "The Prince William Sound oil slick may be headed this way." In Homer most people viewed the spill as a catastrophe that happened 250 miles away. The National Oceanic and Atmospheric Administration was still predicting that only small amounts of oil would escape into the Gulf of Alaska.

However, a week after the grounding, a thick sea of crude oil escaped the sound and hovered off the outer coast of the Kenai Peninsula. It began to look as if offshore currents and the prevailing northerly winds might carry most of it toward Kodiak and the Katmai coast. Then the forecast changed to winds out of the Bering Sea, winds that could conceivably push the oil into Cook Inlet, toward Kachemak Bay and toward Homer.

HOMER BRACES; OIL ENTERS COOK INLET read the Homer *News* headline on April 13. Throughout that weekend, frustration focused on Exxon. The company hadn't made it to Homer yet. "Exxon's absence reflects a larger problem," wrote Tom Kizzia, the newspaper's managing editor. "The Homer area's plight, however serious, is not ranked by officials elsewhere with the crisis in Valdez, Seward, and even Kodiak."

Two days later the first sheets of oily sheen and patches of mousse rounded the corner of the Kenai Peninsula and entered Kachemak Bay, one of the most productive and scenic coastal areas in the world. Here, glaciered peaks rise from green waters containing an abundance of crabs, shrimps, herring, and salmon. The bay has been called the Big Sur of Alaska, both for its landscape and because of the many artists who are drawn to its shores. Seldovia and the small villages of Port Graham and English Bay are tucked into coves along thickly wooded slopes leading back to glaciers and high mountain ridges.

Homer, with a population of 3500, is the largest town on Kachemak Bay, and it's literally the end of the road: get on a highway anywhere in the United States and you can't drive any farther than Homer. Over the years it has become a sanctuary for people who want to be part of a small community set in one of the most inspiring landscapes on earth. Now the residents of Homer and the people of Kachemak Bay had oil from the *Exxon Valdez* heading their way.

"Nobody knew how frightened we were," said Marge Tillion, an energetic young woman who combines motherhood with work as a medical aide, volunteer fire fighter, and commercial fisherwoman. She began compiling a list of fishermen willing to combat the oil, and within forty-eight hours she had more than a hundred signed up.

Following an approach that had worked in Seward, Homer formed its own Multiagency Advisory Committee (MAC) to organize the local response. Borough mayor Don Gillman appointed Loren Flagg, a fisheries biologist, to be the group's first chairman. "We set our priorities at that first MAC meeting: thirty thousand feet of boom was needed immediately to protect the major salmon streams and critical habitats," Flagg said. "But we couldn't get any boom from Exxon. And this prompted area residents to take matters into their own hands."

By the third week in April fishermen and loggers banded together to build their own boom from logs. They worked in volunteer shifts throughout the night, limbing and notching spruce trees on the beach near the harbor. In Seldovia, people began making a boom to string across the mouth of Seldovia Bay, which sheltered their town. Junior high and high school students were let out of school to help fill sandbags for anchors.

Meanwhile, Mayor Gillman secured funds from Exxon and the state for the Homer MAC group to defend Kachemak Bay. "That's when we knew for sure that Exxon had been giving us the runaround," Loren Flagg said. "Exxon had told us there was no boom available. But when we got the money, we ordered boom and got five thousand feet within two days. They just hadn't tried to get it."

The people of Kachemak Bay were so incensed with Exxon that they tried to get Alaska Congressman Don Young and Senator Ted

Stevens to eliminate Exxon from the cleanup and have the state or federal government take over the spill. When that didn't work, John Mickelson, a fisherman from Seldovia, tried to make a citizen's arrest of the Exxon representative during a MAC meeting.

As Mickelson recalled, "It's a federal misdemeanor to convey or impart false information with reckless disregard for human life. The chaotic response to this oil spill was definitely endangering lives, and the Exxon representatives were intentionally giving misleading facts. If you see a crime being committed and don't intervene, then you're guilty too. So on a moral basis I had to go ahead and arrest that Exxon man. He said, 'Okay, you do what you have to do.' I think he'd been instructed on how to respond, so I didn't have to wrestle him down. However, I couldn't get an officer of the law to take him to jail, so he went free."

BY APRIL 24 gale-force winds had broken open containment boom on the outer Kenai coast. Oil rushed onto the beaches, coating the estuaries of salmon-spawning streams. When the storm cleared, sheen and chunks of emulsified oil were seen near Seldovia, and sheets of oil were approaching Port Graham and English Bay. A combination of commercial and handmade log booms was stretched between the coves and streams and the advancing oil. However, the oil took its toll on the vast stretches of unprotected coast.

By mid-May globs of oil were washing up on Homer Spit, a sliver of land extending into Kachemak Bay. Within hours volunteers and Exxon workers were combing the beach for tar balls. Exxon announced that about 500 feet of beach had been hit, but officials at the Homer Center for Disaster Assistance reported oil on more than two miles of beach.

Meanwhile, Kachemak Bay area residents were becoming increasingly incensed with Exxon's lack of resolve to clean up the hard-hit beaches of the outer coast. Gore Point became the focus of their frustration. As Gore Point was oiled and reoiled, the Homer MAC group pleaded again and again for Exxon to clean it up. However, by the end of May the area was still heavily oiled, and Vice Admiral Clyde E. Robbins and DEC commissioner Dennis Kelso came to Homer to demand an explanation from Exxon.

"I'm tired of hearing about Gore Point," Robbins told Exxon. "I want it clean—whatever it takes," he said, sensing that Exxon was more interested in stilling local criticism than in collecting oil. "I want to see a plan. The last time I came down here, there were a thousand excuses why it wasn't done."

Cleaning Gore Beach was difficult because the waves had buried oil in the sand and gravel. To remove it, Exxon would have had to resort to a cleanup in which heavy equipment is used to dig down into the beach substrata. Exxon resisted this costly method. "I cannot give you a better answer on whether we will dig up Gore Beach or not, because I don't have it," responded Exxon representative Dean Peeler at the May 31 Homer MAC meeting. "And I don't know where we're going by continuing to ask the same questions over and over."

When Peeler presented a new plan for sending workers out to Gore Beach and other area beaches, a Homer man said, "We would all like to be optimistic about your new plan. However, this is about the fifth reorganization we've seen. We all know the level that needs to be done. One beach at a time. A hundred men."

"This has been a problem for all the people here in Homer," said another resident. "We get something like cleaning Gore Beach approved, then we walk up to Exxon's door and it's locked. There are other people, from Seldovia and Port Graham, who have innovative beach-cleaning techniques. We all run into the same problem."

By this time Mike Hedrick, a former manager of the Kenai National Wildlife Refuge, had replaced Loren Flagg as chairman of the MAC group. "You know, I've watched Exxon in the Homer zone start out with shovels, giving a twenty-person crew shovels to pick up oil from the beach," Hedrick recalled. "Then Exxon took their shovels away and gave them garden trowels, because they were picking up too much sand. The sand was giving them oily waste they simply weren't committed to handle."

Exxon had wanted to burn oily waste from the beaches, but restrictions by DEC forced them to haul it away in boats. Since Exxon didn't have enough waste-disposal boats, they began cutting back on the amount of waste being picked up. At Windy Bay, on the south side of the Kenai Peninsula, beach cleaners had been using shovels effectively until Exxon took the shovels away. "Now we can only use our hands," said Ephim Anahonak, of Port Graham.

Some workers were fired simply for working too hard. "People who work really hard disappear," said a man who cleaned beaches on the outer Kenai coast. "A foreman will wander over and say, 'Pack up.' In two hours they're gone. One time a foreman even told us, 'We're not here to get everything off the beach. We just want to spray it with water. Make it look like it's been touched. Check another one off the list. Go on to the next one.' "

Disillusionment with the cleanup added to the frustration people were feeling. In Homer, a mental health worker described the vortex of emotions that were pulling many down. "They feel betrayed—not just by Exxon but by the state and federal governments, which are supposed to be looking out for them. Their sense of self-worth has been reduced because people in authority don't appreciate their knowledge and love of this area. This is their home, and it's been violated—so *they* feel violated. We're seeing a lot of intense anger, a lot of uncontrollable crying."

Because Marge Tillion had had emergency medical training, she helped counsel those who were overstressed. In confidential sessions she helped people share their emotions with one another and begin working through the stages of grieving. "By the time a session is through, many people are crying," Tillion said. "There's fist pounding. People are consoling each other. This helps people know that someone is looking out for them, that they are cared for. Unfortunately, in disasters the worst stress is often felt years later."

Some Homer people found that volunteering—doing something constructive—was a way to work through their frustration. Billy Day, a young Homer man, became a driving force in the area's unusual volunteer response to the spill. Day noticed that once Exxon came to town, most people stopped making their own decisions. "We sat back and decided we'd let them take care of it for us, tell us what to do," he said. "But we soon found out they didn't have any answers." So when Alaska's division of Parks and Outdoor Recreation offered Day the job of patrolling for dead birds and animals near Gore Point, he took it, eager for a chance to help.

"There was nobody out there, just a lot of bird and animal car-casses," Day recalled. "As far as I could see along the beach, there was a thick layer of oil, maybe four feet deep, waves of it splashing ashore. It was obvious to me that until we got this stuff picked up, we were going to have more and more dead birds." The oil had not yet sunk into the substrata and was easy to reach. "In five days a friend and I cleaned it up, using shovels and buckets," Day said. "I stacked up about two hundred bags of oily debris. There was probably four miles of beach that could have been cleaned this way, but three weeks passed with no sign of Exxon."

After Day had been there for a month, an Exxon beach-assessment team flew in at high tide in a helicopter. They walked a few hundred feet of the beach and categorized it as lightly oiled. They said they weren't going to recommend any cleanup. "That's a mistake," Day told them. "Why don't you guys wait until the tide goes out."

"They stayed," Day recalled, "and as the tide went out, their assessment of the beach went from lightly oiled to heavily oiled and needing attention right away. So I thought, Oh, good, they'll get a hundred workers out here and clean this beach up. But after those guys left, two more weeks passed without anyone coming out."

Billy Day and a couple of companions continued to shovel up as much oil as they could, and gradually the stacks of debris bags got higher. When an Exxon-chartered barge came by, Day asked its skipper to take away the bags. The captain radioed his Exxon supervisor for approval, but was told no, he was supposed to be standing by elsewhere. However, the captain defied orders and, under cover of darkness, came ashore to hand-load the debris. It weighed in at 35,000 pounds.

"It was kind of a turning point," said Day. "As boats passed by, more and more guys started coming in to help shovel oil. They weren't supposed to be recovering oil. But we realized that if we didn't take care of this beach, nobody was going to."

By July 1, Day was no longer working for Parks and Outdoor Recreation, but had become a full-time organizer of an all-volunteer cleaning effort. To cover the volunteers' expenses, people in Homer raised money by holding bake sales, passing the hat in bars, and making pleas over the radio. Eventually, Exxon sent out a crew of beach cleaners; they came with shovels and buckets and started cleaning tidal pools. "They cleaned them up real well. I give them a lot of credit," Day said. "Then they hit the beaches, where there were larger cobbles. Exxon ordered them to stop using shovels, to reduce the amount of material being picked up. I watched these people crawl around on their hands and knees and wipe rocks with absorbent towels, which came apart and stuck to the rocks. Everyone's morale was just devastated.

"There had to be an alternative. I kept thinking Exxon would show up with a big machine to wash the rocks, but it never came," Day said. "My last week out there I got very angry. I didn't even want the oil company people there anymore. I felt like they were belittling the place with a token effort."

After Exxon's crews went home in mid-September, the volunteers, who came from distant places as well as from Kachemak Bay, kept working long hours in the numbing cold. Their most successful technique was brilliant in its simplicity. When the tide went out, they worked a single patch of beach. First, they dug down to the deepest penetration of oil, usually about 18 inches. Then they lined this pit with a heavy waterproof tarp and shoveled the oiled rocks and sand into their handmade pond. Stirring and scrubbing with hands, shovels, and high-pressure hoses, they lifted oil from the rocks and siphoned it off with an adapted vacuum cleaner. When no more oil floated to the surface, they pulled out the tarp and went on to the next section of beach.

By the end of October the volunteers had cleaned a quarter mile of beach. This was only a tiny portion of the hundreds of miles of beach where oil remained. But this handful of people working without pay had done something that one of the world's largest corporations had been unable or unwilling to do. Their ingenuity and refusal to quit demonstrated that a badly oiled beach could be cleaned.

FOUR hundred miles southwest of Bligh Reef, the green hills of Kodiak Island rise above the deep, cold waters of the Aleutian Trench. The men and women who fish out of the town of Kodiak are among the toughest in the world. They have a saying: Kodiak may not be the end of the earth, but you sure as hell can see it from here. Beyond the safety of the harbors lie a wilderness of ocean, fog, cyclonic winds, 80-foot waves, and a wealth of marine and bird life.

In 1988 Kodiak was the nation's highest-producing fishing port. The bulk of the catch was king crab and salmon—reds, silvers, pinks, and kings. The 5000 residents are mainly fishing men and women, and others related to the fishing industry. The *Exxon Valdez* oil spill seemed, at first, far removed from their lives.

"Seeing the oil come closer and closer was a painful process for everyone," said Kodiak borough mayor Jerome Selby. "We had to face the reality that we couldn't boom off the entire island. No matter what we did, a part of Kodiak Island, which all of us love so much, was going to get destroyed."

While Valdez and Cordova were ground zero, Kodiak was at the far end of the spill and had a hard time getting the attention of Exxon and government agencies. But the oil was headed toward Kodiak, and someone had to deal with it. "Rather than sit here and wait for the oil to get to us, the spirit of Kodiak is Let's go attack it," said a resident. "We couldn't do anything about that Exxon tanker captain, but we could get after the oil."

Some built a log boom for the Afognak hatchery and for the key fishing bays. Others set up shop in an empty barn to make oil-absorbent boom from a synthetic material. Town meetings were held every morning. "We were calling Exxon almost daily, asking them to send somebody and let us know their plans for the defense of Kodiak Island," Selby said. "But they waited until the oil actually hit the island."

When Exxon arrived in Kodiak, three weeks after the spill, many local residents felt control was being taken away from the community. "When we had the first oil spill meeting here, there was a tremendous amount of energy," said Brian Johnson, a Kodiak fisherman. "People were coming out of the woodwork, and we felt there was a lot we could do. Then Exxon walked in and took over the town. We completely lost control.

"It was hard to sit here and see all this oil on the beach and know that no one was going to go out and pick it up," Johnson said. "We could look down through the water and see oil on the bottom. The stuff was plastered all over the place."

Johnson and several friends went out with old nets and picked up 1000 pounds of oily gunk. "It doesn't take a genius to come up with ideas," said one of Johnson's companions. "Any fisherman can do it." A group of draggers—fishermen who trawl with long nets—also went after oil. With no previous experience and no promise of payment, the draggers collected emulsified oil from the water for several days—as much as 20,000 gallons a day.

At fisherman Ed Monkiwiecz's house, a half mile above the harbor, fishing men and women spent many hours sipping coffee and agonizing over the spill. In a dark corner, a cardboard box with an army jacket flung over the top held a frightened gull Monkiwiecz had rescued from the oil. The fishermen themselves felt boxed in. They were seiners who wanted to be out catching salmon, but their fishing season had been lost. Many had no alternative ways to earn money. "Initially, we were led to believe that Exxon was going to do well by us. They didn't, and we have no reason to believe they will," Monkiwiecz said. "But ultimately, I think we're all at fault. We've got to have our cars. We use the fossil fuels. Maybe if we put more value on our environment, this wouldn't have happened."

THE Shelikof Lodge, a split-level hotel with a chrome-and-formica restaurant and bar, is five minutes' drive from Kodiak's boat harbor. This is one of the places where Kodiak residents gather to vent frustrations and relax. Becky Westbrook, a popular bartender at the Shelikof, said, "I hear stories from across the bar about Exxon trying to cover this up. It makes me so angry. Sometimes you don't know what to do with this incredible anger."

Every time the people of Kodiak thought they had experienced the full magnitude of the oil spill, it seemed to get worse. First there were dead birds and otters. Cherished beaches and coves were blackened. Fishing seasons were closed. And then came an unending chain of reverberations within the community—fear, jealousy, selfishness, disillusionment. "Some people have made marvelous money off the spill," Becky Westbrook said, "and others are going under completely. This creates a lot of anger and tension. My fiancé finally went down to VECO and stomped his foot and said, 'I'm not from New York, and I'm not from Wisconsin. I'm from Alaska and I'm starving to death. Put me to work.'

"When VECO first got here," Westbrook continued, "a lot of people were quitting their jobs to go work for it, which left a lot of the small businesses in town up in the air. It has affected the entire economy of Kodiak. A false economy has been created, and once they pull out, the repercussions could be absolutely incredible. Exxon is a multinational corporation, so there isn't any one person you can shake your finger at. I wish those executives in their glass towers who make hundreds of thousands of dollars a year could see the people here who are real scared about their futures."

REFLECTIONS

I WATCH spring return to Prince William Sound. Along the shoreline, snow begins to melt. In places, eagles soar on the wind. Flocks of gulls fly low along the green, white-capped waves. Soon the great migrations of birds and whales will begin; salmon will search for their spawning streams.

Prince William Sound is certainly not dead. But the sound and the Alaska coast southwest to Kodiak and Katmai are not as wild and abundant as they were. Winter storms lashed sea cliffs, but more than 140 miles of exposed shoreline remain oiled. In more sheltered coves, oil still clings to rocks, and patches of bright iridescent sheen still leach into the sea.

Exxon officials insist that the oil did not create an ecological crisis. Indeed, on the spectrum of toxicity, oil is far from our most destructive pollutant. And the planet's air and water systems do have recuperative powers. The sea will continue ceaselessly to clean the shores. The impulse of animal species is toward regeneration, so barring further oil spills, the bird, otter, and other animal populations are likely to return to their prespill abundance. Nevertheless, available evidence confirms that the *Exxon Valdez* spill was the most devastating one ever.

One thousand and sixteen dead otters were retrieved, making this spill the most deadly in history for marine mammals. And no one knows how many otters and other sea creatures actually died. The U.S. Fish and Wildlife Service officially counted 36,460 dead marine birds—again, far more than in any other spill. Moreover, scientists believe that this number represents only between 10 and 30 percent of the total mortality—that 100,000 to 350,000 birds might have died.

The oil also affected clams, mussels, sea urchins, fish, and a multitude of organisms in the intertidal areas. Furthermore, an ecological disaster is not defined just in terms of fatalities. Sublethal effects of the oil spill diminished the reproductive potential of species and rendered habitats virtually sterile. There was a tremendous loss of tiny invertebrates, an essential link in the food chain. The oil upset the balance among species and set off chain reactions whose ultimate effects may not be detectable for many years.

The social impacts of the spill are even more difficult to quantify than the ecological effects. Native Alaskans depend upon resources of the sea; hunting and fishing make up their way of life and are essential to their cultural identity and survival. It can be very hard to live a normal life when you fear that at any moment an enormous swath of oil could sweep through it.

Another almost inexpressible loss is that of wilderness value, the sense that a region's landscape and ecology is as it was created, utterly undisturbed by human beings. This coast of Alaska was wild in ways that it will never be again. It remains beautiful, but it will never again be pristine. No one will be able to return to a favorite cove or fjord, in memory or in person, without sensing the oil buried in the sand. This loss of pure wilderness alone marks the wreck of the *Exxon Valdez* as a tragedy of global significance.

For all this destructiveness and loss, what is the extent of Exxon's responsibility? Certainly it is responsible for the grounding of its tanker. Yet the company responded faster than any government agency and marshaled enormous resources to fight the oil. Lightering 40 million gallons of oil from the stricken tanker was a major accomplishment. Moreover, Exxon mounted its response amid the confusion of state and federal officials trying to determine their roles.

Also to Exxon's credit, the company promptly established a claims process, which no law required. In one year Exxon spent close to $2 billion, making this the most costly oil spill in history by more than a billion dollars. Exxon, with profits of $5.3 billion in 1988, is one of the few companies in the world capable of actually paying the costs of the spill, which could reach $4 billion by the time all the claims are in.

However, according to government surveys, for all its efforts Exxon recovered only 3 to 13 percent of the spilled oil. Regardless of all the efforts to divert, contain, disperse, and recover it, the massive slick inexorably ran its course.

The fact that Exxon did mount an extensive response makes the wreck of the *Exxon Valdez* a highly instructive case study. Experts and observers worldwide learned that no amount of money spent or personnel deployed can control a large oil spill.

"The public, particularly in America, has been misled for many years," said Dr. Ian White, managing director of the International Tanker Owners Pollution Federation. "A myth has been perpetuated that a large oil spill is solvable. A ten percent recovery of spilled oil is tremendous, and dispersants are no panacea. There is no magic solution or cure. Contingency plans must address this fact."

Offshore oil leases continue to be sold in Alaska, and with their sale other people become vulnerable to the myth of oil spill safety. "After all these years of hearing the oil industry tell us that it could clean up oil spills in even the most extreme marine environments, we're finally seeing more than ten million gallons of truth spread across Prince William Sound," said a state representative from the Bristol Bay region, where offshore oil leases in the midst of the world's largest salmon fishery were sold in 1988. "The plainest—and the blackest—truth of all is that the oil companies have lied to Alaskans for years about their ability to clean up oil spills."

Given the fact that there is no way to control a large oil spill, what kind of response should be mounted for the next one?

Six months after the spill, Frank Iarossi said, "If I'm ever faced with a situation like this again, I'll head for Mexico when the phone rings." Although speaking in jest, Iarossi raised the distinct possibility that another industry executive faced with a large oil spill might not initiate a response at all. "We need to recognize that there are some absolute limits to what a commercial company can do. We should be ready to fulfill our legal obligation to pay for the cleanup. But my personal conclusion is that a spill like this is clearly beyond any commercial company. A company should stand ready to support the federal government, but they've got the baton."

The Alaska Oil Spill Commission reached exactly the same conclusion. "The spiller should not be in charge of a major spill. A spiller should be obligated to respond with all the resources it can summon, but government should command that response."

Putting the government in charge does not guarantee an adequate response, but it would prevent the confusion of authority that paralyzed the initial response to the *Exxon Valdez* spill and that slowed down activity throughout the cleanup. The next crisis will not be managed any more effectively unless someone has the authority to act very quickly and decisively. "I don't care if you call him oil spill response dictator or casualty response dictator," says Iarossi. "But if his title doesn't include the word dictator, we will miss the whole purpose of having this individual."

In the end, prevention is the only real defense against large oil spills. As the oil spill commission concluded, "This disaster could have been prevented—not by tanker captains and crews who are only fallible human beings, but by an advanced oil transportation system designed to minimize human error. It could have been prevented if Alaskans, state and federal governments, the oil industry, and the American public had insisted on stringent safeguards."

Admittedly, the tools of prevention—double-hulled tankers, the best electronics, highly trained crews, and heightened coast guard surveillance—are imperfect. Shipping oil in tankers will never be risk free, but being mindful of this fact will reduce the risk. Realizing that there will be accidents is the first essential step in avoiding them.

Once the pipeline was built, tankers loaded with North Slope crude transited Prince William Sound 8700 times without accident. This very success fostered the complacency that added substantially to the danger. The way to prevent another accident is to fight the complacency, and to do that, we must bear in mind two irrefutable facts— *major spills happen, and when they do, they cannot be controlled.*

Knowing that this oil spill could have been prevented makes the suffering and devastation all the more painful. Many share the blame. And yet my own experience with the spill brought me into contact with a wide range of people who rose to the occasion and did whatever they could to help.

Kelly Weaverling fought one obstacle after another to rescue wildlife. Valdez mayor John Devens risked a recall vote when he started criticizing Alyeska. Dennis Kelso, of DEC, was indefatigable in his efforts to ride herd on Exxon. Jack Lamb and the Cordova fishing fleet spared no effort to save the hatcheries. Suzanne Marinelli and others volunteered to work under rigorous conditions. Many state and federal employees put in overtime, and some Exxon people pushed themselves to exhaustion trying to contain the oil.

It was, of course, a losing battle, and no one was more aware of this than Dr. Jim Scott. By summer's end he had treated only a handful of bald eagles, and he knew that hundreds had died. "You still have to save as many as you can," he said. "You do it for the creatures. And you do it for yourself, for who you are inside. I feel we are less human if we don't try to save other creatures, regardless of their numbers."

Individual acts of conscience like Dr. Scott's may seem to have little effect on larger environmental problems. But this spill showed that those who cared and decided to act did make a difference, whether in saving a hatchery or saving a single bird.

THERE is no arguing the fact that, as a nation, we will need large amounts of oil for some time. Tankers will continue plying the waters off Canadian provinces and every coastal state in the United States. Our need for oil and our reliance on oil companies are not going to disappear overnight. Nevertheless, certain quite achievable objectives in both energy conservation and in alternate-energy development would reduce the risk to such sensitive regions as the Arctic National Wildlife Refuge, in Alaska, and coastal areas of California and Florida, and the fisheries-rich Georges Bank, off New England—all targeted by the industry as drilling sites.

But who's going to set the objectives and work toward the goals? Not the industry itself—that much we can be sure of. The responsibility for careful, environmentally sound development ultimately lies with the consumers. "It wasn't Hazelwood's driving, but the driving of a hundred million Americans that put the tanker on the reef," went one quip that emerged from the spill.

It's difficult for most of us to connect the consumption of energy with disasters like that of the *Exxon Valdez*. One who tried is Mark Holdren, of Honeoye Falls, New York. "Who is to blame for the nation's worst oil spill? I am," he wrote to the Homer *News* after the spill. "You see, I am your typical person living in an affluent suburb. And my life-style is choking our planet to death. I rely almost totally on my car to meet my every need. I commute more than fifty miles a day to work. My wife, in her own car, travels hundreds of miles every week. My children, in their own cars, seem to spend more time at a distant shopping mall than they do at home. I am at oil's mercy."

Individually, it's easy to feel that one's effort to use less oil or live in a more energy-efficient house has little overall effect. But improvements in home and business heating efficiency could save as much oil as is delivered by the Trans-Alaska Pipeline—about 2 million barrels a day. Every one-mile-per-gallon improvement in automobile fuel efficiency saves about 500,000 barrels of oil a day. Brooks Yeager, author of *Wasted Energy*, concludes that "If the United States could achieve the same energy efficiency per unit of economic output enjoyed by our

Western European competitors, our annual energy bill would fall by an astounding $200 billion."

This is $200 billion the oil companies would like to keep on their balance sheets. For the public, the fact that they do so represents not only a considerable monetary cost but a tremendous cost to wild places like Prince William Sound as well.

I REMEMBER sitting in the living room of Jack and Paula Lamb, in Cordova, after the Mosquito Fleet's struggle to save the salmon hatcheries. "We ought to be able to trust our government to protect us from this kind of mess," Paula said. "It breaks my heart the way the whole thing was handled. Look at us—the richest country in the world, and we don't invest enough to clean up our own mess. We have to be willing to give up enough to take care of our part of the world."

I hope this tragedy prompts more of us to have some long-overdue conversations with ourselves about our personal choices and their consequences for our planet. If we do, more of us might start to see the connection between our life-style and an environmental crisis thousands of miles away. I'd like the oil company executives of this world to look in the mirror and see business leaders who are responsible for far more than a company's annual profit. And I'd like Alaskans, myself included, to take more time to appreciate how fortunate we are to live in one of the most spectacular and abundant natural environments on earth. This land is good to us—we have to find ways to be more responsible to it.

The process of change starts with one person. And it starts with a personal decision. Says Dolly Reft, an Alaskan who lives on Kodiak Island, "The environment is a reflection of who we are. We can't ignore the reflection we see. We have to live with it—today, tomorrow, and forever."

MURDE
of
INNOCEN

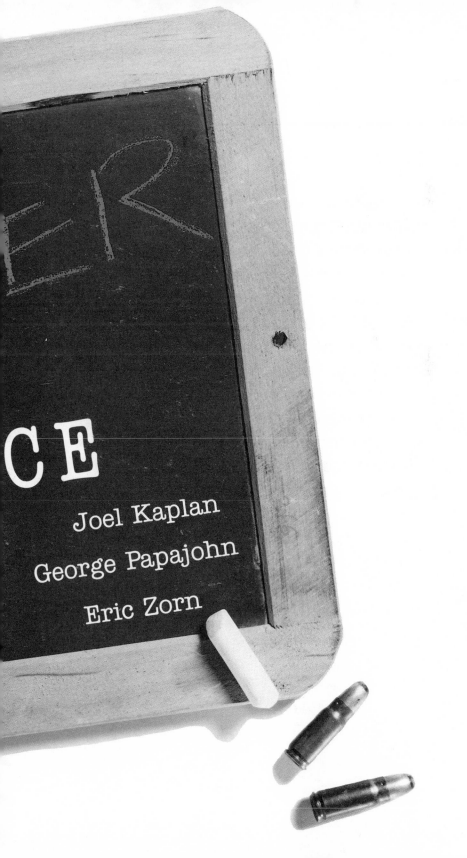

. . . Laurie had awakened shortly
after 5:00 a.m. to begin her final
preparations for the day. The demons
in her past—her parents, her
ex-husband and his relatives and
friends, the men who hadn't loved
her, the men who had loved her
badly, her baby-sitting clients and
her doctors—they would never
underestimate her again.

Her bedroom at that hour was
a veritable pantry of fruit juice
packets, Rice Krispies Treats and
popcorn. For the next fifty minutes,
as Glencoe awakened to a gorgeous
spring day, she loaded her syringe
with arsenic and carefully injected
the foil pouches of juice.

—Murder of Innocence

1.

A BEAUTIFUL DAY FOR A CARNIVAL

LAURIE the baby-sitter had let herself go to hell. Her body, which only five months earlier had been trim and shapely, was swollen with fat—her eyes looked tired and her hair was clumsily cut above the shoulder in a way that lent unflattering emphasis to her drooping jaw. Her admirers had once compared her to a Barbie doll and remarked on how young and fresh she always looked, but now every trouble in her life seemed to have caught up with her at once.

Yet Marian Rushe, one of Laurie's best clients, was not inclined to judge her harshly. Marian was an accepting person, open to everyone, and she already had plenty to concern herself with that morning. She'd just hustled her daughters, Mary Rose and Jennifer, and her son Robert off to school, and at the moment Laurie showed up at the door, Marian was simultaneously trying to clean up the breakfast mess and find Windbreakers and shoes for her two youngest sons, Patrick, six, and Carl, four. The boys were giddy and chattering with excitement. Laurie, their favorite sitter, was taking them to a kiddie carnival.

It was a brilliant spring morning in Winnetka, Illinois, an exclusive suburb of thirteen thousand on the shores of Lake Michigan, seventeen miles north of downtown Chicago. Skies were clear and the temperature was on its way up to the mid-seventies. Laurie was wearing white Bermuda shorts and a tan T-shirt from the University of Arizona

College of Medicine, with a skeleton in the logo. She was carrying a plastic Mickey Mouse mug and a paper plate filled with baked Rice Krispies Treats.

She'd been a regular sitter for the Rushes for more than a year, then had mysteriously vanished after the previous Christmas. Her disappearance more or less coincided with the arrival from Ireland of Marian's sister, who came on an extended visit and took over most of the baby-sitting chores. The few times Marian had called Laurie to fill in, no one answered the phone at her house or else an older man picked up and said simply, "Laurie is out of town."

It had been a surprise, then, two days before this bright morning, when Laurie showed up unannounced at the door.

Marian had invited her in for a visit. "How have you been?" she asked.

"So-so," Laurie said. There had been a death in her family, she said, and her allergies were kicking up. But otherwise she was okay— working as a nurse at Evanston Hospital and living at home. "I missed you and the kids," she said. "I thought I'd stop by and catch up."

"Well, it's great to see you," Marian said enthusiastically. "Are you still planning to get married in June?"

Laurie nodded. "I'm having my engagement ring reset again," she said, apologetically fluttering her bare left hand. "The first time didn't work out. It wasn't right."

"That was his mother's ring," Marian said, recalling their conversations from many months earlier.

"Yeah, it's like an heirloom."

The women sat and talked for about an hour. Toward the end of the desultory conversation Laurie said that the real reason she had come over was to ask if she could take Patrick and Carl to a carnival at her hospital Friday morning. "It's especially for younger kids," she said. "I'm sure they'd enjoy it."

Marian went along with the plan. Laurie had always been somewhat quiet and awkward, but the kids loved her. She'd taken them to the park, out for ice cream and even on excursions to her parents' house in the nearby suburb of Glencoe. Things had gone so well that Marian had enthusiastically recommended Laurie to friends who were engaged in the always difficult search for reliable baby-sitters in the North Shore suburbs.

So on the morning of May 20, 1988, shortly before 9:00 a.m., Laurie rang the front doorbell. Marian let her in, watched her carry the Rice Krispies Treats and the Mickey Mouse cup to the kitchen and set them down. When Marian left the room to help Patrick and Carl get ready, Laurie picked up a gallon jug of milk and filled the cup, sealing it again with the no-spill lid.

"I'm taking along some milk, in case the boys get thirsty," she called.

Marian thought this was a peculiar choice of beverage—milk would spoil on a hot day and she had juice in the fridge—but she said nothing.

She shepherded the children out to Laurie's car—not the old blue Honda she usually drove, but a white, spanking-clean 1986 Toyota Cressida. Vanity license plates—her father's initials followed by three zeros. Marian belted Patrick and Carl into the back seat and waved as Laurie pulled out of the driveway.

She walked back into the house and went to the kitchen to continue cleaning up. Dishes. Bowls. Silverware. And the milk was still out! It looked weird, a little orangy, as though one of the kids had spilled his juice into it. She smelled the milk. Nothing. She took a small taste. Normal. She put the milk away and went about the rest of her chores.

And Laurie, who was supposed to be heading south with the kids toward Evanston, was instead, at that moment, racing north.

2.

LAURIE GROWS

I N 1955 NORM Wasserman, a lean and meticulous young accountant, took out a $14,000 mortgage and built a house on a vacant plot of land given to him by his wife's relatives. It was a long, sturdy bungalow with an uninterrupted expanse of windows across the front room opening on a street lined with shade trees. The day that Norm, his wife and young son moved into their own home marked the realization of his parents' immigrant dream.

His father, Morris, and mother, Betty, had come over from Russia when they were young and childless. Morris found work as a truck driver, and the Wassermans ended up in North Lawndale, a middle-income neighborhood where nearly half of Chicago's Jewish population lived after World War I. It was a quiet residential area graced by

elaborately landscaped parks and dotted with more than a dozen syna-
gogues. Idele, the couple's first child, was born in 1926, followed three
years later by Norm.

In the 1940s the upwardly mobile Jews dispersed into the higher-
status neighborhoods that had opened up to them. The Wassermans
rode one of these migratory waves to the prestigious white-collar
South Shore neighborhood, where they took the top floor of a three-
story on South Phillips Avenue.

Norm had just started attending South Shore High when Morris
Wasserman died of a heart attack. Suddenly Norm, a studious, soft-
spoken kid, was the man of the house.

He graduated from high school and lived at home while going to
the University of Illinois in Chicago. The school offered only a two-
year program of study, and Norm completed sixty-seven credit hours
in a liberal arts curriculum between January of 1947 and December of
1948. He transferred to Roosevelt University, in downtown Chicago,
where he studied business for a year before leaving school in 1950
without a degree.

That same year he married Edith Joy Lewis, a quiet, curly-haired
redhead who'd been a year behind him at South Shore High and
grown up in an apartment building on the next block. The newlyweds
moved into an apartment over a row of stores on Colfax Avenue.
Norm studied to take the certification exam to become a public
accountant.

He passed the exam in July of 1952, when Edith was pregnant with
their first child. Mark Ira Wasserman was born in October, in Michael
Reese Hospital.

The Colfax Avenue apartment was neither big enough nor in a
suitable location for a growing family, so Norm and Edith eagerly took
the opportunity to put up a house on Lewis family land in the Stony
Island Heights neighborhood.

Norm's accountancy practice thrived, and he and Edith decided to
have one more child. On October 18, 1957, Laurie Ann Wasserman
was born.

The Wassermans became an archetypal 1950s nuclear family—the
hardworking dad, the stay-at-home mom and the pair of well-behaved
children. The next wave of Jewish migration was to the suburbs,
almost exclusively northward along Lake Michigan. The more success-

ful families went to the old-money North Shore communities of Winnetka, Glencoe and Highland Park, where large mansions and homes of vintage elegance lined the distinctive ravines.

Norm and Edith Wasserman naturally looked to the best of these suburbs in 1963 when they decided it was time to leave the South Shore. They were not yet able to afford one of the grand homes near the lake in Highland Park, so they settled for a brick tri-level on Sumac Lane, on the southwest side of the city.

They occupied the last house on the block, and other families noticed that they didn't seem inclined to have much to do with them. They often drove out the long way—the way that would not put them in the position of having to pass any of their neighbors or wave to them. When Edith did drive by, she usually stared straight up the road or turned her head away.

Mark, who was nearly a teenager, was older than most of the neighborhood children. He was known on the block as that shy, quiet boy who was doing very well in junior high. Laurie, on the other hand, was often outside with the kids. They were mostly boys, and they played lineball, kickball, hopscotch, army, and hide-and-seek.

Laurie was a reticent, funny-looking little girl, with an oversized nose and sailboat ears. She was always a follower in the group, never suggesting anything and never arguing. The kids accepted her, but it sometimes bothered them that she almost never smiled and every so often would fix them with a blank stare that seemed to come from a million miles away.

"Laurie!" they would tease her. "Are you still there? Laurie!"

Once in a while her mother allowed her to invite a few of the younger girls into the pristine interior of the Wasserman home to play with Laurie's huge collection of fashion dolls. Entering the house was always a little intimidating, though—Edith's nickname among some of the kids was "the Bitch," for the way she would peremptorily call Laurie inside. "You forgot to clean your room!" she'd say. "Come set the table!" Laurie then wouldn't emerge for days except to get in the car to go out to eat. The Wassermans went out to dinner more than anybody. Edith hated to cook so much, Laurie used to tell people, that she didn't even own a can opener.

Norm's favorite leisure activity was tennis, which he played on mornings and weekends at the Highland Park Racquet Club. Edith, much less athletic, was known to go bowling in the afternoons with the sisterhood of B'nai Torah.

Laurie went to West Ridge Elementary School and there, too, was known for being shy and basically serious, though not the exceptional student her brother was. In the fourth grade she showed up with surgical bandages on both sides of her head. After they came off, her ears didn't stick out anymore.

For sixth through eighth grade she went to Red Oak Junior High. She was a reasonably good student, and most of her schoolmates had no idea that she also attended special classes for troubled and learning-disabled children held at Washburne Junior High in nearby Winnetka. The classes, which were more or less modified group-counseling sessions, attracted a grab bag of kids from the North Shore. They were the loners, the low achievers, the behavior problems, the oddballs.

The North Shore has always been a pressure cooker for adolescents. The high schools there are among the best in the nation. The students come from affluent families, where the expectations for social, athletic and particularly academic success are extremely high, and an average kid can easily feel as if he's a disappointment to everyone. Teens on the North Shore take their own lives at a rate three times higher than the national average, and local therapists call the area the Suicide Belt.

When Laurie got up the nerve to speak to the others in the special education class, she told them she didn't feel she was good at anything, that she couldn't communicate with her parents, and that she felt like an outcast in her own family because she didn't feel loved or needed.

She'd already shown several signs that there might be more to her introversion and sense of worthlessness than just a garden-variety dissatisfaction with family life. When she was five years old, she'd adopted peculiar rituals, touching the same objects over and over and fixating on good numbers and bad numbers. These rituals disappeared as she got older, but her family history suggested the possibility of future mental problems—both Edith's mother and Norm's grandmother suffered from clinical depression, an ailment with a strong genetic component.

THE 1971 Red Oak Junior High yearbook included a prophecy for each graduate. Laurie's prophecy—"Laurie Wasserman grows"— referred to how short and physically undeveloped she was.

Beginning in September of 1971 she attended Highland Park High School. She struggled, earning grades that were a terrible disappointment to her parents—her brother, Mark, had also been a mild and unmemorable kid in high school, but he had made National Honor Society.

Laurie, on the other hand, had achieved almost nothing except to live up to her junior high yearbook prophecy—she'd grown. Her body, so recently childish, had developed pleasing amplitudes, and the boys were starting to pay attention. Chuck Brotman, a popular sophomore, noticed Laurie right off and thought she might be worth making a play for. One day in the cafeteria he turned to her and said, "You're going out with me."

Laurie's eyes widened. "Okay," she said.

Chuck dated her for two months and introduced her to heavy petting. Still, the whole relationship started to embarrass him. He didn't care much for how bland she was, and seeing her did nothing to enhance his image, so he made it a point to keep his distance at school. He finally called off the romance, and she hated him for it. He was surprised that such a mousy girl was capable of showing such intense contempt with just her eyes.

AT THE start of Christmas vacation her sophomore year, Laurie met Barry Gallup at a departure gate at O'Hare International Airport. Their families were taking the same ten-day package tour to Hawaii, and Saul, Barry's father, recognized Norm from their high school days together on the South Shore.

The Gallups were then living in Glenview, a middle-income suburb due west of the North Shore, and Barry was a senior at Maine North High School. He and Laurie had plenty of opportunity to ease into a friendship on the flight to Honolulu and, later, at the Holiday Inn on Waikiki Beach, where they all were staying. While their parents went sight-seeing and dining, Barry and Laurie walked together by the ocean and stole unsupervised moments alone in the hotel corridors and, when they could manage it, the bedrooms.

The relationship continued back home. They dated every weekend and went to movies, concerts and school dances. They never spoke directly of marriage, but Laurie talked abstractly about having children. Barry graduated in June and Laurie wrote in his yearbook:

I know you'll have a good time in college and I'll come see you even if you don't want me. I'll always love you.

Love you,
Laurie

BARRY'S impression was that Norm and Edith were too busy with other things in their lives to pay much attention to their daughter. Norm appeared to be totally wrapped up in work and tennis. Edith seemed concerned only with appearances—whether Laurie was dressed right, whether she would be able to get into a proper college.

He noticed that when Laurie approached her mother with a problem, no matter what it was, Edith seemed to trivialize it, as though she couldn't be bothered. "Oh, Laurie," she would say.

Edith was focused at the time on the family's impending move one town south to Glencoe, the second wealthiest village on the North Shore. She had located a $105,000 single-story house on the west side of Sheridan Road. The L-shaped 2600-square-foot five-bedroom ranch was on a half-acre lot. A modest home by Glencoe standards, it was a big step up for the Wassermans.

While many teenagers would have found switching high schools midway through a hardship, the move offered opportunities for Laurie. She'd leave behind the unpleasant memories of Highland Park, where she'd made few friends. Academically, her sophomore year had been disastrous. Maybe at New Trier High School she could turn things around.

As part of her new beginning she had plastic surgery to reduce the size of her nose. The transformation was nearly miraculous. She was suddenly a beautiful young woman. Her big smile became her most noticeable facial feature.

WADE Keats could hardly believe his good luck. He was attending a hockey camp in Aspen, Colorado, in August 1973 when, one day, lying out by the pool at the condominium complex, he saw a girl to die for. She was about his age, darkly tanned and eye-catching in a yellow bikini. He stared at her longingly, and she returned the look.

When they began talking, they discovered they were both from the North Shore. Wade was from Winnetka and was pleased to discover that this quiet but friendly girl was going to be a new student at New

Trier, his high school, that fall. "Small world," he said. "Maybe I can show you around."

Again a vacation romance blossomed for Laurie, and again it transferred back home. Even though she was still technically seeing Barry Gallup, Laurie and Wade were virtually going steady by the time the school year began. Wade would pick her up at home every morning in his gold 1965 Ford Mustang, and she would run out to the car wearing his army jacket.

She was nervous during her first weeks at New Trier, and happy to have Wade around to ease the transition for her. Perhaps her need for him was unhealthy, but Wade didn't mind. The result, though, was that Laurie made a bad impression on the other girls and was unable to ingratiate herself into any of the cliques. She tried out for cheerleading and Girls Club—a social organization that sponsored pep rallies and athletic fund-raisers—but didn't make the cut.

When she wasn't with Wade, she took to lurking on the periphery of groups of girls, and she even picked out one particularly pretty classmate and brought her gifts of candy and earrings so she would be allowed to stand nearby.

During classes she sat slumped indifferently in her chair. She remained an academic lightweight, and her schoolmates noticed with disdain that she sometimes cheated on tests.

Barry Gallup was also going through a rough period of adjustment as a freshman at the University of Illinois. He was not happy with the new friends he was making, and he missed Laurie.

One weekend she went down to visit. When he tried to explain his problems to her, she brushed him off in almost the same way he'd seen Edith brush her off so many times in the past.

"Don't tell me," she said impatiently. "I can't help you with that."

LAURIE gave Wade Keats his army jacket back around homecoming in October and told him she wanted to break up and date other boys. Barry was still in the picture and her other romances continued to overlap.

Rob Heidelberger—a strapping athlete who drove a hot 1968 LeMans convertible—saw her several times standing alone in the hallways looking heartbreakingly lost and friendless. He introduced himself to her one day and asked her out.

They went to dinner a couple of times and cruised around after school in the LeMans listening to the Beach Boys. Laurie had a job at the Highland Park K mart, and didn't hesitate one time to slide items through for free for her new boyfriend. Once, when she was told to restock shelves, she punched in on the clock and left the store. When she returned at quitting time to punch out, the manager fired her.

Rob asked her to the junior prom, which was held at the elegant Orrington Hotel in nearby Evanston. He borrowed his father's car, but on the way to pick her up he was distracted trying to tune the radio and hit the brakes too late to prevent a minor collision that knocked a small hole in the radiator.

He had to call his father, who came and got him and took him home so he could drive the LeMans instead, all of which made him well over a half hour late to the Wassermans'.

"God, you're late," Laurie seethed when he finally arrived.

"I was in an accident," Rob said.

"Well, hurry up," she said. "I can't believe you're so late."

She didn't ask him if he had been hurt, and she held on to her anger most of the evening. Rob took her home before midnight and went off with friends to a sunrise party on the beach in Wilmette.

Back in school the next week Rob approached Laurie. "We should break it off," he said. "This isn't going anywhere."

She didn't argue.

3.

PLAYING HOUSE

DESPITE Laurie's mediocre high school record she was able to get into Drake University, a small private school in Des Moines, Iowa, known as one of the colleges of last resort for underachievers among the overachieving scions of the North Shore.

She enrolled in the fall of 1975, carried a full fifteen-hour load and earned A's, B's and C's, working uncharacteristically hard in an effort to get her grades up so she might transfer to a school like the University of Arizona, with a climate and social atmosphere more to her liking.

At Drake she ran across Chuck Brotman, the boy who'd dumped her when she was a freshman at Highland Park High School. He was pleasantly surprised to see her and thought nothing of calling out a friendly greeting.

She said nothing, but fixed him instead with a hard, malevolent stare. He would feel that same stare nearly ten years later when he saw her at the wedding reception of a mutual friend.

"Don't you look at me," she snapped at him then. "Don't you ever look at me."

THE University of Arizona accepted her after freshman year into the college of liberal arts, where she signed up for education courses. Later she switched to the home economics department to study the merchandising of clothing and textiles. With such a specialty a student could expect to land a middle-management job in retail clothing sales, a field Laurie already knew a great deal about from the consumer end. She had a particular passion in those days for the crisp, understated preppie styles that quietly revealed her family's wealth.

Her wardrobe made a good impression when she went through sorority rush at Alpha Delta Pi, where she was one of thirty women accepted into the pledge class that fall. She was five feet three inches tall by then, weighed a little under a hundred pounds, and always had a deep, smooth tan. Her hair was straight and silky, parted down the middle and falling just over her shoulders in back.

She didn't earn a C average her first semester and so was on academic probation at the sorority second semester when the pledge class went on "Walkout," a traditional wilderness retreat to build spirit and deepen friendships. When the time came to leave for the trip, Laurie didn't show.

Her Pledge Mom, an upperclasswoman, finally confronted her. "You don't seem interested in being part of the group," she said. "Why don't you resign now so we don't have to kick you out?"

Laurie quit.

The summer after her first year in Tucson she took a two-credit home economics course at the University of Wisconsin in Madison. She leased a room in the Towers, a private luxury dorm.

She went back to Arizona in the fall and took a room in a town house at Euclid Terrace—a complex known variously as the Zoo or Animal House because it was occupied by some of the hardest partyers on campus. Since Laurie didn't really take to crazy partying, she was happy to find a soul mate in Pearl Gelb, a quiet, plain but friendly girl from Northbrook, a suburb near the North Shore.

Pearl and Laurie met while sunning themselves by the pool at Euclid Terrace, and they soon were playing tennis, going out to dinner, and seeing movies together. Laurie made it clear to Pearl that academics weren't particularly important to her—she was looking for a husband. Her search took her through a variety of run-of-the-mill boyfriends until she reported the next fall that she'd found a live one, Stephen Witt, a handsome Jewish premed student with dark hair and an athletic build.

They had met at a party one Friday night, and he'd asked her out to a football game the following afternoon. The more they got to know each other, the more they seemed like an ideal match—they were both attractive but somewhat insecure people who had gone from mate to mate with almost no interruption, and they shared a desire that bordered on need for frequent, overt displays of affection.

The new couple took swing-dance lessons, tried all the new restaurants, and went to loud clubs. Steve always paid, even though she was the rich girl and he was the pharmacist's son.

Pearl took a dim view of the relationship as it became more serious. Laurie was far too clingy and dependent, and she seemed easily manipulated by Steve. He also reserved the right to date other girls, and this, Laurie said, made her crazy. She was so obsessed by the progress of the relationship that she dropped out of school for the balance of the semester.

She reenrolled for winter term, and when she came back from Christmas vacation, she told Steve she wanted their relationship to be exclusive. He agreed, but the arrangement seemed to do nothing to calm her insecurities. She raged at Steve whenever he spoke to another woman. His friendships suffered because she never gave him time to see anyone else.

He kept the romance going partly out of convenience. Between keeping up with classes and trying to prepare for the Medical College Admission Test, he had neither the time nor the inclination to engineer a new social life.

He drove Laurie the eighteen hundred miles from Tucson home to Glencoe at the start of the summer and stayed four days at the Wassermans'. Steve returned to Tucson with the impression that Laurie's father was an extremely strong-willed, controlling figure compared to her subdued mother.

In the fall Steve and Laurie moved into separate furnished units in the Colony Apartments. Technically, Laurie was sharing an apartment with three other girls, but she almost never spent time with them. She never talked to them about school, she never talked to them about her friends, she never even talked about herself. Everything was Steve, Steve, Steve.

She virtually lived with him. She did his laundry, she folded his clothes, she cooked and cleaned, all of which allowed him to focus on getting into medical school the next year. It was great for Steve, but he had the horrible feeling she'd be a millstone in the long run.

Early in the winter semester Steve sat Laurie down and told her that because he hadn't been admitted to medical school yet, he'd decided to go away to the University of Southern California for dental school in the fall. He didn't want her to come.

She was crushed. "But why?" she wailed.

"I've lost all my friends here already," he said. "I don't want to go somewhere and not make any friends because of you wanting to spend so much time with me."

Laurie tried anger, tears and promises. "I'll try to be less possessive," she said. "I won't do it anymore."

He was nervous nearly all spring. It was true that he'd been accepted at Southern Cal, but he was actually holding out for the Arizona College of Medicine, where he was on the waiting list. When he cleared the wait list, he didn't tell Laurie, since she was already making plans to leave town.

She was shattered by the end of the affair. She called her mother for consolation.

"You'll find another boyfriend," Edith said.

When it was too late for Laurie to change her plans, Steve told her that he had, in fact, been admitted to medical school at Arizona and he would be staying in Tucson after all.

In July of 1980, with only a promise from Steve that they would get together in Boca Raton, Florida, at her parents' new vacation condominium during Christmas vacation, to see how things stood, Laurie withdrew from Arizona. She was twenty-two credit hours shy of the hundred and twenty-five hours required for a degree, and she hoped to finish up at Northwestern University, on the North Shore, while living at home. She clung to the hope that she and Steve would end up together if only she could get herself straightened out.

Laurie and Steve continued to talk on the phone and she continued to tell herself that things would work out during the reunion in Boca Raton. But when the big week finally came, the feelings were gone, nothing was the same. He'd gone on with his life and she was stuck in hers. The realization sank in that it was really really over.

A few weeks later Steve called Laurie and made it official. "This isn't working out," he said. "We really have to break up."

In the weeks and months that followed, Laurie hounded him by telephone with weepy pleas to give her another chance. But Steve felt no temptation, only relief. He was happy to put the whole thing forever behind him.

Laurie Wasserman was history.

THE summer following her breakup with Steve, Laurie signed up for courses at Northwestern's continuing education program, but then withdrew. In September 1980 she shifted directions and started courses in dance, acting and playwriting. She couldn't finish those classes either.

Nevertheless, to her friends she seemed to be thriving. Those who met her at restaurants and bars in those days thought she was prettier and more self-confident than ever.

She continued to crave the college experience and so moved into the Lake Shore Club, a Northwestern dormitory. She helped support herself by working as a cocktail waitress at Green Acres, an all-Jewish golf-and-tennis club in Northbrook. On one particularly crowded night in the spring of 1981 she was flattered by the attentions of a bright-eyed, mischievous guy with a round face and slightly lopsided grin who'd been giving her the eye as he ate dinner in the restaurant.

"What's your name?" he asked.

"Laurie," she said, but so softly he misunderstood.

"Well, Linda," he said. "What do you say sometime I call you and we get together?"

Laurie smiled. "I'd like that," she said.

He touched her lightly on the end of her perfect nose and said, "See you later, cutie."

THE FLIRT WAS RUSSEL DANN, a twenty-five-year-old sales executive at his family's Northbrook-based insurance company. He was cocky, outgoing, ingenuous, and, Laurie thought, he looked a lot like Davy Jones, one of the Monkees.

Russell and Laurie were similar in some respects. They were both the youngest children of well-to-do Jewish families. They both had trouble early on in school—Russell's problems were attributed to a mild dyslexia. They had both gone to Highland Park High School at one time, and then on to private, less competitive colleges.

But where Laurie had been a reclusive, insecure child, Russell had been rambunctious and popular. Everyone in school called him Rusty. In elementary school music class he and his friends were the ones who screamed and bumped heads together dancing the cancan. By junior high he was riding his minibike hell-for-leather through the streets. One time he crashed into a wall at a friend's house and put his head through a pane of glass. The cuts all along his neck and under his chin were severe and very bloody. His friend was frantic.

"Don't you get worried," Rusty ordered, pressing his hands against his throat to stanch the blood and hold the skin together. "Stay calm."

He got to a phone and reached his mother. "Mom," he said evenly. "Is Dad home?"

The cuts took a hundred and fifty stitches to close and left tiny scars that nicked his face into adulthood.

At Highland Park High, Rusty was happy-go-lucky, a good-time kid who was so lively he could be a teacher's favorite even though he was no better than an average student. In his senior year a private academic counselor directed him to Ithaca College, in upstate New York. He dropped Rusty, a nickname he thought made him sound like a three-year-old, in favor of Russell, and began working toward a liberal arts degree. After his sophomore year he decided to transfer to the University of Denver because the skiing was better out there. In his senior year he returned to Ithaca.

Russell felt a little aimless after graduation, which was good news as far as his father, Armand, was concerned. Armand had always hoped that his charismatic younger son would lend his energies to the Dann Brothers Insurance Company, where Scott, his older son, was already working and doing well. Russell signed on after graduation and started as a clerk, filing claim forms.

He was not brilliant by any measure. He wasn't well read or up on current events and he was not a great conversationalist, but he had self-confidence, a competitive drive, a tireless capacity for work and an insistent, unmistakable sincerity. When he moved into the sales end of the business, he quickly became one of the firm's most prolific account executives.

He bought a condominium in Northbrook. It was a one-bedroom duplex, with a spiral staircase, and a Ping-Pong table in the rec room. He settled into a comfortable life of working long hours, playing in softball and touch-football leagues, and dating the tempting variety of eligible women available to a wealthy and affable guy who bore a slight resemblance to Davy Jones.

He never did follow up with a call to that cocktail waitress, "Linda." He was reminded of this social error one night several months later when he was cruising with friends at a bar named Bennigan's. Russell's group had latched on to two women, one of whom looked a lot like Linda. Different hair, slightly different attitude—her sister, probably.

"What's your name?" he asked cautiously.

"Laurie," she said.

Talk about an awkward moment. Laurie was clearly the prettier and more poised of the sisters, yet technically he had asked Linda out first. Should he say anything? He decided not to mention that he knew Linda at all.

They spoke for a while longer; then Russell asked Laurie and her friend for a ride home. During the ride he got Laurie's phone number, and this time he followed up with a call. Several days later he took her into the city for dinner at a small, trendy French restaurant.

"I feel really bad," he confessed once they entered the place and were seated. "See, I asked your sister out and then I stood her up. Now I'm going out with you. I mean, it could be terrible if I ever have to meet her."

Laurie shrugged uncomfortably. "Don't worry about it," she said.

Their first date was followed by several more. But he was still bothered by what Linda was going to think when she found out. "I'm probably going to meet her sooner or later," he began one night. "And I don't know what I'm going to say."

"That was me both times," she said. "You asked *me* out, you goofhead."

Russell was embarrassed, but he admired her ability to pull a fast one. He also felt that in getting beyond this misunderstanding, they'd broken through that first awkward layer of caution and reserve and were headed toward a serious relationship. She seemed very impressive at first blush—she said she was a graduate student in hospital administration at Northwestern.

Russell Dann fell in love. Laurie was just about the sweetest, most fetching girl he'd ever met—demure, devoted and, when the lights were out, passionate. She also came from a proper family. By coincidence, at the time that Laurie and Russell were first beginning to date, Russell was in charge of making an insurance presentation to a chain of women's clothing stores for which Norm Wasserman was the accountant.

He and Norm got along well. They shared an interest in tennis and finance, and though their relationship was always superficial and distant by Dann family standards, Russell realized after a while that Norm treated him the way everyone in the Wasserman family treated everyone else. They were very controlled people.

Russell's relatives and friends had their doubts about the burgeoning romance. Russell's uncle Charles thought Laurie lacked vivacity and was altogether too reserved for a live wire like his nephew. Beth Kamin, whose boyfriend, Noah Rosen, was one of Russell's best friends, was struck by Laurie's single-mindedness. She seemed totally wrapped up in Russell's world, to the point of not seeming to have a life of her own. She hung on him constantly, holding his hand at all times, kissing him and making almost no effort to socialize with anyone else.

When Beth and Noah parted company with Russell and Laurie after an introductory get-together, Beth turned and shuddered. "That girl's weird," she said. "That girl is really weird."

RUSSELL's brother, Scott, and sister, Susie, were both married, and most of his contemporaries were either engaged or married. Though Russell acted rebellious at times, deep down he was more attracted than anyone knew to the idea of a house, a wife, a big dog and a couple of kids. He figured that in Laurie he'd found a woman who would complement him yet let him be; a woman who would make a good wife and mother.

Nine months after they began dating, Russell and Laurie went to Boca Raton to spend the winter holidays with her parents. They took a long, late afternoon walk together along South Ocean Boulevard and around the condo building. They talked about how happy they were and what the future might hold, and Russell said, well, he'd been thinking maybe they should get married. They let the idea hang in the air between them for a minute; then Laurie decided, yeah, that would be really cool.

Edith was feeling sick and lying flat on her back in the master bedroom when the happy couple returned. Laurie was giggling and fidgeting, trying to figure how best to phrase the announcement.

"What is it?" said Norm, who was standing by impatiently. "You're late."

"We're engaged!" Laurie said.

"That's great. Congratulations," Russell recalls Norm saying with little enthusiasm. "Now can we go eat?"

IN RUSSELL, Laurie found a purpose. When he gave her a Dann family heirloom for an engagement ring, she felt, for the first time, like a success.

"Look! I'm engaged," she bubbled to her childhood playmate Jeanne Nelson when she and Russell ran into her working as a sales-clerk at a North Shore clothing store. "So how's it going with you? What are you up to?"

Jeanne wasn't surprised to see Laurie again after so many years, but she found her attitude startling. In the old days Laurie had always been so flat and faraway. Now here she was, carrying on as if the two of them were best friends.

But the truth was that Laurie really didn't have many friends. Her focus on boys since the early years of high school, combined with her lack of social confidence and initiative, had left her in the humiliating position of having very few people she even knew well enough to invite to her own wedding.

Russell did not have the same problem. He could have filled both sides of the aisle easily, but he knew Laurie would find that embarrassing. The only manageable compromise was for him to invite just ten of his very closest friends and explain to everyone else that it was going to be a small wedding.

In the interest of good family relations, Russell's sister, Susie Taylor, Scott's twin, agreed to stand up at the wedding, loan Laurie her wedding gown, and host the engagement party. She and her husband, Jeff, put together a big spread of appetizers and fried chicken at their house in Highland Park and invited five dozen people, most of whom were Russell's friends.

Susie was holding off judgment on Laurie. She seemed nice enough, but it did strike her as peculiar that Laurie never made any comment about the party or thanked them for hosting it.

Five of Russell's friends took him up to the resort town of Lake Geneva, Wisconsin, for a weekend-long bachelor party at the end of the summer. Laurie, meanwhile, was gearing up for the wedding, to be held on September 11, 1982. One of her tasks was to practice reading a short speech Russell had written for her to deliver at the rehearsal dinner. In it she was to say how grateful she was to her parents for all they had done for her, and that she loved them very much.

It was a speech much more in the Dann tradition of open expressions of family affection than in the Wasserman tradition, and when the time came, Laurie was dumbstruck. She stood, she fumbled, she hemmed. The people around her said, "Come on, it's okay, it's okay."

Laurie sat down. She simply could not say the words.

RUSSELL felt like an ice-cream man in his white tuxedo. At the end of the wedding ceremony he triumphantly broke a glass with his foot, in keeping with Jewish tradition; then, because he was a tidy person, he bent down to pick the shards up off the floor.

Rabbi Sholom Singer stopped him with a smile. "It's okay," he said. "You can leave it."

Everyone laughed.

The reception, which included a sit-down dinner for sixty-five guests, was at Green Acres, where the bride and groom had met. Everyone danced the hora, and Russell's friends hoisted him in a chair and danced around the room waving him aloft.

The newlyweds spent their honeymoon in Virgin Gorda, in the British Virgin Islands, where they had reservations at the Little Dix Bay resort. They stayed two weeks on the white-sand crescent bay. Russell spent his days sunning, snorkeling, scuba diving and sailing, but Laurie often preferred to stay in the room. She was generally more withdrawn and less self-confident than he had expected, but it was not so bad that he doubted his decision to marry her. It would clearly take time for her to blossom under his care and guidance.

When they returned home and moved into Russell's town house, Laurie gradually began adopting superstitions and little rituals—something Russell hadn't seen from her before. Every so often she would open the car door at a stoplight and tap her foot on the pavement or walk down a street hopping deliberately over cracks in the sidewalk. She refused to let Russell leave for work in the morning until she had put her hand on the sofa. "Something bad will happen if I don't," she explained.

"Whatever you say," Russell answered with a shrug. It wasn't so hard to humor her.

Such ritualistic behavior often arises in response to stress and feelings of helplessness, psychiatrists say. It can indicate that a person is attempting to gain a feeling of control over life.

Laurie admitted on several occasions that she felt badly outclassed by the other women in her husband's life. Susie, his sister, was poised, generous and outgoing, a former schoolteacher and a mother of three. Elaine, Russell's mother, was a successful commodities broker. These and other formidable North Shore women had set the standard against which Laurie knew she would be judged. The pressure of knowing she had to measure up professionally, socially and domestically seemed to bring on the quirky behavior that had plagued her briefly when she was a child. The unintended, maddening result for Laurie was that the rituals became part of the problem, making it difficult for her to tend to the normal requirements of life.

One of the first things Russell noticed was the appalling condition of the linen closet. Laurie threw all her clothes—new, old, clean and dirty—inside on the floor, and filled the rest of the space with household objects. Russell would open the closet and then have to dance backwards to avoid the falling debris. He built her a second closet downstairs, but that one got to be even worse.

Such aggressive sloppiness struck a sharp contrast both to the way Laurie had enjoyed "playing house" with Steve Witt in Arizona, cooking and cleaning for him, and to her own upbringing. Guests of Norm and Edith Wasserman's used to remark on the lack of clutter, dirt and

LAURIE GROWS. Below, Laurie Wasserman (bottom right) with her sixth-grade class, at Red Oak Junior High School. Right, Laurie's high school yearbook picture.

Right, Laurie at the University of Arizona in 1976 as a pledge at the Alpha Delta Pi sorority (bottom row, third from left). Below, Russell Dann and Laurie at their engagement party, in 1982.

dust in the house. The knickknacks were placed in a studied array, as though in a museum. From the looks of Laurie's closets, though, you would have thought she had been raised by bag ladies.

It was particularly upsetting for Russell, who had always been something of a neatnik. His initial reaction to his bride's fractured domestic sensibilities was to sit her down and help her devise step-by-step plans to organize her clothing. First she was to pick up what was on the floor and put it into piles. Then sort the piles. Then fold what she couldn't put on hangers, and put the hanger clothes in the closet.

He would be firm and unavoidably patronizing. She would be chastened and compliant. For one or two days afterward things would get a little better; then she would once again find herself slipping back into her old, careless ways.

Laurie's inattentiveness, lack of motivation and other emerging peculiarities made it impossible for her to keep a steady job. Several months after the wedding she began working as a waitress at Langtry's, a restaurant and sports bar in nearby Glenview. Russell stopped by for a drink after tennis at the club and wondered why he didn't see Laurie, who had told him she was working that evening.

The manager, who knew Russell, came over to the bar. "I . . . I'm sure you're here because of what happened with Laurie the other day," he began awkwardly.

Russell didn't know what he was talking about, but played along. "Yeah," he said. "But I want to hear it from you."

"Well, there was a table of girls," the manager said. "They were rowdy and changing their drink orders all the time, so Laurie, she just blew up. I had to fire her on the spot."

Russell tested Laurie when he got home. "How was work?"

"Fine," she said. "Everything was great."

"Well, how come when I was over there, they told me you got fired?" he asked.

She buried her face in her hands and wept. "I'm doing the best I can," she said. "I'm just trying to please my dad. I'm just trying to show him how I can work and do stuff. I didn't want anyone to know I got fired."

"You need to be honest with me," Russell said. "Talk to me. Tell me what happened."

But again Laurie offered no explanations, only excuses.

SHE TRIED AGAIN IN THE EARLY spring, this time at Glenbrook Hospital, in Glenview. She wrote on her application that she'd worked as a volunteer at Northwestern and Evanston hospitals in 1981. She claimed to have graduated from Drake University with a bachelor's degree in general studies.

Her résumé looked good and she was hired. She started in the admitting/business-services department as a full-time patient-services representative in central registration. After she completed her three-week training period, her supervisor concluded that Laurie had almost no interpersonal skills when dealing with outpatients. She also mishandled cash receipts. She was fired almost immediately.

On and on it went, job after job. Russell would return home after a long day at Dann Brothers and there would be Laurie, fuming. The jerks fired her again. She'd done nothing wrong. Luck was against her. It was an outrage.

After she'd been through nearly a dozen employers, Russell sat her down. "You know," he said, "you don't have to work. I make enough money for both of us."

"But I've got to do something," she said.

Russell swallowed the bitter response that came to mind—she could start by learning to take care of herself and her belongings. "Why do you have to have a job?" he said instead.

She shrugged. "You're supposed to have a job," she said. "I mean, people think you should have a job, right?"

"Don't work to impress everybody else," he said. "Do something you like. You like to help people, right?" She nodded. "Well, then you should volunteer with a charity," he went on. "There's no pressure, and you're going to get a good feeling. You start your day by doing something nice for somebody else."

Laurie embraced the idea in theory, but after her initial flurry of activity in volunteer positions, she quit. After that she killed her days by shopping, going to lunch with her mom, sleeping, watching TV and worrying that her own failings would destroy the marriage she had wanted so badly.

RUSSELL and Laurie often played cards with Noah and Beth Rosen, who had gotten married the summer after the Dann wedding. Laurie was such a careless cardplayer that she and Russell lost consistently at spades and it stopped being fun for him after a while. So they regrouped and made it the women against the men. Laurie and Beth, who otherwise didn't have a whole lot in common, built a friendship on the bond they formed trying to beat their husbands.

The women would occasionally go off together to talk, and it was on one of their walks that Laurie confessed her growing worries about her place in the Dann family. "They're so warm and outgoing," she fretted. "My family is kind of introverted. We don't get together and laugh and have fun. And his mom is so great, and his sister is so great. I just don't fit in."

Beth tried to be upbeat. "I'm sure they accept you," she said. "I'm sure they love you. Give it time."

"I know I should," Laurie said abjectly. "But Russ is the first person who gave me a lot of warmth and a lot of love. I don't even know how to deal with it."

"What do you mean?"

"Well, like, if he asks me to do something tomorrow, I'll be so nervous that I won't be able to remember to do it that I stay up all night; then I fall asleep and sleep all day and forget what I was supposed to do. Is that crazy?" Before Beth could answer, Laurie rambled on. "And I've gotten real superstitious. Like I'm afraid if I close the cabinets in the kitchen, he's going to stop loving me. It seems like the more time I have, the more I worry."

"Don't," said Beth. "Don't worry. Russ loves you. Things will be okay."

SUSIE Taylor tried to be generous in her assessment of her brother's wife, but she was quietly entertaining doubts. Laurie came off as immature and unfriendly, and it became a point of interest at every family gathering whether she would say thank you to the hosts or, if she was particularly out of it, say anything at all. Once in a while she seemed normal; other times she seemed impenetrable.

Susie had also been annoyed at the way Laurie treated the Taylor children. When she saw Susie's kids at the Green Acres Country Club swimming pool, she would walk right past and not even acknowledge them. Susie had even asked Russell if he would please mention to Laurie that it might be nice if she would say hi to the kids. The next thing she heard, Laurie was furious at her for talking behind her back.

WHEN RUSSELL AND LAURIE INVITED friends over, Russell usually did all the setting up and all the cleaning. When he once put her in charge of the snacks for a party, she got so worried that she wouldn't have the pretzels and potato chips ready in time that she set them out on the buffet a week in advance. They were soggy and stale when the guests arrived.

4.

OVERWHELMED

L AURIE knew Russell wanted to have children and re-create the vibrant family life he remembered from his own youth, and for her part, Laurie wanted to fashion a life for a child like the life she'd never had. He used to say he wanted two, and she had said she wanted one. They even made a deal—if Laurie would agree to have more than one kid, Russell would allow her to adopt a lapdog instead of the big dog he wanted.

Laurie went along with the plan in theory, but the reality of little children seemed to confuse her. When she visited her college friend Pearl Gelb, she was often brought face to face with Pearl's three-year-old niece, Samantha. The girl was always ready to play or jump into Laurie's lap.

"Oh, how darling," Laurie would say, drawing back and keeping her distance. She appeared uncomfortable.

"I'm afraid to have kids," she confided to Pearl. "I wouldn't know what to do with them. It's such an incredible responsibility."

"You'd handle it," Pearl promised her. "It's an instinct people have."

"Not me," Laurie said.

RUSSELL found that lecturing Laurie was like talking to a cat—she looked at him, seemed to listen, then went off and did whatever she felt like. The messiness in her closets spilled over into the kitchen, where she started storing pots, pans, plates and cutlery together in any old drawer.

He tried encouraging her with praise, he tried ranting and raving, but nothing worked for long. After about a year and a half of marriage it was clear that Laurie wouldn't be able to solve her own problems. She decided to see a psychiatrist.

She began going to psychiatrist Dr. Robert Greendale, in Highland Park. She visited his office three times in the first month, and he put her on thioridazine.

Greendale has never revealed his specific diagnosis, but the drug he prescribed is a major tranquilizer—distinct from such minor tranquilizers as Valium—and is administered for short-term treatment of depression that is accompanied by anxiety and agitation. It is also used to treat psychosis, in which the patient is out of touch with reality.

Russell noticed that the thioridazine helped flatten out Laurie's increasingly unpredictable mood swings. Unfortunately, it didn't provide the instantaneous cure for her deeper problems both she and Russell were hoping for. He went with her to one of the early therapy sessions. Laurie repeated to Greendale some of the things she had told Russell about her feelings for her parents—a confused love-hate having to do with what she saw as a lack of genuine support and affection.

Laurie did not like therapy—it was difficult and the results were far from immediate. She missed her fourth appointment and called the following Monday to tell Greendale she wasn't coming back. He was so alarmed that he wrote her immediately:

> I felt compelled to send you a letter as a follow-up to our very brief discussion today. I am genuinely concerned about your ability to cope with the problems that you have been struggling with. I think it is important for you to realize that the nature of your problems goes back long before you married your husband and it relates very much to your childhood upbringing.

When Russell read the letter, he was not surprised that Greendale had zeroed in on Laurie's family life as the source of her troubles. He himself had already noticed that Laurie's behavior improved dramatically whenever Norm and Edith were vacationing in Florida. She would begin to feel better about herself and show some small signs of being able to cope. When Russell and Laurie visited Norm and Edith in Florida, Laurie decided she couldn't step on the rug in the entryway and so tiptoed around it, her back to the wall. She insisted on using only one hand on the handlebars when they all went bike riding, and she nearly fell off going over a bridge. Russell hoped Norm and Edith would find this startling and troubling, but it didn't seem to bother them.

Responsibilities and expectations had weighed upon Norm Wasserman ever since his father died when he was young, and he'd become a methodical, purposeful man. Laurie complained to Russell that a desire for organization seemed to rule her father's life. Emotional highs and lows made him nervous, she said. When a large, old tree fell over in his yard once, he seemed nearly paralyzed with anxiety: Who would take care of it? How long would it take? How much would it cost?

"He's frantic," Laurie reported to Pearl Gelb. "This is the worst thing that's ever happened in his life. I hope nothing bad ever really happens. I don't know what he'd do."

Edith was no help in such situations. She was the kind of person who wouldn't drive at night or in the rain because of her uncertainty as to where to find the lights and the switch for the windshield wipers, Russell remembered. She never worked. As far as he could tell, she spent her days shopping, going to the beauty parlor, watching television, working crossword puzzles and waiting for Norm to come home.

Laurie told Russell that her mother had given her no sympathy when she was a child. Mark had always been her favorite child anyway—people said they could just tell. Laurie always envied and admired her brother. "I could tell him everything," she once said. "It was really awful when he moved away."

RUSSELL took the letter from Dr. Greendale with him when he and Norm went fishing at a little lake west of Highland Park. During a quiet moment he produced the letter and read it aloud, laying careful stress on the words "the nature of your problems goes back long before you married your husband and it relates very much to your childhood upbringing."

Norm had no response at first, and bit his lower lip contemplatively. "What do you think?" Russell said.

"I think," Norm said, "that there's really not that much of a problem here. It's a nonissue. I don't believe in psychiatry."

Neither did Laurie. She would not go back into therapy.

RUSSELL thought he had another solution. He and Laurie would move from the condo into a real house, where she would have more room to store things and less of an excuse to jam everything into the nearest drawer or closet. They began looking in late 1984, eventually settling on a five-bedroom house on Hastings Street, in one of Highland Park's less wealthy neighborhoods. The house was conspicuously large, even ostentatious, for a childless couple in their mid-twenties.

But even on their first day in the new house Russell could see how foolish he'd been to think the shift in address was going to change things. As the movers brought furniture in the door and asked Laurie where the pieces should go, she said she couldn't decide; she had no idea, no opinion. There was no new beginning for her. Rather than concentrate her energies on self-improvement, she brooded on the apparent inequity that had her and Russell paying $178,500 for their house, while a family on a street behind them had bought a similar house for $20,000 less.

"Let's walk over there so we can see the house," Laurie suggested to Beth Rosen when she came for a visit. "I want to see if it's nicer than ours."

Beth agreed, and over they went. Laurie was polite but frosty to the homeowners, and turned increasingly grim as she realized the house was in better shape than her own.

"Damn it!" she said as she and Beth were walking home.

"What?"

"They got a great deal," Laurie complained.

"So did you," Beth said.

"Not compared to them. I didn't like them," Laurie said, her voice taking on a hard edge. "They were jerks." Her anger stuck with her, not just for days but for months and years. She nurtured every grievance, saved it, recalling it frequently, allowing it to grow.

LAURIE refused to use the "unlucky" back staircase down to the family room and developed an aversion to casual physical contact that was so strong she was unable to simply pass an object to someone else without dropping or tossing it at the last second. She began leaving money in the oven and the freezer, canned food in the dishwasher, and makeup in the microwave. As startling as these new unconventionalities might have been to outsiders, Russell was only slightly put out. After two years he was worn down, almost immune. His wife was kooky; maybe she was just looking for attention.

Russell was in way way over his head. He had married—perhaps hastily, in retrospect—a beautiful, unassuming woman who seemed to share his values. And slowly she had become the victim of some sort of mental condition. He didn't know what to do about it, and so a lot of the time he just tried to pretend that it wasn't so bad. He was not a genius. He was not a hero. He was not an idiot. He was just an ordinary guy in trouble.

SUSIE, Russell's sister, decided she wanted to give away the last of her baby clothes, so she called him and asked if maybe he'd like to take them and put them away for the day he would be a father.

"That's the furthest thing from my mind right now," he said miserably. "I doubt Laurie will ever be able to raise kids, Susie. She can barely get through the day as it is."

"You're kidding."

He broke down and told his sister everything—about the trash all over the house, the belongings stashed in queer places, the superstitions that ruled Laurie's existence. "She's overwhelmed," he said. "She's overwhelmed by life."

Susie gently suggested to him the possibility of a divorce. "It's not such a bad thing," she said.

"I don't believe in it," he said. "I won't divorce her."

"But she's not the person you thought she was," Susie said. "You don't have to feel responsible."

"You don't understand," Russell said. "I do feel responsible."

He became Rusty Dann all over again—his face cut to shreds after a minibike accident, holding it all together. Just holding it together.

ALL Laurie Wasserman Dann ever wanted, really, was to be someone else—a girl from a happy family, popular, a good student, a college graduate and a presentable housewife. She had no idea what to do with the person she was, and she simply sank further and further into isolation and despair.

She began leaving food out to spoil on the counter, storing new clothes with the tags still on them in piles in the back seat of her car, and refusing to close cabinets or drawers she had opened. She would sleep all day. When Russell pulled into the garage after work, he would hear her get out of bed and turn on the shower.

"What's wrong?" she asked him once, reading the irritation and frustration on his face at the end of a long day.

"What's wrong?" he exploded. "I'll tell you what's wrong. I get home from work and you're in bed. Then you get in the shower and I go around picking up all the garbage off the floor; then I gotta close every cabinet, every drawer, everything you've touched. Laurie, I don't have a wife. I've got a f------ daughter!"

"These are part of my problems," she said contritely. "I've got to work them through."

He'd about had it with her problems. He gave her an ultimatum: either she return to Dr. Greendale or he would leave her.

"I'll go," she said wretchedly. "Don't leave. You're the only person who ever cared for me. Where would I go if I lost you?"

"You won't lose me," he said, calming down. "It'll be okay."

But it wasn't okay. Laurie's visits to Greendale were erratic, and she was unable to keep on schedule with the thioridazine, because it nauseated her. Her own shortcomings and a looming realization that she might have inherited or developed a serious mental illness turned her into an even darker character. She began staying in bed even when guests would drop by, in an almost zombielike state, petrified at even the thought of leaving her room.

Russell's patience expired. Their verbal battles over her behavior and her refusal to seek help became more heated and would end when he stormed out of the house in frustration. The more she felt his anger and despair, the more scared she became that he would reject her, and the further she deteriorated.

By October of 1985 Russell was too weary to continue. He decided to ask Laurie for a separation, but went first to warn Norm and Edith before they took their first big trip of the winter to Florida. "It's getting crazy," he said. "I don't think it's going to last much longer."

Norm pondered for a moment. "We should still go," he said, speaking to Russell through Edith. "Laurie knows we're supposed to go, and she'd know something terrible was wrong if we didn't go. We can come back if you decide to do it."

"I'll hang on as long as possible," Russell said. For her twenty-eighth birthday a week later he bought her a pink warm-up suit and a bouquet of flowers. She carried the flowers around for several weeks after they died, and virtually refused to take the sweat suit off. She told Beth she was convinced that Russell would never leave her as long as she had the suit on.

When Russell finally told her he was leaving her, she was devastated but not surprised. "Where am I going to go from here?" she sobbed.

She wept and he held her. They tried to call Norm and Edith in Boca Raton, but they were out. In the evening they finally reached the Wassermans. Laurie was so torn apart with sorrow that she couldn't speak, and handed the phone to Russell. He broke the news.

"Okay, Laurie, hang in there," Norm said when Russell put his daughter back on the phone. "We'll be back in a couple of weeks and we'll talk then."

Laurie hung up and fell back into Russell's arms.

Russell seethed. No wonder the poor girl was all screwed up! He hadn't calmed down when he called the Wassermans back. "Norm, you son of a bitch," he said. "Do you have any idea what your daughter's going through?"

He slammed down the phone. A few minutes later Norm called back. He and Edith would return the next morning.

5.

WAR

AFTER the separation, in the fall of 1985, Laurie lived at her parents' house whenever Norm and Edith were out of town and with Russell whenever they were in town. It was an uneasy arrangement, in which the lines of responsibility and affection were blurred. Russell continued to give her money, usually $50 and $100 bills.

They slept in different bedrooms but still had sex now and then. Russell justified it by telling himself that making love was a way of showing Laurie he didn't hate her.

The separation tore Laurie apart. Beth Rosen was shocked by her appearance when she met her for lunch not long after the announcement. She was thin and haggard, and said she hadn't been able to eat.

"I don't know how we're going to do this," she said. "I don't know how we can possibly divide everything up."

Beth was matter-of-fact. "It's easier than you think," she said. "When you don't have any kids, it's very easy."

"Oh, no, it's not," Laurie said, suddenly bitter. "It's not going to be easy. I'm not going to let Russ get away with this. I want him to suffer. I want him to know what I feel like."

"It doesn't have to be that way," Beth said. "You can just get on with your life. You can get better—work through this problem—and start dating again. Have you thought about that?"

"No, no, no," Laurie said. "I've got to get Russell. I'm going to take him to the cleaners. My dad and I have been talking to the lawyers, and they think we can really screw him."

Beth changed the subject. She worried about Laurie, but her loyalties and sympathies lay with Russell. At the end of lunch she assured Laurie they would speak again soon. But she never did have another conversation with her.

LAURIE'S next idea was that she could get Russell to stay with her if she could convince him she was pregnant.

His first response was to slough off her claim with exaggerated patience, but she saw how the very suggestion got under his skin and she kept on with it.

Such conversations invariably turned ugly. "You're never going to have kids," Russell sneered once. "You wouldn't know how to take care of them."

She would scream, cry and rage at him. He swore, threw a deck of cards at her, changed the locks on the house. Several times she called for the Highland Park police to come mediate their disputes, though the department kept no written reports on the calls, as they were resolved without charges being filed.

In her loneliness and desperation Laurie took to the telephone and fought back in a new way: for hours every day she called Russell, his family and his friends, waited for them to answer, and then, after a sinister pause, hung up. When her targets compared notes, they figured out who was behind the calls, but how were they going to prove it?

A month after the separation she called Steve Witt's father's pharmacy, in Arizona, and told the clerk she was an old friend who wanted to get in touch again. The clerk told her Steve was at a hospital in New York City doing his medical residency, and she called the hospital immediately. She approached the conversation with Steve cautiously. When she found out he was married, she told him she was married, too. It was all very normal, Steve thought, and he was pleased that she was doing well.

RUSSELL'S FATHER AND LAURIE'S father had taken the lead in the divorce negotiations, but progress was slow and tensions high. Armand finally gave Norm a deadline of January 3, 1986, to come up with a mutually acceptable proposal, which they would file in the Lake County court system because Highland Park, where Russell and Laurie had been living, was in Lake County.

But the day before the deadline Laurie filed for dissolution of the marriage as a resident of Glencoe, in neighboring Cook County. She confided her reason to her lawyer. Because of the huge backlog of divorce cases in Cook County, which includes the city of Chicago, she hoped the proceedings would drag out for two to three years.

SUSIE had no doubts about the wisdom of the breakup of her brother's marriage, and she called frequently to reassure him.

In one conversation with his sister Russell outlined various ways to split up the marital assets, several of which were less than favorable for Laurie. He was then surprised when Laurie confronted him the following day, asking how he could be so ruthless and unfair.

Russell blew up at Susie. "What are you telling people about my plans for?" he raged.

Susie yelled back at him. She hadn't told a soul.

Not long afterward the mystery was solved when Russell heard an unusual click while talking to a friend on the phone one Saturday morning. "Hang on a second," he said.

Methodically he searched the house. Finally he found Laurie, who was supposedly living at her parents' home, crouched in a pile of birdseed in her old closet, huddled up to the cordless telephone.

He called Norm in Florida. "Laurie is in a bad way," he said. "She needs your help."

"I understand," Norm said. "Tell her I'll be back in about five weeks."

"Norm, you can turn your back on this, but it's only going to get worse," Russell said. "It's not going to go away."

LAURIE sought a temporary restraining order against Russell on the last day of January, 1986. Her attorney charged that Russell had started closing out various bank accounts and that Laurie was afraid he was about to "dispose of" marital assets.

A week later Russell's attorney filed a counterpetition for dissolution of the marriage, and the gloves were off.

On April 8 Laurie called the Highland Park police to the Hastings Street house to report that Russell had spit on her, slapped her on the face, kicked her in the stomach, and struck her on the back. She showed no physical signs of having been assaulted and declined to sign a complaint form. Russell, who was standing by, told the responding officers he hadn't touched her.

A little more than two weeks later Laurie drove to the Glencoe Department of Public Safety and reported that burglars had torn apart her parents' home. She said she had left the house at 10:45 in the morning and returned an hour later to find the TV set sitting on the front steps. She carried the set into the house, she said, and noticed that the interior had been ransacked, so she left.

Officers later went through the house. Laurie told them that a $500 fourteen-karat chain with gold letters spelling out Laurie was missing, along with $2130 in cash, various stereo and video equipment, clothing, and other pieces of jewelry.

Evidence technicians found no forcible signs of entry, and they noted that most of the mayhem seemed to have occurred in Laurie's bedroom. Her wedding album had been pulled out of a closet drawer and all of her wedding pictures were thrown about the floor. Pictures of Laurie were ripped up.

The Glencoe detective put in charge of the investigation was Floyd Mohr. Mohr was thirty-one. He had started with the department as a patrolman in August of 1979 and was quickly recognized as being a different breed of cop, lacking that cynical, bravura exterior common to policemen. He was thickly built but had a soft, gentle voice and a deliberative manner that caused other officers to remark that he had something of the social worker in him. He was a listener and a negotiator, qualities that served him well in Glencoe. Police in North Shore communities weren't called upon to handle violent crime very often; mostly their jobs entailed mediating neighborhood and family spats, stopping rich kids speeding in sports cars, and investigating property crimes like the Wasserman burglary.

Detective Mohr figured right away that he was being dragged into the middle of a vicious divorce battle. Any police officer who's been around—especially in well-off areas where a lot of money is at stake in divorce settlements—knows there's almost nothing battling spouses won't do to make each other look bad. Mohr's gut feeling was that the burglary was an inside job and that Laurie had done it in order to gain leverage in court. She told him that she was under the psychiatric care of Dr. Robert Greendale, and with her permission Mohr called Greendale. But the doctor could only relay what Laurie had told him.

Just to be thorough, Mohr asked Russell for an interview. Russell was defensive at first. He said he'd been in the western suburb of La Grange on business at the time of the burglary, and he could prove it. "Come on, we'll go to the house," he said. "You can search the whole place, see if there's any of her stuff around."

The search of Russell's house turned up nothing, and when Laurie's parents returned from Florida several weeks later, Mohr shared his suspicions with Norm that the burglary was a fake.

"It's possible," Norm said. "But I don't think so. I think Russell is behind this."

"Something happened here," Mohr said. "I just don't know what."

Not long after the reported burglary at the Wassermans', Russell came home from work to find his shirts drenched with water and Laurie crouched again in a closet.

"This is war," she told him, her eyes narrowing in hatred. "You have no idea how miserable I can make your life."

"Laurie, let's put this behind us," he begged.

"Why?" she said as she stood. "I don't have any reason to go on living. And if I go, you're coming with me."

The threat was barely veiled. "What are you talking about?" he said.

Torment flickered briefly on her face; then her gaze turned hollow and she smiled. "This is the worst thing that's ever happened to you, isn't it?" she said.

LAURIE went to buy a gun on the fifth of May, half a year into the separation. She walked into the Marksman Police & Shooters Supply, in Glenview, and explained to the salesman that she needed something for protection. She eventually settled on the heavy artillery—a $275 nickel-plated Smith & Wesson .357 Magnum with a four-inch barrel.

She also picked out two fifty-count boxes of ammunition, then filled out an application for an Illinois Firearm Owner's Identification Card.

The card required no examination; an applicant simply paid $5 and filled out a questionnaire that asked only eight questions:

Are you an illegal alien?
Have you renounced your citizenship?
Are you under indictment?
Have you been convicted of a felony?
Are you a fugitive?
Do you use illegal drugs?
Have you ever been in a mental institution?
Were you dishonorably discharged from the Armed Forces?

Laurie truthfully answered no to each, and the salesman told her to return after the state's mandatory three-day cooling-off period.

When she returned, Eugene Miller, a friend of the Dann family, happened to be at the shop, and he recognized Laurie. When he saw a salesman showing her how to work her new gun, he recalled conversations he had had with Armand and Elaine Dann about the bitterness of the divorce and Laurie's apparent emotional instability. As soon as he got home, he called the Danns.

Armand Dann was so upset that he immediately called Russell. Russell went directly to the Highland Park police department to tell Detective John Burns and Lieutenant John McKeever that his estranged wife was now armed.

"She's trouble," he said. "Call Floyd Mohr, in Glencoe. He knows all about it."

Burns called Floyd Mohr. Mohr considered this a serious development. He telephoned Norm Wasserman, in Florida.

"I'll talk to her," Norm said. "I'll call you right back."

A few minutes later Norm was on the line again. "She's planning to move to an apartment in Evanston," he explained. "It's a rough town. She wants protection."

"I don't think that's a wise idea," Mohr said. "What's she going to do? Shoot at a cop coming to help her?"

"I don't like guns either," Norm said. "But she does have a right to have it. Well, I'll be home in the next few days. We'll talk about it then."

But before Norm returned to Illinois, Mohr called Laurie directly.

"It bothers me that you have a gun," he said, trying the gentle approach. "I want it."

"No," she said. "I have the card that says I can have a gun. Don't worry. I'm not going to hurt anybody."

Russell was not so sure. He felt so vulnerable that he had Susie find a town house for him on Green Bay Road in Highland Park, and he signed the lease before he even saw the place.

Mohr again called Dr. Greendale for help.

"I can't say anything more unless Laurie agrees to let me," Greendale said.

"But you've got to tell me this much," Mohr said. "She just bought a handgun. Do you think she's violent? Could she be suicidal? Or homicidal?"

"I haven't seen her lately," Greendale said, "but I'd say no, I don't think she's suicidal or homicidal."

Mohr was only slightly reassured, and he continued to raise the issue with the Wassermans. Norm finally appeared to give in—he promised that he and Laurie had agreed to store the gun in a safe-deposit box.

When Mohr asked to look inside the safe-deposit box just to be sure the gun was there, both Norm and Laurie refused.

THE theme of Laurie's complaints to her parents, the police, and the lawyers who were handling her divorce was that she was the helpless victim of a demented man. She told a good story, full of indignation and sorrow, and they attributed her occasional weird behavior to the ordinary emotional distress of divorce.

At a June 1986 temporary-support hearing, the lawyers introduced allegations that Russell had physically abused Laurie during both the marriage and the separation.

Russell filed a petition with the court the following month to force Laurie to cooperate in the sale of the Hastings Street house. She was refusing to sign a real estate listing agreement.

The divorce negotiations proceeded slowly and with extreme ill will. Norm's demands were steep: he wanted Russell to support Laurie for ten years with $20,000-a-year alimony payments after an initial $100,000 settlement.

Russell's attorneys subpoenaed Laurie's records from Northwestern to show that she was an educated woman who could support herself, and it was only then that Russell discovered that she hadn't been a graduate student when he met her and that she hadn't even completed her degree requirements at Arizona.

In light of that, Russell offered twenty-four months of support at $1500 a month, along with the agreed-upon $100,000 payment as Laurie's half of the marital property.

But Norm said no. He claimed the offer was unfair, and that if Russell didn't settle quickly, he would see to it that Laurie was put into a mental institution and that Russell would be stuck supporting her for the rest of his life. "If Laurie is crazy," Norm said, "then Russell is responsible. He ruined her."

The rhetoric was escalating, and Russell decided he just wanted out quickly. He clung to only two specific demands. The first was for the return of the engagement ring. It had sentimental value to the family. The second was for Laurie to change her legal name back to Laurie Wasserman and dissociate herself completely from the Dann family. He would pay extra, he said, for the return of his name.

But the ring was important to her, she said, and she liked Russell's last name.

Once again negotiations stalled.

In August, Steve Witt got another call from Laurie. She said she had something serious to tell him—she had a five-year-old daughter he had fathered during their last sexual encounter, in late 1980. She was telling him now, she said, because she and her husband had decided to adopt the child legally, and she wanted him to come to Chicago to sign the papers.

Steve took her very seriously, as did his wife, Barbara. But in talking further with Laurie, he began noticing inconsistencies as to where and when his daughter had supposedly been born. He finally did some checking with the likely hospitals and determined that no such child existed.

He called and confronted her. "There is no child, is there?" he said.

"No," she said.

"I know it's not my business," he said, "but I think you should seek professional help."

In September an anonymous female caller contacted Steve's New York hospital and claimed that he had raped her in the emergency room. The charge lacked substance—he hadn't even done an emergency-room rotation yet—but Steve felt so threatened that he arranged immediately to transfer back to Arizona to finish his residency there.

Barbara Witt stayed behind, and Laurie bombarded her with late-night phone calls. "You'd better get used to me," she said. "I'll follow you. I'll go to Arizona."

The Witts had their attorney write a letter to Laurie and threaten to bring legal action if the harassment did not cease, and the calls stopped—for a time.

RUSSELL was never sure how it happened, but Laurie got her hands on a key to his town house in the summer of 1986. Little things—notes and pictures—started turning up missing. Files on Russell's home computer mysteriously disappeared from the hard-disk drive.

A little after 3:00 a.m. on September 30, Russell called the operator and had her patch him through to the Highland Park police department. "I've been stabbed!" he cried.

Three officers and an ambulance arrived at his town house several minutes later. He hurriedly told his story: He'd been sound asleep when he suddenly awoke to the sound of his own scream of agony. He felt a sharp, stinging pain in his chest and jumped out of bed.

He walked around the bed, looked in the mirror over his bureau, and saw a reddish purple wound in his chest just above his heart. By the time he got back to the bed he was having trouble breathing. As he stood over the telephone by the nightstand, he looked down and saw an ice pick lying between the bed and the unattached oak headboard.

He knew the ice pick wasn't his, he said. The only logical conclusion was that his wife had tried to kill him, as she had threatened.

The responding officers were more than a little skeptical. The stab wound did not look particularly serious—the hole was just where a right-handed person might stab himself if he wanted to make it look as if he'd been attacked. Russell said he hadn't seen his attacker, and when he showed the officers an assortment of suspicious items on the first-floor couch, including a ski mask and a glass cutter, they figured he could have planted them there.

"Are you sure you haven't had a party here?" one of the cops asked. "Or maybe a friend who would play a practical joke on you?"

"You've gotta believe me," Russell insisted. "She broke in here and stabbed me."

He excused himself to call his brother, Scott, to have him come over to help; then he returned to the policemen and their increasingly sly questions. "Can we take a picture?" one of them asked, producing a Polaroid camera.

"Why don't you get the f--- out of here?" Russell said.

The open hostility and mistrust on both sides left them at an impasse. The officers had Russell sign a release to let the ambulance go without him; then they tagged along when Scott drove him to Highland Park Hospital.

In the emergency room, Dr. Mart Jalakas found that the pick had pierced muscle tissue and gone one inch into Russell's chest, where it caused a ten percent collapse of his left lung.

Highland Park police officer Daniel Dahlberg and Sergeant Edward Armitage stayed in the intensive care unit, where Russell had been placed for observation, to ask him if he would be willing to take a lie detector test. "Gladly," Russell said. He also pressed on them a set of keys to the Hastings Street house where Laurie was living and asked them to please go look around.

At 6:00 a.m. Dahlberg and Armitage checked inside and outside the unlocked Hastings Street house. Laurie wasn't home and hadn't been for two weeks, judging by the mail in the box. They found nothing unusual inside.

When Detective Jack McCafferty contacted Floyd Mohr in Glencoe to get background, Mohr told him the story of the strange burglary at the Wassermans' the previous spring and his suspicion that Laurie was responsible.

Russell was released from Highland Park Hospital at 1:30 that afternoon. Several hours later he called Detective John Burns to ask if he would meet him and his brother over at Hastings Street to go through the house.

Burns and Detective Henry Hoban met Russell and Scott a few minutes later at the house.

"Did you guys come down here and go through the house today?" Russell asked.

"I personally didn't, no," Burns said.

"It would seem to me that would be the first thing you'd do," Russell said disgustedly. His lack of regard for the authorities was palpable.

With ill will casting a pall over all of them, Russell entered the front door and led the way into the foyer. He called out for Laurie.

Two lights were on, but no one answered his calls. The men searched through the house and ended up in the master bedroom. The covers were tossed and clothes were scattered on the floor amid Laurie's Firearm Owner's Identification Card, a pair of brown paper bags and other detritus.

"What's inside that bag?" Scott asked Burns.

"Don't patronize me," Burns said. "I'm probably going to lose my job for an illegal search as it is."

Burns looked inside the first bag and saw a paper receipt and a small amount of cash. He took the receipt out and saw it was from Eckart Hardware, in Winnetka, dated September 22, 1986.

"Where is that receipt from?" Russell asked.

"You guys better get out of here," Burns said. "We've already contaminated the evidence."

"Aren't you going to check this other bag?" Scott asked. He picked up the second bag. "Look what we found in this other bag. See . . . we're doing your job for you." He presented Burns with a package for a Foley brand ice pick. The package had an Eckart Hardware store tag.

"I knew it was her," Russell told Burns. "She did it. This is the ice pick she used. Is that enough for you?"

Burns shook his head. "This evidence won't be admissible in court."

Russell locked the house as they left, and Burns eyed him suspiciously. The stuff with the receipt seemed awfully coincidental. "When was the last time you were over here?" he asked.

"It's been two weeks at least," Russell said quickly. "I couldn't have come back to the house today, because you guys had my keys. I want you to remember that."

THE morning after the search of the Hastings Street house, Detective McCafferty interviewed Norm. He told McCafferty that, as far as he knew, Laurie was home sleeping the night before, when Russell said he was attacked.

"I'm really getting tired of all these problems," he said dismissively. "My daughter isn't capable of stabbing anyone."

"Okay, but we need your help," McCafferty said. "Laurie's got to

cooperate. We need hair samples and fingerprints, and it would probably be a good idea if she took a lie detector test."

"We'll talk to a lawyer and get back to you."

McCafferty then went to Eckart Hardware to interview a salesclerk
who said he remembered selling a glass cutter to a striking young
woman. McCafferty had asked Russell for a photo of Laurie, and the
salesclerk identified Laurie as the woman.

The case against Laurie was looking stronger, but everything crum-
bled on Thursday, two days after the stabbing, when Russell failed his
lie detector test.

Detective Burns was in charge of the test, which put Russell on edge
immediately. He could barely contain his resentment. He was the
victim here, and yet he was being treated like a criminal. He shrugged,
shifted in his seat, and fidgeted through nearly an hour of such questions as "Have you ever lied to authorities?" and "Have you ever
stabbed yourself?"

Burns took note of Russell's discomfort, and though the instrument
readings were ambiguous, his summary statement said:

> The subject of the polygraph examination has indicated he is en-
> gaged in the purposeful act of non-cooperation. The effect has been to
> distort the test response. It has been the experience of the examiner
> that when the subject attempts to distort the polygraph examination
> record by purposeful non-cooperation, they do so to avoid detection
> regarding one or more of the underlying investigations.

McCafferty was contacted by Laurie's attorney, who said he would
not allow Laurie to be tested on the polygraph.

That afternoon Lake County assistant state's attorney Joe Calina
decided there wasn't enough evidence to charge anyone in the case.

The incident remains the only real criminal mystery tucked inside
the larger psychological mystery of Laurie Dann's life. What really
happened in Russell Dann's town house on the morning of September
30, 1986? Did Laurie try to kill Russell? Or did Russell stab himself in
an effort to frame Laurie?

It was certainly not unreasonable for the police to doubt Russell's
story. At the time of the incident Laurie had never hurt or attacked
anyone. And Russell seemed to have a clear motive for faking the
attack. Laurie had been harassing him and his family, and he was very

worried that she owned a .357 Magnum. Had she been convicted of stabbing him, she would have lost her permit to own a gun.

What also must be considered is the suspicious way the Dann brothers found the ice-pick receipt at the Hastings Street house and Russell's failure of the polygraph test.

Yet it's also clear that the Highland Park police allowed Russell's abrasive manner and foul language to get in the way of conducting a thorough investigation.

What matters about the ice-pick incident is not who did the stabbing. What matters is that the events in the immediate aftermath of the crime poisoned Russell's relationship with the Highland Park police department and made it even harder for him and for Laurie's other targets to make their case later that she was a truly dangerous woman.

In exasperation Russell called Laurie from his car phone. "I don't even know where to start with you," he said when she answered. "You can hate me for trying to divorce you. But to try to kill me? You're sick. You need help."

"I know," Laurie said. "What do we do?"

"We've got to get you help," Russell said.

"How?" Laurie said.

Static brushed across their conversation. "Someone's listening in!" Laurie cried. She hung up.

6.
FEAR AND FRUSTRATION

THE harassing phone calls had started again, thirteen and fourteen a day at 4:00, 5:00, 6:00 a.m. Laurie had found a way to control people, and no one in Russell's circle was safe from her power play, not even those with unlisted numbers.

When Jeff and Susie Taylor bought a new house in Highland Park, they kept their old phone number in hope that Laurie would never realize they had moved. But Laurie was a clever snoop, and one day she called Russell at work. "Why do Susie and Jeff have my outdoor furniture in their new backyard?" she said, referring to a set of lawn chairs Russell had passed along to his sister.

Susie, chilled by the realization that Laurie was on their tail, immediately had the furniture shipped back to her. She warned her children that if Aunt Laurie ever came to the door, they were not to let her in.

Susie also went to Ravinia Elementary and the Young Men's Jewish Council day-care center, where her children were enrolled, and alerted administrators that under no circumstances should anyone be allowed to take the children from school without a note from her.

The officials raised their eyebrows dubiously.

It was more or less the same reaction Beth Rosen got when, alarmed by a sudden increase in the number of hang-up calls she was getting, she went to the Deerfield police station to complain.

"Are you sure it's not children in the neighborhood?" the desk officer said.

"Yes, I'm sure," Beth said. "It's definitely Laurie Dann. Listen, this woman stabbed her husband in the chest with an ice pick. Didn't you hear about that?"

"No," said the officer impatiently. "I didn't hear about it."

Eventually both the Rosens and the Taylors paid Illinois Bell $20 a month to install tracing devices on their lines. In early December the traps successfully tracked two of the Taylors' hang-up calls to the telephone in the house on Hastings Street.

The Highland Park police wrote out an arrest warrant for Laurie. On a freezing, blustery December afternoon McCafferty and Detective Myles Bell went to the house to get her.

"I didn't make any calls," she said as they were leading her away. "A lot of people have keys to this place, you know. My husband told me he was going to have me arrested for making silent phone calls, because the divorce is taking so long."

McCafferty was glad to finally get the chance to ask Laurie about the ice-pick stabbing. She and her parents had been stonewalling him for months.

Laurie insisted that she was home on the night of the stabbing.

"What about the ice pick?" McCafferty said. "A week before the stabbing you bought one at Eckart Hardware, didn't you?"

"Yeah," she said slowly. "I was having problems with the ice maker in my freezer. It clogs up all the time."

"Well then, tell me about—"

"I have nothing else to say," she said. "Just give me the phone. I'll call someone to come bail me out."

As usual, Laurie's parents were out of town. She really had no one to go to but her old school friend Pearl Gelb and Pearl's mother, Betty.

"I have nobody else to call," Laurie said apologetically to Betty when she reached her. "I've been arrested and I need a hundred dollars to get out. Can you lend it to me?"

"My God, of course!" Betty said. She drove to the Highland Park police station to get Laurie. On their way back to the Hastings Street house, Betty could not resist asking what the arrest was all about.

Laurie sighed heavily. "For making phone calls," she said. "They called them harassing phone calls."

"Well, did you do it?" Betty said.

"Yeah, but I didn't ever *say* anything," Laurie said, still aggrieved. "I would just hang up when they answered."

"Why on earth would you do that?" Betty said. "That's the kind of thing a ten-year-old does."

"Because that Susie Taylor's given me a lot of aggravation. But can you believe it? She's calling the police for such a stupid thing?"

EVERYTHING was someone else's fault with Laurie, Pearl noticed.

"My mom and dad don't know how to love me," Laurie complained to her. "I don't think they know how to help me. They won't listen and they don't understand. All they can give me is money. All we do is fight, so I just try not to talk to them."

"That's terrible," Pearl said.

Laurie boasted to Pearl that she had gone to numerous psychiatrists, and each time she'd given them a phony name and address. "It's really funny," she said. "I tell them I'm coming back; then I never come back."

"Why are you making up names?" Pearl asked.

"I don't want them to know who I am," Laurie said.

The deceptions bothered Pearl. She found herself caught between Laurie and Russell, with whom she'd become friends. The stories of his heartless cruelty were obviously false to anyone who knew him, which meant that Pearl couldn't trust Laurie as a friend anymore.

It was tough, because Laurie needed a friend more than anything.

DIRECTLY after the Lake County prosecutors decided not to proceed with the ice-pick case, Russell got in touch with attorney Rick Kessler, a former prosecutor who had gone into private practice. Russell hired him to help build a case against Laurie.

Kessler thought Russell should try to get a court order allowing him to be wired with a secret recording device so he could meet with Laurie and try to get her to confess explicitly to the ice-pick stabbing. But the county prosecutor in charge of felony review told him there wasn't enough evidence to support a wire.

For protection Russell hired Frank Bullock, a private detective. Bullock was a gumshoe straight out of central casting—a beefy, tobacco-chewing forty-six-year-old with red hair, a mustache and a tattoo on his left arm. Bullock's assignment was twofold: to try to gather additional information to force the police and prosecutors to take a more aggressive position, and to figure out just how much danger Russell and his family might be in.

LAURIE desperately needed something to do, and began answering baby-sitting ads in the help-wanted section of the local newspaper. As long as the children weren't too young, she found that she could connect with them and that they simply accepted her for who she was.

She impressed her first few clients with her reliability and maturity, her prices and her gentle manner. The Rushe family of Winnetka—to whom she identified herself as Laurie Porter for no reason she ever explained to anyone—was happy to recommend her to friends. She eagerly took the Rushes' five children on outings such as a trip to the park on the Fourth of July to see the Winnetka fireworks. The kids adored her, and Marian Rushe was thrilled to have found a sitter who was willing to work weekends.

Laurie at last had found a challenge she could meet. It was as if Laurie Porter truly was a different person from Laurie Dann.

LAKE County prosecutors dropped telephone harassment charges against Laurie on February 25, 1987, a little more than two months after her arrest. The prosecutors knew that any judge would dismiss the charges in a second because none of the victims had ever heard the caller's voice and several people had access to the telephone in the Hastings Street house from which most of the calls were coming.

RUSSELL and Laurie finally agreed to split the money from selling the Hastings Street house. Russell said he would pay Laurie $1250 a month for thirty-six months and $10,000 for her attorney's fees. She would keep his name and the engagement ring. As soon as they could get everyone together in court, it would be over.

Laurie's harassing phone calls diminished for a while over the winter, but when spring arrived, she returned with a vengeance. The Highland Park police grew so tired of the same old allegations that they became more and more lax about returning phone calls to the Taylors and others who complained. Jeff and Susie, in frustration, wrote an angry letter to Lake County state's attorney Fred Foreman expressing disappointment at what they saw as Foreman's insensitivity to their plight.

Foreman did not get back to them.

ON APRIL 20 Laurie invited her neighbor, Dean Pappas, a man four years her senior who was also living at home with his parents, over to her parents' house. She asked him to bring over his copy of the Stephen King movie *Christine* to watch on the VCR.

They watched the movie; then Dean told Laurie he was getting tired and should head home. She said she, too, was feeling tired. She didn't lock the door behind him as he left.

Later, in the early hours of the next morning, Laurie related the following tale to police:

> I took a shower and then a bath after Dean left. It was about one in the morning when I got out of the tub, and I heard noises in the other room. So I put on a sweatshirt, underwear and a dress and went into my father's office. Russell was standing there, wearing surgical gloves and going through drawers.
>
> He told me, "I want the f------ ring."
>
> I told him, "It's not yours."
>
> He said, "It's mine and it belongs to my family. I want it back." Then he grabbed me, dragged me into my parents' bedroom and began going through more drawers.
>
> After he realized he wasn't going to find the ring, he threw me onto the bed. He pulled off my dress and my panties with one yank, and started saying how much he hated me and how he wanted to see me dead or at least a paraplegic so I would suffer. He pulled out a little steak knife and put it up against my neck.
>
> I said, "You're not going to hurt me with that."
>
> He said, "I'm not stupid enough to leave any marks."

He pulled the knife away from my neck and put it in his back pocket. "You're looking pretty good," he said.

Then he started to get mad again and he told me I'd better sign the divorce papers by Friday or else. He pulled the knife from his pocket again and stuck it into my vagina. He said, "You sign the papers or I cut you all the way up, bitch."

Then he unzipped his pants and began to masturbate with his right hand while trying to hold me down with his left. I grabbed for his groin, but I missed and ripped out some pubic hair.

He yelled out, "I ought to kill you, bitch!" Then he started to leave and said, "The police aren't going to believe you."

Glencoe officers found an eight-inch cut in the screen of a porch door. They also found bloodstains on the sheet and two clumps of dark, curly hair. They drove Laurie to Highland Park Hospital, where a doctor examined her and found only a very small scratch on her vaginal wall. Laurie said she was too frightened to sign a complaint.

Floyd Mohr took the case the next morning. He called Laurie to ask her to meet with him and sign the complaint.

"I just can't handle it today, Detective," she said. "And I don't know if I'm going to press charges."

Mohr then called Russell, who said he had been home sound asleep at the time Laurie said she was attacked. Hadn't Mohr gotten the picture by now? Nothing surprised Russell anymore, not even Mohr's apparently chronic inability to sort out fact from fiction. Russell said he wasn't going to answer any more questions until he talked to his attorney, Rick Kessler. Kessler advised Russell not to cooperate.

Floyd Mohr didn't know whom to believe. The knife rape seemed impossible, on the surface. How could a man hold a woman down, insert a knife into her with one hand, masturbate with the other and leave no bruises and only the tiniest scratch? But then, to further confuse him, Laurie took and passed two separate polygraph tests. Mohr decided to get a warrant to obtain a sample of Russell's pubic hair.

ON APRIL 27, 1987, a Cook County circuit court judge signed off on the divorce. The marriage of Russell Dann and Laurie Wasserman had lasted a little more than four and a half years, including a year and a half of separation.

The very next day Laurie told Mohr that she was frightened about the knife rape and she had decided to prosecute. Mohr drove Laurie down to meet with Cook County assistant state's attorney Edward Vienuzis at his office in suburban Des Plaines two days later.

During the meeting Laurie went over the knife-rape story again; Vienuzis took it all in, thought it over and made a preliminary decision not to file charges against Russell. The evidence was inconclusive and a jury would never buy it.

Norm and Edith were genuinely frightened by what they believed was Russell's escalating campaign to harass their daughter. Through Mohr they arranged for a hearing with Nancy Sidote, supervisor of felony review for the Skokie branch office of the Cook County state's attorney. Sidote had the power to override the original decision not to prosecute, and Mohr drove Norm, Edith and Laurie to her office.

The lack of significant injury to Laurie was what stuck out, Sidote told them. Everything was very neat in the bedroom where the attack supposedly took place, there were no fingerprints, and given the previous allegations against Laurie—the phone calls and the ice-pick stabbing—she wasn't going to make a terribly credible witness.

"But we have to do something," Norm insisted. "Can't something be done to stop him?"

"Your only real hope is the pubic-hair evidence, which hasn't been gathered and tested yet," Sidote said. "And hair usually comes back, at best, morphologically similar, which means it could come from the suspect, but it could also come from hundreds of thousands of other people."

Afterward Norm was very upset when he spoke to Mohr one-on-one. "Laurie's the victim again," he said. "Russell has no right."

"Is she still seeing a doctor?"

"We have her seeing someone new," Norm said. "Dr. Phillip Epstein at Rush-Presbyterian."

Mohr called Dr. Epstein and told him about the burglary, the gun, and the knife rape, and Epstein said coolly, "I wasn't aware of that."

"Well, maybe you'd better be aware," Mohr said. He asked him the same questions he'd asked of Dr. Greendale: Do you think she's violent? Homicidal? Suicidal?

"I don't know enough about her," Epstein said. "But I don't see anything that would say she's violent."

AFTER THE DIVORCE LAURIE LIVED at home for a short time, but soon she began planning to get back into a new school setting, her customary way to start fresh. She'd met a lot of men in college, and campuses had been the scene of many of her social triumphs. She also might be able to pick up a few classes and get her life back on track.

She drove the eight miles south to Evanston one afternoon and walked around the main campus of Northwestern University, a distinguished assortment of brick and limestone classroom buildings, fraternities and ivy-shrouded dormitories. Laurie posted notices on bulletin boards that she was interested in a summer sublet. Derek Christopher, a student, saw her handbill and offered to lease his half of an apartment suite in the Kellogg Living/Learning Center.

When she moved in, on June 15, she found the other half of the suite occupied by another nonstudent sublettor, Andy Gallagher. His presence enraged Laurie right from the start.

She complained to building manager Marc Boney that she had been under the impression that the other side of the suite was not going to be occupied. "He misled me," she said, referring to Christopher, who was working that summer in New York City. "So I'm not going to keep my side of the agreement. All I want is my deposit and first month's rent back."

"It's between you and him," Boney said. "This is not a university matter."

"But I'm not safe in there," Laurie said. "My suitemate is very strange."

Boney was dutifully concerned. "If I were you," he said, "I'd call Derek and appeal to his conscience; then I'd leave and hope to get my money back."

Laurie said that was probably what she was going to do, and left. Boney, whose office was in another building on campus, didn't hear from or about her again for two months.

Andy Gallagher wasn't exactly thrilled with the setup either, especially when he discovered what a terrible slob his new suitemate was. She left newspapers and food wrappers strewn all over the floor of her room and the hallway. She left meat drippings in the oven whenever she tried to cook.

And there were the other oddities: Laurie never used her bare hands to touch anything, so when she opened a door, she used a towel wrapped around her hands. She went in and out of the suite a lot at odd hours, but she never seemed to go anywhere. Andy would see her riding the elevators up and down the seven-story building all afternoon or sitting transfixed in front of the TV in the downstairs lounge, often watching without the sound on.

Laurie told Andy that she worked in the admitting office of a hospital, but she told another summer resident that she was in the nursing program. Over and over again, Laurie reinvented her life, projecting new and better identities onto herself. She began to show a disturbing fascination with meat—her mother would bring groceries to the dorm and Laurie would unwrap the raw meat and put it on a plate in the refrigerator, where it would drip down onto the other food.

Maintenance supervisor David Campbell first got acquainted with Laurie through the prodigious amounts of junk she left behind in the TV room—cookie wrappers, empty pop bottles and other trash—but he went from angry to concerned when he noticed she was wearing rubber gloves as she wandered the hallways. Then Campbell began finding uncooked slabs of prime-cut beef hidden in peculiar places throughout the dorm. He found the first piece stashed under a carpet; then he turned up several pieces behind chair cushions in the main hallway and another stuffed inside a chair in the TV lounge.

THAT summer Detective Floyd Mohr obtained a search warrant for a sample of Russell Dann's pubic hair. A male nurse at Evanston Hospital snipped approximately twenty-five hairs from Russell's crotch and another twenty-five from his head. The conclusion of the lab report, which came back two weeks later, was just as prosecutor Nancy Sidote had predicted—the hairs were only morphologically similar and thus meaningless as evidence.

For Russell the marital nightmare was legally over, but when would it end? The harassing hang-up phone calls had started again after a hiatus of several months. Russell moved out of his town house when he learned that Frank Bullock had temporarily lost Laurie's trail. He took a unit in the Americana Apartments on busy Lake-Cook Road, got an unlisted phone number and had his mail delivered to a post office box so Laurie wouldn't be able to find him. He never drove straight home from work, and always kept a close eye behind him to be sure Laurie wasn't in his rearview mirror.

Then early one morning he looked out the window of his new home as his girlfriend, Patricia Cassell, was leaving and saw Laurie standing menacingly on the sidewalk. He called Bullock at home, but by the time Bullock could get to the house, Laurie was gone.

Then Patricia started getting hang-up calls.

IN THE meantime Laurie's curious activities in the Kellogg apartments had escalated into the realm of the quasicriminal. Building personnel kept seeing her wandering through rooms and areas to which she was not supposed to have access, and the front-desk clerks caught her trying to break into other people's mailboxes.

The residents complained to building director Marc Boney. Then Boney's student manager, Andrew Burke, told him that one of the spare building passkeys was missing, which might explain how Laurie was getting into unauthorized areas.

Boney and Burke went to Laurie's room to demand the key. She wasn't there, but in the process of searching her fetid quarters they found a luggage cart that was missing from the front desk, a stash of rubber gloves and a large collection of *Penthouse* magazines. When they opened up the refrigerator, they reeled at the ghoulish sight and smell of thick, dripping cuts of spoiled meat stuffed into every corner.

"We've got a problem," Boney said dryly.

He called a psychiatrist he knew socially and asked him what Laurie's fixation might mean. The doctor told him her behavior was symptomatic of inner rage—the slashing and hiding of meat was symbolic of the way someone would kill a person and hide the corpse.

But Boney could not easily evict Laurie for strange expressions of rage. Besides, he knew that formal eviction proceedings would take sixty days minimum. By that time the summer would be over. His best shot, he figured, was to catch her with the passkey and use the threat to press criminal charges as leverage to get her to leave.

LAURIE'S sometime boyfriend at the time was Stephen Greene, from the second floor. They'd met while watching TV in the lounge. They went out for pizza a couple of times, and once she came to his apartment to watch videos. She told him she really enjoyed the movie *Black Widow*, a violent thriller, because she was intrigued by the idea of plotting to get back at people.

One afternoon, when Greene took Laurie to the Lincoln Park Zoo, Marc Boney went to her room to search for the passkey. He didn't find it, but he did find the room key that Derek Christopher had given her. He knew then, if she returned and let herself in with a key, it almost certainly had to be a passkey.

At 4:00 a desk clerk saw Laurie use a key in the front door of the complex, so she asked to inspect the key. Laurie then left the lobby and went back outside, where Boney and Burke caught up with her.

"Give me that key," Boney said.

"No way," she said.

"The game's over," Boney said. "That key is university property, therefore you are committing a criminal act. We don't want to prosecute you. We just want you to leave."

"F--- you," she said, and walked away.

When Laurie returned to her room and saw that it had been searched, she filed a burglary report with the Evanston police. The report put Frank Bullock back on Laurie's trail. Hang-up calls to Patricia Cassell's telephone had been traced back to somewhere at Northwestern, so he'd left word with contacts in Evanston to call him if Laurie's name ever turned up. After they notified him, Bullock discovered the sickening stories of her behavior and reported back to Russell and his attorney, Rick Kessler.

NORM called Marc Boney on September 6, demanding to know why he had singled out his daughter for harassment. Boney said he would meet with Norm and Laurie at 3:00 the next afternoon to explain.

The proceedings took place in one of the meeting rooms on the first floor of the Living/Learning Center. Laurie sat next to her father across from Boney, Andrew Burke and two uniformed campus security officers. The university personnel laid out the case that Laurie was in possession of a master key. Boney offered not to press charges if Laurie would return the key and leave that very afternoon.

Norm looked gravely to Laurie. "Do you have that key?" he said.

"No, Dad," she said.

"Did you ever have that key?"

"No, Dad," she said. "I've never had the key."

Norm turned to Boney, his palms up. "She doesn't have the key," he said simply.

"What about the time we found you in rooms that are locked for the summer?" Boney asked Laurie.

"They were unlocked," she said.

"But—"

"Listen here," Norm flared. "My daughter hasn't done anything wrong. You heard her. I thought people had their rights. What kind of a Nazi are you?"

Boney started. "Look, Mr. Wasserman, I didn't want to bring this up, but you've given me no choice. We've seen your daughter wandering the halls wearing rubber gloves and trying to break into mailboxes. She's been leaving garbage and big, bloody pieces of meat stuffed in strange places all over."

Norm was silent for a moment. Then he took a breath and said, "Laurie has some emotional problems. We're getting her medical attention."

One of the security officers interrupted. "We can talk about this for hours, but the fact remains that if your daughter doesn't leave, we're going to press charges."

"Okay, okay," Norm said.

The group went upstairs en masse to check Laurie's room. The conditions were appalling, but if Norm was surprised, he did not show it. He and Laurie packed up the room by heaping her belongings into several large boxes.

When Laurie left the building for the last time, Boney and Burke kicked back in the lounge and sighed with relief.

"Man!" said Boney.

"You're not kidding," said Burke. "You know, I wouldn't be surprised if that girl's in the headlines someday. Like a John Hinckley."

7.

TAKING CARE OF LAURIE

L AURIE Dann had failed at everything. She'd been a rotten student, an awful wife, a disappointing daughter and an unreliable employee. She couldn't even live on her own. The single thing she seemed to have an aptitude for was child care.

The only trouble she had early on was with Katie and Matt Williamson, who lived two blocks north of the Wassermans. In May the

Williamsons came home to find knife slashes on their leather couches and chairs.

Laurie's vague excuse was that a young man who said he was a neighbor had knocked on the door and asked to use the telephone. She said she went upstairs to get one of the Williamson children to identify the man, but when she returned, he was gone.

The Williamsons estimated the damage at $1700 and reported the incident to the Glencoe police, who pointed out that proving a case against Laurie would be difficult without witnesses.

Detective Mohr called Laurie to the station for an interview, but she stuck to the story about the intruder. "I know Russell was behind this," she said. "He hired the guy. Why is he trying to make me look bad?" A sob caught in her throat. Her lip began to quiver and tears poured down her cheeks. Mohr sat uncomfortably by, as confused as ever. She was either one of the most tragic victims he had ever encountered or one of the best actresses.

The Williamson family ultimately let the matter drop and simply stopped hiring Laurie. She responded by pestering them for several weeks with hang-up phone calls.

WHEN Laurie left Evanston and moved back in with her parents, baby-sitting went from an occasional thing she did to make a little spending money to being her sole purpose in life. She posted hand-written notices on bulletin boards in libraries and grocery stores on the North Shore:

> Experienced babysitter, 25 years old, just finished college, living at home in Glencoe, has own car, references, $2.50 an hour. Call me.

Pam Berman saw Laurie's ad in the Glencoe Public Library. She called the number given, and Laurie agreed to come sit for Jennifer, age seven, and Colin, age five, on the nights of September 17 and 18, 1987.

Laurie looked fresh and collegiate in her crewneck sweater and corduroy pants, but she seemed a little weird to Pam Berman. She smiled very strangely and asked unusually direct questions about such things as Stan Berman's medical specialty. Yet the kids had no complaints and everything seemed fine when the parents returned from their evening out.

But the next night, after Laurie had gone home, the Bermans found $50 worth of gourmet frozen foods missing, along with a new pair of shoes, a bottle of shampoo and a bottle of perfume. Colin said he saw Laurie take the items from the house, and Stan Berman called the police.

He did not care to press charges, he told the officers. He was worried, rather, that a woman who stole frozen food—as opposed to jewelry—was so emotionally unbalanced that people shouldn't be entrusting her with their children.

He said he was going to take out an advertisement in the local weekly newspaper warning other North Shore parents about Laurie, but the police cautioned him strongly against it—maybe there would be trouble. Maybe she would sue. Instead, Pam Berman settled for pulling down Laurie's advertising signs whenever she saw a new one up at the library.

On September 24 Florence and Bruce Montrose called Laurie to baby-sit, although they had become increasingly uneasy with her. She had told them that she'd been married and divorced, that she had been a nursery school teacher, and that she was about to go back to school at Northwestern. They noticed that she wasn't comfortable talking to adults but that she immediately sat down on the floor with the children, Jennifer and Peter, and began putting together puzzles.

Laurie came to sit for the Montroses a few mornings later. After the children had gone outside to play, Laurie went into the deep freeze and pulled out hundreds of dollars' worth of steak and shrimp, which she stuffed into a large plastic garbage bag. She heaped various gourmet canned goods on top of the meat, and with considerable effort hauled the bag out to her car. She put the bag inside the trunk and returned to the house.

She then wandered upstairs to the bathroom, opened the medicine chest, and withdrew a bottle of prescription tranquilizers. She swallowed a great handful of them and went back down to the kitchen, where the children had left peanut-butter-and-jelly sandwiches half eaten on their plates.

She threw the sandwiches down on the counter and smeared the peanut butter and jelly all across it. Meanwhile, outside in the yard, a stray dog was romping excitedly with the Montroses' dog. Laurie let both dogs inside and they tore crazily through the house. One of them had urinated on the living-room carpet by the time a neighbor came to take control of the situation.

When Florence arrived home, she found Laurie sitting catatonically in front of the snowing television set.

She's really a nut, Florence thought.

When she and her husband discovered all the food that was missing and talked to a neighbor who had seen Laurie hauling away a filled garbage bag, they reported the incident to the Glencoe police.

Mohr sought out Norm this time. "It seems strange," he said. "She baby-sits in two places and things are missing, things are cut up, people say she acts weird."

"I don't think she'd steal," Norm said. "But I want to take care of it financially."

Mohr went back to the Montroses and dropped some heavy hints. They had a difficult court case, at best, and the alleged offenses were only misdemeanors anyway. Maybe, he said, the Wassermans would offer some form of restitution.

Bruce Montrose telephoned Norm and suggested they could work something out.

"There's no way you know she did it," Norm said.

"The neighbor saw her," Montrose said.

The discussion went back and forth, with Norm attempting to establish Laurie's innocence before offering to pay the Montroses for the missing food. In the end he wrote out and mailed a check for $400.

Shortly afterward the Montroses received numerous hang-up calls after midnight—the same kind of calls that Northwestern housing administrator Marc Boney was getting.

Finally, after more official complaints about theft of food and clothing, Floyd Mohr reached an agreement with Norm Wasserman— Laurie would not seek new baby-sitting clients, but could keep working for the families who liked her.

THE various bizarre fragments of Laurie's life were starting to come together, and Rick Kessler arranged for a meeting to review Laurie's case on October 27 in the Waukegan office of Mike Waller, Lake County chief deputy state's attorney. At the meeting were Kessler, Waller, Detective McCafferty and private eye Frank Bullock.

Bullock had the new information about Laurie's behavior at North-

western, and when he laid it out alongside the other reports, allegations and charges, the pattern was unmistakable and compelling.

But Waller could only shrug. The facts of the ice-pick case remained
as inconclusive and circumstantial as ever, he said. No matter how
peculiar she was, she hadn't done anything that could lead to a
conviction.

Afterward McCafferty, who was no fan of Russell's, said to Bullock,
"I don't know what's going to happen, but it's going to happen."

On November 7 Laurie returned to the Marksman supply store and
bought a .32-caliber Smith & Wesson Terrier revolver for $245.

OBSESSIVE-COMPULSIVE disorder, or OCD, was one of the most
widely publicized mental ailments of the year 1987. Newspapers, magazines and television documentaries offered scores of features on the
related bizarre ritual behavior such as repeated hand washing, hoard-
ing of useless materials, vacuuming of family pets and uncontrollable
thoughts of aggression. New research showed that the syndrome was
up to sixty times more prevalent than doctors had previously thought.

On the bright side, however, people with OCD were never known to
be dangerous, and many of them could learn to lead outwardly normal lives. Medical science was also coming around to the conclusion
that OCD could be treated by certain types of antidepressant medica-
tions. The most promising was the then experimental drug clomipramine, which suppressed or eliminated the unusual urges of more than
two thirds of all OCD patients. Reporters were referring to clomipramine as a miracle drug.

The Wassermans were just one of thousands of families for whom
the emerging information about OCD seemed to be very good news.
Laurie's preoccupation with good and bad numbers, her tendency to
collect junk and her fetish for wearing rubber gloves all squared perfectly with a diagnosis of this eminently treatable condition.

Norm arranged that year for her to see Dr. Phillip Epstein, who sent
her for cognitive testing to Dr. Allen Hirsch at the Mercy Medical
Center. Hirsch's only solid conclusion, he wrote to Epstein, was that
Laurie was not good at telling her left from her right. Perhaps, he
suggested, she had a motivational problem. He prescribed alprazolam,
a central nervous system depressant commonly used to manage anxiety disorders.

Epstein's billing records show that he saw her four times for therapy. He apparently concluded that Laurie did in fact suffer from OCD and that she could benefit from clomipramine. But Epstein was unable to write Laurie a direct prescription. The drug was still undergoing clinical trials in the United States and was approved for use only by selected doctors. Epstein, not being one of those doctors, prescribed it instead through a pharmacy in Montreal. The pharmacy took the order, along with Norm's credit card number, and mailed the pills to Laurie.

The Food and Drug Administration has said that Epstein's use of a Canadian connection was a technical violation of that agency's guidelines. His writing of the prescription through Montreal would later cause him to be named in a civil lawsuit and be the subject of an investigation by the Illinois Department of Professional Regulation.

After Laurie began getting clomipramine in the mail, she typed up a letter to the OCD Foundation, an organization in Connecticut that informed patients of the latest information on therapies. The letter requested a list of nearby treatment centers.

The foundation wrote back and recommended Dr. John Greist, co-director of the Anxiety Disorder Center and the Center for Affective Disorders at the University of Wisconsin Hospital, in Madison. His clinic was one of twenty-one institutions in the country officially dispensing clomipramine.

On November 9 Norm Wasserman wrote to Greist that he had a thirty-year-old daughter suffering from OCD. She was unable to live any kind of normal life. Could he help?

Greist agreed to treat Laurie, and Laurie was enthusiastic about moving back to Madison, where she had spent the summer of 1977. Late in November she packed up her Honda hatchback and left Glencoe.

Laurie rented a room on the isolated far western edge of campus, near the university hospital, for her first month and almost immediately had her first appointment with Dr. Greist and his assistant, Yoram Shwager, an Israeli graduate student.

Shwager, who was assigned to be Laurie's primary therapist, helped Greist conduct the formal intake interview with her and her parents on November 30. She told him that the ritualistic behavior that had troubled her as a little girl disappeared and didn't return until she reached her twenties. Her most prominent obsession, she said, was that something bad was going to happen to her, and she had developed a number of rituals to allay her anxiety. She brushed her teeth over and over, pulled her hair out by the strand, and found herself compelled to go back and touch people who had touched her, even if they had only brushed past accidentally. The numbers three and thirteen were very bad luck for her.

Shwager and Greist concluded that Laurie's OCD was centered on aggressive obsessions and that her compulsions were a reaction to the fear that something terrible would happen and she would be responsible. She might have been a candidate for the trials, but she revealed that she was already taking clomipramine obtained through Montreal. Greist nevertheless suggested the dosage Laurie ought to be taking: one 50-mg tablet each evening and, if the side effects were mild, two and then three tablets each evening.

Greist believed that the most effective treatment for OCD combined drug therapy with behavioral therapy that required confronting fears and eliminating ritualistic behavior.

In her first session alone with Shwager, on December 3, Laurie created a hierarchy of her problems from easiest (getting dressed, talking on the phone) to most difficult (touching people, shopping). He gave her short lists of tasks and goals, and Laurie also wrote little instructional Post-it notes, which she put up in her room to help her accomplish normal tasks in a methodical fashion: "Shoes, keys, chair," said one.

Norm Wasserman and Dr. Greist sat in with Laurie and Shwager for a thirty-five-minute conference four days later. Laurie said the clomipramine had at first given her a tremor and caused her whole body to go rigid, but those problems went away and didn't come back even when she doubled the dose. Greist told her to triple her original dose and to begin seeing Shwager three or four times a week.

During the next session Laurie practiced touching objects that didn't belong to her. Her hands quivered, but she was able to do everything Shwager asked her to. She also reported that she'd been able to walk a mile without engaging in her usual rituals of avoiding cracks.

She spoke at length during the next two sessions about her feelings of wanting to hurt herself. When she complained that the clomipramine was not helping, Greist suggested she continue trying to increase her dosage until the drug began to have its desired effect. Just as she seemed to be making progress, it was time for the three-week winter holiday vacation.

On Laurie's first day back home, December 20, she suffered a severe reaction to the clomipramine—perhaps related to an accidental overdose—and began vomiting every ten minutes for nearly twelve hours.

Norm called Highland Park Hospital at 4:42 the next morning. At 8:51 a.m. he finally reached a family physician, who prescribed Compazine suppositories. Compazine is one of a number of antipsychotic drugs in the phenothiazine class, but one of its major uses is for the treatment of severe nausea. The *United States Pharmacopeia: Drug Information for the Consumer* guide and the *Physicians' Desk Reference* both warn against taking such drugs along with central nervous system depressants such as alprazolam, which Dr. Hirsch had prescribed for Laurie. The Compazine stopped Laurie's retching but apparently caused her hallucinations throughout the next night.

Norm spoke long-distance to Greist for seventeen minutes that evening. Greist instructed him to take Laurie off all medication. But not long afterward Laurie's jaw went rigid, and Norm took her to the emergency room at Highland Park, where doctors administered benztropine, an antipalsy medication often used to counter severe reactions to phenothiazines such as Compazine. It rapidly relieved her symptoms.

When Laurie came home, she sequestered herself with the telephone and made fourteen quick hang-up calls. Her list of victims now included Jeff Taylor's father, Sidney, and numerous friends of the Taylors' and Russell Dann's.

She called Greist early the next morning for a three-minute consultation, during which Greist suggested she try again to resume taking the clomipramine.

On the Monday after Christmas, Laurie made a third trip to the Marksman. This time she picked out a .22-caliber semiautomatic Beretta for $209.15.

Late afternoon the next day she placed two hang-up calls to Russell's office at Dann Brothers. Then in the six hours after midnight she made fifty-five more hang-up calls.

Norm was apparently unaware of what Laurie was up to. His letter to Greist on New Year's Eve was uncharacteristically buoyant. Though Laurie was still seriously ill, Norm wrote, she seemed to be taking the first steps toward recovery.

Laurie returned to Madison after the holiday break very depressed. She told Yoram Shwager that her relationship with her parents was very troubled; he noted that she was back to square one, collecting objects, layering her life with rituals and superstitions.

At Greist's suggestion Laurie increased her dosage of clomipramine to 200 mg a day. She reported that the new, high dosage helped cut down on the duration of her obsessions but that it gave her tremors and made it hard for her to remember things. Greist decided to add 600 mg a day of lithium carbonate to the pharmaceutical mix to try to help balance her brain chemistry.

Laurie was also taking birth control pills—known to be associated with depression—as well as lorazepam, an antianxiety medication prescribed to her by Dr. Epstein. The drug is a commonly used tranquilizer, and the *Physicians' Desk Reference* warns against using it on psychotic patients or those suffering from depressive disorder.

LAW-ENFORCEMENT investigators and medical authorities who have studied Laurie's life have been particularly interested in her pharmaceutical habits in Madison because she took so many different drugs in such a short time. The effects of combined psychoactive drugs on an individual are impossible to predict, doctors say, especially when a diagnosis is not sharp. Psychiatry is an inexact science under the best of circumstances, and the notion that Laurie suffered primarily from OCD came from doctors—Epstein and Greist—who apparently never communicated with each other and who had not treated her at length. They did not consult with Dr. Greendale, who had seen her off and on for several years, but relied for their information on Laurie, a chronic liar, and her father, a man of leonine protective instincts.

Laurie's interest in guns, her carving up of furniture, her stealing and her maniacal telephone harassment all suggest a mental condition far more serious than simple OCD—perhaps manic-depression, schizophrenia or borderline personality disorder.

But whatever was the matter with Laurie Dann, the fact remains that the longer she stayed in Madison, the further she swirled downward into madness.

LAURIE MOVED FROM HER ROOM near the hospital to the Towers, the private luxury dormitory she was familiar with from her summer there eleven years earlier.

She was assigned to the vacant half of suite 610, a room with spare, blond wood furnishings and a shared bathroom. The girl on the other side was Jolie Pollock, a freshman from Highland Park.

Laurie told Jolie that she was a sophomore scholarship student and that she'd transferred from Northwestern. They got along fine, but Jolie could tell that there was something a little off center about her new roommate. Laurie's clothes were out of fashion and her room had no personality—no art prints, no rock posters, nothing on the walls.

In the first few weeks of the semester, Jolie began to pick up on some of Laurie's other peculiarities. She made no friends, never went to class and never studied. Laurie's side of the suite started to smell slightly of urine, and her unwashed, greasy hair often stuck out from her head at odd angles. Sometimes she would run the shower for several hours while lying in her bed. Other times she would wander aimlessly through the halls of the dorm, peering into people's rooms, jiggling locked doorknobs, and riding the elevators.

All hours of the day and night, residents would see the elevator doors open and there would be Laurie Dann, just standing in the cab. She usually looked dazed, and she refused to get off when the elevator reached the top floor. "I'm going higher," she said. Jolie found a note on Laurie's desk that appeared to be a schedule for riding the elevators: "2 in, 6 out, 6 in, 2 out . . ." Students began referring to her as the Psycho Elevator Lady.

TWICE each day, just before the cafeteria opened for lunch and again for dinner, Laurie put on gloves and went down to be first in the meal line.

"Why do you wear gloves to eat?" Jolie asked her.

"It's the metal," Laurie improvised. "I'm sensitive to hot and cold metal."

Usually they were red, light-woolen winter gloves with leather palm pads, but sometimes she chose kitchen gloves or surgical gloves. She often wore a red sweat suit or the pink one Russell had given her, but once she attracted attention by coming down to eat dressed in pajamas and fuzzy slippers.

Inside the cafeteria she placed cutlery on the conveyor belt and stared at it as it traveled down the line. When other students crossed her path in the serving area, she would sometimes move backwards robotically, pacing out exactly two tile squares; other times she would move only along the lines of the tiles, making ninety-degree turns.

Early in the semester she often ate alone, looking forlorn and exhausted. Haley Bareck, an effervescent freshman, noticed Laurie and felt sorry for her. Haley almost always ate with the same chatty group of six young women, and one day she asked Laurie to join their table.

Laurie accepted this gesture of friendship, and she soon became a regular member of the mealtime crew. She listened intently to every conversation and was always quick with questions about boyfriends, classes, dates, jobs and social events that had been mentioned at previous meals. The other women at the table were quietly surprised that the Psycho Elevator Lady was actually extremely lucid and sometimes very talkative and upbeat.

One day Laurie came to lunch carrying a photograph of a lovely woman with long, pretty hair. "This is me!" she said.

It seemed incredible at first, but upon close inspection the girls could see that the woman in the picture was, indeed, their weird cafeteria friend in better days.

"Your hair . . ." Haley said, groping for a tactful way to compliment the photograph without insulting Laurie. "It's great. Why did—"

"One day I just felt like cutting it off." Laurie shrugged.

Not only had her hair become greasy, short and uneven, she had started to dye it a dark, unflattering shade of red. Her face was taking on a rosy cast and she was shoveling in enormous quantities of food. She would go back to the cafeteria line six or seven times during the ninety-minute lunch period and the nearly two-hour dinner period, filling her tray with each of the four entrées and grabbing dozens of cookies.

In order to satisfy her compulsion to eat—probably a side effect of the clomipramine—Laurie had to leave the cafeteria periodically to vomit in the bathroom.

FOR much of that winter and spring of 1988, Norm and Edith were in Boca Raton, where they kept track of Laurie by telephone and through the mail. Norm wrote Laurie a note in late January telling her he thought about her all the time and was frustrated that he could not do more for her. She also was getting periodic letters of support from her brother, Mark.

LATE in February, Laurie rooted through Jolie Pollock's trash and found an empty Colgate toothpaste box. She took the box, set one end on fire, and shoved the burning end under the door of the suite occupied by a freshman from Ohio who was part of a small group that had reportedly been teasing her earlier in the day.

The smoke triggered fire alarms, and the entire building was evacuated. Damage to the student's carpet and door was minor, and no one could really prove who had set the blaze.

Then in early March, Jolie found Coca-Cola spilled onto the keyboard of her new Macintosh computer. She went to the next room to confront Laurie. "Did you use my computer?" she said. "Do you know why there would be Coke spilled into it?"

"Oh, no," Laurie said innocently. "I don't even drink Coke."

Jolie began locking the door that led into her room. Laurie started doing the same.

AMONG Laurie's favorite haunts were the pay telephones in the lobby and outside the dorm. Without a phone in her room, the public phones were her only instruments for continuing her campaign against her enemies in the Chicago area.

Early in the spring Laurie called Bruce and Florence Montrose, the couple who had hired her to baby-sit and later accused her of stealing food. "Your children are going to die," she said, and hung up. Shortly thereafter she called Susie Taylor and sang in a falsetto, "Susie, Susie, you're going to die. I'm a psychopath."

These and other spoken threats marked a major change in Laurie's behavior; until then she had done nothing but hang up on her targets.

On March 10 Beth Rosen received four threatening phone calls, two of which were hang-ups. In the other two, the caller, whose muffled voice sounded a lot like Laurie's, said, "Beth is going to die."

Beth called Robert Bonneville, director of the Glencoe Department of Public Safety. She remembers him saying, "We know all about her. She's a very sick girl." He suggested that Beth call Floyd Mohr, which she did. Mohr, however, was not nearly as sympathetic.

"You can't positively ID the voice if she muffled it," Mohr said. "So you can't prove the threat came from her."

"I'm pretty sure it did," Beth said.

"We've talked to her psychiatrists," Mohr said, referring to Dr. Greendale and Dr. Epstein. "They say she's harmless."

"I hate to say it," Beth said, "but this is not going to end until somebody really gets hurt."

Mohr sighed. "I can only repeat what the psychiatrist said: she's not harmful to herself or others."

"Well, I disagree," said Beth. She hung up.

8.

MAKING PLANS

As Laurie sank further into her closed, paranoid world, she began plotting to accomplish what she had told her doctors was her worst fear: she was going to make something terrible happen.

On Saturday, March 12, 1988, she slipped into a lab across the hallway from Greist's office at the University of Wisconsin Hospital and Clinics Building. A technician saw her looking into a cabinet where chemicals were stored. Three days later employees discovered arsenic and lead solutions missing from the cabinet, along with several beakers filled with stannous chloride. The employees were struck by what an unusual sort of theft it was. Such chemicals were useful only for performing mercury-level analysis on urine specimens—or for killing something.

Laurie had already been to the Madison City Library and stolen a 1974 book, *Handbook of Poisoning;* a 1962 book, *Poisoning by Drugs and Chemicals;* and a 1977 book, *Poison Antidotes and Anecdotes.*

She went looking for disguises at Madison's West Towne Mall on March 14, where she shoplifted four wigs and two hair clips off the mannequins at JC Penney. She stuffed her take into the sleeve of the winter coat draped over her arm. Two teenage boys saw her plundering the mannequins and told store employees. The store detective marched her to the office, where he called the police.

She bit her lip as she posed for her mug shot down at police headquarters. The police released her on $200 bond, and ultimately the court assigned her to a first-time-offender program.

LATER THAT WEEK LAURIE TRACKED down her old college boyfriend Steve Witt, who had left New York to finish his residency in Arizona in order to escape the cloud of the anonymous allegation that he had molested a woman in the emergency room. Laurie called collect and identified herself as Sarah. Steve refused the charges the first time she called, but several days later decided to see what the caller wanted.

"Stephen Howard Witt," Laurie said, snapping off her words. "You f------ bastard, I'm going to kill you."

Steve hung up and told his wife, Barbara, what he had just heard. "It's her," he said. "She found us again."

Barbara, who had just come home from the hospital after delivering the couple's first child, went hysterical with fear. The Witts changed to a new unlisted number, but Laurie got it the same way she had obtained the first number, by wheedling it out of a clerk at Steve's father's pharmacy. The clerk also volunteered information about the new baby.

"You don't have to change your phone number," Laurie said to Barbara in her next call. "That won't stop me from killing you. I know where you are and you don't know where I am. And you might as well take your little baby and throw him in the garbage can."

Laurie's phone calls to her usual Chicago-area victims had become similarly aberrant. At the beginning of April, when Jeff and Susie Taylor were vacationing in New York and their kids were home with the housekeeper, Laurie called and told the housekeeper, "Susie is a stinking bitch! Tell her I'm going to kill her."

The calls continued when Susie and Jeff returned. Laurie started off muffling her voice or trying to disguise it by screeching, but she gradually began using her own voice. "You have to die!" she said to Susie.

The Taylors were, by then, seriously frightened. They called Detective Jack McCafferty to tell him what had been happening and to ask him to tell the department to watch their house.

IN LATE March, Laurie had taken three pairs of pants into the dressing room at Worth's, a women's clothing store across from the Towers, and come back out with only two.

The assistant manager confronted her. "Where's the other pants?" she said. "We gave you three and—"

Laurie removed the green pants from inside her jacket and flung them onto the rack. "I will never shop here again," she said, stalking out. "You people are really rude."

Laurie was so indignant that she brought up the incident over dinner. When word got back to Jolie Pollock that her roommate was involved in still more oddball activities—crimes now, even—she finally decided she'd had enough.

"I'm moving out," Jolie said to Laurie. "There are just too many weird things that have gone on."

Laurie nodded. "Yeah," she said.

And on April 2 Jolie packed up and took her belongings to a vacant room on the eighth floor. Laurie was alone.

HER calls to Arizona continued—up to thirty in an hour on one memorable afternoon—and Steve Witt called his old high school friend and college roommate Lou Spivack for advice. Lou was an assistant county prosecutor in Arizona. He told Steve that such calls were felonies under federal law and he might have luck getting the FBI to investigate and help bring federal charges against Laurie.

So Steve called the FBI. The person who took the information over the telephone was brusque and unenthusiastic. Not enough evidence. Maybe if he had taped the conversations . . .

IN THE middle of April a group of students at the Towers got together to watch a televised interview with cult slayer Charles Manson. Half a dozen of them gathered afterward to tell their own eerie-but-true stories of murder and intrigue. Laurie, who had been rambling through the halls again, sat quietly for a time listening to the vivid and increasingly gory narratives. Then she spoke up. "I've got a story to tell," she said.

It was about a divorcée—a woman out of control—who had harassed her ex-husband for months with various threats, then finally broke into his home and stabbed him with an ice pick. One student remembered later that the husband died at the end of the story; others who were there remember that the husband lived. But everyone remembers particularly how Laurie told the story in a flat, uninflected voice, as though she were relating the details of an unsurprising news event.

"Y'know," one of the boys said, making a collegiate attempt to be cosmic, "there are so many crazy people out there, maybe there's a murderer among us."

BY THEN Laurie had ditched Shwager and Dr. Greist. Her last visit to Greist's office was March 18. Shwager had been pushing her hard, forcing her to perform otherwise simple tasks that she found unpleasant and urging her to make lists of goals.

To hell with it. She didn't need the grief. Her life had found another purpose anyway. She continued taking her drugs, however, and in the first week of April she received five hundred more clomipramine tablets, as prescribed by Dr. Epstein, and one hundred more lithium carbonate pills, prescribed by Dr. Greist.

On April 10 she, Shwager and her father had a three-way telephone call in which Norm told Laurie to stop breaking her appointments and to go to see Greist the very next day. She agreed, but then didn't show up.

Greist was worried. Laurie's condition was deteriorating and her problems were more serious than he could address in sporadic office visits. She needed full-time supervision and intensive therapy as a hospital inpatient if she was to improve. But she reacted badly whenever either he or Shwager even came close to broaching the subject.

To commit a patient involuntarily in Wisconsin, a doctor has to establish first that the patient is mentally ill—which wouldn't have been a problem in Laurie's case—and second that the patient is a danger either to himself or to others. Greist was unsure on that point. Laurie was a very strange young woman, certainly, but he had never known her to speak of violence.

But then again his knowledge of her life wasn't really all that deep. All he could do was ask Laurie's father for advice, which he did during a face-to-face meeting two days later.

Greist probed Norm for information that might help him decide whether to try to have Laurie hospitalized against her will. According to Greist, Norm answered quite firmly that Laurie was not dangerous. Greist could not recall Norm mentioning that the police had accused Laurie of harassing her enemies by telephone for years, that she was a suspect in the ice-pick stabbing of her ex-husband, that she was suspected of having stolen and defaced the property of her baby-sitting clients, that she had exhibited an eerie fascination with raw meat, or that she owned handguns.

Norm saw Laurie the following Sunday, April 17, and returned to Boca Raton on Tuesday. From Florida he composed an anguished letter that he told Laurie was "the most important and hardest" he would ever write. He asked for a favor: Would she allow herself to be hospitalized by Dr. Greist? She could not, he wrote, continue to miss appointments with the doctors in the belief that the drugs alone would cure her. Hospitalization, he said, was the only way she would recover. "See Greist," he wrote; "do it for me."

Susie Taylor answered the phone in early May, 1988, and heard Laurie's maniacal singsong on the other end: "Susie, are you all getting together on Mother's Day? You shall die."

Mother's Day was the following Sunday, and Susie was so terrified that she didn't even want to walk through the kitchen to the TV room, because of the number of windows she had to pass. She had visions of Laurie prowling through the house, popping out from around a corner, her gun at the ready.

"You've got to do something," she complained to Detective McCafferty. "Anybody who can stand over a sleeping person and stab him with an ice pick is capable of doing anything."

"Well," said McCafferty. "Let's just hope not."

THE FBI had finally entered the case in Arizona. Steve Witt's prosecutor friend Lou Spivack had called the FBI himself, and a few days later FBI Special Agent Perry Cole met with Spivack and Steve and Barbara Witt. He listened to the disturbing tales of threats and harassments. Recently Laurie had been calling to brag that she was going to walk into Steve's dermatology office someday and blow his brains out. They had tried to make home recordings of the calls, they explained, but the little suction-cup microphone they'd used had picked up only their end of the conversations.

Cole set them up with a better taping device, but reassured them that sick people make such calls all the time, and ninety-nine times out of a hundred nothing ever comes of it.

Several days after the FBI meeting Spivack looked up Laurie's police records from Illinois. He was startled at the variety of alleged offenses. He called both Detectives Mohr and McCafferty, and found out the whole story from guns to meat. The lawmen told him that they knew they had a problem with Laurie, but they still had trouble knowing how much stock to put in the complaints of Russell Dann and his family and friends.

OF COURSE, as luck would have it, immediately after the FBI recorder had been installed at the Witts', Laurie stopped making threats. But finally, on May 9, the phone rang and it was collect from Laurie. Steve accepted the charges with a mixture of dread and anticipation.

"What do you want?" he asked.

"Stevie!" Laurie began with a whine, her voice high, trembling, cartoonish. "You know what I want."

"What do you want?" he said again, trying to sound disgusted.

"You know. And I'm going to annoy you until I get it." The threat had an almost pleasant lilt.

"First of all, I can't even tell your voice. But I assume this is Laurie."

"Of course."

"So what do you want?"

"You know," Laurie said. She was teasing him as a big sister might torment a little brother. "You know what I'm going to do."

"No, I don't," Steve said, trying to draw the threat out of her.

"Yeah," she said. "And I always get what I want."

"You know, I think you need to get help."

"Uh-huh, I do," she said, the inflection so strangely upbeat it was hard to tell if she meant it.

"I mean seriously," Steve said. "You need help so you can get on with your life and we can get on with our lives."

"It's not going to be that way, though," she said. "I can guarantee you one thing . . ."

"What's that?"

"You won't live to see your baby grow up."

"So you're threatening my life, huh?"

"No, I'm going to do it. I think you deserve it."

"Yeah, and how many other people are you going to take along with you?"

"Does it matter?"

"Why don't you go get help?"

"I don't want to."

"I think that would be best. I think you're having some problems here, okay? But, you know, making threats about killing me and my family is not going to solve your problems."

"It will. It will make me feel a lot better."

"No, it won't."

"You'll be surprised what I'll do."

Steve hung up the phone and switched off the tape recorder. Bingo. He thought about calling the Wassermans, but he decided against it because he didn't want to tip them off to the FBI investigation.

Instead, he bought a gun and put it under his bed.

Lou Spivack dictated a three-page letter on May 10 to FBI Agent Cole. Writing on official county letterhead, he related everything he had learned about the hang-up calls, the death threats, Laurie's strange superstitions, the ice-pick stabbing and the rituals involving meat.

When Cole read the letter and heard the clear, unambiguous threat recorded off the Witts' telephone, he agreed that it was time to press for an indictment.

Haley Bareck went to resident adviser Tonya Neumeier, at the Towers, to ask if she was aware of Laurie's eating habits, her gorging, her vomiting.

"We're taking care of it," Tonya told her. "She's seeing someone. The best thing you can do is just be a friend to her."

But the mealtime crew was getting tired of Laurie. She'd started talking too much, interrupting everyone, dominating conversations. Finally Haley and the other women started eating at a smaller table, where there would be no room for an unwanted guest.

Their purpose was not lost on Laurie, who would find a seat nearby and gaze with cool, blank hatred at Haley, often so intently that she didn't touch her food. Up in her room, Laurie scrawled on the back of an envelope, "Hell on Earth would be having to live with Haley."

Meanwhile, Laurie was compiling a list that included the names of her resident adviser; six residents of the Towers; five friends of Russell Dann's; a friend of Russell's girlfriend, Patricia; the son of an employee at Glenbrook Hospital, where she was fired in 1983; a neighbor of her parents'; her former boyfriend Steve Witt; and the notation "School both Ravinia Clavey Kennedy," a reference to the Ravinia School in Highland Park and the Kennedy School on Clavey Road. The Kennedy School was being used at the time by the Young Men's Jewish Council as a day-care center and preschool.

Jeff and Susie Taylor's kids were enrolled at both facilities.

FBI Agent Cole, Assistant U.S. Attorney Janet Johnson and deputy county prosecutor Lou Spivack made a firm decision on Thursday, May 12, to seek an indictment against Laurie in front of a federal grand jury. The next regularly scheduled grand jury session was for the following Wednesday, May 18. Cole sent out a Telex that day asking police departments across the country for additional information on Laurie Dann.

On Friday, May 13, the Telex was faxed to the Madison FBI office. FBI Agent Kent Miller was asked to find and question Laurie about the threats and to arrest her as soon as the indictment came down.

The Telex did not list an address for Laurie, and the only phone number they had for her traced back to the office of Dr. John Greist. Miller left word with the Madison police department to let him know if they came across her, then secured an appointment with Greist for 4:00 that afternoon. Greist told him that Laurie was under his care, but that he could say nothing else because he had to respect her right to confidentiality.

Miller argued that this was important. He told Greist that not only was Laurie wanted for making vicious threats but she owned a .357 Magnum and was a suspect in the ice-pick stabbing of her ex-husband. Greist said he was surprised by the information, but he could add nothing else until he talked to the University of Wisconsin legal staff. He would have to get back to Miller on Monday.

SUNDAY was the last day before summer break for most of the students in the Towers. That night student staff member Dixon Gahnz was checking the hallways and utility rooms. At 9:00 he looked inside a fifth-floor garbage room and saw, to his horror, that Laurie had burrowed into the refuse and was curled up into a ball in a corner. She was wrapped in a plastic bag and dripping with sweat.

"What are you doing in here?" he asked.

She stirred. "I'm, uh, just looking for things," she said. She stood, shed the bag, and rushed from the room.

Gahnz went downstairs and told several co-workers what he'd seen. They went to her room and pounded on the door for several minutes, then opened it with a passkey. Inside they found a stinking hovel, a toilet filled with excrement, a carpet soaked with urine, garbage everywhere, and Laurie, apparently naked, sleeping soundly under a blanket on a bed.

What could they do? They left the room and found building manager William Levy, who decided to call the Madison police department and Norm Wasserman. Madison officers Mike Koval and Therese MacKenzie responded. When they heard the name Laurie Dann, they contacted FBI Agent Miller.

Miller declined to come out that evening. The officers proceeded to check the suite and found nothing to indicate any danger. Officer MacKenzie talked to Laurie as she lay on her bed. She was groggy but said she was okay. The room was a mess only because she was moving.

And indeed, she was. Shortly after the officers left, she threw a few of her belongings into a couple of suitcases and went back to the North Shore.

Agent Miller waited until the next afternoon to go to the Towers to question Laurie, but by then she was long gone. In her room were fragments from a troubled life—a threatening letter addressed to Steve Witt, a copy of a 1933 book, *Famous Feats of Detection and Deduction,* and a newspaper clipping. The clipping was an Associated Press story out of New York from the February 24, 1988, Chicago *Tribune,* and it described how a man suffering from OCD was cured after he shot himself in the mouth. The headline said FAILED SUICIDE PROVIDES PATIENT WITH A CURE.

Laurie also left behind numerous pages from a writing tablet. The notations within were written at all angles and in a sometimes illegible scrawl. The first page was a sheet stolen from Russell Dann's town house: a note from his girlfriend, Patricia, telling him what clothes to bring on a weekend trip to Detroit. The remaining pages, all in Laurie's handwriting, relate to her relationship with Russell. To read them is to peek into a twisted, paranoid mind: "hate pain . . . abuse. spit, hurt, spat . . . why gun. Threw away wedding tape. . . . terrified I was helpless. I'll deny it. suffer forever. . . . Harm children to pay a bill."

Also in the room was a brown mailing envelope addressed to Dr. Greist containing a V8 juice box stamped SAMPLE and a photo of Laurie and Russell standing side by side, beaming.

DR. GREIST spoke to university attorney Gail Snowden on Monday and asked her what steps he should take given what he now knew about Laurie. He and Snowden agreed that since Greist had learned of the threats only through the FBI and not through Laurie, he could do nothing. They discussed the possibility of contacting Norm Wasserman and telling him that Laurie hadn't been showing up for treatment and was being sought by federal agents. But Greist decided such a move would violate Laurie's confidentiality.

THE figurative net that was tightening around Laurie broke open on Monday when Steve Witt said he was backing off on the effort to seek the federal indictment. He and his wife had decided they didn't want to go it alone against Laurie. They envisioned her being arrested, posting bond, and flying immediately to Arizona with her gun in her suitcase. He figured it would be best to wait and try to coordinate the indictment with other charges back in Illinois.

At noon the next day Laurie called the Young Men's Jewish Council, one of the schools on the list she had compiled in Madison. Shortly afterward she called Ravinia Elementary, the other school. At both places she asked what time the children arrived in the morning.

At 7:05 that evening, she began making nuisance phone calls. At 8:51 she reached Dr. Gail Levee, a friend from the time when she was first dating Russell. Gail said she would be coming to visit from Los Angeles soon, and Laurie said they should get together.

"Life is beautiful," Laurie added. "I've got a package I'll be sending you. Look for it."

The next morning, Laurie mailed the Levees a package of Rice Krispies Treats laced with arsenic. She put the Towers in Madison for the return address. Then she took a drive down to see Marian Rushe in Winnetka and set up a little outing on Friday morning with her children Patrick and Carl.

Wednesday was also the day Norm and Edith arrived home from Florida.

Meanwhile, Russell was in something of a panic. The FBI had told him that they had lost track of Laurie.

Thursday night Laurie and her mother spent several hours in the kitchen making up yet another batch of Rice Krispies Treats. Laurie was so happy, Edith noticed. She was really psyched for the carnival.

9.

FREE SAMPLES

LIGHTS were burning early at the Wassermans' on the morning of May 20, 1988.

Laurie had awakened shortly after 5:00 a.m. to begin her final preparations for the day. The demons in her past—her parents, her ex-husband and his relatives and friends, her tormentors in Evanston and Madison, the men who hadn't loved her, the men who had loved her badly, the women who had shunned her, her baby-sitting clients and her doctors—they would never underestimate her again.

Her bedroom at that hour was a veritable pantry of fruit juice packets, Rice Krispies Treats and popcorn. For approximately the next fifty minutes, as Glencoe awakened to a gorgeous spring day, she loaded her syringe with the arsenic solution she had stolen from the lab at the University of Wisconsin, and carefully injected the foil pouches of juice. Some of the pouches she then placed into long brown envelopes onto which she had written FREE SAMPLE and the addresses of Dr. Greist; Russell Dann; Peter Smith, a former baby-sitting client; and others. The rest of the pouches went into a plastic garbage bag.

Her movements through the North Shore suburbs in the following two hours have been reconstructed by examining the addresses she visited and talking to the people who saw her.

At about 6:30 she walked next door to a house owned by William and Iris Garmisa, friends of Norm and Edith's, and left a poisoned juice pouch in the mailbox. Then she returned home and, because her Honda was in the body shop, loaded up her father's Cressida. She put her handguns, jars and bottles of incendiary chemicals, and ammunition in the trunk, placed the poisoned food on the passenger seat, and threw in an extra garbage bag.

She proceeded south on Sheridan Road, driving five blocks to

Woodlawn Avenue, where she turned right. She stopped at the home of former baby-sitting clients Sam and Debi Oakner and dropped off a leaking container of Hawaiian Punch.

She drove west on Woodlawn, then south on Glenwood Street to where Old Green Bay Road and Scott Avenue come together. There she placed six padded envelopes in the mailbox.

At 6:45 she headed southeast on Scott Avenue to Green Bay Road, which she took north through Glencoe and into Highland Park. She turned left into Charal Lane, part of the neighborhood where she and Russell had lived before their separation.

Steven Lapata heard his screen door open and close at 6:55. He found a juice pouch between the doors. Lapata's wife, Jodi, had known Laurie slightly when she lived nearby, but it seems possible that Laurie mistook the Lapata house for the house two doors away that had angered her several years earlier when she was convinced that the owners had gotten a better deal than she and Russell had.

She drove next to Stonegate Drive and left juice at the home of John Eilian. He knew Laurie through a friend. She headed west and turned right onto Hastings Street. She placed Hawaiian Punch in the rack under the mailbox at the house of Steven Sider. He was a close friend of Jeff and Susie Taylor's. She then slipped a juice packet between the screen door and the front door of the Kalish house. She and Marla Kalish had talked over the back fence from time to time. Her last stop on the block was at the house of another former neighbor, Steven Jazinsky, where she placed a juice pouch in the mailbox.

She then drove west a mile to U.S. Highway 41 south, which took her to Winnetka. She was carrying a slip of paper with an address on DeWindt Road, and she arrived at a little past 7:00 a.m., left a juice pouch in the mailbox, and rang the bell.

Homeowner Nancy Mowry answered the door and saw a woman getting into her car and heading away. Mowry didn't know Laurie; police investigators ultimately discovered that Henry Angston had owned the house up until 1984. He had four children, one of whom had evidently slighted Laurie in a way she never forgot or forgave.

Then she drove south into Evanston and proceeded to the Northwestern campus. At around 8:00 she left a few plates of Rice Krispies Treats sitting on the landing of the stairs at the west entrance of the Alpha Tau Omega fraternity house. ATO was on her list because the previous summer the brothers had forced Donna McDonough to give up her puppy. McDonough, who rented a room at the fraternity for the summer and was employed as a desk clerk at the Kellogg Living/ Learning Center, brought the puppy to work several times, and Laurie grew very attached to it.

At 8:30 Laurie entered the east door of the Psi Upsilon house, next to ATO on Lincoln Street, and on a bench in the foyer set three paper plates of Rice Krispies Treats laced with arsenic; a juice pouch; an open bag of Jolly Time popcorn that later tested positive for a high concentration of lead, which masks the presence of arsenic; and a bottle labeled ARSENIC. She left a note signed, "Love, your little sisters. Enjoy." The note seemed odd to the residents, because they referred to sorority women as daughters, not little sisters. The bottle, which actually did contain arsenic, seemed at the time like a silly and not very funny joke.

She also left Rice Krispies Treats at the Kappa Sigma fraternity house and in the vestibule of Leverone Hall, headquarters of the Kellogg business school.

Laurie turned north toward the Rushe house in Winnetka.

THE very first day that a young boy gets to ride his bike to school is a big day indeed, and as Laurie Dann drove with stone-faced purpose into Winnetka, eight-year-old Nicky Corwin was hurrying to pull on his Chicago Bears souvenir jersey and sweatpants for school, running late but excited.

He had been studying bicycle safety for the previous two weeks at school, and that morning he and his second-grade classmates at Hubbard Woods Elementary would be taking both outdoor and indoor tests. If he passed, he would be allowed to ride the five blocks to school every day for the rest of the year.

His older brother, Michael, eleven, was astride his own bike waiting at the edge of the driveway.

"Go on ahead!" their mother called.

"It's okay, Mom!" he called back. "I want to ride with Nicky."

It was, in many ways, like a scene from a corny 1950s TV show. The Corwins lived in a red brick house on a street shrouded by towering oaks. Nicky was a mop top, with bright hazel eyes, freckles across his nose and a gap-toothed grin. Although Linda Corwin held a master's degree in public affairs, she was a full-time mother to Nicky, Michael and Johnny, a five-year-old. Her husband, Joel, was a corporate lawyer in a Chicago firm and commissioner of the local junior baseball league.

Nicky Corwin was born at Evanston Hospital on April 9, 1980, at 2:48 a.m., just three minutes after his parents had driven up to the emergency-room door. The delivery, Linda later remembered, was totally painless.

Nicky's athletic prowess showed itself early—he was already throwing a ball with accuracy by the time he was just a year old—and soon he climbed trees and jungle gyms absolutely without fear. He went on to excel in soccer, baseball and football. His athletic grace was matched by an artistic talent and academic aptitude already heralded by his teachers.

But what set Nicky apart from many other pint-size whiz kids was a certain humility. Instead of lording his abilities over the other kids, he became their helper and leader, and was known as much for his sense of fair play and camaraderie as his skills. In the first grade he'd been voted "most supportive" by his classmates for his conduct on the athletic field and in the classroom.

He was the center of the family, Linda said. When they posed for a studio photograph, Nicky sat right in the middle. Similarly, when his second-grade class posed for its annual group photo, he was sitting out in front of everyone, all by himself, grinning hugely.

But for all his poise and independence, he still liked to crawl in bed with his mom in the morning after his father got up. Joel Corwin tried to leave the house early for work so he could come home early in the evening, and on the morning of May 20 his last glimpse of Nicky was of the boy curled up against his mother, both of them sleeping contentedly.

"My favorite color is blue," Nicky had written in the journal he kept at school. "My favorite letter is N. My favorite number is 3." He also listed the things he was most thankful for: "Mom, Dad, little brother, older brother, house, bed, money, doctor, grandma, school, my friends, my life, and me."

HE RACED for his bike and streaked down the concrete driveway to join his brother. It was such a perfect day to ride your bike; such a perfect day to be a kid.

THE SCENE AT THE RUSHE household that morning was a sharp reminder to Laurie Dann of what she never was and never had. Marian was thirty-five years old, married, a mother of five great kids, outgoing, involved. Her children were self-assured and talented. Their happiness, and Marian's achievement, was an insult.

The Rice Krispies Treats Laurie left behind on the counter were laced with arsenic. Similarly, the orange tint to the milk was the result of several drops of arsenic solution she had surreptitiously poured into the jug.

After leaving the Rushes' with the two boys, Laurie headed north to Highland Park, then proceeded to Ravinia Elementary, a classic dark brick three-story school for two hundred and eighty students, where she arrived shortly before 9:00 a.m. Jeff and Susie Taylor's nine-year-old boy, Brian, attended the school.

Laurie parked the car and told Patrick and Carl she would be right back. She removed a yellow plastic bag with a drawstring top from the trunk and carried it into the school, the glass jars and bottles inside tinkling against one another.

Upon entering the school, she almost immediately came upon a cardboard refrigerator box that had been cut up and decorated to look like a house. The box was all that was left of Cardboard City, a social studies project in which the second graders earned play money for doing their homework, then purchased toy houses with mortgages from third-grade "bankers." It was a perfect exercise for the children of the well-to-do and, Laurie thought, the perfect hiding spot for her bomb.

She placed the bag inside the playhouse and set fire to the drawstring. The sealed bottles contained such stolen flammable liquid compounds as heptane, butanol, etching acid and pyridine. Laurie had calculated that when they ignited together, they would cause an explosion that would rip through the school.

The bag began to burn, and Laurie backed toward the door.

Fifty feet away, second-grade teacher Paul Grant was leading a line of his students to the library. As Grant looked down the hallway he saw a woman stagger back into the exit door, hit the crash bar noisily, and run away.

Strange. What was her big hurry? Grant and all eighteen students filed past the cardboard house. Two sharp-eyed boys near the end of the line happened to look into a window and see the flicker of the flame. The boys raced ahead and caught up to Grant. "There's something burning in the box!" they said.

Grant smiled. "Well, then, call the Cardboard City Fire Department," he said.

"No!" they said. "Something's really burning!"

"Class, go on ahead to the library," said Grant, still calm. He and the two boys walked back to the house. Grant bent down, opened the door, and saw flames eating the top half of a plastic bag.

LAURIE jumped back into her father's car and sped off. She passed the Mickey Mouse cup filled with arsenic-laced milk into the back seat and told the boys to drink. They both had a taste. It was awful—sour or spoiled, they thought. They set the cup aside.

Laurie drove them half a mile to the Young Men's Jewish Council day-care center. She knew that Lisa Taylor, Jeff and Susie's five-year-old, was enrolled at the center, though she probably did not know that Lisa was an afternoon student and not due to arrive until 12:45 p.m.

When she pulled into the parking lot, Laurie told the Rushe boys they should come with her. The boys threw the Mickey Mouse cup out onto the grass while Laurie withdrew a red plastic gasoline container from the trunk. Leaving the gas can on the sidewalk, she led Patrick and Carl into the building. School director Jean Leivick, who had seen Laurie approaching, went to the foyer to intercept her. Laurie explained that her children—she nodded at Patrick and Carl—were going to attend a summer program at the school and she wanted to look around. Leivick let her go, and Laurie led the boys from classroom to classroom.

Lisa Taylor wasn't there. Laurie returned to the front of the school, where she sent Patrick and Carl off to play on the swing sets and picked up the gasoline container again. When she tried to reenter the school, Leivick stopped her.

"You can't bring that into the building," Leivick said, gesturing at the can.

"I'm out of gas," Laurie explained in mock distress.

"Do you need help putting the gas into the tank?"

Laurie hesitated. "Um . . . yes," she said. Leivick accompanied her to the Toyota and helped her pour the gasoline in.

Right about then, in Evanston, a brother at the Alpha Tau Omega house was taking a big bite of one of the Rice Krispies Treats found on the doorstep that morning. It tasted nasty, he thought. He threw the rest of the plate into the Dumpster.

At the Ravinia School, Highland Park police officers and fire fighters had been summoned after teacher Paul Grant had blown out the fire in the cardboard house. They were examining the vicious combination of chemicals that had been in the plastic bag and wondering if, considering the heavy Jewish population in the area, they had an anti-Semitic terrorist action on their hands.

NICKY Corwin's regular teacher was taking a personal day Friday, but the sub was Amy Moses, who had filled in a lot that year and even knew all the kids' names. She took them outside right at 9:00 a.m. for the first half of the bicycle safety test.

Everyone passed the test. Moses then led them back to the classroom for the written half of the exam. Before getting down to it, she led a group discussion about what a big accomplishment it was going to be to win the right to ride to school every day . . . for the rest of their lives, if they wanted.

LAURIE summoned Patrick and Carl and drove south through residential Glencoe to a neighborhood where she had done a lot of baby-sitting.

First she stopped at the home of Paul Lederer, on Bluff Street, where she left fruit juice in the mailbox. The packet was marked SAMPLE in blue ink. On Milton Street she stopped in front of the home of Julie and Mike Alt and left them poisoned juice. Then she drove to Park Avenue and stopped to leave juice in the mailbox of David and Rosemarie Hawkins, former baby-sitting clients.

Laurie's link with the Hawkins family was apparent. But for some of the other targets—Paul Lederer, for instance—the connections have been impossible to determine. Any one member of the family either did something to Laurie or didn't do something for her, said something, looked a certain way, failed to wave hello, honked a car horn in anger—anything.

But whatever her tangled motivations, Laurie was done, out of poison. Patrick and Carl were still very much alive, prattling away in the back seat, so she decided to take them back home and deal with them there.

A little past 10:00 she arrived back at the Rushe house. "I'm sorry," she said to Marian, who was surprised to see her. "I had the wrong date for the carnival. We went to the park instead."

Patrick and Carl did not appear bothered by the change in plans, so Marian took it in stride. She invited Laurie to stay and keep the children company while she did laundry.

Laurie was carrying a pack of matches and a brown shopping bag rattling with bottles. She followed Marian and the children down a central staircase to the basement laundry room.

"So," Laurie said, as she set the bag down next to a table. "Are Mary Rose and Robert coming home for lunch?"

Marian shook her head. "They're on a school field trip down in Chicago today," she said.

"Oh," said Laurie. Another hitch.

She hoisted the plastic bag. "I have to get something from the car," she said.

Halfway up to the landing Laurie pulled out a large flask filled with gasoline and poured it on the carpeted treads at her feet. She opened a second container and set it on top of the spill. Then she tore a match free, struck it, and touched the lighted end to the soaked fibers. Flames danced up off the stairs in a silent flash of blue and orange.

Marian Rushe was occupied with the laundry when she heard the smoke detector go off. She heard a sound coming from the stairwell that reminded her of a gas grill being lighted—*woof!* The second container of gasoline had ignited.

"Fire!" Laurie yelled. She hurried to the back door and locked it, the better to impede rescue efforts, then locked the front door behind her as she hurried out.

By the time Marian reached the bottom of the stairs to investigate, the fire was furious, creeping down toward her with black, choking smoke. She cried out to her boys, and led them toward the far corner of the basement away from the fire. In the back of her mind she worried for Laurie. Had she escaped?

The southeast window, six feet high against the wall, offered their only way out. It wouldn't open easily, so Marian snapped a leg off an old crib and broke the glass with several smart blows. She pulled shards and fragments out of the frame, cutting her hands and arms badly. With the opening clear, she hoisted Patrick on her shoulders so he could crawl through the opening and into the window well. The boy then pushed out the grate over the well and escaped into the yard. Carl wriggled out behind him.

"Go get help next door!" Marian shouted.

Getting herself out would not be so easy. She had no light, and the smoke was moving toward her in a pernicious cloud. She looked around in a panic for old suitcases and anything else she could pile up to make a platform for herself. When that was done, she climbed upon the rickety pile and pulled herself through the opening into fresh air and daylight.

She was bloodied but safe.

DETECTIVE Floyd Mohr wasn't scheduled to work until 3:00 that afternoon, but to get a jump on his paperwork, he'd come in early and then headed out in his blue, unmarked Ford Fairmont. He was turning north onto Vernon Drive at 10:21 a.m. when he heard the report on his radio of a fire in Winnetka and shook his head sympathetically— what bad timing. Winnetka was shorthanded, he knew, because most of the department was attending the funeral of retired fire fighter Lawrence Carney.

Mohr figured that the men on duty could probably use an extra hand, so he headed south toward the fire fifteen blocks away. When he arrived at the Rushe house, smoke was swirling ominously out of the vents in the attic.

10.

MURDER OF INNOCENCE

AFTER Laurie left Marian Rushe and her two youngest children to burn alive in their own basement, she opened the trunk of her father's car and removed her three handguns and some ammunition. She placed them on the passenger seat next to her and drove four blocks to Hubbard Woods Elementary, a one-story brick school with homey white wooden window frames.

She parked the Toyota on Chatfield Road at the front of the school, facing toward Interstate 94, a mile and a half away.

It was 10:25 a.m. The doors were unlocked. No one even saw Laurie as she pushed through the double doors at the back entrance and slipped quickly into a boys' bathroom. There she probably looked in a mirror to be sure that her guns were tucked safely into the waistband of her shorts and that her T-shirt fell over the bulges to hide them. She reentered the hallway. The school had three hundred and twenty-five students, but fully a third of them, including the elder Rushe children, her likely targets, were off on field trips that day, so foot traffic in the halls was light.

Kindergarten teacher Phyllis McMillan, whose classroom was next to the bathroom, happened to poke her head into the hall at just that moment. As Laurie passed, McMillan thought she could be a nanny, but she had never seen her before. It was odd that she should be emerging from the boys' bathroom.

As Laurie continued up the hallway she passed Ann Hardy, a teacher who was on break, standing in the hall.

"Hello," Hardy said.

Laurie didn't answer, and kept walking, past the small wooden coat carrels, the wall murals, the gaily decorated doorways, the knee-high drinking fountains.

McMillan hurried over to Hardy. "Something very strange just happened," she said. "That woman just came out of the boys' bathroom. I've got to stay with my kids, but would you mind checking on her?"

"Sure," Hardy said. She went toward the front of the school and saw nothing. She knocked on the door of another boys' bathroom.

"Can I help someone?" she called.

No answer. Hardy went back to report to McMillan. "She must be gone."

When Laurie heard Hardy's footsteps receding, she resumed breathing. She stashed her Magnum and a bag of ammunition in the left-hand sink, where she could retrieve them, then left the bathroom and entered the corridor again. Ahead of her across the hall was the closed door of classroom 7. Seven was one of her lucky numbers.

At a little past 10:30 she opened the door and walked in. Twenty-four children were sitting at tables and desks listening to Amy Moses brief them on what they would have to know for the written portion of their bicycle safety test.

On one wall was a bulletin board labeled THE WRITING PLACE, where the regular teacher, Amy Deuble, tacked up short stories and compositions. On the west wall was a series of silhouette cutouts of all the kids. The room had a computer terminal up front and, more traditionally, the alphabet running across the top of the main blackboard.

Laurie walked over and stood next to Moses, who was three inches shorter than Laurie and forty pounds lighter.

Moses interrupted her lesson. "May I help you?" she said politely.

"No," Laurie said.

"Are you here to observe?" Moses asked. Hubbard Woods was informal in this respect. Parents felt free to drop in anytime, and students from Northwestern or the National College of Education, in Evanston, frequently came to watch teachers in action. Laurie didn't answer; instead she simply sat down at a table in the front of the room. Moses continued with her lesson, but she was bothered by the hard, lifeless expression of the stranger. She gave Laurie a copy of the test she was about to hand out.

Laurie maintained eye contact when Moses directed remarks her way, but her face remained blank as her mind roiled with conflicting impulses, plans, strategies. After several minutes she stood suddenly, dropped the bicycle information on the floor, and left the room.

SHE headed back into the hall, where she saw Robert Trossman, six, at a drinking fountain. He was returning from the reading lab to his first-grade class. Suddenly she found her courage.

"Don't you have to go to the bathroom, little boy?" she said.

Robert was too confused to cry out. Laurie dragged him into the boys' bathroom, withdrew the Beretta from her waistband, and fired virtually point-blank. She was so nervous that her first shot missed and slammed into the tile between two urinals. With the second shot she hit him in the right upper chest with a bullet that exited through his lower back. He dropped to the floor.

As she turned to leave, she saw to her surprise that two other little boys had walked in behind her and seen what had happened. She pointed the Beretta at them and pulled the trigger, but the gun didn't fire. They fled.

The two young witnesses ran wildly across the hall to their teacher, Mary Lind, who was in the classroom right next door to classroom 7.

"There's a woman in the bathroom with a gun!" they said.

Lind had heard the percussive popping sounds and assumed they were part of a science experiment in another class. She dropped the papers she was holding and ran across to the bathroom. There she found Robert on the floor, bleeding from the chest. "I've been shot," he cried. "Am I going to die?"

Lind told one of the boys who had been in the bathroom with Laurie to stay with Robert, and she turned and ran, screaming, toward the principal's office. "Call the police! Call the paramedics!"

LAURIE had returned to classroom 7 with fury and resolve. Amy Moses was answering the question of a child who had come to the front of the room.

"Put the children in a corner," Laurie ordered.

"What?" she said.

"Put the children in a corner," Laurie repeated.

"No," Moses replied, more surprised than frightened.

Laurie drew her Beretta. "This is a gun," she said. "And I have another one."

Moses saw the tiny pistol and thought it looked like a toy.

"It's real," Laurie said, reading the doubt in Moses' expression. "I'll show you."

Amy suddenly realized by the tone of Laurie's voice that the gun was indeed real. Instinctively she grabbed Laurie's right wrist and began wrestling with her. During the brief struggle Moses forced a pair of live .22-caliber rounds to eject from the Beretta.

Laurie broke free and pulled the .32 out of her shorts, drawing like a gunslinger. She waved her weapons at the children. "Get in the corner," she said.

They were struck motionless by a combination of fear and confusion. "Why?" one of them asked.

Laurie didn't wait. She moved quickly up to a group of three children against the east wall and held one gun out. Expressionlessly she pulled the trigger.

When the first child, eight-year-old Mark Teborek, went down, Moses thought, They're filming a movie and they forgot to tell me. They just forgot to tell me.

The bullet had hit Mark on the left side of the neck and exited through the right side of the chest.

Laurie walked swiftly past the students who were sitting along the east wall of the classroom, toward the door that led outside. She fired her guns as she went, point-blank.

Nicky Corwin turned away from Laurie toward the blackboard as she came at him. The bullet hit him in his left upper back, penetrated his left lung and pulmonary artery, and exited through the right side of his chest. He fell face down atop a large throw pillow that leaned against a blackboard.

Peter Munro, an eight-year-old, held out his hand to try to stop the bullet, but it ripped through the hand, hit him in the abdomen, and exited through his lower back. He fell near Mark Teborek.

Lindsay Fisher, also eight and an avid soccer player, took a .32-caliber bullet in the right upper chest. It ricocheted downward off a bone and lodged in her lower left hip.

Laurie's last victim was Kathryn Ann Miller, seven. The bullet hit her in the left side of the chest, hit a rib, and exited through her stomach.

And then the madwoman was gone, leaving behind a room filled with blood, screaming children and the acrid smell of gunpowder.

Laurie ran back to the Toyota, guns in both hands. She drove quickly half a block west on Chatfield Road and swung hard into a right turn on Gordon Terrace. But at the intersection of Tower Road a police squad car was blocking the way ahead of her, its mars lights revolving. How quickly she was trapped!

Actually, Officer Rich Carlson was on the corner by coincidence. His humdrum assignment that morning was to clear traffic for the Carney funeral cortege as it came out of Sacred Heart Catholic Church a few blocks east.

But Laurie must have thought the roadblock was already there for her. She pulled a U-turn in a blind panic and sped off down Hamptondale Road, a dead-end street. At the end of the road she drove past a STREET ENDS sign and a stone monument reading 1200, indicating that the pavement from there on belonged to the sprawling Tudor home hidden back among the trees.

The driveway formed a small circle, and Laurie was going far too fast to make the full turn successfully. The car swept wide and ended up with its back end lodged on a large rock. From the distance came the sound of sirens, one, two, three, more.

She reloaded the Beretta and the Smith & Wesson; then she took off her shorts and wrapped her midsection in a light blue plastic trash bag. She got out of the car and took off on foot.

The engine of the Toyota was still running. She left behind a pair of white shorts, two boxes of matches, eighteen rounds of .22-caliber ammunition, one box of .32-caliber ammunition with six rounds missing, a can of gasoline, and Styrofoam strips soaked in an accelerant.

SCHOOL secretary Eva Mendelson had lunged for the telephone as soon as she'd heard Mary Lind's screams. She knew school policy: call for help first and ask questions later.

At 10:41 a.m. Winnetka police department dispatcher Bill Saunders picked up the 911 emergency line and heard a frantic cry. "We've got a shooting at Hubbard Woods School! A child!"

His voice broke with incredulity. "A shooting?"

"Yes!"

"And there's an injury there, ma'am?"

"Yes!" Mendelson said.

"Okay," said Saunders. "We'll get somebody on the way."

Saunders called for Winnetka ambulance 71 to respond. He got no immediate answer, so he called for Glencoe ambulance 81.

But paramedics Michael Roeder and Lee Fanslow, in Winnetka 71, had heard the call and were already on their way.

MARY Lind turned as soon as she saw help had been called and began running back to the boys' bathroom. As she ran, she heard a fusillade of shots fired in classroom 7.

First-grade teacher Alice Horevitz, who was in classroom 11 across the hall from classroom 7, was annoyed by the disruptive popping sounds. The noise reminded her of bursting balloons, and Horevitz figured the screaming was just the kids whooping it up because it was Bike Day and they'd all passed their tests.

Then she heard the sound of running in the hall and still more screaming, this time unmistakably hysterical. The door to her classroom opened, and her student Robert Trossman staggered in. He had made the ten-yard walk from the bathroom unassisted. "I've just been shot by a crazy girl," he said.

The children who had escaped classroom 7 raced straight for the office of principal Dick Streedain. After Mary Lind had sounded the alarm, Streedain placed a quick call to his superintendent, Don Monroe.

Amy Moses ran into the hallway yelling, "Call the police! Children have been shot!"

She and Streedain passed each other as he headed toward Mary Lind's classroom, where shooting victim Peter Munro had run to hide. Streedain was almost there when he heard Alice Horevitz call out for help.

She had set Robert Trossman on a cushion, removed his blood-soaked shirt, and lifted up his T-shirt to get at his wounds.

"She shot me," Robert moaned. "Why did she do it?"

No sooner had Streedain looked in on Horevitz than another teacher grabbed him by the shoulder. "We have several more children shot across the hall," she said.

Streedain's first thought was similar to that of officials in Highland Park that morning—terrorists were on the loose. "Be sure the school is secure," he ordered.

In the hallway, a teacher handed Streedain the limp body of Lindsay Fisher, who had run from the classroom after being shot and fallen before she could get to the office. Teacher's aide Jacqueline Slavick was cradling Kathryn Miller, who'd made it all the way to the office before collapsing, her white shirt spotted and spattered with blood. She and Streedain carried the girls to the main entrance to wait for paramedics. They heard far-off ambulances wailing, and time stood still as the color drained from the faces of the little girls.

Amy Moses was back inside classroom 7, trying to administer first aid to Mark Teborek. Mary Lind had also rushed to the classroom and, holding Nicky Corwin's arm, was soothing him. "It'll be okay," she said. "Hang on." She thought she had a pulse. Later she realized it was just her own hands shaking.

AT THE scene of the fire at the Rushe house, Floyd Mohr heard his hip radio crackle. "Did they say a shooting?" he asked Winnetka animal warden Craig Tisdale, who was also helping fight the fire.

"Yeah," said Tisdale, as puzzled as Mohr. "At Hubbard Woods School."

"I'm getting over there," Mohr said.

WINNETKA CHIEF OF DETECTIVES Patty McConnell was waiting at the drive-up window of the Winnetka Bank on Spruce Street with her partner, Bob Kerner, when she first heard reports of shots fired at the school. They were putting their paychecks in the bank at the end of a fairly slow morning. She was in sweatshirt and jeans, her undercover grubbies.

"Winnetka units, we have a report of a shooting at Hubbard Woods School."

Sergeant McConnell envisioned a BB gun incident. A Winnetka cop never thought in terms of murder. There hadn't been one in the village since 1957.

McConnell and Kerner sped to the school. There they pulled up at the curb, jumped out, and ran for the entrance, where they saw Streedain and Slavick, covered with blood, holding the bodies of two unconscious children.

Streedain looked wanly up at McConnell. "There are more inside," he said.

SCHOOL superintendent Don Monroe drove up to Hubbard Woods literally seconds ahead of the first ambulance, Winnetka 71, which pulled in around the back of the school. A teacher waved paramedics Fanslow and Roeder around to the outer door of classroom 7.

Glencoe ambulance 81 was half a minute behind and pulled up to the main entrance.

In classroom 7, Roeder raced for Nicky Corwin, and Fanslow went for Mark Teborek. Everyone was yelling and screaming.

LAURIE Dann, wrapped in plastic and running hard, had cut down a path through a break in the trees and bushes at the back of the driveway at 1200 Hamptondale Road. After twenty feet she found herself in yet another driveway leading to yet another enormous house. A ten-foot stockade fence rose up to her right, and looming trees blocked the sky all around. She was lost inside a thicket of adjoining estates built into the forest—there was no clue which way led to freedom.

She ran down the curving asphalt driveway, turned left when she got to the street, then took another hard left into the driveway of Two Kent Road, an eight-bedroom stucco mansion. A high wall extended from the front of the house across the side yard to a large garage. A black wooden gate led from the front yard into the back, and on the driveway eighty-three-year-old Vincent Wolf was sitting in the sun in a lawn chair, attended by a nurse.

"My car broke down, I need to use the phone," Laurie panted, running by. She entered the backyard through the gate and turned right into a door that led directly into the kitchen. It was unlocked, and she burst in unannounced. Vincent Wolf's daughter, Ruth Ann Andrew, fifty, was washing a few dishes at the sink.

Ruth Ann was talking to her son Phil Andrew, twenty. He had come home just the day before from his first year at the University of Illinois, where he was a member of the relay swim teams. He was dressed in a white T-shirt and red gym shorts.

Laurie, drenched with sweat, was wearing only her Arizona College of Medicine T-shirt and the trash bag, which she held together in front with the same hand that was carrying both guns.

TEACHER Mary Lind was still hovering over Nicky Corwin. "I've lost the pulse!" she cried to Winnetka paramedic Michael Roeder.

Roeder knelt down and saw immediately how bad it was. "DOA," he said.

Lind didn't move.

Roeder stood. "DOA," he said sharply. "Get away!"

Roeder's partner, Lee Fanslow, broke across the hall to the right, looking for the rest of the wounded. Fanslow found Peter Munro, then retrieved Robert Trossman from classroom 11. All the wounded were laid out on the floor near Nicky Corwin.

WINNETKA police chief Herbert Timm arrived and entered the school, where the hallways were becoming increasingly chaotic as confusion spread. He found classroom 7 and saw the bloodstained floor, the wounded children and the kicked-over desks. Patty McConnell and Bob Kerner were helping other arriving paramedics sort the victims by the severity of their wounds.

"My tummy hurts so bad," Robert Trossman groaned. "I can't breathe. Am I going to die, mister?"

"No, no," Timm said. "You're going to be fine."

A fire department paramedic pressed on the gaping wound in

Robert's chest. "I bet this is more attention than you've gotten in a long time," he said to the boy.

Robert smiled.

Dick Streedain, the principal, returned to the classroom, and the paramedics told him Nicky Corwin was dead.

JOEL Corwin received a call at his law office in Chicago from a woman at the school. She told him in a voice ragged with emotion that there had been an emergency and that he and his wife should get there as soon as possible. Nothing else. Just "an emergency."

He remembered that Linda was at a golf clinic at the nearby public course, and he called the clubhouse. She was in a group practicing sand-trap shots when a man ran out to get her, saying her husband was on the phone. As soon as she heard the panic in Joel's voice, she knew something serious had happened—maybe one of the school's boilers had blown. The school board had just been talking about replacing the boilers.

She ran to her car, and Joel hailed a taxi for the half-hour trip home—there was no time to catch the train.

Meanwhile, no one knew for sure if the gunwoman was still hiding in the school or if she was headed to another school. Superintendent Don Monroe began calling other districts and telling them to lock the doors to their schools, protect their children.

OFFICER Rich Carlson, who had left his post directing traffic and run to the school, took Amy Moses over to Sergeant McConnell. "Patty," he said, "this is the teacher. She was in the room."

"Who did this?" McConnell said, assuming that the attacker would be someone known to the school community.

"I don't know," Moses said. "It's a woman. She's about thirty years old—"

McConnell interrupted. "Would you know her if you saw her again?"

"I'll never forget her," Moses said. "She had red hair, cut kind of short, and—"

"We're going to try to find her," McConnell interrupted again. "Can you come with us?"

"Absolutely," Moses said.

McConnell and her partner, Bob Kerner, took Moses out to the squad car. She kept repeating over and over, "My God, I wish she had shot me and not my children. I wish she had shot me."

"YOU'RE my hostages," Laurie said to Ruth Ann Andrew and her son Phil, her voice steady, her eyes calm. "Get over to the other side of the room. I have a gun."

They didn't take her seriously. "What's going on?" Phil asked.

"I'm running from the police," Laurie said, once again assuming the role of the victim. "I was raped in my car and I shot at the guy who did it. I ran here."

"Did you hit him?" Phil wanted to know.

"I don't know," Laurie said. "I just ran because I was scared."

"Where did you get those guns?"

"My car," Laurie said. "They were in the glove compartment."

Phil tried to get a closer look at the guns to see if they were real. Suddenly he caught a glimpse of the slugs in the chamber of the .32. He paused. "Why don't you give me the guns?" he said.

"No," said Laurie. She recoiled slightly. "I'm afraid."

"Do you think we should call the police?"

"I'm afraid of the police," she said.

Phil could see her point. If she had shot her attacker, he could be telling the police anything—that she was simply a crazy person who had gone after him for no reason. On the other hand, Phil thought, the story was pretty incredible.

Phil was standing close to Laurie, who was not brandishing her guns but holding them by the handles, down at her side. He could have grabbed and subdued her, but he worried that doing so might just further traumatize her. "Do you want my mom to go get you a pair of pants?" he asked.

"No," she said. "I don't want you leaving the room. You'll call the police."

"You should get on the phone, then," Phil said. "Isn't there someone you could call?"

"I could call my mother," Laurie said. "She lives in Glencoe."

"Go ahead," Phil said. "Then you'll be on the phone so my mom can get something for you to wear. Okay?"

"Okay," she said. She took the phone from its cradle on the wall and dialed. Ruth Ann Andrew left the room. She had every chance to use the second line, a children's telephone, but didn't. The girl with the guns seemed frightened, not dangerous. Phil had everything under control, and her husband was expected home any minute.

Edith answered the telephone at 10:57. "Hello," she said.

"Mom," Laurie said. "I've done something terrible. People won't understand. I'm going to have to kill myself."

11.

THE SUSPECT

AT HUBBARD Woods, the classmates of the children who had been shot were locked inside the principal's office, shaking, crying, asking for their mothers and fathers.

Streedain opened the door and looked in on them several times, and each time they jumped up and said, "We're going to be shot! We're going to be shot!"

He was doing his best to intercept shocked and grieving parents who were starting to arrive at the school, and he had the sad duty of being the first to talk to Linda Corwin. She had parked beyond the fire engines and run to the front entrance of the school. She'd noticed as she passed inside that people were turning their heads away from her, avoiding eye contact.

"What happened?" she cried. "What happened?"

No one said anything. Streedain hurried over to her, his shirt stained brightly with Lindsay Fisher's blood. "It's the worst possible thing that could ever happen," he said. "This crazy person came in the school and started shooting kids." He paused only half a second. "And I hate to tell you this, but she shot Nicky."

"Is he dead?"

Streedain said yes, he was.

Linda cried, "Oh, Nicky! Nicky! No!" Streedain embraced her; then Chief Timm led her to a bench to sit down.

"I'm very very sorry," he said.

One of Timm's officers came up beside him. "Do you want someone to go talk to the reporters?" he asked.

Timm snapped to. He went to a window and looked out. Scores of journalists were waiting outside, beyond the yellow police barriers. The news had raced literally around the world—calls were even then coming in from Australia, Germany and England. Could this horrible story possibly be true?

FLOYD Mohr drove to the school, where he walked in for a look at the mess inside classroom 7, then wandered back outside to see how the investigation was proceeding. Chief Timm and Winnetka fire chief Ron Colpaert were discussing the fire at the Rushe house, and how it still appeared possible that the baby-sitter was trapped inside. Her name was Laurie something; that was all they knew.

The words baby-sitter and Laurie clicked immediately in Mohr's mind. He excused himself and broke for his car, jumped in, and drove quickly back to the Rushes'.

"Who's the homeowner here?" he asked as he approached a group gathered around the back of a paramedic van.

"I am," said Marian Rushe. Her hands and arms were bandaged. After she had run away from the house and looked back, she realized that Laurie was probably not still inside—her car was gone. She was beginning to confront the terrible possibility that her baby-sitter had tried to kill her.

Mohr had the same theory. He identified himself to Marian and began grilling her. "Now, what's your baby-sitter's name?"

"Laurie Porter."

Mohr was relieved for a moment, but pressed ahead. "Do you know her phone number?" he asked. "Is it 835-1263?"

"Yes. How did you know?"

"What kind of car does this lady drive?"

"She was driving a white—"

"Toyota?"

"Yes. How did you know?"

Mohr felt as though his beating heart were going to pop through his bulletproof vest. "Was the license number NW zero zero zero?"

"Yes. How did you know?"

At 11:04 an agonized Floyd Mohr broke into the police radio traffic. "The suspect's name is Laurie Porter. Her real identity I believe to be Laurie Dann. She lives at Three four six Sheridan. She's driving a white Japanese car." He paused to breathe hard, then continued. "It has a registered plate of NW zero zero zero."

MURDER OF INNOCENCE. Left, Laurie Dann in a March 1988 mug shot taken after her arrest for shoplifting. Below, teacher Amy Moses shows how she tried to restrain Laurie in classroom 7. A bloodstained Dick Streedain, principal of the Hubbard Woods School, after the rampage.

Above, devastated parents comfort one another outside the school. Right, Nicky Corwin, age eight.

Five minutes later Officer Rich Carlson found the getaway car in the driveway at 1200 Hamptondale, its engine still running. The initial suspicion was that she was inside that particular house, but a phone call there reached a trio of domestic servants, one of whom told police that she had seen and heard nothing.

THE Evanston Hospital emergency room had been placed on full alert as soon as the call came that critically wounded shooting victims from a Winnetka school were on their way.

Lindsay Fisher, the most seriously wounded of the survivors, was all but dead. The bullet had punctured her right lung, her liver and her stomach. Her heart was empty but still beating, and she registered no appreciable blood pressure. Nurses tried to insert intravenous lines but could find no blood vessels that hadn't collapsed. A team of surgeons led by Drs. John Alexander and Stephen Sener put an adult-size 16-gauge intravenous tube straight into her left atrium and transfused blood directly into her heart.

Dr. David Winchester, the hospital's chief of surgery, and Dr. Richard Larson took Kathryn Miller; Drs. Charles Drueck and John Golan tended to Mark Teborek; and Dr. Willard Fry began operating on Robert Trossman.

The chaos was less pronounced six miles away at Highland Park Hospital. Peter Munro had come severely wounded in the abdomen but conscious. Paramedics trying to treat Nicky Corwin in the ambulance had put a tube into his lung to try to get him breathing, and had started heart massage, but he showed no signs of life when he arrived in the emergency room. Dr. Mart Jalakas, the same physician who had treated Russell Dann's ice-pick wound, put in a second tube to drain blood from the boy's chest and continued heart massage.

As THE story spread, it grew. When the news reached the Skokie office of Cook County felony prosecutor Nancy Sidote, the number of children killed was reported as eleven. She rounded up two assistants and headed for the school.

AFTER several unsuccessful passes through the neighborhood, Sergeant Patty McConnell and Amy Moses dropped off Bob Kerner at the intersection of Kent and Hibbard roads so that he could make his way back east toward the school through the overgrown backyards. The two women then returned to the school.

A mug shot of Laurie Dann was rushed to Hubbard Woods from the Glencoe police department, and Amy Moses identified her immediately as the woman who had been in her classroom.

At 11:30 a.m., dog teams began arriving on the scene at the end of Hamptondale Road, where Lieutenant Joe Sumner was preparing to search the house at 1200. He had other teams of officers combing the backyards to the west of the house. Floyd Mohr, who had hurried back to the school, was part of the hunt, and was side by side with Bob Kerner and Lieutenant George Carpenter from Winnetka.

It was 11:46. Suddenly an excited voice broke into the radio traffic: Forget the house on Hamptondale; a nearby resident was reporting a hostage situation at Two Kent Road. A woman was holding the family prisoner.

The officers began heading through the yard toward Two Kent when the air rocked with the shattering report of a gunshot. There was nothing to do but run toward it.

Within thirty seconds Mohr and Kerner were in the front yard of Two Kent. They saw Vincent Wolf and his nurse sitting out next to the gate, so Carpenter provided cover while Mohr and Kerner hurried to the old man's side.

They dragged Wolf in his chair along the asphalt. Mohr crashed into the garage door with his back and the door swung open. They hid the old man behind a car and took up positions in the bushes by the gate, their guns drawn.

THE shot had come from Laurie's .32, a sudden, unexpected explosion. Phil Andrew could not believe she had done it. After all he had tried to do for her . . .

She had been distraught when she reached her mother on the phone around 11:00. "Mom, I've done something terrible," she said again. "These are nice people here. I don't want to hurt them."

After several minutes of listening to Laurie's bewildered babble, Phil could tell she wasn't getting anywhere with her mother. He asked for the phone, and she handed it to him.

"My name is Phil Andrew," he said. "Your daughter is here. She came in with two guns and told us we're her hostages. She said she was attacked, she shot her assailant, and now she's afraid of the police."

"Really," Edith Wasserman said.

Phil was stunned that she seemed so detached.

"Has she ever done anything like this before?" Phil asked.

"No," Edith said. Then she paused. "Would you please see that my daughter gets home safely?"

It was the kind of situation Norm would usually handle, but he was even at that moment driving Edith's car up to Madison to clear out Laurie's room in the Towers.

"I'll do what I can," Phil said.

He hung up and looked at Laurie, who was, in turn, looking hard at him. His mother returned to the kitchen carrying a pair of cutoff sweatpants. Laurie set both guns on the kitchen counter in order to pull the shorts on.

Phil saw his opportunity to take the guns away, and he reached out quickly and got his hand on the .22 Beretta. As he grabbed it Laurie snatched up the .32 and brandished it. "Give me that back," she said.

"No, I'm going to keep it," Phil said. He made an obvious show of removing the cartridge and putting it into one pocket of his shorts while putting the gun itself into the opposite pocket.

Phil then heard his father, Raymond, fifty-one, come into the house. Phil met him at the door of the kitchen. "We have a situation here," he said tightly. "This woman has a gun. She says she's been attacked and she shot her assailant."

Raymond took a seat at the counter. "That explains the police cars," he said. "They're all over the place. I almost thought they weren't going to let me come down the road."

Heightened panic showed in Laurie's eyes.

"We've talked to her mother," Phil said. "She's in Glencoe."

"Is she coming over?" Raymond asked.

"No," Phil said. He turned to Laurie. "Maybe we should get her on the phone again?"

At 11:07 Laurie called Edith back. "No one will understand," she told her mother. "It's terrible." She was pacing, wielding her gun, her finger on the trigger. Phil beckoned again and again for her to hand him the receiver. Finally she gave it to him.

"Can't you come over?" he pleaded.

"I don't have a car," Edith said. "My husband has the car."

"Can't you take a cab? Borrow a neighbor's car?" Phil said.

"No, I just can't," Edith said. "I can't."

Phil passed the phone to his father, who spoke sharply to Edith. "Tell your daughter to give up her gun," he said. "We're all in danger here."

Laurie clamped down on the switch hook, cutting off the call.

"We're not through," Raymond said, taking the same stern tone with Laurie he had taken with Edith. "Call her back."

Laurie complied, and Raymond continued his harangue. "She's got to give up the gun," he said to Laurie's mother.

Finally, exasperated at Edith's bland and noncommittal responses, he handed the phone back to Laurie. She commenced again with her miserable yet unspecific apologies. "I'm sorry to both of you, Mom and Dad," she said.

Their conversation went on and on. "Good-bye," Laurie said at last. "I'm sorry. This is it. Good-bye."

Right after she hung up, Ruth Ann threw up her hands. "Listen," she said, almost scolding Laurie. "My daughters are coming home from school soon, and we don't need any more people involved in this. Anyway, the police will follow them in."

"Oh, that's no good," Laurie said. "We need to keep them out."

"We'll send my mother outside," Phil said. "She'll be there so the girls won't come in."

"Okay," Laurie said. "Fine."

Ruth Ann hurried out the front door. Down the block, a policeman was guarding the entrance to Kent Road as the manhunt through the neighborhood continued. She ran up and told him what was happening in her house.

BACK in the kitchen, Phil was still working at calming Laurie down. "My summer job is in the state's attorney's office," he told her. "I know how the system works. If you give me the gun, I'll go to the police with you and be sure they don't hurt you."

His sincerity was improvised, and Laurie wasn't buying it. She knew Phil had no idea of the enormity of what she had done and how impossible it was going to be to save her.

"You've got to give up the gun," Raymond said. His main worry was not that Laurie would discharge her gun but that the police would storm the house and he and Phil would get caught in the cross fire.

"Look, this is no good," Phil said. "You're endangering us, so we're going to leave." He and Raymond headed for the door.

"No!" Laurie cried, pointing the gun at them. "Stop!"

Phil and Raymond Andrew stopped at Laurie's command.

"How about if just I stay?" Phil said.

She nodded. "Okay," she said.

Raymond left and Phil remained. "You've got to give me the gun," he said again. "It's going to be all right. I promise."

She was five feet away from him, looking around the kitchen and out the windows distractedly. She seemed worried but somehow calm, with the gun pointed toward the floor, her finger still on the trigger.

Phil could not take his eyes off its black barrel. How fast am I? he thought. Can I get that gun from her?

He hesitated. He still had time. His parents were safe. Laurie could be manipulated.

She quickly looked out the window and straight back at her hostage. Without saying a word or changing expression, she raised the .32 and fired it into his chest.

Phil spun with the force of impact. As he staggered and fell, he dived around a corner into the pantry.

She knows she didn't kill me, he thought as he closed the pantry door with his foot. She's going to try to shoot me again.

Phil had yet to feel the pain of the bullet, which had ripped through his lung and lodged a fraction of an inch from his heart, but he quickly found himself having trouble breathing. Concentrating hard, he took the gun and cartridge out of his pockets and assembled them, then pulled himself to his feet. He stood by the entryway of the pantry and listened. No sound. She could be hiding. She could be right on the other side of the wall.

He opened the door, peered out, then led the way into the kitchen with the Beretta. He was prepared just to shoot it out with her. But she had vanished. He backed out of the kitchen cautiously, waiting for the ambush that never came.

Laurie was on the stairs to the second floor. As soon as she'd shot Phil, she scurried from the kitchen. At the landing she turned to the right and wandered down a hall.

Phil, meanwhile, had backed all the way out of the kitchen and through the door leading into the yard. As soon as he was clear, he made a break for the gate that led out through the side wall and to the driveway. His run turned into a stagger.

"I've been hit!" he yelled, waving the gun in his left hand.

Mohr and Kerner, still in position near the gate, were startled by the sudden, bloody apparition. "Police officers!" they screamed, training their guns on Phil as he threw down the gun and collapsed in front of them. "Don't move!"

Kerner advanced on Phil. The kid was sucking for air, so he and Mohr dragged him off behind a tree. A paramedic stanched the flow of blood with a four- by five-inch bandage.

The life was draining out of Phil. "Am I going to make it?" he asked.

"Yeah, you're going to be fine," said Mohr, trying to sound as though he meant it.

The day was still beautiful, with flowers everywhere and buds on the trees. Mohr could smell freshly cut grass in the air; he could smell the soap on Phil Andrew's body and the tangy odor of the blood flowing out of the awful wound. Time for him was creeping along, virtually suspended at this peculiar and horrifying moment. Laurie Dann, he thought. Jesus. All the times he had talked to her, listened to her, *believed* her. Why? he said to himself. Why, Laurie? Why?

It was 11:49. An ambulance was on the way.

UPSTAIRS, Laurie reached the end of the hallway and turned left. Ahead of her was a bedroom shared by two teenage girls—Kathy and Trish Andrew.

Laurie walked past the boom box on the floor and the curling iron and the answering machine on the dresser, and picked her way past a few scattered clothes on the gold-green-and-yellow shag carpet. She stood there at the foot of one of the twin beds and listened to sirens close in around her.

AN AMBULANCE pulled up to the roadblock at the corner of Kent and Hibbard roads at 11:55, but could not go in after Phil. Both the paramedics and Winnetka lieutenant Joe Sumner worried that the ambulance would be an easy target as it passed the Andrews'. They wanted to wait until a large contingent of officers could cover the front of the house.

Mohr couldn't wait. He ran past the house as fast as he could and headed for the ambulance. "Go down there," he said. "The guy's dying!"

"You're crazy," the driver answered.

The paramedic in the passenger seat climbed out, and Mohr got in. "Just drive," he said.

"No way. I'm not going to get killed."

"Get down, then," Mohr said. "You run the gas and the brake. I'll steer. We're going in."

The driver crouched on the floor and worked the accelerator pedal with his hand. Mohr guided the ambulance with his left hand and held his gun out the window with his right, training it on the windows of the big white house.

They passed the windows without incident and parked where they were safely shielded by the garage.

"Give me the stretcher," Mohr said. "We'll bring him to you."

The officers quickly hoisted Phil onto the stretcher and ran him to the back entrance of the ambulance. Once he was inside, they pounded on the side and yelled, "Go! Go!"

Phil was on his way to Highland Park Hospital. It was 12:09 p.m., more than twenty minutes after he'd been shot.

One minute later Edith called the Highland Park police department.

EMERGENCY-ROOM doctors at Highland Park Hospital continued without success for the better part of an hour to stimulate Nicky Corwin's heart and make it beat again, but the effort proved futile. Just past noon Dr. Jalakas decided there was nothing more to do. The boy was dead.

He went to the private grieving area and told Joel and Linda Corwin that resuscitation efforts had been stopped. Jalakas said it looked as though the bullet had gone right through the boy's heart.

It had to be a short conversation because Jalakas was needed to treat yet another shooting victim, a college-age male with a slug from a .32 in his chest.

LAW-ENFORCEMENT officials swarmed Kent Road. The perimeter of the Andrew house was surrounded by the emergency services team of the Northern Illinois Police Alarm System (NIPAS)—a crack unit of twenty-nine officers from twelve local police departments that had been activated only three weeks earlier—along with approximately eighty backup officers. They sealed off the residence from all angles, and sharpshooters in camouflage moved into place in surrounding homes.

It looked as if a perfect web had been thrown up around the killer, but there was still a nagging doubt. The police calculated that a full ten seconds had elapsed between the time Laurie fired the shot that hit Phil Andrew and the time the backyard of the Andrew house had been covered. Not a long time, but enough.

Lieutenant Sumner oversaw the establishment of a command post in the Berghorst home at Twelve Kent Road, two doors east of the Andrew home.

LAURIE's ex-husband, Russell, was having lunch at the Green Acres Country Club with his brother, his father and an insurance client when a Highland Park police officer tracked him down by phone. He told him about the shooting in Winnetka and that the police thought Laurie was probably responsible. She seemed to be holed up in a house, the officer said, and Russell should probably get down to Winnetka as fast as he could in case they needed him to talk her into surrendering.

He had to collect his thoughts, which were alternating between shock and a certain cool feeling of vindication. Now maybe they would believe him—Laurie was out of her mind, a lunatic. They had let it come to this, the goddamned cops. He went back to the table and finished his soup. Then he left for the offices of Dann Brothers, where he found his sister, Susie, crying hysterically.

She had been watching TV at 11:30 that morning when a special bulletin announced the incident at Hubbard Woods School. Details were sketchy, and Susie called Jeff. "Doesn't that sound like something Laurie would do?" she said.

Jeff didn't laugh. It did.

Susie got in her car and headed out for a golf lesson. She kept the radio tuned to the all-news station. The announcer had another bulletin. "Authorities in Winnetka have just announced a tentative identification of the suspect," he said portentously. "She is Laurie Dann, also known as Laurie Porter."

Susie had immediately headed for Russell's office, nearby. She was shaking so badly she could hardly drive.

"I know" were Russell's first words when he saw her. "I'm on my way there."

EVEN though Laurie was thought to be safely pinned inside the Andrew house, police departments up and down the North Shore stationed officers outside schools, where shades were being pulled down and large windows barricaded with cafeteria tables. In Glencoe, the superintendent ordered all students bused home, even though half of them normally walked. All elementary schools in Wilmette went on immediate lockdown, posting custodians to intercept strangers at all doors and canceling recess.

In Evanston, several elementary school students sat at their desks and secretly wrote out their wills.

OFFICIALS inside Hubbard Woods School were facing a huge, unprecedented problem of crisis management. Parents were demanding to be let inside to see their children. Reporters and cameramen were at every corner of the building shouting for the latest news, and evidence technicians were sifting through the crime scene, shooting videotape, gathering up whatever they might need in the event of a trial.

After consulting with police, social workers, and Cook County felony prosecutor Nancy Sidote, school officials decided it would be best to keep the children inside until the end of the normal school day at 3:15—the only exceptions would be the children from classroom 7, who would be reunited with their parents after they had been interviewed by investigators. They wanted to keep the students in the safest possible location and away from the hysterical ministrations of their parents, to reinforce the idea that school was still a safe place and to be sure that their testimony as witnesses was not corrupted. District employees and counselors met parents at the door and directed them to cordoned-off areas where they could talk to one another and to social workers.

Principal Dick Streedain, superintendent Don Monroe and other district officials congratulated themselves for this decision in the aftermath of May 20, but it was far from popular that afternoon. Shouting, weeping parents insisted that the mental health of their children ought to come first and that they should have the right to take their children home.

Dick Streedain took it upon himself to go from room to room along with Dr. Mary Giffen, a psychiatrist from a Northbrook clinic and an expert on death and loss, and explain what had happened as best he knew. He began with the children from classroom 7, who had been moved into a fourth-grade classroom. They were seated together on a carpet remnant where students usually gathered when their teacher read to them.

Streedain started by telling them the story of *Alexander and the Terrible, Horrible, No Good, Very Bad Day,* a book by Judith Viorst about coping with misfortune. "Well, we have had a terrible, horrible day here," Streedain said. "A woman came into our school, went to the bathroom, shot Robert Trossman, and then came to your room and she shot at some of you. Everyone who was hurt is getting the best possible care at the hospital. But Nick has died. Nick was shot and he died. He was a friend to everyone."

AT HIGHLAND Park Hospital, Joel and Linda Corwin were taken into the emergency room to see Nicky one last time and say good-bye. Linda touched him—he was still warm. It was so confusing. She just wanted to pick him up and carry him home and tell him everything was okay.

"What a beautiful child," she said through her tears.

IN THE yard at Hubbard Woods School, much of the initial fear had subsided, replaced with a wrenching grief, confusion and anger— some of which was directed at the media. A neighborhood resident tried to charge a reporter a parking fee for a space in front of his house, and other residents shouted at cameramen to stay off their property.

Many of the parents turned away from photographers and declined interviews. To many, the attention was grotesque and the fascination with their pain sickening and ghoulish. What, after all, was there to say? The unthinkable had happened. A killer had violated the sanctuary of an elementary school classroom. Children had been shot. The world was mad.

12.
NO ANSWER

A SMALL army of police officers bunkered around the Andrew house and awaited further orders. Lieutenant Sumner, who was in charge of the standoff while Chief Timm worked at Hubbard Woods, chose a cautious plan. Laurie was alone and—unless she had slipped out during the ten-second gap in police coverage of the house—totally surrounded.

If he sent members of the emergency services team to storm the house, they would undoubtedly capture or kill Laurie. But at what cost? Perhaps one life. Perhaps two or more if she was lying in wait. Under the circumstances, as long as things were calm, Sumner decided it was better to wait. They could coax her out, make her surrender, get some answers.

So the standoff continued. The police called to her through bullhorns— "Laurie, let's get it over with," said their tinny voices. "You need help"—and placed numerous calls to the Andrew residence, hoping she would answer.

The phone rang and rang and rang.

WHEN Russell Dann arrived, he was taken to the interior command center at the Berghorst home and put in the den. He told the commanders that they might be in for a very long day if they intended to simply wait, because Laurie could easily hide in a closet and not say a word for days.

For a time, then, everything was quiet. Russell paced nervously, then stepped out onto the back patio, where he caught sight of Floyd Mohr, also pacing.

The lull in activity had forced Mohr to feel the full force of his combined shock, fear, anger, sorrow and guilt. He had talked to Laurie dozens of times, counseled her, and, at a certain level, trusted her.

Mohr's commanding officers had briefly discussed removing him from the scene. He was obviously distraught, and the situation called for calmness. They chose to let him stay, but were keeping him out of the way until he was needed.

When he saw Russell, he felt a surge of compassion and self-pity.

"I'm sorry," he said, his voice breaking. "You were right. I was wrong."

"She fooled a lot of people," Russell said.

"My own kids, they mean more to me than anything," Mohr said. "I don't know what I'd do if anything happened to them." He could barely bring himself to look at Russell. "How can you ever forgive me? I feel terrible."

"It's okay, it's okay," Russell said. "If you can learn from your mistakes and prevent this from happening again, you'll be a better man."

"I've learned a lot from all this," Mohr said. He gave Russell a clumsy bear hug. "I owe you one."

The police soon determined that Russell's relationship with Laurie was so poisoned that he was unlikely to be of much use, so they left him to his own devices.

He entertained himself watching the earnest affectations of the suburban commando cops all done up like Vietnam. The whole thing reminded him of kids playing G.I. Joe.

"Are Laurie's parents supposed to come over?" Russell asked Floyd Mohr.

"I hear they'll be here anytime."

"I don't want to see them," Russell said.

"That's fair," Mohr said. He went into the Berghorst house, arranged for Russell to have the den to himself, and the two of them turned on the television to watch the news reports.

NORM Wasserman was driving toward Madison when he heard the radio bulletins about what his daughter had done. He returned to Glencoe to pick up Edith, and they arrived together at Kent Road shortly after 2:00 p.m. Both parents were crying. Norm was wearing a white golf shirt and jeans, and walking with both hands jammed into his front pockets. Edith, in slacks and sweater, had looped her left arm through her husband's right. The police led them to the living room of the Berghorst home.

"She's my little girl," Norm said, highly agitated as he looked out the window. "And they're treating her like a wild animal. Look at these people with army outfits and guns."

He said he felt faint, and Mohr insisted he be checked over by paramedics to see if he was having a heart attack. "If this is Laurie and she did these things," Norm said, "my life is over."

Mohr interviewed Norm briefly and found out Laurie had been seeing Dr. Greist in Madison. He then tracked down Greist to ask him the now familiar question he had asked of Dr. Greendale and Dr. Epstein: "Do you think Laurie could be homicidal or suicidal?"

"She never showed any signs of violence," Greist answered. "I never could have visualized her committing this large an act of violence. She was a very quiet little girl."

JEFF and Susie Taylor and their three children were placed under police guard at the Highland Park police station while bomb squads swept their home for explosives.

Susie went from being frightened to being angry. "I told them so," she said loudly. "I told them this was going to happen. Why didn't they listen to us?"

Jeff told her to hush.

At Carmela and Company, the beauty salon where Edith always had her hair done, the employees were shocked. All those years, and they didn't even know she had a daughter.

NORM was frustrated by the standoff and responded eagerly when Mohr relayed a request from Sergeant Gary Stryker, commander of the Northern Illinois Police Alarm System, that Norm help get Laurie out of the house.

"I'm going in there," Norm said.

"No, you're not," Mohr said. "We'd just have another hostage situation. And if you try to go in, I'm going to have to do whatever I can do to restrain you."

"I'm not the kind of person that fights," Norm said, suddenly mild-mannered.

But just to be sure, Mohr found the only suitable tether handy—a cocker spaniel's leash in the hall closet at the command center—and looped it around Norm's waist. And so the cameras recorded the pathetic spectacle of Norm Wasserman on a leash, walking with his head down toward the Andrew house.

He began shouting. "Laurie," he cried, his ragged and distorted voice echoing through the trees. "Get on the phone. Let me know you're all right. Everything's going to be okay."

Back in the command center, though, Edith was not so sure. After her husband had left with Mohr, she turned to county prosecutor Nancy Sidote.

"I feel so sorry," Edith said. "I feel very sorry for all the mothers of the other children. I had no idea Laurie was like this. How could she ever hurt kids? Last night she was so excited about being with those children. She made Rice Krispies Treats and she brought them special drinks and she was practically dancing around the kitchen. She was so excited about going to this fair."

"I'm a mother, too," Sidote said. "I have a son in grade school. Do you have any other children?"

"Yes, I have a son in Texas," Edith said. "He's doing very well. We have grandchildren and we're really happy about them. I just . . . we just don't know what happened with Laurie." Edith paused. "This sounds terrible for a mother to say. But you know, she's in so much trouble, I think it would be better if she didn't come out of this alive."

AT THE end of the regularly scheduled school day at Hubbard Woods, parents were called into the school, classroom by classroom, to be reunited with their children. Administrators encouraged them to take a back exit to avoid the crush of cameramen still out front.

At 3:40, when all the children had gone home, Chief Timm left to join Lieutenant Sumner, NIPAS team leader Gary Stryker, Nancy Sidote and FBI Agent James Bogner at Kent Road. They took their small group to another house on the street to figure out their next move. As time went on, they were more and more sure that Laurie was still inside the Andrew house.

One way to roust her was to launch tear gas into the house, but after some discussion they ruled it out because tear gas sometimes has no effect on people with mental illness, and to use enough gas to saturate such a large home might start a fire or an explosion. And given that Laurie had set a fire in one school and torched the Rushe house, it was possible she had a bomb with her inside the house. It seemed unwise at that point to underestimate her or hurry her along if she didn't want to be hurried.

But by 5:15 Timm had started to worry. Night was beginning to fall over Winnetka. Darkness was Laurie's one chance of slipping out of the house undetected and into the dense woods all around. They couldn't wait forever.

A LITTLE BEFORE 7:00 SERGEANT Stryker asked Norm to try to talk to Laurie again. Mohr tied him to the leash, walked him to the front of the Andrew house, and this time gave him the bullhorn.

Norm began pleading. "Please, come out of there," he said. His voice broke with sorrow. "If you can hear me, please. Pick up the phone. Laurie. Please come out. Laurie."

He didn't know it, but he was simply a diversion, meant to hold his daughter's attention while a twelve-man assault team accompanied by a police dog and two handlers from Northbrook entered from the rear of the house.

The team, dressed in black and led by Deerfield patrolman Eric Lundahl, got in through basement windows at 7:10. It took the officers ten minutes to check and secure the basement and first floor. Norm Wasserman's wretched appeals were still sounding out front.

The dog went ahead to reconnoiter, and when it returned almost immediately from the second floor, Lundahl turned with alarm to one of the handlers. "Is that bad?"

"That's good," the handler said. "It probably means there's a dead body up there."

At 7:23 four members of the entry team went into the bedroom of Trish and Kathy Andrew and found Laurie lying face down in a small pool of her own blood, the .32 at her feet, her head turned to the left and resting on her right arm where she fell on it, her left arm extended. A single bullet had gone through the back of her mouth and through her brain stem. Her eyes were open, her face was slightly swollen, and the tip of her tongue was clenched between her teeth.

Chief Timm was summoned quickly. Is this it? he thought. All this mayhem and she takes the easy way out?

Patty McConnell, who was back at the police station with Amy Moses, felt relief when she heard that the crisis was over, but also anger that she would never get to talk to Laurie and find out why she did what she did.

POLICE escorted Norm back to the command center at the Berghorst home. He was standing several feet away from his wife when Nancy Sidote came into the living room and put her arms around Edith.

"I'm very sorry," Nancy said quietly. "She took her own life."

Simultaneously, Floyd Mohr told Norm, "She's dead. She killed herself. Shot herself."

Edith seemed relieved, Sidote thought. Norm, however, buried his face in his hands, then cried out, "Why? Why? Why didn't she wait for me? Why didn't she talk?"

Edith turned to Mohr. "Did she suffer?"

"No," he said. "It was quick."

"I WANT to go home," said Russell when he heard that his ex-wife was dead. He tried to imagine the pain she must have been feeling inside—the hurt, the hate, the alienation. He felt an unexpected sorrow. "I just want to go home," he said again.

LAURIE'S parents wept, and embraced each other. After a tactful minute had passed, Mohr approached them. He said he didn't think they should drive themselves home, given how they were feeling.

Mohr put them in the back seat of his Fairmont sedan, and they escaped unnoticed by the media.

It was 8:00 p.m. when they arrived at the house on Sheridan Road. Mohr walked Norm and Edith to the door and, at the last minute, asked if he could come in. "I need to look in her room," he said. "I think it's real important to see if there's any evidence for the case."

"What case?" said Norm, suddenly angry. "She's dead. Leave us alone."

Mohr pressed him. "There could be a danger to you, a bomb or maybe evidence of a danger for someone else."

"I'll give you five minutes," Norm said.

They walked down the hallway to her room. "Please don't disrupt things," Edith told him. "The maid was just here today. Be as neat as you can be."

Inside Laurie's closet were a dozen *Penthouse* magazines. On her dresser were bottles of pills, toiletries, an appointment book, a used bus ticket from Madison to Northbrook and a bag from the Marksman gun shop. Inside the bag was the box for the .357 Magnum. Mohr picked up the bag, and Norm began to remonstrate: "I want you out!"

"I need more time," Mohr said.

In a drawer Mohr found the syringe that, he would learn later, Laurie had used to shoot poison into the fruit juice packets. He put the

THE SUSPECT. Laurie held hostages in the Andrew mansion, right, while police mounted a siege outside, below.

Left, Norm and Edith Wasserman being led to the police command post during the standoff. Below, in the end, Laurie took her own life.

syringe into the Marksman bag, then lifted up the mattress. There he found another *Penthouse* magazine, which seemed to enrage Norm.

"What are you doing?" he cried. "Take whatever you have and get out of my house."

The doorbell rang, and Edith went to let in those who were arriving to comfort them, including Norm's sister, Idele, and her husband, Harry. Mohr moved over to the dresser to grab the appointment book and the bus ticket, but Norm stopped him. "No!" he said. "That was Laurie's and you can't have it. You need to leave now, please, leave my house." He began to weep. "And my daughter, my baby . . ."

One of the guests came over to Mohr. "Mr. Wasserman wants you to leave," he said firmly.

And so Mohr left. Later he would come under much criticism for not making any effort to freeze Laurie's room as part of the crime scene. If he had been less emotionally involved in the case, other policemen said, he would have considered more strongly the possibility that there was important evidence hidden somewhere in the room that Norm and Edith might later have reason to destroy or dispose of.

When he left the Wassermans', Mohr put his gun and badge away, went to Bennigan's, and put back eight bottles of Miller Lite in half an hour. He was not usually a drinker.

LINDSAY Fisher survived two hours of surgery and a total blood transfusion but remained in critical and unstable condition Friday night in Evanston Hospital. She was conscious but on a respirator. Kathryn Miller was in critical but stable condition, as were Mark Teborek and Robert Trossman.

Peter Munro was at Highland Park in serious but stable condition.

13.

THE AFTERMATH

THE morning after the shooting spree, a call came to the Winnetka police department for Lieutenant Sumner.

"I am an attorney representing Norman Wasserman," said the man on the other end, "and we are demanding that you return the Toyota today."

"We're done with it," said Sumner. "Come and get it." He was puzzled by the demand. The entire nation had been rocked by Friday's juxtaposition of school, suburbia and murder. Newspapers coast to coast were splashing the story prominently on the front page—the classroom, the last sanctuary, had been violated. A certain innocence was gone, murdered by a wealthy young baby-sitter gone mad. No parent would ever feel quite the same way again about seeing children off to school.

And, Sumner thought, Norm Wasserman was worried about his car.

LINDSAY Fisher underwent two more operations Saturday, one to stop ongoing bleeding in her diaphragm and the other to clear fluid out of her lungs. She remained in critical and unstable condition. Robert Trossman and Mark Teborek were upgraded to serious condition and moved out of intensive care to pediatric wards. Peter Munro, Kathryn Miller and Phil Andrew were also reported in serious but stable condition.

SCHOOL district superintendent Don Monroe held a special gathering for parents and students at Hubbard Woods on Saturday. His purpose was to get the children back across the threshold of the schoolhouse as soon as possible and to reestablish the classroom as a safe place in their minds.

Some two hundred and fifty of the school's three hundred children came, nearly all with at least one parent. The program opened with a general assembly during which Dick Streedain gave condition reports on all the injured and assured the children that the events of the previous day were freakish and unusual—such a thing had never happened before.

Amy Moses was there. Media accounts were hailing her as a hero who had saved untold numbers of lives by fighting with Laurie and refusing to gather the children in the corner when, Laurie ordered her to do so. Yet a quieter sentiment said that Nicky Corwin was dead and five other children were in the hospital because Moses hadn't recognized Laurie for a dangerous outsider and challenged her immediately. Moses could read the heartless second-guessing in the contemptuous eyes of some of the parents. Her fault.

When the large assembly broke up, the students went with their parents to their homerooms, where they were met by teachers and counselors who encouraged them to talk about what they were feeling.

A fifth-grade girl asked why people were praying for Laurie. The Reverend Michael Weston, a priest at Sacred Heart Catholic Church in Winnetka, later answered her question in a homily. "What she did she could not have done if she were in her right mind," he said. "She certainly was not humanly responsible for what she did. Jesus said, 'Pray for your persecutors,' and we pray for Laurie Dann."

A mother reported that her daughter had playacted putting on a bulletproof vest and shooting Laurie. Many other children had looked in their closets and under their beds to see if Laurie had come back to life and was after them again.

And, in a sense, Laurie did come back to life on Saturday.

After the assembly at the school concluded, Sergeant McConnell and Lieutenant Sumner waited on the curb in front of the school while Chief Timm crossed the street to tell the gathered media what had been said.

A Glencoe police officer drove his squad car right up in front of McConnell and Sumner and jumped out. "Patty, we had a little girl poisoned in Glencoe today," he said. "It was a juice package left on her door, stamped 'sample.' "

McConnell listened with growing alarm as the officer explained how this and other reports of tainted juice in Glencoe appeared related to Laurie's baby-sitting.

"Oh, my God," she said.

Within hours the true scope of Laurie's attack on the North Shore was starting to become clear, and word went out that people should not eat or drink any food samples found in their mailboxes and that the schools Laurie had visited should throw away all their snack foods.

The warnings were only partially successful—well over a dozen people ultimately ate or drank the poisoned treats. Fortunately, Laurie had not taken into account that the arsenic solution she had stolen was highly diluted. Her most seriously affected victim was Northwestern University sophomore Greg McCullough, a member of Alpha Tau Omega fraternity, who had eaten a Rice Krispies Treat. He was hospitalized for tests and released in good condition.

Laurie's enormous ineptitude had dogged her to the end. If she had been successful in all she wanted to do on May 20, she would have fatally poisoned at least fifty people, shot to death at least a dozen schoolchildren, incinerated three members of the Rushe family in their home, and burned down two schools with four hundred and forty children inside.

The Rushe family, whose house was uninhabitable for the rest of their time in Winnetka because of smoke and fire damage, moved in with David and Rosemarie Hawkins, friends to whom they had recommended Laurie as a baby-sitter. Young Patrick and Carl were upset that Laurie was dead. They couldn't comprehend what she had done, only that they had loved her.

THE churches were packed Sunday morning in Winnetka as residents looked for solace and meaning through God.

"We gather as a community whose heart has been ripped out," said the Reverend David Goodman, preaching at the Winnetka Bible Church.

After services, many people simply wandered the streets of Winnetka with their families, as though Nicky Corwin's death had reminded them of something they had forgotten.

Shooting victim Lindsay Fisher's condition stabilized after she'd undergone three nearly total blood transfusions. She was still on the respirator, but wrote a note to her father asking if she had missed a soccer game.

Robert Trossman, Kathryn Miller and Mark Teborek remained in serious but stable condition; Peter Munro was upgraded to fair. Phil Andrew, also upgraded to fair, was able to walk eighty feet down a hospital corridor.

Johnny and Michael Corwin wanted to see their brother Nicky one more time. Linda had promised, but couldn't bring herself to take them to the funeral home, so Joel took them.

The boys each slipped a note into the coffin. Michael, the older boy, wrote, "Nick was the greatest brother anyone could ever have. He was always so nice to everyone and was always helping them. He didn't ever deserve any of this. We love you Nick."

Johnny, who was just learning his letters, drew a picture of a baseball player and wrote "I love Nick" all over it.

A STEADY drizzle started at dawn Monday and turned into a downpour shortly before 10:00 a.m., when funeral services for Nicky Corwin began at Temple Jeremiah in nearby Northfield. Some fifteen hundred mourners filled every seat in the huge, modern sanctuary and stood two and three deep along the outer walls. A small, closed coffin rested at the head of the central aisle.

"We're here this morning with hearts heavy, confused and troubled," said Rabbi Robert Schreibman. "We ask ourselves, 'Why?' We wonder what we could possibly say to relieve such inconsolable grief. We search for words of explanation, but we find none. Nicky is gone long before his time."

The rabbi praised Nicky as "a wonderful and promising child with so much to give," and noted that "the pain is great because the joy was immense."

Referring to the torrents of rain falling outside, he said, "So deep is our sorrow, so great is this loss, that we know that God, too, is weeping."

The funeral cortege led by a silver hearse wound wearily for seven miles to the grave site at Memorial Park Cemetery in Skokie. Several hundred of the mourners reconvened at the maroon awning over the grave.

"God gave, and God has taken away," Rabbi Schreibman intoned. "The dust returns to earth as it was; the spirit returns to God who made us. . . . The spirit itself cannot die."

Linda Corwin was doubled over in grief, and Joel held her in his arms.

LAURIE Dann was also supposed to be buried Monday in Skokie, but to avoid controversy or the appearance of insensitivity, her burial was moved to suburban Palatine. It was a private ceremony, attended by perhaps a dozen family friends. Her body was lowered into an unmarked grave.

Floyd Mohr returned to the Wassermans' on Monday. Edith was home, and she let Mohr search Laurie's Honda. She would not allow him back into Laurie's room.

"We totally cleaned it out, anyway," she said.

The appointment book Mohr had seen Friday night was gone forever.

THIRTEEN bicycles were still locked in the racks at Hubbard Woods School, as they had been all weekend, left behind and temporarily forgotten.

The doors opened at 1:00 p.m. for an abbreviated school day. Most parents walked their children to the front doors.

Patty McConnell had been put in charge of a twenty-six-member multijurisdictional task force to investigate the tragedy. One of the first things the task force did was to establish a hot-line number for people to call with any relevant information about Laurie, to find out if she had acted alone and, if so, what her motivation might have been. McConnell needed all the leads she could get, and wanted to talk to anyone who had anything to say.

Lindsay Fisher remained in critical condition. She had been weaned from the respirator, and her doctors reported with some amazement that her injured right lung, liver and stomach showed signs that they would heal completely. Kathryn Miller, Robert Trossman and Mark Teborek were upgraded to fair condition.

RUSSELL Dann would talk on the record only to *Nightline*. Host Ted Koppel circled Russell carefully in their live interview that night, starting with the ice-pick incident, moving on to the harassing telephone calls, then returning to the ice pick with an unexpectedly hard question: "At some point, you were asked to take a lie detector test, right?"

Russell faltered. He admitted to failing the test, then—mistakenly— admitted that Laurie had passed a lie detector test on the same incident.

"That either says something about lie detector tests," Koppel offered, "or it says something very bizarre about the two of you."

Russell answered that lie detectors don't work, and he went on to ramble about the need for gun control, but the damage was irreversible. He'd looked awful—shifty, defensive, untrustworthy.

Glencoe chief Robert Bonneville followed Russell on the hot seat and looked magnificent in comparison. "Given the same set of circumstances," he told Koppel, "without changes in law or our freedoms we cherish so much, I can't sit here and honestly tell you, Ted, that anything would be different."

PHIL Andrew was moved out of intensive care in the very early hours of Tuesday morning. Lindsay Fisher was upgraded from critical to serious condition.

The normal school schedule resumed at Hubbard Woods, but two police officers stood guard at the entryways. Unfamiliar adults, even parents, would not be allowed into the building. Additional officers were assigned to other schools in the district for the rest of the week.

Regular classroom 7 teacher Amy Deuble was given a full-time aide and the assistance of a teacher from the National College of Education to help her tend to the special needs of the second graders who had watched their classmates being gunned down. They planned to devote a large part of every day to writing, acting and talking about the incident and corresponding with those in the hospital.

LATE Tuesday, Joe Sumner and Bob Kerner of the Winnetka police department and Detective Martin Paulson of the Wilmette police department left for Madison as part of the task force investigation.

They met with Dr. Greist on Wednesday afternoon after searching Laurie's room at the Towers, and played a four-and-a-half-hour game of cat and mouse. Sumner questioned Greist specifically and hypothetically, trying to pry out information. Greist, who was accompanied by a hospital lawyer, didn't say anything particularly enlightening.

Sumner was finally able to compel Greist to hand over his records. But when Sumner got the files, he saw that Greist was as much in the dark as everyone else. He'd seen her only a few times. The graduate student, Yoram Shwager, had done most of the work.

ON THURSDAY, Mark Teborek was quietly discharged from Evanston Hospital and became the first of the shooting victims to go home. Lindsay Fisher was listed in fair condition.

The following day, exactly one week after Laurie Dann had shot him in the chest, Robert Trossman was released. He was two days shy of seven years old. Lindsay's remarkable recovery continued, and she was upgraded to good condition.

The shootings came up in class discussion every day at Hubbard Woods for the rest of the school year. The kids seemed to need to talk about them, and the teachers would sometimes just say, "I have a bad memory. Can you tell me again what happened?" The kids from classroom 7 reenacted the rampage in the form of a play over and over. Children who hadn't witnessed the shooting turned it into a playground game, taking turns assuming the roles of Laurie Dann and her victims. The fears and sleepless nights persisted. One girl suggested that her father quit his job and become a policeman in order to better protect the family.

PATTY McConnell's task force kept scratching for clues. Their files were filling up with minutiae—citizens reporting that they thought they'd seen Laurie once shopping at the White Hen Pantry and so on—but it was slow to add up and the people who might have been able to help the most weren't talking. Russell wanted little to do with the North Shore police and remained virtually in seclusion after the *Nightline* debacle. Norm and Edith made several appointments to speak to Lieutenant Sumner in Winnetka but always backed out at the last minute, saying they were too distraught to be interviewed.

The results of Laurie's autopsy, released June 2, weren't particularly revealing either. The report showed therapeutic levels of clomipramine and lithium carbonate in her blood, but no alcohol or illegal drugs. The Canadian connection through which Laurie got the clomipramine piqued the interest of the Illinois Department of Professional Regulation, which said that it was investigating Dr. Epstein's conduct.

That night shooting victim Peter Munro was released from Highland Park Hospital. Mark Teborek was already riding his bicycle to and from school.

Phil Andrew was released from Highland Park Hospital on June 5. Two days later, during the height of public speculation about the role of prescription drugs in Laurie's mad rampage, the U.S. Food and Drug Administration removed some of the shadow from clomipramine by approving it for wider use. An FDA spokesman said the agency action was unrelated to Laurie's case.

That Friday, on the last day of school, Lindsay Fisher was allowed to take a special excursion to Hubbard Woods to spend a half hour at Book Club Breakfast. She was discharged from Evanston Hospital the next afternoon, three weeks and one day after she'd been wheeled in without blood pressure or vital signs.

AFTER examining the information gathered by the Winnetka police department task force, Chief Timm was prepared to harshly criticize Norm and Edith Wasserman for what he saw as their failure to recognize the threat that Laurie's condition posed to the community. But when he ran a sharply worded draft by the village lawyers, he was advised to tone it down.

As far as Chief Timm was concerned, the final draft, released June 15, forced the public to read between the lines:

> We are . . . convinced that opportunities existed prior to May 20th for Ms. Dann's condition to have been successfully addressed. Unfortunately, it is apparent these opportunities were missed because critical information was not provided to police authorities or mental health practitioners. It was also apparent that many opportunities for prosecution were lost either through withdrawal of criminal complaints, insufficient evidence or lack of cooperation from Ms. Dann or other interested parties.

The report did not include any hint of the obsession the investigators had with trying to figure out what exactly was in Laurie's mind that day, or of the hours they spent with one another playing the "what if?" game.

What if Dr. John Greist had contacted Norm before May 20 and told him that he had learned the FBI was looking into allegations that Laurie was threatening the life of an Arizona doctor? Would Norm have taken his daughter's guns away? Would he have agreed to take immediate steps to have her hospitalized?

What if Officer Carlson had not happened to be directing traffic on the corner of Tower Road and Gordon Terrace? What if Laurie had successfully found her way out of the neighborhood? She would have been long gone by the time the police arrived—where would she have gone? The office of Dann Brothers? It was right off the highway. Home? She had no money and no extra clothes in the car. She might have returned to Glencoe and gathered supplies, dumped her guns, and attempted to flee the state.

And what if Phil Andrew had wrestled both guns away from her and she had been arrested? Would there have even been a trial? And what would it have revealed?

On June 26 two hundred North Shore residents met in Temple Jeremiah to discuss how to go about banning handguns in their communities. Phil Andrew spoke to the assembly.

"I am here as a victim, not as a representative of an organization," he said. "I am here because I was shot in my kitchen, and the necessity of gun control hit home to me."

George Fisher, Lindsay's father, became co-founder of Winnetka Citizens for Handgun Control.

MORE than three thousand letters of sympathy from around the world were mailed to Joel and Linda Corwin. At first Linda was going to try to answer each one of them personally, but the pain became too great and the letters just sat.

She felt embraced and supported by the community for the most part, but there were times when she saw people turn away from her and avert their eyes, as they had that terrible morning at school.

"Winnetka was a town that liked to think of itself as perfect," she reflected later. "This incident was the stain on the white linen tablecloth that you try to cover up."

The great symbol of this internal civic struggle was the debate in late August over the idea of renaming Edgewood Park, eight blocks from the school, after Nicky Corwin. Proponents of the idea, including Joel and Linda, said it would be a fitting memorial gesture, because Nicky used to play there all the time. Those who opposed the idea were less vocal, but they felt that renaming the park would serve to prolong the memories of a terrible incident.

In the end, the Winnetka Park District bowed to the loud faction of those who wanted the park renamed. Those who felt it necessary to remember won a victory over those who wanted to forget.

HUBBARD Woods sponsored three group-counseling meetings for parents and teachers over the summer and had a social worker on duty for private counseling. Before the school year started again, teachers, children and parents met at dawn on a Saturday morning in a lakefront park. They sang songs, talked, and watched the sunrise. Everyone in attendance wore a bright yellow button that said HUBBARD WOODS SCHOOL—NEW BEGINNINGS.

School opened on September 6, a day every bit as sunny and warm as May 20 had been. All exterior doors were locked except for the main entrance, where a monitor checked all visitors and issued them visitor tags—some schools had taken to calling them Laurie Labels.

Former substitute teacher Amy Moses was not back in the classroom.

She had expected to land the full-time position that had opened up at Hubbard Woods, and was discouraged not to have been given an offer. The reason, she heard, was that a small group of parents had lobbied quietly with the district against hiring her, on the grounds that her presence would be an unpleasant everyday reminder of Laurie Dann for the children. Disgusted, Moses gave up on teaching altogether and began looking for work in publishing.

Lisa Taylor's teacher contacted Susie and Jeff early in the school year. She was worried because all of Lisa's art projects concerned guns and people getting killed, and whenever her turn came to tell part of a progressive story, she would kill off the main character.

JUST as it looked as though the nation could write off Laurie Dann's attack as the result of a unique and unrepeatable chain of circumstances, nineteen-year-old former mental patient James William Wilson opened fire inside Oakland Elementary School in Greenwood, South Carolina.

His September 26 shooting spree killed two children and wounded seven children and two adults. After he was arrested he said that in the months before his rampage he had read the *People* magazine cover story on Laurie Dann every day.

"I could understand where she was coming from," he said. "I think I may have copied her in a way."

WINNETKA police chief Timm had trouble for months sleeping through the night. One of his recurring nightmares was that he would be walking down a street, turn a corner and come face to face with Laurie Dann.

In Floyd Mohr's nightmares his own car had a vanity license plate bearing the question that continued to haunt him: Y LORI Y?

ON JANUARY 17, 1989, crazed drifter Patrick Purdy opened fire with an AK-47 automatic rifle on an elementary school playground in Stockton, California. He killed five and wounded twenty-eight before taking his own life. It was a far more brutal crime than Laurie Dann's, but, in a sad way, it was not as shocking.

The children at Hubbard Woods School found voice for some of their feelings in writing letters to the children in Stockton; principal

Dick Streedain and teacher Amy Deuble were summoned to California
to help the Stockton administrators handle their crisis.

Norm and Edith Wasserman sold their home on Sheridan Road and
retired permanently to their vacation condominium, in Boca Raton.

On February 28 Joel Corwin filed a wrongful-death lawsuit against
the Wassermans. His complaint, later amended to include Dr. Phillip
Epstein, charged specifically that Norm and Edith helped buy Laurie's
guns with their credit cards, that they promised the police they would
keep the guns away from her and didn't, that they deliberately withheld crucial information from Dr. Greist, and that they and Epstein
undertook to provide her with an experimental drug that can cause
violent behavior in psychotic individuals. Because Laurie's parents
managed her finances, arranged for her treatments, and acted on her
behalf in almost all ways, the complaint went on to say, they should be
held responsible for the death of Nicky Corwin.

The families of five of the six other shooting victims also filed suit
against Norm and Edith Wasserman; they settled out of court in late
1989 and received undisclosed sums. The Corwin suit survived initial
attempts by the Wassermans' attorneys for summary dismissal on the
grounds that Laurie was an adult. At this writing the suit seems likely
to be in litigation for many years.

THE ceremony to rename Edgewood Park after Nicky Corwin was
held on April 22. The granite marker placed on the site reads:

> Nick Corwin's years were full of life and enthusiasm. His kindness,
> willingness to help others and sense of humor made him a cherished
> member of our community. Winnetka places great value on its chil-
> dren and the loss of any one of them is a loss to us all. Nick Corwin
> Park is dedicated to all the children in the community, past, present
> and future.

As for Laurie Dann, her legacy was gun control.

Prior to her attack on the children of Hubbard Woods School, three
Chicago suburbs had outlawed the sale and possession of handguns.
In the year after, Deerfield trustees banned the local manufacture and
sale of handguns; trustees in Wilmette, Highland Park and Winnetka
banned their sale and possession. Later in 1989 the Illinois General
Assembly amended state firearms laws to prohibit "violent, suicidal,

threatening or assaultive" individuals from obtaining or holding Firearm Owner's Identification Cards.

Laurie Dann should not have had guns—that much is clear. The rest of her life remains a patchwork of didn'ts, couldn'ts, and might-have-beens. Her problems, given the history of depression in her family, may well have had their roots in genetics. Her capacity for distortion and lies made it impossible for those close to her and even her doctors to discover what exactly had created this tortured mind.

She was a lonely child who grew into an unhappy young woman, starved for affection she evidently felt she never got from her family or other women, unable to forge friendships and close relationships, and deeply resentful of the success of others. She both found and lost herself in romantic love, and ended up a helpless, overmedicated emotional wreck who controlled her own life through bizarre rituals, and the lives of others through intimidation.

Behind her mask of evil is a pathetic face.

LATE on a sunny weekend morning in Winnetka almost a year and a half after Laurie's rampage, a stranger stood at a distance from Hubbard Woods School taking it in: the outer door to classroom 7, the entryway made famous in hundreds of TV news reports and photographs, the sidewalk Laurie ran down as she made her desperate bid to escape.

A small group of children hung on the jungle gym and ran across the yard under the vigilant eyes of their parents. A mother left the playground area holding the hand of her daughter, a girl of perhaps three or four with wispy blond hair and a clown's face on her sweatshirt. As they crossed twenty yards in front of the stranger, the mother gave him a quick, hard look—a new look. It said:

Who are you? What do you want? Go away.

IN ALL HIS

The Life of

CBS

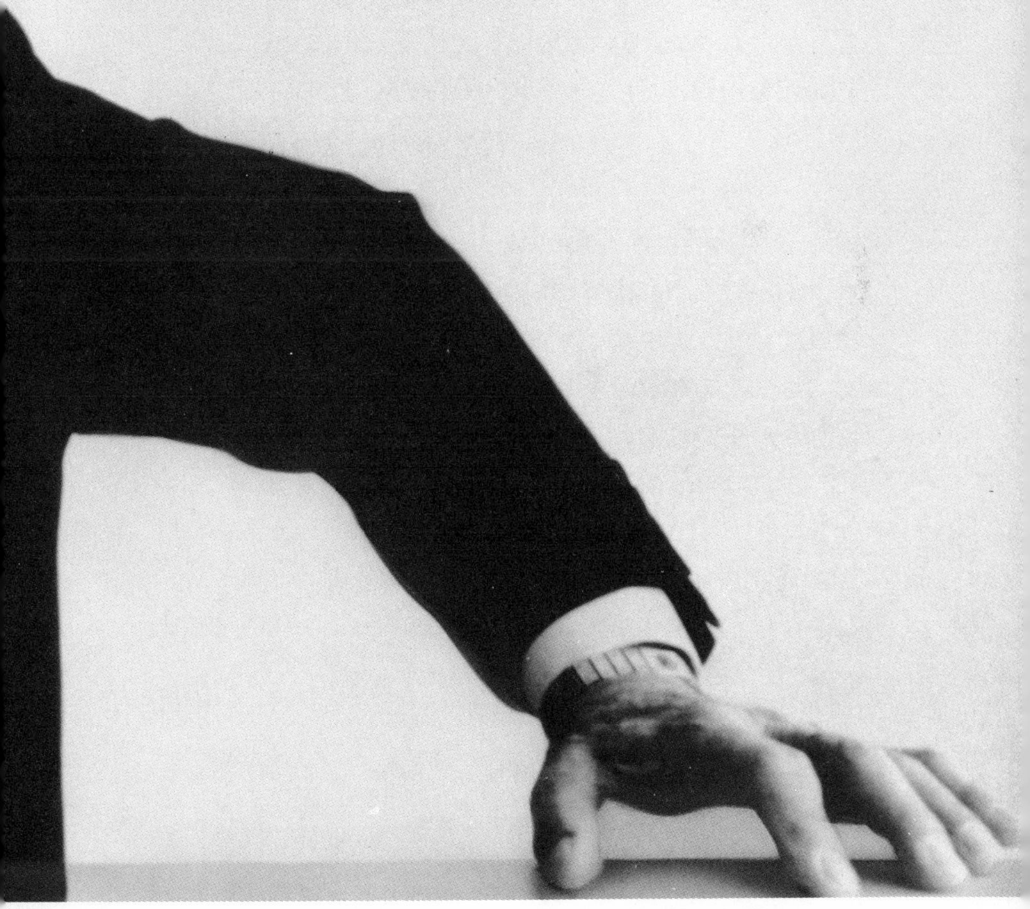

GLORY

Sally Bedell Smith

William S. Paley

. . . "He is to American broadcasting as Carnegie was to steel, Ford to automobiles, Luce to publishing and Ruth to baseball."

—*The New York Times*

. . . Paley had become the ultimate stylish tycoon, living the glamorous highlife. He was charming in society and iron-willed, even ruthless, around CBS. As he grew older Paley relied more on his instincts, although he was far more cautious than his legend would have it. "Rat smart," CBS executives called him behind his back, mindful of the rat's cunning resourcefulness and sense of survival.

—*In All His Glory*

PROLOGUE

THE one they all wanted to see arrived late, as was his custom. To most of them he was "Mr. Paley" or "The Chairman." To a select few he was "Bill." But to everyone in the room he was CBS—the "Tiffany Network"—the tycoon who seemed to have invented the idea of style. Although the party was to honor *60 Minutes,* one of television's most successful shows, center stage belonged to William Paley, now just a few months shy of his eighty-sixth birthday. On this cool spring evening in 1987, all eyes turned to the man who had led the Columbia Broadcasting System for nearly sixty years.

Over a hundred members of New York's broadcasting elite circled the ornate Louis XVI Room at the St. Regis Hotel, on Fifth Avenue, that night. The women sipped Moët et Chandon Champagne and made small talk. The men stood in small knots, trading gossip about their business. "I wouldn't give a nickel for Fox Broadcasting," Laurence Tisch, president of CBS, confided to RCA's former chairman Thornton Bradshaw. Tisch was doubtless the richest man in the room; his fortune—an estimated $1 billion—was double Paley's. But Tisch lacked Paley's panache.

Paley, whose title was little more than an honorific now, had spent much of the day in his elegant office on the thirty-fifth floor of Black Rock, the CBS headquarters on Sixth Avenue. In the late afternoon he had taken a special express elevator to his waiting limousine—a maroon Cadillac Fleetwood, with a television and compact-disc player—and was driven to his duplex apartment on Fifth Avenue by

Charles Noble, his chauffeur for eighteen years. After an hour with his exercise instructor he dressed for dinner, assisted by his valet, John Dean, once an equerry to Prince Philip. Then Paley headed out the door, timing his arrival to miss the cocktail hour. The pain from a lifelong back ailment had become so persistent that he could no longer stand comfortably.

After some photographs with Tisch and the *60 Minutes* contingent, Paley made his way to one of the Versailles Room's round dining tables. Standing at his dinner place, he grasped his chair for support. His thick white hair gleamed in the candlelight. His face was tanned—a deep tan had been a Paley signature since the 1920s—and creased with age; his small brown eyes were nearly overwhelmed by pouches of skin. But the eyes still glittered with life. His pug nose lent him an air of toughness, somewhat softened by his smile, a slightly crooked little-boy grin that promised mischief and mirth. He was not classically handsome, never had been, but his face was virile and sensuous. Despite his advancing years, he appeared nearly as vigorous as twenty years before, when Truman Capote once murmured, "He looks like a man who has just swallowed an entire human being."

Paley, *Mister* Paley. "He is to American broadcasting as Carnegie was to steel, Ford to automobiles, Luce to publishing and Ruth to baseball," *The New York Times* had once written.

William S. Paley had an insatiable appetite for power. But he was not outwardly dynamic in the style of Chrysler's Lee Iacocca. Paley didn't stride through the corridors in a commanding way or pound tables or bark orders. He was much more subtle. His office didn't even look as if it was intended for work; it seemed organized for fun, with an antique card table as its centerpiece instead of a desk.

Like Alice's Cheshire Cat, who lingered only as a wide smile, Paley was often a shadow presence at CBS. He had the disconcerting habit of going away and letting others manage the network for long stretches of time. But somewhat paradoxically, his absences reinforced his power. No one knew exactly when he might appear—or to what effect.

The Paley legend transcended broadcasting. He was a lion in high society. In 1987 *People* magazine listed him as one of a half-dozen "sex symbols for a Corporate Age." Indeed, Paley grabbed everything he could from life—two beautiful trendsetting wives, a string of lovers, an extensive collection of art, and exquisite homes. All the while he took pains to stay above ordinary mortals, managing to be simultaneously visible and invisible.

He cultivated a mystique of privacy but relished his influential role. And Paley was influential. CBS programs shaped and reflected American society to a greater degree than those of its rivals. CBS told us in immediate and revealing terms about war—first through the voice of newsman Edward R. Murrow in bombed-out London during World War II, and later through a series of grim images from Vietnam. It instructed us about the abuses of power by Senator Joseph McCarthy and President Richard Nixon.

Bill Paley associated himself and his network with "a certain standard of taste." He knew how to transform prestige into profits with a legerdemain that frustrated his rivals. That was his genius. He managed to reconcile programs like *The Beverly Hillbillies* with the "Tiffany Network" image, which was sustained by a dignified superior news organization, a sprinkling of classy entertainment programs, and an elegant headquarters building. These stylish touches helped preserve the CBS mantle of quality and fostered the illusion that CBS radio—and later, television—was better than it was.

By the late spring of 1987 the CBS-TV network was no longer either first or best. Paley's power had diminished too. But at the St. Regis that night, Paley was still the star, though his empire—or what was left of it—now belonged to Larry Tisch, a man he did not choose.

Paley, of course, betrayed nothing of this in the hotel dining room as he shook hands with well-wishers. His smile widened at the approach of each woman. Even as an octogenarian he remained the most flirtatious of men, always on the prowl, always looking for a conquest. His eyes twinkled and focused on the moment's object of his attention as if she were the only woman in the room.

His charm was part natural, part learned—a potent combination of power, grace, and enthusiasm. "He listens. He responds. He is affectionate. He is flattering. He laughs a great deal. He knows a great deal. It is an enormous power," said Marietta Tree, a longtime friend.

Paley had a restless energy, a prodigious appetite for pleasure of all kinds. Once something caught his eye, whether it was a painting or a woman, he pursued the quarry relentlessly.

An outward sign of Paley's energy was a tic—a rapid, almost violent involuntary blinking of his eyes. Each spasm would last several seconds, accompanied by a companion tic in his lower jaw—a sort of munching motion. The tic quickened when he was under stress.

Paley had chosen a business with uncommon pressures. Every day millions of Americans judged his programs at the flip of a switch. A drop of one point in the audience ratings could mean tens of millions of dollars in revenues. Paley made no secret of how keenly he felt these demands. But there was another burden that far exceeded ratings points or corporate revenues: Bill Paley constantly strove to live up to his own image. A succession of public relations men had succeeded in portraying him as nearly invincible. He was the man with a magic touch, able to spot hits where others saw flops, to spot stars where others saw journeymen. Paley was determined that others believe his press clips, but it is by no means clear that he believed them himself. To smother his insecurities, Paley resorted to tranquilizers and sleeping pills. Indeed, Paley had always been a hopeless hypochondriac, and as he got older he acquired enough nurses, doctors, and other attendants to staff a small hospital.

On this evening at the St. Regis, Bill Paley was in peak form when he rose to salute *60 Minutes*.

"When *60 Minutes* first went on the air, in 1968, I'm sure that Don Hewitt didn't expect to be producing it nearly twenty years later," he said, reading from note cards through half-glasses. "I'm sure his first correspondents, Harry Reasoner and Mike Wallace, didn't expect to be his correspondents nearly twenty years later. As a matter of fact, the chairman of CBS in 1968"—rising laughter around the room—"didn't expect to be here"—more laughter—"as chairman nearly twenty years later."

When he finished, the applause was loud and heartfelt. Everyone exchanged smiles and admiring glances. "Remarkable," said Eric Sevareid. "What vigor."

It was particularly remarkable under the circumstances. Only three months earlier Paley had nearly died of pneumonia. But miraculously, he bounced back. As was so often the case with Bill Paley, he had the power to surprise. Just when people began to count him out, he would gather his energies and prove them wrong.

CHAPTER 1

WILLIAM Paley was born on September 28, 1901, in a dark, cramped apartment behind a small cigar shop in the Jewish ghetto on Chicago's crowded West Side. Willie Paley's parents, Sam and Goldie, were Russian immigrants, who arrived in Chicago in the late 1880s. Sam had been born near Kiev, in the Ukraine. (The family's name was actually Paley, pronounced Paylay, but German Jews who later looked down on William Paley's Russian origins used to whisper that his name had really been Palinski.)

Sam Paley's father, Isaac, had owned a lumber business in Russia. In 1888, eager to escape religious persecution, Isaac took his wife, Zelda; his sons, Sam, William, Jacob, and Benjamin; and his daughters, Sophie, Sarah, and Celia, on the four-week transatlantic crossing.

Most of the hundreds of thousands of Jews who immigrated to the United States in the 1880s settled in the port cities of New York, Boston, and Baltimore, but Isaac and his family tried their luck in Chicago, drawn by its boomtown atmosphere. The lakeside city was a magnet for trade and an intersection of water routes and railroads; new factories and shops promised jobs and investment opportunities.

A proud man with aristocratic pretensions, Isaac Paley dreamed of investing his money in stocks and living off the income. But it was left to his wife, Zelda, to make sure the family had food and shelter.

Zelda was a small, handsome woman, who proved a powerful if prickly matriarch. "Zelda was impossible," said one of her grandchildren. "She had a lot of fire and spark. She was a devil, a mean old lady, a troublemaker." In later life, while visiting her daughter, she poured a handful of salt into a pot of soup as it was cooking to ruin her daughter's efforts. Bill Paley chose to see beyond his grandmother's mean-spiritedness and admired her strength. He said he believed that he had inherited her spirit. It may be that he inherited her ruthlessness as well.

In Russia, Zelda had been a milliner, but in Chicago, like other matriarchs, she supervised the household and the work of her sons, who assumed the burden of financial support.

Many immigrants found themselves jobless and destitute. But Sam

Paley, still a teenager, moved through several jobs—selling newspapers, laboring in a piano factory—until he found a niche making cigars in a West Side factory.

Cigar making was wet, messy, and monotonous. But if one had skill and ambition, as Sam did, it brought a decent wage. Before long Sam Paley took on a second job, selling cigars from baskets, which he lugged around to cigar stores, saloons, and restaurants. He had every reason to push himself. He and the eight other members of his family were crowded into a four-room apartment.

By 1896, at age twenty-one, Sam Paley had amassed "a few hundred dollars" in savings, with which he founded Samuel Paley & Company, cigarmakers. Two years later he married Goldie Drell, who was sixteen. She too had been born in the Ukraine.

Goldie had a sweet smile and was spirited and plump. Sam was short and stocky, with a moon face, thick features, and a heavy black mustache. Goldie did not consider him good-looking, but she was drawn to his sincerity.

Neither Goldie nor Sam had much formal education. Yet they made an effective team, parlaying their small stake through diligence and cooperation. Goldie was the driving force—more energetic, outgoing, and self-assured than her husband. But Sam had a quick, native intelligence. He was also exceedingly shrewd and a hard worker.

The economic boom of the early twentieth century helped propel Sam Paley toward middle-class comfort. In 1904 Sam took in his brother Jacob "Jay" Paley as a partner. The following year, when Bill Paley was only four years old, Sam moved his family to a row house on Marshfield Avenue, a prime residential street for Jewish immigrants on the rise. With this move he left the retail business to concentrate on cigar manufacturing. He established a factory in a barn behind the house and concentrated on one brand, called La Palina.

Shortly after they began the new operation, Sam and Jacob uprooted their families and transferred the business to Detroit, where they changed the name to the Congress Cigar Company. At first they prospered. But a depression hit in 1908, and their biggest wholesaler went bankrupt, nearly forcing Congress Cigar out of business. In 1909 Sam and Jacob returned to Chicago. They incorporated Congress Cigar and started over. The general economic conditions improved and so did the cigar business. The next year the brothers moved into large-scale manufacturing, employing some sixty people.

Bill Paley professed to have had a happy childhood, but in many ways it could not have been. At one point his family was affluent enough to have a nurse. But when he was only eight, the nurse disappeared after one of Sam's financial reversals. As an adult, Paley spoke of the times he stood outside the ballpark where the Chicago Cubs played, hoping to shag a foul ball and earn the admission that his parents could not afford.

Willie was a quiet and somewhat troubled child. Physically, he resembled his father. He had a plump, round face, and he was short. (A late bloomer, he would not sprout until his senior year in high school.) For most of his childhood he suffered from a severe inferiority complex. In part his insecurity stemmed from being forced to sit at the back of his elementary school classroom—a Siberia for dullards. He lived up to expectations and performed badly.

He also deeply resented his sister, Blanche, who was born in 1905. At the outset the sibling rivalry seemed rather ordinary—a three-year-old jabbing his finger in the eye of the new baby. But when Blanche was two, she fell ill with a lung infection. Goldie devoted nearly all her

Young "Willie" Paley, below, greets the camera. Right, at age nine (front row, right), with neighborhood children in Chicago.

Right, his parents, later in life. Goldie was "the driving force," while Sam "praised and indulged him."

attention to her daughter. Even after Blanche recovered, Goldie's absorption with her daughter continued. Meanwhile, Willie burned with jealousy as he watched his mother cater to Blanche's every need. He felt rejected and unloved. But when he tried to get close to his mother, she reacted indifferently.

Paley felt that Goldie not only froze him out but ran him down. She constantly complained that other children were better-looking, dressed more neatly, or performed better. In later years he said that he believed her "haranguing" fueled his ambition as an adult. He was determined, he often said, "to show her," to prove himself not only to her but to "anybody else who found fault with me."

But Willie was adored by his father, who encouraged, praised, and indulged him. And Willie lived for his father's approval. He thought of his father as a king, and he admired him unconditionally.

As a boy, Willie Paley led a sheltered existence. It was a world of his own kind—a large, extended family, along with neighborhood and school friends who were predominantly Jewish. Paley later professed not to have experienced daily prejudice while growing up, but one incident terrified him and stayed with him. He was only nine or ten at the time and was en route to the library when he encountered what he later called a Jew-hunting gang. When Willie began to run, the boys chased him—all the way to the library. He cowered inside while they waited for him to emerge. Too proud to ask for help, he lingered until after dark, when the library was about to close. Then he bolted out the door and ran home, imagining that the gang still pursued him.

A little bit of luck helped put Willie on the right track in school. His teacher finally shifted him to the front of the classroom. That encouraging move was enough to prod him to apply himself and become a star student.

As a symbol of his new status, he decided at the age of twelve to give himself a middle initial. Everyone else in his class had a middle name, and he felt self-conscious without one. So when school officials asked the students how their names should appear on their elementary school diplomas, Willie impulsively added an S. It stood for nothing, although everyone assumed it was for Samuel, after his father.

After Bill Paley's sophomore year in high school his parents decided to send him away for his final two years. Several of Sam and Goldie's friends had dispatched their sons to Western Military Academy, where the boys had acquired discipline as well as polish; they had also gained a slight edge over students from Chicago's public schools in securing admission to prestigious colleges. At Western Military Academy, Bill Paley found himself in a non-Jewish world for the first time. But it was so regimented that there was little room for prejudice to seep through. Set among tall trees on a hill above the Mississippi River, in Alton, Illinois, the school brought Paley a new sense of independence; he later called his year there "a turning point in my life."

Academically he excelled and managed to compress two years' worth of high school into one year. At seventeen he entered the University of Chicago. During his first semester he applied himself. But he also found a welcome at the top-ranked Jewish fraternity, Zeta Beta Tau, and he gradually became what one of his fraternity brothers called "a good-time Charlie. He chased the girls." Paley's studies suffered, and he barely squeezed through his freshman year.

It was at Zeta Beta Tau that he had his first brush with the snobbery of fraternity brothers who looked down on him. He overcame the prejudice, as he did so often afterwards, with his charm. "One quickly warmed up to him," said a fraternity brother, "although his background was from the other side of the tracks [the West Side] and most of us came from the South Side."

Paley never doubted he would follow his father into the cigar business. "I used to dream about being a salesman," he once said, "going to cigar stores and making them buy *his* cigar."

Along with other cigar manufacturers Sam Paley introduced new machines into his factories to standardize and double output. But the machines also contributed to labor unrest. The members of the Cigarmakers International Union, who considered themselves craftsmen, called strikes to protest the new machines. By 1919 the strikes proved too much for Sam Paley. Faced with a demand by workers for a 50 percent increase in wages, he decided to move his operation to New York or Pennsylvania. Sam took his son, Bill, with him on what was to be a short but portentous trip.

IN THE summer of 1919 the New York skyline lacked the majesty it would achieve with the skyscraper boom of the coming decade. But its avenues were bigger and busier than anything a seventeen-year-old immigrant's son from the Second City had ever seen before.

For much of their stay in New York young Bill Paley tagged along with his father, watching as Sam negotiated for factory sites. In his free time the boy prowled the streets. He longed for a life of riches and leisure, dreamed of living in Manhattan and enjoying all its pleasures.

But Sam eventually settled on Philadelphia as the site for his factory. On his eighteenth birthday Bill enrolled at the University of Pennsylvania's Wharton School of Finance. He immediately hooked up with Zeta Beta Tau and plunged into campus social life.

Paley was well enough liked by his peers to earn the nickname Pop, for popular. In his senior year he was voted president of the fraternity. He was chosen, friends said, because he was a natural leader.

He served on the business staff of the yearbook and for a time sold button-down shirts—a new sartorial style. His sales strategy became an important element in the Paley legend: he recruited football players and other campus heroes as salesmen, figuring their popularity would generate business. His profit was a tidy $1000.

His friends remember him for his amiability and ease. "I would never have expected he would be a big tycoon," said Henry Gerstley, a friend from a leading family in the Philadelphia German Jewish elite. "It was only after he was successful that he became dynamic." Another fraternity brother recalled that Paley was "ambitious in all his actions. He seemed to know what he wanted and go after it, socially and every other way. He liked to go with nice people."

One of the "nice people" Paley befriended at Penn was Ben Gimbel, of the Philadelphia department-store family. The Gimbels were among the most prominent of the city's German Jewish families, none of whom wanted anything to do with Russian arrivistes like Sam and Goldie Paley.

The Paleys did what they could to be accepted in Philadelphia society. They were not so ambitious for themselves, but they wanted the best for their children. Not long after their arrival in Philadelphia, Goldie decided to give a party and invited some members of the Jewish elite. None accepted her invitation. Bill, only nineteen, tried to soothe her feelings. "They don't really count," he said. "I'm going to New York, and I'll not only make lots of money, I'll marry a Vanderbilt."

Bill Paley spent his days in Philadelphia training conscientiously to take over the business. Upon his graduation from Penn he was hired by his father for a modest salary of $1300 a year (about $10,000 in

today's dollars). He had no title and moved among various departments under the tutelage of uncles and trusted lieutenants.

Congress Cigar was thriving. From 1921 to 1926 net earnings went
from $75,000 to $1.7 million. In 1926 the investment firm Goldman
Sachs sold 70,000 of the company's 350,000 shares to the public,
netting the Paley family nearly $3 million. Later that year the family
made a killing by selling 200,000 shares to the Porto Rican–American
Tobacco Company for $13,750,000. Bill's cut was $1 million.

There were some worrisome signs, however. Cigarette smoking was
becoming the rage of the Roaring Twenties. By mid-decade national
cigar consumption had begun to decline.

Bill concentrated on advertising La Palina cigars. Congress Cigar
based its reputation on a cigar that was high grade but priced
moderately. As soon as sales reached a million cigars a day, its
advertising slogan announced, "America's largest-selling high-grade
cigar." That slogan, mingling mass marketing with aspirations to
quality, became Bill Paley's talisman.

Outside the office, Paley pursued a footloose bachelor life. After the
family sold its holdings in 1926 and became very rich, he moved to a
penthouse apartment on the twentieth floor of the Warwick Hotel, on
fashionable Rittenhouse Square. Here Paley gave dinner parties and
entertained his girlfriends.

By this time Sam and Goldie were also ready to indulge themselves.
In 1924 they had moved to a modest home in Mount Airy, an
undistinctive middle-class neighborhood. Several years later, however,
after their son and daughter had left the nest, they made the big leap
to an impressive home in Chestnut Hill, one of Philadelphia's most
prestigious addresses.

Sam and Goldie had few pretensions and led a quiet life. Goldie
spoke directly and simply, sometimes ungrammatically, with an
Eastern European accent that had faded only slightly with time. She
filled her Chestnut Hill mansion with antiques and was always
practical about what money could buy. As Bill was embarking on his
career she advised him, "Never do anything for yourself that someone
else could do better," and then she treated him to his first valet.

Goldie was intelligent and determined to improve herself. She took
art lessons and went to lectures and classes. She was a learner. Yet her
personal secretary suspected that Goldie remained only minimally

literate, because she always insisted that her mail be read aloud to her.

Late in life Goldie took up horseback riding, over protests from Sam, who feared that horses were too high-spirited. And she loved driving her own Lincoln Continental, sometimes wildly, just to assert herself. Still, the Paley household clearly revolved around Sam.

With his guttural voice, a cigar clamped perpetually in his mouth, and a thick accent, Sam Paley seemed hard-boiled and coarse. But he was unassuming and friendly with people, whatever their station. While observers often remarked on his sweetness, he could be tough and tightfisted as well. Sam loved making money and always carried a little notebook in which he kept track of his investments.

Paley came to believe that he had inherited more traits from his mother than his father. Above all, he believed he had inherited his mother's determination. "She would never say no. She just went ahead and did what she wanted to do."

After the Paleys sold their stock in Congress Cigar, Bill Paley became noticeably restless. His social aspirations drove him hardest. He pined for the high life in New York City. He used to leaf through the pages of *Vogue* and *Harper's Bazaar* and admire the delicate, ivory-skinned beauties in the photographs. At bottom, he felt uncomfortable and insecure in Philadelphia, never quite at ease with the Jewish elite and shut out by the old-society Establishment.

Outside Philadelphia, a new spirit of openness had taken hold. No place symbolized this new freedom more than New York City, with its cosmopolitan air and promise of social mobility. In Manhattan it seemed that anyone with style and ambition could win acceptance. But Paley felt that manufacturing cigars was not an impressive enough career for a rising Manhattanite. What Bill Paley needed was a business that was lucrative, glamorous, and, above all, respectable.

CHAPTER 2

WILLIAM Paley heard the first sounds of radio through earphones attached to a primitive crystal set at a friend's apartment in Philadelphia. The year was 1925, and at first Paley couldn't believe that music was actually coming through the air without benefit of wires. He immediately had a set made for the extravagant sum of $100. Night after night, until three or four in the morning, the twenty-four-year-old Paley sat transfixed, trying to pick up signals from points as distant as Pittsburgh or even Kansas City.

The first commercial radio station, Westinghouse Corporation's KDKA, in Pittsburgh, had gone on the air in 1920 with the simple goal of provoking listeners to buy Westinghouse receivers; by 1923 two and a half million radios had been sold. As radio's popularity spread, the number of stations grew. By 1924—a full year before Paley caught up with the fad—fourteen hundred broadcasting licenses had been issued by the Department of Commerce, which was charged with regulating the infant industry, a task taken over by the Federal Radio Commission in 1927.

Stations popped up in all sorts of unlikely places. To entice customers, Wanamaker's, Gimbels, and a score of other department stores set up transmitting studios on their sales floors. There were stations at hotels, newspaper offices, and universities. Stations even beamed from laundries, stockyards, and poultry farms. The programming was often amateurish and gimmicky.

At first no one envisioned using this new medium for advertising. But the American Telephone & Telegraph Company, then in the business of selling radio transmitters, had another idea. In August 1922 AT&T had launched WEAF (for Wind, Earth, Air, and Fire), an experimental station in New York City, and offered advertisers the opportunity to buy time on the station. AT&T called its approach toll broadcasting. AT&T also put together the first rudimentary network, using long-distance phone lines to connect stations around the country to remote broadcast locations such as football stadiums. The phone company made a $150,000 profit from its baby network in 1925. Soon it became clear that advertising could provide revenue to pay top performers and make the medium more professional.

By 1926 the principal broadcasting and radio manufacturing companies were squabbling about who had which rights to profits from the sale of radios. At the same time, the federal government accused these companies of antitrust activities. A settlement was finally fashioned by David Sarnoff, a hard-driving executive at the Radio Corporation of America. RCA was then the largest distributor of radios, which were manufactured by General Electric and Westinghouse but sold under the RCA name. Sarnoff's plan called for creation of a new entity—the National Broadcasting Company—that would link stations around the country to present programs simultaneously to a national audience.

The new "chain" would be owned by RCA, General Electric, and Westinghouse. AT&T would sell its network to NBC for $1 million and lease telephone lines to NBC to connect its affiliated stations. The new network would not aim to make money through its broadcasts but rather would do so by stimulating radio sales. NBC's stated purpose— to serve and uplift the public with "better programs permanently assured"—sounded almost philanthropic.

It was a brilliant stroke for the man with whom Bill Paley would match wits. Ten years older than Paley, Sarnoff also came from a Russian Jewish background. But unlike Paley, he was born in the mother country, in a *shtetl* near Minsk. As a child he suffered through cossack raids, the ordeal of traveling by steerage to the United States, and grinding poverty on arrival in the Lower East Side ghetto, in Manhattan. There Sarnoff sold Yiddish newspapers, ran his own newsstand, and dashed through the streets as a telegraph messenger. He studied English by reading New York newspapers picked out of garbage bins. Soon he was speaking without a trace of an accent. By 1906 he joined the Marconi Wireless Telegraph Company, where he started as an office boy and worked his way up to telegraph operator. He achieved his first fame at age twenty-one on the night of April 14, 1912. As manager of the wireless station in Wanamaker's department store, he was in touch with the sinking luxury liner *Titanic* for seventy-two hours. His coolness under pressure impressed Marconi executives, and his responsibilities grew accordingly.

But Sarnoff was more than a young employee on the rise. In a 1916 memorandum to his superior at Marconi, the twenty-five-year-old visionary described how the wireless could become "a 'household utility,' a 'radio music box' which can be placed in the parlor or living room to enjoy concerts, lectures, music, recitals, etc." His superior rejected the idea as harebrained.

Three years later Marconi was swallowed up by RCA. Junior executive Sarnoff wasted no time dusting off his "radio music box" memo and getting it to the new RCA chairman, Owen D. Young. Sarnoff succeeded not only in pushing RCA into selling radios but into radio broadcasting as well, and Young made him the company's general manager. By the mid-1920s the burly and balding immigrant with piercing blue eyes was being hailed as a prophet of the radio age. Sarnoff's radio brainchild, NBC, burst on the air on November 15, 1926. The inaugural program was a four-hour extravaganza transmitted live from the Grand Ballroom of The Waldorf-Astoria hotel. Walter Damrosch conducted the New York Symphony Orchestra, the Metropolitan Opera's Tito Ruffo sang arias, and Will Rogers impersonated Calvin Coolidge. It was an unqualified success. By 1927 NBC had two networks—the Red and the Blue—comprising twenty-five stations. RCA's monopoly on broadcasting was on its way.

Newcomer stations in cities already covered by NBC had no prospect for a network affiliation. One of those left out of the new network was a shoestring station in Philadelphia called WCAU. It was owned by two enterprising brothers, Isaac and Leon Levy, who had bought it in 1924 for $25,000. Isaac, known as Ike, was a lawyer. He handled most of the business deals. Leon, a dentist, divided his time between filling teeth and programming the station.

The station was making little headway selling advertising against its two entrenched competitors—stations owned by the Wanamaker and Lit department stores and affiliated with the NBC Red and Blue networks. Ike and Leon needed the prestige of a network. So when a fast-talking promoter named George Coats came to call one day in the spring of 1927, Leon listened eagerly.

Coats and his two partners had just organized United Independent Broadcasters, a new network to rival NBC. Leon Levy had nothing to lose, so he named his terms. United Independent had to pay his station $500 a week to carry ten hours of network programming. During those ten hours the network was free to sell advertising and pocket the proceeds. The rest of the time, the station would make money by selling advertising locally. They had an agreement.

Leon was so taken with the new network that he helped Coats sign fifteen additional stations to United Independent on similar terms. A guaranteed weekly income was irresistible to stations when advertising revenue was scarce. But that arrangement proved a crushing burden to the fledgling network. Coats could not find sponsors to cover the $8000 in weekly compensation to sixteen stations.

In April 1927 an angel materialized. The Columbia Phonograph Company was alarmed that a rival manufacturer of record players, the

Victor Company, was poised to merge with RCA. Coats persuaded Columbia executives that an investment in United Independent could be used to promote Columbia records and record players on the new network. The investment came to $163,000—enough to cover United Independent's debts. Columbia stipulated that the network be called the Columbia Phonograph Broadcasting System. In return, Columbia had to pay the stations and performers, and find advertisers to buy time during the ten hours of network programming. As *Fortune* magazine noted a few years later, Columbia "bought the operating rights of United Independent, which wasn't even operating."

Fortified by its new backer, United Independent organized a program schedule for the ten weekly hours: five would be filled by an orchestra, the other five by a dance band. The Columbia network made its debut on September 18, 1927. But the program being broadcast was nearly drowned out by dreadful static and ran more than an hour long. It was remarkable that anything got transmitted at all; a men's lavatory served as the makeshift control center. It was the only soundproof room at WOR, the flagship station for the Columbia network in New York.

Columbia Phonograph lost $100,000 in the first month and decided to bow out. Once again United Independent turned to the Levys. Ike Levy couldn't bear that Columbia was about to go under so quickly. But he did not have enough money to help on his own.

He knew, however, that the newly prosperous Sam Paley had plenty of capital. Sam's daughter, Blanche, had married Leon Levy only weeks earlier. Sam Paley was now family, so in October 1927 Ike approached him with his proposal: Ike would put up $50,000 if Sam would contribute another $50,000 to rescue the ailing Columbia network. Sam agreed.

That evening Ike went to play poker at the Locust Club, a gathering place for Philadelphia's Jewish elite. But he appeared preoccupied. Walking home afterwards, Ike confided in his friend Jerome Louchheim, a millionaire sportsman and builder of bridges and subways. "Jerry, I'm worried," he said. "I'm concerned whether I made a wise move in asking Sam Paley to come along with me. Should this venture fail, it might be embarrassing to Leon." Louchheim replied, "You've got a nerve asking him to come in and not inviting me." Ike was surprised by his friend's eagerness. The next day he told Sam he would like Louchheim to assume Sam's stake. "Anything you do suits me," said Sam, who wanted to keep peace with his in-laws.

Why had Sam Paley so readily agreed to part with $50,000 for a shaky enterprise like the Columbia network? He knew the power of radio. Several months earlier he had signed the Levy station, WCAU, to advertise La Palina cigars. The program starred Harry Link, the composer of "I've Got a Feelin' I'm Falling." He thumped the piano, sang, and plugged La Palina cigars. After a few weeks it became clear that the radio exposure was boosting sales of the cigars.

Sam Paley bowed out gracefully when Ike Levy turned to Louchheim to finance Sam's half of the Columbia network. But still keen on the potential of radio, Sam agreed to spend $6500 a week on a network program advertising La Palina cigars. He was also receptive when Louchheim proposed that Bill, then twenty-six, run Columbia in the fall of 1927. The Levy brothers agreed that Bill Paley was ideal for the job. He was energetic. He was restless. But he refused. "I don't want anything to do with this pip-squeak radio network, this phony chain," Bill said. Reluctantly Louchheim took on the job himself.

At his father's insistence, however, Bill agreed to supervise the half-hour program that Sam had bought on the Columbia network. Bill felt that Harry Link lacked pizzazz, so he concocted the glamorous and sultry-voiced Miss La Palina, the sole female guest at a smoker— an all-male gathering, fashionable at the time. Surrounded by her pack of admirers, Miss La Palina sang, accompanied by an orchestra. Four months after *The La Palina Smoker* began on the Columbia network, Congress cigar sales—which had dipped from six hundred thousand to four hundred thousand a day with the advent of cigarettes—jumped to one million a day. "It was one of radio's earliest spectacular achievements," *Fortune* magazine reported.

Once *The La Palina Smoker* took off, Bill Paley was hooked on radio. Producing the show took him to New York once a week, where he fell in love with programming and made connections in the show-business world. For the next ten months he watched intently as United Independent struggled to keep the Columbia network afloat. Louchheim and the Levys had paid $235,000 initially to buy control of Columbia, with Louchheim supplying the bulk of the money. Subsequently the investors poured more money into the enterprise. Advertisers came in—Bromo-Seltzer, Chrysler, *True Story* magazine—

but slowly. The new owners did achieve an early breakthrough in November 1927, when all of Columbia's affiliated stations agreed to accept new contracts that cut network costs. Instead of paying each station $500 a week to carry ten hours of network programs—whether Columbia had found sponsors or not—Columbia would only pay the affiliated stations for sponsored shows that they broadcast.

Finally, in August 1928, the Columbia network broke into the black. Soon after, Louchheim fractured his hip. Unable to travel to New York to supervise the network, he wanted out. Levy and Louchheim knew that Bill Paley was captivated with radio, so they suggested that Sam buy the network for his son. While Sam would not agree to buy Columbia for Bill, he did tell his son that the network was for sale.

Bill Paley leaped at the bait. He had $1 million from the sale of Congress Cigar shares to Porto Rican–American Tobacco stock two years earlier, and Columbia seemed the ideal place to invest. Louchheim's price for his stock was $200 a share—a total of $503,000 for the 50.3 percent of the company Paley needed to assume control. Since he was using half of his million-dollar fortune, he felt obligated to secure his father's approval. Sam not only gave his blessing but offered to kick in some of his own money.

On September 25, 1928, the Paleys assumed control of United Independent and its Columbia network. Bill Paley was elected president on the twenty-sixth, just two days shy of his twenty-seventh birthday. He put up $417,000, which gave him 41 percent of the company. The remaining 9.3 percent of the Paley holdings was controlled by Sam; his brothers Ben and Jay; and Jay's wife, Lillian.

Sam Paley reasoned that if his son succeeded, he would build a bigger and more important business than the cigar trade. If he failed, he would return to Congress Cigar with broadened experience.

CHAPTER 3

I T IS said that anyone can invent himself in America. In the case of Bill Paley, the process began on October 1, 1928, the day he entered his office at United Independent Broadcasters, in Manhattan. An ambitious but inexperienced twenty-seven-year-old, he was determined to make his mark on the world. Paley had the ability to absorb the best of what he saw around him—whether it was management techniques, bargaining tricks, elegant tailoring, taste in art, ways to charm a woman, the manners of high society. As he watched and absorbed, the Paley of legend began to take shape. Like many people who invent themselves, he came to venerate the invention.

The headquarters of United Independent occupied a four-room suite near the top of the Paramount Building, on Times Square. From there Paley could take in the glittering sweep of Broadway, bathed in the glow of one million electric lights. Enormous signs blazed advertisements for Lucky Strike, Squibb's Dental Cream, Maxwell House coffee, Chevrolet. Everywhere he looked he saw reminders of the commerce he sought to exploit with his tiny network. The people were out there, ready to listen; NBC was proving that every day by attracting audiences as large as fifteen million.

United Independent's dozen employees were hardly impressed by the sight of their new boss: a full six feet but a bit hefty, with a slight "cocktail slouch." His smooth, round face and shy air made him seem immature. "Bill Paley was like a polite Fuller Brush salesman," recalled Edward Bernays, who became his public relations adviser in 1929. "He was actually bashful. In a roomful of people he would appear to be an inarticulate young man."

Paley was, in fact, scared. He was also self-conscious about his youthful appearance—David Sarnoff called him "the Kid"—and tried to rectify it. He ordered a custom-made wardrobe of dark suits to project a more worldly image. He succeeded in looking old-fashioned and a bit fussy, like a youngster impersonating J. P. Morgan. But Paley quickly impressed skeptical underlings by immersing himself in every aspect of the business. "There was nothing remarkable about Paley when he took over the company, nothing in his past career that might throw a light on this remarkable ability in the broadcasting world. His grasp of the new picture was amazing," Ralph Colin, Paley's lawyer at the time, recalled several years later.

He took in everything. He directed one executive, Julius Seebach, to sit at his elbow and coach him on what to say about broadcast problems and policies when station owners called. An engineer named Paul Green tutored him in radio engineering. Major Andrew White, the well-known radio announcer who was the nominal head of the Columbia network, taught him how to deal with affiliates.

At the outset Paley correctly calculated that Columbia had to own its flagship station—the facility where it produced programs for distribution to the network—if it was going to expand significantly. Before Paley's arrival the network leased time from two stations—WOR and WABC—to originate programming. Paley made overtures to both stations and in December 1928 bought WABC because its $390,000 price was lower. Paley now had a transmitter, a license, and an outmoded production studio in Steinway Hall, on Fifty-seventh Street.

For correct soundproofing, a studio needed ceilings reaching as high as two stories. On the advice of a real estate agent Paley looked at a building under construction at the southeast corner of Madison Avenue and Fifty-second Street. He liked its location on the street synonymous with advertising. The architect agreed to modify his plans to construct two floors of windowless studios, and Paley signed a lease for the twentieth through twenty-fourth floors at 485 Madison Avenue. "If Paley had not done this, the new company never could have clicked," Ralph Colin said years later.

Luck was crucial in Paley's early days. He could concentrate on building his network because advertising revenue was taking care of itself. He was fortunate to take over during a presidential election contest between Herbert Hoover and Alfred E. Smith—the first national election in which radio had a critical role. To advertise their candidates, both political parties poured money into radio—nearly $600,000 in October and November 1928 alone. NBC received the bulk of that money, but Columbia received an infusion of close to $200,000.

Early in 1929 Paley hired Edward L. Bernays, the nation's foremost public relations man. Paley had already extracted as much as he could from the executives he had inherited. Now it was time for the advice of a professional. And Bernays was the best. The nephew of Sigmund Freud, he was regarded as the father of public relations. He had been in business since the end of World War I, with such prestigious clients as the U.S. War Department, Procter & Gamble, and Enrico Caruso.

Bernays gave Paley ideas not only about publicity but about organizational structure, sales techniques, and scouting talent. He told Paley that the company was disorganized because of overlapping departments. In the publicity department Bernays set standards for headlines and brevity. He established a procedure to ensure that newspapers printed correct radio listings. He gave Paley a long list of possible humor writers for the network, including Ring Lardner, P. G. Wodehouse, and Don Marquis. He urged that prospective performers be considered not only for their talent but for their potential public relations value.

Around the time he hired Bernays, Paley also brought in Sam Pickard, the brightest man on the Federal Radio Commission, in Washington, D.C., as vice president of station relations for Columbia. Working the telephones in tandem, Pickard and Paley expanded Columbia to seventy-six stations by the end of 1929.

Paley was following his father's advice to "hire smart people and then have the good sense to listen to them." He showed confidence in his employees. Only later would his impulse to take credit for the good ideas of his subordinates cost him the respect of his executives.

Even in the early days Paley relished—and fiercely protected—his power. His actions began to betray his ruthlessness. For whatever reason, some of the original Columbia executives became disenchanted with Paley's leadership early in his tenure. Julius Seebach and Paul Green—two of the men who tutored Paley in his first months—joined forces with a third executive. Their purpose, according to rumors swirling around the company, was to seize control. When Paley heard of it, he demoted Seebach and fired Green and the other executive. Needless to say, the swiftness and severity of Paley's response impressed the survivors.

At the end of 1928 Paley had merged United Independent and the Columbia network and renamed the company Columbia Broadcasting System, Incorporated. He made himself president and appointed Major White managing director. White would concentrate on putting programs together and exploiting his contacts with Broadway celebrities to help Paley sign famous performers. But by mid-1930 White's usefulness would be over, and Paley would fire him.

At first the emphasis at Columbia was on classical music, and in the early days Paley was pleased with this approach and used the cachet of programs featuring opera stars and symphonies to attract advertisers. But in time Paley began to reshape Columbia's programming philosophy along more practical and lowbrow lines.

A more lofty philosophy of broadcasting held sway at rival NBC at this time. Led by Owen Young and David Sarnoff, NBC emphasized its role as a guardian of the public trust. NBC's schedule of cultural, educational, and public-service programs included lessons in music appreciation, concerts, productions of Shakespeare, political debates, and sermons. Millions of listeners tuned in, and advertisers eagerly bought time. NBC made its first profit in 1928.

But forces began working against NBC's high purpose. The most important was the impact of *Amos 'n' Andy*, a comedy series about a pair of black buffoons. It was performed by Freeman Gosden and Charles Correll, two white comedians in blackface who used heavy Negro dialect ("I's regusted") and shameless stereotyping. The show, which began in Chicago in 1928, was radio's first light entertainment. It was a huge hit and soon attracted forty million listeners—an audience far larger than that for any cultural fare. Advertisers clamored for more shows like *Amos 'n' Andy*.

The trend was not lost on Bill Paley. He began the drive toward more popular entertainment. He had decided that the quickest route to making the biggest profits was by appealing to the largest possible audience, which in turn would attract more advertisers. Increasingly Paley filled his airwaves with popular musicians, comedians, and soap operas. He did not ignore cultural programs, but clearly he was changing the emphasis of network broadcasting.

THIS was a time of peak creativity, of enormous energy, for Bill Paley. He was working overtime to shape a new network, but he was also playing hard, dating film stars and socialites featured in the pages of *Vogue,* nightclub hopping, theatergoing. He seemed to be testing his limits, personally as well as professionally.

Nothing symbolized his dual preoccupations—his devotion to Columbia Broadcasting and to high living—so clearly as the apartment he moved into in January 1930. The first in a series of Paley pleasure palaces, the apartment occupied the top three floors of a newly completed building at the corner of Park Avenue and Fifty-eighth Street. Yielding to his impulse for flash, Paley hired a Broadway set designer to turn the apartment into a grown man's playpen. The master bedroom, on the first floor, was sleek, austere, and dark. Its centerpiece was a customized bed, set at an angle as in a stage set. The bed was equipped with remote controls that switched on a radio and various combinations of lights.

The high-ceilinged third-floor barroom was even more urgently modernistic. Its walls were painted silver, with diagonal red and blue stripes. A winding aluminum staircase rose to a silver-painted balcony. French doors led to a terrace and a roof garden.

A guest bedroom on the first floor was decorated with traditional furniture. On the second floor were the living and dining rooms, richly paneled in oak. The decor was beige and brown, with proper English furnishings and Paley's humdrum collection of sporting prints of herrings, pelicans, and other unremarkable fauna.

When Paley moved into his new home, he felt uncomfortable sleeping on his stage set. Two days later he moved into the conventionally decorated guest room; he never spent another night in the opulent master bedroom.

Paley's social life was that of a free-swinging, extravagant tycoon. He threw numerous parties. He hired the best chef in New York. His English butler-valet arranged elaborate dinners on a few hours' notice. Another servant was hired to drag Paley out of bed each morning, lead him through calisthenics, and give him a massage. Paley—who often stayed out until three or four in the morning—would fire his man each day on awakening and then rehire him after his morning shower.

Compared to the tightly stratified society of Philadelphia, New York was refreshingly open. By the '20s, when Paley arrived, many of the distinctions between old money and new money had vanished. It was the heyday of café society, the elite cross section of socialites, financiers, actors, show girls, singers, writers, sportsmen, and tycoons united in pursuit of pleasure. The mood was giddy and hedonistic, fueled by a runaway bull market on Wall Street. Parties began in the early evening and ended after dawn. Café society was gaudy and glamorous. But above all it was not governed by bloodlines. Membership was open to anyone with money, power, charm, or celebrity.

After a year in New York, Bill Paley had plenty of each. He had become a certified member of the smart set. He dined at speakeasies like the exclusive "21" Club. He also frequented the city's nightclubs (there were more than seventy of them), seeking diversion and scouting talent for his network. Even more important, Paley gained membership to the Mayfair Club Dance. Each Saturday night in the

Crystal Room of The Ritz-Carlton hotel, the Mayfair Club held a dance designed to introduce debutantes to eligible young bachelors.

By jumping so enthusiastically into café society, Paley vaulted over Our Crowd, the German Jewish elite of New York. These families were not impressed by the likes of Bill Paley. To them show business was a bit vulgar, barely more respectable than cigar making. Paley would have liked to be accepted by Our Crowd, but when he was not, his resolve to move in WASP circles intensified.

Paley's first link to WASP society, ironically enough, was through his friend Lawrence Lowman, who came from a prominent German Jewish family in Philadelphia. When Paley said good-bye to Philadelphia, he also said good-bye to all his friends with the exception of Lowman, who joined him at CBS. Lowman occupied the office next to Paley's. One of his first jobs was to set up the company's accounting system, but he was also Paley's confidant and right-hand man. Outside the office, he and Paley were inseparable playmates. Lowman was smart and cultivated, with a keen sense of humor and a graceful manner—the sort of amusing man Paley was drawn to all his life. Significantly, at the time Paley hired him, Lowman was courting Cathleen Vanderbilt Cushing, half sister to Gloria Vanderbilt. With that sort of connection Paley's social contacts quickly multiplied.

Still, Paley never really penetrated the WASP Establishment. He was not welcomed as a member by the Union, Racquet and Tennis, or any other old-line WASP clubs. The Vanderbilts would slum in café society for thrills and diversion, but in the end they withdrew behind their exclusive heritage. In later years Paley would achieve tokens of WASP recognition—membership in the fashionable National Golf Links, in Southampton, for example—but all his life he would remain caught between two worlds, WASP and Jewish, firmly rooted in neither.

Paley chased women with the same ardor that he chased success. Both pursuits involved conquest and drew on his legendary persistence. He was usually seen with stunning women, from show girls to socialites. They were of a type—fine-featured, chic, and WASP from head to manicured toe.

THE late 1920s and early 1930s were the pivotal years of Bill Paley's life. With every success his confidence grew. At work the admiration of his subordinates became tinged with awe. They were impressed by his brainpower, dynamism, and winning way with people. "He was always glad to see you. He would look at you in a frank, happy way," said Helen Sioussat, an early recruit for the public affairs department. His enthusiasm infected everybody, and they worked hard to please him.

Not a day seemed to pass at CBS without Paley making some sort of deal with a performer or affiliate or advertiser. These were the building years, the happiest years of his life, he often said. "They gave me more day-by-day pleasure than I've ever had. It was easy because we had a very small organization, and I had to make almost all the decisions, and that was very easy and very quick and it wasn't very complicated." Even though he worked anywhere from twelve to sixteen hours most days, he was continuously invigorated. "Sleep didn't mean anything to me," he said. "There was a drive, a kind of aspiration to succeed. It never has been the same. You undertook the impossible and found that it worked."

Columbia's total revenue for 1928 was $1.6 million. However, revenues could not possibly keep pace with Paley's rapid expansion. Although Columbia had broken into the black in August, it ended the

Below, CBS president Bill Paley addresses a radio audience in the early '30s.

Above, Paley with radio stars he would bring from NBC to CBS in the 1940s. From left, George Burns, Paley, Gracie Allen, Mary Livingston, and Jack Benny.

year with a deficit of $172,655. Paley needed additional funds to keep his dream going.

Initially he drew from his family and friends and his own fortune. At the end of 1928 he bought an additional 1000 shares of Columbia stock for $200,000, bringing his ownership to 61 percent. With another $300,000 from the Paleys and the Levys, he bought WABC and financed his expanded program schedule. Still, it was not enough.

Strapped for cash, Paley was receptive when the head of Paramount-Famous-Lasky Corporation, Adolph Zukor, sent an emissary in the late spring of 1929 to talk about a partnership. For several years the big Hollywood studios had been simultaneously intrigued by and apprehensive about radio. As its popularity grew, movie moguls worried that prospective moviegoers might prefer listening to the box in their living rooms. If only in self-defense, Zukor and other moguls were eager to have an alliance with radio.

In his dealings with Zukor, Paley showed not only an aptitude for high finance but a relentless and fearless negotiating style. Paley's gambit was demanding $5 million for a half interest in Columbia and then refusing to negotiate. His uncle Jay and his father called him stubborn and arrogant for rebuffing a Paramount offer of $4.5 million. But Bill Paley, who had meekly sought his father's approval to buy the Columbia network less than a year earlier, had become defiant, infected by the power of ownership. "I have the right to say yes or no to Paramount," Paley told his father, "and my answer is no."

Finally, Zukor agreed to try negotiating with Paley himself. Zukor was twice Paley's age and the most powerful of the Hollywood moguls. Paramount controlled such stars as Mary Pickford, Douglas Fairbanks, and Rudolph Valentino, as well as a chain of a thousand theaters. Zukor brought a dozen staff members to his meeting with Paley. The Columbia president came alone. Paley delighted in recalling his surprise to see that his adversary was no more than five feet tall and "walked with his feet turned in." Zukor tried flattery and cajolery, but Paley stuck with his price. In the end Zukor agreed to pay $5 million for Paramount's half interest in Columbia.

By Paley's account he triumphed over Zukor in every way. In fact, their agreement, signed in June 1929, was evenly balanced. Since Columbia stock was privately held—it would not be listed on the New York Stock Exchange until 1937—Paley deserves credit for forcing

Paramount to place a value on the company far greater than what he had paid the previous year. But Zukor prevailed with his insistence on paying with Paramount stock rather than cash. Paramount gave Columbia 58,823 shares of Paramount stock—then valued at $65 a share, or $3.8 million. On March 1, 1932, Zukor would buy back that stock at $85 a share, or $5 million. The deal in effect permitted Paramount to delay paying for its half of CBS for nearly three years.

There was one additional condition. During the period from September 8, 1929, through September 6, 1931, Columbia had to earn a net profit of at least $2 million. If Columbia fell short of the goal, Paramount would not have to buy back its stock; Columbia could keep the Paramount stock and sell it for whatever price it could fetch on the open market. Whether Paramount paid the $5 million to Columbia or not, Paramount would still control half of Columbia's 150,000 shares of stock.

Although he didn't say so at the time, Paley was nervous enough about having "all our eggs in one basket if something went wrong with radio" to welcome the security of associating with a larger, more successful company. That Paley would have agreed to sell half of Columbia a mere nine months after buying it shows he was unwilling to chance much in those days. Yet the fact remains that on a crucial day in June, 1929, Paley risked losing control of his fledgling network and with it his broadcasting dreams.

CHAPTER 4

THE stock market crash four months later intensified the pressure on Paley to earn $2 million in profits by 1931. The market value of Paramount stock had fallen to $10 a share. If CBS had to sell that stock on the open market, it would realize only about $600,000 instead of the $5 million the company stood to make under the agreement with Paramount. The clock was ticking. Paley's overriding goal was to make as much money as he could, as fast as possible. He pandered to listeners with more and more mindless programs, from fortune-tellers to gory thrillers, and he permitted commercials on CBS to become louder, more insistent, and more numerous.

These were desperate times of rising unemployment and plummeting wages. Yet radio was proving itself one of the few Depression-proof businesses. Listeners flocked to escapist entertainment, and advertisers saw in the radio audience an opportunity to build demand for their products and prop up sagging profits.

In 1931 advertising sales for the CBS network were $14.5 million. By the autumn of that year it was clear that Paley would meet the terms of the $2 million in net profits specified in the contract with Paramount. However, Paley knew that Paramount, after its terrible dive in the Depression, could not possibly afford to pay $85 a share to buy back its stock. Earlier he had sold off $1 million worth of the Paramount stock to raise capital, so Paramount now had to come up with $4 million for the remaining 48,000 shares held by CBS.

At first Paramount asked for a three-year extension, and Paley nearly buckled under Adolph Zukor's insistence. Then Zukor made an offer Paley could not refuse. CBS could buy back the 63,250 shares of CBS stock owned by Paramount for $5.2 million. Paramount would thereby have the $4 million necessary to buy its own stock back from CBS, with a tidy $1.2 million profit besides. Most important for Bill Paley, he would regain operating control of CBS.

With the help of several prominent investment bankers Paley raised the money needed to buy back the CBS stock. Paley profited handsomely from the deal. He now personally owned 40 percent of CBS' stock—itself worth $4 million.

Throughout this period Paley's counterparts at NBC were learning how slippery an opponent he could be. In 1935 he plucked off some choice NBC affiliated stations, violating an understanding between the networks not to raid each other's stations. This gentleman's agreement between Paley and David Sarnoff had been advantageous to NBC, the older of the networks, with the more powerful string of stations. The raid, in Paley's view, was a necessity. When Sarnoff eventually complained to Paley about CBS' conduct, Paley could only say, "Mr. Sarnoff, radio broadcasting is a highly competitive business."

When Paley wasn't wooing advertisers and NBC stations, he prowled nightclubs and theaters for performers to put on his network. Although relatively inexperienced, he had good instincts about what made a program work and who could draw a large radio audience.

Paley's prize catch was Bing Crosby. Although the baritone crooner was a star on Decca Records at the time, Paley had not heard him until

June 1931, when Paley was traveling to Europe on the S.S. *Europa*. Restless as always, he had a habit of pacing the deck each morning. On one of his rounds he heard Crosby's voice on a portable phonograph. He sent a wire to CBS with orders to sign up Crosby. But when Paley returned to New York later that summer, his program executives had failed to act. Crosby had a drinking problem, they explained, and was considered unreliable. Paley overrode them all, hired Crosby to do six broadcasts a week at eleven p.m., and agreed to pay him an extravagant $1500 a week, when $100 was customary.

True to predictions, Crosby failed to appear for his first broadcast. At Paley's insistence CBS nervously rescheduled Crosby a few days later. That evening Paley was on Long Island in a rented home without a radio. Out in the garage he tuned in from his car. "Crosby was awful," he recalled. Paley dashed back to the house and called the studio. Crosby was drunk, as Paley suspected, and two men were holding him up as he tried pathetically to sing. "Change the program. Get him off," Paley shouted. The power he felt at that moment made him giddy. Years later he would say, "Think of it. I could even change a program while it was on the air!" But Paley refused to let Crosby go. He assigned the singer a round-the-clock guard to prevent him from drinking. "It worked," said Paley. "He knew his job was at stake."

The most popular programs at the time were still those featuring comedians, and CBS introduced many of the best: George Burns and Gracie Allen, Jack Benny, Fred Allen. More often than not, once a comedian established himself on CBS, the advertiser would take him over to the larger and more powerful NBC networks.

For all of Paley's efforts NBC still had the five most popular shows in the 1934–35 season. In 1936 Paley staged his first talent raid. He captured Al Jolson, Nelson Eddy, and Major Edward Bowes, three of NBC's top performers. While it was considered fair play when an advertiser took its star to a better position on NBC, Paley's raids violated an understanding between CBS and NBC not to make direct approaches to each other's personnel.

Paley's scheme to capture Bowes was typical. Bowes ran an amateur hour that had become a national sensation. To cultivate the Major, the CBS president became a regular at the NBC studio where Bowes broadcast his show. While NBC executives could guess Paley's intention, they could hardly eject him from the premises. Whenever Bowes threw a party, Paley was there. Before long his persistence paid off, and Paley persuaded Bowes that he could do better on CBS. Paley knew Bowes was about to switch his sponsorship to the Chrysler Corporation, and he began dropping in on Walter Chrysler as well. Gently but insistently Paley convinced Chrysler that Bowes belonged on CBS, which was more ambitious and fast-moving than NBC.

Paley had become a bona fide impresario. He entertained his performers at dinner parties. He greatly preferred the company of those on the creative side to that of his executives. But his attentiveness was also calculated: keep them happy and keep them on CBS.

WHEN Bill Paley, a man of instant infatuations, first saw Dorothy Hart Hearst across a luncheon table one Sunday afternoon in 1931, he fell hopelessly in love. She had a dazzling, dimpled smile, wide brown eyes that sparkled with intelligence and spirit, and brown wavy hair that brushed the nape of her neck. She had a perfectly proportioned figure, with a tiny waist and narrow hips. Not only was Dorothy ravishing, she was breathtakingly chic.

Just twenty-three, Dorothy had been married for three years to John Randolph Hearst, the third son of the publisher William Randolph Hearst. Typically, Paley viewed her marriage as a trifling impediment once he determined he would have her.

Born in Los Angeles, Dorothy attended Marlboro, at that time the city's most exclusive girls' school, and then spent one year at Bennett College, a fancy eastern finishing school. Her passion was art, and she took as many art history courses as she could.

Back in Los Angeles, Dorothy Hart became the belle of her social set. The summer after her eighteenth birthday she met Jack Hearst. He was as slender and handsome as she was beautiful. He captivated her with his shy charm, and they began seeing each other. Jack's brainpower was substantially less than Dorothy's. At a time when a fortune of Hearst magnitude could easily secure a spot in an Ivy League college for an underachieving son, the best W.R. could do for Jack was Oglethorpe University, in Atlanta. Before he left for his freshman year, Jack proposed and Dorothy accepted.

The couple were married in New York, in December 1927. Within a year Jack dropped out of college and joined the Hearst Corporation in New York to learn about magazines. But soon he began to sink at his father's company. He had entered at too high a level and felt uncomfortable. He started to drink heavily and worked less and less.

In an effort to shame him into applying himself, Dorothy found a job at *Harper's Bazaar*. She was in her element. She had her own office and an assistant, and she wrote a monthly column. But her success only made Jack's condition worse. From the time she began working, he rarely got up in the morning, and when he did, he was hung over.

Dorothy's marriage was shaky, to say the least, when she met Bill Paley. While he didn't sweep her off her feet, she was struck by his curiosity, enthusiasm, and attentiveness. Here, she thought, was a man with enormous sex appeal. His only problem was he needed a new tailor—"I thought he dressed like a one-hundred-and-five-year-old man."

In June 1931 Dorothy and Jack sailed for a European vacation on the S.S. *Europa*. Joining them on board were Dorothy's close friend Marjorie Oelrichs (a New York beauty who would later marry the pianist Eddy Duchin), Larry Lowman—and Bill Paley. "He got on that boat and didn't get off," said Irene Selznick. "I don't even know if he had any luggage. He was that determined to marry her."

In London they all stayed at The Savoy. Dorothy arranged for Bill to visit a new tailor on Savile Row—Kilgore & French. Once suitably outfitted, "he looked divine." The Hearsts took an impressive detour by visiting the Churchill family at Chartwell, their country home. Dorothy had met Winston and his son, Randolph, on a trip to New York, and she and Randolph had become good friends.

From England the Hearsts journeyed to Berlin, where they rejoined Paley and his friends. The five travelers drove to Salzburg, where they stayed with the theater director Max Reinhardt, a friend of Dorothy's. There, in Reinhardt's baroque castle on a lake, with its dark halls illuminated only by candles, things began coming apart. It was obvious to everyone, including Jack, that Dorothy and Bill were crazy about each other. Paley was constantly attentive to Dorothy. Jack turned to the bottle. Dorothy felt simultaneously drawn to Paley and guilt-stricken. Her nerves stretched to the breaking point, she collapsed and entered a Salzburg hospital.

When Dorothy and Jack returned to New York, she began sleeping with Paley. On any number of occasions she and Paley could be seen dancing to Eddy Duchin's music at the Central Park Casino. Jack didn't protest, but he insisted that she stay married to him. He was drunk constantly, which in turn drained her emotionally. "You have to get out of this," her doctor finally advised her. Dorothy took a train to Las Vegas to begin divorce proceedings.

On May 12, 1932, Dorothy and Bill Paley flew to Kingman, Arizona, where one could obtain a license—and marry on the spot—without publicity. After a stop in Santa Barbara the couple sailed for Hawaii, where Dorothy wept through the first few days of their honeymoon. She was still torn apart by the breakup with Jack. She knew Jack's alcoholism was serious, and she felt she had deserted him. Paley tried to make the best of it, offering sympathy and understanding.

There had been many beautiful women in Bill Paley's life by the time he settled down at age thirty with Dorothy. He was known to cool on his women as quickly as he was inflamed by their first glance. What was it about Dorothy that carried him to the altar? Part of the attraction was her connections. Also, she had self-confidence, a strong sense of likes and dislikes, and a clear and enviable style.

Although seven years his junior, Dorothy was more worldly than Bill Paley. She knew her way around in sophisticated circles; friend-

Left, Paley with his
first wife, Dorothy, during
their Hawaiian honeymoon.
Below, Dorothy in a
fashion photograph.

ships with men like Randolph Churchill counted a great deal to the ambitious Paley. She was brainy, and Paley admired her inquiring mind and strong opinions.

Over the years Dorothy would have a significant impact on her husband—her political leanings, appetite for news, taste in art, and sense of style. She supported Franklin D. Roosevelt and embraced his proposals for social welfare. Both Dorothy and Bill had been raised Republican. But Paley's political preferences became situational. He drifted toward what was convenient. When confronted with Dorothy's views, he quickly fell into line. "I can't imagine he would have voted Democrat without me," she said. As a wealthy entrepreneur, Paley believed in big business as unencumbered by regulation as possible. But he could feel comfortable with the Democratic Party in the early 1930s. The Depression had discredited the Republicans. All his friends in the theater and others he admired, like Averell Harriman, the aristocratic banker, were die-hard Roosevelt supporters.

Dorothy's most enduring impact was on Bill Paley's taste. When she first saw his glossy apartment, with its insipid collection of sporting prints, she was appalled. She could not believe how little cultural education he had. With her passion for art history Dorothy set to work to help fill in the gaps.

Like other business tycoons before him, Paley wanted to use some of his fortune to collect paintings; it was the most respected and socially prestigious hobby one could have. In the beginning he relied on those more knowledgeable—professional art buyers as well as his own wife—to direct him. But just as in business, Paley was reluctant to credit those who helped mold his taste, and he has never acknowledged Dorothy's role.

On a trip to Paris in the summer of 1935, Bill and Dorothy saw works by Cézanne, Derain, Picasso, Renoir, and Gauguin. Paley took a plunge by buying his first Cézanne, entitled L'Estaque, for $25,000. With each purchase Paley's taste became more refined, although he was never a dedicated student along the lines of collectors such as Norton Simon. "He didn't always make the easiest selections, but I don't think he was adventurous," said Dorothy. He lacked the daring to find a brilliant unknown. Clearly he loved the range of Impressionists and Postimpressionists; years later he said that he felt a sensuous connection to them.

Dorothy elevated and rarefied Paley's style of living. She got him out of his triplex apartment at the end of 1932, when they rented a five-story town house at 35 Beekman Place, a fashionable and quiet enclave in the East Fifties. The Paleys were so fond of Beekman Place that in 1934 they tore down another town house, Number 29, and erected a six-story home in its place. Paley supervised the architecture, and Dorothy oversaw the interior design.

In 1937 they moved into what Irene Selznick called "that crazy narrow crystal house," a lavish, eclectic, and thoroughly modern home. One side of the small entrance hall was mirrored, as was one wall along the second-floor landing, to create an illusion of spaciousness. The gracefully curving staircase was covered with carpet made of zebra skins. The drawing room had a maple floor, stained black and defined by thin lines of brass inlay. The room was decorated entirely in a pale gray-blue and was filled with eighteenth-century English furniture. The Paleys' newly acquired paintings were illuminated by small spotlights concealed in moldings.

After only three years at 29 Beekman Place, Paley grew tired of the house and decided they should leave. Dorothy was crushed, but he was unyielding. In 1940 the Paleys moved to The Waldorf until they could find a home more to his liking.

Of great importance to Paley was Dorothy's image as a trendsetter. She headed the list of the world's ten best-dressed women, and her photograph appeared in Paley's favorite magazines, *Vogue* and *Harper's Bazaar*. Dorothy's friends were devoted to her and marveled at her cleverness. Dorothy became a mentor to Marietta Tree, granddaughter of Endicott Peabody, the rector of Groton School, and to Irene Mayer, who had recently married Hollywood producer David O. Selznick. "She lavished knowledge and affection on me," said Irene Selznick. "She put me down a few pegs and enlightened me at the same time."

That method applied to Bill as well. Dorothy always appeared slightly superior in her attitude toward him. "There were warning signs from year one," Irene Selznick recalled. "She could be charming and say, 'Darling,' and do everything superbly, but she was also domineering and opinionated." But Paley was so keen to learn and so enchanted with Dorothy that he scarcely seemed to notice that she patronized him.

CHAPTER 5

To ALL outward appearances Dorothy and Bill Paley were a dream couple—bright, handsome, young, eager, and very much in love. They shared boundless energy and restlessness. They seemed to be in a race with life—virtually every night of the week they were at Broadway openings, nightclubs, and dinner parties. Their energy charged the atmosphere around them. At El Morocco they came to see and be seen amid the white palms and zebra-striped banquettes. Marietta Tree recalled that the first evening she saw Paley at El Morocco "he couldn't stop smiling. He was surrounded by beautiful women. He danced with all the women there. I remember him absolutely flying around the room as he danced."

The couple stormed Hollywood too. Paley established a friendship with Sam Goldwyn and his wife, Frances, who entertained Dorothy and Bill at lavish dinner parties. But of all the movie producers Paley met, he had the most rapport with David O. Selznick. Like Paley, Selznick was a son of Russian Jewish immigrants; his father had been a jeweler in Pittsburgh. Selznick was bespectacled, curly-haired, earthy, impulsive, a nonstop talker who routinely convulsed Paley with laughter. "They had a lot in common," said Irene Selznick. "They were two Jewish fellows with big success, great talent and energy, great appetites. They traded information and stimulated one another."

Bill Paley liked to be around creative people so he could pick their brains. He was drawn to style, accomplishment, glamour, power, and money—all of which he found at the home of Herbert Bayard Swope, an acknowledged leader of café society. In the late '20s, when Swope quit as editor of the New York *World,* a series of shrewd stock market plays had already made him a millionaire. His thirty-room apartment, on West Fifty-eighth Street in Manhattan, was open house to a diverse group of theatrical and literary figures as well as wealthy socialites. The Paleys routinely dropped in after the theater for an impromptu party. They attended nonstop house parties nearly every weekend at the Swopes' sprawling home in Sands Point, Long Island, a most fashionable retreat for the city's wealthy elite.

A large red-haired man who talked all the time, Swope fostered a kind of manic congeniality among his guests. A typical weekend might include playwrights George S. Kaufman and Robert Sherwood; FDR's special aide, Harry Hopkins, might drop by, as well as comedian Harpo Marx, columnist Walter Lippmann, or publisher Condé Nast.

The Swope weekends were said to have been the model for F. Scott Fitzgerald's party scenes in *The Great Gatsby*. Guests drifted in and out, some staying for weeks at a time. Herbert Swope and his wife, Maggie, entertained on a scale that made a mockery of the Depression. Everyone played games incessantly: poker, mah-jongg, backgammon, hearts, and bridge. Outdoors, Swope and his guests took up croquet with ferocious intensity. And there were always parlor games. Boisterous, often frantic, these contests attracted large crowds.

Swope was fifty years old and Paley only thirty-one when they first met. Yet the two men developed a lively friendship that deepened when Paley invited Swope to join the CBS board of directors in the mid-'30s. Paley was stimulated by Swope, who had a talent for bringing out the best in his friends.

In 1938 the Paleys bought their own country estate in Manhasset, down the road from Sands Point. Called Kiluna Farm, it was set on eighty-five acres that included a saltwater pool, indoor tennis court, barns, greenhouses, and gardens. Built of white clapboard in the late nineteenth century, the house itself had more than twenty rooms, including servants' quarters. Set on a rise, Kiluna offered a fine view of the distant Long Island Sound.

Although Paley always said he was drawn to Kiluna's simplicity, he and Dorothy added a columned portico that made the house look more grand. Dorothy also redid every room in the house. The white sitting room overflowed with cheerful red-and-green English chintz. On the walls were a Lautrec, a Gauguin, and a Cézanne.

The Paleys became renowned for their entertaining. Less freewheeling than the Swopes', house parties at Kiluna set new standards of elegance and luxury. Kiluna, said Horace Kelland, a visitor in the '30s, "was polite and pretty, rather like a nice stylish country club." Twenty-two servants were on hand to keep everything perfect.

The food at the Paleys' was exquisite. In the afternoon there would be high tea, with an assortment of delicate pastries, cinnamon toast, and tiny sandwiches. Partly to cater to Bill's constant craving for food, orange juice and sandwiches were often served at ten thirty in the evening, only an hour or so after the formal dinner had concluded.

The Sands Point and Manhasset social whirl was an essential part of Bill Paley's existence. It established him as a formidable social presence, exposing him to a wide array of talented and provocative people. In addition to the North Shore regulars, the Paleys included numerous guests from the motion picture world, artistic and literary types, and titled Europeans.

Bill Paley's social life was elitist but not exclusive. Jews such as the Swopes and Kaufmans mixed comfortably with Vanderbilts and other super-WASPs. People were valued for their talent, their liveliness, their accomplishment, not their ethnic origin. Yet overt displays of ethnicity were unwelcome. Bill Paley subtly adopted WASP ways. He never actually tried to hide his Jewishness. But he never flaunted it and in large measure withdrew from it.

For all of Paley's social accomplishments, one pinnacle remained. Living next door to the Paleys in Manhasset was John Hay "Jock" Whitney, the millionaire sportsman and publisher. Jock was a true American patrician, who stood at the apex of social position, and Paley could not get to first base with him—even though Paley and Whitney shared a friend in David Selznick. Whitney had invested in Selznick International Pictures in 1935 and served as chairman of the board and East Coast manager. Primarily through Selznick, Paley and Whitney would periodically cross paths. In 1939 the Paleys and the Whitneys were among the guests who traveled to Atlanta, Georgia, for the world premiere of *Gone With the Wind,* which Selznick produced and Whitney financed. Still, Jock and Bill never became intimate. When the Selznicks came east, they visited the Paleys and the Whitneys separately. Dorothy had little in common with Jock's wife, Liz, a socialite horsewoman uninterested in the world of books and ideas. Nor did she have much use for Jock, whom she considered a stuffed shirt. But in those days Jock showed little affinity for Bill Paley either. With time this situation would become more and more aggravating for Paley—a nagging symbol that until he was embraced by the consummate American gentleman, he still had not quite arrived.

By 1936 CBS had made Bill Paley rich and powerful. His talent for salesmanship had paid off handsomely. From 1929 through 1936 CBS' net profit rose from $480,000 to $3.9 million.

During the same years Paley found the burden of leading the network was lightened by two key executives who came to CBS in 1930—an enormously talented yin-and-yang pair who embodied the poles of Paley's contradictory nature. They were Edward Klauber, the unimaginative straight arrow who put CBS News on the map, and Paul Kesten, the brilliant imagemaker, an aesthete who helped refine Paley's taste. Each man resented the other and vied for Paley's attention.

Bill Paley's first reaction to Ed Klauber was thorough dislike. Charmless and utterly lacking in humor, Klauber seemed the antithesis of everything Paley valued in a man. Klauber had been night city editor at *The New York Times,* where he was a rigid enforcer of objectivity and fairness. He had subsequently worked for an advertising agency and for Edward Bernays, CBS' public relations man, who recommended him to Paley. Klauber's blend of experience in journalism, advertising, and public relations, Bernays told Paley, could help CBS enormously.

Only after Bernays praised Klauber's superior executive ability and sound judgment did Paley overcome his initial aversion and hire him

Edward Klauber, left, who was Paley's second-in-command, and Paul Kesten, below, head of CBS promotion. The two men "embodied the poles of Paley's contradictory nature."

as his administrative assistant. But Klauber was widely disliked at CBS and grew increasingly tyrannical as he assumed greater day-to-day responsibilities. Although every executive in those days called Paley "Bill" to his face, Klauber decreed that they refer to the president only as "Mr. Paley" when they discussed him out of his presence. Paley found that he liked this formal gesture of respect.

Executives dreaded the summons to Klauber's forbidding office. He decorated it entirely in dark brown—rugs, upholstery, and draperies—and always kept the venetian blinds nearly closed. Wearing double-breasted suits that accentuated his stockiness, he sat stiffly behind a massive desk, peering over his pince-nez and smoking a cigarette in a long holder. Periodically he dropped ash over his shoulder onto the carpet as he growled his commands.

As Dorothy did in his personal life, Klauber imposed discipline and organization on Paley at work. He insisted that Paley have only male secretaries, and he streamlined CBS operations, which had been too loose and informal. An extra door connected Paley's corner office to Klauber's adjacent office, allowing Klauber unlimited access to his boss. Klauber became Paley's gatekeeper. Paley chose to ignore Klauber's difficult personality because of his usefulness. Paley preferred to avoid confrontations, and Klauber eagerly took them on, allowing the boss to remain comfortably above it all. Thus, late in 1930 Klauber summarily fired Bernays over lunch. Despite the fact that Bernays was a man who had done much for CBS, Paley looked the other way. Klauber said it cost too much to retain an outside public relations firm. But soon afterwards he hired a publicist from the Ivy Lee Company, which was better connected than Bernays to the WASP Establishment to which Paley aspired.

It was Klauber who, toward the end of 1930, hired Paul Kesten to direct CBS' promotion. Kesten was a brilliant advertising copywriter and was as clever and affable as Klauber was earnest and dour. Thin to the point of frailty, Kesten was already so plagued by arthritis at thirty-one that he had difficulty turning a doorknob. He wore his dark blond hair slicked back from a high, intelligent forehead and dressed stylishly in fashionable suits nipped at the waist.

Paley loved Kesten's cleverness and charm. Both men brimmed with ideas and were adept at figures. In meetings they were so in sync that they finished each other's sentences. Kesten's interest in design fueled Paley's growing fascination with the symbols of quality—the best typeface, the best paper, the best graphics. "Kesten had a feeling for elegance and taste, along with a touch of majesty," said Paley.

Kesten was a popular and amiable executive—perhaps too much so. He was sensitive and solicitous, and could not bring himself to fire anyone. If he wanted something done, he rarely gave an order. Rather, he would politely note, "I am turning this over to you." With Paley he was often obsequious.

Between the iron fist of Klauber and the delicate felicity of Kesten, Paley's executive style took shape. He dressed conservatively in bespoke blue serge suits. He continued to drive himself hard. He smoked four packs of Chesterfields a day and was always nervous and tense, his tic already in evidence. Yet in a crucial negotiation he could appear cool and relaxed—the result, apparently, of his powers of intense concentration.

His days were so crowded that he often held meetings while he ate breakfast—long before the power breakfast came into fashion. He wrote few memos. A man of action rather than ideas, he preferred to conduct business face to face or on the telephone. He kept a radio going continuously from seven thirty in the morning until midnight. He rarely left the office before seven p.m.

In these years Paley was steadily moving away from the informality that had characterized his earliest days at CBS. No longer an easygoing stripling, he had presence and a quiet confidence that grew from his achievements. He acquired imperial trappings, such as the dining room he opened near his office, complete with private chef and waiters. When Paley wanted to change for the evening, his valet would arrive at the office with fresh clothing.

And with Klauber firmly in charge, Paley grew more aloof. Subordinates began to take note of Paley's absences from the office. "He was away quite frequently," said H. V. Kaltenborn, former reporter for the Brooklyn *Eagle* and a pioneer of radio news. "He got a great deal of pleasure out of outside things." But Paley never totally disengaged from the office, even when he was frolicking through Europe for months at a time. Klauber assiduously kept him informed by telephone and by "yard-long telegrams" sent every few days. "There was never business per se on those trips," recalled Dorothy. "But there was no question that CBS was always on his mind."

CHAPTER 6

NEW skyscraper spires glistened against the clear sky when Frank Nicholas Stanton turned his black Model A Ford toward the Holland Tunnel, into Manhattan. It was a crisp Saturday afternoon in early October, 1935. Twenty-seven years old, with a newly minted Ph.D. from Ohio State University, he had driven the five hundred and sixty miles from Columbus, Ohio, to New York City, where he would begin his career at CBS.

Frank Stanton was every city slicker's dream of a corn-fed midwestern lad. Compact and muscular, he stood five feet eleven inches. His straight flaxen hair was neatly parted and perfectly combed. He had a strong jaw, straight nose, and intense blue eyes. At his side was Ruth, his wife of four years. She had a pretty, open face, with flashing dark eyes and brunette hair styled in a long bob.

The Stantons settled into the Pickwick Arms Hotel, on Fifty-sixth Street, between Second and Third avenues. On Monday morning, less than two days after leaving Ohio, Frank walked the four blocks to CBS headquarters, on Madison Avenue, carrying the black aluminum box that was his ticket to the world of network radio broadcasting.

Understanding the role of Frank Stanton at CBS is crucial to understanding William Paley and the success of the network. Stanton was everything Paley was not. Like many great entrepreneurs, Paley was long on creative spark but short on follow-through. It would be Paley's good fortune that Stanton was one of the great corporate builders of the era. The young midwesterner combined Klauber's discipline, executive ability, and high principles with Kesten's taste and instinct for promotion. Stanton was to prove the perfect man at the perfect place at the perfect time.

He was born on March 20, 1908, in Muskegon, Michigan. When he was three months old, his parents moved from Muskegon to Dayton, Ohio, where his father, Frank senior, accepted a job supervising the industrial arts instruction in Dayton's schools.

While still in elementary school, Stanton showed a flair for art and graphics. Later he became fascinated by architecture. He was even offered a scholarship in architecture at Cornell University, but he did not pursue it. "It was a fork in the road," Stanton said years later. "I might have taken the wrong turn." He ended up at Ohio Wesleyan, a small Methodist university ninety miles outside Dayton, because his best friend was there and it was close to his childhood sweetheart, Ruth Stephenson, who was attending Western College for Women.

At college Stanton concentrated in psychology, through which he was eventually drawn into studying radio. In his junior year he wrote a paper on the development of radio as an advertising medium. The library had no information on commercial radio, so Stanton wrote to scores of advertisers inquiring how programs were chosen for sponsorship and how the effectiveness of commercials was tested. He spent months cataloguing the number of sets and stations in use. The outcome was what he later called a gaudy paper, superficial but chockablock with statistics, charts, and graphs. It earned him an A.

Although he became known as the resident expert on radio in the psychology department, he still had not set himself on a broadcasting career. He had no job prospects at all, in fact, when he graduated in 1930. To pay bills, he worked for the next year teaching typography and typesetting at Roosevelt High School in Dayton. He and Ruth were engaged by then; they were married on New Year's Eve, 1930.

In the meantime Stanton blanketed graduate schools with applications for fellowships in psychology. Ohio State finally offered him a post as teaching assistant in the industrial psychology laboratory, where he planned to earn an advanced degree. Stanton became intrigued by the psychology of mass communications, specifically why and how people react to the information they receive.

It was the studies leading to his doctoral dissertation that firmly planted Frank Stanton in radio. He believed the impact of radio was more profound than print, yet few people had bothered to analyze why. He wrote to NBC and CBS describing his views not only on how audiences were measured but on how radio affected attitudes toward purchasing and politics. NBC sent a polite, perfunctory reply, but Paul Kesten, at CBS, weighed in with a three-page letter. He said that CBS was keenly interested in many of the same questions, and he would be eager to see any information Stanton could produce. Stanton responded "like a puppy who finally got attention," he recalled later.

In his thesis Stanton focused on the way networks measured the size of the audience by use of postcards and telephone calls. He catalogued the advantages and disadvantages of each approach. Something was needed, he reasoned, a mechanism to measure viewing patterns without bias or reliance on memory. So Stanton, the lifelong tinkerer, invented a device, a black box that he could plug into a radio—a crude antecedent of the Nielsen Audimeter that would become the primary measurement of broadcast audiences for more than four decades. Inside the box was a small motor, and connected to the motor was a moving waxed-paper tape and a stylus that would scratch across the tape to show which station was tuned in during given time periods.

He built fifty of the boxes and went door to door, persuading families to plug in the device. Every few days he would visit the families and quiz them on what they had heard the previous evening; then he unspooled the rolls and studied the tapes. He discovered that the memories of listeners were often faulty.

After two years of this research Stanton wrote to Kesten describing his results. Kesten was intrigued by the recording device and offered to pay Stanton's railway ticket to New York; instead, Stanton bundled Ruth into the Model A and headed for New York on an icy day in February, 1933, for his first face-to-face meeting at CBS.

Stanton took his black box to CBS headquarters and met with Kesten and two other executives. One of them, Ed Cohan, the chief engineer for CBS, was contemptuous. Kesten, however, was enthusiastic. He told Stanton to return to Columbus, conduct further experiments, and send in all his studies.

The two men kept in close contact. When Stanton sent Kesten his dissertation—an analysis of his work with the recording devices entitled "A Critique of Present Methods and a New Plan for Studying Radio Listening Behavior"—Kesten knew he must hire the young man. Without hesitation Stanton accepted an offer of $55 a week, and in October 1935 he joined CBS' two-man research department.

Frank Stanton brought a prestigious credential to CBS: the world of show business could boast few doctors of philosophy. Midway through the 1930s, when CBS was avidly upgrading its image, it was very useful to have a doctor in the house.

IN LATER years CBS would glory in its reputation as the "Tiffany Network." The public perceived CBS as an organization seeking excellence in every facet of its operation—from its programming to the decor of its offices. CBS' image was no accident. It was spurred by the government's efforts in the 1930s to tighten regulations on radio. Bill Paley and his key executives recognized that unless they created a medium that seemed above reproach, they faced strict regulations, restricted operations, and diminished profits.

Guided first by Edward Bernays, then Klauber and Kesten, Paley decorated the CBS schedule with superior educational, cultural, and news programs. Although these offerings constituted a tiny portion of CBS programming, the network publicized them aggressively— even deceptively—so that in the public's mind they overshadowed the endless hours of middlebrow and lowbrow entertainment.

Paley had learned his lessons from Bernays well. He knew how to maintain a façade of quality by announcing highbrow programs with great fanfare. While NBC spent far more money to develop its cultural programs—$2 million in 1932 versus CBS' $827,000—CBS was widely thought to be the leader. In the autumn of 1930 Paley signed the New York Philharmonic, then conducted by Arturo Toscanini, for a series of unsponsored broadcasts on Sunday afternoons. That same year Paley tried to lure the Metropolitan Opera for a series of Sunday concerts. But NBC executives convinced Met officials that their productions would be better served on NBC. The maneuver infuriated Paley: "It was a bitter blow and one that I resented for a long time." He could console himself, however, that his Philharmonic broadcasts cost him only $35,000 a year, while the Met cost NBC $191,000.

Paley's motivation for his cultural venture was not only to build CBS but to enhance William Paley. "There was a twofold impetus on Bill Paley for cultural programs," said William Fineshriber, who joined CBS' publicity department in the 1930s. "He had to show Washington a record for public service. But he also had a genuine desire not to be a cigar salesman."

Despite such high-profile ornaments as the Philharmonic, Paley was steadily reducing the number of classical music programs on CBS. By the mid-'30s they comprised only 10 percent of the unsponsored schedule, compared with 26 percent in 1930.

Nevertheless, because of CBS' superior promotional skills, Paley established himself as a public-spirited broadcaster; by 1935 he had emerged as the industry leader.

Throughout the late '30s NBC's David Sarnoff continually harangued his executives to match CBS' tactics. "We simply cannot ignore Columbia's consistent and persistent claims to leadership in network broadcasting," he complained to another NBC official in 1939. "We must meet it with facts and with skill."

CBS' aggressiveness eventually forced NBC to play by CBS rules. Just as in the early wars for affiliated stations and ratings, NBC joined CBS in hand-to-hand combat over programs and promotions. In 1937 NBC launched a campaign to sign Toscanini—who had left the New York Philharmonic in a dispute the year before—as conductor of a new NBC Symphony. Sarnoff was every bit as relentless in his pursuit of the maestro as Paley had been in courting such middlebrows as Major Bowes. Sarnoff's success brought NBC wide acclaim.

That summer the two networks found themselves in a pointless competition dubbed the Shakespeare War. CBS announced a series of Shakespeare plays starring Burgess Meredith, Walter Huston, and Edward G. Robinson; Sarnoff countered with a similar series showcasing John Barrymore.

With these highly publicized contests a personal rivalry between Paley and Sarnoff burst into public view. In Paley's early years at the network, NBC executives declined even to meet with the upstart broadcaster for fear of dignifying his enterprise. But with every Paley success Sarnoff grew more jealous not only of Paley's professional achievements but of his social advancement as well. Sarnoff had a bright and fashionable French wife, Lizette, yet he was uncomfortable in the world of high society, where Paley now moved so easily.

"He couldn't understand why women were so attracted to Bill," Frank Stanton said. "He couldn't understand why Bill spent so much time on social events. He didn't think Bill worked very hard, and he really resented the attention Bill got."

Although Sarnoff had the superior intellect, he was deliberate and methodical, and in his eyes everything Paley achieved came too easily. To Sarnoff, Paley was a child of privilege. Yet he also envied Paley's operation. Once, in the 1930s, Sarnoff even tried to lure Paley to run NBC—a tacit recognition of Paley's superiority in programming. But Paley spurned the offer quickly. Not only was it patronizing, it confirmed to Paley that he had the upper hand.

Sarnoff shared some of Paley's traits—an enormous ego, a hunger for publicity, a growing contempt for underlings. Yet Sarnoff lacked Paley's feel for popular culture. When his wife tuned in to *Amos 'n' Andy*, Sarnoff left the room. He had nothing but contempt for comedians. As one of his executives said, "His outlook on life was simply too serious to accommodate to popular taste."

Paley, on the other hand, had a genius for mass programming, mainly because it mirrored his own taste. He also understood that it was the path to big money.

More than anything, it galled Sarnoff—the broadcasting pioneer, the medium's idealist—that Paley was referred to as "radio's restless conscience." When *Time* magazine ran a cover story on the radio boom in the late '30s, a broadly grinning Paley, wearing a snappy glen-plaid suit, was the cover boy. In Sarnoff's view Paley was an opportunist who lacked any long-range vision for the industry. "He thought Paley had no concern with advancing broadcasting," said David Adams, an NBC executive and Sarnoff intimate.

Then on June 7, 1937, Paley brought CBS into the big-time corporate world: the company went public. CBS common stock was listed for the first time on the New York Stock Exchange. Before that date Paley's share of the company had dropped to 26.3 percent of the stock, which was worth $7.6 million by year's end, when the price was $17 per share (nearly $80 million in today's dollars). In 1940 he cashed in again, selling 100,000 of his shares to the public. He netted $2.4 million (approximately $22 million in today's dollars) and retained 20.3 percent of the company—half of his original stake of 41 percent.

This began a steady erosion in Paley's share of CBS—a course that would continue and that reflected Paley's anxieties about putting all his eggs in his own company's basket. Despite his confidence in CBS, he always had an underlying fear, perhaps even a superstition, that the network's prosperity could not last. He would willingly pare down his holdings gradually so that he could invest in other moneymaking schemes—real estate, oil wells—unencumbered by the public interest and other restraints. However, the decline in his stake had no effect on Paley's proprietary view of CBS. He continued to run the company as if he owned it entirely.

Paley frequently lamented taking the company public. He would say to friends and colleagues that CBS could have better served the public without accountability to shareholders and the constant pressure from Wall Street to increase profits. Yet he had ample resources to buy more stock and run the company privately. He chose not to. The fact was that Paley savored the barometer of Wall Street as a measure of his success. And even without shareholders he would doubtless have made the same bottom-line demands. "He had a rapacious attitude about money and profit that was second to none in his time," said a former high-level CBS executive.

CHAPTER 7

ALTHOUGH Frank Stanton and William Paley had only glancing contact during the '30s and early '40s, Stanton was making his mark and moving up fast. Since his arrival in the autumn of 1935, the self-effacing midwesterner had been building a power base from his tiny research department.

A diligent, energetic worker and a stickler for detail, Stanton was increasingly called on to buttress what one CBS executive called Paul Kesten's lightning intuitions. Stanton had his department churning out facts and figures on listeners' habits to salesmen trying to lure advertisers and choice affiliates from NBC. Advertisers were bemused by his elaborate stratifications of the audience according to age, sex, and education, but Stanton showed them better than anyone else how radio was reaching the groups that sponsors wanted to buy their products. Before long his research was used in almost every facet of CBS' business—to help attract advertisers and audiences, to select programs, and to help coax affiliates to switch from NBC to CBS. By 1938 he was research director with a staff of one hundred.

Stanton was not content to remain pigeonholed in the research department, however. He was terrifically ambitious and made himself indispensable throughout the company.

From the standpoint of the network's prosperity Stanton's biggest contribution was in the service he gave to advertisers. NBC had a great advantage in its stronger stations, better positions on the radio dial, and more popular programs. To attract advertisers, CBS had to overcome this edge. One way was to generate goodwill by providing advertising agencies and clients with information they could not obtain elsewhere.

"NBC was a sleepy organization," said Stanton. "If we wanted business, we had to give our all. In research I wouldn't let our people leave until the traffic died down. NBC closed at four thirty every day. We would work our hearts out. We got business that way."

At meetings Stanton occasionally caught a glimpse of Bill Paley, but he sensed that it was wise not to get too close. Stanton was content to work for Kesten, to learn what he could, to meet new challenges. In 1942 Stanton was named a vice president in charge not only of research but of advertising, sales promotion, public relations, building construction, operations and maintenance, and of supervising the seven radio stations owned and run by CBS. In seven years he had become one of CBS' handful of top executives. Still, he had never had a single one-on-one meeting with Paley. If he advanced further at CBS, Stanton knew that would change. But he was in no hurry.

CBS NEWS was organized more by fluke than by design. Back in 1931, CBS press releases had been emblazoned with the slogan, Columbia—the news network. Yet at that time CBS News had neither editors nor correspondents. Instead, a half-dozen public relations men rewrote wire copy for announcers who had been selected for the quality of their voices.

Behind the promotional façade, however, CBS was steadily increasing its commitment to news. In 1931, for example, CBS broadcast four hundred and fifteen special events as compared to two hundred and fifty-six on NBC's two networks. These stirrings were the first evidence of Ed Klauber's most important role at CBS.

"Ed Klauber was an intolerant man," said Edward R. Murrow many years later, "intolerant of deceit, deception, distortion, and double-talk. If there be standards of integrity, responsibility, and restraint in American radio news, Ed Klauber, more than any other man, is responsible for them." Klauber's presence at CBS doubtless prevented the network from following the banal model of the movie newsreels, filled with puffery and self-promotion, that Paley's friends in Hollywood were churning out.

In the early days Klauber and Paley gave commentators considerable leeway in expressing their opinions, which were usually liberal. Except for a brief three months, news commentator H. V. Kaltenborn had appeared on CBS since 1930 only in unsponsored time. Kaltenborn was allowed to endorse Roosevelt. In 1936 and 1937 he broadcast reports on the Spanish civil war that pointedly reflected his sympathies. Because the government of Spain was socialist, many American newspapers decried the government forces as the Red faction and termed the insurgents the Franco regime. Kaltenborn called the government Loyalists, and the Franco forces Fascists and rebels.

Paley's initial tolerance of partisanship on the air can be traced partly to the influence of Dorothy Paley, who frequently urged him to permit bolder news broadcasts. Like many liberals, she enthusiastically supported the Loyalists, and Paley respected her position.

But in time both Paley and Klauber grew uncomfortable with editorializing on the CBS airwaves. Too much controversy upset advertisers and affiliates, and created an overheated environment that weakened or obscured the commercials on which CBS depended. Objectivity and neutrality became the network's goals.

In December 1937 CBS unveiled its code of ethics, which had been developed by Klauber. CBS, Paley declared, would be "wholly, honestly, and militantly nonpartisan. We must never have an editorial page. We must never seek to maintain views of our own, and discussion must never be one-sided." Nor would sponsors be allowed to buy time for propaganda—except during election campaigns, when politicians could pay for time to present their views.

ONE of the great ironies of CBS is that what started as a public relations ploy by Paley and Klauber eventually became one of the most prestigious news organizations in the world. Paley created a full-scale news organization not out of idealism but as a pragmatic response to circumstances. The turning point came when Edward R. Murrow's broadcasts from blitz-ravaged London filled America's living rooms and helped bring the nation out of its isolationist mood.

To Bill Paley, Murrow was a magical combination of star quality and unquestioned integrity. His high principles tempered Paley's hard pragmatism. A lean six-footer, Murrow was as handsome as a matinee idol. He was also a heavy-smoking brooder, who periodically plunged into dark moods. Paley didn't like gloomy types, but Murrow was an exception. The eloquence of his voice, the glints of wit, his swashbuckling love of adventure, and his Savile Row style were irresistible to Paley. Murrow had dramatic flair, a quality Paley valued highly.

Murrow's first position at CBS was as director of Talks—the executive responsible for lining up prominent speakers to appear on the network. He signed on in September 1935, arriving only weeks before Frank Stanton, who would be his chief rival for Paley's favor. Like Stanton, Murrow was an ambitious overachiever in high school and college. After graduating from Washington State University, Murrow worked for the National Student Federation, which represented student governments around the country. In 1929 he helped organize a Student Federation program on CBS. It was as host of this program that Murrow first appeared on CBS, in September 1930.

Around the time of Murrow's arrival at CBS, demand for radio news began to increase as America nervously watched the Fascist dictators in Europe consolidate their power. In 1936, as Mussolini completed his invasion of Ethiopia, Hitler marched into the Rhineland and Franco launched his uprising in Spain. Observing the coming crisis in Europe, Klauber decided CBS needed someone in charge who would understand the significance of what was to come. He offered the job to Murrow in late February, 1939. Three months later Murrow was in London. He had just turned twenty-nine.

Paley did not at the time conceive of Murrow as a star broadcaster. The post in London was purely administrative. Murrow would continue to find politicians and other guests, and he would continue to organize broadcasts, using newspaper reporters as hosts on the air. Murrow hired William Shirer, a reporter for International News Service, to help him make the arrangements. But as Hitler tightened his grip in the autumn of 1937 Murrow and Shirer became increasingly frustrated that they were unable to broadcast on CBS themselves. Shirer later wrote that Paley believed "for us to do the reporting ourselves would be to commit CBS editorially."

However, events forced CBS into making a commitment to full-fledged news broadcasting. Throughout the early months of 1938 Hitler brought increasing pressure on the leaders of Austria to submit to Germany. Shirer correctly saw that if Hitler achieved annexation of his native land, it would be the end of Austria for the duration of the Third Reich. By now stationed in Vienna, Shirer had inside information on Hitler's machinations, which he tried repeatedly to get on the air. Each time he was rebuffed.

On March 11, 1938, the German army marched into Austria. Shirer called Murrow from Vienna to tell him that "the opposing team has just crossed the goal line." Max Jordan, NBC's man in Vienna, was out of the country, so Shirer knew he had a shot at the only eyewitness report of the event. He raced to London, while Murrow flew to Vienna to follow up on the story. This time CBS agreed to give Shirer some time. His account, broadcast from London late on Saturday night, March 12, marked the first time a CBS News staff member was allowed on the air with a report from the field.

In the following hours Paul White, head of CBS' corps of news reporters, and his small staff in New York improvised wildly to cover the story. There was no studio for news broadcasting at CBS, only a suite of offices on the seventeenth floor for the Special Events and Talks staff. White ordered a makeshift studio in the office next door by having blankets tacked to the walls for soundproofing. Newspaper reporters in Europe were contacted by CBS for periodic updates.

Meanwhile, NBC's Max Jordan had rushed back to Vienna, where he was scooping CBS with on-the-scene stories. Murrow was unable to secure a facility in the city to transmit his own report.

In bed with a fever back in New York, Paley was frantic that CBS was being trounced by NBC so conspicuously. He concluded that CBS needed a way to "not only get the news but dramatize it." At that moment, as he has recounted many times, "out of necessity and competition I invented the *World News Roundup*"—the model for broadcast newscasts for decades to come. By his recollection Paley called Klauber at CBS headquarters to describe his vision of a series of reports from European capitals, switching quickly from one to the next. But Robert Trout, CBS' main news announcer at the time, recalled that the idea for the roundup emerged from an impromptu seventeenth-floor discussion on Sunday morning, March 13.

Whether or not Paley deserves the credit for thinking of it, he seized on the idea. That Sunday night, March 13, at eight p.m., Trout introduced the first roundup, with live reports from Murrow in Vienna, Shirer in London, and newspaper correspondents moonlighting as CBS broadcasters in Paris and Berlin. The broadcast made a huge splash. Paley was elated. He asked for a second roundup two days later and still more after that. But he was unwilling at that stage to commit to a regular, much less a daily, roundup.

In September 1938 the Nazis partitioned Czechoslovakia. This time

Kaltenborn was at the anchor desk in New York. Before a microphone in CBS' studio 9 he stitched together nearly two hundred reports from European capitals for eighteen straight days. American listeners were riveted. Murrow and Shirer seeped into the national consciousness with their on-scene coverage. Murrow emerged from his thirty-five broadcasts during the Munich crisis as a bona fide broadcaster.

Suddenly news was in demand. Listeners couldn't get enough of it. Advertisers wanted to be identified with it. Paley authorized Klauber and Paul White in New York and Murrow overseas to build a staff capable of covering the widening story. They turned to eloquent, sophisticated newspaper writers. Eric Sevareid, twenty-six years old, was an editor at both United Press and the Paris edition of the New York *Herald Tribune*. Elmer Davis, a free-lance writer, and Charles Collingwood and Howard K. Smith, of United Press, had all been Rhodes scholars. If these men did not have the necessary sonority for radio, they would learn. Most of them emulated Murrow's calm and dignified delivery and became known as Murrow's Boys.

In early 1939 the *World News Roundup*, appearing twice daily by then, acquired its first sponsor. "From now on we will be sponsored by Sinclair Oil," Murrow announced to his troops. "You will get seventy-five dollars each time we are on the air." Replied Sevareid, "Ed, we are recording this great human story. Is this right to take money from this oil company?" There was a moment of abashed silence. Then Murrow said, "You'll get used to it."

The CBS newsmen in London were helped by the fact that the nighttime bombings coincided with CBS' live broadcasts at one a.m. London time. Murrow created indelible portraits of war for his listeners. He was known for his theatrical touches—the fat pause in his introductory "This . . . is London," the microphones placed at the feet of Londoners as they descended into air-raid shelters. Masterful at evoking a mood, he could analyze incisively as well.

At CBS, news was now as lucrative as it was prestigious, and Paley became its most ardent booster. He permitted newscasts to be scheduled across the board at the same time each day, while newscasts on NBC suffered from poor time periods and erratic scheduling. "He had a real instinct for it," said Dorothy Paley. "The correspondents were really stimulated and encouraged by him. He talked about it a lot. He was excited about it. It was very important to him."

DOROTHY PALEY HAD NO IDEA OF her husband's unfaithfulness. He had strayed early in their marriage, indulging his old taste for show girls. Other flings followed. But Bill's peccadilloes weren't the only symptom of trouble ahead. Other hairline cracks were showing in the Paley marriage. When Dorothy corrected him in public, she was brisk and impatient, not gentle. Sarcasm had crept into her manner.

Dorothy had grown resentful of her husband's need to control virtually every aspect of their relationship. All decisions about the household had to be his. He also dictated their friendships; whoever displeased him was banished. For instance, Paley banned the Swopes after he had a falling out with Herbert. Not only did Paley prohibit them from visiting Kiluna, he instructed Dorothy to cut off Maggie, one of her closest friends.

Dorothy's discovery that she was unable to have children disappointed both Paleys and exacerbated the tension between them. In 1938 they adopted a newborn boy named Jeffrey and a year later an infant girl named Hilary. Paley was an indifferent father. Dorothy was not overwhelmingly maternal. She tended to be severe and held to the prevailing arm's-length approach to child rearing.

While Dorothy catered to Paley and ran her various households exquisitely, she was not quite attentive enough. "I never behaved as if the world revolved around him," she said. Paley needed a woman who was slavishly devoted and who worked constantly to enhance him.

Dorothy learned the truth about her husband's philandering in the most publicly humiliating fashion. On March 8, 1940, a woman known as Johanna Stoddard committed suicide by leaping from the seventeenth floor of the Book-Cadillac Hotel, in Detroit. Behind her she left $700 in cash and checks, fragments of romantic poetry, and costly gowns strewn on the bed. On the table a solitaire game showed the ace of spades—sometimes known as death's card—placed prominently in the center. A florist's card read, "You're still lovely." On one wall she had scrawled in red letters four inches high EXIT SMILING. There was also a note:

Dearest Bill,

I just wanted to thank you for your kindness. You know how things were with me. I may have said things in desperation that I didn't mean. I hope you do not hate me, and, I mean, I'm sorry. I know you will understand and forgive me. I'm not well. My lungs are in a precarious state, where I have to be so careful.

I still love you, but I guess you were right. I only fought so hard because my heart hurt so. You've been very white about everything. I can only hope to emulate you and try to do something good with my life. I am very tired.

Goodbye darling.

Johanna

It was addressed to William S. Paley, of New York, president of the Columbia Broadcasting Company.

When news of the suicide reached New York that day, Paley was distraught. First he went home to Dorothy and confessed: Johanna Stoddard had presented herself as an aspiring actress. They had had a brief affair, which she had tried to keep going despite his rebuffs.

Her real name (which Paley did not know) was Geraldine Kenyon Bourque. She had left her husband, an autoworker in Pontiac, Michigan, as well as an infant daughter, in 1931. Bill "was dreadfully upset, first because his unfaithfulness had been revealed and second that it was a scandal," Dorothy recalled. "He didn't have any feeling about her, but he did feel bad."

The CBS public relations machinery moved into high gear. Klauber spent the day composing a cover story for the press. In a statement that appeared the next day in newspapers across the country, Paley admitted to having met the woman a year earlier in a restaurant with a group of people. He said she had later written to him to say she had tuberculosis and needed help finding a job as an entertainer. He made a point of saying that he and Dorothy had talked to her several times, "trying to straighten her out, but she became more mentally disturbed all the time. Finally she began to write letters to me, declaring that she had developed an emotional attachment for me."

Dorothy's trust was shattered. So she did some detective work and discovered that Paley was a compulsive womanizer. "I don't know how tortured she was about his roving eye, but there was plenty of it," said Irene Selznick. "She covered up, and he covered up. Dorothy tried to take a detached view, reasoning that his philandering was a symptom of his insecurity. Each new conquest, she thought, reaffirmed his attractiveness and desirability."

She continued to cling to their marriage, difficult though it was. The Paleys never had any public spats. Nor did Dorothy ever contemplate seeking a divorce. "I did confront him on a couple of occasions," Dorothy said. "I didn't like what he was doing, but I also recognized the inevitability in him. He could never be different."

CHAPTER 8

WILLIAM Paley, the man most associated with the power and glitter of television, at first mistrusted the new medium of picture and sound. He failed to grasp its potential and uses, and actively obstructed its development. Television appeared as a relentless expense that would end by draining attention and resources from radio, his true love. If it had not been for the Paramount merger, Paley's competition with Sarnoff, and the prodding of several executives, CBS might have stayed out of television altogether.

But the Paramount connection forced Paley to come to grips with television. A main reason for Paramount's interest in CBS was to control the industry as it emerged from its experimental stage. To moguls such as Adolph Zukor television in the home seemed as threatening as radio. But if television could be used by movie theaters, it might prove useful to the studios.

Paley's first pronouncements took this line: "It's hard to tell just how television will be handled." Sarnoff, on the other hand, understood television. As early as 1923 he had informed his superiors at Marconi that television would be "the ultimate and greatest step in mass communications." At his urging, in 1928 RCA and NBC received a government permit for the first experimental television station in New York. With the futuristic call letters W2XBS, the station went on the air in July 1930 showing a fuzzy picture of Felix the Cat.

Sarnoff was dissatisfied with the technology, which relied on a whirling mechanical disc that frequently malfunctioned. He committed $1 million from NBC's radio earnings to develop an all-electronic television system. When the new technology was ready, in 1936, NBC put on a public demonstration, using studios in the RCA Building and a powerful transmitter atop the Empire State Building.

CBS' first experimental station, W2XAB, went on the air Tuesday,

July 21, 1931, a year after NBC's first television broadcast. CBS' inaugural variety show ran from ten fifteen to eleven that night. New York mayor Jimmy Walker made the opening remarks, Kate Smith sang "When the Moon Comes over the Mountain," and George Gershwin performed several of his famous songs. Significantly, Bill Paley was vacationing in Venice at the time.

Over the next two years CBS telecast programs to approximately seventy-five hundred crude television sets in the New York metropolitan area. But in February 1933 CBS discontinued its experimental effort. Paley decided to sit on the sidelines until it was clear that Sarnoff's promise of an electronic system could be fulfilled, which wouldn't happen until 1936.

All through the '30s Paley made his moves in television solely to keep pace with his rival across the street. "Sarnoff, at RCA, had his wary eye glued to the television future and grandly predicted moving pictures in every home; Paley was keeping his eye on Sarnoff," said Peter Goldmark, the brilliant Hungarian inventor hired in 1935 by Paul Kesten to develop television at CBS. Kesten, nicknamed "vice president for the future" by his CBS colleagues, was eager to revitalize

Left, Paley with Edward R. Murrow (left) and Frank Stanton (right). Paley "at first mistrusted the new medium" of television. Murrow would go on to host the acclaimed TV series *See It Now.*

Right, Paley with another CBS radio star, Lucille Ball, who also made a successful switch to television in the early '50s the network's interest in the medium. But Paley, Goldmark knew, "had mixed feelings about television." Only later did Goldmark learn that it was Kesten who "ultimately helped convince Paley to keep the company in television."

In July 1937 Paley decided to build his own new television transmitter. His only instruction was that it was to be "bigger and better than RCA's" and that it was to top the magnificent art deco spire of the Chrysler Building. He also ordered construction of a television studio in Grand Central station. Still, Paley and most of his executives remained skeptical of television's moneymaking potential.

Sarnoff forged ahead. In April 1939 NBC began a regular program service with a telecast of President Franklin D. Roosevelt opening the New York World's Fair, where new television sets, with screens ranging from five to twelve inches across, were on display at RCA's Hall of Television. Every day visitors crowded around the sets to watch NBC's eclectic mix of programs transmitted to the fairgrounds from its studio in the RCA Building: operas, cartoons, travelogues, even live pictures of baseball games and skaters at Rockefeller Center. Consumers began buying RCA sets, richly priced from $200 to $600 ($1900 to $5600 in today's dollars). Six months later CBS launched regular broadcasts when its transmitter was completed. There were still fewer than ten thousand television sets in the New York City area.

To cut costs, CBS concentrated on showing films instead of live programs. But among the fifteen hours transmitted each week was a scattering of programs featuring news, special events, documentaries, and sports. By the early 1940s some thirty staffers at CBS were at work on television. "Before the war we did the minimum to keep our television license," recalled Frank Stanton. "NBC was way ahead of us. Sarnoff was the visionary. He had the guts."

In 1941 the Federal Communications Commission (FCC) permitted the sale of advertising time on television. By then, even Paley grudgingly recognized the commercial possibilities of television.

World War II abruptly halted television's progress. Manufacture of sets was suspended to ensure that electronic components could be used for national defense. Paley, who was still fearful that television would kill radio, was relieved. In 1928 Paley had seized on radio because he grasped its commercial power when the La Palina program pushed cigar sales to new heights. The CBS radio network had a shape that he could mold to suit his purpose. But television was more complicated, and its application was difficult to imagine for a man who always demanded concrete proof that something would work. Like the movie men, Paley could not see beyond the obvious inferiority of the television picture to the theatrical screen.

David Sarnoff was an electronics man. He knew that the technology was at hand to make television a fixture in America's living rooms. Later he would bitterly resent the adulation and power that Paley derived from television. Paley was just plain lucky. When the time was right, he had both a system in place—a prosperous radio network— and a farsighted executive in Frank Stanton that together made it possible for him to rush into television.

On September 3, 1939, England and France declared war on Germany. The White House warned that radio was a "rookie" in handling war stories and must behave as a "good child." This patronizing yet ominous warning prompted Paley, Sarnoff, and their chief executives to meet to discuss the networks' role in wartime.

After the meeting Klauber issued a statement outlining CBS' policies on war coverage. The United States was, of course, still a neutral country. Klauber emphasized the need for objectivity, fairness, and factual accuracy. Newscasters, he said, should read calmly, without showing emotion or prejudice. The task of news analysts would be "to help the listener to understand, to weigh, and to judge, but not do the judging for him."

Kaltenborn, however, was incapable of curbing his outrage over Hitler. Kaltenborn's excesses worried Paley, although the commentator's sponsor, the Pure Oil Company, had few complaints. Pure Oil's sales were booming as a result of its association on radio with Kaltenborn, who had risen to folk-hero status. Yet late in 1939 CBS told Pure Oil that there was no longer broadcast time available during the evening, when male listeners likely to buy the company's products would be tuning in. CBS was relieved when Pure Oil began negotiating with NBC. In April 1940 Kaltenborn shifted networks.

Paley was less inclined to curb Murrow than he was other commentators. Murrow had begun to feel strongly that the United States should join the battle in Europe. In a March 9, 1941, broadcast he was explicit:

"The course of Anglo-American relations will be smooth on the surface, but many people over here will express regret that they believe America is making the same mistakes that Britain made. For you must understand that the idea of America being more help as a nonbelligerent than as a fighting ally has been discarded even by those who advanced it originally."

Despite Murrow's undisguised effort to influence opinion, Paley issued no rebuke, because Murrow was his fair-haired boy. What is more, opinion had begun to shift toward intervention, at least among the nation's movers and shakers along the Eastern Seaboard. Murrow's reports helped turn the broader American public in that direction. By December 1941, when Murrow was honored by Paley at a star-studded formal dinner at The Waldorf-Astoria hotel, in New York City, the CBS commentator's views were so widely accepted that he could comfortably declare that the war in Europe would be decided "along the banks of the Potomac." It was already clear that Murrow's image as a man of conscience honored CBS and Paley.

Barely a week later the Japanese bombed Pearl Harbor. America's declaration of war resulted in tensions over commentary at CBS. Top network executives joined the war effort, enlisting the services of CBS personnel to produce government programs. Inevitably the line between authorized and forbidden opinion became blurred.

Throughout this period, when Paley was often subjected to public criticism over the definition of editorial opinion, Klauber continued to dedicate himself completely to Paley and CBS. But Paley had come to begrudge Klauber, who had become overbearing. Paley began listening more closely to complaints that Klauber's coldness and intimidation were undermining morale. "You've got to get rid of Klauber," said Paley's attorney, Ralph Colin. "He's evil." Paul Kesten made no secret of detesting Klauber either. For more than a decade Klauber and Kesten had been locked in a power struggle over who would run CBS under Paley.

By 1942 Kesten prevailed over Klauber at last. That March, Paley quietly stripped Klauber of his executive vice president's stripes, appointed him to the meaningless post of chairman of the executive committee of the board of directors, and made Kesten first general manager of CBS. A year and a half later, without consulting the board of directors, Paley called Klauber, then fifty-six, to his office late one August afternoon and fired him. After Klauber left, Paley permanently sealed the door connecting their two offices.

The day Paley gave him notice, Klauber invited Frank Stanton to his apartment. As the two men talked, Klauber's eyes filled with tears. "I gave my life to Bill," he said with a tremor in his voice, "and he never once invited me across the threshold."

By THE beginning of 1942 the radio networks began to operate under a policy of wartime censorship. CBS rarely needed to submit a script to the Office of Censorship; the network simply incorporated various government restrictions into its news broadcasts—bans on weather reports, troop movements, war production, and casualties.

To see how these rules were working in the field, Paley decided to spend a month in London—without Dorothy—in August 1942. Paley was met at Heathrow Airport by Randolph Churchill, who swept him into London for dinner with his stunning wife, Pamela. The daughter of a minor English peer, the eleventh Lord Digby, Pamela Churchill (whose second and third husbands would be theatrical producer Leland Hayward and Averell Harriman) was already a legend at twenty-one. She had dark auburn hair, deep sapphire eyes, a shapely figure, and creamy skin. Men were bewitched by her. Unhappily married for less than three years, she and Randolph Churchill had been leading separate lives since the birth of their son, Winston II, in December 1940. For Bill Paley the evening was the beginning of a long friendship with Pamela that would include one brief passionate interlude.

After dinner the Churchills took Paley to a nightclub, where they encountered Jock Whitney, Paley's neighbor in Manhasset, who was an air force captain by then. Whitney and Paley walked back together through the dark London streets to their hotel. Listening to Whitney talk that night, Paley felt that as a civilian he was left out.

The next morning Paley was no longer the kid with his nose pressed against the glass. Harry Butcher—a former CBS lobbyist, now an aide to Dwight Eisenhower, Supreme Commander of the Allied Expeditionary Force—invited Paley for lunch with the general.

Their talk in Ike's apartment at the Dorchester Hotel was entirely casual. But Paley came away deeply impressed with the general. "He was one of the most effective men I had ever known in small groups," Paley said later. Eisenhower, in turn, understood how to ingratiate himself with Paley, giving the CBS chief a car and driver and papers that enabled him to travel freely throughout England.

For the next three weeks Ed Murrow, Paley's star newsman, whirled his boss through London for breakfast, lunch, and dinner with various dignitaries. Murrow put on a big luncheon for Paley at The Savoy and brought him around to his apartment on Hallam Street to converse with "the boys," his talented cadre of correspondents.

Inevitably, Paley and Murrow drew together. The clear-cut nature of World War II made the ideal connection. Murrow and Paley could sit comfortably on the same side of an issue when the fascism and anti-Semitism of Hitler and Mussolini were so loathsome. They could unite in CBS' role as the beacon for all right-thinking citizens.

In ordinary circumstances Murrow would have had little interest in a man so steeped in the values of business as Bill Paley. Murrow had an empathy for the impoverished that Paley admired only up to a point. But during these years Paley needed Murrow, and he brought all his charm to bear on furthering their friendship.

On the day in September when Paley was due to leave England, Paley had one more quick meeting with Eisenhower. The general took the opportunity to underscore the importance of radio in shaping public opinion to back up the United States Army. Afterwards Paley confided to Butcher that he had decided to enlist, "no matter how important other people think the broadcasting business."

Paley knew that he could perform a valuable service by heeding Eisenhower's plea and directing wartime broadcasting at CBS. He did in fact redouble the network's propaganda activities on his return. But his visit to London had convinced him that his service would only be properly recognized if he enlisted.

"Don't be an idiot," Dorothy said when Paley revealed his plan. "You are not a common soldier. There are other things in which you have expertise." Paley took his wife's advice and sought a post befitting his position. He called on his old friend playwright Robert Sherwood, who now headed international operations for the Office of War Information (OWI). Nearly a year later, in the summer of 1943, Sherwood created an enticing position: consultant to the psychological warfare branch of the Office of War Information. Paley would wear the uniform of honorary colonel and be sent to Algiers, Eisenhower's headquarters for his North African campaign and for the planned invasion of Italy. Paley was due in Algiers in mid-November.

With only a few months to prepare, Paley determined that he would leave CBS in the hands of Paul Kesten. Indeed, it had been this need for haste that had prompted the abrupt firing of Klauber that August. He then dived into preparing for his departure.

Paley was not subjected to boot camp with ordinary GIs. For one week in November, 1943, he trained at the sprawling Long Island estate where the OWI had set up its indoctrination school. There Paley pursued courses on pamphleteering, intelligence gathering, and short-wave receiving, along with gentle drills in muscle building. By the time he finished, a gold dog tag from Cartier and bespoke uniforms from London were ready.

CHAPTER 9

PALEY was intrigued by what he called the "lush, strange charm" of Algiers. He shared a lovely home on the outskirts of the city with C. D. Jackson, a Time-Life executive serving as American director of OWI in Algiers; and Edward W. Barrett, editor of *Newsweek,* who was Jackson's deputy. An Arab boy arranged for a barber to visit each morning to shave the men; a Frenchwoman known as Madame bought their groceries and prepared their meals.

At OWI headquarters, Paley occupied a makeshift office with a crate as a desk and boxes for filing cabinets. Jackson assigned him to help establish a radio network in Italy to transmit broadcasts from Armed Forces Radio. The purpose of the network was to lure Italian listeners with entertaining programs interspersed with propaganda.

As in his first days at United Independent Broadcasters, in New York, Paley had a reputation to overcome. This time he was a big shot, who was expected to chafe under orders. But as before, Paley surprised them all. At forty-two he took on the air of an unassuming young man. His colleagues were impressed by his eagerness, by how quickly he caught on to any task he was assigned, and by his way of discreetly pushing to get a job done.

In late January, 1944, Paley arranged for a transfer to London, where Eisenhower was moving his headquarters. There Paley joined the psychological warfare group that would help prepare for Operation Overlord, the planned invasion of France across the English Channel. His new position would be chief of broadcasting within the Psychological Warfare Division of the Supreme Headquarters, Allied Expeditionary Force (SHAEF).

Shortly after Paley's arrival in England a young officer named Guy Della Cioppa appeared in his suite at Claridge's Hotel to brief him on Overlord. Della Cioppa carried secret documents—maps of planned landings at Omaha and Utah beaches, as well as the phony landings designed to deceive the Germans—which he spread out on the floor. Paley nearly overwhelmed him with questions. Several weeks later Della Cioppa was named chief of tactical warfare for radio operations for the First Army, reporting to Paley.

Paley's first two principal tasks in London were to supervise broadcasts to Germany and occupied European countries and to prepare radio messages to accompany the Allied invasion of France on D-day. He was involved in both "black" and "white" propaganda that accompanied the advancing Allied armies.

Black propaganda was information sent out under false pretenses: misrepresented facts and outright lies. It was transmitted by a phony German radio station located in a secret compound outside London. At first the station broadcast accurate information to gain the confidence of the Germans. The information came from intelligence operations and often got on the air before bona fide German stations broadcast it. Announcers on the phony station built up their credibility by reading letters to loved ones seized from captured German soldiers. Only after the invasion, when battle action disrupted communications, would the bogus German station start to broadcast lies.

No stranger to the art of shading truth, Paley was fascinated by black propaganda. He worked closely with Richard Crossman, a brilliant Englishman who would later serve as a member of Parliament and editor of the *New Statesman.*

"One of the basic elements in all successful propaganda is the skillful use of the truth," Paley recalled. "If your listener ever catches you in a lie, you are ruined." Paley discovered that "the truth was useless if it was not believable. An Allied leaflet early in the war told German soldiers about the good conditions in American prisoner-of-war camps. Although it was entirely truthful, the Germans found it preposterous."

As D-day approached, Eisenhower realized he needed more help in planning for radio broadcasting. He asked for the best communications expert in America, and the War Department summoned David Sarnoff to Europe. Sarnoff arrived in London on March 20, 1944—a full two months after Paley—and checked into a fine suite at Claridge's, the elegant Mayfair hotel that accommodated so many American officers it became known as Little America. His pleasure in his new surroundings disappeared, however, when he heard that the suite's previous occupant had been Paley, who had moved into an even more impressive one in the same hotel. Still, Sarnoff could take comfort in knowing he was a genuine colonel, while Paley was only a civilian working as an "assimilated" colonel.

"Colonel" Paley adored the camaraderie he found in London, and once he had all his staff in place, he played more and worked less. Paley expanded his circle of friends among the English aristocracy, New York socialites, and American army brass circulating through London. New acquaintances were enchanted by him. "He was easy, warm, full of energy and curiosity," recalled Simon Michael Bessie, who was also attached to the Psychological Warfare Division.

London was "a romantic place, very romantic," Paley confessed years later. "It was sort of like the normal, conventional morals of the time were just turned on their ear because of the urgency. The normal barriers, you know, to having an affair with somebody were thrown to the four winds."

For someone as powerful and wealthy as Paley, it was hard to know where to begin the amorous adventures. But an obvious start in those days was with Pamela Churchill, by then all of twenty-four years old. Randolph, from whom she was separated, was serving with the British army, leaving her free to work her charms on a succession of American men. She set up a salon in London, where she entertained generals, prominent journalists, politicians, and other dignitaries.

Paley was doubtless as keen on seducing Pamela as she was eager to add him to her list of conquests. They had a short-lived affair that was more convenient than romantic, and it readily settled into a long-standing relationship of mutual admiration.

After Paley, Pamela Churchill flitted to Ed Murrow. Rather than suffer the humiliation, Janet Murrow returned to America. Her coolness, coupled with her husband's guilty conscience, eventually brought the Murrows back together—a profound defeat for Pamela, who was in love with the dashing CBS correspondent.

Paley, meanwhile, had hooked up with Edwina Mountbatten, whose husband, Louis, was in Burma as Supreme Allied Commander in Southeast Asia. Spirited and independent, Edwina presided over a salon that surpassed Pamela Churchill's gatherings in importance. Because of Mountbatten's position, matters of state were routinely discussed by Edwina's guests, who included Winston Churchill, Max Beaverbrook, and Dwight Eisenhower. The well-connected Paley, by now involved in the Overlord mission, fit in perfectly. It is easy to see how a fling with Edwina would appeal to Paley. Like Paley, she was hedonistic and promiscuous; she threw herself into pleasure.

Paley and Edwina were frequently seen together, often over dinner in the fashionable Mayfair section of London. Given Paley's high profile and the important position of Edwina's husband, some high-level members of the British government finally told her that the affair was getting too well known. They broke it off, but Paley still maintained an affection for her; later, after returning to the United States, he would send her lipstick, perfume, and other luxury items.

In mid-June, a few weeks after D-day, Paley went to France with a psychological warfare contingent. There he learned that OWI needed additional loudspeakers to call German troops to surrender. He was sent to Washington, D.C., to secure the equipment.

While stateside that summer of 1944, Paley traveled home to New York. His mission, as he later recounted it, was to ask Dorothy for a divorce. Paley recalled that when he broached the subject with Dorothy, she would not agree.

By Dorothy's account, her husband did not ask her for a divorce during his three-week visit that summer, but it was obvious to her that he was in an agitated state. "He was depressed," she recalled. "He said, 'I'm not sure I want to go back to CBS.' I said, 'This is not the time to make a decision. You are going back to England.'"

PALEY's life was at loose ends when he returned to London that August. From there he traveled to Paris, the new headquarters for psychological warfare, where he took a suite at the George V Hotel.

He had even greater responsibilities in Paris than in London. He continued to supervise black propaganda, which by then was being broadcast from the powerful transmitter of Radio Luxembourg, liberated by the Allies in September 1944. And he was put in charge of drawing up guidelines for German newspapers, magazines, radio, book publishing, film, theater, and concerts after the anticipated Nazi surrender.

Paley's unit worked sixteen-to-eighteen-hour days preparing the German Information Services Manual. He delegated the main job of assembling the chapters to two aides, Guy Della Cioppa and John Minary, an attorney from Chicago with the rank of captain. Minary impressed Paley with his care in drafting documents and his understanding of the political implications of the words he was attributing to Paley. He was bright, with a sense of humor, endless patience, discretion, intense loyalty, and self-effacement to the point of invisibility. Here was a man, Paley realized, with the requisite qualities to be his majordomo after the war. In fact, for four decades Minary would devote his life to serving Paley's interests.

By mid-March, 1945, the manual had been approved. Around the same time, Paley was offered a colonel's commission. By all appearances he was delighted with his new status. However, his mood fell short of complete satisfaction: David Sarnoff had been commissioned a brigadier general the previous December.

As the German troops retreated, the psychological warfare contingent pushed into Germany. On V-E Day, Paley was in a small hotel in Heidelberg with Richard Crossman. They cooled a bottle of wine under a water tap and drank to the victory. The next day, May 9, 1945, sobered them beyond their worst imagining when they reached the Dachau concentration camp shortly after it was liberated.

The truth about the camps was well known by then. Murrow's broadcasts from Buchenwald the previous month had described the horrors in stomach-wrenching detail. But witnessing it firsthand was for Paley a "terrible trauma." At the crematorium he saw some two hundred bodies "piled up like garbage." Years later he vividly described seeing an SS officer try to escape and watching a young American army captain hand his pistol to a camp survivor. The survivor raised his thin arm but could not fire the gun, so the captain took it back and executed the SS man. "I had seven people, at least, die right in front of me while they were walking to get some food," Paley said. "You couldn't describe it. It was awful."

Not long afterwards the Psychological Warfare Division settled into a school compound in Bad Homburg, outside Frankfurt. Although Paley spoke no German, he had enormous control over the populace as supervisor of the denazification of all German media. "I was in charge of every newspaper, magazine, radio station, and theater in occupied Germany," he said. "The Germans were so hungry for information and entertainment that my empire made a fortune for the army. It was the most exciting period of my life as we weeded the Nazis out of the communications media, pumped in fresh democratic ideas and personnel, and generally remade the German mind until we felt they could take over their communications themselves."

The power infected Paley; it fueled him to work harder than ever. "He was a prodigious worker," said his junior officer, Phillips Davison. "He was there all the time. I rarely went to his office and didn't find him. He wasn't a playboy at all in this period, as he was before."

WORLD War II left Paley feeling that "life had never been so exciting and immediate and never would be again." As he neared the end of his wartime rite of passage, he resolved to change the way he worked and lived. Because of his network's role in reporting the war— particularly through the words of Edward R. Murrow—Paley had been lionized as never before, and he intended to build on that prestige. The upper-class English way of life deeply impressed him. He had been able to examine it at close range during his stint in London. Now he wished to perfect the genteel, graceful style for himself. His life would be more rarefied and subtle, but less stimulating than in prewar years. And Dorothy, whose challenging ways had proved too vexing, would have to go.

DOROTHY Paley was shocked by her husband's behavior when she welcomed him home in September 1945. "He had always had a tic, but it was exaggerated to an extraordinary degree," she recalled. "He was extremely depressed. He just sat and made faces. He was a very different person." His two children, Jeffrey and Hilary, by then seven and six, hadn't seen their father for nearly two years. They were at once fascinated and frightened by the way his face moved, and rapidly learned that the violent twitch meant tension, which could burst into anger. When Dorothy consulted a doctor for advice, he suggested that she prod her husband to get out among his friends. So the Paleys went through the motions of a social life.

But only days later Paley was off to Colorado Springs, where he set out to reshape his life in solitude. The first step, he decided, would be to insist on a divorce from Dorothy. With that decided, he went to California to visit David Selznick, his closest friend. Selznick had separated from his wife, Irene, just a few weeks earlier.

Selznick's zest bolstered Paley. Here was a kindred spirit who had made the same decision about his personal life. The two men laughed and caroused. Once again Paley felt happy. He left California with his resolve strengthened.

Back in New York, he pulled himself together and told Dorothy he no longer wanted to be married. Dorothy refused to free him, and the Paleys entered a stalemate. Behind closed doors they argued, but they maintained a polite façade for company.

After several weeks Paley finally left. He took an apartment at the St. Regis and avidly pursued his pleasures—squiring show girls and socialites.

But behind the vivacity Paley was depressed and distracted. His wartime aide, Guy Della Cioppa, who had joined him at CBS, recalled his boss's moodiness: "He was a lonely man then. He would ask me occasionally to go to dinner with him. For the first six months after he was back, my impression of him was disintegration. He didn't seem to have the old spirit. He was faced with problems at CBS. And he was beginning to worry about television heavily."

While abroad, Paley had decided to permit Paul Kesten, by then forty-seven years old, to continue running the business day to day. Kesten would be promoted from executive vice president to president, and Paley, at age forty-four, would become chairman, thus removing himself from the daily headaches.

On the very day of his return to CBS from Europe, September 4, 1945, Paley gave Kesten the news. To Paley's astonishment Kesten not only turned him down, he wanted to leave CBS. Paley ascribed Kesten's response to health problems. Paley later recalled that Kesten "just shook his head and said, 'I'm not up to it, but I have someone who I think is.' "

In fact, in addition to his arthritis, Kesten had the beginnings of emphysema, which he concealed from everyone. But his health was a minor element in his thinking. Kesten had decided he could no longer work with Paley. Their views of the company's future were too much at odds.

Kesten had been spoiled by his wartime tenure. He had been running CBS with the assistance of Frank Stanton. The two executives had taken radio advertising to new highs; fully two thirds of the network's time was sold commercially, compared with one third before the war. They had also developed a strong plan for television, which they recognized would be even more lucrative than radio.

Shortly after V-E Day, Kesten had sent Paley a fifteen-page letter outlining his vision. CBS, he said, should abandon mass programming and concentrate instead on catering to an elite audience of highly educated and cultivated listeners. Kesten's plan was profoundly pragmatic, since he knew that NBC would maintain the edge in pursuing the mass audience because its stations could reach so many more listeners.

Paley, however, thought Kesten's plan amounted to "giving up the fight against NBC." Anything less than winning the largest audience represented defeatism to Paley. His own plan was a scheme based on control of talent and programming. In the summer of 1945 he had sent Kesten a handwritten letter from Germany that he began while riding in the military command car. The "command car letter" laid out the broad outlines of his principles for programming.

Instead of buying programs produced by advertising agencies—as CBS had done before the war—the network would develop the programs on its own. This would require substantial financing, but Paley felt that the payoff would give CBS a new kind of stability by preventing the defections that had thwarted his success before the war. As with many of Paley's ideas, it was simple yet revolutionary.

According to Frank Stanton, Paley's rebuff of Kesten's scheme must have figured in Kesten's refusal of the CBS presidency. "It was the kind of thing that would have cut him deeply," said Stanton, "although he never mentioned that as a reason he didn't want to stay on."

With Kesten out of the running, Paley offered the job to Frank Stanton. He accepted, and at the CBS board meeting in early January, 1946, he was officially named president of CBS.

CHAPTER 10

MRS. MORTIMER JR. HEADS CHOICE OF TEN BEST DRESSED WOMEN, announced the New York *Daily News* on January 21, 1945. The article gushed that a "home-bred heiress, Mrs. Stanley Grafton Mortimer Jr," had come "out of nowhere, as it were, to cop the great clothes-horse sweepstakes." Two years later Mrs. Mortimer was destined to win another contest, with an even bigger prize: Bill Paley.

The fashion upstart was called, incongruously, Babe—a name readily associated with blowsy blondes. But this Babe was delicate, the ultimate in refinement. She was tall (five feet eight inches) and graceful, her posture perfect. Her voice was gentle and touched with a New England crispness. She could look meltingly sweet or icily elegant. Taken separately, her features were imperfect: the lips too thin, the nose sharply aquiline, the jaw a trifle large. But with her dark, flashing eyes, sculpted bone structure, luminous skin, and long, Modigliani neck, the elements came together as a work of art.

Barbara Cushing was born in Boston, Massachusetts, on July 5, 1915, the fifth of five children. She had two sisters: Mary "Minnie" Benedict, ten years her senior, and Betsey, seven years older. There were two brothers as well: William, born in 1903, and Henry, born in 1910.

Although Babe grew up in Boston, her parents, Katharine Stone Crowell and Harvey Williams Cushing, came from Cleveland, Ohio. Harvey Cushing, a prominent surgeon, had pioneered neurosurgery at Johns Hopkins University before becoming a professor at the Harvard Medical School and surgeon in chief at Peter Bent Brigham, Harvard's teaching hospital. Cushing's skills were legendary, and his discoveries greatly advanced the study of neurology. When he began operating on brains, in the early 1900s, 70 percent of his patients died; at the end of his career the mortality rate was 7.3 percent.

Cushing expected his children to be as precise and disciplined as he was. "Perfectionism," said Betsey, "was drummed into us." He insisted the children take cold showers each morning and hung NO SMOKING signs in their rooms. (He, however, chain-smoked two packs daily.) His wife, Kate—or Gogs, as she was always known—was the buffer whenever Harvey came down too hard on the children.

The Cushings lived in a large yellow house in the shady Boston suburb of Brookline. Over all, the household was spirited and happy. The Cushings never lacked material comforts or sufficient funds for vacations, private schooling, or a small staff of servants. But they were not rich. Harvey earned good fees from his practice and inherited a comfortable stipend from his father's and grandfather's real estate investments. However, he plowed a substantial amount of his earnings back into the clinic and laboratory he operated at Harvard.

It has been said that Gogs Cushing once announced, "My girls will all marry wealth in this country or titles abroad." Whether she so baldly articulated it or not, she had one overriding mission in life: to prepare her daughters to marry well, to create a world for their husbands, to keep their men happy by doting on them.

Of the three Cushing girls, Barbara held the most promise. She was a pretty child, but her looks stopped short of beauty because her teeth were a trifle prominent. After she had her teeth straightened in her early teens, she emerged as a stunning young woman and developed a dignified reserve. She studied conscientiously at the Winsor School, in Brookline. At fifteen she moved on to Westover, a fashionable finishing school in Connecticut. Her only spark of misbehavior—a smoking habit developed in her teens—was approved of by her mother and carried out behind her father's back.

Babe graduated from Westover in 1933 and made her debut at The Ritz Carlton in Boston the following year. The hostess for the affair, attended by four hundred guests, was her sister Betsey, who by then could afford such an extravagance. Betsey had been the first Cushing girl to make an illustrious match. In 1930, at age twenty-two, she had married James Roosevelt, a Harvard Law School student and the eldest son of the then governor of New York, Franklin D. Roosevelt.

At eighteen Babe flew into the social whirl of debutante parties and evenings in New York. "You might tell son, Franklin, that the next time he takes Barbara to a night club, whether or not he allows photographs of the fact to be taken, all will be over between us," Harvey Cushing wrote to FDR. "When will you ever become old enough to realize that the new generation goes to a Night Club instead of Sunday School?" Roosevelt replied.

In 1935 Babe, wanting to be with her sisters in New York, secured an entry-level job at *Glamour* magazine. She moved into a Manhattan apartment that she shared with a friend, Priscilla Weld, another well-bred Boston girl, who worked at *Good Housekeeping*.

Babe quickly became a sensation in New York, but not exclusively on her own. Rather, she was part of a powerful trio. Babe, Betsey, and Minnie were known throughout Manhattan as the Fabulous Cushing Sisters. Babe by then was in her early twenties, Betsey in her late twenties, and Minnie in her early thirties. With their dark wavy hair parted identically on the left and falling just below the neck, the sisters were seen everywhere together. All three displayed a carefully cultivated ability to please men. They dressed smartly, projected an air of elegance, and knew how to enter into the fun. Their breeding showed in every way.

The first to bolt from Boston, Minnie pioneered New York as a career girl. In 1935 she became the mistress of Vincent Astor, the forty-four-year-old heir to a $70 million real estate fortune, one of the richest men in the world. Astor owned a Georgian house at 130 East Eightieth Street, a villa in Bermuda, and Ferncliff, a three-thousand-acre estate in Rhinebeck, New York.

It was Babe who was the most beautiful and glamorous of the Cushings. In 1939 she moved to *Vogue* magazine, where she worked under the legendary fashion editors Edna Woolman Chase and Carmel Snow. She also befriended Diana Vreeland, fashion editor at rival *Harper's Bazaar*.

Like Bill Paley, Babe Cushing was a keen student. She set out to pick the brains of those who knew about things that would improve her. "She wanted to know all about fashion and things in Paris," recalled the fashion photographer Horst, who used to dine with Babe regularly. Paris was the center of the fashionable world, and Babe needed to understand it. "Tell me," she would say, "why is it that Chanel dresses look the way they do?"

If a refined, stylish woman could have street smarts, Babe fit the bill. When her friend Susan Mary Jay (later to marry the prominent newspaper columnist Joseph Alsop) wanted to work at *Vogue* in 1939, Babe shrewdly advised her on how to shape her writing sample. The somewhat preposterous topic was "The Future of the Open-toed Shoe." After discovering that Edna Woolman Chase, *Vogue*'s editor in chief, was partial to open-toed shoes, Babe dictated an enthusiastic essay to Susan Mary, who got a job as a receptionist.

Babe was no intellectual. "I don't think she read," recalled Connie Devins, her secretary. "But she was smart enough to be a very good listener, and she asked good questions."

She kept some distance from her many male admirers. She had a certain wariness about men, and may have understood that a lot of men simply loved being seen with her; her attention fanned their egos. "She was savvy. She knew how to please a man, how to make him think he was the most attractive man who ever walked," said Connie Devins. "I used to listen to her talk to all the beaux. It was like listening to Garbo. She had more men in love with her."

The man who succeeded in capturing her was as clean-cut and chiseled as a Greek god. Stanley Grafton Mortimer, Jr., was high-WASP aristocracy. His mother was the daughter of Henry Morgan Tilford, founder of Standard Oil of California. Through her, Stanley stood to inherit at least $3 million.

Stanley Mortimer was a party boy, who put in time working for an advertising agency and spent many afternoons at the exclusive Racquet and Tennis Club, on Park Avenue. Babe was captivated by his good looks and charm; by all accounts she genuinely loved him. As a couple, Babe and Stanley turned heads.

The Mortimer-Cushing wedding, on September 21, 1940, one of the big events of the social season, was held at a home Gogs Cushing rented in Easthampton, Long Island. Harvey Cushing never lived to see Babe marry. He had suffered a fatal heart attack in 1939.

Babe and Stanley settled into a small triplex apartment in an East Side brownstone. They didn't have heaps of money. However, there was enough to hire a maid and a cook, and they entertained frequently and well. Babe abhorred cocktail parties, preferring dinner followed by songs around a piano. Right on schedule, she "retired" from her glamorous job to have a son, Stanley III, in 1942, and a daughter, Amanda, in 1944.

During these years the well-married Cushing sisters took off. Minnie had finally landed Vincent Astor, who agreed to a small wedding at Gogs' house only six days after the Cushing-Mortimer ceremony. It was Gogs who had put her foot down and persuaded Vincent Astor to make an honest woman of her eldest daughter.

When Betsey's marriage to James Roosevelt broke up, in 1940, Gogs set her up in the building next to her own apartment, on East Eighty-sixth Street. Each week she would have Betsey and her two daughters over for dinner with Minnie, Babe, and her children. Gogs sat in a chair and read everyone fairy tales. One fairy tale came true in 1942, when Betsey wed the fabulously wealthy Jock Whitney.

In 1943 Stanley Mortimer joined the navy and went to the Pacific. On his return, in 1945, he had changed. He was drinking heavily and was subject to sharp mood swings. "Babe was still crazy about him," recalled Connie Devins, "but she couldn't handle it." She divorced him in May 1946. He gave her a $40,000 trust fund to support their two children, who remained in Babe's custody.

Well before her divorce became final, Babe had taken up with the recently separated Bill Paley. He always professed to have first noticed Babe at a dinner party in the fall of 1946. But according to Dorothy, in 1942 and 1943 Babe and Stanley took a house in Manhasset near Kiluna. Minnie and Vincent lived up the road as well. "Babe and Stanley were at the house quite often," said Dorothy.

By April 1946 Babe was seeing Paley regularly. When she had an

Above, sisters Babe, Betsey, and Minnie Cushing in 1937. Right, Babe in 1945, as one of the world's ten best-dressed women.

attack of phlebitis and was hospitalized for a month, he visited her every evening. She sat in bed wrapped in tulle, looking like a portrait by Watteau, and he arrived with dinner for two in a warming container. For each visit he consulted with a chef from one of his favorite restaurants to concoct the perfect menu. When Babe recovered, Paley picked out a Cadillac for her.

Babe was flattered by Paley's attentiveness, but she was never madly in love with him. Rather, she found him fascinating. He wasn't as classically handsome as Stanley Mortimer, but he was attractive enough. She was drawn to Paley's vitality, which she found alluring compared to Stanley's simplicity.

Not long after his ardent courtship began, Babe wrote to her friend Susan Mary Alsop in Paris saying that she was going to marry Bill Paley: "In he comes at the end of a hard day. He always has something new to tell me or a little present to cheer me up."

But no marriage plans were made until suddenly, on July 24, 1947, word leaked out that Bill Paley had granted Dorothy a $1.5 million divorce settlement. The settlement—and the size of the check—came as a surprise. Dorothy and Bill had been in a nasty struggle over their

Above, the Paley children on a European vacation in 1953. From left, Billie, Amanda, Kate, and Tony.

Below, Bill and Babe at their New Hampshire vacation camp, Kiluna North

separation. "He was cold as ice," recalled Dorothy. "He couldn't have been more unpleasant." Once, when Dorothy had taken the children to Florida for a holiday, Paley dispatched a truck to their home on Seventy-fourth Street and removed most of the paintings.

Dorothy, who retained custody of Jeffrey, nine, and Hilary, eight, was devastated by the divorce. However, she pulled herself together quite effectively. She married (and later divorced) a Wall Street stockbroker named Walter Hirshon, and she dedicated herself to philanthropic causes.

Bill and Babe were married on July 28, 1947—three weeks after Babe's thirty-second birthday. Bill Paley was forty-five years old, and one newspaper account of the wedding noted that he was "the first Cushing son-in-law who is not socially prominent." The ceremony was at Chester House, Gogs Cushing's "cottage" on the Whitney estate. The guest list was short: Babe's family and in-laws; Goldie and Sam; Bill's sister, Blanche Levy (Leon was on a business trip); Ed and Janet Murrow; Paley's faithful factotum, John Minary; and a few other friends.

Four days later, on August 1, Bill and Babe set sail on the *Queen Elizabeth* for a honeymoon in Europe. To friends who saw them that summer they seemed the dream couple. Each time Bill looked Babe's way, he beamed with pride. He was simply thrilled to be married to her. They took genuine joy in each other's company.

On March 30, 1948—eight months after Bill and Babe's hurry-up marriage—Babe bore their first child, William Cushing Paley. The infant weighed six pounds, and there was no mention of his being premature. The arrival of the Paleys' son, however, seemed to indicate what had only been hinted at the previous July: that Babe had been pregnant by Paley when they were married. (Two years later they would have a second child, Kate.)

The wedding signified destiny fulfilled on both sides. Babe had found the wealthy and powerful man she had been bred to marry. And Paley had found the perfect antidote to Dorothy. Babe's beauty and social standing greatly enhanced his position in life. (In his memoir, he entitled the chapter about his courtship and marriage to Babe "Triumph.") Babe was also trained to look up to her man, to flatter him.

Had Dorothy Paley thought about it back in 1942, she might have imagined what a woman like Babe could offer a man like Bill Paley. That year, when the Paleys heard about Jock Whitney's marriage to Betsey Cushing Roosevelt, Dorothy said, "Oh, he will be so bored."

"No, he won't," responded Paley. "He will have everything the way he wants it."

CHAPTER 11

As a broadcaster, Bill Paley had a simple formula for financial success in radio. He believed that a network should be independent. Its shows should appeal to a wide popular audience. Plots should be believable and uncomplicated, and audiences should identify with the characters. Above all, the network should do everything it could to find and nurture stars.

Paley's 1945 letter to Paul Kesten had revealed his determination to be first in the ratings by gaining control over stars and shows. By the mid-1940s, with Frank Stanton, as president, running the company day by day, Paley was free to pursue his vision with single-minded zeal. He established a programming department to develop mass-appeal shows, especially comedies—the core of NBC's success.

It took Paley's programmers less than a year to come up with their first hits and potential stars. CBS programming executive Harry Ackerman discovered a red-haired comedian named Lucille Ball at the Stork Club, in New York, and signed her to star in *My Favorite Husband*. Ackerman also put Eve Arden in *Our Miss Brooks,* a comedy about a wisecracking high school teacher.

CBS steadily inched up on NBC, which still lacked a programming department. "NBC just sat there," recalled Stanton. "They would take this or that program produced by the advertisers." NBC executives continued to believe that their network's stronger stations and greater reach were sufficient to attract the best programming.

At year's end in 1947, two new CBS shows had joined radio's top ten—*Arthur Godfrey's Talent Scouts* and *My Friend Irma*. But Paley felt impatient. "I know a good comedian when I hear one," he told an interviewer that year. "The only trouble is that too many are on NBC." In May 1948 Paley decided to go on the offensive. It was time to raid NBC, as he had done in the '30s.

Paley's first targets were two of NBC's most popular stars, Freeman Gosden and Charles Correll, the creators of *Amos 'n' Andy*. Paley could have the show, their agent Lew Wasserman said, for $2 million plus a share of the profits from future shows. Paley agreed, and in September 1948 he triumphantly announced that *Amos 'n' Andy* had joined CBS after nineteen years on NBC. At that moment Wasserman returned to Paley and suggested the same sort of deal for the king of radio, Jack Benny.

Although Benny had been a mainstay on NBC since 1932, he was not entirely happy. He felt NBC took him for granted. "Jack is a loyal guy," recalled his former agent, Irving Fein. "He once said to me, 'If I had dinner with Sarnoff once in a while and lunch once a year, I never would have wanted to leave NBC.' "

The price for Benny's departure was steep: $4 million. The news sent shock waves through the broadcasting industry. "Getting Benny away from NBC seemed like getting Quebec away from Canada, so fixed had he been, and for so long, in the heaven of that richer and bigger network," wrote CBS radio dramatist Norman Corwin at the time.

After snatching Benny, Paley plucked off more NBC stars, some of whom had begun on CBS in the early 1930s: Bing Crosby, George Burns and Gracie Allen, Edgar Bergen, and Red Skelton.

By the end of 1949, CBS Radio had twelve of the top fifteen radio programs. For the first time in twenty years CBS led in the audience ratings. *Variety* called the achievement "Paley's Comet." Without a doubt it was the biggest upheaval in broadcasting since Paley's purchase of CBS, in 1928.

Sarnoff responded by earmarking $1.5 million to develop some thirty new radio programs to replace NBC's losses. He sensibly locked in his biggest star, Bob Hope, with a fat contract, but NBC never regained its leadership in radio.

Starting a program department to develop shows in-house was one of the smartest moves Bill Paley ever made. Likewise, the Paley raids of 1948 and 1949 were a brilliant strategic maneuver. For an initial investment of less than $6 million to win over Gosden, Correll, Benny, and Crosby, Paley provoked a small stampede of other valuable personalities. In the space of five months he nearly wiped out NBC's roster of top talent. The raids displayed more vividly than ever Paley's persistence, his cunning, and his refusal to play by the book. They gave CBS a leadership position that meant greater profits and power.

Paley's talent raids were intended, however, to strengthen radio, not to push CBS into television. They were designed to establish him, at last, as the undisputed leader—in radio. "I never heard Bill talk about using the stars for television at all," recalled Frank Stanton. "For him in those days it was all radio. His postwar idea was simply to get control of radio programming. He never talked about television. He didn't see the light until well after the early days."

Paley knew television was coming. But as in the '30s, he wanted to delay its arrival as long as possible. "Bill did not want television," said Stanton. "He thought it would hurt radio. It was also a question of money, as far as he was concerned. He didn't see any profit in TV at all. Bill was concerned about the bottom line, that we couldn't afford television, that it was too costly."

Paley credits himself with more vision than anyone noticed at the time. "I had a very strong feeling that television was right behind us, and we started to think about how we could make the transition," he told one interviewer in the mid-1970s.

This recollection crumbles on the record. In 1948 Ed Sullivan's famous television variety show, originally named *Toast of the Town,* was the brainchild not of Paley but of Charlie Underhill, the chief of programming for television at CBS. Sullivan, a celebrated columnist for the New York *Daily News,* was an artless performer. Paley objected immediately to his high-pitched nasal voice, awkward gestures, bungled introductions, and peculiar grimaces, and wanted to remove the show after the first week. But he deferred to Underhill and the president of the television network, Jack Van Volkenburg. The CBS chairman bought their argument that with Sullivan's extensive show-business contacts, there would be an endless supply of new talent. They were right. As time passed, Sullivan's odd chemistry caught the viewers, and his show became a national institution.

Late in 1951 Jack Van Volkenburg arrived unannounced at Frank Stanton's door. "I have a helluva piece of talent in my office," the CBS Television president said. "I need your authorization to sign him." Stanton had an important luncheon appointment and asked if he could see the performer after lunch. "No," said Van Volkenburg. "It's Jackie Gleason, and he is drinking heavily, and I'm afraid he's going to pass out." The comedian wanted to come to CBS. But it would cost CBS at least $50,000 a week per show, for thirteen weeks guaranteed—later raised to $66,175, making it the network's most expensive show at the time. In other words, CBS would have to pay Gleason more than a half million dollars even if it could not sell the time to an advertiser.

"My God, what if we can't sell him?" exclaimed Stanton. But Stanton had seen Gleason's variety show, *Cavalcade of Stars*, on the Dumont Network—an independent broadcaster—during the previous two years, and he understood Gleason's star potential. "Okay," Stanton said, and went to lunch.

The deal was sealed without Paley, who was away from the office for long stretches in those days. When he returned, he asked Stanton, "What's new?" Stanton replied, "We've signed a helluva talent, Jackie Gleason." "Who's he?" asked Paley. Stanton described the portly comedian's galaxy of memorable characters, such as Ralph Kramden and Joe the Bartender. Paley asked which sponsor had bought him. "We haven't sold him yet," Stanton said quietly. "I suppose if we don't sell him, we can pay him off," Paley said. "No," replied Stanton. "We have to play him even if we don't sell him." "Who was so stupid to make that deal!" Paley thundered.

When Gleason became the most watched man on television during the 1950s, Paley gave him the store—starting with an $11 million deal for two years that included a house in Peekskill, New York. During his lunchtime negotiations with Paley and Stanton, Gleason was usually so drunk he would drop his head on the table and fall asleep before the entrée. But on the air he was a winner, and Paley indulged him. When Gleason wanted to take the show to Miami so he could play golf every day, CBS financed the move.

Bill Paley adored Lucille Ball's radio show, *My Favorite Husband*, but he nearly lost her in the switch to television. When CBS executive Harry Ackerman suggested that Lucy consider television, Lucy and her husband, Desi Arnaz, a Cuban bandleader, decided to set up a company to produce television programs on their own. Naturally, they wanted to share in the rights to any televised adaptation of *My Favorite Husband*, which portrayed Lucy as the zany wife of a midwestern banker. Lucy wanted Desi to play her husband in the TV version. Ackerman conveyed their wishes to Paley, who turned them down, claiming that Lucy had worked in radio for a salary and could continue to do so in television. Paley also had little confidence that Desi could act.

Lucy and Desi proceeded to develop a television situation comedy, *I Love Lucy*, on their own, spending $5000 to fund the pilot in 1951. The plot revolved around the antics of a harebrained housewife constantly scheming to show her husband, a Cuban bandleader, that she belonged in show business too.

Philip Morris bought the show through Milton Biouw, of the Biouw advertising agency. "I have Lucy under lock and key for television," Biouw said when he called Frank Stanton one morning. Biouw was looking for the best possible time period and television-station lineup for his client. "We'll put it on Monday night," said Stanton impulsively. "You don't have any stations," said Biouw. At the time many cities had only one television station, an NBC affiliate. Stanton managed to pull together a string of strong stations that he offered Biouw in a handshake deal that afternoon.

The following autumn *I Love Lucy* zoomed into third place in the television ratings; by October 1952 it held first place. For more than two decades Lucille Ball would triumph as the screwball queen of television comedy—wide-eyed, wacky, hilarious.

According to Paley's account, Lucy's TV show was hatched one day in 1950, when he met with the actress. While that meeting doubtless took place, Paley's role doesn't square with the recollections of others involved. "Bill Paley took credit for starting Lucy—as if he did the work," said Harry Ackerman. "He did make the decision to go ahead. But I can't think of his discovering a piece of talent or buying an idea."

PALEY'S concern about the high cost of shifting from radio to television gave CBS a curiously schizophrenic character in the late '40s and early '50s. Mighty radio and infant television inhabited different worlds at the company.

"Television wasn't on Bill's plate," said Stanton. "It was more electronics and stations than programming in the beginning, and someone had to look after it." Stanton had grown passionate about television's possibilities during the war as he watched the reactions of visitors to CBS' experimental station in Grand Central Terminal. When Kesten retired, in August 1946, Stanton became the new CBS man "in charge of the future." Thus Paley continued to rule radio, and Stanton oversaw television.

But Stanton's efforts to develop a television network foundered on his simultaneous quest for color. CBS had developed its own color system. In September 1946 CBS asked the FCC for permission to broadcast its system commercially. At the same time, because of bad advice from the FCC, the network dropped its applications for key television-station licenses. The FCC ruling on color came in March 1947. To the utter amazement of CBS network officials the FCC vetoed CBS' request. No color system, in the view of the commissioners, was yet ready for approval.

The man behind CBS' stunning setback was Paley's archrival, David Sarnoff. CBS' bold move to bypass black-and-white television and plunge headlong into color threatened his master plan for developing television in America. The stakes were huge: by the end of World War II, Sarnoff had spent $50 million to develop his own all-electronic system for black-and-white television. He wanted first to saturate the market with his black-and-white sets, then years later to introduce sophisticated all-electronic color sets.

Concerned over a growing positive perception of CBS color in the press, Sarnoff had launched an aggressive negative campaign in 1946. He complained about the inferiority of the CBS color system, calling it a horse-and-buggy technology. It may be that Sarnoff planted sufficient seeds of doubt among the FCC commissioners to explain their decision in March 1947 against CBS color. But Sarnoff also appeared to benefit from a special pleading inside the commission as well. The following autumn the chairman of the FCC, Charles Denny, moved to RCA as vice president. "It smelled," said Stanton.

CBS, meanwhile, struggled to catch up. It trimmed its color research and scrambled to reapply for station licenses in San Francisco, Boston, and Chicago. But in September 1948 the FCC dealt CBS yet another blow. Inundated with applications, the commission froze the licensing and building of new television stations. CBS' reapplications were caught in the huge backlog. The company was left with just one company-owned station, in New York, and a short string of television affiliates. Forty-nine television stations were then operating around the country, most of them allied with NBC. The prospects for television at CBS looked grim indeed.

While CBS had its hands tied, NBC operated a thriving television network. Understandably, much of Stanton's time during those years was consumed by scrounging for affiliates and trying to find stations for CBS to buy.

At first he bought part interest in several stations owned by newspapers in Washington, D.C., Los Angeles, San Francisco, and Minneapolis to establish some strategic footholds. Late in 1950 he bought KTSL, in Los Angeles, which CBS renamed KNXT.

Amid its setbacks in television the growing company scuttled its plans to develop its color technology, which was rapidly becoming outmoded. Meanwhile, David Sarnoff prodded his engineers to work eighteen-hour days, seven days a week, perfecting an electronic RCA color system to present to the FCC. In December 1953 the commission fixed the RCA system as the standard.

That same year, however, CBS saw its first profit from the television network that Frank Stanton had assembled piece by piece. After buying the Los Angeles station late in 1950, Stanton coaxed Paley into buying a station in Chicago. As soon as the FCC lifted its four-year freeze on television-station licenses, in April 1952, CBS lost no time in assembling a network equal in size and strength to NBC's. CBS dedicated its new $7 million Hollywood production-and-office facility—Television City—on November 15, 1952, and broke ground on a $2 million TV headquarters in Washington, D.C.

With a year or so of the television network's first black ink, Paley embraced the medium wholeheartedly. By 1956 the CBS Radio network—Paley's pride—was losing money. But the strapping television network was making a profit, and CBS was riding high, with twelve out of the top fifteen shows. Two years later CBS finally had its full complement of the five television stations that the FCC permitted each network to own—for a total cost of $30 million. The final two purchases were KMOX-TV, in St. Louis, and WCAU, in Philadelphia. Many critics charged that CBS had paid inflated prices for its stations. In retrospect, $30 million ($135 million in today's dollars) for four stations seems like a bargain—especially given CBS' subsequent gusher of television profits. Moreover, CBS picked up stations after they had begun showing a profit; most television stations broke into the black in 1951. Had CBS built the stations on its own, it would have had to absorb several years of deficits. So while

NBC had a head start with its own stations, in the end its advantage didn't count for much. CBS' programming flair took the network to first place, where it stayed.

Paley, as so often, had the last laugh. He and Sarnoff had each returned from World War II to pursue an obsession. Paley's was to master his network's fate by controlling radio programs. Sarnoff's was to make television a reality. As it turned out, Paley's talent raids and program development ended by saving CBS Television. He may have thought he was building radio, but by following his gut—the visceral, even primitive love for stars and shows that figured in every move he made—he gave his fledgling television network an advantage Sarnoff would never match.

CHAPTER 12

MORE conspicuously than ever, Paley was the absentee landlord at CBS, taking longer and more frequent vacations during the postwar years. As Paley approached his fifties he seemed in the throes of a mid-life crisis. Although he was as hard-driving as ever, he had been feeling the stresses of the broadcasting business for two decades.

Paley might logically have found new stimulation at his company's emerging television network. Instead, he directed his energy toward lighter pursuits: decorating, collecting furniture and art, and hobnobbing with high society.

The importance of these sidelines to Bill Paley cannot be underestimated. "When he talks about his attainments, he talks not in professional terms but in terms of satisfaction with his social achievements," said novelist Truman Capote, a confidant of Bill and Babe Paley's during that period. "He is a bit of a name-dropper—royalty, for example." Paley was known to display his photo albums to guests, ostensibly to show his prowess as a photographer, but the names could not fail to impress: Picasso and Babe; former British prime minister Anthony Eden with Bill and Babe at Cap d'Antibes; Bill taking a stroll with Queen Elizabeth and Prince Philip.

The CBS chairman grew fabulously rich in those years. Since much of his evolving identity—at least among his friends—derived from his wealth and its stylish emblems, making money became a kind of religion for him. Fleur Cowles, widow of *Look* publisher Gardner Cowles and a friend from those days, compared Paley to "one of the cats of the jungle. He prowled around in search of money-making."

With Dorothy before the war, Paley had sought fun and escape; but his companions were chosen for their cleverness, intelligence, or talent. As he grew richer his world grew smaller. In the postwar years he seemed to concentrate on climbing the social ladder in America and Britain. His world was the realm of Jock Whitney and Alfred Gwynne Vanderbilt, of dukes and viscounts, of beautiful, decorous women and dashing gentlemen, where bloodlines and social standing were all.

Most of Paley's postwar friends fell short of him in intelligence and achievement. Some were not even that rich. But all had high social positions and a certain degree of stylishness. Paley's new acquaintances shared his material and social preoccupations, and he could dominate them. They were drawn by his magnetism, not to mention his money and power. He was a tycoon, not a boring businessman but a glamorous gentleman—a breed apart.

By his early fifties Paley's black hair was streaked with gray at the temples. But he remained vigorous and attractive, and his dark brown eyes and brilliant smile flashed as disarmingly as ever. He appeared a good ten years younger than he was. Thanks to his time spent in London and the example of his brother-in-law Jock Whitney, the fine points of upper-class manners were now second nature.

Appearances became paramount. "The Paleys were social climbers," said Charlotte Curtis, once the society columnist for *The New York Times,* who watched their ascent. "They began to live on a predictable circuit. They went to all the right functions in New York." They became the most-sought-after but unapproachable couple in New York. They cultivated their aloofness. No one but close friends could reach them on the phone; otherwise, a letter was mandatory.

The focal point of the Paleys' social life continued to be Kiluna, where every weekend was a house party for four or five couples. "If I don't keep the house full on weekends, I couldn't live with him," Babe once indiscreetly confided to a CBS executive. Each Saturday morning Paley would rise early and eat breakfast alone in his room. (His guests generally preferred to sleep in.) Sitting on his bed amid newspapers and a bulging briefcase, he would work the phones for several hours before disappearing with his chums for a round of golf at the exclusive National Golf Links, in Southampton, Long Island.

Jock Whitney, of course, stood at the top of Paley's list of weekend cronies. Just being around Whitney exhilarated Paley. "My brother-in-law Jock Whitney," he would say, running the words together as if they were one, whenever he brought Jock around CBS. For his part, Jock Whitney greatly admired success in business.

To Paley, Jock Whitney embodied the ultimate in American masculine style. Yet Whitney's influence was less in matters of taste than in the way he operated. "Bill," summed up. Walter Thayer, an attorney and business associate of Whitney's, "liked the way Jock lived."

A gentle rivalry flecked their relationship as a result. Once, while watching television with Whitney at Greentree, the Whitney's Manhasset estate, Paley wanted to change the channel. "Where's your clicker?" Paley asked, figuring Jock would have a remote-control switch at his fingertips. Jock calmly pressed a buzzer, and his butler walked up to the TV set to make the switch.

Prominent among Paley's friends on the other side of the Atlantic was Loel Guinness, scion of the well-known British banking family. The Paleys spent a month each summer with Loel and his wife, Gloria, at Piencort, the Guinness home near Deauville, France, and cruised the Mediterranean on the Guinness yacht. Other stops on the Paley summer itinerary included Mautry, home of Baron and Baroness Guy de Rothschild in Normandy, and vacation homes owned by assorted friends in France and the Greek Isles.

In America, Paley "had a shield around him, a number of men who had to give top performances," noted M. Donald Grant, former chairman of the New York Mets. They were the court jesters, ever ready to complete a golf foursome, quick with the badinage and practical jokes. They usually had little money of their own; they existed to make bored rich men laugh.

The most notorious jester was Truman Capote, who befriended the Paleys in January 1955 on a trip to Jamaica. Their only intimate drawn from the literary world, he was thirty years old at the time—twenty-four years younger than Bill and nine years younger than Babe. The southern-born writer had been widely celebrated for his short stories and first novel, *Other Voices, Other Rooms*. A flamboyant homosexual,

Capote had a knack for self-promotion and social advancement; he cozied up to a group of high-society women, idolizing them and calling them his "swans" for their grace and beauty.

Capote belonged more to Babe than to Bill, serving as her intellectual mentor, telling her what books to read (Proust, Wharton, Henry James), sharpening her conversational skills, boosting her self-confidence. His charm and intellect impressed her; she considered him a soul mate, a refuge from the banality of Long Island society.

"At first Bill was appalled by Capote," said Irene Selznick, recalling the writer's fey mannerisms, pronounced lisp, and baby face with its fringe of blond bangs. "Then he was amused." Paley called him Tru-boy and appreciated his ability to keep the conversation sizzling at dinner parties, with caustic gossip and unconventional pronouncements delivered in his best high-pitched manner. "Capote," said one friend, "was a rich man's Pekingese."

Capote had an open invitation to Kiluna and for some two decades accompanied Babe and Bill on countless trips to the Caribbean and Europe. Most of the time Paley paid his way.

Capote's relationship to the Paleys was almost too peculiar to be categorized, though it was part entertainer, part psychiatrist, and part intimate friend. He cultivated them, they cultivated him, and each side milked the relationship to the hilt. Yet Capote was also very much the indulged child who, incidentally, took up more of the Paleys' time than their own children did. He thought nothing of having the great Bill Paley curl up on his bed for a chat.

The admiration of his high-status friends meant a great deal to Bill Paley. His extravagant favors were legendary. When Leland Hayward's son Bill had to be flown to Menninger, the famous psychiatric clinic in Kansas, Paley offered the use of the CBS airplane—which he called "my airplane"—a DC-3 equipped with a bar and plush seats. Once, during one of David Selznick's financial crises, Paley gave his friend a signed blank check and said, "You fill in the amount."

It was to please his friends as much as himself that he lavished extraordinary time and attention on his homes. After he and Babe were married, they began a series of Kiluna redecorations that continued over the years—with the assistance of interior designers Syrie Maugham, Billy Baldwin, and Sister Parish, among others. Baldwin also had a hand in the New York pied-à-terre kept by the

Paleys for more than two decades. The three-room suite on the tenth floor of the St. Regis Hotel had a sweeping vista up Fifth Avenue. The drawing-room walls were covered in shirred brown-and-pink chintz. The French furniture was upholstered in apple-green velvet and pale stripes, with needlepoint pillows scattered about. A Venetian bronze clock hung from the ceiling, over a needlepoint rug.

In the early 1950s the Paleys paid $120,000 for a vacation house in Round Hill, a fashionable resort in Jamaica where Noël Coward also had a home. The day before they arrived for one of their two or three prolonged winter visits, a butler would bring their luggage, unpack, fill the house with flowers, and arrange the latest magazines on tables.

The Paleys spent the least amount of time—usually several weeks during the summer—at their camp on Squam Lake, in New Hampshire, which they called Kiluna North.

Some members of high-WASP society continued to eye Bill Paley suspiciously as an outsider. Anti-Semitism was more overt in this rarefied world than in Paley's prewar crowd. The patter on the golf courses where Paley played included ethnic and racist jokes sometimes told within his hearing. "Many of those men reeked of intolerance and

Left, Babe in the Paleys' St. Regis Hotel pied-à-terre. Below, the Paleys with a young Truman Capote in the 1950s.

racism," said one intimate of Paley's. "That he put up with that showed how badly he wanted to be accepted."

Despite his prominence, Paley had problems with exclusive clubs. Although Jock Whitney was his sponsor, Paley was turned down for membership in the golf and tennis club on posh Fishers Island, on Long Island Sound, where the Whitneys had a vacation home. "One reason for Squam Lake was that they couldn't go anywhere else," said Jeanne Thayer, wife of Walter Thayer. "That has to affect someone with long antennae like Bill."

Some hurts Paley never knew about. One summer Babe asked her friend Susan Mary Alsop to help the Paleys get established in fashionable Bar Harbor, Maine. Susan Mary made some inquiries but never heard anything back. Only later did she find out that her own mother and Marietta Tree's father, the Right Reverend Malcolm Peabody, had prevented the Paleys from being admitted to the Bar Harbor Club. Susan Mary was furious when she heard her mother say, "But we can't have Jews." Babe was gracious enough never to bring up the matter again.

Still, Bill and Babe were accepted in some highly desirable places.

"He wore her like a medal." Left, the Paleys on a Manhattan street. Below, Babe in the dell garden at Kiluna, their Long Island estate.

He belonged to the River Club, in New York City, and the National Golf Links, on Long Island, where he was one of the few non-Gentile members. Either by choice or self-protection, Paley never became much of a clubman. His reaction to anti-Semitism continued to be denial and deflection. Had Paley confronted anti-Semitism, he would have upset the odd equilibrium he had created for himself. Paley did not, after all, overtly deny being Jewish. He simply assumed the WASP mantle and left it to others to draw their own conclusions.

In the end the closed doors did not matter. The Paleys were exclusive enough to transcend club memberships. In Kiluna, Round Hill, and Squam Lake they created their own club with their own rules. They determined who could belong, and they could take solace in leaving behind those who spurned them. With Paley's money and power, and Babe's captivating glamour, there were few limits.

PROPELLED by Paley's power, Babe became a legend in her own right. She, in turn, devoted her life to creating a perfect world for her husband. But the role was an immense strain, and she became progressively unhappy. It was not easy to please a man as demanding as Bill Paley. "She had the wisdom to know that Bill Paley wanted control and order around him—and that it should look effortless," said John "Tex" McCrary, a public relations consultant and radio personality who lived next to Kiluna.

She ran Kiluna with extraordinary precision and organization, supervising a staff of twelve. Babe pampered guests even more elaborately than Dorothy. No one had to unpack or pack. Baths were drawn by servants, and any item of soiled clothing was whisked away, washed, ironed, and folded neatly in the guest's dresser. The bedrooms offered every comfort and convenience: fruit and flowers, piles of new books and magazines, and three newspapers each morning.

Babe understood full well that, as her friend Leonora Hornblow put it, "Bill Paley lived for his stomach." He woke up thinking about what he was going to eat. He was voracious at breakfast, often tucking into steak or lamb chops. Wherever he was (at home, on the CBS plane, or in the office), Paley snacked incessantly. On an average day he might consume as many as eight meals—breakfast, lunch, and dinner, as well as five mini-meals.

Babe worked hard at anticipating her husband's needs. She made time to read books and briefed him on what was current and choice. She was never a minute late when meeting him. "Mrs. Paley didn't want any loose ends," said one former employee. "She wanted to keep Mr. Paley happy. He wanted everything to run smoothly."

Because Babe was so preoccupied with order and calm, her rare expressions of strong opinion raised eyebrows. After seeing the musical *My Fair Lady*, in which CBS had a sizable investment, Babe announced that she found it old-fashioned and boring; the criticism vexed Paley. Perhaps as a consequence of such misfires, Babe feared intellectual discussions. There were no reproaches or discouraging words from Babe to Bill in the presence of others. She avoided comments or situations that might diminish him—quite the opposite of Dorothy's bursts of superiority. "Babe always built him up, told him how wonderful he was," recalled her friend Natalie Davenport, an interior designer.

Babe followed Bill's lead. When he tired of their house in Jamaica, in the late 1960s, he sold it and built a new one next to the exclusive club at Lyford Cay, in the Bahamas. Whatever Babe's reaction to losing her adored home in Round Hill, she turned her attention to making their new "cottage" even more beautiful. She even planted tuberoses around the outside of the house so that the tropical breeze would fill the air with their fragrance.

The Paleys were proud enough of their surroundings to permit an occasional magazine photo spread. But otherwise, the details of their private life were protected. Bill and Babe shared a penchant for privacy, which suited their purposes. From afar they appeared larger than life. Indeed, to strangers they seemed like Nick and Nora Charles, of *The Thin Man* series—witty, urbane, wonderfully romantic.

Babe was not permitted to speak to reporters except about the most inconsequential subjects—her favorite flower or the designer of a given dress—and then only infrequently. Her role was to remain a goddess in the public eye, aloof and mysterious.

Babe knew that her looks were of paramount importance to Paley. When strands of gray began to appear in her hair, she agonized about what to do. Kenneth, her hairdresser at the time, advised her to stay natural, using only a rinse to prevent yellowing. Envying her distinctive silver tones, droves of women imitated the look.

More than her beauty, it was Babe's style that elevated her above her peers. On her way to lunch at La Grenouille one day, she removed her scarf because it was too warm and tied it casually to the side of her purse. Within a month this "look" was copied everywhere.

Beginning in 1950, when Bill set up a trust fund of CBS stock in her name, Babe had an annual income—at its peak, in 1977, it was $157,000—to spend on herself, primarily for her wardrobe and costume jewelry. When it came to real jewels, however, Paley paid. He bought Babe more than $1 million worth of baubles from New York's finest jewelers. But his gifts to Babe, including two full-length coats of Russian sable, were calculated to underline his stature and image. Bill Paley wanted a wife without equal, to show how successful he was. He wore her like a medal.

Her attempts to please him were poignant. "She always had a little gold pad next to her place at dinner," said Carter Burden, who was married for a time to Babe's daughter Amanda. "If someone mentioned a book, or if something went wrong with the service or meal, she would jot it down." Leonora Hornblow, wife of Hollywood producer Arthur Hornblow, recalled that sometimes after a dinner party Babe would approach the women who flanked her husband. "You were sitting next to Bill," she would say. "What did he eat? Did he like it? What did he say?"

Yet somehow her efforts were never enough. Bill Paley was as spoiled as a man could be. "He took everything for granted," said Natalie Davenport. "His every little wish was taken care of. He knew Babe would keep trouble from him." This pampering made him even more self-absorbed. But like Paley's employees, Babe dared not cross the master. He did everything he wanted and rarely had to do anything he disliked. Nobody had his way more than Bill Paley.

CHAPTER 13

PALEY'S charm masked his narcissism—and underlying insecurities. He appeared to be easygoing but was not. His efforts to keep his private life under wraps stemmed from a fear of exposure. "He needed to control everything, because if he couldn't control, he was afraid," said one Paley family friend.

Paley would carefully hold his thoughts in reserve, counting on others to weigh in first. He would be unlikely to say, for example, "I think the CBS program schedule is in terrible trouble. I am so stumped about what to do. What is it that you would do?" Instead, he might say, "CBS' program schedule doesn't seem very good to me. The programs just don't seem up to par." His indirect approach was self-protective and somewhat manipulative, but it had the benefit of seeming polite and socially correct.

Paley's inability to share credit was another reflection of his narcissism. It did not occur to him that anyone else could have had a role in his success. His convenient memory and capacity for self-delusion screened out contradictory details. If anyone took him on, Paley was never at fault. "He was not a self-analytical basket case," said a former girlfriend. "It was all steel. He wanted what he wanted, but if he didn't get it, you were the selfish one."

One tip-off to Paley's insecurity was his deep-seated suspiciousness. "He didn't trust a lot of people. He would always think someone wanted something," said Frank Stanton. This may have bothered him; he marveled at the easygoing ways of Jock Whitney. "I've often wondered how that came about," Paley said. "When you have that much money, you're apt to be suspicious all the time of others' motives."

Paley revealed his vulnerability through defensiveness and anger. "He could hide his peculiarity with some people," said Irene Selznick, "but others saw views of him neither you nor I can imagine. I think there must have been moments of rage that I tremble to think of . . . the anger from his vitality and drive and will . . . or when he was being contradicted." Another intimate of the Paley family observed that the trip wires for his anger could be surprising: "He would latch onto something casual in conversation and make a big deal out of it. It was hard to figure. He obviously felt threatened. His image seemed in danger of being tarnished, which is important to someone so dependent on others for his self-worth."

The real casualties of Paley's narcissism were his children. Superficially, the Paley family had a nice symmetry—three girls and three boys, arranged in three sets of pairs. There were Jeffrey and Hilary, the two children Bill and Dorothy had adopted; Amanda and Tony, Babe's two children from her first marriage; and the two children by Bill and Babe—Billie, born in 1948, and his younger sister, Kate, born two years later. Jeffrey and Hilary lived with Dorothy, but they saw their father every other weekend for Sunday luncheon and spent several weeks each summer at Kiluna.

Bill Paley treated his children much as he dealt with his top executives. In each case their absolute dependence shaped his manner toward them. He had little concern about the effect he was having on them. What counted was that they knew he was in charge.

"The temper," said one family intimate, "made the children careful. He could be mellow and comfortable at one time or explosive and terrible another. It was terrifying for those who were dependent on him emotionally or economically. They just wanted to please him."

Babe did not oppose Paley's insistence that the children grow up at Kiluna. Bill and Babe spent most weekdays at their Manhattan pied-à-terre. Its small size made it strictly for adults. Even growing up at Kiluna, Tony, Amanda, Billie, and Kate lived apart from their parents, occupying a five-bedroom cottage that was separated from the main house by a game room.

When Bill and Babe were in residence, they remained remote from the activities of the cottage. Most of the time the main house overflowed with guests. If the Paleys happened to be at home and no guests had alighted, they would have an occasional family meal.

Conversation at these gatherings was circumscribed and superficial. And always, the television competed with the children for Paley's attention; he kept the set in his library going all the time.

A stern, distant father, Paley tolerated his children, but he was not affectionate toward them or involved in their day-to-day lives. Many years later he would admit, "I put much more attention on Babe."

Paley stressed the need for self-discipline, hard work, and the folly of taking money for granted—a noble but decidedly mixed message from such a lover of luxury. Unlike his own father, who had helped his son's career in every way, Paley did all he could to discourage his sons from working at CBS. His rationale, he would say to friends, was, "If one of my sons succeeded, they would say it was because of me. If not, people would be nice to him for the wrong reasons, and it would hurt the company."

Paley's inconsistency—charm one minute, toughness the next— kept his children off balance and strained his relations with all of them. They never knew what to expect. In emotional situations he absented himself. Ironically, however, Paley fancied himself as pater-familias, not family dictator. In his own mind he did the right things as a father. As the children grew older and went away to school he never forgot a birthday. His secretary would send the birthday card, or Babe would send the gift. But Paley himself could not be counted on to pick up the phone and call with a birthday wish.

Jeffrey and Hilary, who came to Kiluna as visitors, were the least touched by their father's presence. Still, relations were strained between Jeffrey and Bill. During his prep school years at Taft, Jeffrey competed on championship basketball teams; his achievements were even mentioned in accounts in *The New York Times*. Yet Paley saw his son play basketball only once, when he attended a Father's Day. Otherwise, Paley's sole visit to Taft—a mere two-hour drive from New York City—was for graduation.

Paley tried to fulfill his duty by guiding Jeffrey in choosing a college. Father and son visited Harvard and Yale together, and Jeffrey selected Harvard, where he performed well, graduating with a B-minus average. But after a year at Harvard Law School, Jeffrey decided to drop out. Paley was furious. He told his son he lacked discipline and the ability to see something through.

Jeffrey's decision to pursue a career in journalism only intensified the friction with his father. Although CBS polished its image with broadcast journalism, probing reporters always made Paley nervous— and Jeffrey was just that sort of reporter. He worked for five years on the *International Herald Tribune*, in Paris, which was owned in part by Jock Whitney. Jeffrey tried to use his newspaper experience, plus a year he spent with Granada Television, in London, as a springboard to join CBS News in the early 1960s.

When Jeffrey asked for help, Paley promised to find him a position. Months went by until Jeffrey discovered that his father had "forgotten" the request. Paley finally placed Jeffrey for a summer in the news department at WCBS, the network's flagship station in New York City. It was a disaster. "He heard nothing but criticism from Bill," said Dorothy. "It was clear Bill didn't want him there."

After that, Jeffrey withdrew further from his father. He turned from journalism to take a master's degree in economics at the New School for Social Research, then lived a quiet, almost ascetic life in New York working as an investment adviser.

Hilary Paley had a somewhat easier time with her father. She was a picture-book child, with blond hair and an upturned nose. "Her beauty pleased Bill enormously," recalled Dorothy. After attending the Riverdale Country School, in New York, Hilary went away to the fashionable Shipley School, on Philadelphia's Main Line. Like her mother, she attended Bennett College for just one year.

Hilary worshipped her father, but she could never be certain how much he loved her. More than anything, she wanted to be Babe Paley. In fact, she was closer to her stepmother than to her own mother. "She would talk about Babe as if she were talking about the queen, whose affection and esteem she sought but was not sure she had," said a friend of Hilary's. Emulating Babe, Hilary took a job with *Vogue* magazine after college and married a stunningly handsome man, J. Frederic Byers III, whose blood ran nearly as blue as that of Stanley Mortimer. Byers was descended from the founders of Byers Steel and W. R. Grace & Company—a WASP pedigree that brought Paley's wholehearted approval.

Of the four children who lived with Bill and Babe, her two children by her marriage to Stanley Mortimer were the easiest. Young Stanley, nicknamed Tony, was handsome and blessed with a sweet disposition. He was Babe's favorite, the child with whom she had the closest relationship. He was a good student, graduating from Harvard and receiving a law degree from the University of Virginia, as well as an M.B.A. from Columbia University. Yet for all of Tony's achievements, he never drew close to Paley. Their dealings were edgy at best, in large measure because of the closeness of mother and son.

Amanda was two years younger than Tony, who gave her the nickname Ba when he was unable to pronounce baby. Raven-haired and dark-eyed, she inherited her mother's looks. "Babe worried about Ba," said Susan Mary Alsop. "She was so beautiful." Perhaps too beautiful. The relationship was difficult and aloof. Babe dictated, and Amanda retreated into shyness.

After graduating from Westover, where she was sent in Babe's footsteps, Amanda went on to Wellesley College. Three days after her arrival there, she had a blind date with Shirley Carter Burden, Jr., a Harvard senior and the great-great-great-grandson of Cornelius "Commodore" Vanderbilt. Burden was tall, blond, and handsome. He was not only rich and social but glamorous as well. His mother was

Flobelle Fairbanks, a former actress and first cousin to the dashing Douglas Fairbanks, Jr.; his father was an investment banker and photographer who lost his Social Register listing when he married Flobelle. Carter Burden had grown up in a Beverly Hills mansion, surrounded by movie stars and dating their daughters.

Amanda and Carter were married on June 14, 1964, at St. Mary's Roman Catholic Church in Roslyn, Long Island. Amanda adopted Carter's Catholic faith. He was twenty-three; she was twenty. It was an enormous wedding, with a dozen bridesmaids and nineteen ushers. Mainbocher designed Amanda's wedding dress, and Cecil Beaton took the photographs. The Kiluna reception took place under a pistachio-green tent filled with pink and white flowers. Babe adjusted her own and Amanda's makeup to counteract the unflattering green glow that made every other woman feel vaguely unattractive.

The Burdens burst onto the New York social scene with one party after another at their elegant apartment in the Dakota, on Central Park West. On weekends they had the run of the Kiluna cottage, where they would entertain their own houseguests. Less than two years after the marriage *Vogue* ran a ten-page feature on the Burdens in their Dakota digs entitled "The Young Joyous Life." Halston called Amanda "the most beautiful girl going." She nudged out Jacqueline Kennedy at the top of the best-dressed list, and she became a fixture in *Women's Wear Daily*.

With her marriage to Burden, Amanda soared in her stepfather's estimation. Bill Paley was crazy about Carter, who had enormous charm, not to mention social prominence. "I never saw anything like Bill's infatuation with Carter," said Irene Selznick. "Carter loved Bill too. Suddenly Bill was a great stepfather, and Amanda blossomed."

In many respects it was a marriage that mirrored Bill and Babe's, with Amanda devoting herself to her husband's well-being. Fueled by Carter's ambitions, the Burdens lived at a level of luxury unlike that of any of their contemporaries—even down to the somewhat bizarre butler who accompanied them on weekend visits. "They simply had an overabundance of taste," Truman Capote told a reporter in 1972. "The truth of the matter was that most of those tastes were Carter's. Carter was the one who was saturated with the Paley way of life." But somehow Amanda and Carter did not quite carry it off. After several years on the New York social scene they seemed shallow and silly.

They had violated Bill and Babe's cardinal rule. Amanda and Carter were overexposed.

To protect their deteriorating reputation, they made a one-hundred-and-eighty-degree turn toward the serious pursuit of noblesse oblige. Amanda dedicated herself to volunteer work. Carter graduated from law school at Columbia University and quickly became one of New York's brightest young liberal politicians. Wearing a pin that said I AM CARTER BURDEN'S WIFE, Amanda campaigned avidly when he waged a successful race for the New York City Council.

Throughout these years Amanda's friends could see that Babe was jealous of her dazzling daughter. "Her mother was extremely competitive with Amanda," said one source close to the Paleys. "When Amanda started doing all the things Babe did, it made it worse between them." And even with her beauty, Amanda had found it difficult growing up in the shadow of the great Babe Paley. Whenever Babe would come to visit her daughter at Westover, Amanda's awestruck friends would wait by their dormitory windows for the Paleys' chocolate-brown Bentley to arrive: first a long, slender arm would emerge, a lighted cigarette curling smoke from the holder

Clockwise from right: Carter and Amanda Burden; Tony Mortimer; Paley with his daughter, Hilary, from his first marriage

poised in hand, and then the long legs would swing out the door as the girls stood wide-eyed.

In due course Amanda was expected to be her mother's daughter in every way—especially by her young husband. On the first day of their honeymoon in Paris, Carter was upset when their room had not been stocked with Perrier. It was only the beginning of the considerable strain Amanda would feel from Carter Burden's expectations.

But Amanda's problems paled compared to those of her half sister, Kate. "She is the most wounded of all the birds," commented one friend. Kate resembled her father, but what was rugged and appealing in a man was merely plain in a girl. Still, she was lively and responsive, and during her earliest years Bill Paley doted on Kate. Then when she was three years old, fate dealt her a cruel blow. During a family vacation in Cap d'Antibes, Kate began to lose her hair. By the autumn every hair on Kate's body had fallen out. She was a victim of alopecia universalis, a rare disorder often associated with severe stress.

The Paleys consulted one specialist after another. "Babe went crazy," said Tex McCrary. "She turned to everything— faith healing, you name it. She was horrified, terrified, mystified."

Above, Kate Paley with her father. Top right, son Jeffrey with his wife, Valerie. Lower right, son William "Billie" Paley.

Babe did what she could to mitigate the trauma. She hired James Masterson, a leading psychiatrist, to work with Kate. She found the best wigs money could buy. Understandably, however, Kate was self-conscious about her affliction. She became shy and acutely sensitive. If someone patted her on the head, she would instinctively pull away.

Kate was very bright, and promisingly artistic, with a strong hand and a keen eye. After graduating from Madeira, a posh girls' boarding school in Virginia, she enrolled at the Rhode Island School of Design, but she never completed her course of studies.

Inevitably, a gulf grew between Babe and Kate. How could a daughter so afflicted have failed to resent a mother who embodied such perfection? For the next seven years Kate had virtually nothing to do with her mother or father. She traveled a great deal, dabbled in painting, and joined the demimonde of Manhattan's downtown artistic community. She seemed to grow more comfortable with her condition; she even painted portraits of herself without her wig. Occasionally Kate would call home and Babe would invite her for tea. But at the appointed time Kate would fail to show up.

Kate's older brother, Billie, suffered in his own way and brought his parents just as much heartache as Kate did. He was a handsome, appealing child, with black hair and Babe's flashing dark eyes, but without quite realizing it, Bill and Babe made him feel he was odd—a sense that Babe compounded when she sent him away at age seven to a special camp to correct his left-handedness. Shy and nervous, Billie bit his nails to the quick. Babe tended to indulge him and forgive his misbehavior too readily. Billie's bids for attention, like those of his siblings, were largely ignored.

"I was a strange child," Billie himself admitted in 1977. "My parents thought I was crazy. I was sent to a psychiatrist when I was ten, got kicked out of schools, started smoking dope when I was sixteen, and didn't have many friends. My father and I never really got along. I was too weird for them to believe. And of course, I wasn't a success. I was different, that's all. I didn't want to alienate my parents. I love my parents, but I hated them, you know? I just left."

As a combat cinematographer in Vietnam in the late 1960s, Billie became a heroin user. Back in the States, Billie dropped out of sight—the most extreme gesture in his lifelong effort to avoid being associated publicly with his famous father. He rebuilt an old sailboat with a friend and sailed around the Florida Keys working as a dolphin trainer, yacht broker, construction worker, photographer, and door-to-door salesman—sustained all the while by two trust funds.

Had she asserted herself, Babe might have made a difference in the lives of the Paley children. But she kept her distance—a genuine weakness in her character. "Bill put pressure on Babe," said one man close to the Paleys. "Every decision had to do with being with the children or with him. One or the other. It was no secret that he was willful."

"She wanted to be a good parent, but I don't think children interested Bill," said Marietta Tree. "She was always ready to do what he wanted to do. She often felt she was neglecting the children."

When trouble arose, her first instinct was to send them to psychiatrists rather than to confront the problems on her own. "She once told me she did all the wrong things," said one of her friends. "There were too many Christmas gifts to compensate for the guilt."

Behind the platonic and publicized ideal of Babe Paley was the private Babe, disappointed and unappreciated, pained and self-pitying. One of Babe's problems, in the view of Leonora Hornblow, was that "she was extra supersensitive. Criticism was painful to her."

Disillusion with her marriage set in quite early, according to her friends. "She wanted Bill heart and soul, and he didn't give himself heart and soul," said Marietta Tree. "He loved Babe and always will, but she wasn't the focus of his life. Nor was anybody. That was very hard for Babe to accept." Her feelings, according to Capote, boiled down to betrayal. "After three years of the marriage she really almost wanted out," Capote once confided. "She thought that he'd married her more for her sister and brother-in-law than for herself, the idea that with her came, you know, Mrs. Whitney and Mrs. Astor. I mean, he was getting the whole family." She was his possession, the most valued among the precious objects in his ever expanding collection.

"There was a streak in everybody's mind about that marriage," said Diana Vreeland. "They weren't born for each other. They were not ideal. But happiness like sun blazing in a room was not Babe's disposition. She was private and didn't radiate that easily. And if she were troubled, there was no way she wore it on her sleeve."

But the signs of strain poked through. Babe suffered from severe migraine headaches that lasted two or three days. She once told Marietta Tree that she thought the headaches resulted from her anxiety about neglecting the children. To smooth out the edges, Babe took Miltown tranquilizers, and she regularly saw a psychiatrist.

Much of the time Paley's infidelities were the source of Babe's unhappiness. "Bill was always flirting with everyone," recalled Babe's friend Jeanne Murray Vanderbilt. "He was on the make. Babe was so nice. She always tried to invite pretty women he would like to look at. But I guess he never stopped—on the side, during the week."

Babe had little choice but to keep her reserve and take pleasure from the freedom and wealth that came with being Bill Paley's wife. She lived luxuriously, and most of the time this was enough. "I think he gave her joy," said Leonora Hornblow, "and he took joy from her company." Said Babe's close friend Slim Keith, "She loved him. She saw him as a riveting man."

CHAPTER 14

LARGELY in Paley's absence, CBS Television grew apace. And as top entertainment shows shifted from radio to television, so did the news operation. TV News at CBS expanded from fourteen full-time staffers in 1950 to three hundred and seventy-six just six years later. During that time the annual budget rose to $7 million. Television, with its complicated electronic equipment, simply required more personnel and cost more than radio.

Like Paley, Ed Murrow, the radio man, had mistrusted television at first. But Paley's wariness stemmed from commercial considerations. He had never harbored any doubts about television as a medium for news. Back in 1948 he had written in *The New York Times* that "television offers keener insights than printed or spoken words alone can provide." He predicted that "if tomorrow's politician's words are honeyed and plausible, we shall know whether his facial expression contradicts them."

Murrow never shared Paley's optimism on this score. While recognizing the potential power of television, Murrow fretted about its inherent deficiencies. He understood that the radio audience was forced to concentrate on words and ideas without the distraction of images. The television camera served to limit rather than expand news coverage, to put a premium on visuals instead of on explanation and analysis. He saw radio's superiority as a medium of greater intellectual force—a distinction that eluded Paley.

Murrow made the jump to television in the autumn of 1951, when he converted his radio program, *Hear It Now*, to *See It Now*. The new weekly half-hour program was designed to be a *Life* magazine of the airwaves, capturing significant stories in documentary style.

See It Now was created by Murrow and his producer, Fred Friendly, who came out of radio in Providence, Rhode Island. A big man of oversized appetites and enthusiasms, Friendly was creative, passionate, and energetic—as much a dramatist as a journalist.

See It Now won high praise, although it did not attract a large audience. Each week it delved into one or two stories, homing in on what Friendly liked to call "the little picture" to explain larger issues. In December 1951, shortly after its debut, *See It Now* took a swipe at Senator Joseph McCarthy in a piece showing the Senator as a haranguing interrogator. But otherwise, the program avoided the subject of McCarthy and his charges of widespread communist infiltration in government, concentrating instead on safe topics.

Prodded by colleagues, Murrow finally focused on witch-hunting in October 1953 with a program on Milo Radulovich, an air force lieutenant who had been asked to resign as a security risk because his father and sister were supposedly subversive. *See It Now* found no evidence for the accusation, and Radulovich kept his commission. Five months later Murrow and Friendly decided to take on McCarthy, whose influence and popularity were at their peak.

In the postwar period Paley and Murrow had kept up the social link they had formed during the glamorous war years. Virile, magnetic Ed Murrow, a man who could make smoking a cigarette seem like the height of romance, became in a way another bauble for Paley. Like Paley, he wasn't to the manner born, but Murrow acquired the bearing—as well as the bespoke suits from Anderson & Sheppard, of Savile Row, shirts from Bertollini, in Rome, and shoes from Scotland—to shine in the most elegant of social circles. The Murrows visited Kiluna periodically for house-party weekends, and Babe and Bill also visited the Murrow country home in Pawling, New York. At work Murrow and Paley had lunch together every two weeks. "He never made a move without talking to me about it," Paley boasted.

Close as he was to Paley, Murrow cunningly kept quiet about his plans to unmask McCarthy. Since the Radulovich broadcast, Alcoa Aluminum, the sponsor of *See It Now,* had come under pressure to drop Murrow, who had been attacked by conservative columnists for one-sided reporting. Affiliates of CBS had also complained about the newsman's supposed liberal bias. Murrow could not be sure how Paley and Stanton would react to a McCarthy report. "We tried to keep it a secret until the last minute," said Friendly.

Memories vary on exactly when Murrow called Paley to brief him on the McCarthy broadcast. Friendly and Paley said it was March 8, 1954, the day before the scheduled Tuesday night program; Stanton and another executive, Louis Cowan, insisted it was the afternoon of the broadcast. "Are you satisfied it is accurate?" Paley asked after Murrow outlined the program. Murrow assured him that it was. "Will it cause a big stink?" asked Paley. "Yes," answered Murrow, who offered to screen the program for Paley before it went on the air. Paley declined, but he added that McCarthy might want time for a reply. "Why don't you offer McCarthy the time yourself?" Paley said. "That way it won't look like you are bending in to him." Paley's suggestion was really a command in shrewd psychological disguise. Before airtime Paley called Murrow. "I'm with you today, and I'll be with you tomorrow," he said.

Despite his brave words, Paley was nervous. He knew McCarthy was capable of coming after Murrow—and CBS. Paley watched the program that Tuesday night in his pied-à-terre, at the St. Regis Hotel, with Babe and theatrical producer Leland Hayward and his then wife, Slim Keith. "His support of Ed was total," recalled Slim. When Murrow signed off, the Paleys called him. But it was Babe, not Bill, who spoke to Murrow and told him how good the program was. Cautious as ever, Paley was putting some distance between himself and Murrow. Paley did talk directly to Stanton. The two men agreed that while it had been a fine show, they had to "batten down the hatches."

The program exposed McCarthy by hanging him on his own words through footage skillfully edited to show the pattern of his demagoguery. Murrow concluded by stating that "this is no time for men who oppose Senator McCarthy's methods to keep silent. The actions of the junior Senator from Wisconsin have caused alarm and dismay amongst our allies abroad and given considerable comfort to our enemies." It was all-out advocacy journalism.

As such, it was enormously effective—the most dramatic evidence to date of television's power. In the aftermath CBS logged some fifteen thousand letters and an equal number of phone calls over-whelmingly supporting Murrow. Thousands of telegrams to Alcoa also sided with Murrow. But McCarthy wrote to the sponsor as well, to threaten an investigation. Conservative columnists lashed out at Murrow, alleging communist connections in his youth.

"The day after the broadcast they tore the roof off the building," said Paley, who called Murrow to say, "We're in for a helluva fight. Is there anything he can get you on?" Murrow assured him there was not, but Paley wanted to be safe. "Let's get our own people to dig into everything you ever did and find out if there is anything vulnerable," Paley told him. With Murrow's assent CBS hired a prestigious law firm to conduct the probe. The lawyers found no skeletons.

Paley also suggested that when Murrow spoke after McCarthy's reply, he should say that history would judge whether he or McCarthy had better served his country. It was a suggestion in which Paley would take justifiable pride.

The televised reply damaged McCarthy even more than the original Murrow attack. Looking awkward and pasty in poorly applied stage makeup, McCarthy raged about Murrow's alleged subversion and repeated his accusations of communist influence in government. Recalled Paley of the Senator's response, "You saw him in action, and you knew he was a very wild sort of guy and not very fair, and you sort of got the feeling, like, God, we've been following this guy and just look at him now. It was the beginning of McCarthy's downfall."

In the following months McCarthy went over the line by accusing the army of harboring Communists as well. The Senate held televised hearings in which McCarthy's irresponsible charges fell apart, costing him the support of his colleagues.

The McCarthy broadcast marked the peak of Murrow's postwar influence at CBS. But while Paley did not waver in his support, the experience made him uneasy. He worried about protests from advertisers. "Bill Paley was proud of the broadcast but more retroac-tively," Fred Friendly recalled. "It was inevitable that Paley would make sure Murrow could never again put the network on the line."

In the fourteen months following the McCarthy broadcast Murrow went out of his way to test Paley's resolve by continuing to report on controversial topics, including book burning and the involvement of the Texas statehouse in a land scandal. In May 1955 Irving Wilson, president of Alcoa Aluminum, told Paley and Stanton that Alcoa wanted to reach more consumers by advertising on entertainment shows rather than on public affairs programming. "My very private reaction was that Alcoa didn't want to take the heat," said Stanton.

Paley was eager to minimize the political controversies stirred up by *See It Now*. The program occupied a valuable slot in prime time that could fetch far more revenue if filled with an entertainment show. In early July, 1955, Paley invited Murrow and Friendly to his office, ostensibly to tell them of a wonderful new opportunity. He offered to expand *See It Now* to a full hour and give them more resources. Of course, such an ambitious effort needed more preparation time as well. It would be better, Paley said, if the program ran eight to ten times a year. Friendly and Murrow, exhausted by their battles with sponsors and the front office, acquiesced.

See It Now (now mockingly known on Broadcast Row as *See It Now and Then*) could not hold a sponsor. In 1956, after a year in the new format, Paley shifted the program from prime time to Sunday afternoon.

In March 1958 Paley and Murrow had their final rupture over *See It Now*. It involved a trivial provocation that Paley took far too seriously. In fact, Paley's response reflected his cumulative ill will toward *See It Now*—and toward Ed Murrow. The program addressed the prospect of statehood for Alaska and Hawaii, an innocuous enough subject. But perhaps for the sake of drama, it focused on the views of right-wingers who saw the two prospective states as havens for Communists. One proponent of statehood called an obscure Republican Congressman from upstate New York, John Pillion, crazy for holding such beliefs. Pillion asked for equal time to refute.

Sig Mickelson, news director at the time, considered the request unwarranted. In a meeting with Paley he argued that the program was sufficiently balanced. But Paley disagreed, insisting that the program flagrantly violated CBS' standards of fairness. In fact, far more was at stake. "Paley was distressed by Edward R. Murrow and wanted to let him have it," recalled Mickelson. Paley ordered Mickelson to tell Murrow and Friendly that Pillion's request would be granted.

Murrow wrote an angry letter demanding to be let out of *See It Now* by the end of the year. In May 1958 Murrow and Friendly met with Paley in the rarefied surroundings of the chairman's office.

The three men talked about ways to avoid a Pillion situation again. But the discussion heated up quickly. Abruptly Paley told Murrow and Friendly that *See It Now* was being taken off the air. When Murrow asked incredulously whether Paley really wanted to destroy such a valuable program, the CBS chairman punched his own stomach and uttered one of his most celebrated lines: "I don't want this constant stomachache every time you do a controversial subject." Countered Murrow, "It goes with the job."

Paley's displeasure went deeper than stomach pains, real or metaphorical. Although Paley never said so explicitly, Murrow—and to a lesser extent fellow news correspondents Howard K. Smith and Eric Sevareid—angered the CBS chairman because they so consistently nettled the Eisenhower administration. Not only were Eisenhower and Paley friends of long standing, but Paley had a political ambition that Eisenhower had the power to fulfill: a prestigious ambassadorship in Europe.

PALEY'S admiration for his amiable former commander had continued unabated after the war. Both men shared a simple, unintellectual approach to problems and relied on the force of personality—quiet charm and confident optimism—to get their way. Eisenhower, like Paley, was far more calculating than he appeared.

When Eisenhower kicked off his campaign with a press conference in his hometown of Abilene, Kansas, Paley made one of his few overt interventions in CBS' coverage of his friends and ordered CBS News to televise the press conference live. During the campaign Paley was a visibly enthusiastic supporter of the Republican cause. Jock Whitney, who contributed significant funds to the campaign, served as finance chairman of Citizens for Eisenhower. Although Paley did not actively raise funds, he was an informal consultant. Paley's private advice was especially valuable because 1952 marked the first television campaign. Eisenhower's use of media events, stressing images over substance, was crucial to his victory over Adlai Stevenson, whose fondness for words and ideas was incompatible with television.

Bill Paley felt far more comfortable as an Eisenhower booster than he had as a New Deal poseur before the war. A man of wealth and a businessman to the core, Paley settled easily into the moderate wing of the Grand Old Party. "He was very much under the political influence of Jock Whitney," recalled CBS newsman Walter Cronkite. But Paley kept his partisanship quiet.

Shortly after Eisenhower's victory that November, the President-elect offered Paley a job as secretary to the Cabinet. But the post evidently didn't measure up to Paley's expectations, and he declined, explaining that he was too busy. The newly elected President felt bruised.

Still, Paley considered Eisenhower to be a true friend. They played golf and bridge together, and Paley dutifully sent birthday telegrams, long-playing CBS records, and words of encouragement.

After Eisenhower was reelected, in 1956, he nominated Jock Whitney as ambassador to the Court of St. James's, the plum coveted by Paley. At the same time, the President sent word to Paley that he was thinking of naming him ambassador to France. Paley expressed interest. Quietly he hired a tutor and began taking French lessons. Then, recalled Stanton, "the circuits went dead." Eisenhower had retreated because he feared criticism over having brothers-in-law in two critical European posts. Paley was crushed.

Paley's frustration was felt at CBS. The men at CBS News knew that Paley blamed their liberalism at least in part for his inability to become an ambassador. Murrow continued to have the most liberal profile of all. In the 1956 campaign Murrow had lost his journalistic bearings by secretly coaching Adlai Stevenson on television techniques. "Bill Paley disapproved of Ed because Ed angered Eisenhower," said Howard K. Smith. "Paley expected much for himself with the Eisenhower administration, and it did not happen."

CHAPTER 15

I F *See It Now* signified television at its best, the quiz show represented the worst of the new medium. The first big-money show, *The $64,000 Question*, surfaced on CBS in early June, 1955.

There was nothing about the start of *The $64,000 Question* that could have allowed anyone to predict the hold it would have on the national consciousness. It was unabashedly crass. Two contestants vied to answer increasingly difficult questions for ever greater amounts of money, beginning at two dollars and going to a $64,000 jackpot. The contestants were ordinary people with unlikely specialties: the cobbler who was an opera aficionado, the jockey with expertise in art.

Louis Cowan, the show's producer, believed that it would celebrate knowledge and give people an incentive to learn. But the show's genuine appeal was the glorification of greed.

The $64,000 Question was an instant success, supplanting *I Love Lucy* as the top-rated show. Sales for its sponsor, Revlon, rocketed as well. Quiz shows sprang up on all three networks. (In 1943 NBC had sold its Blue Network, which was rechristened ABC—the third network.) NBC's hottest version, *Twenty-One,* launched in 1956, raised the stakes by removing the limit on prize winnings.

For the networks all this activity translated into huge advertising revenues. At CBS net revenues had increased more than fourfold since the beginning of the decade—from $87 million in 1950 to $354 million in 1956. But the quiz shows nearly did the networks in.

The seeds of the trouble were planted in 1956, when the Justice Department threatened antitrust action against the networks. After the war, at Paley's direction, control over programming was taken away from advertising agencies, but now CBS felt pressured to hand that control to independent program producers. In so doing, CBS hoped to defuse government criticism that the networks had become too powerful.

The first hints of quiz-show improprieties came in a *Time* article in April 1957 that the networks chose to ignore. Five months later Herbert Stempel, a disaffected contestant on *Twenty-One,* told NBC officials that his opponent, Charles Van Doren, had been fed questions in advance and that the producers had told Stempel to give wrong answers. The producers denied the charges to the NBC executives, who chose not to mention the accusations to their superiors.

In August 1958—three months after Paley had canceled *See It Now*—the quiz-show scandal blew open when Edward Hilgemeier, a standby contestant on CBS' *Dotto,* revealed that one of the show's contestants had been coached. Stanton immediately launched an investigation and kicked *Dotto* off the air—actions that Paley heard about after the fact.

Both the Manhattan District Attorney's Office and the U.S. House of Representatives followed with their own probes. The next fourteen months brought one revelation after another of widespread quiz-show rigging by the independent producers. These were dark days for the networks, casting the integrity of television into doubt.

In the middle of this crisis, on October 15, 1958, Edward R. Murrow threw an incendiary bomb. Speaking to the annual convention of the Radio and Television News Directors Association, in Chicago, Murrow cited the "decadence, escapism, and insulation from the realities of the world" that characterized television. He castigated the networks for squandering their "powerful instrument of communication" in the pursuit of profits. To make up for their sins, Murrow urged the networks to make a "tiny tithe" to increase news and public affairs programs. "This instrument can teach; it can illuminate," he said. "Yes, and it can even inspire. But it can do so only to the extent that humans are determined to use it to those ends. Otherwise, it is merely wires and lights in a box." Murrow's words exposed the hypocrisy of Paley's effort to have it both ways—to cut back on news and public affairs in the push for greater profits while expecting CBS to be regarded as the premier news network.

Paley was deeply hurt by the speech. He had known Murrow's beliefs for a long time. But for the man who symbolized CBS to most viewers to hit the networks when they were down seemed an unforgivable act of disloyalty—regardless of how wounded he was over Paley's cancellation of *See It Now*. "It was a direct attack on me," Paley would say.

Years later Paley described his subsequent treatment of Murrow as "very peculiar." In fact, it was completely in character. He knew Murrow expected, even desired, a showdown. Paley refused to give it to him. He said nothing then, or ever. Paley's silence only deepened Murrow's bitterness. Except for one poignant visit some years afterwards, Bill Paley and Ed Murrow "never had a civil conversation after October 1958," said Fred Friendly.

Firing Murrow would have been too messy, but Paley could freeze him out. When assignments were given for election-night coverage, Murrow learned that he was demoted to reporting regional returns. "He got an office memo telling him what he was to do," recalled fellow newsman Robert Trout. "It was absurd. It was an insult. But he was like a soldier. 'I'm a reporter,' he said. 'I'll accept my assignment.' It was a public humiliation."

Early in 1959 Murrow was granted a leave of absence at his request, amid speculation in the press about his standing at CBS.

THAT May, Paley, who had earned a reputation as a hypochondriac, decided that a chest cold was actually lung cancer. It began quite innocently when Paley came down with a cold. Fretful about his condition, he called his Manhasset physician, William Messinger, who ordered an X ray and later told Paley he saw a shadow on the film. Paley flew into a swivet about the possibility of cancer. He called Babe's doctor, Connie Guion, who assembled a team of specialists at New York Hospital.

A biopsy revealed that Paley's lungs—after some forty-four years of four packs of unfiltered cigarettes a day—were dark purple instead of glistening pink. One of the doctors told Paley that if he could see his own lungs, he would never smoke again. At that moment Paley had a cigarette cupped in his hand. He held it up to the doctor, announced that it would be his last, and dropped it into a bowl of water. Paley was so frightened that he kept his pledge.

Several days later he returned to New York Hospital for further examination by a lung specialist, who ordered additional X rays. All the X rays showed the same shadow. Meanwhile, the biopsy had shown no evidence of malignancy.

It was recommended, however, that Paley's chest be opened and explored (today a CAT scan would have served the same purpose). If a tumor was present, it would be removed.

The surgery involved a huge incision across Paley's chest and the removal of three ribs. The doctors found no tumor; they did discover that Paley's diaphragm was paralyzed on the right side and had pushed up his right lung, resulting in the shadow on the X ray.

Instead of feeling relieved, Paley plunged into a depression that would last a year. He went to Biarritz, France, with Babe for the summer to convalesce. But rounds of golf and festive luncheons with friends failed to cheer him. With Babe, he was frequently irascible and sometimes downright nasty. To explain his behavior, he decided that he was really two Bill Paleys: when he was feeling chipper, he was William; when he was depressed, he called himself Guillaume.

The following fall Paley, still caught in the grip of his depression, was even further removed psychologically from CBS than usual. He remained in the shadows, acquiescing to nearly every decision made by Stanton.

The quiz-show imbroglio finally wound down in November 1959, after Charles Van Doren made a dramatic confession at a congressional hearing. The following month Lou Cowan, whose quiz-show success had propelled him to the presidency of CBS Television, resigned from CBS under intense pressure from Stanton. Because of a flare-up of phlebitis, Cowan had not appeared before the congressional committee, and Stanton had borne the brunt of the congressional wrath instead. Stanton was convinced that Cowan had to have known about the crooked goings-on at *The $64,000 Question* and that he had purposely avoided testifying about it.

Bill Paley believed strongly in Cowan's innocence. But when Stanton told Paley that Cowan had to go, the CBS chairman raised no objection. "Paley vanished to the Bahamas," said Cowan later, "and never returned my phone calls."

As Cowan's replacement, Stanton appointed James Aubrey, whom he had been grooming for months. By now Paley's absence from the company had become so conspicuous that it was the occasion for *Variety* to ask, "Where is Paley?" Former *Variety* reporter Robert Landry noted, "In a crisis Paley was always out of town."

Paley didn't grasp that the quiz scandals stemmed from the very nature of commercial television. More than anything, it had been Paley's insistence on ever higher ratings and profits that pushed the producers over the line. What Paley concluded from the quiz scandals was the need for the networks to reassert control of programming—an idea close to his heart.

Murrow returned to CBS headquarters from his sabbatical in May 1960. In the following months he narrated some notable CBS broadcasts, but he had little contact with Paley. Their social relationship had ended several years earlier. Now, even in the office, they rarely met face to face. No longer was Murrow special; he was just a cog in the CBS news machine.

Murrow's bitterness was palpable. "When Ed was on the way down," recalled Charles Collingwood, perhaps the closest to him of Murrow's Boys, "it was a very poignant time. He felt it bitterly. He told me,

'They'll use you up and burn you out and throw you out.'" Wounded as he was, Murrow declined to criticize Paley directly. "He never lost his fascination with Bill Paley," said Howard K. Smith.

Shortly after the election of John F. Kennedy, in November 1960, Murrow got a call from the President-elect: Would Murrow be interested in heading the United States Information Agency? The newsman was interested, but before he made his final decision, he sought out Paley, as so often in the old days.

Stanton was in Paley's office when Murrow arrived. Murrow explained the job offer and said he was inclined to take it. Without offering any specifics Paley assured Murrow he would have a place at CBS "forever." A week later Kennedy announced the appointment.

Murrow did his last CBS broadcast on January 31, 1961. In the autumn of 1963 he was diagnosed as having lung cancer and underwent a three-hour operation. To ease his recuperation, he and Janet moved to La Jolla, California. Early the following month Bill Paley came to visit. This was the one moment that genuine warmth returned to their relationship. They had lunch together, laughed about old times, and Murrow took Paley sightseeing. Paley offered to take Murrow on as a programming consultant.

Back in New York, doctors found that the cancer had spread to Murrow's brain. They removed a tumor and treated him with radiation. He could barely speak, his body was wasted, and he wore a stocking on his head. Paley dutifully made numerous visits to Murrow's bedside. But it was by no means certain that Murrow had forgiven him. In April 1965 Murrow died.

In later years Paley found comfort by glossing over their estrangement. "We were very close friends to the bitter end," he said. "I guess he was one of the closest friends I ever had." When pressed about what happened between them, Paley preferred to blame Murrow's unhappiness on the necessary restrictions of television and on a nostalgia for the more freewheeling days of radio.

At bottom, the rift occurred because Murrow brought too much controversy and too little money to CBS. "Paley wanted to make a lot of money and keep a lot of money," said newsman Robert Trout. In the end Murrow sensed a gross betrayal of principles on Paley's part, and he was forced to tell Paley precisely what he thought Paley was—a greedy businessman. Nothing could have hurt more.

CHAPTER 16

BILL Paley and Frank Stanton had few common interests, no natural chemistry. Theirs was a relationship built on convenience and necessity: each instinctively recognized that his own weaknesses were the other's strengths. They were wary of one another, each privately disapproving of how the other lived. Without their shared devotion to CBS, Paley and Stanton might well have disliked one another.

Each used the other for his own ends. Stanton wanted operating control of CBS, and Paley wanted someone to operate it for him while he maintained ultimate authority. To Paley, Stanton was a corporate Jeeves, the man who took care of the details, cleaned up messes, and could be counted on always to do the correct thing.

Superficially, Paley and Stanton cut handsome figures as CBS chiefs in the early '50s. Paley was now in his fifties, Stanton in his mid-forties. They were nearly identical in height, and both had resonant, broadcast-quality voices. Stanton had the edge in meticulousness: his closely cropped flaxen hair was so perfectly parted that he was jokingly referred to as the Veronica Lake of CBS. Paley's dark, English-tailored suits tended to be more conservative, while Stanton favored flashy touches like shirts of robin's-egg blue. His jaw often clamped on a pipe that he miraculously kept glowing with a single light. But Stanton carefully balanced the flash with a professorial mien.

Temperamentally, the two men were opposites: Paley had a restless, readily satisfied curiosity; Stanton was more brainy, more sensitive, more orderly, and decidedly more intellectual than Paley.

CBS was Frank Stanton's life. On trips to England he would sit in a room at Claridge's and watch British television for several days, taking notes. His social life was curtailed by his willingness to work every weekend. His wife, Ruth, often joined him at the office on those quiet days. She would sit and read, and they would have dinner together at a nearby restaurant.

Paley had become the ultimate stylish tycoon, living the glamorous highlife. He was charming in society and iron-willed, even ruthless, around CBS. As he grew older Paley relied more on his instincts, although he was far more cautious than his legend would have it. "Rat smart," CBS executives called him behind his back, mindful of the rat's cunning resourcefulness and sense of survival. He grew more and more arbitrary. Stanton knew, along with everyone else at CBS, that one flick from Paley could whip him into line.

It was in business meetings that the contrasts between Paley and Stanton were most noticeable. Stanton's approach to problems was rigorously logical. He made decisions quickly, dissecting them piece by piece in orderly fashion.

Paley's approach seemed undisciplined and haphazard. Paley, recalled programming executive Harry Ackerman, "was the kind of man who came in each morning and would reach into his pockets and put on the table twenty-four pieces of paper, including napkins. I think of him not so much as nervous, as having the quickest intelligence—constantly on the alert, constantly thinking, one jump ahead, with crinkling, shining eyes, zeroing in on the next question."

Both Paley and Stanton shied away from simple comparisons casting Stanton as analytical, cerebral, and intellectual, and Paley as instinctive, intuitive, and impulsive. Those characterizations contained truth, but Stanton said they were "overstatements in both directions. We were closer than many people realize." Both men chose to emphasize their mutual concern with taste and quality for CBS. Paley often said he respected Stanton's organizational ability, his equanimity, and his relentless commitment to CBS.

Stanton was awestruck by the magic of Paley's charm; for some time it obscured his appreciation of Paley's shrewdness and brilliance. "He had such facility in his personal relations in business. He was a smooth piece of work," Stanton remarked. "He could charm the birds right out of the trees. I used to think there was an awful lot of luck in what he did. But I learned that there was a lot more skill than I first gave him credit for."

Paley believed that Stanton did not know how to live. To Paley, Stanton was hopelessly square. Paley was forever making suggestions to Stanton about leisure. Take time off, he'd advise, visit this or that European capital. When Paley urged Stanton to build a home near Kiluna, the Stantons declined. "I made it a condition when I agreed to be president of CBS that I not socialize with Bill," Stanton would say years later. "I told him he could have me anytime during business hours but not after. I didn't want to be part of that world."

Stanton never felt comfortable with Paley's crowd. Both men had arrived in New York lacking connections to the schools, clubs, and resorts that were the touchstones to "the right people." But Paley shut the door on his modest origins and transformed himself through invention and determination into a facsimile of the eastern Establishment. Stanton could not; he was unable to escape being the son of a high school woodworking teacher. It was easier for Stanton to retreat than risk rejection or, even worse, mockery.

Stanton's rebuffs of Paley's various social overtures deeply annoyed Paley. The emperor of CBS would benevolently extend his hand, and Stanton would turn away. But nothing rankled Paley more than Stanton's refusal to invite him to his home.

The Stanton town house, on East Ninety-second Street in Manhattan, was a sacred hideaway. His stubborn insistence on not including Paley among the select few guests—even after Paley had entertained the Stantons in his home any number of times—was an obvious cut. Over the years Paley bitterly complained to others about the slight.

At bottom, Paley and Stanton's relationship was "always at arm's length," said Dorothy Paley. They could never openly acknowledge the unbridgeable distance between them. Had they been genuinely fond of one another, they might well have averted the power struggle that would entangle them both in the years to come.

PALEY and Stanton did not assume the classic Mr. Inside–Mr. Outside relationship so common between corporate presidents and chairmen, where one man operates inside the company and the other deals with the outside world. At CBS each man was Mr. Outside in his sphere of influence—Paley in Hollywood, Stanton in corporate and political circles. William Leonard, a longtime CBS News executive, said that "Frank seemed to handle Paley in much the way a wily prime minister would deal with an equally shrewd, erratic—but absolute— monarch."

Stanton's first rule for dealing with Paley was to keep him informed, but not too deeply. With a careful eye toward controlling the information, Stanton had all areas of the company reporting to him; programming executives reported to both Paley and Stanton. In meetings Stanton submerged his ego, never taking issue with Paley.

When Stanton expressed his own opinion, it was to agree with the boss.

While Paley was inaccessible, Stanton kept an open door. He was generous with both his time and his advice, always ready to offer a warm ear to unhappy subordinates. It mattered little to Paley that he remained distant from so many at the company he built. If something failed, Stanton was the fall guy; if it was a success, Paley could take credit—an astute but not terribly admirable strategy.

Both Paley and Stanton were quite content at first with their relationship. "I let Frank Stanton run the company," Paley would say years later with imperial certitude. "I had complete confidence in him and allowed him to get recognition. I think he felt he got it."

Paley had carved out a life for himself that was not too demanding—a kind of semiretirement, with enormous leisure and just enough anxiety to keep it spicy. Paley did exactly as he pleased. He knew that the stimulus of the small amount of responsibility he carried was enough. He also knew he could count on Frank Stanton.

To much of the outside world Frank Stanton—not Bill Paley—was Mr. CBS. In Washington, D.C., Stanton made headlines fighting for broadcasters' independence and got favorable treatment for CBS. He knew every Senator and Congressman. His speech, conduct, and look gave CBS a personal dignity that had little to do with what was appearing on living-room TV screens. Stanton's contribution to CBS' image was incalculable.

Significantly, for the first decade of Stanton's presidency he drew a higher salary and bonus than Paley. In 1946, Stanton's first year in office, he made $94,010 in salary to Paley's $65,000. By 1955 Stanton's salary and bonus had risen to $281,522, compared to Paley's $225,000. But because of his CBS holdings, worth $19.2 million by the mid-'50s, Paley made considerably more than Stanton in stock dividends: $786,132 in 1955. By that year Stanton also had a comfortable CBS stake, worth nearly $4 million, that yielded $151,168 in dividends.

During the first decade that Stanton and Paley had worked together, the true nature of their partnership was masked. Paley allowed Frank Stanton to build an entirely new business at CBS. As Stanton recalled years later, "Who else had the opportunity to take a new medium—television—and plot its future and be there at each step of the way? Some days it was so interesting that if they had not paid me, I would have almost paid them to do it."

By the mid-1950s, however, Paley began to suffer in comparison to his dynamo president. Because he was so often absent, Paley began to be regarded by CBS executives as a dilettante seriously out of touch with his own company and lacking Stanton's dedication.

Paley found himself in a box. He needed Stanton; Stanton made the machine run and understood many of the complexities that eluded Paley. But as Paley recognized this dependence he grew to resent Stanton. Paley hated to admit being dependent on anyone.

Paley had come out of World War II as a true statesman of broadcasting, on the strength of the contributions of Murrow and his colleagues at CBS News. Yet in Paley's quest for pleasure and convenience he had allowed that reputation to dissipate. He had gone beyond delegating; he had abdicated. He gave Stanton too much running room and ceded too much power and prestige—outside CBS and within it as well.

Thus the CBS proxy statement for 1956 contained a small but telling number—a glimmer of an essential turning point in the relationship between Bill Paley and Frank Stanton a decade after it began. That year, for the first time, the two men had identical salaries—$300,000. From that time on, Paley began insisting on symbolic equality with Stanton. Their offices were designed to measure the same square footage down to the inch. They were driven around town in identical limousines.

Still, Paley's work habits continued much as before, and Stanton continued to pilot the company in the chief's absence. Stanton persevered at CBS because he assumed that when Paley reached the mandatory retirement age of sixty-five, in 1966, he would hand over the reins to his number two. Stanton was confident that one day CBS would be his to run on his own.

CHAPTER 17

WHEN Paley emerged from his postoperative depression late in 1960, he was fifty-nine years old. Like Rip Van Winkle, he found the world had changed at CBS. James Aubrey, Jr., the youthful TV network president appointed a year earlier, following the quiz-show scandal, had taken over programming, and Stanton controlled everything else. Paley saw that in effect he had become a supernumerary, and he was determined to reclaim his empire.

"It was a difficult relationship with Bill," recalled Stanton. "As he got older he reentered the company. He had not been involved for years. Also, he discovered what an important force television had become, and he wanted to be part of it."

To his surprise Paley found himself virtually excluded from programming by James Aubrey. Once, in Aubrey's first year, Paley had made a halfhearted stab at reasserting his influence over the entertainment schedule. In a long memo in August 1960, Paley complained that Aubrey had failed to include any cultural programs on his list for the 1960–61 television season. He reminded Aubrey that CBS had always highlighted a few such offerings to reaffirm its reputation as the quality network.

Aubrey ignored the memo—a response Paley would later rationalize by saying, "I was in my recessive period after the operation. It may be that I did not altogether get my way for some time."

That was an understatement. For the next four years Paley seemed in thrall to Aubrey—the embodiment of WASP traits he so revered. Born to privilege and wealth, James Aubrey grew up in prosperous Lake Forest, north of Chicago, where his father was a successful advertising executive. He went to Exeter and Princeton, and served as an air force test pilot in World War II.

In 1948 he got a job at CBS' radio station in Los Angeles. He advanced quickly and joined the network's West Coast programming department. In 1956 he jumped to ABC, where he helped devise a string of action shows that gave the third-ranked television network its first successful programming lineup. In 1958 he sent a message to Frank Stanton: he wanted to return to CBS. Stanton immediately hired him as his executive assistant.

Aubrey occupied an office between Stanton's and Paley's, and he dazzled the entire twentieth floor with his intelligence and ability. Whether by design or by instinct, Aubrey mirrored many of Paley's traits. His luminous smile gave him unstoppable charm, but this outward affability masked a steely interior. He was consumed with winning. Above all, he focused obsessively on the heart and soul of network television—programming.

By the time Paley had bounced back from his surgery and

depression, Aubrey was so entrenched and so manifestly capable that Paley could not afford to intrude. The Aubrey juggernaut was making CBS and Paley richer than the CBS chairman had dreamed. From 1959 to 1964 CBS profits nearly doubled—from $25.2 million to $49.6 million. During the same period Paley's CBS holdings grew in value from $38.6 million to $87 million.

Paley's programming catechism found its most ardent advocate in Aubrey, whose formula for success was simple—and simpleminded: "broads, bosoms, and fun" was the way a colleague put it. Aubrey jettisoned all live drama and moved entirely to filmed weekly series in two categories: inane comedy and fast-action adventure. With hits like *The Beverly Hillbillies, Petticoat Junction, Green Acres,* and *My Favorite Martian,* CBS surged ahead of NBC in popularity. In the 1962–63 television season CBS had eight of the top ten television programs, seven of them comedies. It was CBS' most shameless excursion down the low road.

At first Aubrey and Paley got on well. They played golf together, and Paley invited him to Kiluna. They shared a penchant for philandering as well, prowling together in New York and Hollywood. By 1963 Aubrey had divorced his wife of nearly twenty years. Paley, of course, continued to have it both ways by staying married to Babe.

As Aubrey grew more successful and powerful he became insufferably arrogant. "Once he got a strong power base in the company, he went bananas," said Stanton. "He was rude to affiliates, showed contempt for advertisers, and was rude to talent."

Eventually Aubrey began mistreating Bill Paley. One producer recalled being in Aubrey's office when Paley called to question a show. In the most superior manner Aubrey said, "Billy, you worry about the finances, I'll worry about the programs," and hung up. Remarkably, Paley tolerated the impoliteness for a time. He felt he could not afford to cross someone who was riding so high.

By the spring of 1964 Aubrey was taking credit for single-handedly masterminding CBS' success. At the same time, the Hollywood gossip mill began raising questions about Aubrey's personal and professional behavior. He was notorious for his girlfriends, wild parties, and drunk driving.

On April 16, 1964, *Hollywood Closeup,* a scandal sheet, alleged in an "Open Letter to William S. Paley" that Aubrey was taking kickbacks from producers. Stanton hired a New York City police detective to tail Aubrey. He discovered that Aubrey used a chauffeured limousine that was owned by Filmways, a television producer, and that he was sharing an apartment on Central Park South, paid for in part by Filmways. However, although Stanton was disturbed by the conflicts of interest, they fell shy of illegal kickbacks.

But doubts lingered. Mindful of the questions raised about Aubrey, Paley had already begun to make some noises about programming. He was tired of winning high ratings with cheap shows.

Meanwhile, there were rumors of Aubrey's larger ambitions at CBS. In November 1964 the *Gallagher Report* said that Aubrey was angling to take Stanton's job. A few weeks later Stanton and Aubrey were both working late. As they left the office they decided to walk up Fifth Avenue together. Passing by The Pierre hotel, Aubrey suggested a nightcap. There Aubrey dropped a bomb. He had been talking, he said, with some Wall Street investors who were willing to buy CBS, installing Stanton as chairman and Aubrey as president. "It's time to kick the old man out," Aubrey said. Stanton was shocked. "I'm not the guy to play that game," he said. As they walked home Stanton felt that he and Paley had been betrayed. "Aubrey had to go," recalled Stanton.

Aubrey had already started to self-destruct. His fall schedule was in tatters as NBC and ABC pulled even in the ratings with CBS. In late January, 1965, Paley and Stanton accompanied Aubrey to Hollywood to set the 1965–66 schedule. After those assembled watched the pilots together, Aubrey, acting as ringmaster, displayed the new schedule on a big magnetic board and then declined to take questions. From the back of the room Paley said, "Aren't we going to discuss anything?" Aubrey said, "No. That's our programming for the year." Paley had never before been humiliated in front of his staff. Driving to the airport with Stanton, the CBS chairman was livid. "We've got to get him out of there," he said. Stanton—who had not told Paley what he had heard at The Pierre hotel bar—knew he was free to oust Aubrey.

Aubrey was fired in late February, 1965. For his replacement, Stanton settled on John "Jack" Schneider, who had shown good leadership as the head of CBS stations in Philadelphia and New York. Like Aubrey, he was handsome and charming, but his geniality was genuine.

PALEY HURLED HIMSELF BACK INTO CBS' programming schedule, which Aubrey had left in shambles. "From 1965 on, Bill Paley became the living, acting, vital force I knew him to be," recalled programming vice president Mike Dann. "Every single night or morning he would be on the phone with me about ratings and how we were doing."

Jim Aubrey had instituted the custom of marathon screening sessions—reviewing dozens of pilots—for several days each February, prior to setting the new prime-time schedule. During Aubrey's reign Paley had been a bystander. Now he was a presence. The screenings would begin at nine a.m. and end at six p.m. Paley suffered from back problems. When his back hurt, he would lie down on a special sofa installed in the screening room. On his lap he kept a bound book containing photos and story lines for each show. Paley liked to scribble in the book, glancing only occasionally at the screen. Close by, Mike Dann placed a heap of Paley's favorite deli sandwiches—served warm on the best bread available.

"If Mr. Paley didn't like a show, he would fidget a lot," recalled one programmer. "If he liked it, he was quiet and took notes." Paley thought nothing of talking through a show that bored him, or if he was really bored, walking around, grabbing a pickle, and chewing on it. Mysteries with complicated plots often confounded him.

"If something was bad, he would go through the roof," recalled Mike Dann. Once in a while Paley would proclaim, "Good job," but he would never say, "You've got a winner." The worst judgment was when he left the room.

Programmers were unnerved by Paley's instinct for the bull's-eye. "If there were a show, for example, where you had done nothing but fight with the director and you were unhappy with the direction," recalled Oscar Katz, one of Dann's associates, "you would screen it for Bill Paley, and the first thing he would say would be a criticism of the direction. You would think to yourself, How did he know?"

Paley's instincts about performers were more unshakable than ever. In September 1965 he tuned in the opening episode of *Rawhide*, a six-year-old show about a cattle drive in the wild West, and was incensed by what he saw. Eric Fleming, the star of the series, had died earlier that year. Instead of replacing Fleming, one of Dann's subordinates promoted Clint Eastwood, the second-in-command, to trail boss. Paley called Mike Dann in his Hollywood office to say he couldn't stand Eastwood in the lead. The viewers didn't like the changes any more than Paley did, and *Rawhide* had to be canceled at the season's end.

Paley could be paternal about hit CBS shows, defending them to the end. By 1967 *Gunsmoke,* the long-running CBS western, had lost its appeal to the Saturday night audience, and Dann recommended its cancellation. Paley resisted but finally capitulated. Several days later he called Dann from the Bahamas. "I haven't been able to sleep at night," he said. "We've got to get *Gunsmoke* back. Let's switch it to Monday night." Recalled Dann, "Shows became like a part of his family if they were successful." Dann made the switch, and *Gunsmoke* held a place in the top ten for five more years.

For all of Paley's demands, his programmers relished the attention he gave them and their work. "He was good at supporting you," said Mike Dann. "If I had a problem, the first thing he would tell me was, 'Settle down. We can lick it. Just relax. It isn't that bad.' You never got into trouble with Bill by telling him about a problem you were having, but God help you if he discovered it on his own."

In meetings with his performers Paley was suitably attentive. A few performers, however, declined to have much to do with the CBS chairman. Bing Crosby kept his distance. Some CBS stars pointed to the case of Arthur Godfrey to demonstrate that one stood up to Paley at one's peril. Back in the early days of television, when Paley criticized Godfrey's television show as too static, Godfrey mockingly read Paley's comments on the air. Then he turned to the camera, wiggled, and said, "Is this movement enough, Mr. Paley?" Paley later got his revenge by having Godfrey fired.

A radio man at heart, Paley stayed close to the stars who came out of radio after the war. Lucille Ball was an enduring favorite, as was George Burns. Even after *Amos 'n' Andy* left the air, Freeman Gosden—the more urbane of the pair—remained a friend of Paley's. What Paley's pets had in common, besides their popularity, was an ability to make him howl with laughter.

Because of Paley's image of showmanship, top writers and producers gravitated to CBS, where they knew that programming was a high priority. Those who met Paley were struck by his level of involvement, his knowledge of such arcana as scheduling and plot lines. Instead of budgets, he talked about character believability, always keeping the focus on what would work for the viewer. "That part of the world lives on impressions," said Stanton. "Bill sprinkled magic dust on CBS."

By late 1966 CBS had bounced back smartly from the discomfiting moment in April 1965 after Aubrey's dismissal, when Paley faced his shareholders to explain why CBS' earnings had dipped. Now CBS revenues and net income were once again on the increase, and CBS had eight out of the top ten prime-time shows.

Wall Street was not as impressed as it should have been. These were the go-go years of corporate diversification, and the moneymen were eager to see CBS earn its stripes as a full-fledged conglomerate. All three networks felt pressure to expand their horizons and move away from businesses subject to big profit swings. CBS also had large amounts of cash that it had to invest to avoid heavy taxes. Paley knew that acquisitions could fuel CBS' growth and add to its stock price. What was more, buying companies would take him back to the heady deal-making atmosphere of his early years at CBS.

Stanton and Paley had been looking into ways to diversify since the early 1960s. Stanton made overtures to a handful of communications companies, including Paramount, McGraw-Hill, and Curtis Publishing. Each time Paley declined to bite. By the end of 1963 CBS had $85 million in cash on hand, and it had considered and rejected some seventy-five possible purchases.

In July 1964 Paley stunned Stanton with the news that he had decided on CBS' first acquisition. He wanted to buy 80 percent of the New York Yankees for $11.2 million. (CBS would eventually buy out the remaining 20 percent for $2 million.)

Why did a man as prone to caution as Paley make such an odd first move? At the time of the purchase Paley said regally, "It's a good investment." When pressed, he added, "There's more leisure time in this country and a percentage of it will be spent at ballparks." Sometime later Paley told Fred Friendly that his motivations were rooted in his childhood, when he shagged balls for free tickets to Chicago Cubs games. "All my life," he told Friendly, "I wanted to own a baseball team, and that's why I bought the Yankees."

Most of all, Paley wanted the Yankees because they had class. In the previous decade they had won the American League pennant nine times. The Yankees' aura of quality fit CBS' self-image.

Paley's next few acquisitions were as unlikely as the Yankees. In

1965 CBS paid $13 million for the Fender electric guitar company, and in July 1966 CBS bought Creative Playthings, a manufacturer of expertly crafted educational toys, for $13.5 million. In each case Paley emphasized that CBS was pursuing its goal of buying top-quality companies in their fields.

The investment in the Yankees would go completely sour. In 1966 the once dominant team had dropped to last place; it finished fifth the next two years. Only in 1969, when the Yankees climbed to second, did the team make a profit. In 1973 CBS finally sold the ball club for $10 million to a group headed by George Steinbrenner.

Throughout their acquisition dances, Paley and Stanton kept a discreet distance and avoided stepping on each other's toes. If Stanton was disappointed that Paley declined to act on his proposals, he didn't show it. He played loyal soldier on the Yankee purchase.

Close aides saw small indications of Stanton's unease, however. Paley was becoming more vigilant about his power, and Stanton's frustration began to show: he started to growl. Slowly, almost imperceptibly, Paley did to Stanton what he did to so many executives throughout his career—he wore Stanton down and made him smaller.

THE most bitter battle between Bill Paley and Frank Stanton had nothing to do with any CBS programs, or even with a proposed expansion of the company. Rather, it concerned a new headquarters for CBS. The building was to be a sleek, sophisticated symbol of CBS quality, and it was enormously important to both Paley and Stanton. For four straight years it consumed the two men. They squabbled over the smallest details. They wounded and infuriated each other. The outcome of the struggle served to deepen the divisions between them.

Stanton had been pushing for a new CBS building since the mid-1950s. After scouting a number of sites, he had persuaded Paley to buy a piece of land on Sixth Avenue and Fifty-second Street. Stanton, the onetime aspiring architect, also had definite ideas about the building. He wanted to avoid the skyscraper cliché, a "Coca-Cola bottle with setbacks," and he was set on having Finnish-born architect Eero Saarinen do the design.

In March 1961 Saarinen presented a mock-up of the building to Paley and Stanton. It was restrained and orderly, simple and modern. Paley hated it. In every respect the design reflected Stanton's taste. A dispirited Saarinen started over, but Paley's continued indifference gnawed at Stanton—and at Saarinen, a perfectionist who took his work very seriously.

Finally, Stanton invited Paley for a talk in his office on Easter Sunday. Stanton pressed for a decision, but Paley wouldn't commit himself. "If I could assure you that *Vogue* magazine would shoot a spread with its models in front of the building, would you do it?" Stanton asked in exasperation. Paley brightened. "Yes!" he said, then took it back. But in Paley's instinctive response Stanton understood one source of Paley's indecision: he worried that the building would not get the kind of attention he wanted it to have.

Not long after, Paley called Stanton. "Let's talk some more," he said. Paley had decided he liked Saarinen's original design. What Paley had dismissed as too austere was now strong, beautiful, and timeless. Why the turnaround? Stanton never knew, and Paley never said.

To lock Paley in, Stanton proposed a shrewd compromise. He would oversee the building's exterior, and Paley would be in charge of the interior. Shortly thereafter Eero Saarinen died. Fortunately, Saarinen's chief designer, Kevin Roche, was able to take over, and the building proceeded as planned. Rising thirty-six stories, it was composed of a series of vertical slabs interrupted by dark-tinted windows. The exterior was sheer, devoid of setbacks.

Naturally, Paley tried to change the terms of his compromise with Stanton. Both Saarinen and Stanton had settled on black granite for the façade, but Paley seemed uneasy. After Paley and Stanton visited the mock-up Roche had built in New Rochelle, New York, Paley said, "I know why Eero wanted it black—because he knew he was dying."

Paley pressed for pink granite, which, Stanton later learned, had been Babe's idea. Stanton finally persuaded Paley that pink simply would not work. After months of searching for the right granite, collecting samples from around the world, Stanton found the ultimate selection—a rough stone of charcoal gray—at a quarry in Quebec.

Although Paley claimed to have visited the mock-up in New Rochelle thirty times, he ended up ceding to Stanton the entire design of what became known as Black Rock.

When it was completed, in 1964, at a cost of $40 million, Black Rock was a triumph of elegance and simplicity, one of New York's most distinctive skyscrapers. But as it won awards and kudos from critics,

CBS executives could sense Paley's resentment. "To my mind the coldness between Frank Stanton and Bill Paley began with the building," said Robert Wood, president of CBS Television.

Eventually Paley overrode his anger by taking the lion's share of the credit for Black Rock. "Bill did what he did to almost everybody who worked for him," said another executive. "What they did became his."

Everyone had always recognized the fundamental differences between the two men, but for more than fifteen years they seemed otherwise complementary. As Paley moved through his seventh decade, however, Stanton's usefulness became threatening to him. The rift between the two men widened as Paley sensed Stanton's growing desire for the top job.

During the year preceding Paley's anticipated retirement in September 1966, his signals to Stanton were conflicting. Then in January 1966 Stanton received a memo from Paley that confirmed Paley's unwillingness to leave the company at sixty-five and Stanton's need for a title to reflect his duties.

The memo, to be ratified at the February 9 board of directors meeting, proposed that at the request of the board Paley remain chairman and devote himself to "planning and development." Stanton would assume Paley's title of chief executive officer, with responsibility for all of CBS' operations.

"It came out of the blue," recalled Stanton. "It took me by surprise." Still, everything seemed set for Stanton to become chief executive officer. On February 9 the CBS directors assembled for lunch in the CBS boardroom, on the thirty-fifth floor of Black Rock. They sat around the long mahogany table, surrounded by paintings by Ben Shahn, Georges Rouault, Jean Dubuffet, and Ben Nicholson. Everyone was in place except Paley. After several minutes Winnie Williams, Stanton's secretary, entered the room and whispered in his ear. Stanton excused himself and told the others to begin eating.

He hurried to the chairman's office, where Paley was waiting. Paley told Stanton that he wanted to table the proposal for Stanton to become chief executive officer because there were still too many details to work out in Stanton's contract. "Let's wait and talk about it later," Paley said. Mystified and disappointed, Stanton nevertheless assented without comment.

The two men then went to the boardroom, where they joined the luncheon. "It was one of the most dramatic things I ever saw," recalled Richard Salant, who as corporate vice president served as secretary to the board. "The only way you could ever tell that Frank Stanton was angry was when the back of his neck was red. That day it was flaming. Afterwards I asked Frank what had happened, and he said, 'Bill couldn't go through with it.' "

Paley never again mentioned the chief executive officer title to Stanton, who was shattered at not getting it. In fact, six years passed before Paley gave a clue as to what he had been thinking. On that occasion Paley and Stanton were discussing several candidates for president of CBS when Stanton said, "I have never come back to the meeting when you were talking about making me CEO."

Paley paused for a beat and said, "I couldn't bring myself to do it."

Years later Stanton would rationalize that the CEO title was not that important to him, but the fact was, his whole career had pointed toward achieving it. After the big letdown, why didn't he simply walk out the door? He was immensely successful in his own right; he could have readily secured a CEO job at another major corporation. And he had plenty of money.

But he was still in thrall to Paley and the glamour of a company he had dreamed about as a boy. When he ran into the wall, he didn't have it in him to leave. He had become the ultimate corporate man. And because of Paley's cunning, Stanton could still delude himself that the boss might yet come around. It was too soon to recognize what later became so obvious: that Paley would hang on forever at CBS.

CHAPTER 18

As BILL Paley became more involved in CBS he drifted further from Babe. By the mid-1960s the Paleys hit a turning point. Not only had he reached sixty-five, but Babe had passed fifty. For both of them it was a period of doubt and searching, a time to set new ground rules for their relationship. They continued to dominate their social circuit, entertaining exquisitely at their various homes. But their routines grew rigid and stale. Increasingly, Bill and Babe led separate lives; they had not had sexual relations for well over a decade. Each of them seemed to be setting the stage for the finale.

At bottom, Babe remained a "nice New England charming girl," in the words of her friend Horace Kelland. But in public she was absorbed with keeping up appearances. She was an icon, Bill Paley's perfect jewel, and the role was a demanding one. "She never changed at heart, but she did a lot on the exterior," said Kelland. The pressure showed in Babe's near incessant smoking; by now she was up to more than two packs of L & M cigarettes a day.

Truman Capote, who knew her faults better than anyone, once wrote that "Mrs. P. had only one fault—she was perfect; otherwise, she was perfect." Perfectionism became an obsession. "She ran establishments, not families," said Jeanne Thayer. "She had to do so much, spend so much time preserving their life-style. Bill wanted the atmosphere to be perfect wherever they were."

Relations with her children weighed on Babe as well. By the late '60s she and her husband were estranged from their two youngest children, Kate and Billie, who were then entering their twenties. Kate was living the bohemian life in lower Manhattan. Billie had entered his drifting and drug phase by this time. Babe remained distant from Amanda, who was a star on the New York social circuit.

Babe did draw closer to Tony. Mother and son spoke every day, and on many evenings he would join her for a drink. But the more she leaned on Tony, the more resentful Paley became. He begrudged not only the time she gave her son but also the confidences that she obviously shared with him. Babe couldn't even enjoy the one strong relationship she had among her children.

Ironically, in 1965, just about the time when the children had all left home, the Paleys bought a new apartment in New York. Unlike the small pied-à-terre at the St. Regis, this apartment had room for all. More to the point, the twenty-room duplex at 820 Fifth Avenue overlooked Central Park and had the scale required for grand entertaining. But what really distinguished the apartment was Paley's treasured art collection. The living room alone held Van Gogh's *Washerwoman at Arles,* Toulouse-Lautrec's *Montmartre Madam,* Bonnard's *Still Life,* Rousseau's *Vase of Flowers,* Monet's *Deux Roses sur une Nappe,* and Gauguin's *Queen of the Areois.*

In her stylish new base of operations Babe fell into a routine quite distant from her husband's. Moments of togetherness were rare. Most mornings she awoke at seven. After she and Bill had eaten breakfast in their separate bedrooms, they would sit down for what amounted to a business meeting to review their agendas for the day. Then Babe would scan the newspapers, call her friends, and take her bath.

Babe went out every morning, usually before ten. Sometimes she was driven to the Art Students League, on West Fifty-seventh Street, where she took classes in drawing, painting, and sculpture. Babe was one of the original "ladies who lunch"—a ritual in which eating takes second billing to gossiping with chums at glamorous restaurants such as La Côte Basque and La Grenouille. In the afternoons she would frequently cruise the city's exclusive stores.

Interspersed throughout each day were tasks and chores dedicated to her husband's well-being. His expectations were always on her mind. In earlier years Babe's devotion had been easier to understand. She was enthralled with Paley, perhaps even genuinely in love with him. But as she reached middle age, love had turned into convenience. The marriage now rested on habit, creature comforts, and a shared social life. Her identity too had changed: to the public she had become Babe *Paley,* and she was content with the status that the name conferred. She craved a tranquil life, a luxury that her fear of Paley's rage made impossible. But Babe Paley knew she had made a Faustian pact. To be admired in public, she had to endure in private her husband's belittling demands as well as his infidelity. Only later would she come to grips with what she had given up.

For companionship, warmth, and fun, Babe counted on a devoted circle of friends, male and female. Those closest to her included fashionable society women such as Jeanne Murray Vanderbilt, Françoise de la Renta, and Slim Keith. Although Irene Selznick had divorced Bill's close friend David, she stayed an intimate friend of Babe's. Babe also had a coterie of single men, platonic companions known for their urbanity and wit. Called variously "walkers" or "laughing men," these friends included Horace Kelland and Truman Capote. She felt safest with Capote, who idolized her and in his odd way wanted to *be* Babe Paley.

Babe was fundamentally old-fashioned: private, circumspect, and proper. Yet Capote ingratiated himself so skillfully that Babe opened up to him as a confidant. She told him everything. He was the magician of gossip. He would disclose deeply revealing facts about himself—many of them, it turned out, untrue—in order to elicit the secrets of others. Babe naïvely trusted him. Capote knew all about the sterility of her marriage. She told him that she and Bill Paley had stopped having sexual relations in the early 1950s.

To Bill Paley, Babe's friends were a relief. They diverted her, kept her at a distance, and afforded him the freedom to chase women.

Paley was as lusty and indefatigable as Babe was cool and proper. His conquests were on the order of models and starlets, even shop girls in expensive stores. But he was discreet about his infidelities. His women tended, according to one friend, to be "sexy but tarty-looking." Brains were certainly not a prerequisite. From time to time a famous name would surface. There were rumors in the '60s that Paley had an affair with Marilyn Monroe. However, the link with Monroe was an instance where Paley's legend as a lothario ran ahead of reality.

In truth, Paley's pursuits had misogynist overtones. Said one friend, "He was not a woman-lover; he was a womanizer."

CHAPTER 19

FROM the moment Bill Paley reneged on his promise to make Frank Stanton CEO, the two men's coexistence was strained. Stanton continued to do his job conscientiously, running much of the company and providing counsel when Paley asked. But those who knew him saw a change. Paley's betrayal had broken Stanton's spirit—at least as far as CBS was concerned. He had learned that in Paley's world, even the president of CBS was a hired hand. He coasted toward retirement, hiding his bitterness from all but a few.

In February 1967, after more than a year of negotiations—amid repeated rumors that he might leave CBS—Stanton signed a new contract designating him a senior executive of CBS until 1971, two years shy of his sixty-fifth birthday. After that, CBS would employ him as a consultant until 1987.

In the years that followed, Stanton would experience one final spurt of hope that he might, if only for a few years, run CBS as his own. But once more Paley was unable to relinquish the title.

One reason Paley briefly reconsidered elevating Stanton to chief executive was his own hope, following Richard Nixon's election in November 1968, that he would finally be rewarded by the Republican

Party with an appointment as ambassador to the Court of St. James's. "It would have been the ultimate ratification," said Jack Schneider. "It would have evened him up with Jock Whitney."

Paley had supported Nelson Rockefeller and not Nixon at the Republican Convention. Nevertheless, after Nixon was elected, Paley felt that his many years of loyal Republican service put him in good position for a patronage prize. It was testimony to how little he understood Nixon or politics. Or perhaps it was something more basic: for a lifetime he had demanded loyalty from others without ever grasping that it might one day be demanded of him. In January 1969 Nixon did what any President would do: he gave the plum London posting to an unwavering friend, supporter, and contributor—in this case, Walter Annenberg, owner of *TV Guide* and *The Racing Form.*

Paley was doubly defeated because he felt himself superior to rough-diamond Annenberg. "He was so galled," recalled a former CBS executive. "He would have been psychologically willing to accept that he didn't get it because he was Jewish. But then that damned Annenberg got it—and he was Jewish."

In 1971 STANTON was forced to step down as president, to become vice-chairman until his retirement, on March 31, 1973. For the next fifteen years he would be a consultant to the network at a salary of $100,000 a year plus office space, a secretary, and other support and services (including a limousine) that he had enjoyed as CBS president.

Paley's contract originally stipulated that he too would continue as a senior executive only until March 31, 1973—six months before his seventy-second birthday—after which he would serve as a consultant, like Stanton. But in 1972 Paley changed the terms of his employment to read: "until such date as Mr. Paley shall cease to be a senior elected officer of CBS." In other words, Paley would continue to lead CBS as long as he wished, while Stanton had to retire on schedule.

Paley would never repent of forcing Stanton out. Decades later he would exclaim imperiously to a writer for *M* magazine, "So what! If he had been made chairman, I would have had to get out. I didn't want to get out. And I guess Frank didn't want to retire. There's no use having these retirement rules unless you act on them accordingly. I'm the only exception."

Starting in 1971, Stanton's principal function was to help Paley find and train his presidential successor. Paley had concluded that CBS needed a different sort from Frank Stanton. Stanton was a good administrator, but he was a mere broadcaster. CBS was now a $1 billion corporation with an array of businesses. Like ITT—the model conglomerate of the day—CBS needed someone who understood diversification and could handle complicated financial machinations.

After considering several Wall Street prospects, Stanton and Paley zeroed in on fifty-year-old Charles T. "Chick" Ireland, a Yale-trained lawyer and senior vice president of ITT. Here was the genuine article, a former marine and a veteran of the acquisitions game who had learned at the feet of the master, ITT's Harold Geneen.

Chick Ireland took over on October 1, 1971, when Stanton officially became vice-chairman—a supernumerary for the first time in his life. In June, after less than a year as president of CBS, Ireland suffered a fatal heart attack. Within days Paley was orchestrating a full-fledged search for a successor.

The leading candidate was Arthur Taylor, the thirty-seven-year-old executive vice president of the International Paper Company and a former investment banker at prestigious First Boston. Stanton met him twice before dispatching him to Paley, who invited Taylor and his wife to Kiluna for lunch. It was, recalled Taylor, "love at first sight. We both knew I would be president of CBS." Paley asked only a couple of questions—about Taylor's views on business planning and his theories of organization—and spoke of his own possible retirement; at that stage Paley's contract still called for his departure along with Stanton's the following year.

They hashed out details in two more meetings and shook hands on July 7, 1972. Paley was completely taken with Taylor, a financial whiz with degrees in Renaissance history and American economic history from Brown University. But even more than Taylor's financial acumen, Paley was drawn to Taylor's youth and easy ways.

With Stanton's retirement approaching, tensions between Paley and Stanton stretched close to the breaking point. That autumn Stanton drew up the specifications for the office he planned to use and the services he would need upon his retirement.

As stipulated in his contract, Stanton asked for office space identical to what he had at CBS. "Too much," thundered Paley to Clarence Hopper, CBS' man in charge of operations. "I won't stand for it." In a meeting in the luxurious Black Rock office that he never intended to relinquish, Paley made clear to Stanton his determination to renege.

"Couldn't you get space in a hotel?" said Paley.

Stanton burned with anger. "That would not satisfy my conditions," he said.

"But you have a lot of money," said Paley (on retirement Stanton's CBS stock alone would be worth more than $9 million). "Why do you need this?"

"You wouldn't have any respect for me if I walked away from this," answered Stanton.

It was hopelessly petty. The money in dispute amounted to something like $20,000 a year for a company that was making nearly $200 million a year in pretax profits. But Paley refused to yield. Utterly dispirited, Stanton asked his friend Cyrus Vance, the prominent New York attorney, to represent him in possible legal action.

The board's finance committee agreed that Stanton's position was justified. Said David Hertz, a management consultant who observed both men at close range, "I'm not sure Paley really cared. But he wanted to show Stanton who was boss."

Eventually Paley calmed down, and the contract remained in effect. "The only question," recalled board member Roswell Gilpatric, "was how much consulting work Frank Stanton would get. The answer would be, Not much."

March 1973 had an almost surreal quality for Paley and Stanton, both still seething. At one point Stanton did ask Paley why he insisted on staying in his job at CBS. "I have to stay in it," Paley said. "I don't know what else I would do."

Stanton stubbornly rebuffed all of Paley's requests for parties and receptions to mark his retirement—rites Stanton found too painful to contemplate. At the CBS board meeting in mid-March, Paley gave Stanton a small sculpture called *Atom Piece* by Henry Moore, an old friend of Stanton's.

It poured all day on March 30, Frank Stanton's final day at CBS after thirty-eight years. Black Rock showed its sadness. "There was a great loyalty a lot of people had," said Emily Greene, a veteran executive assistant. "Everyone felt very sad. Some people cried. People felt CBS would not be the same without him, which was true."

Late that afternoon Stanton had a farewell drink with a group of executives. As the men filed out, *New Yorker* writer Lillian Ross arrived with her seven-year-old son, Eric, and her cocker spaniel, Goldie. While Ross watched and asked questions, her son poked through the boxes being packed by Stanton and his longtime secretary, Winnie Williams. Stanton was determined to get everything organized in time to assume his new job, chairman of the American National Red Cross, two days later. His final visitor was Izzy Seigal, a staff photographer for CBS. Bashfully he presented his humble gift to Stanton: a vintage ceramic holder for kitchen matches.

At six thirty p.m. Stanton prepared to leave his office. He carried photographs of his wife, Ruth, as a girl with braided hair, an oversized book entitled *Homage to Henry Moore,* the *Atom Piece* sculpture, the ceramic match holder, and a brass clock.

Before turning into the elevator, Stanton paused to hug Betty, the receptionist, who was crying. His parting words were recounted by Ross in her *New Yorker* piece a month later: "I think I'll make it home in time for the seven-o'clock news."

CHAPTER 20

IN JANUARY 1974 a small tumor was found on one of Babe Paley's lungs. On January 18—Amanda's thirtieth birthday—doctors removed one third of Babe's right lung. The tumor was malignant, but her doctors were hopeful that surgery had checked the cancer.

Babe managed to keep up their entertaining—less frequently than before but just as perfectly. She even gained weight and ate chocolates avidly. Then in the spring of 1975 another tumor appeared, and the rest of her right lung was removed. That summer the Paleys gave up their customary European travels to stay in the Southampton villa of friends Mica and Ahmet Ertegun. Exhausted and ill, Babe took long naps and visited quietly with friends.

Bill Paley now faced the prospect that his fifty-eight-year-old wife could die, leaving him alone in his old age. His perfectly constructed world threatened to unravel. Paley, so accustomed to controlling his existence, worked furiously to conquer Babe's illness.

He combed the globe for cures, importing experts and traveling abroad to confer with doctors. He read books and articles about cancer and used his position as a trustee at Columbia University to probe every conceivable contact there. Once, he dispatched a CBS newsman in Paris to investigate an obscure clinic in Switzerland.

In the summer of 1976 the Paleys traveled to France. "All serene," Babe wrote to Irene Selznick in mid-July. "Here is perfect life for me. We will have one escapade—St.-Tropez by boat overnight."

Back in New York, Paley became ferociously protective of Babe. He constantly fretted over whether a room was too hot or too cold for her. "I would see the touch of his hand when they were sitting next to each other," recalled his friend Henryk de Kwiatkowski. "The slightest cough from her or the slightest expression of discomfort made his face shrivel with pain."

At the outset Babe was pleasantly surprised at her husband's newfound attentiveness. But after several months she adopted some atypical new attitudes. To close friends she began to question the choices she had made in her life and to contemplate a new course.

Saying her artistic talent had been thwarted, she set up a makeshift studio in their Fifth Avenue apartment. Using friends as models, Babe fashioned small terra-cotta sculptures of heads. But as the months passed, she relegated her art to the sidelines again, reassuming the role of perfect hostess and helpmeet that she had played for three decades. For the first time, however, Babe dropped her propriety and openly criticized her husband. One senior CBS executive was stunned when Babe called him to ask, "What's the old s.o.b. doing today?"

The toll of Babe's illness on Bill Paley was evident to everyone in the upper echelons at CBS. He was away even more than usual, and on the job he often appeared preoccupied. Arthur Taylor did his best to offer support, and Paley was appreciative.

For a time Taylor and Paley seemed downright chummy. Taylor referred to the CBS chairman as his "senior partner." Still, a sense of wariness sharpened their dealings. Even in their first meeting Taylor had detected danger. "I liked him," he once said. "But it was clear I was in the presence of an imperious man with enormous power."

Paley's work life began to disintegrate at the time that he grappled with the horrible trauma at home. After Stanton's departure, in March 1973, Paley lost the buffer he had relied on for nearly three decades. Stanton knew what was best for Paley and protected him, and he had a natural gift for managing and inspiring subordinates. "If the world only knew what Frank Stanton absorbed," said Robert Wood, president of CBS Television. "If Paley was going wild, we caught only a small percentage of it because Frank soaked so much up."

Paley tried desperately to reconnect to a company that had grown too large and too complicated for him to grasp; he had neither the temperament nor the grounding to keep on top of everything, as Stanton had. His effort, however, took on new urgency beginning in 1976, when the linchpin of the network's fortunes—prime-time programming—came unstuck.

Since the beginning of the decade CBS had managed to turn back a series of challenges to its entertainment shows. In 1970 network president Robert Wood had proposed a radical plan to "get the wrinkles out of the face of the network without eroding our popularity." He felt that with its rural comedies CBS appealed primarily to older viewers and that it needed to offer more sophisticated shows to draw in a younger audience. Shocked that CBS would cancel popular shows, Mike Dann heatedly objected to the plan when Wood presented it to top CBS executives. "Lower your voice, Mike," said Paley. Several months later Dann quit CBS.

"Gentlemen," Paley told his executives, "you finally have a network president with a vision of what is absolutely correct." Over the next two years CBS dropped such hits as *Petticoat Junction, Red Skelton, The Beverly Hillbillies,* and *Green Acres.* In their place CBS found success with shows like *All in the Family, Maude, The Mary Tyler Moore Show,* and *M*A*S*H.* The prime architect of the schedule, along with Wood, was Freddie Silverman, an energetic whiz kid who replaced Dann.

Paley went along with the choices made by Wood and Silverman, although he hated Archie Bunker, the bigoted hero of *All in the Family.* Paley found the show vulgar and Bunker's insults—calling Puerto Ricans "spics," Jews "Yids," and blacks "spades"—offensive. However, once *All in the Family* was a hit, it could do no wrong.

By 1974 CBS held nine out of the top ten shows, the best showing by any network in a decade. The new CBS hits, especially *The Mary Tyler Moore Show* and *M*A*S*H,* were top-quality comedies conferring the Tiffany prestige Paley hungered for. But Paley was blind to the internal tensions that threatened to undermine CBS' success.

Although Silverman respected Paley's abilities, he never felt especially close to the chairman. Paley did not bother with the gestures—

the occasional lunch or dinner—that would have given Silverman the pat on the back he sought. When Silverman wanted a bigger title, more money, and a limousine, Paley turned him down.

In May 1975 Silverman jumped to ABC, where he received the status and approval denied him at CBS. That fall CBS' new programs had unusually poor showings. A year later Silverman had taken a handful of incipient hits at ABC—including *Happy Days* and *Welcome Back, Kotter*—to build a schedule that took a lead in the prime-time ratings. CBS fell to third place for the first time in two decades.

The drop in CBS' prestige and fortunes infuriated Paley. He pointed his finger at the "complacency" of his programmers. Paley could not bring himself to acknowledge that CBS had genuine competition from ABC. Moreover, more than a half-dozen key CBS programming people left the network in the year following Silverman's departure.

Meanwhile, tensions between Arthur Taylor and Paley had been growing steadily since early 1975. Unlike Stanton, who took advantage of Paley's lapses of interest in CBS to develop his own style and power base, Taylor never attained the authority that had enabled Stanton to effectively counterbalance Paley. Taylor, whose experience was exclusively in finance, was further hobbled by having to learn on the job.

Still, Taylor proved a dedicated executive and a capable administrator. He imposed much needed financial controls, efficiently tracking every expenditure. Wall Street loved him. CBS profits jumped from $83 million in 1972 to $123 million in 1975.

The following year Paley turned on Taylor—and by most accounts CBS' ratings free-fall played only a small part. "Paley was constantly undoing what we had done for the previous two weeks," recalled Taylor. "It was humiliating—all the second-guessing." Said Taylor, "I had no power. Paley had it all."

Paley never seemed to know what he expected from Taylor. Paley seemed to want someone to assume Stanton's duties, but he did not quite grasp what exactly Stanton had done all those years. At the same time, Paley sought someone in his own image as a successor, but the better he got to know Taylor, the more he realized that the CBS president could not possibly become the next Bill Paley.

The effect of Babe's declining health on Paley cannot be underestimated. The specter of her death was a constant reminder of his own mortality. Taylor's youth—he turned forty in 1975—threatened Paley all the more.

Taylor finally ran aground when he tried to raise his public profile. Taylor was pushing too hard, Paley felt, and getting too big for his britches. Wherever Taylor went, he was trailed by a retinue of assistants—just like Paley. Taylor even popped up on the pages of *Women's Wear Daily*, hobnobbing with Paley's social set.

To friends Taylor openly spoke of aspirations to the White House. Taylor, said William Leonard, CBS' chief lobbyist at the time, "flung himself early and often upon the Washington scene." In 1976 Taylor had a new office built in the CBS Washington headquarters: a grand suite with a dining room, screening room, and bathroom. Paley went to town unannounced in the early summer of 1976 and was shocked by the grandeur of Taylor's quarters. "Both the money spent in decorating it and the way it was decorated pissed Bill off," Leonard recalled. Stanton had had strong ideas about how CBS should be run, and strong tastes that were very different from Paley's. But he had asserted himself only when Paley left a vacuum. Taylor, by contrast, challenged Paley head-on. He was like a man taking over an apartment and redecorating it before the previous tenant had moved out.

Several days after Bill Paley's seventy-fifth birthday, on September 28, 1976, the phone rang in the office of John Backe, president of CBS' publishing group. "Can you come and talk to me?" said Paley. The forty-four-year-old executive had been at CBS nearly four years, recruited by Taylor from General Learning Corporation, a publishing venture run by General Electric and Time Inc. Taylor had charged him with turning around CBS publishing, then in a state of near collapse. Drawn to the challenge, Backe had thrown himself into the reorganization, increasing sales and profits significantly.

Although Paley had little to do with publishing at CBS, he had seen Backe in meetings and had been impressed by his approach: cautious, thoughtful, well prepared. Single-handedly Backe had just reeled in the first promising acquisition in years—Fawcett Publications—for less than $60 million, a lower price than CBS had anticipated paying.

"I find our lives are becoming increasingly entwined," Paley told Backe in his office that Friday evening. "Could you and your bride come to dinner with Babe and me on Monday night?" When Backe said yes, Paley asked him to come an hour earlier—alone.

In the library at 820 Fifth Avenue, Paley poured Backe a glass of wine. Characteristically blunt, Paley said, "How would you like to be president of CBS?" "What about Arthur Taylor?" asked Backe. "That is not a factor," said Paley. "It is not going to work out with Arthur."

Paley was taken aback when Backe seemed blasé about the offer. "How do you feel about being CEO?" Paley asked expectantly. "I haven't the vaguest idea," said Backe. "We are two tough guys and sooner or later we will collide."

Paley was incredulous. "I am offering you the most exciting job in America. How can you turn around and say no?" Backe observed that he didn't know what Paley wanted from the man who would be CBS president. "We want someone to run the company," said Paley—failing to note that he himself wished to remain in charge.

At dinner that night Backe was enchanted by Babe, who functioned well despite her illness. Backe was touched by Paley's solicitude toward his ailing wife. Still, he declined the offer.

Every afternoon for the following week Paley invited Backe to his office to discuss the job. Eventually Paley's powers of persuasion won out. On Friday, October 8, Backe accepted.

The following Wednesday, an hour before the eleven-o'clock board meeting, Paley asked Taylor to his office. The tanned, white-haired CBS chairman sat at his desk, with board members Henry Schacht and Roswell Gilpatric nearby. "We want your resignation," Paley said.

Taylor was dumbstruck. "Why?" he asked. "I thought I was doing a good job." Only fifteen months earlier Paley had publicly signaled Taylor's position as his successor, calling him "outstanding" and "exceptional." Despite the ratings slump, CBS had $400 million in cash and was about to report record sales and earnings for the first nine months of 1976.

"You've done a great—" Paley started to say, but Gilpatric interrupted him. "Don't answer that," said the lawyer. "It's like a marriage gone bad." With that, Taylor knew any argument was futile. He cleaned out his desk and left the building by noon.

As in the past, Bill Paley was brutal and insensitive to his second-in-command, who for all his flaws did not deserve such callous treatment. Arthur Taylor could be faulted for letting CBS go to his head, but he was too young, too eager, and too thin-skinned to cope with a master as relentless and unforgiving as Bill Paley.

CHAPTER 21

ARTHUR Taylor's firing created a mud slide of bad publicity for CBS. *TV Digest,* a widely circulated industry newsletter, hit the right nerve: neither ratings nor financial performance was the cause. Taylor was sacked because of a "personality conflict." Paley, said the piece, was a "jealous old man" who didn't want Taylor to take over.

Paley felt that his reputation had been damaged by the reaction to his handling of Taylor. He was extremely agitated over this latest blot on his reputation.

Until the previous year Paley had carefully maintained an almost spotless façade. He had endured short bursts of bad press, but for the most part he had been lionized and treated with near reverence as the CBS godhead.

Paley had long relied on an efficient public relations machine that included consultants Earl Newsom and Arthur Newmyer. When Newsom died, his New York manager, Arthur Tourtellot, came to CBS to work exclusively for Paley. Along with a CBS staff headed by Kidder Meade, they managed to smother all evidence of Paley's peccadilloes and fan his legend. Press interviews were tape-recorded by CBS, and the transcripts were edited before being sent out to reporters. The publicity men not only wrote Paley's speeches and letters, on occasion they even drafted people outside the company to promote the Paley cause.

However, beginning in 1975, cracks appeared in Paley's artfully constructed image, offering unsavory glimpses of both his professional and private life. Most damaging to Paley's reputation was an *Esquire* piece that hit the newsstands in mid-October, 1975. Entitled "La Côte Basque, 1965," it was the first fragment of Truman Capote's long-awaited (and never finished) novel, *Answered Prayers.* In the story a Capote-like narrator named Jonesy dined at La Côte Basque, the famous Manhattan restaurant, with an American friend, Lady Ina Coolbirth. Across the room, Capote wrote, were Babe Paley and her sister Betsey; the author's mingling of real names with fictitious ones underscored the story's apparent grounding in fact.

As the fascinated Jonesy listened, Ina dished the dirt on high society, much as Capote and his swans had done countless times over the years. Her most egregious tale concerned a man named Sidney Dillon, a "conglomateur" with a "twinkle-grinning tough-Jew face." He was married to Cleo, "the most beautiful creature alive." Dillon longed for acceptance in WASP society. One manifestation of that desire was his attraction to the wife of a former New York governor, a woman, Jonesy said, who "looked as if she wore tweed brassieres and played a lot of golf." The governor's wife, wrote Capote, "was the living incorporation of everything denied him, forbidden to him as a Jew, no matter how beguiling and rich he might be."

It was a scandalous and vindictive piece of writing. Everyone in New York social circles recognized the lusty Bill Paley in the character of Sidney Dillon.

Kidder Meade had obtained a copy of the story before publication. "I told Paley he could read it, but I didn't want to discuss it," recalled Meade. "I recommended that he ignore it, that he not react to it." Meade was right; denying that he was Sidney Dillon would only have called further attention to Paley.

When Capote called, Paley was quintessentially cool. After starting to read it, he told Capote, "I fell asleep. Then a terrible thing happened: the magazine was thrown away." When Capote offered to send another, Paley replied that he was preoccupied. "My wife," he said—pointedly, he didn't refer to Capote's erstwhile dear friend as Babe—"is very ill." That was the end for the Paleys and Capote.

Paley repeated his line about falling asleep all over town and got a good laugh. "Of course he didn't fall asleep," said Kidder Meade. "It was too vile, too filthy. You couldn't fall asleep reading it, especially if it was about you and your wife."

In the view of Capote's biographer, Gerald Clarke, the tale was a twisted form of revenge—for Babe. "Now that she was dying," wrote Clarke, "Capote was avenging her in the one way he knew how: by holding up to ridicule the man who had caused her so much hurt."

Babe, said society columnist Charlotte Curtis, was "devastated" by Capote's treachery. She could never forgive him, explained Babe's friend Jean Stein, because of her ingrained loyalty to family. "Truman didn't understand the kind of woman she was, that she would have to be loyal first to her husband, and that Truman would be left out."

Stein once tried to explain Capote's motivation to Babe. "She heard me," said Stein. "But she was so private and felt that whatever she had told him had been violated."

Capote wrote Babe two long letters that went unanswered. He encountered Babe and Slim Keith at the fashionable Quo Vadis Restaurant. "Hello, Bobalink," said Truman, summoning his favorite pet name for Babe. "Hello, Truman," she replied. Slim cut him cold.

Even as Paley simmered over this embarrassment, he was girding for another negative onslaught. This time the avenging angel was David Halberstam, the celebrated reporter who had proved his adversarial mettle as a correspondent for *The New York Times* during the Vietnam War. In December *The Atlantic Monthly* was due to publish the first of two excerpts from *The Powers That Be,* Halberstam's book-in-progress about CBS, Time Inc., the Washington *Post,* and the Los Angeles *Times.*

After the first *Atlantic* article appeared, an irate Paley went on the attack. Halberstam described the CBS chairman's relentless drive for profits, his abandonment of Murrow, his brutal treatment of various executives, his social climbing, and his sensitivity over his origins. Paley's strongest reaction was to what Halberstam later termed a "neurosis about the Jewish question." The CBS chief took great exception to Halberstam's account of his refusal to back *Fiddler on the Roof,* which Paley had described as "too Jewish."

Paley mustered Meade and a small army of public relations aides to dissect Halberstam's prose for inaccuracies. They prepared a nine-thousand-word reply. "I spent hundreds of hours with Paley going over each of the points," recalled Kidder Meade. Paley was a man obsessed. He tried initially to sell his rebuttal to the *Atlantic* as an article. Editor Robert Manning declined but offered to publish a shorter letter to the editor.

Paley could not grasp why he was attracting such bad press after so many years of laudatory coverage. Others, however, could trace the decline straight to Stanton's departure. "It was widely felt that Frank Stanton should not have left at sixty-five," recalled Meade. "Most of us inside CBS thought it was a crime. He was genetically about forty. He was at his prime, and he had at least five more years of a tremendous contribution. He was a wonderful talent and Bill Paley got rid of him, and that angered many people. There was a lot of resentment, which you cannot bottle up. There was no question that it had a lot to do with the bad publicity. It was a tragic error that Bill Paley made. And all because he was jealous."

Ultimately Paley decided that the best defense was a good offense. In March 1975 he signed on with Doubleday & Company to write his memoirs. His theory, he explained, was to neutralize the Halberstam book with his own account, to be published at the same time.

For his amanuensis Paley chose John McDonald, a veteran writer who had retired from *Fortune* magazine several years earlier and had ghosted Alfred Sloan's memoir, *My Years with General Motors*. McDonald taped more than thirty hours of interviews with Paley; no one else was interviewed except to check certain factual points.

"The problem from the beginning was that Paley wasn't willing to reveal much about himself," recalled one person who worked on the project. "It was extraordinarily difficult to get him to admit he failed at anything."

Paley read the drafts and dictated comments for revisions. Invariably his changes tended to flatten the book, muting strong opinions and tamping down adjectives. When McDonald characterized Paley's dinner parties as glittering, Paley said, "I don't want my dinner parties called glittering."

As the book progressed, McDonald's disillusion grew. Through his comments and corrections on the manuscript Paley inadvertently revealed how his desire for attention and recognition clashed with his instinctive fear of being exposed. He tried to perpetuate his myth by recounting innocuous stories that he told at so many dinner parties. In sanitizing his life story Paley did something even his worst critics couldn't have done: he stripped his life of its richness and texture, and undermined both his power and his accomplishments.

IN DECEMBER 1971 Paley's old rival David Sarnoff died at age eighty after a protracted illness. Several months before the end, when Sarnoff was nearly blind and could barely speak, he invited Paley for a farewell visit. As the CBS chief reminisced with the RCA founder, Sarnoff reached out, found Paley's hand, and clasped it. Later Paley marveled at the strength in the grip of the dying man. He knew that with Sarnoff's passing, he was the last pioneer. The responsibility for preserving the heritage of broadcasting would be his alone.

Earlier that year Paley's aide-de-camp, Arthur Tourtellot, had proposed that Paley set up a broadcasting museum. Paley warmed to the idea of a carefully culled collection of television and radio programs as a way to perpetuate his legacy.

Four years later Paley hired Robert Saudek, a veteran TV producer and instructor at Harvard, to organize the museum. Paley picked out the site, a building on East Fifty-third Street.

The Museum of Broadcasting opened its doors for the first time on November 9, 1976. In its style the museum reflected CBS' spare design. It was an admittedly modest facility—a complex of rooms on three floors for viewing and listening, storage, and administration—and was greeted in the press with respect, if not wild enthusiasm. Still, there was nothing that Paley could be ashamed of.

Why, after leaving so strong an imprint on the place, did he not name it the Paley Museum? By not affixing his name, Paley could get others to help defray the costs (ABC and NBC contributed $50,000 apiece); yet as the prime mover and biggest contributor, he could control the museum's direction. Paley's strategy was practical—and characteristically cunning.

In the autumn of 1976, with the museum on track and his book in the works, Paley again threw himself into CBS, determined to restore the network's programming to its former preeminence. Babe's fragile health curtailed his social life, so he really had nowhere else to turn.

"He couldn't do anything else, so he thought he would plunge in, and he would be the savior," recalled former CBS executive Jack Schneider. "But his touch didn't turn it around. It made it worse."

Part of Paley's problem was that instead of making decisions based on solid information, he was winging it more than ever. And the old magic was gone. Paley was too removed from his audience. For decades he had led a rarefied life. He did not carry cash, never stood in line, and each morning his faithful valet, Dean, knotted his tie. Early in 1977, after CBS acquired *Woman's Day* magazine as part of its Fawcett Publications purchase, Paley asked Jack Purcell, president of CBS Publishing, "Who would buy this? It's nothing but recipes." Purcell told him that eight million women bought the magazine every three weeks. Paley was amazed. "Where do they go to buy it?" he said. "Supermarkets," said Purcell, who could tell by Paley's quizzical look that the CBS chairman had never been in that sort of store. Purcell subsequently took Paley to a supermarket on the West Side. After walking all around the store to inspect the displays, Paley stood transfixed as women moved through the checkout lines buying *Woman's Day* or *Family Circle*.

By contrast, CBS president John Backe was decidedly a man of the people. Midwestern born, he had earned his M.B.A. at night school in Ohio and served in the Strategic Air Command during the 1950s as a bomber pilot. He had an unassuming manner and lived a quiet suburban life.

At CBS he steered away from acquisitions and focused on rebuilding the program schedule. With Paley, Backe trod carefully, watching and listening. After Backe's first month on the job, Arthur Tourtellot invited him to lunch.

"How's it going?" asked Tourtellot, whom Backe knew was Paley's closest confidant.

"Let me try something on you," said Backe. "Bill Paley is very insecure." Tourtellot replied, "You are very perceptive. One thing you should know is that the better you are in your job, the more he will try to tear you down."

"Watching him operate," continued Backe, "the things he worries about amaze me. How could he be so hung up, after all he has achieved and all his money?" Tourtellot answered, "It is so deep-seated. That is why Babe is his front."

In February 1977 Goldie Paley died at age ninety-five (Sam had died in 1963); Bill took the news of his mother's death with noticeable calm. "Goldie had a full life," he told one executive. "She was a helluva woman. From her deathbed she was telling me she was ninety-five. I know she was ninety-six."

In the spring of that year, as promised, Paley relinquished his chief executive title to John Backe. "This is not a charade," Paley said. "I expect Mr. Backe to make the final decisions." Yet after a brief pause the chairman added, "Of course, I'd be surprised and maybe even a little disappointed if I'm not asked about problems as they arise."

Indeed, Paley was quick to stress that he would continue to come to the office virtually every day. Some observers remained appropriately skeptical. Said one former CBS executive to *The Wall Street Journal*, "Bill Paley isn't going to give up control of CBS until he's carried out in an elegant, hand-carved rosewood box."

By autumn 1977 Paley was finding it difficult to concentrate on much of anything at work. Besides Babe's illness, he was preoccupied with his autobiography. Paley, who had squeezed all the juice from the story, predictably found John McDonald's manuscript wanting. "When it was almost finished, he worried that it wasn't snappy enough," recalled one man close to the project. "What he wanted was impossible. He wanted zippy, fast reading, but he wasn't willing to provide the raw material."

Paley secretly brought in a CBS News producer named Perry Wolff to assess the manuscript. After Wolff submitted each revision, Paley would laboriously copy Wolff's corrections in his own hand so McDonald would not know about the existence of a ghost's ghost.

Wolff's principal criticism was Paley's glaring omission of Stanton; in the original manuscript the former CBS president only rated a couple of passing references. When Wolff wrote a chapter praising Stanton, Paley demanded a rewrite. The second version pleased Paley no better; he tore up both of them.

Paley continued to complain that the manuscript was too wooden. Finally, in the spring of 1978, Doubleday called in a new writer, Alvin Moscow, who had worked with Richard Nixon on *Six Crises*. Moscow worked at a furious pace to put a new gloss on the manuscript.

Paley's animus toward Stanton was painfully apparent at CBS. Throughout the 1970s Paley declined to use Stanton's services as a consultant, and the two men kept a chilly distance. Early in his tenure Backe had Stanton in for lunch. Afterwards Paley summoned Backe to his office. "Don't you ever have him here again," said Paley. "He is trying to work against me."

Stanton continued to serve as a director of CBS, but when he turned seventy, early in 1978, Paley forced him off the board. CBS had a policy stipulating that directors retire at that age, although members sitting on the board before the policy went into effect were exempted. Stanton, along with several other directors, including Paley, fell into that category. But Paley insisted that Stanton had to comply because he came from management—conveniently ignoring that the chairman did as well. Backe recalled Stanton's disquieting final board meeting: "We were going into an executive session, and it was time for Frank to leave. He got up and started to walk out. I stood up and shook his hand, and I couldn't believe it: Bill Paley didn't shake his hand or anything."

CHAPTER 22

For a time in 1976 and 1977 it seemed that Babe's cancer had stabilized after Paley pulled strings to have her treated with Interferon, then in the experimental stage. But in the autumn of 1977 she went into a decline. The cancer had invaded her central nervous system, and Paley, determined to supervise her tests and treatments, cut his schedule at CBS, coming in only three to four days a week. Even then he was on the phone with doctors or checking in at home, where he had nurses on round-the-clock shifts. When the Paleys tried to have a dinner party for close friends or family, Paley often presided alone, while Babe ate on a tray in her room. Afterwards the guests would file to her bedside for a visit.

The daughter of a doctor, Babe took a stoic, almost clinical attitude toward her condition. She spoke authoritatively about her treatment and prognosis, all without complaint. Alarmingly thin, she wore knits by Valentino to hide her skeletal appearance. The drugs and radiation made her hair fall out—an awful reminder of what had happened to her youngest daughter. "Oh, God, now I know what Kate went through," she said one day while studying her reflection in the mirror held by her maid. When she wasn't wearing a wig, Babe would knot a chiffon scarf around her head like an exquisite turban.

A stream of friends came to see her. All were moved by her dignity and graciousness even when she was in dreadful pain. "She would make the most terrific effort to get done up and never say a word about her illness," recalled Horace Kelland, a frequent visitor.

Babe stayed in touch with her two sisters, mostly by telephone. Widowed by her second husband, the painter James Fosburgh, Minnie was stricken with cancer too, and Betsey ended up spending more time with her than with Babe. When Minnie felt able, she would come by. Babe's son Tony visited every morning and evening, and for the first time Babe and Amanda drew close.

Amanda's dazzling marriage to Carter Burden had broken up in 1972, when she sued him for divorce on their eighth anniversary. She had been dismayed to find her marriage on the same track as her mother's. "Carter wasn't considerate of Amanda—one of those machismo things," a friend of hers said at the time. "C.B. is highly influenced by Bill Paley. Paley can get away with that sort of thing, but Carter just came on as sort of a bully." So Amanda did what her mother had found impossible. She left—with her mother's blessing.

Still, in the following years, when Amanda was on her own with two school-age children, Babe kept her distance, even after she fell ill. "For a long time she didn't have the desire to see me," recalled Amanda. "It is a very weird thing to have your mother not want to see you. But that changed in the last three months of her life. She waited for my visits. She would walk with me. Those moments were terrific for me."

Babe's stepchildren, Hilary and Jeffrey, also came by, as did Billie, after he realized the gravity of his mother's illness. Only Kate stayed away, resisting written entreaties from both parents.

Aware that her time was limited, Babe had all her jewelry brought to her from the bank vaults. For several days she sat on her bed amid heaps of necklaces, rings, pins, and bracelets examining each piece and making notes about who would get what. She kept a stack of file cards on which she wrote all her bequests—to friends and relatives.

Babe went to Lyford Cay for the last time at Christmas in 1977. By then she was extremely weak. She had to lie down—covered with her new $15,000 full-length blond Russian sable coat—for the entire trip aboard the CBS plane. Her son Billie flew in from Washington, D.C., where he had settled down as a novice restaurateur. She was overjoyed to see him, although his brooding intensity—not to mention his beard, long hair, and gold hoop earring—clearly irritated his father.

At the end of their vacation the Paleys were hit with a horrible shock. Jeff Byers, Hilary's husband, leaped to his death from their Manhattan apartment early in the morning on New Year's Eve. His suicide note mentioned business problems. The handsome and ambitious Byers was deeply in debt, the result of some bad investments and extravagant spending habits. Friends felt that he strove too hard to emulate Bill Paley's way of life. Several times when Byers had come up short, his father-in-law bailed him out. When Paley heard the news, he rushed back to New York and took charge of the arrangements.

As Babe's illness worsened in the early months of 1978, her mood toward her husband became overtly hostile. In his presence she unleashed a flood of recriminations. Those who witnessed her anger were shocked by its bitterness. "She complained that she had knuckled

under, that she had done too many things that he wanted her to do,"
recalled one man close to the Paley family. "Everything that she
harbored against him came out. She knew she was dying. She didn't
have anything to lose."

For the first time in her life Babe Paley had the upper hand in their
marriage. She was the focal point, and Bill receded to the sidelines.
Instead of fleeing or fighting back, he took the abuse. He remained
patient and attentive. The more she abused him, the more devoted he
became. "He was devastated," recalled Amanda. "He was in tears
many times from March to July. He was desperate, frantic, and teary."

Yet his agony could not override his old habits. "He found another
girl during that time," said Charlotte Curtis. "He wasn't visible or
unkind, and he did spend the rest of the time with Babe." The other
girl was half Babe's age—thirty-year-old Jan Cushing, a blond woman-
about-town with intense social ambitions.

Jan Cushing was in the midst of getting a divorce from her husband,
Frederick, who came from a socially prominent Long Island family.
"I was a doctor more than a girlfriend," she claimed years later. "We
talked and talked." One day Paley started talking about Babe's illness,
and to Jan Cushing's amazement he began to cry. "He couldn't believe
Babe was dying," she recalled. "He didn't want to face it. He felt in
a selfish way, How could she leave me when I need her so much, when
I have not yet even retired?" Convinced that he wasn't thinking
properly, she told him in the late spring that they should stop seeing
each other. "I don't think you can continue our friendship when your
wife is that sick," she told him. He agreed, and the relationship ended.

Babe took to her bed that Easter and in the following months spent
much of her time sleeping. She used oxygen to assist her breathing,
but she refused to be hooked up to a lot of tubes. To ease the pain,
she was given frequent shots of morphine. In early June, Babe entered
the terminal stage of her illness. At her request her doctors began
gradually withdrawing nutrition.

Still unwilling to give up his quest, Paley located a doctor in
Philadelphia offering an experimental treatment. The new doctor
ordered Babe's nutrition boosted, and he dispatched his nurses to New
York. They brought glass vials filled with the medication that they
would inject daily. "It was a painful period for everyone," recalled
Amanda. "Before that my mother had been mellow, but when they

started the medication, she had to walk to get her lung working again. She was very brave, but after three weeks we knew it wouldn't work."

In mid-June, Babe made her final visit to Kiluna, accompanied by Bill, Tony, and Amanda. They drove her in a golf cart all over the grounds. Gardening had been a lifelong passion; she had spent years creating a sunken dell of flowering trees, shrubs, and wildflowers. Before her illness Babe had spent hours in the dell, digging, planting, and pruning. Now having savored her artfully planted woodland glen for the last time, she retreated in exhaustion to a sofa in the library.

During her periods of consciousness Babe took care to say good-bye to her friends. She called her former hairdresser, Kenneth, and asked to be remembered to each of his employees. She invited others to tea or lunch at her bedside. "She knew she was dying, but she didn't talk about it," said her friend Aline de Romanones. "She gave me pointers about makeup."

Lying on her floral sheets, she looked as beautiful as ever. "Her face never changed. It didn't get all drawn in," said one Paley family intimate. "It was odd," recalled another friend, "but when she was dying, she had no faith, no religion. She didn't believe in another world or a higher plane. Her death was painful for that reason. She had not a glimmer of having a soul. Still, she was very courageous."

On July 5, 1978, Babe's sixty-third birthday, she hovered close enough to death for her family to summon Kate, who had agreed to come only at the final moment. Babe was semiconscious, but she talked a bit, and she recognized her long-estranged daughter. Babe had wrapped her head in a chiffon turban, and she wore a beautiful lace bed jacket. She uttered no complaint. Even at the very end, with a shaky hand, Babe Paley put on her makeup.

Paley and the children sat on her bed, paralyzed with sadness. Their vigil lasted until early the next morning, when she died with Amanda holding her hand. Moments later Bill Paley picked up the phone to call Steve Ross, the chairman of Warner Communications, who was dating Amanda at the time. In the early days of his career Ross had been an undertaker. "Call me when it is over, and I'll be there," he had said to Amanda. Arriving within minutes, Ross said, "If you go out of the bedroom, I will take care of it all." So the family filed out, leaving a silver-haired movie mogul to tend to Babe Paley's lifeless body.

Several days later four hundred mourners, including three

Rockefellers, a Harriman, and a Vanderbilt, came to pay their respects at Christ Episcopal Church in Manhasset. The family walked in, led by Paley in his dark suit made by Huntsman, of Savile Row. "I don't think I ever saw such a sad face as Bill's," recalled Leonora Hornblow. "He was very controlled—no tears—and he walked straight." The Reverend Frank N. Johnston read the eulogy—a collaborative effort by Paley, Slim Keith, and Irene Selznick—that praised Babe as "a beacon of perfection in this era of casual convenience."

After the forty-minute service of Scripture readings and sturdy hymns, Babe's friends assembled at Kiluna for an alfresco luncheon. Like the service, the gathering had been meticulously planned by Babe. Waiters stood underneath the columned portico holding silver trays of champagne and Babe's favorite wine, Pouilly-Fumé de Ladoucette. The rooms overflowed with flowers, all selected by Babe.

Bill Paley, barely three months from his seventy-seventh birthday, stood for the entire afternoon and greeted guests. He appeared dignified, composed, and strong—the complete American gentleman.

"At the end I looked around to thank Babe for the wonderful afternoon. It was as if she was there," said Slim Keith. But some guests had more than Babe's memory on their minds that day. Sitting at one table was Horst, whose images of Babe in *Vogue* had immortalized her elegant style. As the afternoon wore on, Horst was stunned to hear, not from one but from a succession of women who wandered over and whispered as they glanced at Paley, "I'm going to marry him."

"Poor Bill," said Irene Selznick as she reached the front door of Kiluna after the memorial luncheon for Babe. "He's going to have to walk up that staircase all alone." Paley, however, had no intention of living with Babe's ghost for even one night. Along with his servants and all the flowers from the luncheon, he headed to Keewaydin, the Southampton home of Henry Mortimer, Babe's former brother-in-law. The Paleys had rented the house for the month of July.

Paley spent several weeks there, tended by Kate. It was as if her mother's death had broken a spell; from that day on, Kate became intensely attached to her father.

Although Babe and Bill's marriage may have been hollow at the core, Paley was overwhelmed by the loss of her. Babe's death shattered him in a way that surprised even those closest to him. He started carrying a silver-framed photograph of Babe in his briefcase, and he showed clear signs of depression. Visiting the CBS chairman in his apartment one day, John Backe found him in his pajamas, seated on his bed. "I don't know what to do with my life," said Paley.

Paley put Kiluna up for sale (it would be sold for $6 million in 1985), and late in 1978 he bought an elegant home called Four Fountains, in Southampton.

As 1979 began, Paley was hard at work reconstructing his social life. Many friends remarked that he began inviting people who would never have passed muster with Babe, such as Barbara Walters and Frank Sinatra. Dinner at Bill Paley's was suddenly more merry and more democratic than it had been in the Babe days. And he was turning up everywhere—a maiden visit to Elaine's Restaurant, parties at the Museum of Modern Art, White House galas, openings of the New York City Ballet, private dinners all over town.

In avid pursuit were the women who craved to be the next Mrs. Paley. Evangeline Bruce, widow of David Bruce, former ambassador to Britain, led the pack. Recalled Leonora Hornblow, "I had the feeling Evangeline had already picked out the silver."

"As 1979 began, Paley was hard at work reconstructing his social life." Right, at a dinner party with Henry Kissinger and others. Lower right, with Diane Sawyer. Below, Evangeline Bruce.

Paley hunted as eagerly as he was pursued; one needed a scorecard to track his changing taste. By March 1979 he was fixated on sometime model Barbara Allen—some fifty years his junior. Clearly Paley gloried in his Don Juan bachelorhood—doing in the open what he had been doing on the sly for years.

While his actions denigrated Babe's memory, he seemed intent on idealizing their relationship. His portrait of their life together was one of many false notes in *As It Happened,* the Paley memoir that Doubleday published, in March 1979—only weeks before Halberstam's book was to appear.

The book received a barrage of publicity. Doubleday ran full-page advertisements in *The New York Times* and *Variety.* Paley even submitted to an appearance on NBC's *Today* show with Tom Brokaw, and he talked to reporters from national magazines and top newspapers who wrote glowing interviews laced with praise for the book. All the reporters received gracious thank-you notes from Paley.

Other critics were considerably less favorable. The most scathing review was Nicholas Von Hoffman's in *New York* magazine: "Paley depicts himself as a purse-proud, egotistical, vulgar, grudge-bearing man who is as greedy for praise as he is for pelf."

The sales were respectable, but they fell far short of Paley's expectations. Anything less than best-sellerdom and unanimous praise was complete failure in Paley's eyes. After his dutiful promotional appearances he could not disavow the book fast enough. He spread the word in his crowd that he hated the memoir and rationalized the book—four years and three ghostwriters in the making—as a work rushed out under pressure when, as he said later, "my wife was dying, and I was in a bad mood."

CHAPTER 23

IF ANYONE could find encouragement in *As It Happened,* it should have been John Backe, who was two years into his tenure as the network's CEO. Concluding the book's awkward description of his struggle with heirs apparent, Paley called Backe a "wise choice" and noted his feeling of "pleasure and comfort because my successor is in place."

But in reading the book, Backe took little pleasure or comfort. "It read as if Paley did everything," recalled Backe. "He took credit for anything that was good." Even worse, Paley once again began to reassert himself at CBS. Recalled Backe, "Babe was dead, his book was written, he wanted to be in charge, and there I was."

Backe felt suffocated by Paley's intrusive and mercurial ways. "Paley was always around," recalled executive vice president Jack Purcell. "That meant there was a guy called president and chief executive, and there was a guy called the boss."

Midway through 1979 Backe felt his relationship with Paley had turned. "It became negative," recalled Backe. "He would find things wrong just to find things wrong."

As a defensive measure, Backe started to stonewall Paley by refusing to take his phone calls. Jack Purcell soon found himself carrying messages between the two men. When Paley complained, "Can't you get John to call me?" Purcell went to Backe. "You don't have to agree with the old coot," said Purcell, "but he does deserve a call." Still, Backe dug in his heels.

It was Backe's discourtesy that rankled Paley more than anything, Purcell believed. For all his ruthlessness Paley usually clung to courtesy in awkward or difficult situations. For years CBS executives would recall the time in 1978 when Records president Walter Yetnikoff brought Meat Loaf, a three-hundred-pound CBS rock star with long, stringy hair, to meet Paley in his office. "Yo, Bill," said Meat Loaf. "Good afternoon, Mr. Loaf," said Paley, who then called his steward to set out fine china and cutlery so Meat Loaf could eat his brown-bag lunch of cheese, beer, and a banana while they discussed songwriting and life on the road.

The sharpest disagreement between Paley and Backe over CBS' future concerned a proposed new channel for cable television. In 1979 Ted Turner, the brazen cable entrepreneur from Atlanta, Georgia, began developing a twenty-four-hour video news service. Backe figured that CBS, with its vast news organization, could establish its own news channel and "blow Turner out of the water." Paley, however, favored a channel of cultural programs.

Paley and Backe squabbled about petty matters as well. When Paley wanted CBS to buy a helicopter that he could use to travel to Southampton on weekends, Backe suggested that the chairman, who was worth at least $500 million, could buy one and lease it to CBS when the need arose for executives to use it on business. Backe gave Paley a toy helicopter for Christmas in 1979, but the chairman was not amused. "I was always in the position of saying no," recalled Backe. "I had to because it was in the company's best interests."

On April 24, 1980, Paley held a victory party at the luxurious Four Seasons restaurant, in New York City. CBS had recaptured first place in prime time, and Paley lauded Backe. "I don't think anyone tasted [a victory] as sweet as the one we had the benefit to come by," he said.

Even as he spoke, Paley was plotting to unseat John Backe, a maneuver he accomplished on May 8 largely through his shrewd behind-the-scenes manipulation of his cronies on the CBS board of directors.

Backe's departure set off another wave of bad press for Paley. Wall Street analysts called him erratic and unpredictable, and CBS stock fell to a five-year low. For the first time, the board took some hits in the press for permitting Paley, who now held only 7 percent of CBS stock, such sweeping powers. "The CBS board, it appears, frequently abandons its public responsibilities," one broadcasting industry executive told *New York* magazine.

John Backe's successor was Tom Wyman, the fifty-year-old vice-chairman of the Pillsbury Company, in Minneapolis.

Although Wyman's roots were in St. Louis, he had the solid eastern Establishment credentials and gloss that Backe lacked. Educated at Andover and Amherst, Wyman had lived in Lausanne, Switzerland, and London for five years, rising to vice president of the Switzerland-based Nestlé Company. He had also put in ten years as a senior vice president of Polaroid Corporation, in Boston.

Four days after Backe's dismissal Wyman met with Paley and five key directors: Benno Schmidt, Henry Schacht, Franklin Thomas, Roswell Gilpatric, and Jamie Houghton. "The meeting was an odd piece of geometry," recalled Wyman. "It was the first time Paley and the board had interviewed anyone together." The board members had been bashed in the press as yes-men, and it was clear to Wyman that they were determined not to be patsies this time.

The upshot of the meeting was an understanding that Wyman would be president and chief executive at the outset. Roughly a year later Paley would step down as chairman. Wyman would get a $1 million signing bonus and a salary of $800,000 a year.

Tom Wyman and Paley glided through their honeymoon. Wyman soothed Paley on several of his sorest points with Backe. Wyman agreed to buy a corporate helicopter that Paley could use for his Southampton jaunts. Wyman likewise embraced Paley's cultural cable channel and scheduled its introduction for the fall of 1981.

As for Paley, he was keen to show everyone that he was back in charge. At work he seemed less forgetful and more energetic and alert. He attended all the major program meetings, playing his role more forcefully, if not more effectively. "Everybody felt they were going through the exercise for Mr. Paley," said one CBS executive. "It was a Potemkin process, but we were winning the ratings."

Winning or not, Wall Street wasn't completely enthusiastic about Paley's comeback at CBS. In June 1980 Joseph Fuchs, a broadcast analyst at Kidder Peabody, wrote, "The departure of Mr. Paley, for whatever reason, would undoubtedly be greeted in the financial community with a solid increase in the price of the stock."

In truth, Paley had become an albatross for the network. "A corrosion took place," said ABC chairman Leonard Goldenson. "Bill Paley could not maintain the spirit and drive and morale to keep CBS on top."

Mindful of their deal a year earlier, the most influential members of the board came to Wyman in May 1981. "The time has come to cross the bridge on Bill Paley," they said. But Wyman hung back.

"The consequences would be potentially traumatic if we do it now," Wyman told them. "He would not like it, and there's no possibility of having a graceful transition." They agreed to wait another year before asking Paley to step down as chairman.

CBS launched Paley's cable channel in October 1981 amid great fanfare. The man who had brought America *The Beverly Hillbillies* now reveled in turning out highbrow fare. He immersed himself in the details of the channel's programming for months before the debut. There were ballets, concerts, plays, a miniseries about the life of Giuseppe Verdi. It was, said one reviewer, "a feast for the eye and ear." But Paley seemed apprehensive; he was worried about whether CBS could afford the expenditure.

Tensions between Wyman and Paley surfaced toward the end of

1981, after Wyman made a surprising gaffe. In an interview with *The New York Times,* Wyman said, "I don't think there's any question in anyone's mind that I'm running the company." Sounding more than faintly patronizing, Wyman acknowledged that Paley had been "helpful, particularly in long-range planning, and he is wonderfully tough-minded and asks spectacular questions. But the initiatives have been mine."

Paley bitterly complained about the remark to friends. One who heard his lament most clearly was Frank Stanton, Bill Paley's new best friend. As his troubles with successors deepened, Paley had come to appreciate Stanton's abilities in much the way that his appreciation of Babe grew after her death.

Stanton was enjoying an enviably productive—and apparently lucrative—retirement, working as a member of corporate and non-profit boards and as an investor in an assortment of communications companies. During nearly a decade of Paley-imposed exile from CBS, Stanton had remained quietly loyal to the company.

Paley had first extended the olive branch in 1980, after firing John Backe, inviting Stanton to breakfasts and lunches. Stanton graciously resumed their friendship. Paley needed Stanton's counsel, and Stanton was just as eager to serve. He had hated being on the outside looking in. CBS was still his first love.

Paley tried in various ways to make it all up to Stanton. In 1981 he coaxed the CBS board of directors into approving a $500,000 corporate donation to create the Frank Stanton Professorship of the First Amendment at the John F. Kennedy School of Government, at Harvard. Two years later CBS named Stanton president emeritus. The idea had actually come from Wyman during a discussion with Paley about improving CBS' battered image. Paley's only misgiving, recalled Wyman, was, "Can it be graceful for me? Will I be criticized again for not making him chief executive?" Paley decided the gesture would be a plus for CBS, and the board gave its unanimous approval.

Like their relationship of old, the new bond between Paley and Stanton was more convenient than affectionate. But they did become confidants, closer than they had ever been at CBS. At regular intervals they would sit across from each other at a small table in Paley's exquisite library talking about CBS past and present, and they would find common ground.

Stanton had been Paley's subordinate, but now they were on a more equal footing. If anything, Paley was now dependent on Stanton, who was more vigorous and more widely informed about broadcasting in general. "Whenever I have a problem and need to get some advice, I call him," said Paley several years into their rapprochement.

"They are like a husband and wife who fought like hell when they were beautiful people," said William Leonard, who was CBS News president at the time. "Now they sit together drinking tea and eating toast. They have each other."

Despite another big win in the prime-time ratings, there were signs in the spring of 1982 that CBS was faltering. The company had lost more than $20 million on CBS Cable the previous year—about what had been expected. But losses were accelerating instead of declining in the new year. CBS was taking in only half of what had been projected. *Business Week* noted in March that questions were being raised about Tom Wyman's future. "Paley is reported to be disgruntled," said the magazine.

Ignoring Paley's grumbling about Wyman, the CBS directors stood firmly behind their chief executive. After Jock Whitney's death, in February 1982, the board saw an opportunity to dislodge Paley.

Whitney had been ailing with heart disease for six years, and no brother-in-law could have been more devoted than Paley. Until Whitney lost his voice, Paley called him every morning to fill him in on the latest news. Many Sunday evenings on the way home from Southampton, Paley had his helicopter land at Whitney's home in Manhasset. For several hours Paley would sit with Whitney and watch television, neither of them speaking. "Bill would come to see Jock and adore him," said Irene Selznick.

With Whitney's death Paley and his friend Walter Thayer concocted a plan for Paley to pay $14 million for Whitney's one-third interest in the *International Herald Tribune*, in Paris. Paley wanted to become chairman of the newspaper, buy an apartment in Paris, and live there part time while he oversaw the business.

Seizing on what CBS board member Roswell Gilpatric called a fortuitous pretext, the inner five directors began orchestrating Paley's exit from CBS. "We felt that after two years the future should be clarified, and we should make Mr. Wyman's authority crystal clear," said Gilpatric. "We had to break the syndrome."

But even with the *Herald Tribune* possibility, Paley resisted giving up his position as chairman. "When I step down," Paley asked Wyman, "will I be invited out to dinner? I dread the sense that I might be seen as no longer contributing to CBS' success." The board and Wyman held firm. "Paley was one tough s.o.b.," said one source close to the negotiations. "At the core was a man with an enormous ego and need for recognition and adulation."

Paley's new contract demands included an office and dining room at CBS for his lifetime, personal use of CBS aircraft, as well as a provision requiring his election to the board indefinitely. After several months of wrangling, the board finally gave in on the office and aircraft but stopped short of the lifetime board membership.

Once it became clear that Paley would have to step down as CBS chairman, he launched his campaign for the chairman's job at the *International Herald Tribune*. Both Katharine Graham, chairman of the Washington Post Company, and Arthur Sulzberger, chairman of the New York Times Company—joint publishers of the *Tribune*—had veto power over the Whitney third. With Paley nearing his eighty-first birthday, Graham and Sulzberger felt it would be folly for him to take on the job. They also resented his presumption that he could simply move in, with no prior newspaper experience.

Undaunted, Paley argued his case: "I am a wonderful business-man, I get on well with people, I have the talent and ability to contribute." His involvement in the *Herald Tribune*, he said, was "Jock's great wish." He finally said, "I don't understand. Why would you object to me?"

When it became obvious that his plan would be thwarted, Paley bought into the Whitney stake in the *Herald Tribune* and settled for being a cochairman along with Graham and Sulzberger. In early September, 1982, CBS announced that Paley would relinquish the chairman's job to Wyman in April 1983 so that he could pursue his exciting new venture with the *International Herald Tribune*. Paley would remain chairman of CBS' executive committee, and he would be paid $250,000 a year in retirement benefits plus $200,000 a year as a consultant through 1992, the year of his ninety-first birthday.

Less than a week later CBS announced that Paley's cherished cultural cable service would shut down in December. CBS Cable had posted losses that would amount to more than $60 million since its inception—$12 million more than had been expected. The decision to fold it was Wyman's. Paley had no choice but to agree. "To me it was one of our most hurtful failures," Paley said later.

Tom Wyman walked on eggs until April 20, 1983, when Bill Paley called the CBS annual meeting to order. Wearing a dark suit and white shirt, Paley stood at a podium in the studios of KMOX-TV, CBS' station in St. Louis. "It's difficult to tell you what a jumble of emotions I feel at this time," Paley said, his voice cracking slightly. He cleared his throat. Those standing close to him could detect tears in his eyes. "Wherever CBS goes, my heart will go with it." CBS directors, executives, and shareholders stood and gave him a rousing ovation. It was a seemingly graceful exit, simple and heartfelt, befitting the style and elegance that Bill Paley symbolized.

CHAPTER 24

WITHIN days of Paley's farewell he was the odd man out at CBS. He no longer received management reports, and his name was even removed from the CBS telephone book—technically because he was no longer an employee. The hardest blow came when Wyman told Paley that he could not attend the round of meetings in May to set the prime-time schedule. "The programming department," Wyman recalled, "welcomed the decision." Paley was frantic. He made a dozen fruitless calls to CBS executives asking them to dissuade Wyman. With Paley as leader, the scheduling meetings had usually taken four or five days; that year they ended in two.

For the next two years Paley went to his office every day, but it didn't much matter. "Nobody knew if he came to work or not," said public relations aide William Lilley, whose office was around the corner. In board meetings Paley struggled to follow the discussions. When he disagreed with one of Wyman's initiatives, his questioning seemed halfhearted. But some CBS executives with longer memories than Tom Wyman's sensed that the phoenix was only sleeping.

As in the past, Paley sought distraction outside CBS. Although he was in his eighties, Paley continued to chase women with the gusto of a postpubescent. "He has more charm and clout than Rhett Butler and James Bond rolled into one," gushed the New York *Daily News.*

Paley's most intriguing crush was Diane Sawyer, co-anchor of the *CBS Morning News* since the spring of 1982. By May of that year Sawyer and Paley had made the gossip columns, and they were spotted walking hand in hand. Sawyer attended his dinner parties, met him for lunch at his home, and was his houseguest (along with Oscar de la Renta and the Kissingers) in Southampton. She said her involvement was not romantic, but others thought Paley was truly smitten.

Paley's social life assumed a manic, almost desperate quality. "He says he is so lonely," said his friend Marietta Tree. "He is so restless. He wants to fill up every minute with lots of people."

Paley fought the infirmities of aging as hard as anyone could. His first brush with a life-threatening illness came in January 1985, at age eighty-three. While on vacation in Acapulco, Paley collapsed from a bleeding ulcer. The CBS jet whisked him to New York Hospital. During Paley's six-week convalescence he lost seventeen pounds, and his doctor ordered him to give up liquor. After his hospitalization he always had a nurse nearby, even when traveling.

With his health restored, Paley turned his attention to a task that would prove more rejuvenating than any medicine: getting even with his tormentor Tom Wyman, who was riding high as 1985 began. The previous year CBS profits had been $212.4 million, up smartly from $110.8 million two years earlier.

The man who opened the breach for Paley's attack was North Carolina Senator Jesse Helms, a most unlikely ally. In January, Helms and a group of like-minded conservatives launched a campaign urging citizens to buy CBS stock to "become Dan Rather's boss" and end the "liberal bias" of CBS News.

While that threat eventually lost steam, the Helms effort caught the eye of Wall Street, then in the middle of a takeover frenzy that was fueled in mid-March, when Capital Cities Communications announced it would buy ABC for $3.5 billion. Ivan Boesky, the powerful arbitrageur, quickly gathered 8.7 percent of CBS stock, hoping that a buyer would emerge to drive up the price; by the time his stake was revealed, on April 1, 1985, CBS stock had already jumped to nearly $110 a share from $73 before the Helms scheme came to light.

As soon as it became clear in early March that CBS was "in play," Paley had seen his opportunity to recapture the chairmanship by leading a leveraged buyout to make CBS private. He enlisted James

Wolfensohn, the only investment banker on the CBS board, to study the possibility. Wolfensohn came up with what seemed to be an ideal bid of $162 a share, and Paley pressed the directors to approve the proposal. Instead of leaping at the idea, the board tried to explain to Paley that his bid would hardly be the last.

The much awaited move on CBS came in mid-April from cable television maverick Ted Turner, creator of the successful Cable News Network. Turner offered $5.4 billion, financed by junk bonds—risky securities that offered high interest rates. At a price of $175 a share, Turner's bid was $67 higher than CBS' close that day.

Paley was in a state of high anxiety fretting about the Turner crisis. "He was a wreck," said William Lilley. "He couldn't understand why this was happening—why people like Turner and Boesky and Helms were suddenly in his life."

In midsummer CBS announced that it would borrow nearly $1 billion to buy back 21 percent of the company's stock for $150 a share. Since CBS would pay shareholders in cash and high-grade CBS securities instead of risky junk bonds, the offer swamped Turner.

To pay off the $1 billion debt, Wyman had to sell small pieces of the company and cut staff. He unloaded KMOX-TV, the St. Louis station where Paley had delivered his farewell address, for $140 million. Even worse, from Paley's standpoint, Wyman planned to sell the company's helicopter and corporate jets, which were costing the company $10 million a year.

Paley was enraged. His retirement contract stipulated that he be provided private aircraft. He argued that he needed them because his wealth and status made him a potential kidnap victim. "It is right there in the contract," Paley complained to Stanton, who could only smile inwardly, remembering those dark months before his own retirement, and say to himself, That's what I thought too.

At a time when CBS was grappling with extensive layoffs, Paley bogged down board meetings with his arguments against the aircraft sale. "Do you mean to take away the plane that goes to Southampton too?" grumbled Paley. "Bill, we call that a helicopter," Tom Wyman replied acidly. "You can lease one just as effectively." Wyman was appalled that Paley could be more concerned about his own perks than the future of the company.

After months of wrangling, Paley's new lawyer, Arthur Liman, struck a compromise. Paley bought one CBS airplane for $5.4 million, and CBS sold the helicopter. Instead of paying each time Paley took a helicopter to Southampton, CBS agreed to contribute $150,000 a year to Paley's transportation expenses. The aircraft crisis left scars in the CBS boardroom. "The airplanes became a horror," said director Michel Bergerac. "They were really only a symbol for reducing costs. It was not wise of Tom to go out of his way to irritate Paley."

"Tom was very insecure," said one executive. "His mistake was he overcaged the beast and created resentment." Paley, as Wyman would find out, was not a man who took insult lightly.

Takeover tom-toms began to beat again in July, when Laurence Tisch, chairman of Loews Corporation, a $17.5 billion holding company with interests ranging from insurance to cigarettes, bought 5 percent of CBS stock. Tisch assured Wyman that he was only interested in CBS as an investor. But he continued to accumulate stock. Within weeks he had brought his stake to 10 percent, eclipsing Paley's 8 percent to become the largest shareholder. James Wolfensohn, a tennis partner and close friend of Tisch's, arranged a luncheon

Above, Paley and Frank Stanton (right) outside Black Rock in 1964

Above, Arthur Taylor (left), who became CBS president in 1972, with Paley. Left, John Backe, the first designated chief executive officer of CBS.

to bring together the oldest and the newest CBS power brokers.

In Paley's eyes Tisch came from a lower social order, despite his estimated $1 billion net worth—about twice that of Paley. Short, bald, and unprepossessing, the sixty-one-year-old Tisch was the antithesis of Paley in virtually every way. Tisch drove himself to parties in a Pontiac station wagon, inhabited a bland office, and spent his weekends playing tennis at a suburban country club. Known for his philanthropy, Tisch was also a pillar of the New York Jewish community that Paley had kept at arm's length for nearly sixty years. Each week Tisch and two of his sons gathered with a Hasidic rabbi to study the Bible and the Talmud.

By October 1985 Tisch had raised his stake in CBS to 12 percent. He told Wyman that he intended to buy no more than 25 percent—still, he insisted, acting as a passive investor. After a discussion with the directors, Wyman invited him onto the board. "The assumption," recalled Wyman, "was that he would be less threatening inside the company than outside." Paley welcomed the move; by then he had concluded that Tisch could prove useful in ousting Wyman. At a dinner party Paley told one of Tisch's friends, "That son of a bitch

Above, Tom Wyman (left)—who supplanted Paley as chairman—with Paley before he fell from grace. Right, Laurence Tisch (left), with Paley. Tisch took full control of CBS in 1986.

Tom Wyman. He stole my company, and I want to get it back."

When Tisch slipped into his director's chair for the first time, in November, CBS was in trouble and Paley was emboldened. Paley criticized Wyman's $362.5 million purchase the previous February of twelve magazines owned by Ziff-Davis Publishing. After the deal was announced, the losing bidders revealed that their offers had been some $40 million less, making Wyman seem like a patsy. "Paley was positive when we bought Ziff-Davis," recalled Wyman. "He has quite a capacity to move history around."

Meanwhile, CBS profits for 1985 plunged to $27.4 million— $185 million less than the previous year. To make matters worse, the network dropped once again to second place in prime time in the fall of 1985, prompting Paley's complaints about mismanagement to grow louder. Anything that weakened Wyman strengthened Paley.

And it was Bill Paley who played a key role in shaping one of the most negative among a flood of newspaper and magazine articles about CBS. The November 4 issue of *New York* magazine pummeled Wyman for mishandling CBS and invoked Paley as a symbol of better days. Wyman and his staff had declined to cooperate with the story. So, apparently, had Paley, who was not quoted. But Paley's finger-prints were everywhere. "Paley spent one and a half hours with me," said the writer, Tony Schwartz. "The deal was, I had to disguise his quotes."

Throughout winter and spring Tisch burrowed into CBS far more deeply than the classic "passive investor." He visited Hollywood for wall-to-wall meetings with producers and studio executives. At direc-tors meetings he questioned every decision, with Paley's happy concurrence. "Tisch was in effect running the meetings from the other end of the table," said one director.

Wyman seemed secure despite Tisch, who made the CBS directors apprehensive. They worried that his purchases of CBS stock amounted to a gradual takeover without paying a premium price. But the directors were also annoyed at Paley for causing trouble and trying to obstruct their meetings in his effort to wear Wyman down. Paley's main preoccupation in early 1986 was blocking Wyman's plans to install a company cafeteria on the ground floor of Black Rock.

New predators started circling CBS after the December 1985 announcement that General Electric would buy RCA, and with it

NBC, for $6.4 billion. In February and March, Marvin Davis, of Twentieth Century-Fox, met several times with Wyman to propose buying CBS for $160 a share. After consulting closely with Tisch and informing Paley as a courtesy, Wyman deflected the bid. Several days later Larry Tisch's brother Robert declared his family's intention "to control CBS and operate it as a first-class broadcasting company," and a week later the Tisch stake climbed to nearly 17 percent.

Tisch's audacious move depressed Paley. His most public expression of discontent was boycotting the CBS annual meeting in April—the first one he had missed since 1947.

As he approached his eighty-fifth birthday Paley's thoughts turned to posterity. He launched a campaign to build a new Museum of Broadcasting. The original museum, he felt, was too small. He wanted something grander that would do justice to his reputation—or at least his estimate of it. Paley had found a site, next door to "21" and down the block from Black Rock, and had paid $12 million for the land. However, he wanted to tap other sources for the $40 million to finance the building—starting with $2.5 million from each of the networks. For months Paley had tried to persuade Wyman to authorize CBS' contribution, arguing that its commitment was crucial to prying funds from ABC and NBC. In May, Wyman finally agreed—a gesture that board members saw as a significant peace overture.

When Larry Tisch had pushed his stake toward 20 percent, Wyman and directors Gilpatric, Wolfensohn, and Thomas confronted him before the June board meeting to ask him to sign a "standstill" agreement. Tisch dismissed them, saying he had told them he intended to buy up to 25 percent, and he would not break his word.

From that moment Tisch turned on Wyman. "He [Wyman] knew he had an enemy, and could never have a relationship of trust or confidence," said a close friend of Tisch's. "Taking on Larry Tisch was like closing an umbrella in the rain. It was the beginning of the end."

Tisch criticized Wyman openly for the first time during a dinner at the Links Club before the July board meeting. On a recent trip to Hollywood he had heard an earful from executives about Wyman's softness at the bargaining table. "He's a nice man," said Tisch, "but he's not a good businessman." Paley seconded Tisch in even harsher terms, deriding Wyman's lack of talent in programming.

Most of the directors defended Wyman and dismissed Paley's

tirade. "It was a rehash," said 'one director. "It would have been the same whether it was Tom Wyman or anyone else." The directors expressed their dissatisfaction privately over the way Wyman was running the company, but they were even more vexed at Tisch for buying CBS cheap through a "creeping tender offer." At the board meeting the next day, they raised the prospect of a "poison pill" to stave off a hostile takeover. "If you do that, it's a declaration of war," said Tisch. Soon after, Tisch raised his stake in CBS to 24.9 percent.

In early August it became clear that 1986 broadcasting revenues would amount to only $235 million—$150 million less than projected. The CBS network, which had finished the season in second place the previous spring, saw its lowest prime-time ratings to date on the night of August 2. The *CBS Evening News* with Dan Rather was losing viewers as well.

"Paley cared about the ratings and news, and Tisch cared about the financial shortfall," said William Lilley. "It was a fatal linkage for Tom Wyman, joining the driving concerns of the two most powerful people on the board." Now that Paley and Tisch together controlled more than one third of CBS stock, Paley initiated an alliance to oust Wyman. "There was an inevitable point," said a close friend of Tisch's, "when they got together and said, 'If we act together, we can change management.'" Over a series of lunches at Paley's apartment and in discussions through their tough-minded intermediary, Arthur Liman, Paley and Tisch sketched out scenarios.

Despite their common interest in dislodging Wyman, they were unable to forge a close relationship. Each man had a specific goal— Paley to be chairman and Tisch to be chief executive. Not surprisingly, Paley tried to talk Tisch out of being chief executive, but Liman eventually got Paley to acquiesce.

The prospect of ousting Wyman revitalized Paley. As the September board meeting approached, Paley confided to a friend, "I am not going out anywhere Monday or Tuesday night. I have to be strong. I have to save my company."

Tom Wyman had not been idle during those days either. On September 2 he had lunch with his friend Francis T. Vincent, Jr., chairman and chief executive of Columbia Pictures, to discuss possibly joining forces with its owner, Coca-Cola. Vincent told Wyman that if CBS was interested, Coca-Cola would consider a merger. Having been given a yellow light by Coke, Wyman was busy briefing CBS directors Bergerac, Gilpatric, Thomas, Brown, Houghton, Schacht, Spencer, and Wolfensohn—conspicuously omitting Tisch, Paley, and their allies. Not only did Wyman tell eight men on the board of Coca-Cola's interest, he mentioned that he expected to raise the idea at the September board meeting.

On Tuesday, September 9, 1986, the eve of their September meeting, the board met for dinner at The Ritz Carlton hotel. Neither Tom Wyman nor Larry Tisch was invited. In a private dining room they ate sandwiches from a buffet and talked for five hours about the mess at CBS. Paley, who was accompanied by Liman, passionately made his case. "We have to have a change in management," he said. "Tom Wyman is not right. I have met with Larry Tisch and discussed it, and he feels the same. The two of us have decided we will act together. We are asking you directors to join us."

When the board met the next morning, Wyman, confident that he had the backing of eight directors, presented the Coca-Cola merger idea. The only people who spoke up were Paley and Tisch. "We are not going to sell our stock under any circumstances," they said. Even the good guys were bad guys because "Tom Wyman's friends didn't back him," said a friend of Tisch's. "None of them said a word."

Having watched his proposal slide off the table, Wyman left the boardroom. The directors quizzed Tisch on his intentions and invited Paley to speak. Typically, Paley pulled away from his earlier understanding with Tisch. Instead of making Tisch chief executive, Paley proposed naming him acting chairman of a four-man executive committee, of which Paley would be a member. The chairman of CBS, of course, would be Paley.

Paley, Liman, and Tisch left the room, and the directors hashed over their options. There was no way they could oppose Paley and Tisch to support Wyman's proposal, whatever its merits. They likewise threw out Paley's cockeyed executive committee plan and sensibly decided that one person had to be in charge: Larry Tisch. At first most of the directors strongly resisted reinstating Paley as chairman, fearing they would never get him out again. But when board emissaries passed the word to Paley, he got tearful and petulant.

In the end the board named Paley and Tisch "acting" chairman and "acting" chief executive, respectively—an effort to create the illusion that the titles were subject to change. It suited Tisch perfectly to have Paley as chairman; he knew Paley's continued presence would confer legitimacy on the Tisch regime.

At four p.m. Henry Schacht and Franklin Thomas—the board's emissaries—walked to Wyman's office, where he had been waiting alone for five hours. They told him the board had officially vetoed any proposal to sell the company. Like John Backe before him, they forced Wyman to resign.

The directors gave him a staggering settlement of $3.8 million plus $400,000 a year for life. Tisch was not happy about the magnitude, but he went along. The directors had betrayed Wyman, and their guilt was expressed in dollar signs. Still, Wyman was shaken by his dismissal. Other than sitting on the boards of several companies, he would not soon run another company.

After the meeting adjourned at six fifteen, Paley sat with Liman as the champagne corks popped. Weary but alert, Paley's well-tanned face crinkled in a grin. Only weeks before his eighty-fifth birthday he had used cunning and determination to seize the one job that could sustain him. In another office Larry Tisch talked on the telephone, his mind whirring with the tasks he faced in his glamorous and highly visible new post.

They were by no means equals. Tisch was destined to dominate by virtue of his holdings in CBS—at that moment, $780 million to Paley's $257 million—as well as his physical and mental vigor. Paley had made a classic pact with the devil. He had willingly ceded control of his company in exchange for an honorific and the chance to dive back into programming. But even if Paley was only a figurehead, he clung to the belief that no one would ever again shut the door in his face, as Tom Wyman had done.

CHAPTER 25

PALEY'S friends celebrated his triumph, and so did his children—at a party to mark his eighty-fifth birthday, an elegant family dinner at 820 Fifth Avenue. Everyone rose to give a toast, and each child spoke openly and warmly. Their words evoked laughter and tears. Paley was genuinely touched.

It had taken great effort for the sons to reconcile with their tyrannical father. Tony Mortimer had barely spoken to Paley since Babe's death. Their antagonism had been aggravated by conflicts over Babe's will, but by the mid-'80s he and his stepfather reached an accommodation, helped along by Tony's wife, Siri, whom Paley adored.

Billie had an even more tortuous path to his father's good graces. When Babe died, Billie was operating two restaurants in Washington, D.C. But in January 1979 he was arrested for heroin and marijuana possession. After pleading guilty, he received a suspended three-month prison sentence. He knocked around from job to job and in 1980 married Alison Van Metre, the daughter of a yachtsman and real estate developer. She was pretty, so Paley naturally took a shine to her. She and Billie had two sons, Sam and Max. Billie finally kicked his habit and became a drug counselor.

Even Jeffrey returned to the fold—helped, like his brothers, by the presence of a lovely young wife, the former Valerie Ritter, who also caught Paley's admiring eye. Jeffrey had retreated from the family after Dorothy and Paley divorced. But when Paley was in his eighties, Jeffrey made an effort to get to know his father. Paley responded for the first time by expressing an interest in his eldest son. Jeffrey began showing up at family gatherings and periodically having quiet dinners at 820 Fifth Avenue with Paley.

Both Amanda and Hilary had maintained relatively harmonious relations with Paley. Amanda had married and subsequently divorced Steve Ross. Hilary bounced back from the suicide of her husband to marry Joseph Califano, former Secretary of Health, Education, and Welfare.

Paley's relationship with Kate was, as Carter Burden's new wife Susan put it, "in and out," but always intense. She was, Paley often said, his favorite child. Some months after Babe's death Kate suddenly fled to South Africa, where she became a born-again Christian. Back in New York, she hovered over her father, occasionally serving as his escort to social events.

Paley's first task following his restoration in the autumn of 1986 was "saving" the CBS prime-time schedule. The day after his eighty-fifth birthday he flew to Hollywood for three days of meetings with the programming department. The CBS executives recognized immediately that his short-term memory had degenerated. Occasionally, though, he would startle his subordinates by clarifying a fuzzy program idea with sharp questions.

Tisch, meanwhile, was busy learning the ropes and making contacts in Hollywood—activities that visibly disquieted Paley. Although he would never admit it, Paley had a boss for the first time since he worked for his father sixty years earlier. And the boss treated him very much as an employee. Tisch's flattery often seemed patronizing, and he thought nothing of correcting and even interrupting Paley in meetings. Yet Paley, in his instinctively imperious way, "still doesn't recognize that Larry is running it," said one close friend of Tisch's four months after the September coup. "Paley views Larry as a convenience who brought him back to power and in some way will depart to leave Paley in complete control of his empire."

BILL Paley wanted every last minute from life. In February 1987 he made his customary trip to Lyford Cay. After a few days of nonstop entertaining he came down with a cold that rapidly worsened until one evening he collapsed on the floor of his bedroom. He had pneumonia complicated by emphysema.

He was flown in the CBS jet to New York Hospital, where he spent three touch-and-go days in intensive care. His daughter Kate, frantic, moved in with him for a round-the-clock vigil of Scripture reading.

When Amanda arrived at the hospital several days later, she found Diane Sawyer, wearing a pink angora sweater, sitting opposite Paley at a small table as Paley's valet served them an elegant dinner. The sparkle had returned to Paley's eye, and after six more days he was home, at 820 Fifth Avenue. To ease his breathing, he had to sleep sitting up, and he needed oxygen.

By the end of March, Paley was back in his office at Black Rock, in the words of one observer, "thrashing about because he was unhappy about programming at CBS."

On May 11 and 12 Tisch sat with Paley for the first time during the annual prime-time scheduling marathon. Paley showed admirable stamina through the long days of meetings, but when Paley awoke on the morning of May 13, he could barely see. A blood vessel had burst in the retina of one eye. Yet he rebounded to wow the crowd at the

60 Minutes tribute, in the St. Regis Hotel, the following month. But over all, his mood began to darken as his ailing back worsened despite daily workouts with a physiotherapist.

By September, Paley had lost sensation in his legs and could only move around by wheelchair. His vision was so bad that he needed a magnifying glass to read, and he was weakened by severe anemia.

Nevertheless, he endured a four-hour board meeting, during which Tisch presented a proposal to sell CBS Records to Sony for $2 billion. At that price, said Roswell Gilpatric, "Paley could make no argument." The following month Tisch sold CBS Publishing for $650 million. His health failing and his empire shrinking, Paley hit bottom. "This is the most unhappy time of Bill's life," said one friend.

Paley's only bright spot was the prospect of better health. Toward the end of the year a nurse started accompanying Paley to Black Rock. She would sit outside his office, and every half hour Paley would summon her by pressing a buzzer. She would enter the room saying, "Excuse me, it's time," and pop a pill into his mouth.

It was an experimental drug called erythropoietin, or EPO—a genetically engineered protein that stimulates production of red blood cells, thereby avoiding the transfusions traditionally used to treat anemia. The federal Food and Drug Administration had not approved the drug in the United States, so Paley used his connection at Genetics Institute—the Cambridge, Massachusetts, biotechnology company, where he was a big investor—to secure government approval to import it from Germany. After several months of treatment Paley was having lunch with Stanton in his office. "Surprise," he said with a twinkling smile as he stood up from his wheelchair and walked across the room.

Once again Paley had the stamina to ply the social circuit. Laser surgery on his left eye arrested his visual trouble, a condition called macular degeneration that results from problems with the blood vessels in the retina. His back still hurt, but by using a cane he could get around with some dignity.

One weekend in early February, 1988, Paley took Kate to Southampton. He was intrigued when she talked eagerly about the healthful properties of cucumbers, and at her urging, his chef served the vegetable raw at several meals. Paley gorged on the cucumbers, eating more than a half dozen. His overindulgence provoked a severe gallbladder attack, and he was flown to New York Hospital for emergency treatment.

After a few days in intensive care Paley's kidneys and already weakened lungs failed. He was hooked up to a respirator, dialysis kept his kidneys working, and four nurses tended him around the clock. Kate was once again the vigilant watchdog. As Paley clung to life he occasionally wrote cryptic notes.

Paley's family and aides kept his illness secret for more than a week. When word finally leaked out, the hospital acknowledged that he had been admitted for gallbladder treatment and was recovering. Four days later another bulletin pronounced Paley in critical condition from respiratory and renal failure, and obituary writers started working overtime. Yet at that very moment Paley was off the respirator, sitting in a chair for the first time and taking food.

In a remarkable turnabout, Paley settled into a luxurious suite in the New York Hospital tower several days later. He signaled his recovery by growling complaints and commands to everyone. His faithful factotum, John Minary, kept Paley abreast of goings-on at CBS, one of which threw the old man into a tizzy: Larry Tisch wanted to nominate his brother Preston to the board of directors. Using Minary and Arthur Liman as messengers, Paley told the directors they should not support the nomination. "My sense is that Bill is concerned about the perception of two Tisches being there," said one director. "That it would look as if they were outweighing him." Under the circumstances the directors deferred the question until the autumn. "Paley was like one of those drug kingpins on Riker's Island," said one friend afterwards. "He got the nomination blocked from afar."

After nearly a month in the hospital Paley was released. On entering his apartment, he asked to be wheeled through all the rooms four times. In each room he stopped to declare how beautiful it looked and how glad he was to be home. Soon he was asking friends such as Henry Kissinger over for lunch.

Paley would greet guests in a wheelchair, sometimes wearing a bright blue dressing gown of heavy silk with a simple monogram. His handshake was strong, but conversation had become disorienting. "It is like listening to a short-wave station when the tuning isn't quite right," said one visitor. "It comes in sharply, then you get another language momentarily, then it comes back clearly."

By now Tisch knew he no longer needed to worry about battling with Paley. And Paley, said Don Hewitt, "had finally concluded that he couldn't beat Tisch." Tisch was now calling every shot, informing Paley after the fact.

Paley felt much more comfortable in the precincts of the Museum of Broadcasting, where he was still the supreme—and often autocratic—commander. At the museum's board of directors meeting in April, he made a dramatic entry in his wheelchair, perfectly attired in one of his $1000 bespoke suits, holding on his lap the black cane that he called Arnold, after the silver dog's head on top. Frank Stanton led the directors in a standing ovation. Afterwards one director remarked to another, sotto voce, "His will is the only one that reads, 'If I die . . .' "

Stanton was Paley's chief consultant on the new broadcasting museum to be built on West Fifty-second Street. As with Black Rock, Paley was plagued by indecision over the architect and the design. Stanton wanted Philip Johnson, but Paley hesitated. After finally selecting Johnson, Paley complained that his design "looked too much like a cathedral." Four versions later the dignified design—seventeen stories of beige limestone with mullioned windows and neoclassic touches such as pillars, arches, and pediments—still resembled a cathedral. That was the point, said Johnson, who believed that "museums have taken the place of the church in lay culture." Although Paley yielded to Stanton once again on the architecture, he got the last word on the façade, which he wanted to look exactly like Bergdorf Goodman's, on Fifth Avenue.

The board decided to call the new building the Museum of Radio and Television, and there was talk of adding Paley's name posthumously. He was now eager to be publicly identified with an elegant symbol of a well-respected cultural institution. In the view of Slim Keith, Paley once again seemed focused on the future.

Paley's big disappointment was the failure of his eyes to improve, even after further laser surgery. His desk was littered with magnifying glasses, but when they proved inadequate, he bought an electronic reader that scanned pages and blew them up on a monitor. He could still identify his beloved paintings, make out the images on a television set at medium range, and recognize a beautiful face next to him at a dinner party. But it was clear that he had lost the one thing that had touched him with genius: the ability to *see* what others could not.

Endless money and a squad of attendants made all the difference, of course. Still, there was real pathos in the decline of the aging dynamo. His three Irish nurses rotated twenty-four-hour shifts and took turns accompanying him on trips. Wherever he went, a nurse brought along a portable supply of oxygen, because he often panicked when he felt breathless. But unlike others, who yield to their infirmity and slip from public view, Paley clung to center stage. He loved the visibility and the awe that he still inspired. If it meant risking making a fool of himself, it was a chance worth taking.

"You know a party isn't a success out there unless I go," Paley said to one old friend, explaining his frequent presence on the Southampton social circuit the summer after his illness. He went to a dance in the autumn given by socialite Anne Bass, and the seventieth-birthday party for choreographer Jerome Robbins. At the Robbins fete he seemed distinctly put out that he was seated next to the well-preserved Claudette Colbert rather than next to a pretty young thing. There was something joyless in Paley's social activity, however. "He had an underlying fear," said one man close to him, "so he was always hanging on, proving something, and living hard to do it."

In December 1988 Paley stood up at a Museum of Broadcasting tribute to Walter Cronkite. He used a bright light, and each page of his speech contained only five lines, with letters one-inch high and words underlined and accented. But he couldn't focus, and for several excruciating minutes he stumbled incoherently, reading sentence fragments, breathing hard. "I'm sorry, I can't read this," he finally said, and then he ad-libbed for several minutes, extolling CBS News and its tradition of integrity. His delivery was fluid, strong, and passionate. He was obviously using every ounce of his strength. The audience shot to its feet and applauded him for thirty-five seconds. "Everyone was dying at the thought he would humiliate himself," said one of the guests that evening. "They wanted him to be *Paley*. When he saved himself, there was a thrill." On returning to his table, Paley grumbled, "I bombed out," but he knew otherwise.

Paley and Tisch continued to operate at arm's length, with lingering resentment on both sides. At a cocktail party in the autumn of 1988 Tisch stunned a group that included *60 Minutes* correspondent Harry Reasoner by saying, "Sometimes people live too long. Everybody's forgotten Bill Paley. They don't realize he is still around. I went to an industry luncheon this afternoon and nobody came up to me and asked, 'How's Bill?' "

When Larry's brother Preston Tisch was elected to the board in the fall of 1988, Paley lodged no further protest. Privately Paley complained that Larry Tisch didn't seem to understand broadcasting.

For a time Paley even schemed to find a buyer for CBS to get rid of Tisch. Paley was particularly distressed when Tisch announced a deal with the K mart discount chain in which CBS shows would be promoted by games and banners at K mart stores—as ignominious a counterpoint to the Tiffany image as one could find. "I made a mistake," Paley said to a colleague at the time. "I wanted to get rid of Tom Wyman so badly I would have done anything."

Frustrated by his diminished role at CBS, Paley asked friends and businessmen where he might find an interesting business to run. In truth, he was physically and mentally incapable of any such thing. "He so wants to be in the center," said one business associate. "He remembers when the world revolved around him."

In his social realm everything still did. Invitations to his home were the most coveted in town. His 1989 Fourth of July party in Southampton was bigger than ever. He still went to dinners and dances, always with his nurse nearby. "All that is left is his wit and the gleam in his eye," said Slim Keith as she watched Paley at a dinner party.

The fall of 1989 was marked by a further deterioration in Paley's mental condition. With increasing frequency he would call meetings and forget their purpose. He often lost track of where he was; he could be sitting in the sunshine and ask if the sun was out, or he would fail to recognize a close friend. It was an especially cruel form of senility, rather like a flickering light bulb. One moment Paley would be bright, witty, and perceptive. Then the light would go out, and when it flipped on again, he would have lost the thread. His moments of clarity were usually focused on a dollar sign. When his partners in the *International Herald Tribune* offered to buy out his stake for roughly $25 million, he demanded twice that amount and refused to budge for many months. He might confuse the details, but the fundamental instincts remained.

By 1990 most of his old friends were gone. Losing Slim Keith, in early 1990, and the deaths of Loel Guinness and Walter Thayer, in

1989, had been particularly tough. By contrast, Paley barely blinked when his sister, Blanche, died, in 1990. On his doctor's orders he did not attend the funeral. When Jeanne Vanderbilt said, "I'm sorry, Will," he launched into his old harangue about how his mother had hated him after "my sister"—he had never called her Blanche—was born. "It always goes back to his mother," said Jeanne Vanderbilt. "Imagine, after all these years."

Each death understandably rattled Paley, reminding him of his own mortality.

As Paley's life shrank, CBS assumed greater meaning once again, Larry Tisch notwithstanding. In his senescence Paley grew closer to Tisch. The lines were clearly drawn. Paley knew now that Tisch, not Bill Paley, made the rules.

Dismembered and stripped to bottom-line efficiency, bereft of its old style, CBS seemed to be someone else's creation. "CBS is just another company with dirty carpets," Frank Stanton said to a friend some months after Tisch's takeover. Perhaps Tisch finally made CBS what it had been all along—a machine of lowbrow mass-market entertainment, now shorn of its pretensions. Yet there had been something uplifting about the Tiffany image. Even if CBS aimed high only intermittently, its news and entertainment programs had been the best in the business.

Despite the changes, CBS was the place where Bill Paley could live his legend as he approached the beginning of his tenth decade. In the halls of Black Rock he would always be great, and he would get respect and admiration. Here his myth had grown, nurtured by repetition and embellishment. Here, in his own mind at least, he remained the wise founder, the television visionary, the seducer of women, the master of style, the toast of high society. In reality, of course, the only thing remaining beneath the myth was Paley's incredible force. As Barry Diller, now the chairman of Twentieth Century-Fox, had said when he first met Paley, "I have seen pure willpower."

In May 1990 the CBS annual shareholders meeting was held in the auditorium at the Museum of Modern Art. Paley entered through a back door and was assisted to the dais. He wore his trademark dark blue suit and white shirt, his white pocket handkerchief crisply folded in his left breast pocket. Paley's only duty was to read seven lines introducing Tisch. He couldn't see the text, and his ability to improvise failed him. "You sound good," he told the audience. "All in all, this is a good day for me"; then he turned the meeting over to Tisch.

During the meeting itself Paley sat through two and a half hours of questions and harangues by an odd assortment of gadflies and eccentrics. Tisch fielded everything while the old man sat impassively, his face free of the vexing twitch. Paley put on two different pairs of glasses, one with red-tinted lenses. When an outrageous remark broke up the audience, he sometimes chuckled along. "I hope you hear this, Mr. Paley," said one questioner. "He hears you," said Tisch, patting Paley patronizingly on the shoulder. But Paley registered no reaction as the speaker continued, "When you have to go to K mart to get viewers, that's the bottom of the barrel."

It didn't much matter what Paley heard or understood. What counted was showing up, going the distance, tapping the amazing reserve of stamina yet again. Those who knew him—especially those who cared about him—told one another that Paley had put on a hell of a show.

He left as quietly as he had come, through the back door, into a waiting wheelchair, and up in the elevator to the ground floor. His pretty brunette nurse wheeled him to the black Cadillac Brougham at the curb. Anybody else would have headed for home and a long nap. Bill Paley rode the half block to CBS headquarters, where he climbed out into the bright spring sunshine. His body listing to the right toward the cane he called Arnold, he walked slowly across the sidewalk, with his nurse guiding his steps. The door to Black Rock opened, and Bill Paley walked in, proudly.

On October 26, 1990, William S. Paley died at his home in New York City at the age of eighty-nine.—THE EDITORS

GUERRILLA PRINCE

PRINCE

———————————

The Untold Story of Fidel Castro

Georgie Anne Geyer

. . . "You can be sure we have no animosity toward the United States and the American people. Above all, we are fighting for a democratic Cuba and an end to the dictatorship."

—Fidel Castro, 1957

. . . "As a child, he was always a terrible liar."

—Father Armando Llorente
Fidel Castro's high school teacher

ONE
The Thirtieth Year

To most of the world, on January 1, 1989, the thirtieth anniversary of the Revolution, Fidel Castro was still the romantic revolutionary hero of the twentieth century. He had smitten the dread and archaic dictator Fulgencio Batista, cuckolded the great and all-powerful United States of America, and "freed" his Cuban people. He had sent his guerrillas sweeping napoleonically from one end of the globe to the other, destroying governments from within and creating new ones, like no power in history.

By the thirtieth anniversary of the Revolution, Castro had more troops around the world than all the other communist leaders put together. The Cuban army numbered 145,000 men, but these were backed by 110,000 ready reserves and more than 1 million men and women in the territorial troops militias. Cuba, with slightly more than 10 million persons, was probably the world's most completely militarized country.

But numbers only sketch the form of the unique, odd power of this modern man. To understand its pervasiveness it is necessary to look at the global consequences of guerrilla warfare in the twentieth century. For although the roots and practice of "little warfare" reach deep into history, it was Castro who invented or perfected every single one of the techniques of guerrilla warfare and of terrorism that would later be expanded upon by the Palestinians, the Iranians, the Central Americans. Without Fidel Castro's advice and support, there would have been no Nicaraguan Sandinistas, no guerrilla movements from

El Salvador to Uruguay to Chile, no Marxist Angola, Mozambique, or Ethiopia. There would have been no supernational "drug state," defended by the leftist guerrillas he had trained, spreading like an evil and consuming Rorschach blot across Latin America. In short, Castro was the century's doctor of distintegration and vicar of breakdown. From 1959 on, whenever the United States had a watershed foreign policy crisis, his formative hand could be found.

But as he stood atop the podium in Havana in the Plaza de la Revolución that January 1, 1989, he was strangely disconsolate, and he was angry. He felt his victories slipping away from him. From his position high above *las masas*—the masses—on that sparkling winter day, he could see the fringe of stark white buildings proudly displaying pictures of Lenin and Che Guevara. The square still looked appropriately martial, clean, revolutionary. But beyond, the once sensuous Spanish colonial city of Havana was literally sinking into its own decay.

Once, Havana had been the exotic, heavenly blooming plant of the Caribbean. Now, sober Havana waited in food lines, waited at restaurants, waited for the minuscule rations of milk, of meat, of shoes. In Fidel's defiantly socialist Cuba a bride still received a bonus ration of a nightgown, and so did a pregnant woman, causing some irreverent wags to note that these were exactly the two times when a woman least needed one.

But in the plaza that day in 1989, Castro's problems fell away from his broad shoulders. Again he breathed deeply of the power that the Cuban people granted him. Again he gazed down on the more than 200,000 heads bobbing and swaying and listening. Yes, his beloved masses were still there. They had not deserted him, for the very simple reason that they could not. It was in the plaza, in the response of the faithful, that he found the only real love he knew.

The speech started.

It was a special speech, marking as it did his three decades of "transformation." Still tall as a palm tree and strong as an oak, he remained mystically capable of grasping *las masas* in his strangely feminine hands and molding them to his whim and will. His harangue was delivered as always in a voice that altered rhythm only occasionally. His right arm swept in great circles, then crashed down, his second finger outstretched for emphasis. Occasionally he cajoled, even joked, even flirted with *las masas*. They loved it. He loved it, too, for the masses not only provided him with the only sure human resonance to his powerful will, they were his only real human contact.

Part of his genius was that while he was projecting this very image of strength, he was able in the same breath to make the people afraid for him. This double imagery of strength and vulnerability bonded the crowd to him even more diabolically. The people in the plaza that New Year's Day of 1989 could see that although he was only sixty-two, he had suddenly started aging very quickly; his beard had grayed and then whitened as a transformation began to overtake the Cuban strongman.

Indeed, a morbid preoccupation with his health had started to grow inside him, although the Cuban people knew nothing about it and the world heard only rumors: a heart attack, lung cancer, rectal cancer. CIA physicians confirmed, in their masked anonymity, that he had lung cancer, a view that gained in credibility when he suddenly gave up smoking his favorite cigars. Even the Russians leaked to the American press that they wanted to talk about Castro's succession.

Then at that crucial moment of the anniversary something unusual and even ominous occurred. Since the birth of the Revolution thirty years before, he had always ended his speeches with the classic, grandiose words of the "Apostle of Cuban salvation," José Martí: "*Patria o muerte* [Fatherland or death]!" But that day, with his gargantuan capacity for confounding, he paused first for dramatic effect; then, in a different voice, he shouted: "*Marxismo-Leninismo o muerte* [Marxism-Leninism or death]!"

What was he doing? Confusion flickered across the Cubans' faces, then passed. Actually, it was quite simple. For thirty years Castro's very favorite game had been to toy with the world over the question of when and if he had become a Communist. First he was, then he wasn't, then he was again. At this moment, as the Russians effectively launched their decommunization, Castro was mockingly, but also seriously, proclaiming Havana as the new Vatican of true Marxism, deliberately relegating his Russian patrons to some shadowy ideological periphery halfway between social democracy and the Republican Party.

Castro had never liked the Russians, but he had trusted them cynically to be there for their own interests. They did not need to be loved, as did the Americans; they only needed him to expand their empire into the Third World that loved him and hated them. Now there was Mikhail Gorbachev—democratizing, liberalizing, reforming. Mother Russia was shedding revolutionary fervor.

Gorbachev had even held elections in the Soviet Union for the first time since Lenin had wisely abolished them in 1917. In historic Leningrad "the people" went out and massively wrote "X" on the ballots to negate the Communist Party chiefs. If that sort of treacherous disobedience had been lurking all this time inside the sober and shrouded Russian people, could it not be lurking too inside those very Cubans who were cheering him in the plaza? If Gorbachev could do these unforgivable things, what rock did Castro himself have to stand on to move the world?

When Gorbachev arrived in Havana, on April 3, 1989, the incredible weave of dramas of that fateful year began its inexorable unraveling. It was the Russian leader now who was the younger man, the new leader with new ideas. As Castro escorted him around decaying Havana, signs quickly accumulated of unhappy rifts. But it was when the Russian leader addressed the Cuban National Assembly that the yawning chasm of ideology opened before the entire watching world.

In his speech to the assembly Gorbachev first praised Castro as a living legend. But living legends are always dangerously close to becoming dead legends. Then Gorbachev spoke against any further aid to the Castroite guerrilla movements, and Castro's cup of rage boiled over. They were threatening his very life's blood. But Gorbachev forged right ahead, calling for "an end to military supplies to Central America from any quarter."

On the immediate level, Gorbachev for the first time revealed to Cubans the reforms that were taking place within the Soviet bloc. In effect, he was forcing his *glasnost* down Castro's throat—and in Castro's own country. On another level, he was informing the Cuban people that Fidel Castro had tied them for thirty years to a failed ideology, and that to survive they now had to mimic the *americanos*.

The aftereffects of Gorbachev's visit flooded over the suddenly beleaguered Castro for months. In the fall of 1989 communist Eastern Europe collapsed like a treacherous house of cards. Castro had depended upon East Germany for intelligence training, upon Czechoslovakia for weaponry. Now where would he go?

From then on, Cuba descended into a hellish chaos and into a realm of cold brutality that the country, even in its worst days, had never before witnessed. When Adolph Hitler saw his Third Reich failing, he launched a last Götterdämmerung from his Berlin bunker. When Fidel Castro saw old age and the failure of communism closing in on him, he turned ruthlessly against his very finest military officers, executing them in the name of "corruption."

There was an even more menacing event to come, in that crucial year of 1989. For over a decade Castro had depended upon unscrupulous governments in Panama to smuggle him technology, drugs, medicines, consumer goods. Since 1981 the clever little pockmarked brute General Manuel Noriega had staunchly stood with Castro against the United States. Together they were sure the *gringos* would never invade Panama. But Noriega began to go quite crazy that fall of 1989, and then, amazingly, on December 20, 1989, it happened—the United States did invade.

As Castro's empire was falling apart politically, so too was he losing intellectual support. Everywhere he looked he found criticisms from former admirers, such as Régis Debray. Castro remembered all too well how the young Frenchman from a powerful upper-class Gaullist family had come to Cuba as the most entranced of acolytes in 1965, when Castro was putting his guerrilla universe in place.

Debray had played with communism in those years, traveled about the world, suffered over revolution while wearing English tweed jackets and dancing in St.-Tropez. Soon Debray was personally chosen by Castro to sit at his feet as he dictated his ideas on a new, indigenous kind of Marxism for Latin America and for the Third World. *Revolución en la Revolución?*, a treatise on guerrilla warfare, was only a small, slim book, but it had a huge impact. At the height of the romance with guerrilladom, the book would stand as the creedification of Castro's own revolutionary experience and the announcement of his intention to impose its form on the rest of Latin America.

But by now Debray was back in Paris, working for a tame and "respectable" socialist president, François Mitterrand, and writing with a most supreme ingratitude that periods of "wars of national liberation" had nearly everywhere drawn to a close.

The ingratitude of foreigners was bad enough, in Castro's view, but far worse was that now, after thirty years, the youth of Cuba were beginning to leave him. They were clearly bored with the sheer inefficiency of Cuba and exhausted by a sacrifice that had become bureaucratized into eternity. These young people even went so far as to dare to make fun of the sacred iconography of the Revolution. A Cuban folk song group released a catchy song, "That Man Is Crazy," supposedly about Ronald Reagan. Instead, Cuban young people began chanting it whenever Castro's image came on the movie or television screen. While Fidel walked back and forth in his high-ceilinged office in the palace, stopping often to stare at the huge mock-up of the Sierra Maestra on one long table—all his great and memoried battles carefully marked on every hillock and mountaintop—these abhorrent young Cubans were haunting the alleys of Old Havana like wild creatures, tormenting their leader by looking for American tourists with dollars to sell.

Then there were those others who were "leaving him," the suicides: revolutionary Cuba's first president, Osvaldo Dorticós; the minister of labor, Augusto Martínez Sánchez; Ambassador Alberto Mora. Suicide had always been part of the surrealist landscape of Cuba, but now it had become the major cause of death for Cubans between the ages of forty-five and forty-nine.

Still, Castro knew his power would last only as long as the world did not really know him. It was ironic, because everyone thought they knew Fidel. In fact, his life was a carefully calculated game, played to keep the truths about him and his psyche at always just the right distance. Indeed, he set up his life so that nobody would really know him at all.

His techniques of wooing, of cajoling, of flattering, were brilliant. He made people his accomplices, and they thought he was their friend. He wooed them with red-carpet treatment, with closeness to absolute power. He dealt with himself in conversation with mocking self-deprecation, and people whispered to one another, "See how sincere, how humble he is. He can't continue his errors, because he always admits them."

But what did any of them really know? What did they know about Mirta, his only wife? Who knew that she lived reclusively now in Madrid with her conservative second husband? Who knew that if she ever dared talk about the "great man" she had loved and married, she would never see their son again?

And what did they know about Celia—the irreplaceable Celia Sánchez? What did they know about the gorgeous, mischievous, voluptuous Naty Revuelta, who helped finance the Revolution and then made the odious mistake of turning down Fidel's proposal of marriage before he came to power? What did they know about Dalia, the "woman from Trinidad," and the five children she had borne Fidel?

The same mystery that Fidel so carefully wove about his affairs he also created about his houses. In the early days Cubans and foreigners knew that he had often stayed at Celia's walk-up apartment in the Vedado section of Havana. They knew he had a spartan room there, with a single bed, a balcony with exercise machinery, and a small study. But most of the Cuban people did not know that their leader, while having no true home, actually had an extraordinary range of houses. There was a mansion in historic Siboney, near Santiago, another in Havana. There was an estate in Candelaria, La Deseada, and a hunting lodge, La Víbora, about ten kilometers away. When Fidel hunted there, he would instruct the Cuban air force to send a small plane to skim the mangroves and scare up the ducks so they could be more easily shot.

He had a complete island, Cayo Piedra, which was reserved for the *líder máximo*'s most intimate and personal affairs. A sophisticated facility that included a heated pool, this "home" served other purposes besides recreation or the ever constant wooing of foreign visitors, pilgrims, and supplicants. Fidel's financial dealings were conducted in total secrecy in places like Cayo Piedra and the strange, isolated Orwellian settlement of Barlovento, which opened to the sea but was wholly closed to Cuba. In these villas by the sea, shadowy international buccaneers like Robert Vesco could come and go in a world without visas, live in clandestine comfort, and provide Fidel Castro with virtually everything he needed, from Apple computers to American machine guns.

Tens of millions of dollars flowed through Cuban "corporations" like CIMEX, a front enabling the Cuban Ministry of the Interior to receive dollars for Cuba in exchange for every sort of "business" from false visas to the illegal use of dead bodies. Indeed, Cuba had become a country in which privileges for the Castro elite spun off from the center in every direction.

But despite all these privileges and all of the extraordinary reaches of his unique power, as the new decade of the '90s began, Castro was afraid. Not only American culture and economics, but the information age was closing in upon him. The Americans had formed the insolently named Radio Martí, to "awaken" the Cuban people, and nothing threatened him more than that. Above all, his dreams of world conquest through his guerrilla warriors—dreams that had shaken the very world in the 1960s and '70s—were falling like wilted leaves around him.

How could it all have happened?

TWO
Gnarled Roots

ON THE westernmost arm of Galicia, that northernmost region of Spain, a mute and mystical regiment of cliffs faces the same sea that led Christopher Columbus to the New World. The cliffs were long ago named Cabo Finisterre. This was the cape where the superstitious *gallegos* believed that the world ends.

Even today Galicia is a place that seems strangely impermanent, a place of farewell and good-bye forever. Many of the farmhouses stand half finished. It is a quiet place, lonely and unchanging, a deceptive—a delusionary—land. It looks all green and fertile, with grazing cows and small plots of soil lovingly staked out, but underneath, the land is rocky, spare and barren and skeletal.

On December 8, 1875, the name of Ángel María Bautista Castro Arguiz was inscribed in the birth register of Láncara, a small village in the beautiful but barren mountains of Galicia. The baby boy was born to typically poor *gallego* peasants, in a gray stone house with dirt floors. Even when new, the house leaned against a small hillock, as though it had been born tired.

Ángel Castro grew up among reserved and secretive people, who liked to nod unsmilingly and say, "A man is owner of his silences and prisoner of his words." During his teens he worked as a day laborer in the fields, and he liked to gamble at cards. But as he approached manhood Ángel realized that there was no future for him in Galicia, and so he decided to become a "soldier of Spain" in faraway Cuba. Poor but adventuresome, he accepted thousands of pesetas in payment from a rich Spanish boy's family to fight in his place against the *americanos*.

Spain had always been religiously, culturally, and emotionally anti-Protestant and anticapitalist. But it was following the war of 1898—when an imperial Spain, in its last, dying breath, lost its most treasured colony, Cuba, to the Yankees of the Americas—that anti-Americanism settled into the Spanish soul like a gnawing cancer. To this day the Spaniards of Galicia refer to the Spanish-American War as *el desastre*—the disaster.

When Ángel Castro sailed away from the Cape of the End of the World, he carried with him that special inner sadness and cynicism, but also that dogged determination, of the historic *gallego* to succeed on foreign shores. Once the war was over, Ángel returned briefly to Galicia, found it still a hopeless land, and went back to Cuba for good.

In those turbulent days of the turn of the century, the Bay of Nipe, on Cuba's rugged northeast coast, was one of the most beautiful corners of Cuba. The bay and its shores were a drowsy area of low and very green rolling land, with meandering rivers and mountain ranges that were friendly and gentle. Ángel chose the area wisely, because this part of Cuba, known as the Oriente or simply the East, was at that very moment on the verge of commercial discovery. But when Ángel arrived—a poor and penniless laborer—it was an open and savage land, as ignored by the fashionable, fun-loving, impeccably white-suited Cubans of Havana as Galicia had been ignored by Madrid.

After the war, power in Cuba remained perversely with the Spanish, who still dominated the economy; with the *americanos*, who now moved to expand their industries everywhere in Cuba; and with the rich Cubans, who had not really even fought for the still unfinished independence.

Once he decided to stay in Cuba, Ángel started out as a simple day laborer for United Fruit Company, that overweening symbol of American expansionism and manifest destiny. But with a seemingly endless capacity for work and unlimited ambition, the wiry little man soon rose to become a sugarcane contractor in charge of fifty to sixty men who did the beastly difficult work of cutting the cane. Ángel was the boss—everyone felt it—but the real boss of the area was sugar itself, and it would be King Sugar, the wealth and bane of Cuba, that would inspire, enrage, and finally bedevil Ángel's son.

In every way, Ángel Castro was an irregular in Cuban society. He was the eternal outsider, a "soldier of Spain" in a Cuba heady with independence. But with rare energy and ruthlessness he soon carved out a place for himself in this strange and hostile land. He bought a farm near the rustic eastern village of Birán. Like many of his neighbors in the "wild east" of Cuba, he was far from meticulous about the manner in which he expanded his dominion. He would go out at night with his men on horseback, and in the dark they would move the fences, thus expanding his land into unclaimed areas. Within a few years his hacienda, Manacas, grew to 10,000 acres and dominated the region. With the sugar boom that followed World War I, Ángel became a wealthy man who had hundreds of men working for him. And when the boom collapsed, he remained wealthy; cautious Ángel Castro kept his money not in the banks, but in his own strongbox.

Ángel's marital life was as self-styled as everything else about him. He first married a respectable schoolteacher named María Louisa Argota, and they had two children, Pedro Emilio and Lidia. But the marriage began to founder when the family brought into their remote and isolated household a new maid, named Lina Ruz. Some years after the arrival of Lina, Ángel and María Louisa were divorced.

Rawboned, with a long nose and with her brown hair pulled back, Lina roved around the Castro plantation on horseback, carrying a pistol and a Winchester, shooting off a round to call the family to meals, wearing high boots under her loose and carelessly revealing dresses. She ran the Castros' store, where their workers could buy supplies with a kind of voucher from Ángel.

While everyone seemed to like Lina, no one ever accused her of being a good housekeeper. The Castro house was of raw wood, round, and stood on stilts. The inside of the house mirrored the chaos that soon became evident in the interworkings of the entire family. Chickens roosted freely on the chairs, without apology. Visitors were astounded because the family liked to eat standing up. After he became ruler of Cuba, nobody could understand why it was that Fidel Castro so often ate standing up! But if the rest of the house was filthy, Ángel's room was meticulous. The table had a cloth on it, and there were often cigars burning somewhere, for Ángel loved cigars.

While Ángel was still officially married to María Louisa, Lina began to bear him a horde of children out of wedlock that would eventually include Raúl, Emma, Juanita, Angelita, Ramón, and on August 13, 1926, Fidel Alejandro Castro Ruz, whose name loosely means faithful. Fidel was born, at least in his later memory, at two in the morning and in the middle of a devastating cyclone. "I was born a guerrilla, because I was born in the night," he said.

There was something very different about the Castros compared with other Cubans: despite their colorful life together, they had no sense of family. Their relations were endlessly conflictive and unharmonious. They were a family without a past, without a religion, without a sense of real Cuban identity, like a little savage tribal band; and yet because of their money they were in an odd way privileged. Certainly Fidel saw it this way when he later told a friend, "I was born into a family of landowners in comfortable circumstances. Everyone lavished attention on me, flattered and treated me differently from other children."

There were, however, many conflicts and influences on him as a boy that Fidel never ever spoke of, and the main one was surely his illegitimacy. Left on their own, Ángel and Lina might never have married, but for their children to be educated in Catholic schools, the couple had to legitimize their union.

Fidel also suffered from the fact that he had been born of a father who had come to Cuba as a soldier of Spain. By all accounts, this tormented him, for the boys in school mocked him as doubly illegitimate—politically as well as personally. Rafael Díaz-Balart, his wife's brother and at one time Fidel's closest friend, recalled that Fidel frequently spoke almost enviously about the Díaz-Balart aristocratic heritage. "Often he told me, 'Rafael, you have a name; I don't have a name. I have a negative name.' And so he hated, without reason." And so, too, this man without a name created one: he made the name of Fidel Castro synonymous with a totally different Cuban culture, a politics, and even the religion he never had.

THE historic age of modern Cuba that would eventually form Fidel Castro had begun in 1868 with the Ten Years' War of independence. Like so much in Cuban life, the war lacked sense and cohesion. It claimed thousands of casualties, but there were almost no large battles.

The Cubans fell back on what they instinctively knew from Mother Spain, *la guerrilla*—the little warfare—that Spain had invented and employed so successfully against Napoleon. Now, under a brilliant and innovative general, Máximo Gómez, Cuban guerrillas taunted and tormented the Spanish regular troops from one end of the island to the other, setting fire to property and destroying everything in the way.

The Cubans lost the Ten Years' War, but the conflict did not end. By 1895, uprisings were intensifying, particularly after the dramatic arrival by sea of José Martí. Here, in one small, black-mustachioed, intellectual man of romance, was the savior—the leader and the inspiration of Cuban independence. It was José Martí—the Apostle— whom Fidel Castro would quote and use and misuse more than any other single person in Cuban history.

Born in Havana in 1853, Martí began speaking out against the Spanish when only sixteen years old. Sent to a Spanish jail, where he was forced to work in the rock pits, he lived a horror he would never forget. After being exiled from Cuba, he roved restlessly from country to country—to Spain, to Mexico, and finally to the United States. It was in his New York exile that he formed his Cuban Revolutionary Party, a name that later parties would repeat.

Martí's landing on the Cuban coast at Cape Maisí, on April 11, 1895, was not unusual. Landings by sea to "free Cuba" were eternal verities in Cuban political life. It all ended in a small skirmish that took place thirty-nine days later. Martí, who had never been in this part of the Cuban countryside, much less in a full-scale guerrilla war, actually headed in the direction of the enemy. He rushed into the midst of the Spaniards, on a white horse, and was, not unexpectedly, shot dead.

As Cuban patriots reeled at Martí's untimely death, war fever started to build up in the United States. Then on February 15, 1898, the U.S.S. *Maine,* a great ship anchored in Havana harbor, was mysteriously blown up, and 260 American seamen were killed. "Remember the *Maine!*" the young American nation cried, and America remembered by going to war.

Not far from where José Martí martyred himself, the only real land battle of the brief war occurred on July 1, 1898. This battle for San Juan Hill, led by Theodore "Teddy" Roosevelt and his Rough Riders, was so greatly enhanced by historic imagination as to be almost unrecognizable in fact. History has the *americanos* riding up the hill courageously against Spanish firepower. In truth, many of the U.S. soldiers had lost their horses and had to straggle up the hill on foot. It didn't matter. The Americans were the supermen of the age, and they reveled even in the chaotic exuberance of it all. "Yesterday we struck the Spaniards and had a brisk fight for two and a half hours," Teddy Roosevelt wrote later of the great day. "The Spaniards shot well, but they did not stand when we rushed. It was a good fight."

Just over a month later an armistice was signed that effectively dissolved this last Latin American outpost of the great Spanish empire.

To celebrate "their" victory, American generals rode alone, without their Cuban allies, into the historic city of Santiago—the city that was the very birthplace of Cuban rebellion and revolt. There, in a scene so humiliating to fragile Cuban nationalism that Cuban nationalists would dwell on it for years to come, the Americans raised their flag—not the Cuban flag—over the governor's palace. Cuban General Calixto García and his men waited in despair and humiliation outside the city while the "anticolonialist" Americans seized not Cuba but Cuban independence.

By the end of the Spanish-American War, any real break between the United States and Cuba was palpably impossible. The United States was Cuba's most important trading partner, with some $30 million invested in Cuba's economy. The end of the war was followed by three years of military occupation, with Cuba becoming ostensibly independent only in 1902.

In the meantime, the United States forced an amendment upon the Cuban constitution. It gave the United States the right to intervene militarily in the island again if civil war erupted or if Cuba was not kept clean and free from dangerous disease—two things eternally threatening to the Americans, the Cubans noted. The amendment further restricted the Cuban government's capacity to incur debts and to enter into treaties with a third power, and it enabled the United States to establish a naval base at Guantánamo.

Four decades later Fidel Castro grew to young manhood in a conflicted Cuban world of bitterly won half freedoms, and he yearned to restore the greatness that he knew must be Cuba's. Above all, his generation of Cubans "knew" that the fault and the guilt for what they were could not be theirs—that would be too terrible, that would be adding a too monumental burden on top of the Sisyphean ones they already carried. No, the fault must be the Americans', and the guilt must accrue to American officiousness and to the American generals who took Santiago for—and thus from—the heroic Cubans.

THREE
Praying to Win

IN THAT remote eastern end of Cuba, in the village of Birán, the Castro children grew up in a sort of happy, rustic chaos. Fidel was from the start an unusually violent child, letting his mind rove in school, where he invented war games for hour after hour. He loved sports and reveled in their competitiveness, but what he enjoyed in strength he lacked in discipline. In baseball, for example, he was a powerful pitcher, but he had little control.

Once, as a teenager, Fidel wanted to use Ángel's car. When Ángel said no, Fidel ran furiously from the house. Shortly thereafter an employee raced into the house, crying urgently, "Don Ángel, Fidel is trying to start the car. He says if he can't start it, he will burn it!" Fidel was stopped in time, but few of the onlookers had any question in their minds that he would indeed have burned the car.

The other children were quite different, especially his younger brother, Raúl. While Fidel was big and brawling and uncontrolled, Raúl was small and closed and logical. Even as a child, Raúl represented culture and family, in sharp contrast to the basically unsocialized Fidel. It was Raúl who was concerned with questions of social justice and of ideological organization, while Fidel was the very embodiment of action and was always exploring the outer limits of personal sovereignty.

It is certain that Fidel got his first feelings for social justice, as amorphous as they were, and his first experience with "democratic" politics, as dirty as it was, on Ángel Castro's farm. He watched as his father paid off the political captains who were running for office, each controlling hundreds of votes.

As a boy, Fidel saw a rural spoils system, with everybody in on the take and the winnings going to the strongest. The fact that his authoritarian father happened to be the strongest man around was both satisfying and disgusting to him. From Ángel he absorbed his contempt for the traditional systems of law—and the supremely successful example of how to create one's own law.

WORLD War I had left 10 million men dead on the blood-soaked soil of Europe, but it had scarcely touched faraway Cuba. Indeed, the early 1920s marked a time when the United States' limited colonialism in Cuba stood in all its puritan glory. Thanks to American and Cuban doctors, yellow fever was wiped out; thanks to American politicians, democratic institutions were supposedly being grafted onto the infirm institutions of the Spanish isle. And all the while, American tourists brought American dollars to the island in windfalls. It was in these years that the great palaces, casinos, and country clubs of Havana were built and that the gleaming white city on the blue Caribbean became one of the most delectable cities of the hemisphere.

Then General Gerardo Machado took power. He was a popular president at the beginning. But it went to his head. He began to repress the newspapers, and he altered the constitution to remain in power. His thugs roamed the country, murdering hundreds. The University of Havana became the center of opposition. It was closed in 1930, along with all high schools and normal schools.

In response to the growing repression, underground organizations of students and professionals were formed, like the ABC, whose name has remained a deliberate secret. As an impressionable Fidel Castro was growing up in Cuba the ABC began to use urban terrorism all over Cuba. They employed the bomb in the street, they killed policemen, and they thought in politically complex enough terms to use terror to try to induce the United States to intervene in Cuba to overthrow a Machado who could not keep the order the North Americans so loved.

To an extraordinary extent many of the later tactics that Castro would employ began with the ABC. The ABC's philosophy was as amorphous as Fidel's would be—the former generation had failed, colonialism must be expunged from the Cuban economy, and Cuba must be independent of the United States. Throughout all the Cuban revolutionary generations, those three simple expositions about told it all.

During this period the United States did nothing. Franklin D.

Roosevelt was President, with his Depression at home and his Good Neighbor Policy abroad in Latin America. In 1933 FDR ordained, to the disappointment of many Cubans, that there was "no possible question of intervention."

In August of 1933 Machado was finally driven from power by a combination of military and popular power. With the end of the brief but bitterly definitive dictatorship, a new generation of Cubans took over. They were to dominate Cuban political life until 1959.

ONE day when Fidel was a teenager at the Colegio Dolores school in Santiago, he sat down and wrote a letter to President Franklin D. Roosevelt. In a style as guileful as the one he would later employ with *las masas,* he told the American President:

> My good friend Roosevelt:
>   I don't know very English, but I know as much as write to you. I like to hear the radio, and I am very happy, because I heard in it, that you will be president of a new era. . . . If you like, give me a ten dollars bill green american, because never, I have not seen a ten dollars bill green american and I would like to have one of them.

He also asked the American President to sign the bill. Soon a letter from Franklin Roosevelt was posted on the bulletin board at the school. In it the President of the United States of America thanked Fidel Castro for his "letter of support and congratulations." But to Fidel's disappointment Roosevelt sent no money.

In 1941 Fidel Castro entered the most prestigious secondary school in Cuba. The Colegio de Belén—College of Bethlehem—in the wealthy suburbs of Havana, stood like a citadel of Spanish culture. Built in 1926, it had a flat, four-storied front, with a powerful baroque façade. Sometimes called a palace of education, it provided a regal, intellectual showcase for the Jesuits. For the young Fidel it was a comfortable and comforting environment.

At Belén, Fidel seemed to have multiple personalities—different, contradictory, and often warring with one another. At times he appeared to be a normal, mischievous, life-loving boy, clumsily searching to find himself. But at other times his darker side would emerge like a suddenly gathered storm cloud.

Father Armando Llorente was his mentor, and to this tough-minded Spanish Jesuit, Fidel showed his first side, that of a boyish lad who loved sports and mountains and adventure, and often seemed quite capable of doing noble things. "I saw him as a boy with many ambitions," Father Llorente told me one morning years later in Miami, looking out across the waters that now separated him from Cuba and from what little was left of Belén—thanks to that same ambitious boy.

But Father Llorente loved the boy then—and he continued, like so many of the people who came under Fidel's spell, to love him in some ways always. Under the guidance of Father Llorente, some of the students at Belén formed a club called the *Exploradores*—Explorers. Seventy boys—and only the best ones—could belong to it. Fidel became the group's chief. Father Llorente organized them like the military, for they would often camp in the mountains, where there was some danger from wild pigs and who knew what else.

On one of their excursions it rained all day, turning a normally complacent river into a tortuous flood. Fidel and the priest found themselves on one side of the river; the younger boys and all their things were on the other. The two of them had to cross it. Fidel got a rope, put it in his mouth, and swam across the dangerous waters. Once he was safe on the other side, Father Llorente started across, hanging fast on to the rope. Suddenly he slipped and fell on the stones and was about to be washed away down the river. Fidel, a strong swimmer, dashed in to save him. When they arrived safely on the bank, he gave the priest a big hug and said, "Father, this is a miracle. Let us say three Ave Marías to the Virgin." Spontaneously the two knelt and said the three Ave Marías underneath the night sky.

Despite moments such as these, Fidel did not ever become really religious. Later in life he confided to the Brazilian leftist priest Frei Betto that "I never came to have a religious faith, because all of my force and attention was consecrated to the acquisition of a political faith."

If his lust for life did not extend to religion or really to any belief, it did extend to other areas—and always with flair. "He knew everything by heart," his school friend José Ignacio Rasco recalled. "In school he used to make a joke with us. He would read the page of a book and throw it out. At the end of the book he was left with the index only. We would ask him, 'Fidel, what does the book of sociology say on page fifty-three?' And Fidel could tell us. He had a really photographic memory."

As for Fidel's violent side, his fights would later become legendary. Indeed, his temper seemed to be always at the ready, waiting to explode against anyone who dared to challenge him. One day at Belén, Fidel was chatting with some girls when a fellow student, Ramón Mestre, provoked him by calling him crazy. Fidel flew into a rage, got into a fistfight with Ramón—and, for one of the few times in his life, lost. Fidel never forgot. Later, when he became ruler of all of Cuba, he sent Mestre to prison, if not only because of the early fight, certainly in large part because of it.

His incessant passion to do and to be, regardless of intent or outcome, was extended to sports. When he first came to Belén, he did not know how to play basketball, but as basketball became a fashionable sport Fidel determined to become the best at it. He began to practice day and night. Finally the priests had to put a light on the court because of *"el loco Fidel."* The school coach admitted that the young man tried his patience. "Fidel drove me crazy," he remembered. "Always asking me what he had to do to be a leader, what he had to do to make himself known. He said he was a greater orator than even the leaders of Cuba, and could do something great."

Fidel tried desperately at Belén to hone his oratorical skill—or, at that time, nonskill. For this man who was later to move millions with his resonant voice was then a notably poor speaker. He wanted to join the oratory group, but in order to join, he had to give a ten-minute speech without notes. After failing several times because of nervousness, he was finally accepted.

At any rate, debating in any form was never desirable to Fidel. He liked even then to state something and have it immediately agreed to, saying repeatedly and with emphasis, *"Porque lo digo yo* [Because I say it]!"

During all of this time, there was another Fidel, a Fidel who was seeking out a philosophy, an ideology, a rationale for the restless power he felt so turbulently inside him. And at that moment in history Fidel found what he was seeking among the European fascists.

He walked soberly around the campus with a copy of Hitler's *Mein Kampf* under his arm; in his room he had a map on his wall upon which he charted the movements and successes of the Axis armies across

Europe; for hours he would stand before a mirror, holding a primitive early recorder and mimicking Mussolini's speeches over and over again.

When Fidel graduated from Belén in the spring of 1945, the entire family came to celebrate. "There was such happiness," Father Llorente recalled. "You never heard an applause so great!" In the yearbook, under a picture of a serious young man with a long *gallego* nose and distant eyes, Father Llorente had written:

> Fidel distinguished himself always in all subjects related to letters. A top student and member of the congregation, he was also an outstanding athlete. . . . He has won the admiration and affection of all. We are sure that, after his law studies, he will make a brilliant name for himself. Fidel has what it takes and will make something of his life.

Father Llorente also recalled the times when, touched, he would see Fidel praying in the chapel. He smiled a canny Jesuit smile and said, "I would see him alone, praying in the chapel. I knew what he was praying for—he was praying to win."

FOUR
The University Years

FIDEL went home to Birán that long and sensuously hot summer of 1945, and both he and his parents realized that it was the last time it was really to be his home. Ironically, his father and mother had decided to send him to the University of Havana because they were convinced that he would become a lawyer and protect their properties. How little they knew their son! In the turbulent and troubled halls of the university Fidel would discover an entirely new world of political action—and of political violence.

That summer Fidel's mother seemed inordinately proud of her son, but it was still another summer of conflict between Ángel and Fidel. This was not unexpected. Throughout his life Fidel retained at best an ambivalent attitude toward his father and at worst one that ranged between cool indifference and angry resentment. Nevertheless, Fidel was usually able to exercise his implacable will. The day before Fidel was to leave for Havana, Ángel gave in to his son's entreaties and, despite his wiser judgment, bought him the new American car he so wanted.

The Fidel who went to the University of Havana that October both attracted and repelled his fellow students. Physically, Fidel stood out. He was markedly tall in a country of generally short men. In his personal habits he was so sloppy that he was almost immediately named *Bola de Churre*—Greaseball. However, on some occasions students would see him meticulously attired in the finest of suits. He seemed to be trying out different versions of himself on the world.

Fidel lived in a boardinghouse in Calle Ele, on the corner of Seventeenth Street. By all accounts, his room mirrored his disorderly and searching ways, except for his growing and beloved library of José Martí, which he guarded with some care.

But if Fidel was a contradictory person in those days, even more so was the University of Havana a place of contradictions. The two-hundred-year-old university was a complex of graceful tropical buildings that sprawled over several hills in the middle of a new commercial and tourist center in the elegant neighborhood of Vedado. By Latin tradition, universities were autonomous in Cuban society. Police were not permitted to enter the campus, which thus provided a sanctuary not only for ideas but also for politicized people of all sorts.

As it happened, in 1944 Ramón Grau San Martín, a leader of the democratic party popularly called the *Auténticos*—Authentic Ones— had won the presidency. The list of his party's promises and intentions was noble and progressive. But then the old curse of corruption raised its ugly head and President Grau, once the professional idealist around whom students flocked, became a despised figure, bloated with vice. And with the government so corrupt, the university became the arena for the most dramatic and symbolic working out of politics.

Fidel loved it; he had found his milieu. And, as ever in Cuban history, there was the shining hope that this time, this generation would find the answer to Cuba's endless searchings for legitimacy.

In this atmosphere Fidel developed a gang of friends who, at first, were good boys, boys from middle-class families—in sharp contrast to the boys he would find, choose, and mold later on, in the first phase of revolution.

It took, as so often in Latin America, something as plebeian as a rise in the bus fares to bring these students to the streets. Fidel made his debut in Cuban politics by organizing the demonstration against Grau and his supposedly innocent increase in the bus fares. That day a large bank of students marched down the streets with a huge Cuban flag. The police stopped them, beating them with sticks and guns. Fidel was wounded the worst. After having his head bandaged at the hospital, he and his brother Raúl made the first of many visits to the newspapers and the radio station. Fidel, as always, knew exactly how to exploit the situation.

Three days later the students announced another demonstration, and this time President Grau grew so alarmed that he agreed to receive their leaders in a delegation. Only at the last minute was it decided that Fidel should also go, because he cut such a wonderfully martyred figure with his head still wound up like a mummy's. They went to the palace to meet the old and always cordially smiling president, and there Fidel revealed one of his amazing predilections.

Since it was particularly warm that day, President Grau invited them to step out onto his balcony to get some fresh air. Meanwhile his assistants had all left, so the moment witnessed a symbolic emptiness of power. At this point Fidel suddenly whispered to his co-conspirators, "I have the formula to take power and once and for all get rid of this old son of a bitch." His comrades were stupefied as he explained, "Now when the old guy returns, let's pick him up, the four of us, and throw him off the balcony. Once the president is dead, we'll proclaim the triumph of the student revolution and speak to the people from the radio."

"*Vamos, guajiro, tú estás 'chiflado'* [Listen, redneck, you're nuts]," Chino Esquivel told him. And when Fidel insisted on his astounding plan, Enrique Ovares finally squelched it by saying, "We came here to ask for a lowering of the fares on the buses, not to commit an assassination." It is important to remember that Grau, for all his faults, was not a dictator but one of Cuba's first democratically elected leaders.

Fidel was remarkably frank about his political ambitions, even in those early days. Perhaps it was that ingenuous quality of his that lulled so many into a sense of unconcern about his motives. "At that time, I loved Fidel Castro," recalled Dr. Mariano Sorí Marín, a Cuban doctor who would help Fidel. "He was like me—a political agitator.

Besides, he was very intelligent. A megalomaniac with a sense of grandiosity! He never could be a democratic president, but he was a man who was personally very attractive and sympathetic."

Above all, Fidel wanted to be president of the Federation of University Students (FEU). It was the antechamber to political power in the country. However, he was not successful at winning any major elective office. At the university he was regarded as an interesting fellow, but he was never really one of the crowd. Fidel would never forget that. One day he would let them know the price of their never having allowed him to be one of them.

Enrique Ovares, who served five years as president of the architecture school and three terms as FEU president, has said the reason for Fidel's unelectability was that he could not work with others. He was too independent. Ovares also said that this was why the Communists, who were small in numbers but well entrenched in the university, if not in Cuba as a whole, did not support Fidel. "Anybody who followed closely Fidel's political process as a student knows that Fidel at no time maintained relations with the Communists," Ovares said. "Fidel was a negative type for the party because he was an individual who would say 'white' today and 'black' tomorrow and 'gray' the day after. He was totally independent; he could not be controlled."

To another college acquaintance Fidel joked that he would become a Communist immediately, but on one condition—"If I can become Stalin."

Despite his failure to win elections, Fidel never gave up. He contacted just about everyone he could in student politics. He would meet with people, discuss, and then meet with more people. One day he got the idea to support his political ambitions by selling *fritas* to the students. *Fritas* were Cuban hamburgers, and this, as far as the records show, represented Fidel's first attempt at capitalism. Unfortunately, he had to close the *frita* stand within a month because there was no profit. "One guy ate all the *fritas*," a classmate sadly summed up.

But if Fidel failed to win elections at the university, he nevertheless took a big leap toward his future. Once he told his friend Rafael Díaz-Balart that Al Capone was a stupid man because he never developed any ideological *traje*—form. If he had, Fidel said, he would be famous, and not remembered only as a gangster. In his second year at the university Fidel became something that to this day very few people will acknowledge and that he has never even remotely spoken of—a classic gangster. But unlike the lamented Al Capone, Fidel had his *traje,* and it was sheer Machiavellian power tactics.

LATE in the afternoon one day in December, 1946, a disheveled Fidel suddenly appeared at the door of Rafael Díaz-Balart's apartment in Havana. "Rafael, let me in," he blurted out. "I just killed Leonel Gómez."

"You what?" Rafael said, stunned. "What are you talking about?"

Only a few weeks before, Rafael recalled, Fidel had told him, as they engaged in a discussion of power and politics, that Leonel Gómez and Manolo Castro (no relation to Fidel), two particularly violent leaders of opposing student gangs, were his obstacles. Rafael had disagreed. "No," he said, "not Manolo. The obstacle is Leonel Gómez because he is going to win the student federation elections." Fidel agreed and insisted suddenly that an attack had to be prepared on Leonel Gómez, but Rafael never dreamed he would do so.

Now, safely inside Rafael's apartment, Fidel insisted that the assassination had not been planned. He had been standing atop a hill at the university with two trusted attachés of Manolo Castro. Suddenly, out of nowhere, they noticed a car down below on Rionda Street. The car belonged to rival gang leader Leonel Gómez. They watched in silence as it moved along Rionda Street, a cul-de-sac. Knowing that Gómez had to return the same way, a kind of blood lust passed over the three men.

"Let's kill him; he has to return," one of them said.

"Fine," Fidel said, and his eyes turned back to the prey.

When the car turned around, the three started to fire wildly. Within minutes the assassination of Leonel Gómez was announced agitatedly on the radio, and Fidel had fled to Rafael's uneasy sanctuary.

OF ALL the periods of Fidel's early life, the most mysterious and most open to dispute is that of his gangster years in the university. Far from being unusual or outside of the norm, violent gangs—also called action groups or happy triggermen—were common at that time. Fidel himself remarked, when he took power in 1959, that his five years at the University of Havana studying law were "much more dangerous than all the time I fought against Batista from the Sierra Maestra."

The seeds of the student gangs had really been sown in the 1920s, during the dictatorship of General Machado, but they were richly fertilized in the ensuing disillusionment with "democracy" that followed the strongman. When subsequent administrations failed to punish those who had abused and killed citizens under the protection of Machado, gangs of young men and women arose across the island to do it themselves. These enraged students prided themselves on their courage and excused their violence because they were revolutionaries.

To understand the extent of the disillusionment Cubans felt with the post-Machado "democracy," one needs to take a closer look at the man who really ran things during this period—a former army sergeant, Fulgencio Batista.

From the time of his birth, Fulgencio Batista Zaldívar seemed strangely destined to be the man—his followers called him *el Hombre,* the Man, denoting his exalted macho—that Fidel Castro would pit himself against. He was born near Birán, in that same Oriente where the Castro children had been born and grew up. He had even at one time worked for Ángel Castro. But Batista was no *gallego;* he was a typical Oriente mix of Indian, black, and Spanish—a fact that tormented him. His largest accomplishment in early life, after joining the new Cuban army, was being named a court sergeant-stenographer. But he really came into his own after the successful Sergeants' Revolution that finally unseated Machado in 1933.

Batista was compellingly handsome in those early days—he had such a sensuous smile that he was nicknamed the "pretty mulatto"— and his dramatic machismo was represented by the dark leather jacket he liked to wear, with, of course, his handgun in his holster. Formally, Batista was army chief of staff from 1934 to 1940 and, as such, was stronger than any president. Then he held the presidency from 1940 to 1944, when he peacefully turned over power. In 1944 his candidate for president lost, and Batista gamely "allowed" Ramón Grau, who had won, to fill the position. Batista then went into comfortable, if temporary, exile in Daytona Beach, Florida.

OCCURRING as it did against this bitter background of disillusionment and frustrated violence, Fidel's stratagem in shooting Leonel Gómez stands as a case study in the understanding of his abilities for grasping power. When Fidel entered the university, he began immediately to scrutinize the leaders of the most important gangs—and they were an impressive lot. Many were men bigger than life and more evil than most. Rolando Masferrer of the *Movimiento Socialista Revolucionario* (MSR)—Socialist Revolutionary Movement—would become Batista's worst henchman and most adept killer. Alongside him in the MSR was Manolo Castro, who headed the student federation during most of Fidel's time at the university. Manolo Castro obsessed Fidel, who did everything possible to win his favor—but Fidel's idea was to become not his friend, but his successor.

The other major gang, the *Unión Insurreccional Revolucionaria* (UIR)—Insurrectional Revolutionary Union, was headed by Emilio Tro, who had fought with the United States forces in the Pacific during World War II. But why did Fidel shoot Leonel Gómez? Fidel shot the UIR leader in order to get the attention of MSR's Manolo Castro, and to ingratiate himself with Manolo in order to enter the MSR and eventually take Manolo's place. But, as is usually the case with Fidel, that rather simple reality did not emerge until much later.

For the truth was that Leonel Gómez did not die. Fidel had shot him in the lung, but he survived after some time in the hospital. Gómez gave Fidel's name to the UIR as one of those responsible for the attack. Indeed, in a special meeting of the UIR, Fidel was accused of the shooting. But now Fidel's luck came into play. His original purpose in shooting Gómez was fulfilled, but with an ironic twist. Fidel did not win over Manolo Castro, nor was he invited to join the MSR. He did, however, gain the friendship of Emilio Tro, head of the UIR, Leonel Gómez's own gang. "It seemed that Emilio Tro had a certain sympathy for Fidel and, far from acting on the consequences of the aggression suffered by one of his men, Tro was converted into a *padrino,* or godfather, of Castro," Fidel's friend Max Lesnick summed up. From that moment Fidel Castro was accepted into the UIR, and he was obviously very pleased.

If he had gained a friend in Emilio Tro, the leaders of the MSR made no secret of their contempt for Fidel. However, their differences with their hot-tempered, impetuous classmate would be temporarily forgotten in an international episode that would, in effect, be a dress rehearsal for dramas yet to be performed by Fidel Castro.

THIS TIME BOTH LINA AND ÁNGEL Castro were enraged with their son. They had sent him to all the best schools; they had worked night and day, as *gallego* parents do, to educate him; they had generously sent him money even while he was playing gangster at the university. But this new development was too much—Fidel, their great hope and their brightest and bravest son, had enlisted in a cockamamy scheme to invade the neighboring Dominican Republic.

The fact that his enemies from the MSR led the Cuban force was not really an obstacle. To ensure his safety, he negotiated a truce with them. It would, however, last only for the duration of the expedition.

The Cayo Confites Expedition, as the invasion came to be known, was headed by Dominican patriot Juan Bosch, an intense and passionate intellectual who had long advocated the overthrow of the despised dictator Rafael Leónidas Trujillo. In 1947, from his head-quarters in a small hotel in Havana, Bosch put together a fascinating and unique political alliance.

Cayo Confites, a key much like any of the other sandy and barren islands in this northern part of the Caribbean, was chosen as the spot where a disparate group of 1200 men would train for invasion under a blazing sun. The expedition marked a historic turning point because never before had Cubans, Dominicans, Venezuelans, and Costa Ricans come together to fight as one. The group was held together by a rabid hatred for Trujillo; for while the rest of the Caribbean was moving with heady new hope toward forms of representative govern-ment, the Dominican Republic under Trujillo stood as *the* horror of the ancient regime.

The strength of the Cayo Confites Expedition—that is, the joining together of men from a number of different countries for a single purpose—was also the source of its failure, for everyone in the Caribbean, including most definitely Trujillo himself, knew just about every detail of the well-advertised plan. The situation approached the ludicrous when Trujillo sent a circular note to the governments of the various other South American nations advising them of the entire invasion-in-preparation and calling for international consultation.

Fidel and the other *expedicionarios* were en route to Santo Domingo when President Grau ordered them back. The expedition had been called off, and Trujillo would remain in power until he was assassinated, in 1961. But for Fidel, who had turned twenty-one on the barren, mosquito-infested key, Cayo Confites was like catnip to an eager tomcat. It was his first step into the gallant world of internationalism that would rule his life and torment the United States for the next four decades.

In the years following Cayo Confites, Fidel began—partly through his supreme intuition and partly through trial and error—to use the power of the newspapers to manipulate the impressionable people of his troubled country. He was to become, among so many new things, the first truly successful media revolutionary.

An activist friend of Fidel's from this period recalls that when staging a protest, Fidel would get hold of a torch, wait until the press and the cameras arrived, and then use the torch to illuminate his face. When the pictures came out in the newspapers the next day, it would of course be Fidel's face that would command the attention of the reader.

In March of 1949 an event occurred that was tailor-made for the talents and anger of Fidel Castro. A small group of drunken and rowdy United States marines clambered boorishly atop the statue of José Martí in the beautiful Central Park of downtown Havana, and one of them urinated on it, defaming the sacred memory of Martí, the inspiration for the great and uncorrupted new Cuba that was being born. The marines barely got out with their lives and were only gingerly rescued by the Cuban police.

It was as if Fidel had been waiting for just this sort of event to occur. Immediately he formed an honor guard, which flanked the statue all night. The next day he called for a protest demonstration at the U.S. embassy. The student protesters walked from the university to the American embassy. When they were about half a block away, they began throwing stones at the windows, creating a huge ruckus, before running to a nearby restaurant, where they watched the police cars rushing to the embassy, their sirens blaring.

In a gesture of apology, the Americans put a wreath of flowers at the statue, and the U.S. ambassador, Robert Butler, agreed to meet with the students. The newspapers covered the meeting and even ran a picture of Butler with some of the young Cubans. This marked the first time that Fidel Castro's name appeared in the Cuban press in a

really important way. It was also the first time Castro used the
anti-American sentiment in Cuba to evoke a response from the hated
americanos.

FIDEL'S courting of Mirta Díaz-Balart, the lovely green-eyed girl with
the dark blond hair and the wistful smile, from one of Cuba's
wealthiest families, marked the period in his life that was closest to a
time when he lived like a relatively normal man, one who felt and
acted on simple and even pure and uncalculated feelings. The
courtship took place at the university, to the staccato of guns and
killings. But there were also lazy, drowsy summer days on the
languorous Puerto Rico Beach in Mirta's hometown of Banes. There
were simple, joyous days—and nights—when this girl from a very
proper, if also troubled family was always chaperoned. In later years
the idea of Fidel Castro being chaperoned could only strike one as the
extreme of the unlikely or the ludicrous, but those were different
times.

Even then, behind the deep love Mirta felt for the vigorous young
"god," with his curly brown hair, his broad shoulders, and his aquiline
nose, there always lurked the warning of the ruin and tragedy he
would bring to her life, as indeed he brought it to nearly all the women
who became close to him.

Fidel met the young Mirta one day when her brother Rafael
Díaz-Balart introduced them at the law school cafeteria. Mirta was
then a pretty and dedicated student of philosophy and letters. Most
observers recall the meeting as love at first sight.

Filled with a lusty sensuality, Fidel was extremely attractive to
women. But on dates he bored them because he would never stop
talking politics. And unlike virtually every other Cuban man of that
time, he never danced. Dancing was revealing, dancing was humaniz-
ing, and Fidel abhorred revealing himself or putting himself on the
same level as others.

Throughout his life Fidel had fiery political ambitions, but his
sexuality was cold and calculating. Women were to be used, coolly and
most often quickly. With Mirta, at least at first, it was different. She
had about her that sweet, languorous, romantic dreaminess that
seemed to cling to all of her family. Mirta and her brothers, Waldo,
Frank, and Rafael, were a handsome brood—but they were not a

happy one, despite the fact and finally because of the fact that their father was the respected mayor of the United Fruit town of Banes, the lawyer of Batista, and a man of substance.

Nothing could have possibly excited all the ambitions, all the complexes, and all the resentments of Fidel more than this single woman. For in her he found personified not only a valiant family of the war for independence, but also the inner nexus of power around Batista and the most egregious extension of American power in Cuba, if not the Caribbean. Only sixty miles away from the rustic and squabbling Birán, where he was born, there existed the world of Banes. It was the very American world of the sugar industry, of the aggressive and triumphant United Fruit Company.

"Few places in Cuba were quite so dominated by the North American presence," one historian has noted. Here, instead of the enveloping dark forests that Ángel had cut away with so much sweat, were luxurious lawns and impressive tropical homes. American and Cuban employees of United Fruit played polo, swam in their swimming pools, and shopped in boutiques for American goods, which arrived regularly by ship. Banes had more ties to New York than to Havana. On the Fourth of July the Americans and the Cubans held a huge picnic at the American Club. Life in Banes in those days was remembered by nearly everyone in later and more troubled years as a rare, halcyon existence, a special era caught in time like a moment of Cuban Camelot.

The problem for the Díaz-Balart children, and especially for Mirta, was Angélica, the classically evil stepmother. The domineering Angélica, with her piercing black eyes and her hair pulled severely back from a strong forehead, kept Mirta tied to her every and most fickle call. Friends would shake their heads in sadness when they saw how Mirta, planning to go out, would be peremptorily called back to care for Angélica when at the last moment the woman predictably would develop "a headache." They talked even then about the possibility that Mirta saw marriage to Fidel as a way out. But Mirta, always the proper lady, never complained.

During their courtship the young couple divided their time between the still savage milieu of the Castros' Birán and Banes. If Mirta actually liked the huge and rustic Castro farm, as she always cheerfully said she did, Fidel by all accounts was in a kind of constant inner—and often enough outer—rage about her Banes. The town represented everything he hated. In Banes lay everything he would smite and destroy.

It can hardly be seen as accidental that all of the women Fidel became deeply involved with were of one precise profile: all were upper class, Americanized, English-speaking, beautiful—most, but not all, were blond—and from "old families" who had fought against the Spaniards. With these women he could act out on both the most refined and the most primitive levels the drama of his personal politics, his vendetta against the United States, and his hatred of the "traitorous" Cuban middle class.

Now, as he visited Mirta in Banes, his rage seemed to focus on United Fruit's Puerto Rico Beach. Along this long, white stretch of pristine beach, partygoers came to play. Fidel was in a constant state of fury because there were fences all around the beach, and gates, maintained and duly overseen by United Fruit. In truth, a key was needed for the first gate only, and almost anyone could get one from the fruit company. But this seemed only to obsess him the more. After he came to power, one of the first things he did was unlock the fences.

Fidel and Mirta were married on October 10, 1948. The marriage looked splendid on the surface: two handsome young people, both of well-to-do families, both educated, very much in love with each other, and filled with idealistic yet realizable hopes. How right it all seemed to those who witnessed the wedding. But the shadows were closing in on this seemingly blessed couple right there in the church. Fidel was being threatened by the gangs in Havana. As Mirta and Fidel spoke their vows, many who watched them were terrified that one of his ever lurking enemies would attack. But not Fidel. As they were leaving on their honeymoon he opened the valise he was carrying. Inside was a pistol. "I'm not worried," he told his friends. "I have this, and I had it with me at the altar."

WHILE the Castros' wedding trip had some of the little eccentric trademarks of Fidel, it also revealed him in a brief and unprecedented fling with bourgeois life—paid for, as everything in his life, by someone else. The senior Rafael Díaz-Balart, Mirta's father, had given the young couple $10,000 for a honeymoon in that most symbolically American of cities, New York. Pocket money in the amount of $1000 had been provided by none other than Fulgencio Batista, who in 1948 was nothing more than a former president in exile, in Daytona Beach, and a friend of both families.

The newlyweds began their honeymoon in Miami, then moved by train to New York in December of 1948. In New York, Fidel used part of the $10,000 to buy a white Lincoln Continental whose doors opened at the touch of a button.

Mirta's brother Rafael had married a lovely, sweet woman, Hilda, only a few months before, and was now living in Manhattan. Fidel and Mirta asked "Rafa" and Hilda to get them a furnished room in the same building where they lived. By all accounts, the honeymoon was happy, if fleetingly so. Fidel tried during this time to learn better English—indeed, he took a dictionary and memorized two hundred words a day—but he never did learn really good English.

Rafael and Hilda returned to Cuba when the honeymooners did, but went from Miami by plane, while Fidel and Mirta took the slower route by ferry from Key West. The young newlyweds watched the coastline of the *americanos* fade slowly out of sight as the boat churned toward Cuba across the narrow channel of those mere but symbolic miles that separated the two peoples.

The newlyweds established themselves in a series of small apartments in Havana and Vedado. Their friends remember Fidel and Mirta at this time as a very happy couple, and they recall that in the beginning Fidel treated Mirta well, even protectively, in the old macho Cuban sense. "They were in love with each other," one friend told me. "Fidel was handsome, and when he wants to be polite, he is the best." But those days were not to last. Fidel never really got around to getting a paying job and continued to rely on money from Mirta's father and monthly checks from Ángel. The fathers were beginning to tire of supporting him, and Mirta began desperately to need money. In addition to that, within three months of their marriage she found herself pregnant.

In 1949, at the end of a lazy summer in Banes, the Castros' first and only son was born. As was Cuban practice, this firstborn was named after his father and immediately nicknamed Fidelito. But as the enchantment with the new child wore off, relations between Mirta and Fidel became strained. Now there was almost no money at all, for Fidel still persistently disdained working. Less and less did he even come home to eat, preferring to have chop suey with his political friends at El Pacifico, a favorite Chinese restaurant. Friends noticed that when he did come home, he would often bring his most distasteful political pals with him and insist that Mirta cater to them until the early hours of the morning.

Mirta struggled valiantly to keep things going, but the fact was that she now often had no milk for the chubby Fidelito and that friends often had to lend her money when the electricity was shut off for lack of payment. It was increasingly humiliating to her quiet pride. She knew that even when Fidel did have money, he never spent it on his family, a trait he shared with many of the charismatic leaders of history.

"Fidel never knew how to love," one observer told me years later. "Giving himself was something he didn't know. He was too worried about his theatrical role."

Which makes it all the more amazing that Fidel ever married Mirta or anyone at all. Certainly Mirta was his only attempt to love any one person, to place his trust and affection in one human creature. "Fidel tried a respectable marriage, which failed; he tried respectable politics, which failed," Dr. Marcelino Feal, the canny Cuban psychiatrist, suggested. "Society ignored him, so he became society—to form it in his own creation."

On Fidel's ability to love, American writer Gene Vier wrote, "Castro demonstrates another characteristic of the charismatic, that no single person represents an absolute value. They are always seeking the universal, which implies a detachment from the particular, a detachment that pervades Castro's friendships. No particular person has an absolute value for him." The charismatic leader cannot have a wife, cannot be seen to care for another individual or for his children, cannot give himself to another person. The true charismatic leader is a vehicle, a human sieve, a purifying agent, through which the soul and spirit of his people passes. There cannot be anyone standing between this sacred exchange and complaining of rent money or milk for the baby.

In his later life Castro would instinctively understand these imperatives of the myth and spell of the charismatic leader—and always act brilliantly upon them. He would hide his marriage from the Cuban people and, indeed, from the world. His early biographers not only accepted but connived in guarding the secret, in part because they too were under the spell of the *líder máximo*.

Yet the mystery of his marriage, like all the mysteries about Fidel, was no mystery at all. The absence of personal information, which would make Fidel a man and not just a myth, made him seem unknowable and therefore omnipotent. That was the idea, of course, and Fidel manipulated it masterfully.

FIVE
Suicide by Microphone

NOT even the close friends and political intimates who were with Eduardo "Eddy" Chibás that terrible Sunday in 1951 noticed anything very unusual about the great leader and singular hope of Cuba as he walked purposefully into radio station CMQ in downtown Havana. Eddy Chibás, although he was a dynamic political figure, wore prim glasses and had thinning mousy hair instead of the usual vibrant black hair of most Cubans. He was tense, emotional, and eccentric. He always wore white, and he was a man who would impress his followers by suddenly fasting for days or even weeks, or frighten them by remaining submerged in his bathwater for long periods of time. As his political genius developed in the turbulent 1940s, some of his followers as well as many observers became more and more concerned that his hortatory speeches were passing from hysteria to incipient madness.

But Chibás was also, in the words of one Cuban writer, "a genuinely honorable man, the heir to a huge fortune but utterly uninterested in money; a political leader controlled and driven by a single obsession—the need for total honesty in public dealings. He knew that Cuba's Augean stables were sorely in need of cleaning. His great error was to designate as his Hercules a man emotionally incapable of the role—himself."

Still, in the late 1940s Chibás seemed to remain generally in control of himself and was increasingly seen as the man most likely to be elected the next president of Cuba. Chibás had been an early supporter of President Ramón Grau, but, like so many, he became disillusioned with the Grau presidency in the years between 1944 and 1948.

In opposition to the Grau government, he created his own party, the *Ortodoxos*—Orthodox Party. When Carlos Prío Socarrás was elected president, in 1948, there was renewed hope that his administration would be an honest one. It was a false hope. Within a short time of taking office, the Prío men were robbing the treasury at every turn and living openly in offensive splendor in a land of many poor.

Chibás—who was recognized by many, including Fidel Castro, as the political genius of the time—came to blows with the Prío government. It began when Aureliano Sánchez Arango, Prío's minister of education, called Chibás a "master of defamation" and "a man of no honor."

Chibás responded by accusing Aureliano of "robbing the funds of the public schools to buy a ranch in Guatemala." The Eddy-Aureliano debate became every day more scandalous; finally it grew into a sordid national pastime, with Chibás using his mastery of the medium of radio to attack his opponent. He began speaking on the radio every Sunday at eight p.m., and few times in history has a leader so spellbound his people. On the streets of Havana his fiery words bounded from every window, tearing at corruption and reiterating "honor, honor, honor."

That Sunday, August 15, 1951, seemed no different from other Sundays. As Chibás began to talk, to exhort, to compel, the masterful manipulator of emotions fell into a theme that eerily preceded Fidel's later hubris about his small country: the potential and thwarted greatness of Cuba. At the very end—of his life as well as his speech—Chibás gave a particularly rousing cry. "Comrades of the orthodoxy, forward! To economic independence, to political liberty, to social justice! Take a broom and sweep away the thieves in the government! People of Cuba, rise up and move! People of Cuba, awaken!"

Then he shot himself in the stomach with his revolver. He was forty-three years old. In the panic that ensued, supporters carried the still alive Eddy Chibás to the street. There, amazingly, Fidel Castro was already waiting for them. Fidel motioned them into a Chevrolet sedan and drove off smartly to the medical center.

Chibás lingered for eleven long days, and during that time it was almost as if the very country itself had stopped breathing. No one spoke of anything but the beloved orator who was now suffering, almost Christ-like, for his people. In the words of one observer, Chibás' "crucifixion took the form of suicide by microphone." On August 26, 1951, Eduardo Chibás, the great hope of Cuba, slipped finally into eternity.

All those days, Fidel had maintained an unwavering vigil at the bedside. In fact, he had been only a minor young supporter of Chibás and one whom Chibás did not even like. But now Fidel stepped in and simply took over. The body must lie in state at the university, he insisted, and in the Great Hall. There actually were good reasons for this. The police could not enter the university, and so the body would be protected from any foul play on the part of the Prío government. The decision also gave Fidel and a few other student leaders control over Chibás' funeral. So it was that Fidel stood for twenty-four hours by the bier, as part of the honor guard. Pictures in the Havana newspapers show him in the first row, fourth from the casket. The man who had once been called Greaseball by his classmates now wore a formal gray suit and tie, while most of the others were dressed in the more informal white guayabera shirt. Fidel appeared by far the greatest and most profound mourner, and perhaps he even was.

When it came time to move Chibás' body to the cemetery—with between 200,000 and 300,000 Cubans waiting outside the university— Fidel approached José Pardo Llada, another student leader. "We're going to make use of this enormous manifestation of grief," Fidel said. "We're going to carry the body to the palace."

Pardo was stunned. "To the palace? What for?"

"To take power," Fidel answered. "You will proclaim yourself president, and I will be chief of the army. We are going to give to Chibás after his death the satisfaction of sweeping away the government of Prío."

As Pardo recalled it, he told Fidel, "Listen, Fidel, forget this madness. Remember that with the burial procession there will march a battalion of the army for the military honors. They are capable of killing thousands of people if we decide to assault the palace."

Fidel, standing there bullishly in his fine suit and sporting a slim pencil mustache, still insisted. "I tell you that they won't do anything. They are all cowards. The president, the army, the police, the government, all of them. Let's take Chibás to the palace and seat the dead in the presidential chair."

It was the "seat the dead in the presidential chair" that made Pardo decide to "cut off the dialogue." He said with finality, "There's nothing more to say, Fidel. I am taking Chibás to the cemetery."

And so the silent multitudes accompanied the great hope of Cuba to still another cemetery of their dreams. But Fidel's idea of carrying bodies to the palace to take over swiftly and forever was not buried with Eddy Chibás. It is a tactic that tells a great deal about his perception of the grasping of power. His genius lay in his ability to seize control not by traditional military coup but by inspiring the masses through brilliant tactical and insurrectional acts.

Years later Pardo Llada discovered that Captain Máximo Rabelo, who accompanied the troops to the burial of Chibás, carried only false bullets and had precise instructions from President Prío *not* to intervene in case of any disorder. Further, the president had packed his bags and ordered a plane readied to carry him from the country in case the burial resulted in a popular insurrection. It was not the first time, nor would it be the last, that Fidel's incredible vision of the tactically possible, which to everyone else was impossible, turned out to be uncannily precise.

FIDEL'S personal life was now becoming as chaotic as his political life. There were occasional peaceful scenes, with Fidel, Mirta, and Fidelito apparently happy at home. But those were growing fewer and fewer. At the time of Chibás' death, Fidel's brother Raúl was living with Mirta and Fidel in a tall building in Havana, where Mirta's younger and closest brother, Waldo, and another brother, Frank, also lived. Waldo found striking differences between the two Castro brothers that would explain a great deal in later years.

"Fidel was very authoritarian and very organized and had followers," Waldo related. "You were either pro-Fidel, or forget it! He was always pursuing what he wanted, and he didn't care about anything else. So I never talked to him. But Raúl was more idealistic. When he arrived in Havana, he was about eighteen years old. Raúl was curious, very interested in sociology, curious about communism, concerned about justice. Raúl had a hunger for knowledge, a hunger for resolving the whole situation, and the Communists gave him everything. For Raúl, Fidel was the vehicle to achieve communism."

Many political analysts like to toy with the idea that, had circumstances turned out differently, Fidel Castro might well have become a democrat or even some kind of capitalist. He did receive his law degree and could have used it to make a good deal of money.

Much has been made of the fact that Fidel practiced law in his little law firm of Azpiazu, Castro y Rosende in the picturesque old section of Havana, near the docks. But the truth is that he tried only a couple of obscure cases and showed an astounding lack of interest in law per se. Even more incongruous was the fact that Azpiazu, Castro y Rosende had a second little company, an American-style insurance company, whose sign in the law office window announced the future "communist" dictator of Cuba as the respectable proprietor of the Protect Home Insurance Company.

It is true, however, that after the death of Chibás, in 1951, Fidel had a brief fling at elective politics. He decided to run for *representante*—congressman—on the Orthodox ticket. The leadership of the Orthodox Party, however, did not support him or put him forward as a candidate, for he was already dubbed too radical and too renegade, so Fidel just reached out with his inexhaustible energy and created his own political world. He began his campaign nearly a full year before the spring of 1952 elections.

"He made a fabulous campaign," his friend Max Lesnick recalled later. Indeed, Fidel was indefatigable. He sent out some 100,000 letters. He spoke at two, three, four meetings a night. He was up at five in the morning, traveling all over Havana province. Women were powerfully attracted to him, as, interestingly enough, were older people, and not only the marginalized or the "outs" that he would later so depend upon. "Why?" Lesnick asked rhetorically. "Because he was young and he appeared to be a man of convictions."

It was at this moment that Fidel also illustrated another part of his tactical brilliance—the manner in which, at each crossroad, he cleared his past, almost like a computer screen being reset for future use. Now it was time to purge his damaging reputation as a gangster. First, he came out publicly and attacked the *pistoleros* in the gangs, naming names and deeds, even in his own UIR. Second, Fidel attacked President Carlos Prío. In one of the most audacious exposés in Cuban history, Fidel set out to show the links between the Prío administration and the *pistolero* groups. As well, he wanted to show the extraordinarily sumptuous elegance in which Prío lived in his notorious villa, La

Chata, described by the writers Warren Hinckle and William W. Turner as "a mini Garden of Eden done with the understatement of a Busby Berkeley production."

In this tropical paradise twenty kilometers from Havana, Fidel, dressed as a gardener, took pictures of the fountains, the shooting range, the waterfall roaring into the huge swimming pool, and of the debonair Prío himself, chatting with his guests. The following week, in mid-February, 1952, the daily *Alerta* published the pictures with the provocative headline THIS IS THE WAY THE PRESIDENT LIVES WITH THE MONEY HE HAS ROBBED FROM THE PEOPLE.

Fidel accused Prío of distributing $18,000 a month to the gangs, and of having "bought and sold assassinations." As Pardo Llada later wrote, "Fidel, the accomplice of all the gangsters, now was accusing those gangsters. In this moment nobody would have given a cent for the life of the young lawyer. But such was the size of Castro's audacity that nobody dared to do anything."

This period from the fall of 1951 to the aborted elections of the spring of 1952 marked a major turning point in Fidel's life. At this juncture he was not only rhetorically but also palpably filling the empty shoes of Eddy Chibás. Almost imperceptibly, Cubans began to transfer their hopes to the young, brilliant, honest fighter.

WHILE all of this was happening, nobody except Fidel himself was watching the machinations of Fulgencio Batista, who had returned from exile. In the end, it was not Chibás' untimely death that tolled the end for democracy in Cuba, it was Batista's coup prior to the elections. Before that March day of 1952 democracy could still have worked in Cuba had a decent man assumed the presidency and been able to deal with the corruption and the floating but angry anomie. After that day Cuban democracy was doomed.

FIDEL was at home asleep in Havana that early morning of March 10, 1952, when a friend rushed into his apartment with news of Batista's unexpected coup. Now, fearing arrest, he fled five blocks in the tense dawn hours to the apartment of his older half sister, Lidia, a calmly dedicated woman who would always remain the sister closest to him. As usual, his feral instincts were impeccable. Only a few hours later, midmorning, with the coup barely consolidated, secret policemen appeared at the Castros' apartment looking for Fidel and Raúl. Both were already gone.

For several days Fidel moved and moved and moved again. The swiftness of his "relocations" certainly saved him from prison and may well have saved his life, but the overwhelmingly important aspect was that from the moment he heard there had been a coup he knew that a new revolutionary cycle had begun in Cuba.

The coup came as a great relief to Fidel, who was frustrated by attempts to run for elective office. The coup catapulted him into a world of conspiracy that he loved and of clandestine organization, at which he so brilliantly excelled. It marked the beginning of the Fidel Castro the world would come to know. From that day he would begin the organization of his own first "movement."

THE coup d'état took place at 2:43 a.m. that Monday, March 10, when General Fulgencio Batista, wearing a leather jacket and packing a .45-caliber pistol, strode into Camp Columbia and took command of the army. In a mere seventy-seven minutes it was all over. By midday Batista was in power and Carlos Prío had fled the palace—and soon the country—to settle in Mexico.

Why did Batista choose this moment to retake the formal power he had held from 1940 to 1944? The truth was that by the winter of 1952 polls showed that Batista had a bare ten percent of the vote. Chibás, before his death, was the clear front-runner. Even after Chibás' death, if elections had been held, not only would Batista have lost ignominiously, he would have looked so unbearably foolish that both his military and his political career would have been finished.

Most observers accept as the most simple of givens that Fidel Castro abhorred Fulgencio Batista—and perhaps he came to. But the relationship between the young, still secretively military revolutionaries of the left and the older, overtly military caudillos of the right, like Batista, were often complicated and contradictory.

In 1951, for instance, when Fidel was still scouting about for revolutionary techniques, he asked his brother-in-law Rafael Díaz-Balart, who by then had joined the Batistiano youth organization, to introduce him to Batista. The meeting occurred at Batista's estate. "Fidel wanted Batista to prepare a coup," Rafael related to me. "Batista would not allow him actually to say it. Finally Fidel walked up and down in the library, looking at the books. 'I don't see a very important book here,' he said to Batista. Batista asked, 'Which one?' Fidel answered, 'Curzio Malaparte's *The Technique of the Coup d'État.*' " But the veiled invitation to discuss a coup evoked nothing in the cynical Batista, and Fidel did not pursue it further. He was never more than cursorily interested in the coup as a mechanism for revolution, believing its roots to be too shallow to mobilize and transform the people in the ways he had in mind. Many years later Rafael recalled that Batista had told him after Fidel left, "Your young friend is very intelligent, but dangerous."

Once the coup had come, however, the two men were from that moment onward total and irreconcilable enemies; it was a fight to the death, in which a complacent and compulsively upward-striving "pretty mulatto" would enormously—and fatally—underestimate his opponent. As for Fidel, he did what he always did: he looked around him with those cannily hooded hawk's eyes and pushed every lever of opposition to the Batista dictatorship that he could find or create. Within days he had filed a brief in the Court of Constitutional Guarantees to try to force what was left of the Cuban legal system to declare Batista's seizure of power to be unconstitutional. He asked "modestly" that the man who in effect held total power in the country be sentenced to 100 years in prison.

Meanwhile, at home, Mirta waited and waited and waited. One night during this time Fidel and a friend stopped at the Castros' apartment to find it in total darkness and three-year-old Fidelito crying piteously with a throat infection and high fever. The electricity had been cut off, since once again Mirta had no money to pay the utilities. Typically, Fidel, on the spot, borrowed five pesos from the friend to give to Mirta, while he himself was carrying 100 pesos in his pocket. And typically also, he justified such parsimoniousness by telling himself that those 100 pesos had been collected for the purchase of weapons—and nothing else!

But now Mirta was confronted with a much more serious and threatening problem. Her name was Natalia, and she was very beautiful.

Fidel still loved Mirta, as much as a man like him could love a woman, but her patient ways, once comforting and consoling, now were becoming trying and tiresome. The dingy apartment, in its darkness and in its silent pleading for his help and presence, had become increasingly unattractive to him. It was at this period, in November of 1952, that he met Natalia "Naty" Revuelta, one of the most exquisitely beautiful women in Cuba and a woman with an abnormally sensuous appetite for revolution and adventure.

Naty lived with her wealthy doctor husband in a modern house that was as glorious and luxuriant as she was. Blond, green-eyed, buxom, and always in exuberant spirits, Naty was the kind of woman who stopped tongues when she entered a room. To make the affair even more delicious to Fidel, she was not only from the Cuban bourgeoisie, she was haute bourgeoisie, an ambitious young woman who proudly belonged to the Havana Yacht Club and the Havana Country Club. Naty was the pride and joy of her upper-middle-class family, a girl who attended the distinguished American-run Ruston Academy in Havana and studied at a Catholic girls' high school in Philadelphia, a young woman who held responsible positions in the U.S. embassy in Havana and later with Esso. When she "married well," to a respected doctor, Dr. Orlando Fernández Ferrer, it seemed that her life was on a straight and flawlessly unmarred track. But this type of affair between a society girl and a revolutionary was far from rare, and Naty fell happily into the time-honored tradition.

AFTER Batista's coup, Fidel began exercising his leadership on two distinct levels. To confuse the government he appeared to be only publicly engaged—a lawyer practicing amateur politics on the side. In truth, underneath that superficial respectability he was also privately engaged—a conspirator, compulsively and tirelessly organizing secret cells. The rehearsals were over now. The years of experimenting and observing had ended. Keys to his approach as he strode through this antechamber of revolution were absolute secrecy, total control of everything and everyone by him, and the constant evoking of valiant old Cuban images.

And so the "movement" started, a collection of Cubans who, as if sleepwalking, obeyed unquestioningly everything Fidel commanded. Rules were stringent, and any indiscretion meant automatic and often traumatizing separation from the group and its dreams. Drinking alcohol was forbidden, and weekly meetings were held to analyze the conduct of each member. Strict sexual morality was the rule—except for Fidel, with Naty. The organization, the secrecy, the impassioned camaraderie of this new underground gave the movement's members a sense of potency that none of them had ever experienced before.

There was secret weapons training for new recruits on the roof of the science building at the university. Then on January 27, 1953, the eve of the centennial of José Martí's birth, Fidel revealed himself—and the totally militarized character of his movement—in a manner that would seem at first almost stunningly foolish. That day thousands of youths paraded in the name of Martí from the school to downtown Havana. But the hundreds of Fidel's followers, who by now had started calling themselves Fidelistas, did more: they created a breath-taking torchlight spectacle as they marched shoulder to shoulder with such discipline that anyone who was really observant would have recognized the beginnings of a protofascist movement.

Why Fidel showed his hand at this moment is open to question, but his acts did fit in with his enjoyment of balancing the obsessively secret with the daringly public. What is more remarkable is that Batista and his men did not take more notice of his parade. They suffered from the fatal sins of dictators: arrogance and greed.

ARTEMISA was a town founded in 1803 on the main highway to the west of Havana, en route to the glorious and dramatic province of Pinar del Río, with its weirdly beautiful giant rock formations looming over dreamy green and fertile valleys. It was here, among the young men of the middle and working classes, that Fidel found many of his first followers. "The traditionally rebellious Artemisa region was an excellent training ground," a Cuban historian later wrote. "It was sufficiently rural to permit military maneuvers. Moreover, it was removed from the prying eyes of Batista's urban secret service, yet close enough to the capital to allow rapid mobilization if necessary."

In addition to Artemisa, the other major meeting place of the budding movement was in Havana, at the little house of Haydée Santamaría—who was devoted to Fidel—and her brother Abel, a calm and committed young man, a second kind of magnet for the alienated youth of Cuba. Soon Fidel and Abel were organizing meetings, and soon the planning boiled over into plotting.

By early summer of 1953 Fidel was almost ready for his debut as a revolutionary. Just twenty-six years old, he had formed a movement of some 1200 men and women. He had been tireless in his efforts. In the year following Batista's coup he traveled some 30,000 miles in his car—more than forty times the length of Cuba itself— searching for money, arms, and men. With his oddly childlike beseeching quality he appealed to people by expressing what they themselves had only groped for in ambiguous and hitherto unfulfilled ramblings.

But his methods of winning people over depended as much on his example as on his evocative words. One afternoon during weapons training on a farm in Pinar del Río, a rifle had been damaged. Fidel immediately began to look for a small spring that had fallen from it into the high grass. Everyone else soon gave up, but Fidel persisted, searching in the rain until he finally found the lost part. He turned then to his weary men and said triumphantly, "See, this shows that perseverance will bring about our victory." That afternoon could have stood as a metaphor for his whole life.

In his search for followers Fidel looked for people he could mold, souls that had been alienated by the old Cuba. And he found them in the margins of Cuban society. They were young, angry, lost, alienated, left behind, both by their governments and by the great but impersonal American companies where a good number of them worked. Indeed, many of their revolutionary tracts were printed on the mimeograph machine of General Motors in Havana! They were like Fidel himself, the outsider from Birán who didn't clean his fingernails. But the most important factor was that each of the men and women in Fidel's movement had to be totally and unequivocally committed to it, and thus totally obedient to him and to him alone. And they were.

In their desperate seeking, they were willing to give themselves over heart and soul to one leader, to one totally and fulfilling truth. From his words, but most important from his actions, one could clearly see his latent forming of not only a new Cuban revolutionary man but, most crucial and breathtaking, a new Cuba: his Cuba. The men and women he chose and trained for Moncada were also the nucleus of *las masas* to come, a people with no past, formed by and passionately loyal to the person and to the spell of Fidel Castro.

IN THOSE pregnant days of the high summer Fidel was, quietly, everywhere. As he traveled across Cuba he decided to give his father, Don Ángel Castro, the opportunity to again support him. He went to

Birán with one of his followers to ask Angel for $3000. Don Ángel was not amused. "You have to be perfect dolts," he said angrily, "to think you would be capable of overthrowing a government like Batista's, with all its tanks, cannons, and planes." Ángel huffed and puffed and finally gave them $140, which Fidel accepted with minimal good grace. When they were leaving, the old man said with gruff feeling, "Good trip, *loco,* and hopefully nothing bad will happen to you."

At about this time Fidel also went to see his old professor, the respected Herminio Portell Vilá. Of the great Cuban historian he asked, "I understand you used to teach the military history of war?"

The professor said, "Yes. Until Batista."

"Did you ever visit the Moncada fortress and barracks?"

"Yes," the professor responded. "Twice."

"Do you think it could be taken by direct assault?"

"You would have the garrison with you?" the professor asked, narrowing his eyes.

"No," Fidel answered. "But young men . . ."

"What weapons?"

When Fidel told him what they had—all they had—the professor was suddenly sick at heart. "You don't have a chance in the world," he told the foolish young man. "It would be a slaughter."

"Yes," Fidel said, strangely calm. "But I'm going to do it."

By July 22 everything was in place. Fidel's followers began closing in on Santiago de Cuba, and thus on the Moncada Barracks. They came in ones and twos from all over the island, like bits of metal drawn to a magnet. It was Carnival time in Santiago, and the gala music and dancing set a grotesque stage for Portell Vilá's "slaughter" that was so soon to come.

SIX
Moncada

O F ALL the graceful and sensuous cities of Cuba, the most aching with memories is Santiago de Cuba, the capital of Fidel's own Oriente. The historic city lies on a wide and mirrored bay, only a few miles from the foothills of the great Sierra Maestra mountains. Founded in 1514, Santiago is filled with lovely Spanish houses and villas that seem to embody the very inner spirit of Old Spain. But Santiago is also known as the most rebellious city of Cuba, most of Cuba's revolts having started or grown to maturity there.

Santiago seems never more itself than at Carnival time, that festival in Cuba that nominally honors the African deities with which the Cubans themselves seem always to be on ambiguous but voluptuous terms. On the two nights of Carnival, Cubans drink and dance until morning to the sounds of tribal instruments venerating the African *Santería* religious rites.

The Carnival of July 1953 occurred in oppressive heat, but it was a happy one, for in truth Cuba felt itself then a happy country. Prosperity lulled the people into a deeply flawed sense of well-being, and though politically the country was arriving at the point of revolution, most Cubans did not realize it. One of the most middle-class countries in Latin America, semi-industrialized, with exports matching imports, with huge gold reserves, and with sugar mills rapidly passing from foreign to Cuban hands, the island was at an economic takeoff point. But at the same time, there was a Third World within Cuba, and it could be seen clearly in the city of Santiago. Obsessed by injustice and neglect, *santiagueros* tended to think they existed only to provide minerals and agricultural products to the more educated people in the capital.

At Carnival time the people of Santiago found release from their problems and forgot the threat of revolution that lurked behind the costumes and masquerades, not knowing that, as in so many masquerades, a gruesome reality was already present among them.

For months the Fidelistas had been obediently planning for Moncada without knowing in the slightest what it was. They simply gathered and talked and practiced shooting, and the women busily sewed Batistiano uniforms for the group. The uniforms were of tremendous importance. They would not only disguise the Fidelistas but also properly dress them for their battle. Fidel loved uniforms; long after the Revolution triumphed, thirty years later he would still be wearing uniforms, totally unlike the leaders of all the other communist regimes.

Even the aristocratic Naty sewed uniforms. Indeed, Naty's closeness to Fidel, as lover and confidante, was shown by the fact that it was she who was chosen by him to type his manifesto and also to select the records for the music they would play over Santiago radio at the moment of their victory. Naty chose the Cuban national anthem, Chopin's A major Polonaise, and Beethoven's "Eroica" symphony. Meanwhile Mirta, as usual, waited patiently at home, having no idea whatsoever of the imminent attack.

As the Fidelistas gathered from all over Cuba some stopped overnight in Havana, where they were somberly given train tickets to Santiago.

At last the group took off for Santiago, many for their deaths. As an omen, perhaps, of things to come, Fidel left his glasses behind, and even though he could barely drive without them, he was afraid to return for them because such a move might arouse suspicions. As a result, the man who was to become Cuba's great revolutionary hero could not see well during his entire first "heroic" episode.

Planning for the attack had begun in February. Leasing an old and roomy farmhouse on a two-acre farm near Santiago, Fidel played one of his delicious little jokes on authority. The farm, which they called El Siboney, was located on the road to the famous Siboney Beach, where the crude and brutal commander of the Moncada army barracks, Colonel Alberto "the Jackal" del Río Chaviano, owned a house. This meant that several times a day Chaviano would drive by Fidel's "chicken farm," soon to be brimming with guns gathered precisely for the purpose of killing Chaviano and his men.

The target of the attack, the 1000-man Moncada Barracks, incongruously resembled a Moroccan fortress, with its white plastered walls and its crenellated moldings. The idea was to assault this fortress in the dawn hours after Carnival, when most good santiagueros would be sleeping. Fidel would broadcast the Revolution over the radio, and the people would rise as one in revolt. Meanwhile there would be a second diversionary attack, on the barracks at Bayamo.

The only two women—Haydée Santamaría and Melba Hernandez, another early recruit to the cause—arrived at the farm on Saturday, July 25. They immediately set out to clean it up, and then they lovingly prepared a fricassee of chicken. It was a night of revolution as strange as any in history. When the men arrived, Melba and Haydée walked among them passing out glasses of milk. Fidel stood towering above them all, a figure now more compelling than ever. Now he told them, somberly, for the first time, exactly what was about to happen to them.

"When I asked you to come to Santiago de Cuba and then to this farm, I could not tell you, for security reasons, what our mission would be," he began. "Now I can tell you that our target is the Moncada Barracks." The group was astounded. "We will attack at dawn," he went on, "when the guards are only half awake and the officers are still sleeping off their drunkenness from last night's Carnival parties. It will be a surprise attack and should not last more than ten minutes.

"We will go by car. The squad in the first car will take advantage of the confusion caused by our uniforms to take the guards at Post Three prisoner. We will remove the chain between the two stanchions at the entrance. We will drive in, leave the cars, and enter the buildings to our left, taking prisoner those in the dormitory who surrender. A second force, of twenty, will seize the hospital, whose back windows open on the fort. They will then provide harassing fire through the windows against the rear of the barracks. A third group, of six, will take the Palace of Justice and from the roof neutralize the machine guns on top of the barracks inside the fort."

The room seemed held in a taut silence that no one dared break. Only one Fidelista, Gustavo Arcos, protested. He said the plan was suicidal. Fidel, his eyes now coldly focused, demanded, "You are afraid? You are not with me?"

"I will go to Moncada even if I die," Arcos retorted, then paused and added, "I hope that you are willing to die, too." This compulsive talk of death was their romance and their resurrection, just as it had been with José Martí.

For some, that final night had elements of the deepest kind of religious experience. "The stars were bigger and brighter," Haydée, always the most lyrical of spirits, rhapsodized. "The palms, taller and greener. The faces of our friends were faces we might never see again but would have with us always. Everything was more beautiful, everything was larger, lovelier, finer."

Her brother Abel, Fidel's second-in-command and the man Fidel would call "the best," spent a lighthearted evening. "Abel was as happy as if nothing were happening," Haydée told me many years later of that night before the fall, when the world gleamed and glittered for a few immensely innocent and idealistic young people. "He laughed and said, 'How surprised they would be if they knew what was going to happen!' He didn't mean just the next day—he meant everything."

In the dark early morning the men spent a lot of time trying on the Batistiano uniforms. Amazingly, Fidel's, which was the largest, did not fit. He stood there, a huge hulk of a man, clean-shaven, without even a mustache, with sleeves too short and pants up around his ankles. "Looking at himself in the mirror," one of the group recalled, "he worried that he would not look like a soldier of the regime, the role we were to play in attacking the garrison. He had the same worry when Abel tried on his uniform. 'Look, Abel,' Fidel said, 'you will at least have to *act* like a military man.' "

Fidel was not the only warrior to display vanity that night. Boris Luis Santa Coloma, Haydée's fiancé, had bought special two-tone shoes to wear into battle. "They were his new shoes," Melba recalled later, "and he was like a child. He went with his new shoes into action."

By three a.m. they were ready, and Fidel gave his last speech. "In a few hours," he told them, "you will be victorious or defeated, but regardless of the outcome—listen well, *compañeros!*—this movement will triumph. If you win today, the aspirations of Martí will be fulfilled sooner. If the contrary occurs, our action will set an example for the Cuban people and from the people will arise young men willing to die for Cuba."

Only one person came forward to voice what most rational people would have said many hours before. Mario Muñoz was the doctor and radio operator they had brought along. "Fidel," Dr. Muñoz said then, "I am ready to die for Cuba, but to think that we can take the Moncada Barracks with a few more than one hundred men, when they have a garrison of more than a thousand soldiers, is to send these boys to a sure suicide."

Fidel was enraged, as he always was when anybody challenged him. Coldly he stood there, not responding. Finally Abel said, "Those who are afraid can stay behind—"

Muñoz did not allow him to finish. "I will be in the vanguard," he interrupted, "but I repeat that this plan seems to me to be madness, even a crime."

Ten of the Fidelistas did then separate themselves from the group and decided not to join in the attack. Fidel scorned them. Then the poet of the group, a sensitive youngster of eighteen years, Raúl Gómez

García, recited in a tremulous voice some verses of a hymn he had composed for the Moncada uprising.

At five a.m. their convoy of twenty-six cars left El Siboney to attack the Moncada Barracks. It was the beginning of the Cuban Revolution.

THE attack on Moncada that early morning of July 26, 1953, remains one of the great military disasters of history. To this day, reports of the exact number of men who took part, the number of cars, and even the exact length of time that the attack involved vary so much that it is impossible to clarify those details. Studying all the accounts, the number of Fidelistas ranges from 87 to 165 men and two women. The number of Batista soldiers on the other side ranges from 262 to 1000. Yet the picture of the attack and the sense and mood of it are very clear indeed.

When the line of cars moved out of El Siboney, the uniformed attackers sat silently inside them. Renato Guitart, the young *santiaguero* who was to lead the assault, was in the first car; Fidel drove the second, which also carried two others. The attack began within fifteen minutes of leaving El Siboney, when Guitart jumped out of his car in front of the Post 3 gate and shouted imperiously at the soldiers on guard, "*Atención, atención, ya viene el general* [Attention, attention, the general is coming]."

In the deceptiveness of dawn the guards thought that this new group was a military band that had been brought in from Havana to perform during Carnival, and so, in that confusion, the insurgents were able to take their arms away from them. The plan had been to rush Post 3 after disarming the guards; then the others would enter the courtyard, disarm the sleeping soldiers inside, and fan out through Moncada with their newly captured weapons. But all of this plan was aborted almost immediately when suddenly there appeared a special patrol that was unknown to the Fidelistas.

Renato Guitart had studied the fort's defenses for weeks, but he had never seen this roving guard, because it had been instituted only for the Carnival period. Furthermore, far from the great majority of the soldiers being safely asleep, as Fidel had expected, most of them had been at the Carnival all night and were just coming home as the insurgents approached.

As Fidel jumped from the car, carrying his submachine gun, wild firing began in all directions. The key element of surprise was lost from the very start.

Now everything seemed to go wrong. Fidel leaped back into the car to move forward, but the car wouldn't start. Gustavo Arcos, half out of his car and about to level his rifle at an army officer, was ludicrously knocked over when a swinging car door hit him.

Several Fidelistas, led by Guitart, actually did get inside the barracks. Here the Cuban Revolution won its first martyrs. As the rebels fired their pathetically small arms—.22-caliber rifles and old shotguns—Batista's soldiers shot back. Within seconds Renato Guitart lay dead at the door of the radio station.

Where were the reserves? Fidel wondered, as the wild shooting continued. Later he would learn the unbelievable truth. It seems that the ten men who had refused to fight did not stay behind as they had been instructed. Instead, they left the house, and, in driving away, they inadvertently drifted into the line of cars heading for Moncada. Making a wrong turn, they led the rebel fighters behind them, who did not know Santiago, into the city. So as the real battle began, the men who were to back up Fidel and his group in the crucial attack on Post 3 were haplessly wandering the streets, trying to find the second largest military garrison in Cuba!

When Raúl and his group realized that the attack had failed and that Fidel had given the order to retreat, he and his men simply took off their outer uniforms, walked casually into the streets of Santiago in their civilian clothes, and disappeared.

Meanwhile a group of twenty Fidelistas, led by Abel Santamaría, occupied the local civilian hospital—the Saturnino Lora—which was strategically situated near the fort. As was the plan, they immediately began to distract the soldiers in the courtyard with diversionary fire.

By the time the insurgents realized no one else was firing, it was too late. At about eight a.m. Abel took the two women, Melba and Haydée, aside. "We've had it," he said. "You know what is going to happen to me, but it's important not to risk you two. Hide in the hospital and just wait. Somebody has to survive to tell what really happened here."

An intern helped all of them put on hospital gowns and bandages. Many of the rebels got into beds, where they lay terrified, pretending to be patients. Haydée and Melba ran into the children's ward, where they tried to impersonate nurses.

When the Batistiano soldiers poured into the hospital, the masquerade came extraordinarily close to working. Indeed, the soldiers were just about to leave when the military's public relations man for the hospital, who happened to be there at the time, whispered to the soldiers what had occurred. Brutally the soldiers grabbed the insurgents from their beds and literally threw them outside.

The last time Melba and Haydée saw Abel alive was in the hospital courtyard, being beaten mercilessly by the soldiers with their rifle butts. Dr. Muñoz, who had argued with Fidel about the suicidal nature of the attack, was shot in the back at point-blank range.

After giving the order to retreat, Fidel and eighteen others took to the Sierra. Brokenhearted and physically exhausted, the little group started out on foot for the rough, heavily forested mountains. Peasants along the way helped them. Even so, Fidel was caught a few days later and imprisoned. But only temporarily.

Meanwhile Raúl began walking across the country, away from Santiago. He slept in a cane field that night, and the next day began walking again. "As I continued walking," he said later, "I was arrested. They took me to the San Luis garrison." Raúl was a captive, but at least he would survive.

Fidel was right when, later, he estimated that the attack "worked" in the long run for one reason and for one reason alone: the barbarities of the Batistiano military. In the horrible aftermath of Moncada the true nature of the regime was revealed for the first time. Orders came from Havana to kill ten insurgents for every soldier killed, and the officers at Moncada went about it with relish.

The two women—the only ones to survive the horrors of the hospital—were captured and then taken to prison, where they were subjected to unspeakable terrors. From their cell they were made to hear the screams of their comrades as they were tortured to death. At one point they heard the soldiers talking about "that one with the two-toned shoes," and Haydée's hopes rose for her fiancé. But Boris did not survive the torture. And Haydée was to suffer still more.

A sergeant came to her in prison and, opening his bloodstained hands, showed her the eye of her brother and demanded that she tell everything or else his other eye would be torn out. Haydée's reply, which every Cuban schoolchild knows by heart was, "If he did not tell you under torture, far less will I tell you."

Gómez García, the young poet who had recited the revolutionary hymn in the last minutes before the rebels left El Siboney, died slowly, of the tortures. In the end, everyone who gave himself up to the police died. Ten for one, as Batista had demanded.

Yet Moncada catapulted Fidel Castro into the leadership role of a Cuba in which every other political possibility had failed—or was failing. "The Moncada attack was a failure from the military point of view," a Cuban writer wrote. "But it was a resounding political success. After July 26, 1953, everything in Cuba became of vast historical moment—brutal, bloody, and inevitable."

WHEN the trial of Fidel Castro and his comrades opened in the Santiago Palace of Justice on Monday, September 21, 1953, Fidel's first act was to grasp domination of the ceremonies. He entered the courtroom wearing his favorite old dark blue striped suit, a white shirt, and a red print necktie. His hair was combed with unusual care, and his new mustache was meticulously trimmed. His physical stature and his defiant demeanor soon had the onlookers whispering in excitement, "This is Fidel! There he is!" It was his first leap onto the public stage of Cuban mass consciousness, and he took full advantage of it.

Holding his manacled hands up toward the judges and offering himself as a metaphor for Cuba, he said in a loud voice, "Mr. President, what guarantees can there be in this trial? Not even the worst criminals are held this way in a hall that calls itself a hall of justice. You cannot judge people who are handcuffed."

The chief judge, who like all the judges was to show himself vastly sympathetic to the insurgents, agreed and immediately ordered the handcuffs removed from all the prisoners. From that moment on, it was not the state's trial against Fidel Castro, it was Fidel Castro's trial against the state.

Fidel began in his clear and resonant voice, "I want to express my desire to make use of my right, as a lawyer, to assume my own defense."

The tribunal agreed, not understanding in the slightest the use Fidel would put it to. He immediately donned a lawyer's imposing black robes. The state, in the person of Colonel Chaviano, the commander of the Moncada Barracks, then read the list of accused, and the charges.

When Fidel was asked if he had participated in the assault on Moncada, he said simply, "Yes, I participated."

Fidel then produced one of the greatest theatrical dramas in a lifetime filled with them. One minute he was defending himself. The next he was cross-examining his accusers. Throughout the trial he shrewdly used what were in effect costumes to confuse, amuse, and mesmerize the courtroom. He would put on the black lawyer's robe when he was acting as lawyer, and then take it off when he went back to being the prisoner and defendant.

As Fidel built his powerful case he very deliberately showed the Cuban people the brutality of the Batista regime. But of even more importance, he used the trial to educate the people of Cuba in a very specific idea that was crucial to the final success of the Revolution. This was the belief that he and his men had not only the right but the duty to take extraconstitutional means to overthrow a dictator who was himself a usurper.

The top leadership group of the Fidelistas, including Raúl Castro, were sentenced to thirteen years in prison. Twenty others received ten years, and three men got three years in jail. Fidel was not yet sentenced. Instead, it was decided that he would be retried separately, in extraordinary secrecy, in the small nurses' lounge in the Saturnino Lora civilian hospital, the same hospital where Abel and his small contingent had suffered so. Once again Fidel asked for and was granted permission to defend himself.

The trial began about nine o'clock on a morning in early October. Fidel was again wearing his blue striped suit. There are many differing versions of his pronouncement that day. It came to be known as the History Will Absolve Me speech. The best proof one can muster tells us that Fidel began with "Honorable Judges, never has a lawyer had to practice his profession under such difficult conditions." He then meticulously reconstructed the attack—its reasons, its rationale, its nobility, and its suffering. He spoke of "sacrifices which had no precedent in the struggles of our republic" and of the "cruelest and most inhuman oppression in all their history."

Programmatically, his ideas centered around five "revolutionary laws." First, Fidel called for the restoration of the Constitution of 1940, a liberal-radical document theretofore little honored. Second, he demanded full ownership of small farms worked by tenants, sharecroppers, and squatters. Third, he spoke for the right of workers and employees to share in the profits of all large industrial enterprises. The fourth law demanded the right of sugar workers on plantations "to share fifty-five percent of the value of the sugarcane produced," and the fifth law called for the confiscation of "all property and wealth secured through politically protected fraud and graft during previous regimes."

In perhaps its most telling section, the speech also clearly rejected "absolute freedom of enterprise" as a guiding principle for an economic solution. It noted especially "that more than half of the most productive land belongs to foreigners"—which was true in 1953. And he particularly singled out the United Fruit Company.

Then came forth the noble words that would go down in Cuban revolutionary history—and, indeed, revolutionary history across the world. With all the considerable dramatic power at his disposal he told the court, "*Condenádme, no importa! La historia me absolvera!* [Condemn me, it does not matter! History will absolve me!]"

The trial was over. Fidel Castro was sentenced to fifteen years and taken to prison on the Isla de Pinos—Isle of Pines—south of Cuba. But he was determined that his History Will Absolve Me speech would not be forgotten and that it would be passed hand to hand across Cuba until it became nothing less than a reverberating revolutionary refrain from seashore to seashore.

In the long days on Isla de Pinos he began to reconstruct the speech, to expand it, and in many ways to change it. Painstakingly and surreptitiously, he coalesced and disseminated his ideas. Between the lines of apparently prosaic letters to friends he inserted passages from his speech, revised, reworked, rethought, written in lime juice so they would not be visible to the prison censor.

When Melba and Haydée were released from prison in February of 1954, they became his chief agents on the outside. They would receive letters from Fidel, often carried from the prison by Mirta; they would perform the delicate work of ironing the sheets of paper to get the lime juice to show; then they would piece them all together. Ever grandiose, Fidel had wanted 100,000 copies of his documents to be printed and distributed. But this was much too ambitious; they only had money for 20,000 copies. Melba recalled that they drove across the island in an old car so loaded down with its revolutionary cargo that the springs almost brushed the ground, and they stopped at every town to leave copies for distribution. For all their efforts, however, the speech did not become popular and hallowed until after the Revolution triumphed in 1959.

THE presidio prison on the Isle of Pines was composed of four circular buildings surrounding a large round dining building. Each building had six floors, with ninety-three cells per floor. There was a tower in the center of the first floor, from which a guard could watch everyone in the circle. Built by General Machado in 1931, the prison had room for 5000 inmates.

If Fidel had turned the state's trial against him into his trial against the state, now he turned the prison cells into a school. The prison became a revolutionary training ground where he created a vanguard of men to be the core of the movement to come.

In sharp contrast to the prisons he would later build, Fidel's cell was large enough for him to walk back and forth. Sometimes he would sit in his rocking chair; sometimes he would cook spaghetti on his small hot plate. But the greatest passion in his life at this time was books. "The prison is a terrific classroom!" he wrote in a letter on December 19, 1953. "I can shape my view of the world in here and figure out the meaning of my life."

Fidel was treated in typical Spanish style as a political prisoner, which meant that he was respected and that he suffered none of the punishments of the common criminal. He was often called Dr. Castro by the other inmates and the prison workers. The little school he began for his men was called the Abel Santamaría Ideological Academy.

"We are permitted to go into the courtyard from 10 to 10:30 a.m. and from 1 to 4 p.m.," he wrote in one of his many letters. "Every morning, I give a talk—philosophy one day, world history the next. Other comrades give lectures on Cuban history, grammar, arithmetic, geography and English."

At this point another mystery occurred in Castro's personal life. One day he wrote letters to both Mirta and Naty. The two letters got mixed up and Mirta got Naty's letter and Naty, Mirta's. This, of course, stunned and finally enraged the usually patient Mirta. Indeed, it was the last unbearable blow. Before that, she had dutifully visited

Fidel at the prison, and she had dutifully carried out his messages to the movement. Now it was all but over. But—accidental? No one who knew Fidel ever thought so.

With her husband in prison Mirta was more personally and financially desperate then ever. Her brother Rafael decided to help her by giving her a *botella*, a no-show government job. By that time Rafael was the number two man in Batista's ministry of the interior under Ramón Hermida, so Mirta's little *botella* came directly from the ministry that Fidel hated above all others.

Once Fidel's single most intimate friend, Rafael was now not only bitterly ideologically opposed to Fidel but also deeply embittered about the way Fidel treated and abused Mirta.

But while Rafael could help Mirta out financially with the *botella*, he could not control his sister's relationship with her husband. One day, not long after the *botella* had been arranged, Rafael got word from a friend that Mirta, acting for her husband, had made an attack on Hermida. The minister immediately gave a press conference and revealed that Mirta had a *botella* in the ministry. Mirta was humiliated, horrified, and ultimately doomed.

At first Fidel assumed that Rafael, for whom he now harbored a smoldering hatred, had made up the story. But soon he knew the truth, and he was coldly unforgiving. Beginning with the letter to Naty and ending with the *botella*, the marriage was finished. A divorce suit was soon filed by Mirta.

ONE night in 1955 Fidel listened to the radio while former president Grau made a speech. In the background he could clearly hear voices in the crowd chanting, "Fidel Castro . . . Fidel Castro!" As he listened, Fidel became exuberant and his dark eyes gleamed.

By 1955 Batista was also feeling confident. He had been "reelected" president, with the great enthusiasm of the United States, though everyone knew that the elections had been fraudulent. Because he felt strong, he gave in to the appeals of the *Ortodoxos* and exchanged seats in the senate with them for an amnesty for the Moncada prisoners.

So on May 15, 1955, Fidel, Raúl, and the others marched victoriously out of the Isla de Pinos prison and rode in a small boat back to the mainland. Fidel, wearing a white shirt and dark trousers, raised his arms victoriously over his head as he disembarked.

SEVEN
The Mexico Years

BACK in Havana, Fidel was greeted with wild enthusiasm. He was carried on the shoulders of worshipful supporters to his sister Lidia's apartment, where the small rooms were mobbed with newspapermen, photographers, relatives, and friends. It was mid-May. By June there were two court warrants against him and he feared for his life. So on July 7 he left Cuba for Mexico. His devoted sister Lidia sold her refrigerator so that he would have enough cash to travel, and as always, he carried many more books than clothes.

But Fidel had not wasted even one moment of those brief weeks in Havana. During that time he began to form his new organization. The somewhat nebulous movement that had marched on Moncada now became the much more focused 26th of July Movement, or M-26-7, as it came to be known. He had already decided to land a rebel force in Oriente province. Meanwhile he prepared about twenty persons to keep the movement alive in Havana. Being Fidel, he left each of the "anointed ones" thinking that he or she was his sole chosen and empowered representative in Cuba.

The Mexico City to which Fidel and his comrades traveled to exile that summer of 1955 was a glorious place, an elegant city of broad boulevards and liquid dusks. But to Fidel, Mexico was merely political exile and a rock to stand on while he prepared to move the universe.

For his followers, those first months in Mexico had about them much of the same magic feeling as that last night at El Siboney before the Moncada attack. Again the men and women arrived secretively, in Mexico City, one by one, two by two, and again there was the tremulous sense of noble expectation and purpose.

A total of sixty to seventy soon were lodged in six rented houses scattered all over the city. The various groups were completely divided, with only Fidel knowing everyone and only his spirit—and spell—holding them together. Discipline was rigorous and monastic, with each of the six houses having its own commander and each group forbidden to visit with the others.

Fidel's real strength came from a core of four men: his brother Raúl; the Spanish Republican general and guerrilla fighter Alberto

Bayo; the brilliant Argentine physician and radical revolutionary, Ernesto "Che" Guevara; and the sober, thoughtful Cuban Baptist revolutionary organizer, Frank País. Each one would, in his own way, become a historic and revered figure—and each one, except Raúl, would eventually be denied or destroyed by Fidel.

When General Bayo first met Fidel, in August of 1955, he knew he had finally met his appointed destiny. "This," he told friends, "is a real revolutionary." The bluff and heavyset Bayo, with his neatly trimmed Vandyke beard, had been born in Camagüey, Cuba, in 1892, and like Fidel was of Spanish parentage. He had fought in the Spanish Republican air force against Generalísimo Francisco Franco, and he had fought in Africa, where he had organized guerrilla warfare operations. Bayo lost his right eye in Africa, then returned to Cuba, and ended up, incongruously, owning a furniture factory in Mexico City.

In the summer of 1955 a friend brought the young Cuban to Bayo's home. Fidel told the old general forthrightly, "I am a Cuban lawyer. I want to fight against Batista. Though I am only twenty-nine years old, I know you have written several textbooks on guerrilla warfare. Please help me train my men."

Bayo asked practically, "How many men do you have?"

And Fidel answered, "Not many yet. But I am going to the United States to get men and money, and I would like to know if you could be the instructor for my men."

"I will do it," Bayo replied, "but I'm afraid I don't have much faith in your possible success. A young man only twenty-nine?"

Fidel answered simply, "I will be successful."

Bayo sold his furniture factory and soon was training Fidel's *guerrilleros*.

At first Bayo moved daily from safe house to safe house, disguised as an English instructor. Then he and several of Fidel's trusted aides found a perfect training spot near the town of Chalco, a ranch called Santa Rosa. Not only was the ranch house roomy, it was surrounded by a nine-foot stone wall, had towers for protection, and looked like a fortress, which in a sense it was. A clever man, Bayo managed to assure the owner he had a millionaire Central American colonel hovering in the wings, eager to buy Santa Rosa for its asking price, but that first the ranch house had to be repaired and painted. Thus, they paid only an interim rent of eight dollars monthly during the repairs.

At Santa Rosa, Bayo trained the men in night fighting, armaments, aviation, explosives, antitank mines. He was as excited as a child again. One day he asked the men if they had toothpaste, soap, shaving cream. Then he took everything away from them, saying harshly, "No guerrilla shaves, nor cleans his teeth, so from now on none of you are going to bathe, nor clean your teeth, nor . . ." Another time he told them—truthfully, as it turned out—"Very few of you will survive in Cuba. You are going to win, but from you there will remain few."

It is probable that Che Guevara met Fidel in early July of 1955. We know the meeting took place at the house of a mutual Cuban friend in Mexico City. It was one of those rare historic meetings of two men whose myriad strengths and weaknesses gripped and fit like the parts of a finely tuned machine. Each man came to the union with his own implacable sense of destiny, but each brought to their strange and fertile collaboration very different gifts. Fidel was ruthless, but he had an amorphous sense of doing what he was doing for *las masas.* Che, the more human on an individual scale, nevertheless was ready to sacrifice everything for *la idea.*

They talked for ten hours, through the warm Mexican summer night. "At dawn," Che would later write proudly, "I was already the physician of the future expedition." He added that he had been "moved by a feeling of romantic, adventurous sympathy and by the conviction that it would be worth dying on an alien beach for such a pure idea."

Ernesto Guevara had been born in the historic Argentine city of Córdoba, just two years after Fidel's birth in Birán, but while Fidel's more common family was rich, Che's aristocratic parents were poor. His mother, Celia, was a beautiful, passionate woman who adored her five children; his father, Ernesto senior, a civil engineer, was the more practical of this very impractical family.

From an early age, like Fidel, Che was incapable of doing anything the ordinary way, and also like Fidel, he liked things *his* way. At twenty-three, already a doctor, he left home, telling his parents jauntily, "Here goes a soldier of the Americas." With those words he started out on an odyssey of Latin America, which he, like Fidel, wanted to save from itself. Already considering himself a free, nonparty Marxist, the more he traveled, the more he became convinced that all the problems of his impoverished and benighted continent were the fault of the native aristocracy and, especially, of the United States. As with Fidel, hatred of America was to be the single most abiding passion of his life, only he would die for it, while Fidel preferred, as always, to live for it.

Once Che and his Peruvian wife, Hilda, had moved to Mexico and met the Castro brothers, Hilda introduced Fidel to her friend, a Venezuelan poetess named Lucila Velásquez. She became Fidel's first romantic interest in Mexico, but it was a brief one, for Lucila soon tired of his incessant talk about politics. Lucila recalled much later how "the Cuban passion of Fidel and the revolutionary ideas of Guevara came together like the flare of a spark, with an intense light. One impulsive, the other reflective. One emotional and optimistic, the other cold and skeptical. Without Ernesto Guevara, Fidel Castro might never have become a Communist. Without Fidel Castro, Ernesto Guevara might never have been more than a Marxist theorist, an intellectual idealist."

Frank País is immeasurably less known today than Che Guevara, but in many ways he was the most extraordinary leader of the 26th of July Movement, other than Fidel himself. A tall, handsome, intensely serious young man, Frank was born on December 7, 1934, to a humble Spanish immigrant and the pastor of Santiago's First Baptist Church. What everyone remembers most about Frank País was his utter and uncompromising seriousness and honesty. His common sense stood in stark juxtaposition to Fidel's impulsive willfulness. Still, it was to Frank's *Acción Nacional Revolucionaria* (ANR) group that Fidel turned in the summer of 1955 to be the in-Cuba wing of the movement. Frank's group began the deadly dangerous work of readying Oriente province for a revolt against the Batista regime, and he came to Mexico to confer with Fidel at least twice. The big question was the timing of the in-Cuba resistance. Fidel insisted that Frank's group must be prepared to stage a diversionary uprising in Santiago before the end of 1956. Frank insisted to the very last that his men would not be ready, but it did him no good.

In the fall of 1955 Fidel began reaching out for support and for funds among the Cubans in exile in the United States. That he had allies among those disaffected, often poor, and always homesick Cubans was obvious. That he was deliberately walking in the shoes of

José Martí, who had pursued his work of revolution almost entirely on North American soil, was unmistakable.

Fidel made his first explicit and unwavering public commitment before an audience of eight hundred Cubans at the Palm Garden, in New York City, on October 30, 1955. From New York, where José Martí had written his articles and proclaimed his beliefs, Fidel moved to woo the cigar makers in Tampa, Florida. From Tampa to Philadelphia; to Union City, New Jersey; to Bridgeport, Connecticut—it was like a moving vaudeville show. And at the end of every performance, cowboy hats were jammed full with dollar bills.

ON CHRISTMAS Eve, Fidel's inner group gathered for a traditional Cuban Christmas feast: rice and black beans—the Cubans called it Moors and Christians—roast pork, and cassava, with the classic Spanish almond dessert. That night Fidel expressed with a startling new clarity his plans for Cuba's future. "He spoke with such certainty that one had the feeling we were already in Cuba, carrying out the process of construction," Che's wife, Hilda, then seven months pregnant with Hildita, recalled. But first this uniquely motivated little group had to get to Cuba.

In January 1956 the real planning for the landing on the Oriente coast—the landing that would follow exactly in the tragic footsteps of Martí—began.

In March, Fidel began to tidy up his own political house. He broke openly with the Orthodox Party under the ruse of a procedural quarrel, and he proclaimed the 26th of July Movement as the only real opposition to Batista.

On March 18 a baby girl was born to Naty Revuelta in Cuba. The baby was Fidel's. Before leaving for Mexico, Fidel had asked her to go with him, but her mother had insisted that she remain in Cuba with her prominent doctor husband, and Naty had dutifully obeyed. Everyone who knew her pitied her, for they knew she was in love with Fidel—it was the talk of the country club.

In April, Fidel watched, first with apprehension and then with relief, from his Mexican redoubt while two attempts were made to overthrow Batista. Both failed dismally. The first, which would come to be known as the Conspiracy of the Pure because it consisted largely of the most honest and liberal military officers, was aborted when the secret police uncovered the plans. The second attempt was waged by none other than former president Carlos Prío, who sent a group of militants to assault the Goicuría army barracks, in Matanzas. It was not unlike the attack on Moncada, and just as fatal.

Despite Fidel's strict insistence on secrecy, Batista knew every single thing that was going on in Mexico, and he basked in his knowledge, supposing himself not only safe but invulnerable. Soon, not surprisingly, he was plotting to get rid of Fidel Castro. In late June, 1956, Fidel was swept up off a street of Mexico City and hustled to prison. In all, more than fifty members of his group were arrested.

Fidel, of course, made the very best of this new "prison opportunity." He wrote letters, he exhorted his fellow prisoners, and he appealed to the nobility of the Mexican soul—not to speak of the legal system—saying to the press, "I trust that Mexico will continue to be loyal to its noble tradition toward the politically persecuted."

It was in prison that Fidel met Teresa "Tete" Casuso, the voluptuously beautiful blond Cuban woman of intelligence and artistic sensibilities who would now play a key role in his life. Her husband, the famous poet and writer Pablo de la Torriente, had been killed fighting in Spain on the Republican side. Tete had smiled bitterly when she saw an editorial referring to some young Cubans, now in prison, who had been training for an expedition to "liberate" her Cuba. Nevertheless, she decided she would like to meet these romantic renegades, and the next day she appeared at the prison—along with a quite gloriously beautiful sixteen-year-old Spanish friend, Isabel Custodio.

A large group of Cubans was gathered in the central courtyard of the prison when Tete and Isabel arrived, and in the middle, standing out as always, was Fidel. While watching the beauteous Isabel from the corner of his eye, Fidel told Tete how honored he was that the widow of the great Pablo should come to see him. Before she left that day, Tete gave Fidel her card and told him to "consider my house your own." Little did she guess how literally he would take her suggestion.

By the end of July all of the Cubans had been released, largely through the help of a leftist former president of Mexico. Two days after his release Fidel asked Tete if she could keep "a few things" for him. The "few things" turned out to be seven carloads of munitions, which filled her house. From then on, Fidel and his group dropped in whenever it pleased them, cleaned their guns in her bedroom, carried away their rifles wrapped in quilts from her beds. But although Tete Casuso, like so many, came to have a deep attachment to Fidel, it never was romantic in a love sense; that relationship began to bloom between Fidel and Isabel Custodio.

Their relationship moved so rapidly that within two months he had done the extraordinarily bourgeois thing of proposing marriage to her. At first she accepted, and Fidel even bought her a trousseau: new clothes, shoes, a large bottle of French perfume. But the engagement passed quickly, the breaking point being his unique invitation to her to come along on the boat for the invasion of Cuba. Almost immediately Isabel married a Mexican businessman and faded out of history as rapidly as she had entered it.

In August, Fidel turned thirty. Ever since his divorce from Mirta, and particularly since Fidelito had come under the influence of her family, the hated Díaz-Balarts, Fidel had brooded about losing control of the chubby, dark-haired, playful little boy. When he heard that Mirta was going to be remarried, to a conservative Cuban, he was incensed even further. So he carried out one more bizarre coup, this time against his former wife. He arranged for Fidelito to be brought to him in Mexico.

"Fidel called Mirta that summer before she remarried," her brother Rafael told me many years later. "Fidel said he would like her to send Fidelito to Mexico for two weeks to visit him. Mirta said, 'Fine.' The only thing she asked was that he give his word of honor that after two weeks he would return her boy to her."

Fidelito was brought to Mexico on September 17, 1956, just at the time when Mirta was marrying Emilio Núñez Portuondo, the son of the Cuban ambassador to the United Nations. Fidel placed Fidelito with two of his patrons—Alfonso Gutiérrez, a Mexican civil engineer; and his wife, a beautiful Cuban nightclub singer. The boy got a new name, Juan Ramírez, and, incongruously, joined the Boy Scouts. Fidelito lived in the Gutiérrezes' gorgeous modern villa, complete with swimming pool and surrounded by a high protective wall. Whenever Fidel came to visit the boy, he would blow the car horn in a special signal and soon the heavy wooden gate would swing open.

But Mirta and her family had no intention of allowing the

seven-year-old boy to stay in Mexico. On December 8, with the help of the Mexican police, Fidelito was taken to the Cuban embassy, where he was duly returned to his mother.

Meanwhile, on October 21 Ángel Castro, the patriarch of the Castro family, died suddenly in Birán, a wealthy and respected man, leaving an estate worth $1 million. While no one really expected Fidel to be at the funeral—and he wasn't—Batista took no chances. The entire town was surrounded by his soldiers. Around midnight something extraordinary happened—out of the darkness came several men of the 26th of July Movement. Padding quietly like cats, they emerged from the shadows of Oriente to pay their respects to the *padre* of their *líder máximo*. Respectfully, they put roses on the bier, and then they left, fading away again into the steamy, hot tropical night.

By November, Fidel was bursting with a sense of urgency; he was determined to leave Mexico and land in Cuba before the end of 1956. He decided that his group of rebels would depart from Tuxpan, a small port on the Gulf of Mexico. There he found a boat, an American-owned yacht named the *Granma*. It could hardly have been more inappropriate. A shabby thirty-eight-foot wooden boat, it could carry no more than twenty-five persons safely and was propelled by two small diesel engines. No matter. Fidel declared confidently, "In this boat, I am going to Cuba." The American owner sold this unlikely revolutionary vehicle to the Cuban "fool" for $20,000.

In later years a model of the *Granma* would be displayed in a small museum in Tuxpan, and pictures of the "great historic expedition" would garnish the walls. But on the rainy night of November 24, 1956, no one there knew of the historic event taking place in their town. As they had before Moncada, Fidel's men began to arrive by ones and twos, staying overnight in different small towns and in those shabby, lightless hotels that have housed revolutionaries from time immemorial.

Once they were all aboard the little boat, with their pitiful weapons and slim provisions, the *Granma* was so overloaded that the water was almost slopping over the sides. As they sailed away from Tuxpan in the moonless early morning of November 25, they passed a ship from the Mexican navy. But the *Granma* went unnoticed because of the rain. On board, Fidel and his men were so crowded that some were forced to sit with their legs doubled up; others couldn't sit at all. Some got seasick.

Then, as the little, overloaded, unlit boat chugged out into the Gulf, these men, most of them soon to die, bedraggled and already exhausted, without even room to move or turn in, spontaneously began to sing the Cuban national anthem. The lights were put on briefly, and they all stood and looked at one another for long, silent minutes.

Then they hugged one another as best they could, turned out the dim lights, and sailed on into the unrelieved and unknown darkness of the Gulf of Mexico—toward Cuba.

EIGHT
The Landing

RUNNING a bare 7.2 knots an hour, the *Granma* headed to sea, tossed by huge waves. But on that dark and awful voyage, the ship battered by winds and repeatedly coming near to sinking, there did emerge a strange and eerie faith in Fidel and their purpose. "The *Granma* was invincible," Faustino Pérez decided as the seas gradually calmed. "Forces other than purely physical ones had resisted the storm and were driving the ship to her destination."

And Fidel, the invincible leader of the invincible ship of the invincible cause, was not even seasick. Indeed, he seemed to be everywhere, his hyper level of intensity heightened even more than usual. He talked only of plans. "Where are we? When do we arrive? Let me see the map!"

Two days into the voyage, however, both Fidel and the men began to realize that they had a bigger problem than the heavy rain and high winds. Instead of the trip taking five days and nights, as he had predicted, it was obvious now that it would take at least seven days. This meant that the *Granma* was not going to arrive in time to take advantage of the uprising in Santiago that Frank País was desperately organizing.

On November 30, five days into their journey, the hapless men on board the *Granma* heard over the ship radio the tragic news of the failure of the Santiago attack. While Frank himself survived, scores of his men lay dead across the silent streets of Santiago. Now there would be no simultaneous attack within Cuba to divert attention from the *Granma* landing.

While their fellow revolutionaries were dying in Santiago, the men of the *Granma* sailed on, adrift in time and tied together only by their *líder máximo*, Fidel. As they neared the Cayman Islands a small plane ominously approached, a momentary reminder of danger. But then the plane swerved away and left them alone.

On December 1 they chugged the last 180 miles toward their disembarkation point at Niquero. Before landing, Fidel checked the rifles, one by one. But the salty seawater had oxidized the steel parts. Then, in that odd ritual of the warrior, the men began to put on their uniforms. From that moment on they did not shave; thus the myth of the *barbudos*—bearded ones—following their Christ-like shaman was born. At five o'clock on the morning of December 2, 1956, the *Granma* touched Cuban soil.

CHE Guevara called the landing a shipwreck. More than a mile from the intended spot on a sandy beach, and near a place appropriately called Purgatory Point, the *Granma* literally became stuck in the mud. The odd little band, so gravely uniformed, was soaking wet and grimed with dirt. Worse, the Batista regime knew exactly where the landing party was.

Despite all this, Fidel remained bursting with spirit. He later spoke of how he had been "moved by the raw beauty of the coastline, with the craggy green mountains of the Sierra Maestra rising straight out of the water." At that very moment he vowed to make the area into a great tourist attraction once he came to power. Meanwhile, however, Purgatory Point was simply a very dangerous area. Within an hour of the landing, airplanes were flying overhead, throwing down bombs at the intruders. But nothing could daunt Fidel. He had fulfilled his promise to land in Cuba in 1956. Now he was, in his own mind, the true son of the Apostle, José Martí.

Meanwhile, up in the mountains, a very clever and powerful old man, Crescencio Pérez, a local producer of marijuana, whom the Batista government called the bandit of the Sierra Maestra, wondered what had become of Fidel Castro. He and Celia Sánchez, a gaunt, raven-haired upper-class young woman who was deeply involved in the urban movement, had waited through the entire day of

November 30, growing more and more alarmed at the inexplicable absence of the *Granma,* which they were to meet with trucks to carry the men to the Sierra. They went to the appointed rendezvous again on December 1. Still no *Granma.* But they never despaired.

"You'd better get going, *compañero,*" Celia told the old bandit on December 2. And on this day Crescencio finally found some of Fidel's men. They were hiding in the unused freezing room of an ice plant in the little port of Niquero. The others had vanished.

In Havana, Batista basked in his supposed initial victory over Fidel, but as always, he made the ultimately fatal mistake of not taking this strange young man seriously enough. Batista was in the house of his prime minister, playing canasta with several officials. When they urged him to send in two naval boats, he said, "I don't want to be accused of the assassination of Fidel Castro." Later Batista would say bitterly, "When I could have been done with Fidel, I didn't want to—and when I wanted to, I couldn't."

Far from being "done with," a very alive Fidel was in the peasant hut of Ángel Pérez Rosabal, regaling the humble family with his unmistakable air of prophecy. "Have no fear. I am Fidel Castro." It was not unlike the revelation that Christ had made to his people when He announced his presence on earth, and it was not supposed to be unlike it, for Fidel, forging his spiritual nexus, was beginning the myth of *los Doce*—the Twelve. In Fidel's version, only twelve of his original rebels survived those first fearful days to get to the Sierra.

After landing on December 2, the men spent the night on a wooded hill. In the morning they began marching eastward. On December 5 they reached a small area called Alegría del Pío, near the actual Sierra. In three days they had covered a bare twenty-two miles. Utterly exhausted, they set up their campsite in a dangerously exposed spot where a low hill jutted out into a cane field.

At four p.m. the rebels were accosted by a barrage of bullets, as Batista soldiers swarmed over them. Che was hit by a bullet in his lower shoulder but escaped with four other men, wandering for days through the forests of the Sierra. As the military dropped napalm on the area, the men found themselves in the most horrible of situations. They had no water and no food. They were forced to drink their own urine and survive on herbs, raw corn, and crabs.

The men had been separated into many small groups, and they

didn't know where they were. But miraculously, among those remaining were most of Fidel's top leadership. As for Fidel, he seemed only to grow in inner confidence and stature. At one point, as he and two others lay hidden in a cane field, communicating only in whispers, Castro cleared his throat and said with force, "We are winning. . . . Victory will be ours."

Whatever the words, it was this confidence, or the unrelenting appearance of such confidence, that time after time would draw Fidel's men back to him and imbue them with the inevitability of victory.

And now he began reaching out to the peasants of the Sierra. Guillermo García, a square-jawed mountain man who was the first peasant to join the Revolution and helped in rounding up the scattered rebels after the bombing at Alegría del Pío, remembered walking through a field of bananas when Fidel suddenly asked, "Are we already in the Sierra Maestra?"

Garcia said that, yes, they were.

Fidel was jubilant. "The Revolution has triumphed!" he cried.

Now, indeed, they were in the Sierra, that abysmally impoverished but magically beautiful world 100 miles long and between twenty and thirty miles wide that was to nourish the savagely reduced but ever more intensely dedicated band of Fidel's. And the Sierra's sheer poverty and its historic sense of injustice soon bonded many of the peasants, most of them squatters without title or security to their land, to the passionate young revolutionaries. For the first time the peasants were being recognized and treated as human beings worthy of attention. The little rebel army began to grow.

On Christmas Eve, Fidel and his handful of followers were actually celebrating, eating roast pig with a sympathetic peasant family. Before leading his men deeper into the mountains, Fidel decided to answer Batista's attack with one of his own. In early January, 1957, he set out for the coastal garrison at La Plata. The column marched for eleven days, gathering new recruits as peasants began to join along the way. By the time they reached La Plata, the army numbered thirty-three men. This time Fidel's battle was brief—and even successful.

The rebels attacked the little garrison directly, leaving behind them two dead soldiers and five wounded. They carried off nine Springfield rifles, a Thompson submachine gun, and a wealth of munitions and supplies. After setting fire to all the buildings, the rebels simply melted back into the devouring jungles of the Sierra.

Attacks from the Batista forces now came fast and furiously. Two weeks after La Plata the rebels barely survived a surprise air attack that came almost directly upon their camp. By accident or miracle, none of them was killed.

The group also had to deal with their first traitor, Eutemio Guerra. This peasant, about thirty years of age, thin and cordial, was a respected guide of the Revolution, and for once Fidel's uncanny sixth sense about people failed him. He liked Eutemio. He even gave him a pass to visit his home away from the Sierra, which was when Eutemio made contact with the Batista army.

When Fidel discovered the betrayal, he confronted the peasant, who confessed and was duly executed on February 17. A small cross carved in a tree in that remote aerie of the Sierra still marks the legendary treachery of Eutemio.

Once again Fidel had survived. This, along with the victory at La Plata, fueled the belief that Fidel was invincible, that he was indeed Cuba's true man of destiny, and that he was even the final fleshly incarnation of the Apostle's grand and unfinished dreams.

ONLY three weeks after Fidel and his men had found a spot deep in the forests of the Sierra to settle and regroup, he sent Faustino Pérez to Havana to "bring back a foreign journalist." Fidel intended to show the world that he was indeed alive and well, and invincible. The confirmer of those facts had to be a foreign journalist for the simple reason that Batista would have censored a Cuban reporter.

Faustino Pérez understood well the mission Fidel had entrusted to him. Dressed like a peasant, he walked out of the Sierra and made his way to Havana, where he enlisted the help of Felipe Pazos, the country's leading economist.

Since Pazos knew the famous and intrepid *New York Times* bureau chief, Ruby Hart Phillips, a big and rawboned woman with an honest and generous spirit, he went immediately to see her in her office. It was not a particularly private place, and that day there were a lot of people milling around outside the small office.

Belying her size and stature, Mrs. Phillips had a high and penetrating voice, and she now squeaked at him, dangerously loud for secrecy, he thought, "Are you telling me that Fidel Castro is alive?" It was the question all Cuba was asking.

She told Pazos that she, as a resident correspondent, should not be the one to go to the Sierra—it was too compromising. But the highly respected *New York Times* foreign correspondent Herbert Matthews was arriving for vacation on February 9, with his wife. Matthews offered the perfect solution.

A tall, graying man of fifty-seven, Matthews had distinguished himself reporting Chiang Kai-shek's triumph in Peking in 1929, the Italian army's horrors in Ethiopia in 1935, the Spanish Republic's tragedies during the '30s. But despite his experiences, Matthews remained a hopeless romantic, who sought desperately to find and believe in causes. As so often in his life, Fidel was to stumble onto the consummately right person at the right moment.

Just before dawn on February 16, Matthews and his party arrived at the appointed place. "The dense vegetation," he later wrote excitedly, "gave the impression of a tropical rain forest." Fidel was not there to greet them, but it was whispered to Matthews that the guerrilla fighter would arrive after a meeting with his general staff. Fidel had ordered his men to make the jungle clearing look as much like a busy command post as possible. The Matthews party actually believed they were in a remote and isolated clearing in the jungle when, in fact, they were a bare twenty-five miles from the city of Manzanillo.

Then out of the mist came Fidel, appearing like a legendary hero. The middle-aged American journalist was immediately smitten. "Here was quite a man," he wrote in the fullness of his exuberance, "a powerful six-footer, olive-skinned, full-faced, with a scraggly beard. The personality of the man is overpowering." For hours, under the dense foliage, the man from the *Times* and the shrewd young Cuban revolutionary sat and talked.

At this point Fidel staged one of the most extraordinary shows of Sierra history, which some have rightly called guerrilla theater. Fidel had instructed his men to adopt martial airs. One by one, then two by two, they marched by Matthews. Then they marched by him again and again and again. One man had no back to his shirt and had to march sideways. Matthews thought he counted approximately forty fighters, where there were no more than twenty, and he was convinced that a much larger force hovered hungrily in the high jungles.

Matthews' long story, the first of three, appeared in *The New York Times* on February 24, 1957. In summing up, Matthews wrote of Fidel Castro:

> He has strong ideas of liberty, democracy, social justice, the need to restore the Constitution, to hold elections. The 26th of July Movement talks of nationalism, anti-colonialism, anti-imperialism. I asked Senor Castro about that. He answered, "You can be sure we have no animosity toward the United States and the American people. Above all, we are fighting for a democratic Cuba and an end to the dictatorship."

The articles electrified the world and caused a sensation inside Cuba. But despite them, Batista would insist that Castro was dead, until Matthews printed the pictures he had taken of Fidel, as well as a sheet of paper signed by Fidel and marked "Sierra Maestra."

After Matthews' historic visit other journalists made their way to the Sierra. Indeed, the Sierra was becoming so crowded that one newspaper correspondent on his way up was crestfallen to discover a reporter from *Boys' Life* on his way down.

THE day before Fidel met Herbert Matthews, he also met twenty-nine-year-old Celia Sánchez for the first time. Celia came from a well-to-do doctor's family in the provincial city of Manzanillo. Her father, as well as other members of the family, fought in the underground against Batista. Despite their political involvements, some relatives were horrified when she "ran away" to the Sierra.

There is no testimony to her meeting with Fidel in the damp jungles of the Sierra, but from that moment on, the two were close. It was one of those romantic friendships between a great man and an ever admiring woman, in which each one's strengths seemed to balance the other's weaknesses. Where Fidel was disorganized and chaotic, Celia was neatly efficient and calm. Where Fidel dealt expansively in grand schemes and dreams, Celia dealt with the details of life. Where Fidel cared for *las masas,* Celia genuinely cared for individuals.

Many who liked and deeply treasured Celia were disparaging about her looks. But this is unfair. Olive-skinned, tough and sweet at the same time, with direct and knowing pitch-black eyes, Celia was a very feminine woman. Even in the Sierra she wore a gold chain around her slim ankle and over her boots.

Celia soon took over the "business" of the Sierra. She ran things; it was she who tended to guerrilla headquarters, to Fidel's voluminous correspondence, and to paying bills. She was his secretary, his guide, his mother, his protective shadow—that one woman in a man's life who will and must always be there because she is the one woman who has made herself indispensable.

IN THOSE early months of 1957 Fidel was constantly on the offensive, organizing new groups and recruiting men from the cities to join the rebels in the hills. At all times Fidel insisted that support for the guerrilla war in the Sierra was the prime priority. In this he met with fierce disagreement from Frank País, disagreement that would eventually lead to a crucially important schism in the movement between the urban revolution and the Sierra.

In fact, the fight in the cities was far more dangerous and brutal than anything that was happening in the relatively peaceful Sierra. The rebels in the Sierra were able simply to move away from the enemy without losing psychological advantage. There, under the skilled direction of Alberto Bayo, they were beginning to view themselves as "citizens of a guerrilla group" rather than citizens of Cuba. And Fidel himself began using the term Free Territory to mark his new nation of guerrilla citizens.

These were months of restructuring. Food was scarce, and the rebels ate mostly vegetables, chicken soup on holidays, and an occasional pig. But their spirits never flagged. Such was their camaraderie that two of the men even wrote ballads celebrating life in the Sierra, and sang them to the group.

For much of 1957 the guerrillas of the Sierra were constantly on the move. Finally Fidel set up a sort of command post at La Plata. As always, he was everywhere—talking, bellowing, thinking, writing, questioning. He wrote his messages, his manifestos, his appeals—to individuals or to the Cuban people—on little scraps of paper, often while sitting in his hammock, his feet hanging out sideways. Celia then put the scraps together into readable form.

That Fidel was the leader among the men of the Sierra was never in question; that he was consistently difficult and contradictory was equally never in question. His iron will did not, however, turn people away from him or even frighten them. It drew them to him. It was almost as though the more rages that he went into, the stronger was his mythic pull on people. Fidel's hold on his men in the Sierra was a microcosm of what his relationship with the people of Cuba would be, an almost amorous bond.

His enemies called him a coward, the leader who almost always disappeared at the moment of danger. To be sure, Fidel did not always lead his men into battle; he directed from the sidelines. He was not lacking in courage, but he was not a willing candidate for martyrdom either. At times Fidel seemed almost a sorcerer in his uncanny ability to determine how to win and how to survive, when to risk and when strategically to withdraw. That he often casually risked others' lives and never mourned them is equally clear, and perhaps never more apparent than in his conflict with Frank País.

From the moment Fidel arrived on Cuban soil, he was dependent on twenty-three-year-old Frank País. The Sierra relied upon Frank for arms, for money, for contacts, and for representation to the outside world. But from the beginning, Frank also challenged Fidel, contradicting him unhesitatingly on strategy and organization. It was only a question of time before the two would clash irrevocably.

Frank's title was National Chief of Action of the 26th of July, and many—probably even Frank—thought that put him on an equal footing with Fidel. After all, under the dangerous eyes of the Batista killers Frank had built up a tight and effective urban movement not only in Santiago but in Manzanillo, Bayamo, Guantánamo, and even remote villages in Oriente. By the spring of 1957 Frank's most cherished objective was to open a second guerrilla front in the Sierra Cristal. This presented a profound political threat to Fidel, as did Frank himself.

As the war in the cities became more ferocious, Frank was forced to move desperately from house to house while the army searched for him with an icy fervor.

At the end of July, Frank moved into the house of a friend in Santiago, Raúl Pujol. He had been there only a short time when the police suddenly surrounded the place. "Peering through a window, País saw several carloads of police and soldiers in the street," an American journalist wrote. "Then, seeing the searchers coming closer, he suddenly decided to leave, alone and on foot." On the street, Frank País died at the hands of a notorious assassin known as *Mano Negra*—Black Hand—who "rushed after the youth and fired a bullet into his back at close range."

Only four people had known that Frank was at the Pujol house that day—his fiancée; Raúl Pujol; a pastor; and Vilma Espín, a Communist who was active in the 26th of July. After evading Batista's men so brilliantly for so long, how did it happen that this day all Frank's meticulous precautions seemed so fatally to vanish?

For months Frank had been working closely with Vilma Espín, a delicately pretty but coldly self-righteous communist girl, whom he did not particularly like. "Vilma was a power grabber," one observer contends. "She had tried to become Frank's girlfriend or mistress, with the thought of being a power behind the throne. Frank put her off and in effect named others to be his eyes and ears. This bothered her very much. Vilma didn't know where Frank was the last week of his life. But she found out. The morning of his death she called him. That afternoon he was killed."

At Fidel's campsite that day there was a celebration of the baptism of a peasant child for whom Fidel was to be godfather. When he heard the news of Frank's death, Fidel called him "the most courageous, useful, and extraordinary of all our fighters," then went on, without observable emotion, partaking in the festivities.

Whether Vilma informed on Frank, or led the police to his hiding place, or whether Fidel simply again exercised his uncanny instinct for leaving people in places long enough so "inevitable" things just happened to them, will never be fully known. But the outcome we know, and after that, any idea of dividing up power within the movement was never revived, ever, by anyone.

NINE
FidelFidelFidelFidelFidel

HAVANA was as enticingly beautiful as ever that Christmas of 1957. The stores were crowded with last-minute shoppers, and the mood was festive and gay. For his part, Fidel did his own kind of Christmas shopping. He visited the village of Veguitas, disarmed the soldiers there, and swiftly returned to the hills with four truckloads of provisions and arms paid for in cash. His rebel guerrilla army was now roaming the Sierra almost at will.

The fall following Frank País' death had been a turning point, for on September 10, at Pino del Agua, Fidel for the first time deliberately lured government troops into an ambush. The hamlet of Pino del Agua was built around a sawmill in the deep forest. Fidel paused there briefly to tell the local inhabitants that he was moving on, knowing that one of them would surely pass this information on to the army. One of them did. When Batista's soldiers arrived, the rebels attacked them. It was a great victory for the Sierra guerrillas.

In November the Fidelistas began sowing terror across the island by burning the sugarcane. Fearful fires raged from one end of Cuba to the other, killing scores of people. One of the very first plantations to be burned was Lina Castro's, an event that marked the beginning of a lasting estrangement between mother and son.

Then, in the cold early months of 1958, something amazing happened. The once despised and remote vastness of the Sierra—where Cuba's dispossessed had lived forgotten in the dense forests—now began filling up. Guerrilla warfare was becoming popular, fashionable, even safe.

In March, Raúl Castro formed a second front, in Oriente. Although he was still under Fidel's command, Raúl was authorized to do most everything in his area, and his performance was to prove little less than brilliant. From March 1 to December 31, 1958, his six guerrilla columns encountered the regular army 247 times, captured six airplanes, intercepted five ships, captured twelve trains, and shot down three air force fighter planes. With 160 casualties of their own, they probably killed 1979 men in Batista's army—or so at least the Castro brothers claimed.

In warfare, the personality differences between the two brothers became especially evident. Fidel existed somewhere out there in political and psychic glory space much of the time, dreaming Napoleonic dreams, pushing his men forward with bold severity and his undimmable faith. Raúl was the organizer, the executor, the far more traditional military man, who depended not upon psychic perceptions but upon pure military strategy.

As the "brothers' show" developed, Fidel carefully nurtured the myth of good brother, bad brother. Whenever he wanted to threaten people with the results of his possible demise, he pointed to Raúl. "He will be much worse than I," he warned repeatedly. And he may have been right.

At this point Raúl began to introduce new guerrilla tactics that would later be carried around the entire globe. One of these new tactics, international kidnapping, proved particularly successful for the rebels. The first kidnapping by the Fidelistas occurred in February of 1958, when the movement in Havana kidnapped the world champion auto racer Juan Manuel Fangio. Actually, Fangio was quite nice about it; taken at pistol point in a downtown hotel, he said, after he had been safely released, that he understood it was "for the Revolution." Then, in retaliation for the delivery of 200 training rockets to the Batista army, from the United States via Guantánamo, Raúl kidnapped a busload of forty-seven American sailors who were returning to Guantánamo Naval Base from special leave.

The sailors would all be released, after a number of meetings between the rebels and U.S. consular officials. But Fidel had again caught the attention of the world. The American public became more aware of the United States' role in the Cuban Revolution. Batista realized he could no longer extend guarantees of personal safety to foreigners, and he was obliged to permit the representatives of a foreign government to conduct negotiations within the republic's territory with the enemies of his own government.

On April 9, 1958, a call to strike was broadcast over several radio stations. Citizens were urged to throw stones and Molotov cocktails at patrol cars. In retaliation, Batista passed a law authorizing anyone to kill anyone associated with the strike. It was a license to kill with absolute impunity, and that is exactly what happened. At least 140 youths died, most of them gunned down on the streets by the followers of the hated police chief, Pilar García.

What really happened that sobering morning of April 9? Basically, the whole country was to have gone on a general revolutionary strike, which was to be carried out primarily by the movement in the cities, backed by guerrilla action in the countryside. Instead, a few shops closed, bombs went off sporadically, electric power was cut off in the old part of Havana and in Vedado, forcing people to use kerosene lamps, and everything seemed to go wrong.

In the bloody aftermath of the strike's dismal miscarriage there were two significant repercussions: the first real meeting of the minds between Fidel and the Communists, and the unequivocal end of the urban movement of M-26-7. Total revolutionary power now gravitated swiftly to the Sierra.

It was in February 1958 that the Communist Party began to adopt Fidel's "armed struggle" tactics. But the real moment of change occurred when the Cuban communist thinker Carlos Rafael Rodríguez traveled to the Sierra sometime in the late spring or early summer. A tall, well-built man, with an extraordinary steel-trap intelligence, he was unquestionably the mind behind the old Communist Party. He remained at Fidel's side for months—a fact still today only barely noted in most histories.

But Fidel was not looking to be absorbed by the Communist Party. Rather, he was seeking disciplined cadres to run the country when he came down from the Sierra. He would then form his own party, which he would call—out of convenience, out of understanding and respect for the revolutionary fashion of the times, and as a final way to revenge himself against the *americanos*—Communist.

As for those *americanos* who so obsessed Fidel, their response to the Cuba of the time was ambiguous. Despite some appearances, the United States no longer wholeheartedly supported Batista. Indeed, outside high diplomatic and military circles, there was a great deal of sympathy for Fidel and his rebels. The consul in Santiago was close to the 26th of July Movement, and a public affairs officer at the embassy in Havana actually helped reporters get to the Sierra to interview Fidel. The movement had cells all over the American base at Guantánamo, and the base itself provided a sanctuary for rebels, who used it to smuggle arms to the mountains.

While American attitudes toward Cuba seemed to take many forms, there was a central policy, agreed upon by the top policymakers. Its main proponent was William Wieland, the State Department's director of Caribbean and Mexican affairs. Wieland, who had lived many years in Cuba, sought a middle way, the way that good Americans always sought. This middle way recommended supporting a third force, made up of persons known to be pro-American, and getting Batista out peacefully.

It was quite simply an exercise in unreality. Here you had a Fidel Castro in the mountains, who was an absolute genius at getting rid of any and all competitors—and you had the distant men of Washington, who believed that, from afar, they could replace him with a new and unnoteworthy group of men of goodwill. Fidel Castro had captured the emotional imagination of his people. There was no way such a connection could be neutralized with goodwill alone. And in its failure to understand the appeal of Fidel Castro, the United States would make the same kinds of mistakes that were to mark its relations with revolutionary movements to follow.

By THIS time the rebel army occupied or controlled most of the mountain regions of the Oriente. Fidel's headquarters at La Plata consisted of a large, rambling wooden house that was open on the sides and gave the impression of hanging over the edge of the mountain.

Celebrities were also being drawn to the Sierra—or to an image of the Sierra, which was all that was really important. By the end of the year Errol Flynn was in Cuba, making a movie appropriately entitled *Rebel Girl*, and the famous Tarzan, Johnny Weissmuller, took part in a celebrity golf tournament in Havana. Weissmuller showed great aplomb when a group of Fidel's rebel soldiers appeared out of nowhere and surrounded him. With all the confidence of one jungle man meeting a few others Weissmuller simply pulled himself up to full height, beat his chest with his fists, and let out a resonant Tarzan yell! After a few seconds the rebels began screaming in delight, "Tarzan! Tarzan! *Bienvenido*. Welcome!"

At about this time the man who was to become one of Fidel's greatest commanders entered his life. Huber Matos was a rugged, small, honestly determined man from a family of teachers and judges. He had been a dedicated teacher and rice farmer before, enraged at the Batista killings, he joined the revolutionary movement and went to Costa Rica, where he picked up a shipment of arms and carried them as an offering to the Sierra. The first meeting between the two men was a propitious one. But although Fidel respected Matos' remarkable leadership and military qualities, the two men never really got along well. The reason for this was very simple: like Frank País, Matos was his own man.

By the time the big summer offensive was started by the Batista army, it was becoming clear to any objective observer that the rebels

Left, Fidel Castro's parents, Lina Ruz and Ángel Castro, at home in Birán

Right, a rare photograph of the youthful Fidel (center), on a speedboat with two friends, reveals a Castro who exists only in a handful of memories.

Left, Fidel and Mirta before their wedding, in 1948. They are standing on Puerto Rico Beach in the "American" town of Banes.

Left, the first family of prerevolutionary Cuba—General Fulgencio Batista with his second wife, Marta, and their children

Right, after swarming down from the Sierra Maestra, Castro's guerrillas pause for a portrait on the streets of conquered Havana.

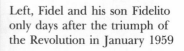

Left, Fidel and his son Fidelito only days after the triumph of the Revolution in January 1959

Right, the core of the Revolution in the early years. Celia Sánchez is, as always, at the right hand of her leader.

Left, Raúl Castro, Fidel's younger brother, a brilliant military strategist and a devoted Marxist

Right, Fidel confers with Ernesto "Che" Guevara, Castro's chief agent of Third World revolution until his death in the Bolivian jungle in 1967.

Castro's relationship with the Soviets was subtle and complex—but always opportunistic. Right, Castro and Nikita Khrushchev in 1963.

Left, in 1989, the thirtieth year of the Revolution, Soviet leader Mikhail Gorbachev visited Havana bearing new and—to Castro—unwelcome ideas.

Right, "the last Communist." Increasingly isolated by history, an aging Castro continues to hold absolute power over the Cuban people.

were, amazingly, winning the war. When the summer offensive failed, Fidel, despite serious mistakes, emerged politically and militarily strengthened.

Rebel attacks now increased on the peripheries of the Sierra, and in September, Che and a comrade, Camilo Cienfuegos, took their men westward to central Cuba. Batista's military machine was melting away, refusing to fight, even going over to the rebels as Fidel's men spread like an inkstain over the absorbent blotter that was now Cuba. By mid-November the rebel army controlled rail and bus transportation in all of Oriente. In December town after town, city after city, and army post after army post fell to Castro's rebels. The turn of the tide, when it came, was as dizzying as a sudden storm at sea, sweeping away everything before it with its unexpected relentless force.

As THE days of both 1958 and the Batista regime dwindled down, Fidel's old Jesuit mentor, Father Armando Llorente, wove his way up and into the Sierra. "One day my superiors in Havana called me," Father Llorente recalled. "They had received a letter from the Vatican, urging us to do a study of what was happening in the Sierra. They were getting contradictory reports. I decided that I would go to the Sierra. It was a picture so different from what you think. First came a peasant, who gave a shout as a sign, saying, 'Don't be afraid, Padre. I have a gun but no bullets.' That was the vanguard of Fidel. These men had nothing. They were almost barefoot. Nobody had bullets—and it was only three weeks to the victory.

"It was two days later that Fidel suddenly appeared. Now he was very effusive. In the evening we listened by radio to all of the battles being won—and they didn't have bullets. The whole world believed they had an army—and people believed that Fidel Castro was fighting all over—and for four days we were having a picnic."

At one point the priest asked Castro flatly if he were communist. "How am I going to be communist?" Fidel replied impatiently. "From where am I going to get communism?"

But then Father Llorente recalled that "as a child, he was always a terrible liar. In fact, at school he would call it his second nature. I would say, 'You are telling me lies,' and he would laugh."

In those weeks Fidel was resting, waiting, thinking. It was a bare two years since he had landed from the *Granma*. In that short time he had defeated the Batista military, brought the city movements under his control, made impotent the old political parties, fooled and neutralized the United States, and used all the disillusioned classes of Cuba to build a mesmerized following that would be his new Cuba. It had been quite a two years!

MOST of the people at President Fulgencio Batista's party to celebrate New Year's Eve of 1959 did not realize what was going to happen. True, the party was smaller than usual. But Batista appeared perfectly normal, displaying complete control over the situation and over his emotions. Then, just before two a.m., he met with his military commanders in a private room, and within minutes the men who had ruled Cuba ruthlessly for almost seven years began to leave the country.

As Batista hurriedly boarded a plane with his wife and three of his children, he turned to the small crowd below and with a smile spoke his last words to the Cuban people: "*Salud! Salud!* [Health! Good luck!]" It was his traditional greeting, but at this point it was outrageously incongruous, especially as a benediction to those thousands of Cubans loyal to him whom he was leaving behind.

He was also leaving behind the largest army he ever had controlled: 46,000 soldiers and large shipments of new arms and equipment. This was the force that had now lost to between 2000 and 3000 in the rebel army. The total defeat of so many by so few is extraordinary in modern history, and the experience would mark Castro's mind and ambitions forever.

MEANWHILE, Castro was spending New Year's Eve at the home of Ramón Ruiz, the chief engineer of a sugar mill near Palma Soriano. Celia Sánchez and a few intimates were with him. They knew that victory was imminent. It was a quiet, wistfully happy night as the protagonists paused to let history take the course they had set for it.

On January 2, without a shot being fired, Fidel entered the historic city of Santiago, home of the Moncada Barracks. But now he entered as liberator, and the inhabitants deliriously welcomed the bearded warrior as though he were a saint out of biblical times. As for his simple and brave men who had fought the battle in the most vaunted Spanish tradition of *la guerrilla,* many seemed almost to be in shock, as if they could not believe that, after so much suffering and against such terrible odds, they had actually won.

Fidel spoke in Céspedes Square to a crowd that seemed hovering close to delirium, and it was here that Castro really began his mass assemblies. At the conclusion of his speech Fidel Castro—who would always remind people that in the year of his grasping power he was the same age as Christ when he was crucified and rose again— proclaimed some of the truest words of his life: "Neither crooks, nor traitors, nor interventionists. This time, yes, it is a revolution!"

With that, deliberately and systematically, Fidel began to move across the country, first in a parade of jeeps, then in a helicopter, and finally and theatrically on a tank. He was a modern-day Hannibal crossing the Cuban "Alps" with his "elephants"; he was the Caesars sweeping home to Rome from the conquered territories; but he was also something new—he was the pure Spanish guerrilla, the virile man of the countryside, marching down onto the sinful cities of modern times. As he moved across the island he paused in every major town and city to be sure the rebel position was fully entrenched, that every fort and city hall was in the hands of one of his most trusted officers.

As THE political control of Cuba was changing, so too were the lives of the revolutionaries. To some, the revolution they had dreamed of brought not glory, but only personal loss and despair. To others, it brought new personal relationships, new partners, new loves.

Castro himself was now inextricably linked to Celia. But seeing the adulation of the beautiful women of Cuba for him, she eschewed a life of passion with him; instead, she would tie him to her in more intricate ways. Naty Revuelta would remain his lover, and now she wanted also to marry him. Everybody around them expected it.

How little they knew Fidel Castro! Not only would he never give in to the woman who had earlier turned down his proposal of marriage but also he now realized that he had moved beyond the possibility of any marriage; it was impermissible in the charismatic leader.

Che, for his part, had met a pretty blond schoolteacher in Santa Clara, a Bible-reading Presbyterian named Aleida March, and they would soon marry. Meanwhile his devoted wife, Hilda, working as a journalist, waited in Peru with their daughter, Hildita. At the moment of triumph she was left behind, abandoned by her husband.

THE FIRST DAY AFTER BATISTA fled, Havana had been eerily quiet. But the following day the city awoke to the roar of angry crowds as the long pent-up emotions of the Cuban *masas* were released. In a raging frenzy that stunned the more sober Cubans, they attacked the parking meters and hacked them to ruins, for the meters had been a symbol of privilege of the old regime. Then the mob rushed the Sevilla Biltmore Hotel and trashed the casino, which was a symbol of the vice and corruption of the Batista thugs, not to speak of the corrupting American influence.

But one casino was spared. George Raft, the famous tough American movie actor, operated the casino at the Capri Hotel, and when the irate mob started up the stairs at the hotel's main entrance, Raft snarled at them in his famous movie-gangster snarl, "Yer not comin' in my casino." Cubans, who were avid aficionados of American gangster films, retreated.

AND then and then and then . . . In the midst of this instantaneous transference of Cuba's leadership from dictator to rebel, Fidel moved upon the city. On the edge of Havana, with great emotion and theatrical planning, he was reunited with Fidelito, the son he had not seen since 1956 and who was now a sturdy, robust nine-year-old boy.

Then Castro, riding in a tank with Fidelito beside him, entered the city at the Shrine of the Virgin of the Road and moved through the crowds of more than a million people. Along the route Fidel's message to the people began to emerge. "We had a quieter life in the hills than we are going to have from now on," he told the Cuban people, few of whom caught the ominous nature of his words. "Now we are going to purify this country."

At last he stood in front of the people in the parade ground at Camp Columbia. As he began speaking to the multitudes several white doves, which had been let go as a peace gesture, fluttered about. One even landed on Fidel's shoulder, while two others perched just before him. Now a kind of spiritual calm fell over the masses. Former Batista soldiers removed their caps, some putting their right hands over their hearts and standing at attention, while others fell to their knees in prayer. Finally the Cuban people had someone who would take care of them—the myth was being born before the people's own wondering eyes.

Castro did not move. He acted as though the doves were not even there as he stared straight ahead, telling the bedazzled crowd, "We cannot become dictators. We shall never need to use force, because we have the people, and because the people shall judge, and because the day the people want, I shall leave."

At one point in his speech he suddenly raised his right hand. He lowered his voice, and in a hoarse and dramatic tone he asked the multitude to open a path for him to walk through, so he could pay his respects to Manuel Urrutia Lleó—a sympathetic judge Castro had chosen to be provisional president of his new government—at the Presidential Palace. Then, one observer wrote in some awe, "like Moses parting the waters, he crossed the sea of people." And always the crowd cried, "FIDELFIDELFIDELFIDELFIDELFIDELFIDEL!"

Just once that day there was a glimpse of Fidel the old guerrilla fighter. As he was entering Havana, Fidel suddenly spotted the hulk of the *Granma* moored in the harbor. Deeply moved at seeing his old friend of the seas again, he rushed over to the scabrous little ship, a Cuban flag now flying from her bow. There, not unexpectedly, he gave a little speech.

"That boat," he said to the crowd, "is like a piece of my life." Then he told the people somberly that he had "the sensation of a person changing jobs. From the role of a warrior, which was what I had been, to the role of a public man." These words were extraordinarily insightful, for this particular man would indeed have a terrible time passing from the guerrilla fighter to public man; from the often jubilant, sometimes playful, and always plotting and ever watchful Fidel of the mountains to the severe Castro of Cuba.

It had been an apocalyptic day of Cuban genesis; from then on, everyone noticed how little he smiled.

TEN
The First Months

AFTER the wild triumph of his entry into Havana, Castro took over the Havana Hilton for his headquarters. He settled in on the top three penthouse floors, where he was guarded night and day by the rebel army and, above all, by Celia. His paymaster and confidante, she also became the portal to his presence for the tens of thousands who now fought to see him. Occasionally he would find a way to escape Celia's vigilance; at those times he would flee to the hotel kitchen to fry steaks or to the hotel lobby to talk with the hundreds of journalists who were always there. At the same time, he took over—for a token fee—the elegant beach house of a Cuban family, in the picturesque village of Cojímar. Here he would hide out when he did not want to see anyone. And he also often stayed at Celia's apartment in Vedado.

It was a magical time. Despite the years of turmoil, the Cuba that Fidel Castro took over was a flourishing national enterprise. Far from being an underdeveloped country, Cuba's national income in 1957 was $2,311,200,000, topped in Latin America only by that of the much larger countries of Argentina, Mexico, and Venezuela.

The key to the changes that would come lay in the fact that the development was uneven; those in the countryside barely shared in the prosperity, and those were the Cubans whom Castro sought for his new Cuba. Beneath the prosperity there was also a structure of vice—prostitution, drug trafficking, and gambling—that was singular in Latin America, and whose nationalist resentments against the United States he would exploit.

Castro was to go after this subterranean structure of vice not so much because of moral reasons but because such corruption clearly corroded his base and made him look less a leader. "We are going to purify this country," Castro had threatened when he marched into Havana. Few realized how profoundly he meant those words.

Always the master political alchemist, Castro now moved swiftly to become the master legal alchemist as well. To give legality to the executions he had planned for the Batistiano war criminals, he grafted his Code of the Sierra Maestra onto existing Cuban law, now allowing capital punishment.

The big trials and executions were, at first, of war criminals like the hated torturer Major Jesús Sosa Blanco, a man notorious for his wanton killings. Sosa Blanco's trial was held in the Sports Palace, where 17,000 riotous and angry Cubans watched. But the strident American criticism of the trials stung Castro, for even though he hated the Americans, he also secretly yearned for their respect.

Actually, far more questionable both morally and legally was the relatively unknown airmen trial. This group of forty-three pilots, bombardiers, and mechanics, accused of carrying out bombings against the rebel army, was tried at the end of February in a military court in Santiago. These men had not attempted to flee the island and indeed had expressed a clear desire to serve under Castro. Since there was no real evidence against the airmen, they were soon acquitted. But Castro would not let the affair end with that. Dramatically declaring them "the worst criminals of the Batista regime," he ordered a retrial. The airmen were thus brought to trial again and sentenced to thirty years in prison and ten years of forced labor.

But it was the trial of Castro's old companion in arms Comandante Huber Matos, in the fall of 1959, that became a true watershed. A stalwart man of honor, Matos was in a position to threaten Castro, or so Castro imagined. Matos was running the economically crucial province of Camagüey, where great cattle ranches dotted the picturesque and fertile landscape. More important, Matos, a brilliant commander who won as much undying respect from his men as Castro did from his, in effect had his own army. Making the threat even worse, Matos was an efficient manager, and Camagüey was thriving, whereas the rest of Castro's Cuba was in chaotic disarray.

In the end, Castro sent the revolutionary leader Camilo Cienfuegos to Camagüey to take command of the province. Cienfuegos found, to Castro's distress, that Matos' forces were loyal to him. So Castro resorted to his old tactic—he would personally mobilize the masses of Camagüey against their *comandante*. Castro went immediately to the province, gathered a mob in the square, and denounced Matos for being in the pay of "foreign embassies" and for having prepared a "barracks revolt."

Matos and thirty-eight of his officers were tried in the gray old rooms of La Cabaña fortress. Castro never looked at the prisoners. He harangued the crowd for three hours. This was no court; it was a psychological lynching. As for Matos, he was not permitted to speak, and when it was over, he was sentenced to twenty years in prison.

But the Matos affair would not die. Were it not for the Matos question, there would not historically be so many questions about the death of the immensely popular Camilo Cienfuegos.

That Camilo was far more a romantic revolutionary than a Communist is beyond question. In those changing months of 1959 he had expressed to several people close to him his concerns about the probable fate of Matos, whom he liked. Additionally, close observers say that Cienfuegos originally refused to accept an order to arrest Matos.

Probably the mystery of what happened to Camilo will never be solved. All that is known is that on October 28 he was returning from Camagüey to Havana in a light plane, when he and the plane disappeared totally from the face of the earth.

At the time many of the "facts" given out by the government were totally false. They said he probably had gone down in a squall, and yet it was a brilliantly clear day. The area where the plane had been flying was crisscrossed with radar.

Meanwhile Castro himself "heroically" and publicly searched for Camilo. He even brought Camilo's mother and father on the search and had them pose for pictures in which, hands cupped over their eyes, they were looking upward into the skies.

But Camilo's plane was never found, nor any sign of it. Without any real evidence his death or disappearance had to be considered an accident.

In sharp contrast to the menacing gravity of the executions and imprisonments that shook that first year of the Revolution was a strange and surreal lightheartedness in other matters. During those first frenetic months Fidel was everywhere—and nowhere. On any one day there would be 800 to 1000 decrees lying in his office, piling up endlessly. Like many Latins, he had the idea that proclaiming something was actually doing it, and he hated bureaucratic demands on him.

In the excitement of the time, the revolutionary family began closing in upon the "new Rome" of revolution, adding still further to the confusion. North American idealists came; European utopists came; fools and charlatans and celebrities of every caste came; democrats hoping the Revolution was not communist and Communists hoping it was not democratic came. All poured into Havana to touch and feel the magic of the new Cuba and the new *hombre.*

Tete Casuso had returned to Cuba and was handling the foreign press for Castro. One day she was preparing him to appear on the American TV show *Person to Person.* The show wanted to picture Castro in domestic relaxation, which was tricky, since it was a mode he had never contemplated in his entire life. When Castro arrived twenty minutes before the show was to start, none of the newly made civilian suits was large enough for him, and by that time he had none of his own. In desperation a pair of pajamas and a finely tailored dressing gown for him to wear over them were found.

"The rage he flew into when he saw that dressing gown was of epic quality," Tete recalled. Finally he agreed to appear in his own striped pajamas, but on the condition that he be shown only from the waist up. "As soon as he came under the lights," she added, "the dragon grew tame. He was another person. What a great actor was lost to the stage!"

On another night, when Castro was scheduled to give one of his long speeches on state-controlled CMQ television, Fidelito was involved in a horrible car accident that necessitated his spleen being removed, and was actually in danger of dying. CMQ television was prepared to cancel the program and to announce the accident. But Fidel said no, that he would go on with the show.

The first question from the panel of journalists came, and Castro talked for about half an hour; the second question came, and again a long answer. At that point the moderator turned to Castro, telling him that they knew his son was badly hurt and publicly inviting him to leave the panel and go immediately to his son. Still Castro hesitated.

By now the audience of forty to fifty was itself restive and even angry, for this was a country where family had always been the most hallowed of concepts. A woman in the audience finally yelled out to the *líder máximo*, "Comandante Castro, who is it who rules in Cuba?"

"The people," Castro shouted back triumphally.

"Then," the woman persisted stubbornly, "the people want you to go and see your son."

At this, but only at this, Castro jumped up, threw back his chair, and left the TV station. He arrived at the hospital at two a.m., and in the lobby, as the doctors operated to save his son's life, he busied himself receiving political sycophants and signing checks for people who passed by and to whom the state owed money.

WHILE Castro was setting up Cuba's political machinery, a river of devoted women was flowing like quicksilver through his life. They were everywhere, fighting to touch him and even eager to be deflowered by him, while Celia stood guard as valiantly as she could, shooing them out of Castro's bed and bedroom.

Amid all these brief liaisons, the exquisitely beautiful Naty Revuelta hovered, never far from the picture. By then divorced, Naty lived in Havana with her two daughters, her doctor husband's Natalia and Fidel's Alina, and though Castro now utterly refused to think of anything so plebeian as marriage, he visited her often.

Naty undoubtedly would have been devastated had she known that there was soon to be yet another woman in Fidel's life. On the anniversary of the Revolution, Castro had instructed his ambassador in Colombia to invite the widow and daughter of the great liberal martyr Jorge Eliecer Gaitán to attend the first 26th of July celebrations in Havana. The daughter, Gloria, was young and blooming. Those halcyon days marked the beginning of a beautiful romantic friendship with Fidel. It was more than a friendship; a feeling flowered between the two that apparently was much deeper than most of his female attachments.

Fidel wooed her with all his impresario's brilliance. Was she going to the 26th of July celebration? The streets were not good enough—he sent a helicopter to carry her to the plaza. "What I remember is a man with an impressive vitality—with a great charisma!" Gloria recalled years later. "Being close to him was like being close to a phenomenon of nature, like a volcano."

IN EARLY spring of that first year, the American Society of Newspaper Editors decided to ask the virile young Cuban leader to speak at their annual meeting on April 17 in Washington. Fidel was ambivalent about a trip to the United States. But finally he decided to accept the invitation, and planning was begun in earnest.

The trip, scheduled for mid-April, would change history, although probably no one except Castro suspected that. For Cuba was no longer the Cuba that America had known for three centuries. Cuba had changed. Castro knew it, because it was he who had so singularly willed it. Castro's new Cuba would no longer be under the tutelage of the *americanos*.

The trip would be a crucial turning point. It would convince Castro's friends that the United States would never help the Cuban Revolution. It would convince his enemies that he was indeed the Communist they sought to make him out, and thus an implacable enemy of *El Norte*. But as always with Castro, the trip had almost nothing to do with what either his friends or his enemies believed.

THE MORNING OF APRIL 15, 1959, was a warm one in Havana. When Castro's economic advisers assembled at the big, ultra-American Havana Hilton before leaving for the airport, they had a sudden and strangely revealing impression of their deliriously popular new leader. There, in the lush modern rooms, the man who was familiarly still called Fidel by just about all the Cuban nation was pacing back and forth in an oddly evocative attire. He was wearing military boots and trousers, but a pajama top hung down over his waist, much like an ancient warrior's tunic.

Cuba's top economist, Felipe Pazos, drew his breath in for a moment because "I had the impression of a king or a monarch." The picture was indeed breathtaking. This man, Fidel Castro, was huge, with powerful shoulders and a coldly withering gaze. That incongruous combination of clothing, along with the luxuriant and unkempt beard, pointed to the disparities that would emerge on the trip just beginning.

The flight that April day was one of the many pauses in Fidel's life linking periods of possibility. For the two hours, the fate of the two countries was suspended in the clouds above the ninety miles of lapis-and-emerald waters that divided them.

At least a thousand Cubans waited at the Washington airport to greet the man who had liberated their country. They unfurled banners and welcomed him with shouts of *"Viva Fidel!"* But Castro was man of the hour to more than Cuban exiles. Everywhere he went, the Americans he feared and hated lionized him. As for Castro, far from being displeased with America, he was, on this trip, enchanted with it. "We have never met Americans like these," he repeated to his group over and over. "We only knew the colonialists."

In Washington, Castro and his party were installed in the elegant old Cuban embassy, where the FBI immediately moved the young Cuban leader into a back room for safety and put economists Ernesto Betancourt and Regino Boti in the front room, in case there was an attack. Economists, apparently, were expendable.

There was no more morally and ethically sterling group of men and women in Cuba than the group that Castro brought with him to Washington. There was not one Communist or old conservative or radical among them. They were the leading economic thinkers and doers. And all of them firmly believed the trip would bring their country freedom and accomplishment. But curiously enough, right from the very start they began to wonder why they, in particular, had been brought along. As a result, some of them began to watch the words and actions of their complicated new leader more carefully.

Meanwhile, contrary to the way he would later describe the trip, Castro was feted, admired, and celebrated everywhere he went. Acting Secretary of State Christian Herter gave an elegant luncheon for him at one of the best hotels in Washington. To some it seemed a rather bizarre lunch, as Castro brought eight of his highly armed guards with him and insisted upon their being seated in the dining room. Finally his men agreed to leave their guns in a neighboring room. They returned and sat on the floor along the walls while the others ate.

Actually, the Herter lunch, proffered to a revolutionary only three months in office and without constitutional power, was a generous gesture. "The State Department went out of its way to provide a cordial welcome," Betancourt insists to this day. And in fact, Castro agreed, although there is some evidence that he was miffed that Eisenhower was playing golf in Atlanta during his visit. Castro regarded Ike as a war hero, and it was for this reason, unnoted by history, that he wanted to meet him.

Far from being slighted in the United States, Fidel Castro was the darling of the hour. He spent five days in Washington, testifying before the Senate Foreign Relations Committee, where he stated that the Cuban revolutionary government would maintain membership in the hemispheric Mutual Defense Treaty for the defense of the Western Hemisphere and would protect foreign private industry in Cuba.

Castro also met with Richard Nixon for more than two hours in the Vice President's office off the Senate floor in the Capitol. In a memo Nixon wrote immediately afterward he stated that "my own appraisal of him as a man is somewhat mixed. The one fact we can be sure of is that he has those indefinable qualities which make him a leader of men. Whatever we may think of him, he is going to be a great factor in the development of Cuba and very possibly in Latin American affairs generally. He is either incredibly naïve about communism or under communist discipline. My guess is the former."

At the American Society of Newspaper Editors' lunch, which was the ostensible reason for his trip, Castro was asked whether it was true that Joe Cambria, who had been a big league baseball scout in Cuba, had once tried to recruit him for a team in the United States.

"Yes," he admitted grandly, "there was some conversation of that. But let me tell you one thing. I always play pitcher, never catcher."

In New York, huge crowds fought to see Fidel, all the way from Grand Central Station to the Statler Hotel. He toured Columbia University, met with U.N. Secretary General Dag Hammarskjöld, visited Yankee Stadium—where according to legend he ate hot dogs and hamburgers—and jumped the barrier at the zoo to approach the lion cage, thus terrifying the FBI agents protecting him.

No Communists had been included in Castro's American contingent, but suddenly a number of prominent Cuban leftists appeared uninvited on the scene, sent by Vilma Espín, the beautiful but cold-spirited guerrilla fighter who was now Raúl Castro's wife. Moreover, Raúl, always the loyal epigone but also the loyal Communist Party member, seemed bent on playing a disruptive role during the New York trip. With considerable distress he watched as Castro enjoyed himself in this city. Raúl began to call his brother nearly every night, warning him that back in Cuba it was appearing as though he was "selling out to the Americans."

Next Castro visited two prestigious American universities, Princeton and Harvard, where he was received by cheering multitudes. But it was at Princeton that he received his most extraordinary reception in all the United States, and it was here, too, that he gave the most extraordinary performance of the trip.

The Princeton visit came about due to the efforts of a wealthy liberal professor, Roland T. Ely, who was writing a history of the Cuban economy and who had high-ranking family in Cuba. Professor Ely had visited Cuba in the first three frenetic months of the Revolution and had been deeply impressed by the great mass demonstrations.

When the Castro entourage arrived at Princeton Junction, there were students perched in trees who unfurled huge Cuban flags. But the truly generous outpouring of love from these students to Fidel took place that night at Princeton University's Woodrow Wilson School.

Castro entered the hall, in his trademark fatigues, through a small and carefully guarded rear door, and soon a row of bearded men in olive-green uniforms, their hair tied in braids, marched up the central aisle. There was a standing ovation when Castro walked toward the stage, calmly acknowledging greetings from all sides. When he reached the front of the room, he turned slowly to face the students— and immediately charmed them.

Basically his speech was a long plea for cooperation between the United States and the new Cuba. He talked about "revolution today" to this group of students whose ancestors were part of the Revolution of yesterday. He lectured them, saying that the Cuban Revolution had not been founded on the Marxist model of class struggle.

In this speech Castro said something extremely significant, had people picked it up. He said that his men had "proved that an army—even a modern army—could be defeated." In his own way he was laying the groundwork for the guerrillas he would train and send around the world to wage war in his name. At the time, however, it seemed a moderate and liberal speech, and the students loved it.

At the end of the lecture, Fidel marched away from the security men waiting at the rear entrance and departed like a victorious hero, through the main door and into the waiting night. The youth of Princeton, cheering and filled with excitement, lifted him shoulder-high and carried him for several minutes, until the frantic security men were able to move in again.

The trip grew in boisterousness as it hurtled toward its end, and Castro's behavior became more problematical as his patience with formality wore thin. He was at his worst in Montreal, where he strewed cigar ashes over the beautiful carpets of the Queen Elizabeth Hotel, pushed all the silverware aside at the formal banquet held in his honor, and downed the glass of sherry, meant for a toast to the queen, in one gulp.

After Fidel had left the United States, the American press scrambled to identify the significance of his visit. But what Fidel Castro did brilliantly on this trip, and what he would do again and again, was to go over the official heads of the government and take his case directly to the people. He had set up a myth of a revolution of "humanism," a revolution of "bread and liberty," a revolution the *americanos* could not fear and thus would not try to overthrow. He had reached out to a new generation.

The two countries, peoples, and ways of life came together for a moment that spring, but they did not meet. They passed like ships on a foggy night, ships that already were moving inexorably in totally different and finally antagonistic sea-lanes. They paused for a moment. That was all.

THE very day after he returned from his trip, Castro announced his agrarian reform. It was really the key to everything, and it was appropriately signed in the highest recesses of the mystical Sierra Maestra, with the kind of drama at which Castro so excelled. Officials and scores of journalists trudged up the savage green mountains to his old headquarters at La Plata. There they were joined by thousands of peasants who had come to see Fidel.

Castro arrived by helicopter with some of the cabinet. "It rained like hell," one observer recalls. "And we were there for about three days. No one could get out." But despite the rain and the lack of food—no one had thought to bring enough—there were moments of transformational beauty. The law was signed by Castro, Provisional President Urrutia, and several ministers by the light of a lantern on an old wooden table, and everyone slept on the floor without blankets, just like the peasants they were going to save with the historic bill.

Basically, the agrarian reform sounded moderate, and it *was* moderate in its wording, but it was radical in its intent. American and Cuban sugar mills were stripped of their cane fields; no foreigner could acquire farmland in Cuba or inherit it; upwards of 200,000 peasants would receive land. In fact, the peasant was simply exchanging the private owner as boss for the government as boss because (1) the land could never be sold or mortgaged and (2) the peasants were to grow crops ordered by the National Agrarian Reform Institute (INRA) and they were to deliver their crops at the price set.

Castro had embarked on his revolutionary transformation of the country. Before anyone realized, INRA became for a crucial period of time the new Cuban state. INRA created its own 100,000-man armed militia with the aid of Raúl and set up its own department of industrialization, headed by Che. INRA built roads, seized private lands, and created tourist resorts. Soon Castro was literally running Cuba through INRA, while the other, formal structures floundered in the spotlight, mere pretenses to power.

Was Fidel already a Communist in this era? If so, when did he become one? Or was he, perhaps, always something else?

The truth is that Fidel Castro never "became" a Communist as one becomes a Mason, a Catholic, or a Hare Krishna. He did not adapt himself to an ideology; he found an ideology to adapt itself to him. His communism was not—could not be—an act of faith, because his only faith lay in himself and his "noble" intentions. He created his own Fidelista Party, which he called communist, in order to stand up against the United States and to gain backing from the Soviet Union. For the first time in history, a national leader converted the Communist Party to himself.

BY THE summer of 1959 Castro had consolidated his power completely. Now he would get rid of the man he personally had groomed to be president. Manuel Urrutia Lleó was a quiet, inconspicuous but honorable judge who for a time really thought he was president of Cuba. When Castro unleashed his full fury against him, it was a storm all Cuba would remember.

Instead of resorting to the usual Latin American–style coup, Castro appealed directly to the people through a series of carefully crafted maneuvers. It all began one morning when the newspaper *Revolución* came out with huge red letters in a ten-inch headline: FIDEL RESIGNS! There were demonstrations everywhere; the entire nation shook and virtually shut down. At this juncture Castro disappeared, making the people, who by now were utterly dependent upon him, wait in fear and trepidation. Like Hitler, like Qaddafi, like so many charismatic leaders, he knew how to use space and time, to use the people's fear of abandonment.

When he returned to Havana after several days, he went first to the TV station, CMQ, and talked calmly on the air for about thirty minutes. Then he zeroed in on the point, stating that "the reason for my resignation is my difficulties with the president of the republic." He went on to accuse Urrutia of treason because he had even mildly spoken out against the Communists. The performance would never be forgotten, for it was Castro's most menacing to date, and many who had been with him up until then were stunned by the ferocity of this attack upon a man who had blindly followed his every wish.

As for Manuel Urrutia, the small modest man with the long Spanish nose hid in his office in the Presidential Palace, staring at his television set as though in shock, while his loyal secretary shouted at Castro's face on the screen, "You lie, you lie. . . ." It was then that Urrutia started to weep uncontrollably.

This was not a simple political maneuver, where one man replaces another, often without any rancor, because it is all simply part of a power game; this was an emotional, a psychological, a charismatic coup d'état on television. Castro, quite simply, no longer had any need for Urrutia, with his moderate views, and so he got rid of him and, with him, anyone else who held similar views.

Finally Urrutia fled, disguised as a milkman, and took asylum in the Venezuelan embassy, where eventually hundreds would seek refuge. No evidence of any kind was ever presented against him. On July 26, Fidel Castro emotionally "bowed" to the demands of the people to return as prime minister, while a Communist of little note, Osvaldo Dorticós, a forty-year-old lawyer, was named president. Castro's coup de television had, for all intents and purposes, destroyed whatever prestige was left of the moderates and democrats.

ELEVEN
An Iron Filing

ON FEBRUARY 4, 1960, Soviet First Deputy Premier Anastas I. Mikoyan landed in Havana with his entourage. It was a trip that, unbeknownst to the Russians, much less to most Cubans, would constitute the first step in the realignment of Cuba from West to East.

Castro made certain that the airport was filled with every celebrity of the Cuban Revolution. He himself stood strong and utterly determined, a Napoleonic figure in uniform. Next to him were President Dorticós, Che Guevara, and the others. Far from coming there with some sure purpose, as the United States supposed, the bewildered Russians had no idea at all what they would find in this faraway land. They stepped hesitantly out of the plane to the strangely juxtaposed sounds of the Cuban and Soviet national anthems.

Ostensibly, the reason for this first Russian visit to Cuba was to inaugurate a major Russian exhibition of goods and machinery. But on a more soulful level, it was a meeting of the Soviet Oriental East with the Latin Christian West. Communism was barely mentioned, or even socialism, during the Mikoyan visit. "It was only during the nine days that my father was there that he began to realize what was happening," recalls Sergo Mikoyan, the son of Anastas Mikoyan and a prominent Russian journalist. "At the time of the Revolution no one knew what kind of man Castro was. In fact, the Russian leaders were surprised at the important results of that visit."

But there were revealing moments. As Castro took the first deputy premier on one of his exhausting whirlwind tours of the interior, showing him cooperative after cooperative, the dark and swarthy Mikoyan kept saying words in Russian to his translator, which Castro finally realized were not being translated. He asked the interpreter, "What is Senor Mikoyan saying each time he sees a cooperative?" The answer was, "He is saying, 'If we had this in Russia, we would call it communism.'"

DURING this unclear period in the realignment of Cuba from West to East, whatever tentative ties Castro still had to his family grew even weaker. His sister Juanita, soon to become his Medusa-like nemesis, began her terrible fights with Castro. Another sister, Angelita, was arrested on his orders. His mother, Lina, was still living on the land that she and Ángel had carved from the heavy jungle, and she did not like her son's new "moving of the fences" over the land. By the time Lina Castro died, on August 6, 1963, she was totally estranged from her Fidel.

But as Castro broke with members of his own family—except, of course, Raúl—he began to create his own new Cuban family. He no longer would have a personal family; the Cuban people would be his family. After the Revolution it was even rumored that he would decree that all the children born were now "children of the Revolution" or "Fidel's children." The boy who was born illegitimate was creating his own legitimacy. To do this, he had to destroy the ties, the bonds, the attachments to the past. "Only the new was good," the prominent Cuban psychiatrist Dr. Marcelino Feal told me. "They began to teach in school that children only have to obey the party and its doctrine, and not their parents. And they began to take the girls and boys at high school age to the fields to do work that they had never done."

In the fields, alone, without their parents, with only their peers and their ideological mentors, the youngsters felt the old strict Spanish cultural norms, traditions, and taboos fall away. Massively, the entire generation lost its inhibitions in the cane fields of Cuba. Many of the girls became pregnant. The authority of the family was replaced by the authority of the government.

As Castro continued to sever ties with the old, he began consolidating ties with the Eastern bloc. From October 1959 Che Guevara began making repeated trips behind the Iron Curtain, signing commercial agreements with the Czechs, the Russians, the Chinese, and even the hermetic North Koreans. But Castro's intent, at this point at least, was not so much even to make friends or do business with the Communists as it was to strengthen Cuba's position vis-à-vis the United States.

Even those who were aware of Cuba's tentative approaches to the Soviet Union were bewildered by how fast relations between the United States and Cuba were deteriorating. For the truth was that when Castro looked out at the world from behind that huge beard and those hooded eyes, he saw everywhere a pervasive sense of threat from the overpowering presence of the *americanos*.

All that was needed to freeze relations between the two countries completely was a handle. Castro had many, but the one he chose was oil. Cuba owed American and European oil companies—Esso, Texaco, and Shell—a little over $50 million in accumulated debts for crude oil. When the Cuban government demanded that the oil companies accept less money, the oil companies grumbled but acquiesced. At first the U.S. government went along with the deal, but then suddenly the Treasury Department urged the oil companies not to accede to Cuban demands, and they did not. On January 29, 1960, the Cuban government "temporarily" took over the management of the three refineries. This gave the Russians the opening they wanted. Almost immediately Russian technicians and Russian crude oil began arriving in Cuba.

It was the point of no return; within months all American properties, from sugar mills to oil refineries to utility companies, were nationalized. Americans filed a staggering 8816 claims of $3,346,406,271.36 against the Cuban government, an amount more than the expropriations of all communist governments in history combined!

Now everything escalated. In March, President Dwight D. Eisenhower, who never could understand a Fidel Castro any more than Castro could understand him, signed an order authorizing the training of Cuban counterrevolutionaries in the United States. With that signature the Bay of Pigs was conceived.

In Castro's dramatic May Day speech, Cubans and the world heard for the first time what was to become the famous *"Cuba sí, Yanqui no!"*

Then on July 6 the United States announced it would not import the remainder of the 1960 Cuban sugar quota and would not buy any Cuban sugar until further notice. Castro called this the Dagger Law— the dagger in the back of the Revolution.

Finally, during the summer of 1960, the Soviet Union began training and equipping the armed forces of Cuba. Nikita Khrushchev himself proclaimed the stunning words, "The U.S.S.R. is raising its voice and extending a helpful hand to the people of Cuba. Speaking figuratively, in case of necessity, Soviet artillerymen can support the Cuban people with rocket fire."

Interestingly enough, Castro was not at all pleased with this rocket rattling on his behalf. Indeed, he was personally and politically incensed by it. He saw it as another attempt to insult and threaten the independence of his country. But he did something that laid the groundwork for the Missile Crisis that was to come in a bare two years: from that moment on, he treated the rocket speech as a commitment made by Russia to defend the Cuban Revolution from any armed attack by the United States.

While the Americans, with their insistence on constitutional government, offered a man like Fidel Castro absolutely nothing he wanted, the Communists offered him every single thing he wanted. The Soviet bloc was not entirely attractive to him. In fact, Castro knew that it would be unattractive to Cubans culturally—which was the area in which the Americans so guilefully attracted them. But there were political similarities between Fidel's vision for Cuba and the government of the Soviets. Both Castro and the Russian Communists were at heart medieval, anti–individual effort, and anticapitalism.

Finally, the alliance with the Soviets gave Castro the possibility of arriving in history as a new political creature—the socialist caudillo, as a Cuban historian put it. The old caudillos of Spain were all-powerful leaders who ruled without question. But in the twentieth century this was no longer enough. The new strongman needed an ideology, a program, a justification for power. Marxist socialism provided Castro with the possibility of total dictatorship, of power undreamed of on a world scale, backed by an ideology accepted by the modern world.

As for the Russians themselves, they came to Castro and Castro to them at an unusually propitious moment. The Soviet Union, in the flush of the postwar period and the end of Stalinism, had only in the decade of the '50s acquired the capability and the willingness to underwrite a revolution 8000 miles from its border. Only now could they take on such a new but delicious burden.

ONE day in the fall of 1960 Castro was taking a stroll, when he paused to talk with a black shoeshine boy who was known as the most expansive gossip in all Havana. With barely restrained drama and a small smile on his lips Castro asked the boy, "What do you say I go up to New York and speak at the U.N.?"

"*Caballo,*" the boy supposedly answered, enthusiastic at this new development. "Get on up there and put it to those damn Yankees!"

And so once again Castro was flying across those legendary and mystical ninety miles. This time, as they took off, he suddenly turned to Ramiro Valdés, his security chief, and asked if there would be an escort plane with them.

When Valdés, nervous and embarrassed at his forgetfulness, stuttered out, "No," Castro shook his head.

"We're in danger," he muttered. "If I were running the CIA, I'd shoot down the plane at sea and report the whole thing as an accident." There was dead silence in the plane. "What a mistake," Castro murmured. Everyone knew by now how graciously he sustained mistakes.

Then, as if on cue, there came a huge roar, and as the Cubans peered out of their small windows they saw an entire squadron of Yankee fighter planes bearing down upon them. But the planes were only an honorary escort. They literally ushered the Cuban party into the Colossus of the North and into what would be Fidel Castro's "greatest show on earth," at the United Nations.

The curtain rose in the lobby of the Shelburne Hotel, at Lexington Avenue and Thirty-seventh Street in New York City, where Fidel railed against the management's supposed unacceptable cash demands for room deposits—$10,000, Castro claimed. Furious at this materialistic outrage, Castro and his *barbudos,* dressed in their olive-green combat fatigues, dramatically left the hotel. Followed by hundreds of reporters and New York police, they clambered into cars and descended upon the U.N. There, Castro told the amenable Dag Hammarskjöld that the revolutionaries were either going to stay at the U.N. or in Central Park, which would be quite all right because "we are used to sleeping in the open air!" Instead, the Fidelistas took off in a caravan for the seedy Hotel Theresa, at Seventh Avenue and 125th Street in Harlem, where with considerable amusement Castro was able to bring the attention of the world.

IN THOSE same days a Russian ship, the *Baltika,* was plowing steadily along in a rough sea, when suddenly her most important passenger slipped on the deck. He might have fallen into the dark and treacherous waters had not a Soviet diplomat caught him. "Right now we aren't too far from Cuba," Nikita Khrushchev joked, "and they'd probably receive me there better than the Americans will in New York."

As he stood at the ship's railing he mused, "I hope that Cuba will become a beacon of socialism in Latin America." Then he veritably smacked his lips and in his deep, gruff peasant's voice spoke prophetic words: "Castro will have to gravitate to us like an iron filing to a magnet."

In New York, against the advice of both Russian and American security agents, Khrushchev determined to go himself to Harlem to meet Fidel Castro for the first time. Castro, in his ever present military uniform, waited for Khrushchev at the door of the Theresa, and there, on September 20, 1960, the two worlds met and mated. Their discussion upstairs in the Theresa lasted only twenty minutes, but Khrushchev made it clear that it was all that was needed for a new axis between the two countries.

As for Castro's speech at the United Nations, it went on and on and on. By the fourth hour even his admirers were falling asleep. In it he linked Cuba deliberately with the oppressed and recently decolonized countries of the world, and he dismissed John F. Kennedy, soon to become President, as "an illiterate and ignorant millionaire."

Back at the Hotel Theresa, Celia, slim to the point of starvation, carefully watched over her uncontrollable charge, preparing his meals, "protecting" him from the hovering, omnipresent women, and overseeing the money. On every floor of the hotel the rough *barbudos* cooked their favorite recipes. They would go down in New York memory as the ones who "plucked chickens in the city's hotels." Very probably the chicken plucking was not just related to their meals. At least some of those *barbudos* were practicing the rites of *Santería,* something that no one in the hotel suspected.

The minute Castro returned to Cuba that fall, he announced he was creating *Comités para la Defensa de la Revolución*—Committees for the Defense of the Revolution—to wage a campaign of collective vigilance. It was a dramatic moment, and an ominous one. These committees were to become infamous in Cuba as they developed into neighborhood spy organizations; now no one could park a strange car in an area without being questioned, no one could come and go without being noted, no one's life was his own.

During this time, one after another the moderates and the democrats continued to leave Cuba. To them it was an alien place. By the time they left disconsolately for foreign shores, many of them were fractured individuals, without following and largely without mourners. And all realized, usually with considerable pain, that somewhere along the way they had lost their country.

TWELVE
The Bay of Pigs

B AHÍA de Cochinos—Bay of Pigs—is a sparkling finger of water that juts into a vast swamp on the southern coast of the province of Matanzas. In the first year of the Revolution, Castro had constructed a small house in the middle of the swampy lake. It was put together with sheets of zinc and aluminum and floated incongruously on barrels. He often retreated to it in the post-triumph days.

With its crocodile-ridden swamps and sinuous coves, Bahía de Cochinos was an ideal place for a guerrilla landing. In fact, Castro himself once said so. Ironically, it would not be Castro's guerrillas who would land there; it would be his enemies.

The Bay of Pigs became the United States' first—but certainly not last—attempt to use traditional regular military power against a brilliant irregular enemy. And it was John F. Kennedy, the vigorous ruling prince of Camelot, to whom history bequeathed the task of dealing creatively with this new period and its new methods of warfare.

Like Castro, Kennedy and many of the men around him had a new vision for their country. While Fidel Castro was creating his own form of Marxist internationalism, Kennedy was trying to sculpt a new, competitive, and ultimately victorious democratic internationalism that would include everything from a Peace Corps to the training of guerrillas.

Actually, the general outline of a Bay of Pigs invasion was decided upon shortly after Castro's visit to the United States in the spring of 1959. By the end of 1959 Cuban exiles were being recruited for training by the CIA in camps in Guatemala and Nicaragua. The purpose of the covert action, approved by Eisenhower in March 1960, was "to bring about the replacement of the Castro regime."

John F. Kennedy inherited the plan in almost a casual way and at first looked on it only as a contingency. Then bureaucratic momentum took over, and the event that was to go down in history as his first major presidential act and premiere policy disaster was acted out with the star-crossed inevitability of a Greek tragedy.

As the planning progressed, the military tactics changed from the much-talked-about new guerrilla or irregular warfare to a traditional Normandy Beach–style landing in the Bay of Pigs. The Americans believed that the Cuban exiles could land there secretly and work their way inland, fleeing to the Escambray Mountains in an emergency. Meanwhile the President barely paid attention when CIA director Allen Dulles briefed him on the change in military strategy for the Bay of Pigs operation—a change that came about largely because the CIA could not bring itself to trust the new irregular type of warfare.

On Friday, April 14, 1961, Castro paced back and forth, in full battle dress, at the national military headquarters in suburban Havana. Knowing that something was coming, he was both anxious and exhilarated, in part because this would be the first time he would stand up directly against the Americans. He was more than ready—his regular army of 25,000 men now was buttressed by some 200,000 militiamen. On that Friday an American ship was spotted off the coast of Oriente. But Castro went to bed; as he rightly suspected, the ship was simply one of many diversions the CIA had planned. The planes that came the next day were not.

Castro awoke at dawn to the ominous noise of B-26 bombers flying low over Havana. The planes, piloted by Cuban exiles, hit Camp Libertad airport, San Antonio, and Santiago de Cuba. An avid student of military history, Castro had assumed that the first step of the invasion would be an attack on his airfields, so he had dispersed the planes in his small air force. This one move meant the difference between victory and defeat. In the bombing raids that Saturday, Castro lost five planes, but he was left with four British Sea Fury light attack bombers, one B-26, and three T-33s. It would be enough.

But it was, as always, in the realm of the psychological and the symbolic that Castro's ramparts were most unbreachable. "On the night of the bombing, thousands of people filed past the row of the bomb victims' coffins at the university," an American journalist recalled. "Revolutionary music blared through loudspeakers. The following day tens of thousands of soldiers, militia people, and women and men, old and young, followed behind the trucks carrying the coffins in a death-cadence march to the cemetery.

"After the burial an enraged Fidel Castro spoke from a jerry-built wooden platform in front of the cemetery's ornate entrance. Fidel's speech was as angry as the sun was hot that day. The people shouted for vengeance over and over again! '*Paredón . . . paredón . . . paredón!*' " And then came a new message, one Castro had long been preparing. "What the imperialists cannot pardon us for," he shouted, "is for making a socialist revolution in the very nostrils of the United States!"

These words marked a historic moment: the first time Castro had referred publicly and openly to the Cuban Revolution as socialist. And this new definition of reality traveled across Cuba like blood through open and receptive veins.

THE 1400 *brigadistas*—the Cuban exiles of Brigade 2506 who left Nicaragua by ship the afternoon of April 14—were in a high state of exaltation. They believed with all their hearts that soon they would succeed in becoming the new rulers of Cuba. Four days earlier John F. Kennedy had stated that no U.S. forces would be involved in their attack, but they simply did not believe he meant it.

Adding to the sorrowful *comedia*, the Nicaraguan dictator Luis Somoza himself saw them off at Puerto Cabezas. Surrounded by his ever present bodyguard, Somoza cried after them, "Bring me a couple of hairs from Castro's beard!" As a crimson sun set over the beckoning Caribbean, American destroyers carried them inexorably to a Cuba they still pitifully thought of as home.

Meanwhile, in Havana, Castro had been wondering what in God's name had happened to them. Why, he kept asking himself, had the invaders not yet attacked? Finally, on Monday, the seventeenth of April, shortly after three in the morning, Fidel, at Celia's apartment, received a report from a militia group in the Bay of Pigs: enemy troops had been seen landing at Playa Larga (Blue Beach) and Playa Girón (Red Beach). As he paced back and forth Castro became ever more certain of what the *americanos* were going to do. His response was direct and uncomplicated: enemy supply ships must be sunk immediately and the beachhead must be made to collapse.

That night Castro was on the phone constantly, alerting all of his troops and sending nearby battalions rushing to the Bay of Pigs. But it was his small air force that won the battle, before the rest of the fighting even began. The American plan had been predicated entirely on the idea that Castro's tiny air force would be destroyed before the invasion force landed. Castro sent his little Sea Furies out from their hiding places to stop the invasion fleet of the United States of America. The amazing and unexpected fact is that they did!

Castro himself arrived in the area that Monday afternoon and set up a command center in an old sugar mill. It was chosen simply because it had the only phone in the region. Behind him Castro had some 20,000 troops and twenty tanks.

The battle was not very old when the surviving American ships began steaming out of the bay, stranding some 1350 *brigadistas*. Virtually abandoned on the beach, they were forced to rely on whatever ammunition and food they carried with them. The CIA had been so certain that Castro's air force would be destroyed that they had not taken even the basic precaution of placing antiaircraft weapons aboard the ships.

In Washington, a unique political and diplomatic minuet was being danced out, in sorrow but also in self-righteousness. The meeting of President Kennedy and his advisers began that Tuesday night at 11:58 and lasted until 2:46 the next morning. Almost all were in white tie and tails, having come to the meeting from a formal White House party, which John Kennedy had entered to the tune of "Mr. Wonderful." They knew the beachhead at the Bay of Pigs was collapsing, and military men like Admiral Arleigh Burke argued that now, certainly, American air cover must be provided to save the men.

President Kennedy finally approved what was in effect the hopeless American middle ground that would doom American policy in all these irregular situations. The American navy would make reconnaissance flights over the Bay of Pigs to evaluate the situation and to determine whether the *brigadistas* had any chance of holding out. The reconnaissance missions were authorized to "return fire if fired on during this humanitarian mission."

From the small hell that Bahía de Cochinos had become, the exile *brigadistas* exploded into hope when six unmarked jets from the *Essex* flew over them just after dawn on Wednesday. But as the men stood cheering on the beach, the planes turned and flew away.

After sinking the initial ships, Castro repeatedly hung back when it came to directly confronting the Americans. The Bay of Pigs, therefore, despite his claims that it was the "first defeat of Yankee imperialism" in Latin America, really represented the first self-defeat of "Yankee imperialism" in Latin America.

It was Robert Kennedy, with his uncanny instinct—which, alone on the American side, matched Castro's—who grasped the next and looming threat. On April 19, as resistance was ending on the beaches, Bobby Kennedy added a prophetic end to a memorandum on the Bay of Pigs failure. "If we don't want Russia to set up missile bases in Cuba," he wrote to his brother, "we had better decide now what we are willing to do to stop it."

In the end, Castro would take 1189 prisoners, including the entire high command of Brigade 2506. Two days after the end of hostilities, Castro began a televised dialogue with his prisoners. It would last four days and become a kind of revolutionary Roman circus. The captives were kept in el Palacio de los Deportes—the Sports Palace—whose symbolism was not accidental. For twenty-one hours a day they sat in serried rows on hard, small chairs, and loudspeakers blared out the names of one after another, ordering them to come forward. Otherwise they were permitted neither to move nor to stretch their legs, and they had to beg for permission to use the toilet. From three to six a.m. they were allowed to lie down on the floor, but the searing white lights were never put out.

Castro began the four days of these marathon performances in a professorial mode, standing tall and victorious before the men and the world as he told the story of the invasion. In everything he said, he lectured the invaders about the Cuban Revolution, reminding them of the abusive past and tying them into it. Although some of the exiles gave in and cooperated with the Cuban government, ninety percent did not. Almost all, however, gained a begrudging respect for Castro. With tireless energy he managed to turn the interrogation around. Soon the prisoners were eagerly asking "Mr. Castro" how he himself would have conducted the invasion. He was happy to oblige; he was now their teacher not only of revolution but also of the war that they had tried so pitifully to wage against him. At one point, in front of a watching world, the prisoners gave the man they had come to kill an ovation. It was exactly what Castro wanted.

THE months passed. That New Year's Eve some of the exiles in prison drank shaving lotion for toasts to the new year, and one man killed himself. The American people, who never had really known very much about these embarrassing men, effectively forgot them. It was not Castro's plan, however, to let the prisoners be forgotten. One night early in 1962 Castro went to the prison gallery, turned on the lights, and announced that he was going to demand a ransom for their lives. "In four months you'll all be gone." He added, "I'm putting a price on your heads."

For once, the American chosen to deal with Castro had some understanding of the situation he was dealing with. James Britt Donovan was a stocky man of medium height, whose prematurely white hair contrasted with his pale blue eyes. A smart, tough lawyer, Donovan had been involved with everything from the development of the atom bomb to the pre-CIA Office of Strategic Services and the Nuremberg Trials. His most recent triumph had been negotiating the trade of Eastern bloc spy Rudolf Abel for U-2 pilot Francis Gary Powers. He now offered to represent, pro bono, the Cuban Families Committee, the group that would try to liberate Brigade 2506.

His first meeting with Fidel Castro was on August 31, 1962, at the Presidential Palace in Havana. The two negotiated directly for four hours, with only interpreters present. Each side had its pride; the Kennedy administration would have no part of any deal in which

Castro received cash, because that would appear too crass. The next day they met again, and Castro gave Donovan a list of goods he would accept in exchange for the prisoners. Donovan returned to the States to see what he could do. He was back in Havana in October.

Then an event occurred that cut off further negotiations: the Missile Crisis. After a two-month hiatus, during which the world hovered on the brink of war, 1113 exiles finally were ransomed for $53 million worth of medicine and equipment, the equivalent of $48,000 a head.

And when the last prisoner was safely aboard the last plane, the compact little Donovan walked up to the huge and husky Castro, who was smoking one of his long cigars, and said resonantly, "You know, Premier, I have been thinking of all the good I have been doing for the people of Cuba these past weeks. I have relieved you of almost twelve hundred liabilities, and I have also helped the children, the sick, the poor, and the elderly. When the next election is held, I'm coming back to run against you. I think I can win."

Castro smiled; he rather liked this Yankee, who was a very different and much smarter *americano* than the others he had known. "You know, doctor, I think you may be right," he answered with a half smile. "So there will be no elections."

PRESIDENT Kennedy was inconsolable about the failure of the invasion, whose prospects in retrospect looked so clearly absurd that he could not believe he could have made such a mistake. But while he agonized in the Oval Office, Bobby Kennedy grew more determined than ever to get rid of Castro. It was Bobby's push, push, push that would lead the Kennedy administration and the CIA to intensify Operation Mongoose, a series of bizarre attempts to poison Castro, to assassinate him, even to make his beard fall off—and to do it with the help of the Mafia.

But there were more—and even more serious—ramifications. John Kennedy wisely tried to learn from the failure of the Bay of Pigs. But ironically, he would directly compensate for his humiliation there by getting into—and stubbornly staying in—Vietnam, not wanting to back down or lose again.

The failed invasion also marked the first great post–World War II disillusionment with American policies for many of the best young

American diplomats, journalists, and intelligence officers, and it laid the bitter basis for disillusionments to come, not only in Vietnam but in Iran, Lebanon, Nicaragua, Cambodia, El Salvador.

From Moscow, Nikita Khrushchev watched the Bay of Pigs first with delight and finally with concern. "We were quite certain that the invasion was only the beginning and that the Americans would not let Cuba alone," Khrushchev wrote in his memoirs. "One thought kept hammering away at my brain: What will happen if we lose Cuba? We had to think up some way of confronting America with more than words. We had to establish a tangible and effective deterrent to American interference in the Caribbean. But what exactly? The logical answer was missiles."

THIRTEEN
The Marxist-Leninist

ON December 1, 1961, Fidel Castro calmly and deliberately spoke the most defining words of his political life: "I am a Marxist-Leninist and shall remain a Marxist-Leninist until the day I die."

As Castro had intended, those historic words made of the still hesitant Russians nervous but now totally responsible "parents" of a young tropical communist state 8000 miles away. And they confirmed American fears of a Russian-Marxist takeover of the Third World.

The reverberating effects of Castro's Marxist-Leninist declaration were all the more remarkable since his words were false. He would transform Cuba all right, but in his own image. This transformation had no greater effect on the lives of ordinary Cubans than in the area of culture. Castro took over the budding Cuban film industry. Then he destroyed the independent *Lunes de Revolución*, the respected weekly literary supplement.

When Castro decided to get rid of *Lunes*, he called together the finest intellectuals in the country for three Sunday meetings at the José Martí National Library in Havana. Before each meeting Castro studiously removed his pistol and carefully laid it on the table. The symbolism was clear. The library became a courtroom, with the intellectuals seated on one side, looking at the government that was both judge and jury. The intellectuals lost. *Lunes* soon was closed.

The steps Castro would take to effect Cuba's political transformation were more complicated. First he announced the formation of a new vanguard party, the Integrated Revolutionary Organizations, which would bring together members of the old 26th of July Movement, the Communists, and what remained of the Student Directorate.

He solidified the educational honeycomb of ideological schools, the Schools of Revolutionary Instruction, that he had begun to put together early in 1960. These were mysterious schools, little known to the people of Cuba. Courses included the Cuban revolutionary experience and the type of centralized planning Cuba would have in the future. At times Fidel would say jokingly that this offered a "master's degree in communism." But from the beginning, if the students knew and learned Fidel's magic Marxism, they learned remarkably little about real, organized, disciplined communism.

The year 1962 was called the Year of Planning, but the planning that existed was totally chaotic. In January, Cuba was expelled from the Organization of American States at the United States' urging. Castro responded to this insult by issuing a revolutionary call to armed struggle throughout the hemisphere. Meanwhile food and consumer goods rationing was imposed in one of the most agriculturally rich countries on earth.

During this time Castro was constantly and endlessly obsessed with the arming of Cuba. Far from being relieved by his victory at the Bay of Pigs, his profound inner need to build a strong Cuban military increased furiously after the invasion.

So it was that Raúl made frequent trips to Eastern bloc countries and to Moscow. In July of 1962, during one of Raúl's visits to the country dacha of Nikita Khrushchev, Castro finally got what he wanted. By now Raúl and the Russian leader had become cozy with each other. As they were engrossed in a long talk about security Khrushchev hit the table suddenly with his tightened fist. His voice had a new pride, and a new arrogance, too, as he declared, "What is more, I am going to give you offensive weapons also, because if you are attacked, then you have a right to attack and defend yourselves."

Bringing missiles and Russian troops to Cuba would mark a breathtaking challenge to history. The very act would break the back of the Americans' prided Monroe Doctrine and open up the heretofore closed Western Hemisphere. The installation of missiles would double the capacity of Russia to strike the United States, and—perhaps most important—these weapons, approaching from the south, would escape the U.S. early-warning system. But where did the idea of establishing missiles in Cuba come from?

Nikita Khrushchev claimed credit for the idea; he believed Kennedy could be intimidated. "My thinking went like this," Khrushchev later wrote. "If we installed the missiles secretly and then if the United States discovered the missiles were there after they were already poised and ready to strike, the Americans would think twice before trying to liquidate our installations by military means." Like so many leaders of countries who had the rotten historic luck to sit astride barbarian invasion routes, he deeply resented America's unique geographical protections. He felt peevishly that "it was high time America learned what it feels like to have her own land and her own people threatened."

But it is also certain that Castro had been cleverly laying the groundwork for just such a possibility. From the Bay of Pigs, in the spring of 1961, to the Missile Crisis, in the fall of 1962, Cuban diplomats all across the Eastern bloc kept hammering away at one single message—the Americans were going to invade Cuba again, this time with American troops.

The stories that Castro would tell later about the Missile Crisis would change with the whim and the wind, but one version unquestionably comes closest to the truth. He told a Mexican reporter, "We planted the idea of an American invasion of Cuba with the Soviets, and the idea of the measures they should take in order to avoid it, because the invasion of Cuba could provoke a world crisis. The proposition was to persuade Washington that they could light the spark that would inflame the world. That was how the idea of establishing missiles in Cuba came about."

Then he sat back to wait. It was a short wait.

Late in August the Russian ships carrying their deadly cargo began slipping out of the Black Sea. Between September 18 and 21, reports began arriving in Washington of inexplicable movements in the mountainous San Cristobal area of Cuba. Nevertheless, without the defection of Soviet military man Oleg Penkovskoy, who brought with him the plans for these missiles, the Americans would never have recognized them. Without the reports from CIA-supported guerrillas in Cuba and from agents, at least one of whom coincidentally lived next door to the prime missile site, they would not have believed it. And without the arrogance of the Russians, who did not even bother to camouflage the missiles from U-2 photography, President Kennedy would never have been fully convinced.

Once the Americans did believe it, a delighted Castro watched as the mood in Washington approached Armageddon. Asked the odds of going to war, Kennedy estimated soberly that he believed they were "between one out of three and even."

But Castro's joy was soon tempered. Suddenly it became clear that something was going very very wrong with his scenario: once the conflict was joined, the name of Fidel Castro almost never entered into the discussions anymore.

The dawning came cruelly for Castro. He had entered the game of nations as croupier, but once the game became serious, it was played out by the casino owners. He responded by dramatically building up the always volatile levels of fear within Cuba. For months he had been preparing the island for the "final battle" with the Americans. Now he began talking in morbid terms of an apocalyptic last stand. Far from appearing triumphant, he began holding meetings at the university during which he told the students, in dark and whispered tones, that they must be prepared to die.

Then, on Saturday, October 27, 1962, an American U-2, piloted by Major Rudolph Anderson, who had brought back the original pictures of the missile installations, was shot down over Cuba. In the White House, preparations now began for war as Bobby Kennedy reported that "the noose was tightening on all of us, and the bridges to escape were crumbling."

Who fired the missile that brought down the U-2 and almost started World War III? Some say it was Castro, who visited one of the Russian rocket bases that day. But the most credible theory is that a Russian commander of one of the missile batteries, most probably without orders from Khrushchev, nervously or by accident shot down the U-2. This was the conclusion of both the Kennedy administration and the Russians.

What was unquestionable was the fact that the shooting down of the U-2 led to the real possibility of the United States attacking Cuba as early as Sunday, October 28, and the Soviets agreeing to pull the missiles out in exchange for an American promise not to invade Cuba.

The crisis was over. Castro watched as the world applauded the Kennedy administration for not humiliating Khrushchev and yet getting the Russian missiles out. He watched as the same Russian troops who had brought the missiles into Cuba now dismantled them and shipped them home.

As the missiles were leaving his island Castro exploded with every curse word he could grasp for. He railed at Khrushchev to the editors of *Revolución*, screaming, "Son of a bitch! Bastard!" Then as Castro swore still more he swung around and kicked a huge mirror that hung on the wall. A veritable shower of glass rained down on the office. But bad feelings pass. They give way, in time, to self-interest. In 1963 Fidel would make a triumphant visit to Russia.

The entire crisis, caused by Fidel Castro, was the closest the world had come to nuclear war. It would be many years before the two superpower protagonists truly realized how Castro had set them against each other and, most disturbing, how easy it had been for a Castro to foment such confrontation because they themselves had so profoundly misunderstood each other.

CASTRO's personal life was practically invisible to the Cuban people now. The notice of his mother's funeral, in August 1963, was the last time Fidel's private life was mentioned in the press. Eccentric sister Juanita's melodramatic defection in 1964 went unreported. Castro instinctively complied with one of the cardinal rules of all dictators: no apparent personal life, no individual loves, no public need for others.

Castro's relationship with Naty Revuelta, however, continued in these years, and she often stayed with him at his Varadero Beach house. Mirta had gone to live in Madrid with her second husband and two daughters, Mirtica and the ironically and daringly named América.

Fidelito remained in Havana for a while, and even appeared with his famous father on the American *Person to Person* television show. But soon Fidelito, too, disappeared from public sight. He was secretly placed in school under a false name, until his later years when he would study in Russia under his nom de guerre, Raúl Martínez.

Tellingly, while Castro felt no or almost no attachment to his family, he often returned sentimentally to the ranch at Birán. Fidel roamed about "his" island at will. But never alone. Specially trained guards traveled everywhere with him. His unpredictable habits—he rarely slept in the same place two nights in a row—made him a deliberately problematic target. In the years following the Bay of Pigs, Castro needed all the protection he could get.

Castro knew that the American government was working with the Mafia to assassinate him; to him it was a replay of the old days in Havana, when he had begun his program to purge the city of vice and the mob had placed a $1 million bounty on his head. Now Castro watched as the United States government broke its own laws, not because of a nuclear threat from Russia but because of Cuba, always little Cuba.

Actually, the CIA's attempts against Castro had started in conjunction with the Bay of Pigs invasion. Mobsters Johnny Roselli and Sam Giancana met in March of 1961 in Miami at the Fountainbleau Hotel with Florida Mafia boss Santos Trafficante. There, heaps of cash were dumped melodramatically into laps and poison capsules were readied. There were two major assassination plots timed to coincide with the invasion—one was with the Mafia and the other was with the Cuban underground. Because of the swiftness of Castro's victory, neither plot was activated, but that fact only created more of a sense of urgency for the postinvasion plans. And in the anger and embarrassment inside Washington after the invasion, the attempts became more "respectable."

Ironically, one of the few men who had criticized the planning of the Bay of Pigs, General Edward Lansdale, was put in charge of Operation Mongoose. A tall, gangly Special Forces army officer, Lansdale had successfully employed irregular warfare in the Philippines to defeat the communist-backed guerrillas.

Lansdale, who was without question a brilliant and innovative man, now seemed to go crazy. He used nonlethal chemicals to incapacitate sugar workers; he hired gangster elements to attack police officials. According to one witness, he even spread the word that Castro was the Antichrist and that the Second Coming was imminent.

There were numerous attempts on Castro's life, but only one came close to succeeding. Castro often stopped for a milk shake at the Havana Libre cafeteria, and a cafeteria employee, who had been hired by the CIA, tried to slip a cyanide capsule into the milk shake. The capsule, however, was frozen, and it broke. The man was too nervous to pick up the pieces and put them in the milk shake.

Soon after the Missile Crisis, Operation Mongoose was disbanded, and it would be only of historic curiosity were it not for the terrible fact that on November 22, 1963, the young American President, John F. Kennedy, was assassinated. For years experts and the public alike have wondered about a connection between Kennedy's death and the attempts on Castro's life. There are so many questions still unanswerable. And yet, there are some clues.

Castro was at Varadero that Friday, talking with the editor of the French journal *L'Express*, Jean Daniel. Ironically, Daniel was there to discuss a possible rapprochement between Kennedy and Castro. It was Óscar Mori, the man who managed the Varadero property for Fidel, who told Castro the astounding news that President Kennedy had been shot.

As Daniel recalled it, the small group at Castro's beach house gathered around the radio to listen to an American station. In time they heard "the fatal announcement: 'President Kennedy is dead,'" Daniel wrote. "Then Fidel stood up and said to me, 'Everything is going to change. At least Kennedy was an enemy to whom we had become accustomed. This is a serious matter, an extremely serious matter.'"

Then something eerily strange occurred. The radio station began somberly playing the American national anthem. There, in the very house of Fidel Castro, a strange circle of men, including those who loved John F. Kennedy and those who hated him, stood quietly for a few seconds listening attentively to "The Star-Spangled Banner."

Castro's first public guess was that the assassin was a Vietnamese come to take revenge for the war. But as he listened further to the radio he heard talk about an American with ties to Cuba through the Fair Play for Cuba Committee. He blew up!

"I know them," Daniel remembered Castro shouting. "They will try to put the blame on us for this thing." Then he went on about how he had always been repelled by assassination, from the viewpoint of political self-interest as well as everything else.

Was Castro to blame? Nearly three decades after the assassination, there is still no proof that Fidel Castro took part in, connived in, or planned John F. Kennedy's death. But there are simply too many "accidents" not to assume that there could have been some involvement. Lee Harvey Oswald had been to the Soviet Union, and once back in the United States, he sought out Cuban connections at every turn. In September 1963 this normally reticent and secretive man took the bus from Houston to Mexico City, and it was as if he were transformed on the bus, talking spiritedly to people about going to Cuba to see the wondrous "accomplishments of the Cuban Revolution." The CIA, listening in on the telephone lines between the Soviet and Cuban embassies in Mexico City, made a recording of a dialogue between Oswald and Ob'edkov, a Soviet guard, on October 1. Oswald was seen at private parties conversing with Mexican Communists and with Cuban diplomats.

Without the existence of Fidel Castro, it is hard to believe that John F. Kennedy would have been assassinated that fateful day in Dallas— with all that would come to mean to the world.

FOURTEEN
Guerrilla to an Age

THEY came from all over, young men and women alienated from their societies and seeking not so much political revolution as personal redemption in Fidel Castro's new Cuba and through his "inspired" word. From 1959 on, this flow of restless young poured into Havana like nervous quicksilver. Not for them the long, patient, imperfect Anglo-Saxon business of economic development and tedious political campaigns—their hope was to forge no less than a new world.

In Cuban training camps from the wilds of Pinar del Río to the seclusion of the Isle of Pines, Castro would train them to overthrow governments not by the traditional methods of military defeat or coup d'état, but by figuratively plunging into the gut and soul of the people from Guatemala to Panama, from Zanzibar to Congo-Brazzaville, from Grenada to Suriname.

The aim of the Cuban leader was clear, although his deliberately obfuscating and contradictory statements obscured it. Orlando Castro Hidalgo, one of Castro's leading intelligence officers, knew what it was from the beginning. Castro wanted nothing less, Hidalgo said, than the "final storming of the imperialist heights: the United States."

Castro poured all of his tactical, strategic, and psychological brilliance into his "guerrilla international." Palestinians, Italians, Germans, French, Spanish Basques, Vietnamese, Iranians, Africans, American blacks, American whites, American Indians—a minimum of 1500 of them a year came to Cuba for training.

As Castro was creating his worldwide apparatus for revolutionary change, the United States was beginning to implement its long-range economic development program, its Alliance for Progress, in Latin America. This led to an epic—although, oddly enough, little known—historic confrontation. Everywhere the United States began a program for economic improvement in Latin America, Castro's tenaciously stuck-together international network opposed it.

By this time Castro had the incalculable benefit of an intelligence system that perfectly fit his authoritarian mind-set. As early as 1961 Cuban agents were being sent to Moscow for training. Cuba's Directorate General of Intelligence (DGI) would come to be considered the fourth most efficient intelligence service in the world, after the CIA, the KGB, and Israel's Mossad.

Soon two Cuban patterns for expansionism evolved. One was to support a leftist government already in place, as in Angola, Mozambique, Chile, Nicaragua. The other was to overthrow an antagonistic government through a guerrilla landing, as in Peru, Venezuela, Bolivia, Guatemala, El Salvador, Colombia.

Venezuela was to be first. Castro's hatred of the effective Venezuelan democratic president, Rómulo Betancourt, led to Cuban support for the Venezuelan guerrillas as early as 1961. Suddenly, in this rich land of Andean peaks and vast jungles, humble policemen were being gunned down on the streets, bombs were exploding in Caracas, and guerrilla operations were spreading. "We almost had a civil war," remembers one Venezuelan official.

Colombia was to be second. Its incessant and incipient violence, its chasmic divisions between the classes made it the perfect country for Castro's guerrillas.

Beautiful but equally tormented little Guatemala was next. With its brutish military and landed gentry caste, with its sixty percent Mayan Indian population, with its constant American intervention over the years, Guatemala was an inviting target.

It seemed, in those heady days, that the long arm of Castro's guerrillas reached everywhere. In Haiti, so close physically to Cuba, Castro air-dropped little radios to the peasants, who complained that they could hear only Havana on them. Guerrillas were organized in El Salvador, Honduras, Costa Rica, and on many of the islands in the Caribbean. Most amazing, groups were even organized in classically democratic countries like Uruguay, Chile, and Argentina.

CASTRO's interest in postcolonial Africa was perfectly in tune with Cuba's black population. In 1961 an office of the revolutionary Zanzibar National Party was opened in Havana, to the confusion of U.S. intelligence officials. Soon Cuban agents and guerrillas were meeting with Zanzibaran rebels in Tanzania. Victory came to the rebels in January 1964, when the brutal John Okello swept into Zanzibar town with a force of six hundred Cuban-trained guerrillas. They handed out weapons and overthrew the pro-Western Arab government of the sultan to form the People's Republic of Zanzibar. Observers were amazed and even a little amused to see the African guerrillas on the streets of the city wearing Fidelista beards and berets, but, as thousands were slaughtered in the aftermath of the coup, the situation proved far from amusing.

Castro's prime agent in Africa was to be the once irreplaceable Che. There was no longer any room for Che in Cuba. He had begun to disturb Castro profoundly with his constant and vociferous anti-Russian pronouncements, in exactly the years that Castro was growing more dependent upon the Russians.

In the late winter of 1965 Che went to Congo-Brazzaville, a steaming hot little enclave huddled at the mouth of the Congo River. There he led his Cuban troops, along with thousands of leftist Congolese fighters, into battle in Castro's name. But the Congo was maniacal madness, and Che, or Comandante Tatu, as he was called by the two hundred Cubans and their Congo-Brazzaville allies, ended up abhorring it. He left within six months and returned secretly to Cuba.

Castro never spoke of Che's failed adventure in the Congo until January 1977, when he introduced it into Cuban history with pride. Why? Because by that time Castro, in his closed nation, could ignore his failures. But also because there was one positive that did come out of the disastrous Congo campaign. It laid the long-term connections for Cuban work with the Marxists in Angola and Mozambique, which would blossom in 1974–75.

When Che returned from the disastrous Congo adventure in the fall of 1965, his pictures were emblazoned all over Cuba. To some, the display seemed eerily more a memorial than a tribute, for Che himself was nowhere to be seen. Then Castro stood up before a stunned group in Havana on October 3, 1965, and read an astonishing "letter from Che." It had been written, Castro declared elliptically, the April before.

Castro's pungent voice and Che's historic words held the assemblage breathless; they were words of the most copious praise for Fidel Castro. " 'My only serious failing was not having trusted more in you from the first moments in the Sierra Maestra,' " the letter said, " 'and not having understood quickly enough your qualities as a leader and a revolutionary. . . .' " Then came the key words: " 'Other nations of the world call for my modest efforts. I can do that which is denied you because of your responsibility as the head of Cuba, and the time has come for us to part.' "

There were tears in many eyes as Castro went on reading what was in fact Che's farewell to Fidel and to the Cuban people he had so heroically helped to liberate. " 'If my final hour finds me under other skies, my first thought will be of this people and especially of you. I embrace you with all my revolutionary fervor, Che.' "

The true believers around Castro tended to take the letter at face value. But to others the letter appeared ominously like the "confessions" in Russia in 1936, after which all the confessors dutifully disappeared forever.

In a very real sense Che followed in the shadows of Frank País, Camilo Cienfuegos, and Huber Matos. Like them, he was viewed by Castro as a competitor for power, and like them, he had to be moved aside—in one manner or another.

The facts about Che's death are known, but the details are far from clear. We know he was back in Cuba, hidden away, for most of 1966, and it is presumed that during this time he and Castro reached agreement on Bolivia as the next step in Che's intercontinental revolution.

So it was that in September 1966 Ernesto Guevara left Cuba for the aridly beautiful highland of Bolivia. Disguised as a balding business-man, he traveled by plane to the capital of La Paz. From there he was whisked away by his few followers to a farm called Ñancahuazú, on the densely forested eastern slopes of the Andes. With seventeen Cubans he began building a small guerrilla movement, one that would remain always more pathetic than threatening and which never reached more than seventy persons.

Che, who should have known better, now put himself and his destiny in the hands of the Bolivian Communist Party. On New Year's Eve of 1966, Mario Monje, the secretary-general of the party, traveled across the snow-covered Andes to meet with Che and to discuss the power structure of his guerrilla operation. Monje explained that the Communist Party would take part if (1) Bolivian Communists who followed the abhorrent Peking line were not allowed to participate, (2) the military and political direction was in the hands of the Soviet-line party, and (3) Che solicited the help of all Communist parties of Latin America.

Che was furious. He was particularly enraged by the impudent leadership demands. Che would never give up direction of the movement, never! And so the Bolivian communist leader left, never to speak to Che again.

And then there was Tania.

Looking at Tania's pictures, one sees a slim, attractive, dark-haired woman, severe, with long legs and a mannish posture. Looking at her intelligence dossier, were that possible, one would see the files of one of the most intriguing female intelligence agents of all time. She had been Che's intimate since they met in 1961, and now in the mountains of Bolivia, she would play a key—probably *the* key—role in whether Che lived or died.

Tania's real name—insofar as she actually had one—was Haydée Tamara Bunke Bider. She had been born in Buenos Aires to a German communist refugee from Nazism. It was Tania who was commissioned by Che to set up the Bolivian "revolution," and it was Tania who was sent into Bolivia ahead of Che. For months she lived in La Paz, and there she showed an ingenuity and a steely dedication that came close to rivaling Fidel's own.

In order to become a citizen and move freely throughout the country, Tania married a hapless Bolivian and then swiftly shipped him off to the Eastern bloc on a scholarship. At one point she gave advice to the lovelorn over the radio, advice that was sometimes unintelligible because it was in reality a coded message to Havana. It was Tania who chose and set up the guerrilla operation for Che at Ñancahuazú. It was Tania who was to seal Che's fate.

In March of 1967, as she accompanied the French Castro supporter Régis Debray and the Argentine artist Roberto Ciro Bustos out to the mountains to meet the guerrilla leader, the three stopped in the dusty little town of Camiri. Against the protests of the two men, she decided to leave their jeep locked up. The men's reasonable fears turned out to be well founded. In a town like Camiri, where nothing had happened since the Spanish conquest, a jeep standing alone, particularly when locked, would draw attention. It did. And in it the police found a rich batch of incriminating documents that Tania had left—an astonishing "lapse" on the part of such an infinitely clever woman.

Among the papers were four small notebooks filled with the names and addresses of leaders and members of Che's urban organization, as well as communist contacts outside Bolivia. There were lists of secret sources of funds reaching from Brazil and Peru all the way to Switzerland.

Who was this woman who planned Che's life with the care of a German-Argentine Celia? After her death in Bolivia, an East German intelligence officer who had defected some years earlier saw her picture in the papers. Stunned, he revealed that she had been under his orders to spy on the Castro people and Che—not only for the East Germans but for the Russian KGB as well.

The only question really is whether Castro knew it. While it would seem that he, with his sorcerer's feel for deception, would have at least suspected that she might have been an agent, the question remains unanswered.

When Debray and Bustos arrived in Ñancahuazú, sent directly by Castro, they were only slightly less ill at ease about being there than Che was about having them. After the two men left, they got as far as the little town of Muyupampa, where they were captured. Without hesitation Debray and Bustos revealed to Bolivian soldiers that Che Guevara was indeed in Bolivia.

Now Che's situation grew steadily worse, and one of the reasons was

Castro himself. It is a little-known fact that toward the end of March, 1967, Castro simply stopped resupplying Che. Nothing ever seemed to arrive. There was almost no contact with Havana after the initial "battles" of March. Che complained of his "isolation" for the first time in his April summary. By May he spoke of "total lack of contact with Manila"—Manila being the code name for Havana. In July, Che received a long message from Havana, but after that, nothing.

On August 11 Castro hailed Che as an Honorary Citizen of Latin America. On August 14, after the guerrillas lost the important and revealing contents of one of their caves, Che wrote, "A black day. It is the hardest blow they have ever given us; somebody talked. Who?"

It would only get worse. By September 28 he was writing, "A day of anguish. At times it seemed as if it would be our last." The men were hallucinating, Che himself was sick, and the peasants, instead of welcoming them as liberators, fled at the very sight of the terrifying bearded strangers.

By October the days had dwindled down to the last.

It was an apparently distraught Castro who went on television to announce to the world the death of his comrade-in-arms Che Guevara. Immediately the Cult of Che was launched in Cuba—and around the world. Posters of El Che became the staple of young revolutionaries and new leftists from Berkeley to Berlin to Baghdad. In Havana's Plaza de la Revolución, portraits of Che and Lenin soared four stories high. Che's body had been burned in the jungles of Vallegrande, but the hands had been cut off to await identification by forensic specialists. So it was in the legend of Che that his hands ended up in Havana, in a sober room in the monument to Martí in the Plaza de la Revolución, framed by the sleeves of his uniform and his major's stars.

The story of Che's hapless capture and death is now well documented. Captured on October 2, 1967, Che was soon face to face with the Bolivian officer in charge, hawk-nosed, American-trained Captain Gary Prado Salmon. "When I captured him, I had to ask him, 'Who are you?' Prado, by then a general, told me many years later. "He said, 'I am El Che.' That was when I started to tell my men to cover the hills. But he said, 'Don't worry, we have failed.' Then after we talked for a while, his spirits seemed to get better."

The order to kill Che came from La Paz by radio, and it was given by the entire top Bolivian army command. He was killed in a small hut, by an officer who shot the revolutionary nine times. Che lay in state on a crude operating table in the town of Vallegrande, and the superstitious Bolivians who saw him there imagined in his face the same frightening likeness to Christ that Castro had always inspired.

People wondered why Castro was so generous with the memory of Che, launching it as he did into a cult that would invade the universities of the world like an intellectual guerrilla campaign. There was really little to wonder at. Now that Che was dead, Castro could make him "live" exactly as he wanted him. In this new, resurrected life, under Castro's transforming fingers, Ernesto Guevara became Che of the heroic poster. But it was a myth.

And that is exactly what it was meant to be.

On January 3, 1966, Castro opened the First Conference of Solidarity of the People of Africa, Asia and Latin America, or more simply, the Tricontinental.

No fewer than 512 delegates, sixty-four observers, and seventy-seven guests, representing eighty-two countries and territories, gathered in the once luxurious Havana Hilton. Russian-backed and Russian-sponsored, Castro's Tricontinental was a veritable carnival of the world's outcasts searching for ways to take power through violence—the Vietcong, Guatemala's rebel armed forces, even the new and relatively unknown Palestine Liberation Organization.

Out of the Tricontinental grew Castro's first really serious attempts to subvert black America and to influence the young in America who had become so alienated by the Vietnam War. Before it was over, 2500 young Americans would be selected to visit Cuba, and black America would be infiltrated at every level. The primary intent was to destabilize the United States and neutralize its will to action.

Castro's tactics, as usual, were flawless. His men would take the young Americans for sessions on a beach near Havana; at night when the moon came up over the Caribbean and a gentle breeze blew, it was a romantic and sensuous place, even for the humorless Eldridge Cleavers, Jerry Rubins, and Bernardine Dohrns of that era. The young *americanos* listened enthralled as the guerrillas of the Sierra Maestra regaled them with wondrous tales of the Revolution. These commanding "new men" of Cuba, dressed in rumpled khakis, were so different from their gray "organization man" fathers back home.

"When we wanted to demoralize the Batista regime," a guerrilla would say, "we threw bombs at guardhouses and in public places, and eventually the whole society stopped." And soon the Americans were being shown how to make Molotov cocktails. They were never exactly told to use them; they were just constantly told how the Cubans had done it.

Thus Cuba became a haven for the radical young. Castro knew how to make them feel important. He flattered them and gave them a heroic alternative. In place of the country they hated, he offered them his country, his creed, and himself.

It was with these radical young Americans that Castro was most successful in helping the North Vietnamese. Throughout the '60s he organized constant meetings between groups like the Weathermen and the Vietcong's chief representative in Havana, who instructed the Americans how to organize more antiwar demonstrations at home, to emphasize the number of American casualties and the number of planes being shot down, and to encourage draft resistance. Such meetings, with their instruction to "bring the war home," had a profound impact on the young American radicals, and as the war continued, on nonradical Americans as well.

If Eldridge Cleaver and many others grew weary of Cuba, it was not before Castro had had an extraordinary historic effect on the United States, an effect that burrowed into the American psyche, into American patriotism, and into American self-confidence in a manner never before seen.

Since the Puritans landed in America, virtually all new ideas flowed from north to south in the Western Hemisphere. Fidel Castro changed all of this. Suddenly, amazingly, there stood a Latin leader who not only dreamed of but was implementing a total change in the currents of influence. If Americans deigned to think about it at all, it frightened them. And it should have. For Fidel Castro had changed the very nature of war.

By 1984 there were no less than forty wars raging across the globe, and relatively few of them took the traditional form of fighting between the regular armed forces of two or more states. It was a new age: the age of the vigilante, of the guerrilla, of the terrorist. It was, in short, the age of Fidel Castro.

FIFTEEN
The Dictator of the Cows

THE years following Che's death should have been a period of new succor and security for the Cuban leader. Castro's friend the Soviet Union was to an extent re-Stalinizing under Leonid Brezhnev. Castro's eternal enemy, the United States, was daily sinking deeper into the worst period of its modern history, with the Vietnam War growing in horrors. But nonetheless, these years were not good for Fidel.

At home, Cuba was beginning to look more and more like her dour cousins in the Eastern bloc. Beautiful Havana perhaps best reflected the growing shabbiness of Cuba; the paint of her lovely buildings peeled away from lack of care, and her gardens fell to weeds. For Cubans there remained now nothing but shortage. A well-known chef, who gave recipes on television, would tell her viewers to get the best meat. Then she would go on to say that if one didn't have that specific cut, well, one could use this or that or even flour. How to present a major Cuban meat dish without meat, that was the challenge of the magical Cuba that Castro was constructing!

Meanwhile Castro deliberately and systematically destroyed every remnant of the wicked past. Statues of former presidents were hammered to bits, books destroyed. The entire contents of an exceptional museum in Cárdenas, which included a world-class collection of shells, butterflies, and Roman coins, were either destroyed or sent to Russia.

Castro's dreams about the economy of Cuba were as extravagant as his dreams of world conquest. He talked of creating a civilization without money and of producing a Camembert better than that of Normandy. A campaign was launched to eradicate all weeds—"a weed-free Cuba" was the call of the day. Another day Castro got the idea of planting an entire cordon of coffee in a circle of land around Havana. Immediately workers were dispatched as if to battle. But the soil there was no good for the delicate coffee plants; within a year unrelenting nature had destroyed that particular dream of Cuba's premier dreamer.

But it was cows that truly riveted him, cows that became the focus of his obsession to control every living thing on his island. With his cows Castro would improve on nature, substituting his planned artificial reproduction for the notably haphazard natural process. He had created a revolution against all the odds; now he would create new life.

Cuba would become a center of genetic engineering and Castro the new Father of Genetics. How? By crossing the Cebú and the Holstein cow to create a wholly new bovine, the F-1, which would provide Cuba with more milk and more meat and dazzle the world. When an English scientist told him that it would work for one generation, but that "the second generation will have the worst defects of the father and the mother," the man was immediately expelled from Cuba. The scientist was right, of course. One cow worked: Castro's "star of cows," *Ubre Blanca*—White Udder. She became so famous that when she died, a distraught Castro stuffed her and placed her in a museum, where "future generations could admire her magnificent udders."

In most ways his cows became more real, and more personal, to Castro than human beings. Not only the cows but all the farm animals had "animal passports"—tiny metal plates identifying what the creature was, when it was purchased, and by whom. Some bulls had air-conditioned stables. When an animal died, there fell upon the owner the sad task of going to the police station to report the demise so the animal could be taken off the police lists.

In these years Castro imported a lineup of foreign scientists who were commanded to be magicians. Dr. René Dumont, a highly respected French agronomist, came to Cuba wanting to believe in Castro's "revolutionary" agriculture. But at every turn the unhappy Dumont found waste and pseudoscience. He saw "mile upon mile of banana plantations where the trees were dying because they had been planted in badly drained soil." In the end, all the experts who failed to recognize the brilliance of the "new genetics" and the "new agriculture" were thrown out, vilified, and excoriated by Castro.

Looming above all these dreams of scientific triumph was Castro's greatest obsession—the "great ten-million-ton sugar harvest." Into this effort he poured those mammoth energies that, for the moment, had been diverted from military expansionism abroad. As he had once militarized his guerrilla international, so now he militarized the harvest and, indeed, the whole of Cuba.

The entire country was called by its master illusionist to the grandiose delusion. In 1969 the harvest lasted 344 days, and everyone participated. Christmas was not celebrated that year, because of "activity in the cane fields," and the revolutionary "holy day" of July 26 was proffered by Castro as the "new Christmas." As it happened, Christmas has never since been celebrated in Cuba. In place of the old holidays, monster rallies, with hundreds of thousands filling the plaza, were held regularly, but there was an almost desperate passion about them, for in truth there was little to celebrate anymore.

And then the harvest failed. Not only was nine million tons the maximum to be expected, but even that figure was misleading because much of the cane was in actuality left over from the previous harvest or prematurely cut from the next one. How would the proud figure of Fidel Castro get out of this one?

On July 26, 1970, the seventeenth anniversary of the Moncada attack, Castro stood before the Cuban people. In the past he had emotionally and psychologically changed places with his *masas,* making them one with him. Now he made himself one with them. The all-knowing macho caudillo transformed himself for the moment into a contrite and humble human being, a man who could no longer perform miracles. They were all responsible for the failure, he told his people, but he more than anyone. He acknowledged his mistakes, and then, brilliantly, he offered to resign.

"No, no, no," the crowd shouted, in its utter dependency upon the *líder máximo.* "No, no, no!"

In the end, Castro actually gained by his mammoth failure. He was not only anointed once again but he emerged stronger than ever. He now held the top leadership posts in the party, state, and armed forces. His power seemed supreme.

CASTRO spent time at Varadero Beach during this period, and he saw to it that his top men had beautiful villas there. Unpredictable as always, Castro would simply arrive unannounced at Varadero, but Óscar Mori, who looked after the property, was always prepared. "There were nights when we had parties," he said, "and we would have some drinks, but I never saw him drinking too much. He liked Courvoisier Cognac. The women of the *comandante* were always about.

There were times when they went to Fidel's house. But only when Fidel sent for them."

Castro's affairs became quietly known. Flowers would suddenly appear on the woman's birthday; and her mother, on her birthday, would receive the rare paella and lobster—all sent by the ever efficient Celia Sánchez. Occasionally a boy in some school would see a picture of Castro and blurt out, "That is my papa." Since Castro was surely the father of the country, this disconcerted few.

During this time, however, Castro did become involved with a woman who was to give him as close to a real family as he was to have. Known by insiders simply as *la mujer de Trinidad*—the woman from the city of Trinidad—Dalia Soto del Valle Jorge was still another of those beautiful black-haired, green-eyed *cubanas* that Fidel liked so well. Dalia came from a well-to-do family, her father, Enrique, having been associated with a large cigar factory. She had worked as a secretary for the sugar workers' union, where she probably met Fidel. When their affair started in 1962 or 1963, Dalia's family considered her a prisoner of Fidel's, and her father told friends that he had "lost a daughter."

By the early '70s Dalia had five children by Castro, all of them boys and four of them bearing Fidel's middle name of Alejandro. Like Fidelito, they would be educated in the Soviet Union, and one was described as having all of Castro's habits—temper tantrums and all. Although it was known that the boys were Fidel's children, Dalia herself remained largely unnoticed. It was Raúl's wife, Vilma, who paraded in public as Cuba's reigning first lady.

DESPITE all the trappings of power in his hands, the enormous failure of the ten-million-ton harvest left Castro dangerously vulnerable to attack in the one area he neither understood intrinsically nor grasped as the looming new power in the world—economics. In December of 1970 Cuba sought to renew the five-year economic treaty with the Soviets. It was this treaty that showed more clearly than anything else the Soviets' disillusionment with their tropical communist revolutionary, as it gave to the Soviets, for the first time, the definitive decision-making voice in Cuban economic affairs.

Superficially, relations between Cuba and Russia looked rather good. In reality they were not. But the world did not see their private disagreements, and in particular, the American intellectuals, journalists, radicals, and liberals who continued to flock to Havana in these years chose not to see them.

IN 1971 CASTRO launched out on still another cycle of revolutionary transformation. On the surface, when he arrived in Santiago de Chile on November 10, he was merely visiting his good friend Chilean president Salvador Allende, the first Marxist elected to that office. But Castro stayed almost a month, and there was much more to the trip beneath the surface. He intended to use Chile as the next venue for fighting the United States.

Castro would see to it that revolutionaries everywhere poured into Chile. "In Chile the problem to us was not Allende, but Fidel Castro," CIA chief William Colby recalled years later. "We took it as rather clear evidence of an alliance between the two countries to carry on the revolution." So the CIA aided the truckers' strikes in Chile and aided the Christian Democrats—to the great criticism of the world. But it did not in truth take any direct part in Allende's assassination, as so many on the left alleged.

When Allende was overthrown by the conservative Chilean army in 1973, socialism died in Chile, and tragically, so did democracy. Under attack in the Presidential Palace, Allende wore a helmet, gas mask, and bulletproof vest as he ran wildly through the emptied rooms; finally, as the soldiers closed in upon him, he shot himself with a submachine gun that had been a gift from Fidel Castro. On it were engraved the words, "To my friend and comrade-in-arms, Salvador." The country was plunged into a rightist military dictatorship; Castro had failed to create socialism in Chile, but he had managed to play a crucial role in the destruction of Chilean democracy.

This setback, interestingly enough, didn't set back Castro. Through the early '70s his foreign policy showed a new and more complex sense of elaboration, of proliferation, and of evolution. He was no longer only fighting dictatorships; he was now offering his aid to fight democracies, not only in Chile but in Costa Rica, Argentina, Uruguay, and particularly in Jamaica.

The luxuriant neighboring island of Jamaica became an obvious place for Castro to exercise his new foreign policy when his friend Michael Manley became prime minister in 1972. Tall, lean, and handsome, Manley started out with all the stars hovering about him. He was the son of the founding father of his country, and he was a man who could move people to tears by his every word. Like Castro, he seemed to think that wealth was manna from heaven and that his God-sent mission was simply to divide it up. And he began to pop in and out of Cuba, often secretly. On one visit he said ecstatically, in what would become a famous quote, that he would go "all the way to the mountaintop with Fidel."

For his part, Castro soon had an astonishing amount of influence and power in Jamaica. The Cuban embassy became the center of activity for what was to be the transformation of the island from British-style parliamentary democracy to Jamaican socialism. Cuban planes and officers began flying in and out of Jamaica through their own private airports, unknown and unseen by the people of Jamaica. Poor and ambitious Jamaican boys were sent to Cuba and came back as *brigadistas* to wait for the uprising. A suppression-of-crime act gave special powers to the security forces, its intent being to take power away from the judiciary, just as Castro had effectively done in Cuba. Parallel structures were being formed.

But Jamaica didn't work, either. After eight years of Third Worldism, instructed by Cuba, things only grew stranger and stranger on the island. Instead of more independence and more riches, Jamaica got poorer and poorer. Michael Manley, under his Cuban spell, was coming perilously close to killing his country economically.

In the end, the Cuban-trained Jamaicans turned to violent street massacres. The bauxite industry collapsed. Jamaicans became so angry at the Cubans that they perched in trees around the embassy to spy on what was going on. What they didn't know was that just before it all fell apart and Edward Seaga became the conservative prime minister, in 1980, Castro had planned to move the Americas Section of Cuban Intelligence to Jamaica. That never happened. But even that failure had virtually no effect on Castro's global plans. There was always a next time in socialism.

IN SEPTEMBER of 1974 a new leftist ruling military junta in Lisbon had begun dissolving the Portuguese empire. Historic, authoritarian, imperial Portugal was falling. But who was it falling to? Around then a curious little event occurred in the southeast African country of

Mozambique. As the Portuguese colonists sat in one of their beloved cafés they suddenly heard a page calling, "Mr. Fidel Castro, telephone, please. . . ." Silence. Then a mirthful voice shouted out jubilantly, "He is not here, but he won't be long."

That voice was all too prophetic. While Mother Portugal was herself paused in confusion, the colonial liberation movements, which had been plotting for years for just this moment, groaned to life to position themselves for final victory. What the world completely missed at the time was the degree to which Fidel Castro, waiting and watching in Havana as Portugal and its empire collapsed, was uniquely prepared for a role in Africa. The hundreds of military advisers Che had left in Congo-Brazzaville in 1965 had been planning and scheming for nearly ten years. Now it was time to ignite those embers into revolution.

Almost directly opposite Mozambique, on Africa's southwest coast, the country of Angola was now emerging from nearly four centuries of Portuguese domination. It was to be a long and costly transition as two pro-Western movements—the National Front for the Liberation of Angola (FNLA) and the National Union for the Total Independence of Angola (UNITA)—and one Marxist movement, the Soviet-supported Popular Movement for the Liberation of Angola (MPLA), became inexorably caught in a final fight for the historic mantle of Portuguese power. But it was to be two outside forces that would win—the Portuguese military's leftist factions and Fidel Castro.

In the murky months of 1974 and 1975 plotters crisscrossed the globe from Lisbon to Havana, from Angola to Congo-Brazzaville, and back to Havana again. The Portuguese military left, in particular, moved with deliberate drama, back and forth to Cuba, making their deals. For Castro the key was the man who would come to be called *O Almirante Vermelho*—the Red Admiral.

Admiral Antonio Rosa Coutinho, named by the Portuguese military junta as the all-powerful commissioner of Angola, found that his tactics fit perfectly with Castro's. From his temporary but powerful perch in Angola he immediately decided and decreed that the Marxist MPLA, with its abundance of doctors, teachers, and intellectuals, "was the only real political force." He would recognize only them, and by giving them money and facilitating the entry of the Cuban troops, he would preclude any other victory.

In the fall of 1975 Castro's own military actions clearly warned of his long-term plans. In late August and early September the top Cuban general staff began suddenly appearing in Angola. And in Cuba itself there were war exercises involving large numbers of troops. All of this would not have been possible without the Russians, who had been backing the MPLA for years.

The Cuban armada that Fidel Castro personally sent off to Angola in the dawn of November 7, 1975, might have reminded a romantic of the original Spanish armada. It was a thing to behold, a new creature from a Third World flexing its muscles in a remarkably new way. First moved a battalion of Castro's own personal Prime Minister's Reserve Troops and the Special Forces of the Commander in Chief, about 650 men sent by air. They flew across a hostile ocean to Guinea-Bissau, then proceeded in secrecy to Congo-Brazzaville, where they landed without lights. Tanned and in summer sportswear, they looked more like tourists than international revolutionaries. They carried their machine guns in their briefcases. Later a number of cargo ships with a normal capacity of eighty crewmen set sail with as many as 1000 soldiers aboard, plus armored cars, armaments, and explosives.

Castro's strategy was clear: with Soviet logistical support he would rout the South African troops who had belatedly entered Angola across the southern Namibian border, and at the same time put the blame for his own new kind of interventionism on the apartheid government of South Africa. Leading the MPLA, he would assure that Angola's capital city, Luanda, would be taken by the MPLA before the independence day the retreating Portuguese had proclaimed for November 11. The MPLA would then be the government in fact of Angola, thus sidestepping the promises of elections.

For years Castro would argue vociferously in the world forums of public opinion that he had entered Angola in response to a legitimate call from the "legitimate government of Angola." But that was palpably absurd and even easily disproven. There *was* no government of Angola when Castro sent in his troops. The city of Luanda was in the throes of anarchy. So it was that on November 11, 1975, with all the other movements successfully kept out of Luanda by the intervention of Cuban troops, the MPLA entered the city and proclaimed the country independent.

CUBA EMERGED TRIUMPHANT from Angola. By spring of 1977 Castro was making a widely publicized tour of Africa—Algeria, Libya, South Yemen, Somalia, Ethiopia, Tanzania, Mozambique, and Angola— much like Caesar inspecting the outer provinces of Rome.

He was indeed a modern-day conqueror. With his move into Angola, Castro made political and military history that was little realized at the time. The invasion showed that the Cubans could now be readied for overseas combat; it illustrated the degree to which Cuba, far from being only some poor surrogate of the Soviet Union, was actually a partner of the superpower. Most of all, Castro was in Angola because it was one of the three places in the world where United States–supported forces were at war with Soviet-supported forces. Angola was simply one more new and far more extravagant place in which to fight the United States.

As he dug in to stay, Castro proceeded to demonstrate that he was able not only to export fighting men but also to export the structures he had created in Cuba. "Liberated" Angola was forced into the same mold as revolutionary Cuba. The Angolan Popular Armed Forces for the Liberation of Angola were structured exactly after the Cuban army. Castro coined a new money for Angola, the *cuanza*, named in homage to a battle the Cubans—not the Angolans—had fought at that river. Hospitals and hotels were reserved exclusively for Cuban officials. The best beaches were for Cubans only and soon had PRIVATE signs just like those placed by the hated United Fruit Company on Puerto Rico Beach in Castro's youth. Cuba even exported its dismal economics: between 1975 and 1977 Angola's gross domestic production and growth rate decreased by fifteen percent.

But for the moment Fidel Castro was reaping the fruits of triumph. Even the General Assembly of the United Nations gave him its approval by recognizing the legitimacy of the struggles for national liberation in Africa. He was at the dizzying height of his powers. And there would be still more to come.

JUST as there could have been no success for the MPLA in Angola without Cuba, so, too, the Marxist Sandinista revolution in Nicaragua would never have existed without Fidel Castro. These were the young Nicaraguans he had wooed to Havana immediately after they formed the Sandinista National Liberation Front (FSLN), in July 1961. The front was named after the famous Nicaraguan guerrilla fighter Augusto Sandino, who had fallen in a guerrilla war against the American-supported Nicaraguan military in the 1930s. Unquestionably, Sandino was one of Castro's inspirations, and now, in turn, Castro became an inspiration to Sandino's namesakes. The FSLN was so politically attuned to Cuba that it even adopted the red-and-black colors of the 26th of July Movement.

It was in the last year before the Sandinistas' triumph, in July 1979, that Castro played his most crucial role in Nicaragua. At the time the Sandinistas were divided into three groups. He called their leaders to Havana for a series of meetings and presented them with dire warnings. He told them that he would support them only if they unified. Political unity, economic moderation, and confrontation avoidance: that was the triumvirate of advice he offered this new generation of revolutionaries.

Castro's moves were largely tactical. He was uncertain that the Soviets would support another revolutionary state in the area. And he knew he could not send massive numbers of armed soldiers to Nicaragua, as he had to Africa, without inviting confrontation with the United States. At the time it seemed to the world that the Cubans were playing a surprisingly minor role. But behind the scenes, Havana was the coordinator of virtually every step of the Nicaraguan revolt. Even during the actual fighting, ever present in the communications center of his Ministry of the Interior, Castro monitored broadcasts from the Nicaraguan army and passed information—and precise orders—on to the Sandinistas.

On July 19 the battle-wearied Sandinistas, with their red-and-black bandannas and their insouciantly noble bearing, marched into Managua and finally overthrew the hated American-supported dictator Anastasio Somoza.

Although it was not generally known, Castro often flew clandestinely that first year to Managua, landing at a special airstrip on what had been one of the large, elegant estates of Somoza. By the first anniversary of the Nicaraguan revolution, however, Castro was no longer keeping his visits to Managua secret. He was now ready to quite openly dare the United States, which was becoming increasingly troubled over the Marxization of the Sandinistas.

In 1980 Castro arrived, to every possible honor, at Managua's international airport, striding confidently down the steps of the plane and embracing everyone in sight with his huge bearlike grasp. Within two years he had 2000 security advisers and 4000 civilian professionals working throughout the country in a wide variety of activities. In 1981 he gave Sandinista Nicaragua $64 million; in 1982, $130 million. Meanwhile he was also bringing 1200 Nicaraguans a year to Cuba for training.

As for the Soviets, they saw the victory in Nicaragua as another U.S. defeat. On October 20, 1980, the Soviet Central Committee formally added the countries of Central America to the list of states in Africa and Asia that could be expected to undergo revolutionary changes of a socialist orientation. They owed their revolutionary son, Fidel Castro, a good deal—and he well knew it.

SIXTEEN
Fidel's Grenada—Death in a Small Place

WHILE the eyes of the world were focused on the sudden triumph of the Sandinistas in Nicaragua, in July 1979, few realized that another Castro-inspired revolution had come to pass in the single most unlikely spot for revolution in the entire Caribbean, Grenada.

That March a small band of only forty men had overthrown the strange government of the island's very strange leader, Sir Eric Gairy, a dark-spirited man who could often be found out in the dark of night vigilantly searching the skies for UFOs, while his brutal Mongoose Gang was out terrorizing the gentle Grenadan people.

How different Castro's young revolutionaries seemed from the evil Gairy. "The revo," as the rebels fondly called the change, announced itself over the local radio station when the reggae music suddenly stopped. The rebels then seized the True Blue Army headquarters, and it was all over in forty-eight hours.

The leader of the coup was a lithely handsome bearded young man, Maurice Bishop. A romantic revolutionary, "Brother Maurice" had been trained as a lawyer—and also in British radical politics—in London. Indeed, Bishop's New Jewel Movement adepts were soon boasting breathlessly that theirs was nothing less than the first Marxist revolution in the English-speaking world!

If the mood of Maurice Bishop was almost always jovial, inspired revolution was joylessly real. To the south, Guyana had turned to the left in the early '70s; Suriname was on the brink; in 1979 St. Lucia also began to move to the left. Now, in Grenada, Castro lost no time in supporting his revolutionary leap into the eastern Caribbean. By November of 1979 he had sent 300 Cuban construction workers to build the new airport Grenada so badly needed, and he agreed to pay half the $50 million construction cost. Rumors spread throughout the island that there were truckloads of Cuban arms hidden somewhere.

For Grenada, Castro was to serve as an intermediary in transfers of Soviet arms, to be delivered at night to hidden depots across the island. In return, Grenada was to provide information on the other liberation movements in the Caribbean. These agreements seemed unimportant, but in truth they provided Castro with his first real opening into the English-speaking Caribbean. For their part, the Cubans introduced the Grenadians to the labyrinth of Soviet international front organizations. Of course, no one could say that all the Cuban help was perfect. At one political bureau meeting it was duly recorded that, "of the ten boats that were donated to us by Cuba, only two are working" and those two "can collapse anytime." But then Castro could not give to Grenada what he could not give to Cuba.

By 1982 the Russians were signing deadly serious, top-secret economic and military treaties, agreements, and protocols with the little island nation of Grenada, as though it had grown into a big country overnight. The amount of military weaponry and equipment they provided was enough to outfit a force of 10,000 men. In addition, the practical Grenadians asked for autobuses, loudspeakers, six English typewriters, and 2000 folding chairs—and four guillotines.

At Pearl's airport, a special little Russian Antonov II plane waited patiently for the right moment to move. The Soviets said the plane was for crop dusting, on an island where there were no crops to dust. In actuality, it was waiting to drop off small paramilitary units on St. Vincent, St. Lucia, Dominica, and Antigua, units that could easily overthrow those unprotected little democratic governments.

As CASTRO expanded his guerrilla activities into Grenada, he was hobbled by realities at home. For the first time, in December 1979, he had to tell the Cuban people what was indeed the truth—that there would be no end to the economic hardship. Forced to liberalize, Castro increased the minimum wage, allowed a certain amount of private business on a limited free-market basis, and issued licenses to crafts-men and entrepreneurs.

At the same time, he created still another alternate military force, the Militia of Territorial Troops. With active-duty armed forces of 225,000, plus 190,000 reservists and 1.2 million persons now being equipped and trained in these new militias, Cuba had not only the best-equipped military force in Latin America but also a force that was larger than the U.S. National Guard and military reserves combined! The militias also served to protect him from his "friends," the Soviets. He was convinced they were plotting to replace him, and at that tense moment he was right.

Most said his turn of mood—his turn of luck—came in 1980 because of the one possibility he had never really believed possible: the death of Celia. This consummately loyal human being, this irreplace-able companion in arms and in life, died of cancer on January 11. Since virtually the moment they had met, that damp, misty early dawn in 1957 in the Sierra, she had been his first and last and at times his only real tie to reality. Now she was suddenly gone.

In his office, he whiled away melancholy hours looking at designs for statues to be built to honor Celia. More and more he was the sole caretaker of the legend that was also singularly Celia's legend as well, for that most beloved and compelling part of his life was the one thing he could share with no other woman.

Then on April 1, less than three months after her death, his fortunes turned even worse when six Cubans seeking political asylum crashed through the gate of the Peruvian embassy in Havana, killing a Cuban policeman who had been guarding it.

Castro was utterly enraged at this challenge to his rule. Now, in order to show that the masses would not really desert him, he chose a typical Castro maneuver: instead of closing the Peruvian embassy, he went on the offense, withdrawing the embassy's Cuban military guard and even going so far as to announce the withdrawal publicly. This time his tactic was terribly wrong. For the next seventy-two hours an astonishing 10,800 Cubans poured into the embassy, desperately seeking escape from their homeland. In the palace, Castro paced, and exploded in waves of anger.

By now Castro no longer depended solely upon his own instinct of the moment. He had crisis-management teams of sociologists and psychologists who recommended relieving the discontent within the country by opening a safety valve. On April 21 Castro announced that those wanting to leave would be permitted to go by boats to Florida from the small Cuban port of Mariel. In the end, 120,000 fled desperately to Miami in the historic boat lift, bringing the number of Cubans who had left Cuba since 1959 to 1.5 million.

Castro's terms were cruel beyond even the expectations of those who hated him. He permitted only one family member to leave on each boat. The others were chosen by the Cuban government, and many were released criminals and known psychopaths. The ships were overcharged at every turn by the Cuban government, and Cuban soldiers brutishly forced the refugees through a ritual of brushing the Cuban soil from their shoes before leaving.

The Mariel boat lift provided illumination on parts of Castro's heretofore closed world. The released prisoners talked for the first time about Castro's prisons, and the world learned of sadistic beatings, of cells flooded so suddenly the prisoners thought they would drown, of political prisoners who refused to be reeducated into Castroism and who were then forced to remain for long periods naked.

Once the Marielito prisoners were released in the United States, American lawmen across the country were almost immediately faced with a crime wave so vicious, so without norms, so desocialized, that even they were stunned. These men of Castro's prisons seemed to believe in nothing and to be living effectively outside civilization.

Accustomed to taking the offensive, Castro began to find himself now constantly fighting to maintain even a reasonable defensive position. In his speeches he now raged endlessly against *incompetentes* and *indolentes*—incompetents and indolents—who were in truth his people. He was raging against a dawning, and he did not recognize the new day.

Castro's position was worsened by the election, that same watershed year of 1980, of Ronald Reagan to the American presidency. President Jimmy Carter's idealistic efforts to make peace with Castro had failed abysmally. The Republicans were far more cynical—some would say realistic—about the possibility of any genuine rapprochement with Castro. But it was after President Reagan sent the shrewd General Vernon Walters—his United Nations ambassador—to Cuba, in 1982, that the administration definitively made up its mind about whether to try anything new with Castro.

Old fox Walters, a hulk of a man with brilliant linguistic abilities and cynical good sense, traveled to Cuba "to see." The content and results of the crucially important meeting were never publicly revealed and indeed remained top secret until now; it would be Walters' judgments that would form the crucial U.S. response to the last years of Castro's unending fight against America.

Reconstructed from several sources, the meeting began when the two men met in Castro's office and then went to dinner. Once Castro realized the American diplomat had not come to threaten him, he relaxed. They talked of communist philosophy and Cuban history, about which Walters knew a good deal.

At one point Walters even joked with the Cuban leader, telling him very seriously that "we do have something in common." Castro's eyebrows raised suspiciously. "We're both graduates of the Jesuits," Walters went on. Castro sat back, nodded his head but without sentiment. "But there is something different between us," Walters added. Castro raised his eyebrows again, this time in curiosity. Walters went on in Spanish, saying, *"Me quedé fiel,"* a play on Castro's name, meaning, But I remained faithful.

Walters left Cuba having impressed Castro, but he also left convinced that nothing could be done about the Cuban leader. He was convinced that the United States had nothing Castro wanted and that if he were to come to our side, he would be only "like the president of a banana republic."

The Walters visit convinced Ronald Reagan to give up even any thought of trying to deal with Castro. It was followed by hostile move after hostile move. The most threatening of all to Castro was the formation of Radio Martí and the beginnings of broadcasts to Cuba from America in 1985. Finally, fair and objective news was made available to the Cuban people—hour after hour after hour and week after week. It was as if Castro himself were being invaded this time; it was an airwaves Bay of Pigs against which his armed legions could not protect him.

In these years Castro began to reveal himself in new and frighteningly paranoid terms: "Cuba is alone. We cannot wait for the help of anyone. They are threatening us with an invasion right now. . . . We should prepare ourselves!"

Those were Castro's words as, once again, he stood in the historic square of Santiago on July 26, 1983, on the thirtieth anniversary of the attack on Moncada Barracks. The emotions, the heat, and his memories that day made a tremendous impression on the crowd.

The invasion scare let down not for a second. All of a sudden Cubans were soberly telling foreign diplomats that all they could do was absorb the first blow; then they would entrap the Americans and wear them down with guerrilla war. Castro's militias trained for "Red Sundays," when the invasion would come. Even the children embarked upon a veritable frenzy of digging air raid trenches.

IT WAS at this point that a bizarre scenario unfolded in Grenada that fulfilled Castro's worst nightmares. The romantic Maurice Bishop came up against the other side of revolution in the figure of the rigid, cold-eyed Soviet-backed Marxist Bernard Coard, a kind of Caribbean Trotsky, who was determined to get rid of Bishop. In the internecine fighting that ensued in the summer of 1983, ideological clouds of difference darkened the once beautiful island with blood.

That fall Castro watched with alarm as the Coard elements put Bishop under house arrest, where he refused to eat for fear of poison. Then on October 19 at least 10,000 of Bishop's "beloved" masses broke in, took Bishop, and carried their tragic and hungry hero— never a killer, always the gallant, ever the bon vivant—to the picturesque Fort Rupert overlooking the exquisite azure bay of St. George's. There Coard coldly gave the order to shoot. Bishop, his lover, five of his closest associates, and a still unknown number of others were lined up against a mural of Che Guevara and wantonly shot to bits. Still worse, Castro realized with growing horror that the Americans were preparing to invade Grenada.

Castro moved carefully. He summoned Colonel Pedro Tórtolo Comas, a husky, able black officer, and sent him to Grenada to command the Cuban troops there. He sent still another 150 to 200 seasoned soldiers with him. Yet in the poor Tórtolo, Castro had called upon one of his true "new men," an officer whose utter fealty and obedience could never be questioned, but a man who lacked combat experience. Tórtolo arrived less than twenty-four hours before the landing of the U.S.–Caribbean Security Forces. This was, in effect, the battle Castro had awaited all his life.

On October 20 the seven member islands of the Organization of Eastern Caribbean States held a meeting and invoked Article 8 of their Treaty of Association to seek American and other friendly aid. President Reagan immediately decided to send troops.

Castro watched with apprehension, but also with a simmering excitement, as on the early morning of October 25 the U.S.– Caribbean Security Forces landed on the beaches of Grenada. He immediately instructed his men that it was their duty to die fighting, "no matter how difficult the circumstances may be."

Despite genuine American attempts to avoid any fighting with the Cubans, there was some halfhearted engagement. In the end, twenty-four Cubans were killed and fifty-nine wounded.

On Grenada the Americans found thousands of infantry weapons with millions of rounds of ammunition, five secret military-assistance agreements not hitherto known—and the extraordinary "Grenada Documents," which were in fact several tons of papers, dog-eared scraps and handwritten notes that detailed the stories of every relationship between Grenada and the Eastern bloc.

When the Grenada Documents of the Bishop regime were discovered, Castro's pride was stripped bare, exploded by the ill-spelled ideological gibberish of these careless "island clowns" he had claimed as his children. Grenada was the turning point. For Castro it was impossible to accept defeat. As one observer put it, "The image of the invincible cracked right there."

Castro's face was grotesquely contorted the day he stood on the tarmac at Havana airport to greet the soldiers who, fighting in his image, had failed even symbolically to resist the enemy. As the men moved slowly off the planes—all sent back to him not by victory, but by the grace of the American army—Castro stood alone, his strong shoulders wilted, for long, silent minutes that frightened his people far more than did his tirades.

All the men were physically dirty, and many were shirtless. The incorrigible Tórtolo, who had run away when fighting began, walked gingerly off the plane wearing a casual sports shirt. He saluted Castro and intoned rhythmically, "*Comandante-en-Jefe* . . . Mission accomplished." An artillery corps band belted out a few appropriate revolutionary hymns, and women militia members duly goose-stepped across the tarmac of the José Martí Airport. But President Fidel Castro said not a single word.

At first Castro tried to pretend that everything was all right. He visited the men in the hospitals, brought them books, and talked with them. Word would get out about how much the *comandante-en-jefe* cared about his soldiers. Subsequently the men were all demoted to lowly positions, and the unfortunate Tórtolo was banished to Angola. Finally, in the court martial, the mood was so bitter that Raúl Castro tore the men's epaulets off their jackets in postured rage.

SEVENTEEN
Él—He

FROM 1983 on, all Castro could do was fight to hold position. Cuba's economic situation worsened to the point where the island nation was unable to produce enough sugar for its quota to Russia. In 1985 Castro tried to recoup by seizing upon the issue of Third World debt to Western banks to stoke the fires of his guerrilla fight against the United States. In the spring and summer of that year no fewer than five international conferences were held in Havana on the debt. Delegates arriving at José Martí Airport were met by Cuban school-children singing "The Debt of Latin America and the Third World Must Be Canceled."

That same year things got even worse for Castro, if they could, as Mikhail Gorbachev came to power in Moscow. So it was that in 1986, Castro's Year of Rage, he struck back and back and back.

He threw veritable tantrums—against waste, against mismanagement, against individual entrepreneurs, against both the United States and the Soviet Union. At the Third Congress of the Cuban Communist Party that year, his mood was bitter, his predictions downbeat, his visage dark and angry. Before 3500 party leaders he berated a farmer making $50,000 a year by privately selling garlic, and he literally rained all the fire and brimstone of his volcanic personality down on the heads of certain enterprising local lads in one Cuban town who had bought the whole supply of toothbrushes and melted them down to produce plastic necklaces. That was what the Revolution had come to—screaming at garlic farmers and the producers of illegal plastic necklaces.

Never mind, he would now step in to rectify things at home so he could continue his expansionism abroad. The Campaign of Rectification of Errors was his first answer to the *glasnost* and *perestroika* reforms that Gorbachev was trying to make. It was to be an "exciting" new program for a people who had already known nothing but twenty-seven years of bruising austerity.

Like so many dictators in their waning years, he sat surrounded by a little group of fulsome and ever changing courtiers, who could be identified by their Rolex watches and foreign cars. While the world spoke trustingly of a Cuban communist apparatus—a politburo, a central committee, a collective leadership—all of that was by then a mirage.

Cuba was being run by Castro's tight little team of fourteen to fifteen persons who hovered ever around him at his beck and call. And they made very sure never to tell Castro anything that would not please him. To arrive at this point of guarded inner-circle perfection, Castro had to purge and purge and purge, and then to replace and replace and replace all of his oldest comrades-in-arms.

If there had been one truly exemplary military officer, it was Arnaldo Ochoa Sánchez, a hawk-nosed, handsome Rommel type who would have stood out for excellence and honor in any army. He had served in the Sierra Maestra with Castro; he had studied at military academies in the Soviet Union. He had fought at the Bay of Pigs, in the Congo, and in Nicaragua, finally becoming the top commander of troops in Fidel's favorite foreign war, Angola. But when the Soviets began forcing Castro to bring home his 57,000 troops from Angola, Ochoa became not only a threat to Castro but *the* threat. Ochoa's house became a gathering place for war veterans frustrated by the quagmirish bureaucracy of the Cuba they returned to. Discontent and disaffection were palpable, and discontent was something that Fidel never countenanced. He lost no time in acting.

The ensuing Ochoa "trial" shocked awake a world that had refused, before, to look with any seriousness at the way Castro used the courts. The handsome, gallant Ochoa sat impassively in the courtroom in his light gray dress uniform. He looked like a man stunned, as he stared vacuously at the floor. When Castro accused him of drug-running,